WORLD CHRISTIAN HANDBOOK
1968 Edition

WORLD
CHRISTIAN
HANDBOOK

1968

Editors

H. WAKELIN COXILL
Chevalier, Belgian Orders of The Crown, Lion and Leopold

SIR KENNETH GRUBB, C.M.G., LL.D.

Assistant Editor

KATHLEEN A. KNAPP

ABINGDON PRESS
NASHVILLE   NEW YORK

Previous issues of
World Christian Handbook
were published in 1949, 1952, 1957 and 1962
by the World Dominion Press
(Survey Application Trust)
and distributed in the United States by the Friendship Press, New York

*Printed in Great Britain
by Ebenezer Baylis and Son, Ltd.
The Trinity Press, Worcester, and London*

TABLE OF CONTENTS

PREFACE

THIS is the fifth edition of the *World Christian Handbook* compiled by the Survey Application Trust. It is published, not in this case by its publishing branch the World Dominion Press, but by Lutterworth Press, for whose ready co-operation the Trust is grateful, in collaboration with Abingdon Press in the United States. After several decades of work in the field of survey, statistics and statistical methods, not to speak of much other activity, the Survey Application Trust has decided to conclude its operations in the near future.

The compilation of the Handbook is a complex and expensive operation, even when the statistical data sought is comparatively simple and straightforward. The present edition has been compiled by the Rev. H. Wakelin Coxill, with the assistance of Mrs. K. A. Knapp, as was the case with the fourth edition. But others on the staff of the Survey Application Trust have assisted from time to time. The Editors also desire to thank particularly the Rev. David Barrett of the Church Missionary Society, who has taken much time and special pains to collect, examine and check the African figures, and they are equally grateful to those who have contributed to the invaluable series of introductory articles. It must be remembered that the Handbook is often ordered by scholars or institutions who have no other ready means to hand of informing themselves of the nature and characteristics of the world mission of the Church.

It is not possible to say whether the Handbook will have a future in any other form. Preliminary conversations have been held designed to lead to the formation of an adequately financed international trust which would arrange for the collection and publication on a larger scale of statistical material of all Christian churches, including, it need hardly be said, the Roman Catholic Church. The expense of this undertaking might be considerable, not least because as Dr. Frank Price shows, the enterprise would require the work of travelling investigators. Should the outline of a satisfactory scheme be adopted, and an international Trust established, with reasonable provisions and due safeguards, the Survey Application Trust might consider the transfer to it of their records, indices, contacts and goodwill. A cautious and moderate scheme, with promise of continuity, would at the start, be preferable to an over-ambitious one. In this field it is easy for vaulting ambition to "o'er-leap itself and fall on the other". However, in the collection of statistics it should be comparatively easy to achieve co-operation between churches. One of the principal difficulties will be the unsolved and intractable one of the definition of terms.

The need for a more rigorous and also more detailed apparatus of statistics is clear both from the material presented in the statistical pages, and from the observations of some of the eminent writers of the prefatory articles. See, by way of illustration, the questions explicitly or implicitly raised in Dr. MacGavran's article on Contrasts in Church Growth. The irony of the matter is precisely that the greater the need the greater the difficulty. The proliferation of Independent Churches in Africa as described by Mr. Barrett is a simple and vivid example of this. There will never be complete statistics of the churches in the world; the best to be hoped for is a constantly improving approximation. With the termination of the work of the Survey Application Trust, grants frequently paid to Christian Councils for the collection of their own figures will cease. Finally the significance and proper interpretation of world Christian statistics has hitherto received but sporadic attention. Statistics are a valley of dry bones . . . "Son of Man, can these bones live?"

Yet, as Dr. Warren points out in his article, by implication, there are tendencies in world culture, population and political and economic attitudes which make it all the more urgent to face the position. The statistics in this edition of the Handbook give by no means an alarming and pessimistic picture. They do, indeed, show the magnitude of "the unfinished task". But they also show that almost everywhere there has been an increase in church membership, but only in a few areas, of which Latin America appears to be the chief, does the advance match the population growth. Proportionately to world population Christians are losing ground heavily.

It is not easy to assess the likely progress of the Gospel in the next decade or two and he would be a bold man who would attempt it. But a few obvious considerations, most of which have been commented upon, sometimes by more than one of our contributors, are worth an extra word here. There are tragic areas of famine and war in the world, but generally speaking, the people of all nations have caught the vision of an age of progress, where war and want shall be no more. But with the vision there is bound to grow much disillusionment. The gap between rich and poor remains and indeed widens. The planning of a balanced economy of production, agricultural and industrial, and the maintenance of stable prices for primary products have proved very tough nuts to crack. Or, perhaps it would be fairer to say that many can plan, but few can execute. In many countries the cloud-capped palaces, the solemn towers, of human achievement require for their erection a degree of talent which simply does not exist. The conquests of science emanate from highly sophisticated societies and their techniques are to be neither taught nor financed overnight. There will be much disillusionment before the "take-off point" of self-generating progress is reached in most countries of Asia and Africa.

Meanwhile, however, the mind of man, aroused and excited by his apparent self-sufficiency—"Drest in a little brief authority, Most ignorant of what he's most assured", will not be readily disposed to listen to a message which declares that all have sinned, and fallen short of the glory of God.

Such is the modern world in which missions have to be carried on. I limit myself here to a few selected comments on topics which other writers in the Handbook have developed more fully.

The statistics in this edition, more perhaps than the articles, illustrate the considerable progress made by the "conservative evangelical" groups. These bodies which often do not fit into any denominational pattern are particularly active in N. America and send out as many, if not more, missionaries, than the "historic" boards and societies. For the most part, they do not co-operate with the World Council of Churches, or its Commission on World Mission and Evangelism (successor to the International Missionary Council). Their agents are fervent and often well-financed and they increasingly possess a higher level of education than formerly, without losing their evangelistic zeal. Their achievements are, therefore, considerable. Their drawbacks are mainly an inadequate appreciation of the Church, a consequently prolonged measure of mission patronage and an unwillingness, by no means however universal, to co-operate with others. It is important for the world mission of the church that all who are conscious of the situation should strive together for closer understanding.

The Laity today are objects of interest almost everywhere in the church. The clergy are a little uncertain how to handle them, and their life and role have been the subject of many treatises. It is felt desirable that they should exist, and I have not seen any proposal for their abolition. The World Council of Churches even publishes a bulletin under the title "Laity" and at intervals it is intelligible, although not very readable. Brevity is not the soul of it. The review *Frontier* is entirely the initiative and work of laymen, and there are other such publications. Vatican Council II took due note of the laity. There has been in many countries much ado about industrial missions. It is natural that in a day when organized religion is hard pressed by secular and humanist thought, and in certain countries churches are very thinly attended, the laity should suddenly be remembered. They must be trained; they must be mobilized; they must be put to work; they must pray; they must produce money. Noble and high-minded clergymen are wrestling gallantly with all this, but I suspect that there is in most communions an inbred tendency to clericalism. The next decade will show.

The corollary of much of this is that the clergy themselves must be better trained. The presentation of the Gospel is not simply a matter of intellectual attainment, but it is not good when professional laymen in the pew have a more rigorous training in their own discipline than the clergy have in theirs. The right not to answer the unanswerable questions about man's destiny depends on the ability to answer the answerable ones.

Dr. Handspicker, drawing largely on Faith and Order reports, has given in this volume, some admirable material about the progress of union negotiations. It is less clear that the union of churches leads to a wider and more effective evangelization. Unity and Mission, we have been told *ad nauseam*, go together. It may be so and to take any other view is to show oneself an unteachable brat, well-birched and none the wiser. But this is a sphere in which facts are better than dreams.

The ecumenical movement forges on steadily. The World Council of Churches now carries the membership of most of the Orthodox and Eastern churches and has accomplished its merger with the International Missionary Council at the same time increasing its membership particularly in Africa. It has lost Dr. Visser 't Hooft, its distinguished and indefatigable chief architect, and, after some hesitation and a little awkwardness, has acquired Dr. Eugene Carson Blake as General Secretary. At the moment therefore, the General Secretary, the Chairman and one of the two Vice-chairmen of the Central and Executive Committees are all Anglo-Saxons, able men accustomed to that peculiar aura of background which, almost unconsciously, attaches to men from nations which largely dominate or have recently dominated, the world. The renewed spirit of reform and *aggiornamiento* which has characterized Vatican Council II necessarily and rightly is of great interest to the World Council of Churches and contacts with Roman Catholic theologians and others, both official and personal, have increased, and have developed mutual understanding without arousing too profound suspicions.

The World Council of Churches is going through a difficult stage, common enough to all such movements. The "first fine careless rapture" has faded. The early generation of pioneers have largely "done their task and ta'en their wages". The actual union of churches is a slow process for "tasks in hours of insight willed, must be through days of gloom fulfilled", and the growth of confessional families all fervently avowing ecumenical loyalties continues with that charming *double entendre* which makes churchmen such delightful and slippery colleagues. The new World Council of Churches' headquarters at Geneva is an imposing building, and the planning of operations is suitably conducted in the pleasant neutrality of Switzerland where great power clashes can be viewed from the spectators' gallery, women have no votes, and all men love their neighbours in the next valley. The temptation to yield to the fascinations of centralized bureaucracy must be strong. A modern Mephistopheles, tempting a modern Faust, would not offer him the sweetness of an innocent Gretchen, but the fascination of a centralized machine.

Meanwhile the World Evangelical Fellowship, much less equipped in general resources, is steadily strengthening its connection, winning friends and influencing people.

Local Councils of Churches and regional bodies have grown in influence in the last quinquennium. There is much still to be worked out in the relationship between them and the world ecumenical organizations. Equally, the relations, if any, of the Pentecostal churches and the Independent African churches, movements whose growth is succinctly dealt with in the articles by Mr. du Plessis and Mr. David Barrett, remain largely a task for tomorrow. Strong central bodies cannot, however, exercise power unless they have steadily acquired authority; if they possess authority they will not need power.

Perhaps I may be pardoned a final personal word. This is the last Handbook with which I shall be actively associated and for which I have been responsible for setting up the arrangements. I owe an unrepayable debt to the Rev. Wakelin Coxill who has worked without ceasing on this issue as well as on the last. Together our joint and concurrent knowledge of the great enterprise of world evangelization, at least in many of its aspects, must total not far short of a hundred years. Many preoccupations and responsibilities in the work of the churches have prevented me from personally giving to the Handbook, the attention I should have desired, but I accept my full share of responsibility for the errors and omissions of this work.

I do not altogether despair of the Church and its mission in the world. I do not think that, at least in the West, we have yet discovered that approach to the presentation of the Gospel which makes it attractive, intelligent and convincing to modern man. I do not think that the customary arrangements of Christian worship fit very readily into the pattern of life of a sophisticated and industrial society, and I think therefore that a considerable adaptation in the life of the churches, has to be made as a prelude to the reconstruction of religion as a living force. I welcome, therefore, with equal respect and gratitude, the great crusades carried on by Dr. Graham, and the discussion group where the two or three meet and pray. It may well be that the words "revival" or "renewal" mean something very different from any of our conceptions today.

KENNETH G. GRUBB
23rd April, 1967

It is now possible and desirable to be a little more precise about the proposal mentioned on page vii. On the initiative of the Institute of Social Studies at The Hague, and with the collaboration of the World Council of Churches and of FERES, a leading Roman Catholic Research Centre concerned hitherto with the publication of the *Bilan du Monde,* a small international body of Trustees has been set up to establish a Documentation Centre on the work of the Churches. I have accepted an invitation to join the Board of Trustees. One of the main tasks of the new centre will probably be an attempt to publish a successor to the *World Christian Handbook* and the *Bilan du Monde* together.

K.G.G.
28th July, 1967

FOREWORD

HUNDREDS of people of scores of nationalities have contributed, either directly or indirectly, to the production of this edition of the *World Christian Handbook*. To all who have given thought and care in providing the information needed we give our sincere thanks.

Special efforts have been made to obtain reliable facts concerning the Christian Church, country by country, throughout the world. Soon after the publication of the 1962 Edition, letters were sent to churches and missions, in each of the six continents, asking for corrections and comments. Those received were noted and filed. Then in 1964 a letter was sent to all concerned giving notice of the intention of the World Dominion Press to publish a new edition of the Handbook in 1967 and giving detailed particulars of the sort of information that would be requested a year or so later. Consultations with Christian leaders were held in London, Paris, Geneva and New York. Following this, the questions to be asked of the Anglican and Protestant churches and Christian organizations, with explanations as to their meaning (see Introduction to Statistical Section, p. 57) were settled.

Five different questionnaires were prepared and sent out with covering letters to all known Protestant churches, missions, Christian organizations and national and international councils and associations. The accuracy or otherwise of the information given in the Handbook reflects, in large measure, the response received, though other means of trying to obtain information have, where necessary, been sought and used.

Some of the difficulties and problems facing the Christian statistician are ably dealt with in the article on page 48 written for us by Dr. F. W. Price. I do not need, therefore, to draw further attention to them. For various reasons, and for some countries at least, it must be admitted that it is impossible, at present, to obtain accurate figures of church membership.

Comparisons between figures now published and those given previously can also be misleading, especially for large areas. For example, some churches, though they have existed for many years, have supplied figures now for the first time. Against this there have been serious cases of overlapping in the past when missions and newly independent churches have both made returns without consultation. We hope such duplication has been eliminated in this edition. The safest and most accurate comparison, showing church growth or otherwise, can generally be obtained by studying the returns of individual churches over a number of years.

We were most fortunate in having in Africa at this time in the person of Dr. David Barrett, one who was in an unique position to check, complete and correct our African statistics. We add our thanks to those expressed elsewhere by Sir Kenneth Grubb. Through the kindness of Dr. David M. Stowe of the National Council of the Churches of Christ, we were able to send all our statistical sheets for the whole of North and South America and for Asia to friends in New York, who helped us with valuable corrections and comments before going to press. We thank them all. Friends in Germany were also able and willing to check and correct some of the figures we had received for that country. We thank them too.

The Directory Section of the Handbook is more comprehensive than that of previous editions. We have endeavoured to bring it up-to-date. There have been many changes of address and not a few new ones to be noted. We have also included, for the first time, telephone numbers, where these have been known. We believe hundreds of users of the Handbook will find this a help.

I am especially grateful to Mrs. K. A. Knapp who has been the Assistant Editor of this work. We worked happily together on the 1962 Edition and I have greatly valued her experienced help on this one. We have appreciated also the assistance given to us from time to time by other members of the Staff of the Survey Application Trust (World Dominion Press).

I would also like to thank Sir Kenneth Grubb himself. It has been a pleasure to work with him. He has been behind previous editions of the Handbook and from his wide knowledge and experience has always given sound advice and encouragement. More than that, he has been willing to share or shoulder criticism that would otherwise rightly have fallen on my head.

The Christian statistician can, I believe, expect to receive more boos than cheers when his ambitious field is the whole world. We therefore are the more grateful to all who have given us sympathetic support.

We hope that this edition of the Handbook will prove to be of real value to the many people who need it in all six continents. To Christian workers, especially, we hope it will bring challenge, encouragement and assistance.

H. WAKELIN COXILL

ACKNOWLEDGMENTS

WE are particularly grateful to those who have contributed articles especially for this edition of the Handbook. They are all experts in the field of which they have written. While most of our contributors hold official positions in Christian organizations the views they express must not be taken to represent the bodies with which they are connected. No attempt has been made to harmonize the views of our contributors.

For the statistics of the Roman Catholic Church which figure in this publication our thanks are due to Mr. A. E. C. W. Spencer, of the ISS-FERES Project.

Thanks are due to the following publishers for permission to use statistical material which has appeared in the publication indicated:

Messrs. Macmillan & Co. Ltd., publishers of the *Statesman's Year Book, 1966* (edited by S. H. Steinberg, Ph.D.)

National Council of the Churches of Christ in the U.S.A., publishers of *Yearbook of American Churches, 1966* (edited by Benson Y. Landis)

American Jewish Committee and Jewish Publication Society of America, publishers of *American Jewish Year Book, 1966* (edited by Morris Fine and Milton Himmelfarb)

United Nations Publishing Service, publishers of the *United Nations Demographic Year Book*

The *Bilan Du Monde, 1964*, published by the Eglise Vivante (Louvain), and the *Britannica Book of the Year, 1966* have both been useful sources of information.

A *Statistical Survey of Protestant Missions in Latin America*, published in 1961 by The Evangelical Foreign Mission Association, U.S.A., while often taking figures from the 1957 edition of our own *World Christian Handbook* has, however, been of help to us in filling some gaps in this later edition. For this too we are grateful.

NOTES ON CONTRIBUTORS

THE REV. DAVID B. BARRETT, Ph.D., Secretary for Research, Church of the Province of East Africa Unit of Research, Nairobi, Kenya.

THE REV. EMILIO CASTRO, Executive Secretary of the Latin American Commission for Christian Unity (UNELAM), Montevideo, Uruguay.

SIR KENNETH GRUBB, C.M.G., LL.D., President of the Church Missionary Society; Chairman of the House of Laity of the Church Assembly; Chairman of the Commission of the Churches on International Affairs; Managing Trustee, Survey Application Trust.

THE REV. M. B. HANDSPICKER, Division of Studies, Commission on Faith and Order, World Council of Churches, Geneva.

THE REV. FR S. MASSON, S.J., Professor of Missiology, Pontificia Universita Gregoriana, Rome.

THE REV. DONALD A. MCGAVRAN, Ph.D., Dean of the School of World Mission and Institute of Church Growth, Fuller Theological Seminary, Pasadena, California.

DAVID J. DU PLESSIS, Lecturer on the Pentecostal Movement in ecumenical and other circles.

PROFESSOR FRANK WILSON PRICE, Director of the Missionary Research Library, New York, until 1961.

THE REV. FR PAUL VERGHESE, Director of the Division of Ecumenical Action, World Council of Churches, Geneva.

THE REV. H. WAKELIN COXILL, formerly General Secretary of the Congo Protestant Council and Representative in Belgium of Protestant Missions.

CANON M. A. C. WARREN, D.D., Sub-Dean of Westminster; General Secretary of Church Missionary Society, 1942–1963.

PROTESTANT AND ANGLICAN CHURCHES AND MISSIONS

A Contemporary review

by

MAX WARREN

FOUR broad developments in the international scene during the last five years may be held to provide the background against which the Church and its Mission have to be studied.

First there has been the end of the "honeymoon" period of political independence as enjoyed by those nations which have escaped from alien control since the end of the Second World War.

The pressure of unsolved economic problems and the increasing difficulty of finding adequate scapegoats have led to widespread disillusionment. There has been a serious set-back in educational pro-grammes, in addition to a dangerous lowering of standards, and con-sequent bitterness of the growing class of "just-failed secondary school graduates". The widening gulf between the rewards enjoyed by the small élite in government service, and the majority with some measure of education, is creating acute tension in many of these nations, par-ticularly in Africa.

One sequel has been the loss of confidence in the western pattern of parliamentary democracy inherited from the previous imperial régime. General unrest has promoted the development of military governments and one-party states.

All this has contributed to a widespread sense of frustration at the inability of such international bodies as the Organization of African Unity, the Arab League, and the Bandung powers, to secure peace and order in their immediate areas of influence, and so to exert an influence at the United Nations comparable with their membership.

Second has been the growth of conflicts within the Communist world. These conflicts do not necessarily presage any change in the direction of Communist policies. They have indeed added to the general unrest of mankind. And, immediately, they have led to adventures designed to distract the attention of the peoples of Communist countries from causes of internal discontent. Rocket-missiles in Cuba and the Chinese invasion of India on the one hand, and aggressive diplomatic and cultural activity in Africa, and the clash of Soviet and Chinese interests there, are illustrations. The riddle of these events is not easy to read.

Third has been the ever-widening gap in material prosperity between

1

the economically developed and under-developed areas of the world. We have seen emerge a North-South division of mankind even more ominous than the East-West division of the world following the end of the war.

Fourth is the Population Explosion, the true facts of which are beginning to impinge on the consciousness of most governments. The fact of world hunger, the threat of famine and disease, and the potential revolutionary sequel are obvious subjects of concern. Less obvious, but as far reaching, is the inevitable sequel to this explosion in the increasing regimentation of all life which must, in due course, profoundly modify the structure of every society, sophisticated no less than primitive.

These four broad developments have been described as the background against which the Church and its Mission must be understood. Perhaps it would be more accurate to describe them as integral elements in the actual involvement of the Church in its Mission to the world. With this reminder, the contemporary scene can be interpreted under six heads. The order under which these are listed is not accidental.

(i) *The rapid development of urbanization.* This phenomenon which is proceeding apace in Asia, Africa and Latin America involves a decisive re-orientation for the Churches of these continents, which have hitherto been overwhelmingly rural in character with an ordained ministry not only drawn from peasant stock but geared mentally to the life of the village community.

This new development possibly outstrips in importance and urgency every other facet of the changing world scene as far as the Church is concerned. For a Church which appears totally irrelevant to the actual situation in which people live in towns, and which appears unable to provide relief from the pressures they endure, is unlikely to command their allegiance for long. The flight from any form of Church membership, which is already a dramatic fact in Western Europe, is being reflected in the vast conurbations of Asia, Africa and Latin America.

To meet this need much adventurous experiment is being made. Thoroughgoing surveys of many local situations have been and are being made. A redeployment of personnel, native and foreign, is everywhere being undertaken. Experiments are being made in the use of visual aids, drama and broadcasting on a more ambitious scale than ever. Specific projects in industrial areas such as Durgapur in India and Port Harcourt in Nigeria are examples of a development in Mission already begun and likely to increase very rapidly in the coming decade.

At the same time it is widely recognized that in all these countries an industrial revolution involving urbanization must be paralleled by an agricultural revolution. Here, albeit as yet on a small scale, the Church and its Mission are pioneering. One very experienced observer has recently spoken of "the vast opportunity facing the Churches if they will help with agricultural training and primary education to equip people for the basic life of a profitable peasantry which must remain the backbone of East Africa's economy". What is true of East Africa is true of other areas where an agricultural revolution is an indispensable complement to an industrial one. Town-dweller and peasant belong together and society in its political, economic and religious expression must express this interdependence if there is to be any kind of stability.

(ii) *The deployment of manpower.* This follows as an indispensable sequel to what has just been considered. It must be reported that nothing commensurate with the real needs of the Church has yet been attempted. Church structures are extremely resistant to change. A traditional pattern of organization is rarely flexible. Theological training, unfortunately, is normally more concerned with *what* has to be taught than with the people to whom the teaching has in due course to be mediated!

This represents a major problem. The Theological Education Fund, established at the Ghana Meeting of the International Missionary Council in 1956, is a serious and responsible attempt to start remedying the situation at the root-problem, which is the training of the ordained ministry. But progress is very slow.

Meanwhile, increasing attention is being paid to a new understanding of the role of the Christian layman as he plays his part in the ordinary activities of secular society. Almost all the traditional Churches are over-clericalized institutions in which the role of the Christian layman is either misunderstood or consistently underestimated. It would be rash, however, to imagine that de-clericalization of the Churches will be rapid.

(iii) *A failure in Missionary vocation.* It is perhaps no accident that at this moment there is reported from almost every Church a serious drop in the numbers of those who are prepared to commit themselves to any kind of a missionary vocation, whether in the ordained ministry or as professional missionaries. Commitment of this kind is uncongenial to the temper of the age and to much in the climate of Christian opinion. It may be surmised that this in some degree reflects what has been said under (ii).

(iv) *Dialogue as a method of encounter.* The shrinking of the world through all the means of communication presents the Church with the enduring prospect of co-existence between the different religions of mankind, assuming that religion is to continue to be a characteristic of mankind. In the nineteenth century, and still in the minds of those who are living in that century, the idea of such co-existence is wholly repugnant. Missionary hymnology, which most accurately expresses traditional Christian missionary thinking, has never envisaged co-existence as more than a very temporary phenomenon.

One direct result of facing this new fact of co-existence has been the increasing attempt to approach the men of other Faiths as being persons with a valid spiritual experience of their own which has to be sympathetically understood. This approach does not in any way involve an abdication of the Christian conviction of the uniqueness of Christ, as both Saviour and Lord. It does not involve anything approaching syncretism. But it does involve a quite new appraisal of the nature of the

3

evangelistic task. Few contemporary developments are more encouraging than the evidence of widespread exploration of this way of "Dialogue".

But Christians need to be aware that creating the conditions for "dialogue" will call for very great restraint in the use of radio and other mass media for which, in some places, Christians possess the resources which others lack.

(v) Of the four features in the contemporary scene outlined above, each points to the urgency of *the movement for Christian unity*. Recent years have seen some arrest in the progress of this movement. In the World Council of Churches, for instance, the need to digest and assimilate the contribution of so many new Churches of such varied traditions has brought to light a new range of problems. Not wholly unconnected with this increase of membership in the World Council has been the fact that at the local level non-theological factors have come to play a more obvious part in halting progress towards unity. Nigeria is a case in point. Recent events in South India, and some uncertainties in North India, point in the same direction.

Meanwhile, certain forces are active in promoting Christian disunity and these are showing no decline in influence.

(vi) Of very far-reaching importance is *the emergence of more and more indigenous Churches*, particularly in Africa, which owe no allegiance to the denominational traditions of the West. Often substantially orthodox in Faith these Churches show a desire of men and women for a Christian community untrammelled by Western organization, a place in which they can feel "at home".

This article would suggest that the present position can best be understood in the light of the inter-relatedness of these six features just listed, themselves seen against the background of the four broad developments of the international scene which provide their present historical context.

THE ROMAN CATHOLIC CHURCH AT THE TIME OF THE SECOND VATICAN COUNCIL

by

S. Masson, S. J.

Statistics

Roman Catholic statistics are compiled in two ways. The first is a straightforward method based on baptism. According to this criterion, Roman Catholics constitute about 18 per cent of the total world population, or a good 60 per cent of all Christians. Statisticians point out, however, that the former percentage is likely to decrease. Because of their higher rate of population growth, the countries of Asia, notably China, are coming to represent an ever increasing proportion of mankind. Since all the Christian denominations are mainly situated in the West, this leads to a corresponding decrease in the proportion of Christians in the world. Despite substantial progress in countries such as Formosa, South Korea or black Africa the missionary effort is not in general able to offset this relative decrease.

The second statistical method is to take baptism for granted and classify Roman Catholics according to their faithfulness in attendance at worship. By this method the statistics can differ both in their criteria and in their results. One may count up the Christians who keep up attendance at mass each Sunday or only on the main festivals, or even those who only go to Easter confession and communion. Whatever criterion is used, the conclusion will emerge clearly enough that, in certain regions, especially the industrial ones, people now only go to church for weddings, baptisms, the children's first communion, and funerals. This basic minimum seems to be still generally observed. The percentage of Catholics attending mass each Sunday can vary considerably: in the worst cases it may be only 8 or 10 per cent, while in some where religious practice is well kept up it may rise as high as 80 or 90 per cent. As a general rule, it must be stated that the number of practising Catholics dropped considerably—in France, for example—at the end of the nineteenth and the beginning of the twentieth century. This drift away from the Church now appears to have been strongly checked. In a number of places, practising Catholics have not only gained in devotion: they are now gaining in numbers. This is true of much of the "free" West (for example, the United States). It is, however, not true of the Communist West (for example, Poland) or Latin

5

America, where a shortage of priests leads to a dearth of instruction and religious services.

There is no indication that the decline in vocations to the priesthood and the religious life is coming to an end; but at the same time, its seriousness must not be exaggerated. Even in France, which has been called a "mission field", there is one priest for every seven or eight hundred inhabitants. The situation in Germany or Portugal is more serious, and some increase in vocation here is essential.

The Vatican Council provided an opportunity to compile statistics of the bishops and heads of the religious Orders: they numbered more than three thousand.

Worship and Catechesis

For a number of years, work for liturgical renewal has been going on, aimed at bringing the liturgy closer to the people. Centres were established such as the *Centre de Pastorale Liturgique* in Paris or the centre at Loppem in Belgium. A number of conferences were held: at Assisi, for instance, and at Uden in Holland. Vatican II's Constitution on the Liturgy, which lays down the double principle of unity in essentials and diversity in their local expression, is the result of research undertaken mainly in north-west Europe; but at the Council it received well-informed support from the missionary bishops.

The same thing goes for catechesis. The Germans and the French have been working hard for its renewal. They wanted a fresh emphasis on the "proclamation". There was some disagreement about the meaning of the word, but all were united in underlining the need to "proclaim" the Gospel to non-believers—and not to proclaim abstract truths, but in the first instance a "history of salvation", based on the event of Christ's coming, and moving towards the end of time. This christological and eschatological perspective has since appeared in the most dynamic documents of the Council—the Constitution *Lumen Gentium*, the Decree on Missionary Work and the Constitution on the Church and the World. It is also clearly seen in recent catechisms.

Relations with the World Council of Churches

As early as 1961, when the World Council of Churches held its Third Assembly at New Delhi, an important Catholic delegation attended the sessions as observers. Catholic observers were also present at the Faith and Order Conference at Montreal (12–26 July, 1963) and at the annual meetings of the Central Committee of the W.C.C. At the Rochester meeting in 1963, the W.C.C. expressed its desire for closer co-operation with the Roman Catholic Church, in view of the change in attitude brought about by the Second Vatican Council. When the Central Committee met again at Enugu, Nigeria, (12–21 January, 1965) with two members of the Secretariat present (Frs Duprey and Hamer) this resolution was put into effect by the setting up of a Commission, or Working Party, to study the problems related to the dialogue between the W.C.C. and the Catholic Church. This Commission has eight members from the W.C.C. and six from the Catholic Church, and has already met twice in 1965, at Bossey (22–24 May), and at Rome (17–20 November).

Catholics also took part in the meeting of the Central Committee in Geneva (4–17 February, 1966) and official delegates of the Secretariat were present at the World Conference on Church and Society at Geneva (12–16 July, 1966).

Relations with the Orthodox Churches

Progress in this field is even more startling and even more indicative of a change of climate. A Catholic delegation (Mgr Charrière and Fr Dumont, O.P.) attended the Golden Jubilee celebrations of Patriarch Alexis of Moscow (14–21 July, 1963). The most outstanding event, however, was the unforgettable meeting of Pope Paul VI and Patriarch Athenagoras in Jerusalem in January 1964. The Panorthodox Conference held at Rhodes from 1 to 15 November, 1964, declared its desire for a dialogue between Orthodoxy and the Catholic Church. It did not, however, fix any date for this. The resolutions of this Conference were reported to the Holy See on 15 February, 1965, by the President, Mgr Meliton, on behalf of Patriarch Athenagoras. Other events worth mentioning are the transfer of the relics of Saint Andrew to Patras on 26 September, 1964, and the formal proceedings with which the Second Vatican Council closed—a joint declaration by the Pope and Patriarch Athenagoras on 7 December, 1965, mutually lifting the ban of excommunication made in 1054.

Visits from the heads of other churches, which were begun under Pope John XXIII, have continued under Pope Paul VI, the most notable being that of the Archbishop of Canterbury, Dr. Ramsey, on 23rd March, 1966.

Social work

Catholic social work in recent years has taken its direction both from specific contemporary needs and from three important documents, the encyclicals *Mater et Magistra* (15 May, 1961), *Pacem in Terris* (11 April, 1963), and the pastoral constitution *Gaudium et Spes* published by the Council on 7 December, 1965.

The problem of manual workers, particularly industrial and agricultural workers, as well as small farmers, has been seen in modern times. It is still a current problem. In respect of the workers' right to form organizations to obtain a more just position in society, the *Confédération Internationale des Syndicats Chrétiens* deserves mention for its steady efforts to obtain freedom for trade unions in the many countries where such freedom does not yet exist, and to promote that freedom in the new countries. Evidence of this can be found in every number of the journal *Labor*. Participation requires preparation; and here the *Jeunesse Ouvrière Catholique Internationale* plays a most important role. Its third International Council was held at Bangkok in 1965; the previous one took place in Rio de Janeiro in 1961.

Some of the workers' movements which have sprung from the efforts of Catholics have decided in future to refrain from any explicit reference to religion (this is illustrated by the change of the French CFTC to CFDT). Others, however, feel it is essential to base social action on explicit religious convictions and, moreover, to widen their horizon to include other religions as well as Christianity (this is the case with the CISC).

There is a steady effort on the part of the employers (chiefly under the aegis of the *Union Internationale Chrétienne des Dirigeants d'Entreprise*) to set up associations, especially in the developing countries. There have been mergers between well-established associations and new organizations. In other respects also, work in aid of the developing countries has become an important aim of Christian associations of employers in recent years and has taken a wide variety of forms.

It has, however, gradually become clear that the "social problem" has wider and more complex dimensions than simply the relations between workers and employers. The encyclical *Mater et Magistra* defined some of them: relations between agriculture and the other sectors of the economy, the balance between different regions of the same country, relations between the developed and the developing countries and the balance between population growth and economic growth. The last two dimensions are particularly important and deserve further mention.

Catholic aid to the developing countries is given in two ways: firstly, through their own ranks—the hierachy and organizations like *Misereor* (the principal ones are mentioned in the March 1966 number of *Justice dans le Monde*, pp. 301–3) and secondly, through non-denominational organizations, both state organizations and otherwise. The fact that the Holy See has been represented at important international meetings on the subject, (notably the International Conference on Commerce and Development at Geneva in 1964), and also the Council's decision to set up, in close touch with the Holy See, a Secretariat for World Justice and Development, are evidence of a desire to encourage this many-sided activity.

The population expansion has been receiving increasing attention in Catholic circles in recent years. This is indicated by the many studies published on the subject and by the formation of such organizations as the *Secretariat (européen) de Liason pour les Etudes de Population*, the Asian Population Research and Information Association and the *Centro Latino-americano de la Población y Familia*, not to mention many national organizations. In this field, too, the Holy See has been represented at international conferences. As is well known, the problem is being examined in all its aspects at the request of Pope Paul VI, by a commission of experts drawn from various related scientific disciplines and coming from all parts of the world. Spokesmen of all the varying shades of doctrinal emphasis were included, and married laymen were strongly represented.

The most world-wide social problem of our time is that of peace among the nations. It is no longer a question of the peace of the established order, but of ceaselessly building a new order, which the increasing unification of mankind and the development of means of mass destruction make more essential than ever before in history. The-visit of Paul VI to the Assembly of the United Nations was a striking indication of the importance which the Church puts on the development of international institutions of a public nature. Meanwhile, in a less spectacular but more continuous fashion, the work of individual witness goes on in many different ways.

Missionary work

Recent years have seen a considerable change in the conditions of missionary work. On the one hand, the field seems more restricted. Decolonization, declarations of independence and the new self-awareness of the peoples of Asia and Africa have led many of them to consider their traditional religion as part of the soul of their nation, and to reject, or at least to view with suspicion, missionary work and missionaries. This is the case in Sudan, Tunisia and Algeria, Burma and Ceylon, to mention but a few; nor should we forget China's pitiless struggle against loyal Catholics.

On the other hand, the mission field has broadened, because a number of countries which might be called Christian in so far as their inhabitants are baptized, have been revealed by sociological research to be places with incomplete local churches still in process of formation. This is the case in many Latin American countries, where there are still insufficient clergy and inadequate places of worship, and where, as a result, the ignorance of baptized Catholics is as great as their attendance in worship is weak. This is particularly so in the suburbs of new towns and in the remote parts of the country. The authors of the *Missionary Decree* acknowledged this situation, and its influence on missionary methods is being increasingly seen in the sending of European and American diocesan priests to Latin America on a temporary or a permanent basis.

Finally, it could perhaps be said that the mission field has deepened. There is a universal realization of the need to take up into Jesus Christ all that is good in the non-Christian cultures and even in the non-Christian religions, so that Christianity in its turn can play its part as "leaven" within them. This policy of respectful approach gave birth, with the Pope's blessing, to the Secretariat for non-Christian Religions and the Secretariat for non-Believers. It is this type of penetration, rather than numerical increase, which is seen as the end of missions;

9

for it allows Christianity truly to take root, and allows for the formation of a local *élite*, especially of native priests. In Japan, Vietnam, India and Ceylon, much progress has been made in building up the number of local priests and in the work carried on by the lay apostolate.

THE ORTHODOX CHURCHES

by

THE Eastern Orthodox Church is now divided into two families. This division dates from the fifth and sixth centuries, following the Council of Chalcedon (A.D. 451) which debated the issue of whether there were one or two "natures" in Christ.

The various Orthodox Churches

The pre-Chalcedonian family, as we may call it, consists of five Churches: (1) the Coptic Orthodox Church of Alexandria (membership *c.* $3\frac{1}{2}$ million, Patriarch Kyrillos, Cairo), and (2) the Ethiopian Orthodox Church (14 million, Patriarch Baselios, Addis Ababa) form the largest units. (3) The Armenian Orthodox Church (3 million, Catholicos Vazken in Etchmiadzin, U.S.S.R.) comes next in size. (4) The Syrian Orthodox Church (Patriarch Ignatius Yakub, Damascus) which continues the Syro-Palestinian traditions of Jerusalem and Antioch, has some 200,000 members in the Middle East and in Western countries. (5) The Syrian Orthodox Church in India (Catholicos Baselios, Kottayam, India) has $1\frac{1}{4}$ million members. This smaller family of the Orthodox Churches thus constitutes some 22 million Christians.

The Chalcedonian family has some 100 million members. Their main strength is in Russia (estimated 50 million members, Patriarch Alexei, Moscow), in Rumania (15 million, Patriarch Justianian, Bucharest), in Greece (8 million, Archbishop, Chrysostomos, Athens), in Bulgaria (6 million, Patriarch Kyril, Sofia), in Serbia (7 million, Patriarch Germanos, Belgrade), and in the U.S.A. jurisdictions are smaller. The Patriarchate of Constantinople (Patriarch Athenagoras, Istanbul) has a few Greeks in Istanbul under his direct episcopal care, but has also a large exarchate in the Greek diaspora. The ancient patriarchates of Alexandria, Antioch and Jerusalem are maintained, but with very small numbers of believers. The ancient Church of Cyprus (Archbishop Makarios) and the newer ones of Poland, Czechoslovakia, Albania and Finland have memberships varying from 400,000 to 70,000.

There is no single administrative head for either of these two families. Among the pre-Chalcedonians, or "Oriental" Orthodox, the Patriarch of Alexandria has seniority of rank and next to him the Patriarch of Antioch, but they do not exercise any co-ordinating function over the whole family. On the Byzantine or "Eastern" Orthodox side, a great deal of the co-ordination comes from the Ecumenical Patriarch though his leadership is difficult to exercise because of conditions imposed on

11

him by the Turkish government, and is often contested by other Orthodox Churches. The heads of Oriental Orthodox Churches met in Addis Ababa in January 1965 under the invitation of Emperor Haile Selassie, and have established a permanent secretariat for co-ordination, with chief headquarters in Addis Ababa. The Pan-Orthodox preparatory commission at Rhodes functions as a co-ordinating body for the Churches in communion with Constantinople, but it lacks adequate office and staff to carry out that co-ordination effectively.

Until the rise of modern "secularism" the Western Church did not have to face a rival religion or a religious crusade. The Orthodox Churches have also had their heyday in the earlier half of the Byzantine Empire (330–1453), and that is the time when they laid the foundations of their liturgy, iconography, music and monasticism. It was also the period when the Byzantine Orthodox became influential in the conversion of the Slavs. The Russian Orthodox had a period of undisputed sway from the eleventh to the beginning of the twentieth century, in much the same way as the Western Church, but without major schisms. But, in general, the Orthodox have had to live under the oppressive yoke of either Islam or Communism.

Apart from the Russian Orthodox, very few of these Eastern Churches have undergone the chastening and unsettling effects of the confrontation with modern rationalism. This is why there is so little of Orthodox theology intelligible to modern readers. In fact the question, "what is the difference in belief between the Orthodox Churches and the Western Churches", is itself characteristic of the Western Church. The question implies that differences between Churches always find their focus in doctrinal formulations. While during the first centuries, and especially in the fourth and fifth centuries of the Christian era, most of the creative output of theology came from the Eastern fathers, in subsequent centuries theological articulation has become more characteristic of the Western Churches.

The Distinctive Quality of Orthodoxy

The distinctness of the Orthodox Churches cannot be located in the different theological formulations. It is to be seen more in the ethos of spirituality that stems from the Eucharist. It is a spirituality which does not minimize the value of truth, but it refuses to maximize intellectual formulations as vehicles of truth. If the notion of original sin, and therefore of the forgiveness of sins, occupies the centre of Western spirituality, it is the vocation to transfigure the body, as well as material creation, in order to express the glory of God that is at the heart of Orthodox spirituality. In the West there has been a strong emphasis on the great gulf between God and man which continues to persist even after the incarnation of Jesus Christ. In the East the assumption is that because God has become man, man can now live in unity with the God-man. To over-simplify, *encounter* is the Western word: *union* is the Eastern norm.

12

This emphasis on the direct personal union with Christ is not totally absent in the Western tradition. One finds it all through the mystical tradition of the Roman Catholic Church and in the tradition of "experience of salvation" in Free Church and sectarian Protestantism. But, quite often, this union with Christ is seen in a much too individualistic way and without the possibility of affirming the goodness of all creation. Orthodox spirituality is a spirituality of the Church united with Christ, in the Holy Spirit, facing the Father. In the Eucharistic encounter the Church takes the whole of history with it into the presence of God. In an authentic Eucharist the Christian community experiences the final return of the Lord when he gathers his people unto himself. But this experience of entering into the Last Day has to result in a transfiguration of every-day life, through simple joy and by the wise and loving utilization of all the powers that God has placed at the disposal of man.

Problems of Orthodoxy

What is suggested above is a description of authentic Orthodox spirituality as it ought to be. The reality of the lives of Orthodox congregations in many parts of the world is far from ideal. Elements alien to Orthodox spirituality have invaded the lives of the congregations. The first among these is a narrow ethnicism. In general the Orthodox congregations are closed communities of a single national or ethnic group.

Even the emigrants from Eastern Europe who have settled down in countries of the West fail to transcend this ethnocentrism. In America, as well as in Western European countries, Churches with the same faith and sometimes with the same liturgical language, insist on remaining separate communities, as in the case, for example, of Russians, Serbians and Bulgarians. America, the melting pot of civilizations, has been till now largely unsuccessful in integrating these various Eastern Orthodox traditions into one single Orthodox Church.

Another alien element in the reality of Orthodox Churches today is their undiscriminating conservatism. Aware of a great heritage to be conserved, they lack the perspicuity of understanding which enables one to discern between the fundamental and the occasional. This undiscriminating conservatism stands in the way of the renewal of the Orthodox Church even in Western countries. In countries like Ethiopia or Greece, this conservatism still has disastrous social consequences. In Eastern Europe, such conservatism leads the Church often to take one of two false positions, total resistance or total conformity to the main currents in society.

The attempt to come to terms with the modern world and with the new ecumenical situation began in the last century with the great Russian theologian, Alexis Khomiakov. When the Orthodox Church first confronted the debate between the Roman Catholic Church and the Reformers, it sought at first to take sides in the debate, now arguing with the Lutherans against the Jesuits, now with the Jesuits against the

13

Lutherans. It was Khomiakov who broke through this and began to question the very issues that were being debated. The greatest contribution that the Orthodox Churches have rendered in the past, and are capable of rendering in the future to the ecumenical movement, lies precisely in this ability to go beyond the issues of a divisive debate in order to find a common ground on which all can stand.

Most of the Orthodox Churches, with the exception of the Albanian Church, have become members of the World Council of Churches. Two families of Orthodox Churches then met each other in an unofficial consultation of theologians in Denmark in 1964 and discovered that they were separated from each other for some fifteen centuries by reasons more cultural than theological.

Within the family of the World Council of Churches, the meeting between East and West has been in process for decades. The difficulty for mutual understanding stems not only from the paucity of Eastern scholars who can communicate in the idioms of the West, but also from the even greater dearth of Western scholars who have devoted a lifetime to study of, and involvement in, the life of the Eastern Churches.

THE WORLD PENTECOSTAL MOVEMENT

by

DAVID J. DU PLESSIS

World Movement

The modern Pentecostal Movement has become a growing and dynamic force in Christendom during the past half century. It has developed into a great evangelistic-missionary surge which has swept to the ends of the earth. Its testimony now stretches from Alaska in the north to Patagonia in the south, from Ghana in the west to Indonesia in the east. The evolution of the Movement, its rapid growth and development, its evangelism and missionary zeal, are now matters of record for all to read. In a Presbyterian Survey, Dr. Charles S. Sydnor Jr. reports: "It is becoming increasingly evident that the Pentecostal Movement we are witnessing—and perhaps have been prone to dismiss contemptuously—is an authentic reformation revival movement of historic significance, equal with those other great movements of centuries past."

The beginnings

This Revival began simultaneously in the United States of America, Scandinavia, Europe, South Africa, Canada, India, China, South America and the Islands of the Sea. The Pentecostal Movement does not owe its origin to any outstanding personality or religious leader, as did the Reformation, the Wesleyan Revival and other great religious awakenings.

"The Pentecostal Movement is a biblicistic-ecstatic movement which sprang into being . . . at the turn of the last century. The most outstanding characteristic of the Movement is the doctrine of Spirit baptism as an experience different from conversion, manifested by speaking with tongues. The movement pretends to represent a restoration of original Christianity, and has above all emphasized the charismatic gifts, such as glossolalia and supernatural healing. The doctrine of sanctification is for the most part nearly the same as that of early Methodism, and concerning Baptism the teaching and practice is Baptistic" (Nils Bloch-Hoell in *The Pentecostal Movement*).

This writer says further that: On the whole, the Pentecostal Movement . . . has evolved rapidly from its charismatically spontaneous beginnings to a dogmatic institutionalism, and now appeals to a higher social stratum than in the beginning. The Puritanism in the larger denominations is decreasing, and these churches are more influenced by the general culture and education. But the distinctive character of the Movement is still very apparent, and the primitive and expansive power of the Pentecostals seems to remain unimpaired.

Missions

While it is true that the Pentecostal Experience is at the very heart of the Movement as a distinctive testimony, it is equally as true that Mission and Evangelism has been its drive from the earliest days. Before "assemblies" of believers had developed, some of those who had first come into the experience were on their way to distant heathen lands as "faith" missionaries.

Without home boards or guarantee of support, many sold all they had and went to the foreign field. Their work became indigenous, for there was no control from any sending church or board.

"The Pentecostal Movement represents, in some sense, the only Christian movement with real indigenous roots here in Latin America," says W. Dayton Roberts in his report on *Pentecost South of the Border, as seen by a Protestant*. He further says: "If indeed we represent the science, the method, the theology, they represent the Spirit, the passion, the incarnation. The first is not worth much without the second."

This indigenous character of the Movement in all nations has been a source of rich initiative in its development. With the transition of "Mission churches" into "mother churches" there was little need for consultation with "home boards" of sending churches. The vast missionary forces of the Pentecostal Movement, which seem to maintain a steady 10 per cent of all Protestant missionaries, work as teachers, consultants and fraternal workers. Almost two-thirds of the Pentecostal community in the world are joined to the Movement as a result of Missions.

Organization

The pioneers of the Movement originally visualized a revival that was to touch and inspire every section of the Christian Church. These men came from those Churches. However, vehement opposition from within the historic Churches compelled them to withdraw and develop new "assemblies". Soon conferences were held and councils were formed. Publishing houses and bible schools were established in many lands. In all this there was no central control nor much co-ordination. The need for "world fellowship" began to be felt by many. The first Pentecostal World Conference was held in 1947 in Zurich, Switzerland. It was resolved to make this a triennial meeting and thus the 8th World Conference will be held in Rio de Janeiro, Brazil, July 18–23, 1967.

Education

"When the Pentecostal Movement began about 1900 it was largely a reaction against arid intellectualism and modernism in the Churches. Consequently a foolish premium was placed upon ignorance. This resulted in widespread fanaticism. Now the pendulum is swinging in the opposite direction, and great emphasis is being placed upon scholastic attainment. Liberal arts colleges are being established and degrees are coveted by a new generation of Pentecostal preachers" (the late Donald Gee in *Christian Life*, July 1966).

The most ambitious scheme of all this is embodied in the new Oral Roberts University in Tulsa, Oklahoma. "This University is dedicated to the promotion of total human excellence: spiritually, intellectually, and also physically, in a Christian environment," says Oral Roberts, the founder and president. *The Tulsa Tribune* reports that "The University has perhaps the best physical plant in the nation for an institution of higher learning only one year old."

Recognition

Contemporaries are rarely capable of assessing the full impact of an historical event upon the life of humanity, but the movement of the current indicates the direction of the stream. Whilst the aloofness of Pentecostals from political and industrial problems has obscured the extent of their spiritual work, yet the absolutely world-wide impact of the Movement, possibly something unique in history, is a remarkable fact which cannot fail to impress open and thoughtful minds.

In recent years this Movement has attained sufficient significance to be called by some a "third force in Christendom". In writing about this "third force" in *Life* magazine, Dr. Henry P. van Dusen, noted Presbyterian and inter-church leader, says: "Until lately, Protestants regarded this movement as a temporary and passing phenomenon, not worth much attention. Now there is a growing, serious recognition of its true dimensions and probable permanence. The tendency to dismiss its Christian message as inadequate is being replaced by a chastened readiness to investigate the secrets of its mighty sweep, especially to learn if it may not have important, neglected elements in a full and true Christian witness." Preaching in St. Paul's Cathedral, London, Dr. Donald Coggan, the Archbishop of York, found reason to say, "To neglect what is one of the most extraordinary features of religious life in the twentieth century is to show lack of responsibility or an unreadiness to face the evidence."

The future

"Though dangers are implicit in the stage of institutional development at hand for the Pentecostal Movement, it will, I believe, emerge stronger and more effective, having kept pace with the times in terms of

17

program and methods, but remaining the same in terms of doctrine and mission. By enlarging their services to meet people's pressing needs yet retaining their fervour, their distinctive characteristics, their mission, the Pentecostal groups will make a unique contribution to modern Christendom" (Klaude Kendrick in *Christian Century*).

The value, then, of the contribution that the Pentecostal Movement can make to the Church Universal seems almost too obvious to need amplification. To recapture the power and presence of the Holy Spirit in the Church as enjoyed by the early Christians is RENEWAL in the best sense of the word, for it means NEW LIFE.

THE CHURCH
IN LATIN AMERICA

by

Emilio Castro

L ATIN AMERICA is living its hour of high tension, on the social, political and economic field. Guerilla-wars, strikes, military *coup d'état*, landing of foreign troops—all these are signs of a situation which is steadily deteriorating and moving towards profound social changes. The growth of the population, which is not accomplished by corresponding and necessary growth in the number of opportunities of personal development, leads to the accumulation of human beings on the fringes of big cities, uprooted masses, living on the margin of society. Estimates maintain that the slums of the Latin American cities are growing at a rate of 17 per cent per year. The attraction of the cities and the exodus from the country are starting to integrate the *indio* into the life of the nation, although this means, in the first instance, placing him on a level of misery which is even lower than the one which he left behind on the "hacienda". This means that there is a growing sector of the population with a strong feeling of social uprootedness which constitutes a great potential for a radical change.

The feeling of uprootedness which we can classify as a symbol of the situation in Latin America is an important factor also in the rapid process of secularization similar, although chronologically retarded, to that in Europe. The traditional routes of conduct are being abandoned whereas there is no clear line as yet to follow in the future. In the sophisticated atmosphere of the universities secularization as the basic attitude and Marxism as the valid philosophy tend to be generally accepted.

In the face of this background of uprootedness, tension and secu-larization we must try to understand the situation of the Christian churches. Roman Catholicism came to Latin America as the religion of the conqueror. That has determined its policy up to the present: the natural defender of the *status quo* with which it is identified. For this reason "religion" always tended to be something superficial, exterior and formalistic, unwilling to question the basic ideas of the current type of Latin American Society. Until a very short time ago the "Christendom" concept reigned in its theology. Nowadays, with the Second Vatican Council, the Church has received a new impulse, and fresh winds are changing the traditional picture. A true invasion of

19

priests and foreign orders has come to cope with the chronic numerical deficiency of the Latin American clergy. More important, however, is the fact that they have also come to contribute to a theological renewal and a new understanding of the sense of Mission.

The traditional form of Catholicism is still to be found in some instances of authoritarian paternalism, but they are employed in the battles of the rearguard, which means that they are practically doomed to disappearance. It does not mean that Roman Catholicism has found a definite line of action, but there is a growing conviction that the traditional style no longer corresponds to our times. The social tensions call for serious thought about the re-structuring of society and this is a task in which the Roman Catholics cannot participate in a conservative attitude. The Roman Catholic "recipes" for the participation of the Christian in the social struggle may be divergent, but they all agree in their rejection of the traditional quietism and traditional conformism.

In the task of renewal and actualization of Latin American Catholicism certain institutions deserve special mention, such as the cultural training centre of Cuernavaca, Mexico, which provides studies concerning the Latin American reality and experiments with new forms of ecumenism; the work of certain orders, such as Dominicans, the Jesuits and the Franciscans, who have launched a true intellectual and spiritual struggle for the renewal of the understanding of the Christian message through theological reflection, and in an attempt to embody it in a genuine form of Christian presence in society.

Considering the geographic and human extension of the areas and the limits of this short article, it is, of course, necessary to make generalizations and to be unfair in the judgment of many persons and orders within the Roman Catholic Church in their striving for renewal in the Latin American context. The groups mentioned are those of which the author has personal knowledge.

Even the hierarchy of the church, on the institutional level, is searching for the formation of a Latin-American conscience by means of the establishment and the work of a number of commissions for the study and promotion of ideas and concerns on a continental scale. The church is showing a rhythm of activity which is completely in keeping with the exigencies of our time. Thus it can again be taken into consideration as a positive factor for social change; it has regained a fair portion of the intellectual respect of those who are concerned with the renewal of structures in these countries.

Protestantism has now gained a little more than 5 per cent of the population in Latin America, and it is a movement in constant growth. Particularly because of the Pentecostal churches, especially suited for evangelism in the slums, the numerical growth does not lose its vigour. It is the only area in the world where a Christian church is growing more rapidly than the population. (In spite of the fact that this is the continent with the highest rate of population-growth.)

Protestantism came to South America in two ways: the immigration of Protestant communities and missionary work. The result, however, has been similar in both cases: the constitution of islands which were religiously as well as culturally separated from the community. There are differences, of course, as the churches of missionary origin have a proselytic zeal which the others lack; in either case, however, the emphasis was laid upon the incorporation of the individual into the church, which meant separating him from the world.

This Protestant sub-culture was possible while the first generation still constituted the model of conduct, and as long as the small number of the Protestants made them an insignificant community with regard to their contribution in the building of the nation. Nowadays we are living, however, in the second and third generations of Latin American Protestants, and their numerical growth as well as the pressure of events urge the church to face the question of its mission in radically new terms. Thus a number of ecumenical groups like ULAJE (Union Latino Americana de Juventudes Evangelicas—Latin American Union of Protestant Youth), the Christian Students' Movements, and, more recently, the Latin American Commission on Church and Society are trying to develop a Latin American consciousness and thus creating a group of leaders who will be able to promote an active participation of Protestant Christians in the building up of the new morrow of our nations.

In this way we have looked upon the birth of a new type of ecumenism on the frontiers of the revolution, where the churches, challenged by the magnitude of their task, have, to their own surprise, found a common source of inspiration and a common purpose.

We are entering a stage full of new possibilities for the development of the churches, united in their common cause with the development of these countries.

At the risk of oversimplification I shall try to outline the lines of action for the future which can be discerned in the churches in Latin America. With regard to the Roman Catholic Church, on the assumption that there will be no return to the pre-conciliar period—although this possibility cannot be altogether discarded, e.g. the situations in Nicaragua and the attitude of some Argentine members of the Hierarchy—the general direction seems to be clear: to accept the position of the church as of a servant to the world. This new option of the church puts it into a position which is totally different from the traditional conservative attitude. The reason is to be found in the different interpretations of the image of the church as servant by Roman Catholic theologians. Whereas it implies for some persons the total acceptation of the secularization and the recognition that the social and political contribution of the Christian have to be made on the secular level, while the church itself renounces the possibility—more or less openly—of access to a position of temporal power, others still see the possibility of establishing a system of values and rules for society, which can be incorporated into programmes like those of the Christian Democratic Parties which are supposed to form the political alternative to the marxist parties. The growth and scope of the Catholic educational system, the attention which is given to the Chilean phenomenon, the work of the Bellarmino-Centre, etc. lead us to think that for the moment this line is going to be dominant. The other line, theologically more radical—purer, perhaps,—will work as a necessary and useful corrective of the first, and may also avoid its inward logical leading to the formation of a new "christendom-situation".

The most acute problem of the Protestant churches will be the nationalization of the church with its inherent ecclesiastical conflicts with the mission boards, especially in the United States. At the same time there is a new phenomenon, which at the beginning bears a source of conflict, but which promises a more genuine participation in the Latin American process of renewal: the encounter between the so-called historical churches and the pentecostal churches. At the beginning the conflict is of a sociological nature. The members of the first group of churches belong to the middle classes, those of the second to a marginal proletariat. Once the lack of understanding between the groups is overcome, then a true dialogue and mutual sharing in their interests in society will have to follow. Protestantism, too, is—on a different numerical level, of course,—confronted with the choice between the formation of a "Christian Front" and total participation as the servant of society. In general terms we may say that, while the incipient theological reflection is leading towards the second possibility, ecclesiastical and social inertia are leading the bulk of the church towards the first: the formulation of principles or social credos which are to set up standards for society. This form of sharing in the Roman Catholic attitude shows that a phenomenon which was already visible within Protestantism—that is to say that theological divisions do not respect the denominational limits—is also appearing between Protestantism and Roman Catholicism.

It is possible to see a common concern and a link of sympathy among Roman Catholic and Protestant sectors even if it were because of an opposition against another sector within one's own confession. At the same time, this new kind of ecumenism produces its counter-effects in the sense that certain sectors, in one group or another, think that this fundamental concern with the witness to be given to the nations leads to the neglect of the problem of truth and the traditional doctrines. In this way, an ecumenism which includes the Roman Catholics, produces divisions and tensions within Protestantism and vice versa.

As regards their institutions, the Protestant churches are trying to meet the challenge of the hour by means of the creation of international and interdenominational associations, like the *Comisión Provisoria Pro-Unidad Evangélica Latinoamericana*, which is trying to include the churches in a process of study and awareness of their mission in the new Latin American reality.

Within the Roman Catholic Church it is the Bishop's Conference which is the highest responsible organ on a continental level, but its activities are accompanied by an immense net of secular and religious organizations which are working with the same concern.

22

The fundamental question with which the Christian Church is confronted at this moment is the following: Are its life and its structure going to be determined by its loyalty to the past, to tradition, or by its commitment towards the present and the future? Or, in other words: Will the Church allow itself to be formed by its history or by its mission, by its present structure or by its calling?

THE AFRICAN INDEPENDENT CHURCHES

by

DAVID B. BARRETT

SIXTEEN centuries ago, the scholar Jerome surveyed the rapid advance of the schismatic Donatist Church among the North African Berber and Punic populations and reported that it had become the religion of "nearly all Africa". Today's observer of the vast proliferation of ecclesiastical schisms in Africa—4,594 at the latest count—might well be excused for reaching a similar conclusion.

A Phenomenon Unprecedented in History

It is in fact the case that schisms from foreign mission bodies in Africa have been taking place for the last hundred years on a scale unparalleled in the entire history of the expansion of Christianity. These independent Church movements, founded either by direct separation from parent Churches or, in a few cases, under the initiative of African leadership outside the missions, are now found in some thirty-three African nations, with a total of almost seven million adherents drawn predominantly from 270 different tribes in all parts of the continent south of the Sahara.

This extraordinary phenomenon, which has thus been observed in one-third of the tribes of Africa, is at present completely absent from the remaining two-thirds. Further, almost all of these known secessions, from the smallest involving a single congregation to the largest involving nearly a million adherents, have arisen out of a remarkably similar pattern of background circumstances in each of the ethnic groups concerned, yet in most cases without conscious links or visible coherence.

Most of these movements have emerged spontaneously in areas that have been subjected to Christian missionary activity for several decades. The tempo of their occurrence and expansion across Africa has been increasing for the last century since 1862, and shows no signs of abating. In fact, the size of the movement as a whole is now comparable to both the entire Protestant and Catholic communities on the continent.

Moreover, this massive proliferation is, figuratively speaking, only the top of the iceberg—hundreds more of such indigenous movements of renewal or protest remain inside the Protestant and Roman Catholic Churches at varying depths without as yet having broken surface in schism. Nevertheless, conditions within the historical Churches remain

24

sufficiently inhospitable for the movements to break off at a present rate of over one hundred per annum.

The Geographical Distribution of Independency

The present distribution of these bodies across Africa may be examined in detail in the two tables in the statistical section (pages 98 and 227). If we divide sub-Saharan Africa into four regions, it will be seen that West, Central and Eastern Africa each has a total of about one million adherents, while Southern Africa has well over three million.

The first of these independent Church movements occurred in West Africa, where today some 572 separatist ecclesiastical bodies exist, each with its own distinct name and organization. Then, since 1872, Southern Africa has produced at least 3,152 such secessions, the greatest proliferation being among the Zulu of South Africa. In Central Africa, some 563 movements have arisen since 1888, almost all in French-speaking territories; in Congo-Kinshasa alone, 200 bodies have emerged since Independence in 1960. The last of the four regions to become involved was Eastern Africa in 1894; although it has at present the smallest number of groups (291), it contains as varied and colourful personalities and as rapidly-growing bodies as anywhere else on the continent.

The remarkable thing about all these Churches is their ability to survive: at least 90 per cent of all the 4,594 secessions since 1862 still exist as organized bodies. Some idea of the present size of individual Churches, and of the dynamic and picturesque Christianity that they represent, may be obtained from the small selection from various nations shown in the table of Membership Statistics (pages 227–8) and from the names in the Directory (pages 254–6).

The Extensive Coverage in the Literature

Such a fascinating phenomenon has naturally attracted numerous observers, and a considerable literature exists of a total of 1,400 books and articles. With a wealth of vivid detail, these describe movements, personalities, prophets and prophetesses, liturgies, healings, dreams and visions, holy cities, and so on. Most of these studies deal with a single body or area, but a handful attempt an overall description and analysis of the whole movement. In general, they give independency sympathetic and impartial treatment. A whole range of terminology for these Churches is used. Some of the terms in vogue are favourable, describing them as spiritual movements, renewals or revivals; others are more properly descriptive, using such adjectives as charismatic, prophetic, separatist, or schismatic; while still others have derogatory connotations—syncretistic, neo-pagan, non-Christian. The reader wishing to assess for himself the theological calibre of these movements and the nature of their dynamism therefore has at his disposal an unusually rich source of primary material.

Disparate Causes or a Common Cause?

A preliminary examination of the independent churches leaves one with the impression that we have here a mass of disparate and unrelated movements, the causes of which are as numerous and different as are the colourful personalities who lead them. Observers have naturally tended to emphasize local causes, which vary widely from case to case—personal friction, racial incidents, ambition, missionary paternalism, political and economic crises, and so on. From such considerations have grown the valuable typologies under which the divergencies of these bodies have been classified, the best known of which is the Ethiopian/Zionist/Messianic scheme.

Closer analysis has revealed, however, that there are several less visible factors common to the entire range of movements. It has been noticed that in each tribe involved, there are always (a) certain factors representing the strength of traditional African society, e.g. the polygamous structure, or the ancestral cult; (b) certain factors representing the strength of the European colonial impact, e.g. high literacy or the presence of white settlers; and (c) certain factors representing the strength of missionary impact, e.g. publication of vernacular translations of the Scriptures, or high missionary density; and so on. The accumulation of these factors is closely correlated with the onset of separatism, which therefore suggests that the basic cause common to the entire movement is the clash of three cultures, the traditional, the colonial and the missionary. The unique factor here, never paralleled in previous Christian expansion, is the vast proliferation of Scriptures in some 411 African vernaculars. Bearing these facts in mind, therefore, one may speak of independency across Africa as both a single phenomenon and one unique in history.

A Provisional Assessment

Within this overall unity, however, there exists a whole vast spectrum of types of movement, ranging from ultra-orthodox bodies at one extreme to definitely syncretistic bodies at the other. But there is one remarkable fact that must be taken into account in any assessment. Almost all these bodies are characterized by a definite acceptance, often under new and original African forms, of the centrality of the historical Jesus as Lord and Saviour. In varying degrees, in fact, three basic ingredients are found in virtually every movement: (1) a central confession of Christ as *Kyrios* (using the traditional vernacular term for chiefship), (2) a marked resurgence of traditional African custom and world-view, and (3) a strong affirmation of their right to be both fully Christian and fully African, independent of foreign pressures.

What seems, therefore, to be happening all over the continent is that the independent Churches, working quite spontaneously and in the main independently, are engaged in a massive attempt to synthesize the apostolic *kerygma* with authentic African insight, based on biblical

26

insights derived from the vernacular translations. Beyond the tragic spectacle of schism after schism, therefore, one can sense the emergence of a genuinely indigenous renewal of Christianity in terms that can be understood by African Society.

Three Significant New Developments

In conclusion, three quite new developments in recent years may be noted, which indicate a fundamental shift in the relations between the separatist Church movement on the one hand, and governments and ecumenical Christianity on the other.

To begin with, determined efforts have recently been made by bodies across Africa to secure government recognition by applying for registration as legitimate societies. In the case of most of the larger bodies, this has already been successful. In Kenya, Nigeria and Congo-Kinshasa, particularly, there have been so many applications recently that the movement as a whole is being treated with a new and marked respect.

Further, a similar determination is being shown to win ecumenical recognition and to work towards Christian unity. Here it seems as though a definite strategy—almost certainly unorganized and spontaneous—is in process of being worked out. In the first place, importunate applications for membership have been made in increasing numbers since 1955 to National Christian Councils across the continent; but in only a handful of cases, notably in Kenya, Cameroon and Rhodesia, has this membership been granted. When, therefore, such efforts prove fruitless, bodies have bypassed national councils and applied direct to the major ecumenical bodies. Here, their reception has been equally cautious. By 1966, the All African Conference of Churches has accepted into membership only four of the many applying bodies— the African Church (Nigeria), the African Brotherhood Church (Kenya), the African Methodist Church (Rhodesia), and the Eglise Protestante Africaine Baptiste (Congo). Likewise, amongst the applications being considered by the World Council of Churches in 1966 was that of the largest of all the African independent Churches—the E.J.C.S.K. (Eglise de Jésus-Christ sur la terre par le Prophète Simon Kimbangu), with 200,000 adult members.

Separatist bodies have next attempted to form themselves into federations with assistance from liberal elements in the historical Churches. The happiest example of this today is the formation of both the A.I.C.A. (African Independent Churches' Association) and the Assembly of Zionist and Apostolic Churches, both in South Africa, which receive assistance (particularly with theological education) from the Christian Institute and the Christian Council of South Africa. But lastly, if all such ecumenical feelers are rebuffed, the separatist Churches have shown that they can organize powerful rival Christian councils: the East African United Churches organizes forty constituent members, and C.O.S.S.E.U.J.A. (Conseil Supérieur des Sacrificateurs pour les

27

Eglises-Unies de Jésus-Christ en Afrique), from Luluabourg, claims to act on behalf of some fifty bodies.

One final development of major significance for the evangelization of Africa is that independency has now taken on a distinctively missionary character. In at least sixteen nations, separatist Churches are growing faster than their Protestant or Roman Catholic counterparts. In West Africa, where the historical Churches are making little headway in the Muslim north, separatist congregations have been established in most of the major Muslim towns and cities. Elsewhere in Africa, numerous bodies have commenced missionary work far distant from their home areas: the E.J.C.S.K. has work in South-west Africa, the Apostolic Church of Johane (Rhodesia) has spread as far west as Luluabourg and Kinshasa, Zionists have moved from South Africa to all adjoining nations, including Mozambique, and so on. The major concern behind this development seems to be genuine evangelization rather than mere proselytism.

Whether or not the historical Churches are able to accept them as partners, it is clear that the African independent Churches are on the crest of a new wave of expansion that is making them a major force in the rooting of Christianity in the soil of Africa.

CONTRASTS IN
CHURCH GROWTH

by

DONALD MCGAVRAN

*M*ISSION *is correctly interested in church growth.* Obedience to
the Lord Who sends us out to disciple the nations, demands
many things, chief among which is church growth. The vast
missionary enterprise has always affirmed its chief purpose to be pro-
claiming Jesus Christ as divine and only Saviour and persuading men to
become His disciples and responsible members of His Church. God
wants His lost children found. He desires the sheer physical extension
of sound Christian churches. Nothing else will redeem the world. Hence
the many ways churches grow and do not grow are of intense interest
to all Christians active in mission.

I. Church Growth is of many Degrees.

*The growth of the Church around the world is marked by great
unevenness.*

In places churches multiply in New Testament fashion; in others little
congregations remain dependent and stagnant. In some lands three
fourths of the population becomes Christian; in others it is difficult to
find one in a thousand who is Christian. Every student of missions is
struck by the amazing contrasts between slow growth and rapid growth.

Notable growth of the Church is to be found in many denominations.
Despite war, schism, and economic disaster, the number of Presby-
terians in Korea doubled between 1953 and 1959. In Uganda, the
Anglicans have grown well and, in Burma, the Baptists. In South India,
between 1920 and 1965 one branch of the Methodist Church grew from
40,000 to 200,000. In Brazil, the Assemblies of God number over a
million communicants. In Chile, Methodist Pentecostals in two
denominations have, in the last fifty years, come to number about eight
per cent of the total population. Miniscule growth of the Church marks
many other denominations.

Variations of growth also occurs within one country. In Panama, one
denomination grows to 12,000 communicants in thirty years, while its
sister denomination during twice that time with far greater resources
stagnates at 600! In one province in India two Churches proclaim the
Gospel; one grows in New Testament fashion, the other, while doing

29

much splendid mission work, establishes a few static congregations. Indeed, in one church, one can readily find two clusters of congregations, the first numbering thousands of full members, the other hundreds. To probe the contrast still further, a greatly growing constellation of congregations usually has in its history a period when it grew very little.

II. Causes of Variation in Rate of Growth.

What are the reasons for slow and rapid growth? Church growth is an extremely complex process. There are tens of thousands of different populations of the world, each marked by its own culture, language, degree of learning, wealth or poverty, city or country surroundings, freedom or oppression, and innumerable other conditioning factors. The Church grows differently in each. Combinations of factors in different proportions, with different time tables, and different outcomes are observable on every hand. Viewing the complex scene, some observers conclude that all the Christian can do is to proclaim the Gospel and leave the outcome to God. Others, fully as dedicated to the sovereignty of God, point out that missionaries always seek to make themselves fit instruments for the Master's use—for example, they learn foreign languages to become better vehicles for the Holy Spirit. Learning the reasons for rapid growth and acting in their light, these others judge, is what any good steward or obedient servant would do. What, then, are some of these reasons?

For most, when there is great growth, "the fullness of time" has come for some segment of the population. Some piece of the mosaic which makes up mankind has turned responsive. Our Lord was speaking of one such piece when He stood by the well in Sychar. Between 1882 and 1889, young *samurai* and other middle-class Japanese became most responsive to the Gospel. The Congregational Church in Japan grew from 1,000 to 10,000 in those seven years. Those who had led the revolt against Spain in the Philippines were, between 1902 and 1920, unusually responsive to the Gospel. What causes such receptivity?

Let us turn, first, to *environmental causes.* Anthropologists say religious change is likely when a population is in tension and crisis. Pastors observe that recent immigrants into a city or countryside are usually open to the Gospel. When war, famine, or pestilence shatters a society, men look for an abiding city. For several years after the Japanese conquest in 1895 the Chinese on Formosa were unusually receptive. The English Presbyterian Church there grew from a few hundreds to three thousand in perhaps four years. Since, in Korea, Christians composed more than half the patriots who in 1919 launched a civil disobedience movement against the Japanese; becoming a Christian appeared a patriotic thing to do. In India, the civil disobedience movement of the same year, led almost exclusively by Hindus, had reverse effects.

Many populations become responsive and others become or continue resistant. The existence of resistant peoples should neither conceal the responsive from us nor determine the main outlines of mission policy. A danger Christian mission faces is that missions to the resistant, to secure the continued evangelization of their peoples, define mission as if the whole world were rejecting Christ. For example, they maintain that mission is Christians simply being there, with a presence willed and determined as a witness to the love of God in Christ. While this may be a plausible definition of mission in Morocco, it is a traitorous definition of mission in Brazil or any other receptive population. Christians must not let resistant populations hide hundreds of millions who are now receptive. Theory of mission should count vast responsiveness a most important aspect of the current scene.

Responsiveness has theological implications. The true and living God, the God of history, acts to turn certain populations responsive. Segments of mankind do not start accepting Jesus Christ accidentally. The Spirit of God moves on the face of the nations. A countryside or city full of potential gospel acceptors has been moved upon by God. His obedient servants, carrying out mission among the two billion who have not accepted the Saviour, might well observe where He is leading.

In addition to environmental, we can observe *missionary causes of contrasts in church growth*. No error in mission is more damaging than to assume that only environmental causes are responsible for rejection of the Gospel. When any church or mission believes its missionary labours are fruitless only because the "field is hard", "the non-Christian pressure is great" or "the hostility is fanatical", it is likely to be mistaken. Most populations have more or less responsive segments in them. Whether these are won or not depends on missionary factors. I list eight of the more important of these.

(a) Populations ripen because, across the years, converts have established a Church and lived full-orbed Christian lives. Frequently, the more churches are planted, the more receptive a population becomes.

(b) Petty expectations of church growth often result in few churches. What the Christian and the missionary expect and pray for, influences what God can give them. Conversely great expectations and great prayers are conducive to church growth.

(c) Hard, bold plans for church growth usually precede and accompany it. Nothing is more likely to prevent growth than good natured "mission work" with vague objectives. If God's messengers do not aim at winning men and nations to faith and obedience (Romans 1:5, 16:26) God is not likely to let them see much church growth.

(d) Lay leadership is a potent element of growth. In most growing denominations we see large numbers of lay witnesses hard at work. Clerical leadership, no matter how competent, when dominant and exclusive, tends to prevent the multiplication of congregations.

(e) Study of church growth, across the denominations and the nations, is a valuable missionary factor. The many branches of the Church demonstrate many varieties of growth and non-growth. When

31

their evidence is neglected, missionaries, missions, and churches achieve less growth than possible. Were they to study other denominations and other patterns through which God is giving growth, they would find they could use many of them.

(f) The sciences of man, notably anthropology and sociology, can be harnessed to the propagation of the Gospel. In themselves neutral, they can be used to discipline the nations.

(g) Great cities are arising throughout the earth. In a few, the Church is growing enormously. In most, it is static and small. The task is not "to reach" the city. The city is already being abundantly "reached" by missionaries—most of them congregate there. The task is to baptize urban multitudes.

(h) Theological training can be a missionary factor of weight, though at present it usually is not. Passage through most theological seminaries turns out ministers who neither feel passionately that the world must be discipled nor have any knowledge as to how it can be. But theological seminaries can reverse this. They can impart passion to reconcile men to God in Jesus Christ and knowledge as to what modes of missionary action God is currently blessing to the multiplication of sound churches.

III. Rich Rewards of Research in Church Growth.

Research is the life blood of most advance. Notable progress in most forms of endeavour follows systematic study of what processes achieve the ends sought. Research in steel and plastic manufacture, air travel, electronics, education of youth, and the diseases and their cures have ushered in a new day.

The hundreds of missions and churches throughout the earth can readily pool existing knowledge about how churches grow and do not grow, search for more, publish findings, ensure that these are read and used, and that mistakes and failures are not repeated. Centres for information and research are an urgent necessity—one in each major area. It may be true, as some assert, that God is withholding His greatest blessing until His faithful servants use adequately the enormous knowledge and experience which He has already given to them. Were missions to devote two per cent, or better five per cent, of their gross income to research in how churches grow, we should, within a few years in many lands, stand in the midst of apostolic growth of Christ's churches.

CHURCH UNION NEGOTIATIONS

by

M. B. HANDSPICKER

UNITY in the Body of Christ is by no means brought about by, nor guaranteed by, institutional amalgamation. However, from the beginning of this century the recognition has grown that institutional separation hampers that process whereby "the whole body ... makes bodily growth and upbuilds itself in love" (Eph. 4:16), since it seems to be the law of separation that it breeds isolation and even misrepresentation of others. There has therefore been a growth in the number of negotiations which seek to overcome separation and aim for organic unity: a unity which seeks to discover the appropriate external forms to nurture and manifest unity in faith and life.

In this essay we arbitrarily take the year 1925 as our starting point since we have more extensive information about developments since that date. We shall mention first some figures indicating the growth of church unions and union negotiations, and then discuss some of the issues which have arisen in the course of such negotiations, particularly as they occur across confessional and polity lines.

Statistics. Since 1925 negotiations have brought 131 *different* churches together into 38 united churches through 44 acts of union. These unions took place in 21 countries on all six continents. The number of acts of union indicates that 5 churches, which together included 16 formerly separate churches engaged in a second act of union. These 5 further unions included 10 additional churches. Of these 38 united churches 12 are at present engaged in further negotiations for organic union. There is much to support the thesis that "union begets further union".

The world-wide character of the movement towards organic union is indicated by the statistics of union negotiations presently under way. There are 121 different churches involved in 46 negotiations in 29 countries, again on all six continents. The more deeply ecumenical character of present negotiations may be seen when one compares the number which seek union transcending confessional differences with the number of unions which have already achieved this. Of the unions since 1925 about one-third transcended confessional differences (14 out of 43). Of negotiations now under way two-thirds seek to cross these barriers (31 out of 56).

33

Issues. In many of the unions, particularly the earlier ones, the major issue was church polity. Congregational, Presbyterian and Methodist churches came together in the United Church of Canada in 1925; similar unions crossing polity lines occurred in China, the Philippines, the United States, and a number of other countries. The polity issue was resolved in different ways; in each instance the united church attempted to forge a form of government, appropriate to its contemporary situation, out of the forms available in its constituent churches.

At the present time the question of the ministry is a central issue for two reasons: (1) Anglican churches are involved in 20 of the 31 transconfessional negotiations at present under way, and they insist that the three-fold ministry of bishop, presbyter and deacon (with bishops in the "historic episcopate") must be the basic form of ministry in a united church; (2) there is a growing awareness that all churches have neglected the "ministry of the laity", so most schemes of union seek to develop a more adequate understanding of the relation between the ministry of the whole Church and the ordained ministry. Another aspect of this issue is the ordination of women: In Asia, Australasia, Europe and North America negotiations are under way between churches which have ordained women presbyters and those who refuse ordination of women. Since there are significant numbers of ordained women in some of these churches the issue will in most instances have to be resolved before union can take place. (In many instances the question of the ministry takes so much energy it can be said that many laymen look upon union negotiations as ministers talking to other ministers about the ministry!)

Another issue which is being discussed in various ways can best be termed "Christian initiation". Churches which practise only believers' baptism (Disciples of Christ and Baptists) are involved in seven negotiations. In some instances the conflict arising with regard to infant baptism has been resolved by suggesting that either kind of baptism will be acceptable in the united church; in other cases a "conscience clause" has been included which would allow a person who has received baptism as an infant, but who later considers this to be no baptism, to receive baptism as an adult. Unfortunately there has to date been too little consideration of the theological questions involved in this conflict. So far, the most extensive discussion in union schemes is contained in the "Joint Report" of the negotiating churches in New Zealand. Even here, although it provides a basis for further discussion, attention is not given to the way in which baptism and confirmation together can be related to the practice of infant dedication and believers' baptism. Until the discussion reaches this stage the various theological ramifications of the issue will not have been confronted.

It should be noted here that theological "spade-work" on these and other problems in church union has been done by the Faith and Order Commission—through its meetings and some of its special studies. These studies, furthermore, are carried out together with Christians from Eastern Orthodox and Roman Catholic churches, giving them the benefit of wider experience and insight. However, the results of these studies need wider circulation and use by the churches. Furthermore, more exchange of ideas and solutions from various negotiations is needed than has heretofore taken place. (While there has been fruitful interchange between Ceylon, North India, Nigeria and Ghana, for instance, the "mother churches" take insufficient interest in what has been achieved in former mission fields.)

Approaches. As experience in unions and union negotiations has increased, many lessons have been learned about the proper ways to go about seeking unity. One of the most important is that negotiations merely at the "top level" of church bureaucracy are out of order at any stage. Increasingly, official negotiating committees seek to involve many people at various levels of the Church in discussion of the points at issue. This is sometimes done by publication of a special journal (like *Church Union News and Views* in North India), or the use of extant denominational periodicals (as in the Consultation on Church Union in the United States), by popular fliers (Ghana), or even by publishing the first drafts of union documents for discussion in congregations (New Zealand).

There is also a tendency towards multi-lateral rather than bi-lateral negotiations. The largest one at present is the Consultation on Church Union in the United States, involving eight churches. In the British Isles, as the result of a resolution passed by the British Council of Churches' Faith and Order Conference at Nottingham in 1964, moves have been made to involve the churches in each nation (England, Scotland, Wales and Ireland) to commit themselves to seek union together. The virtue of this development is that fewer negotiations will be necessary, and the cumbersome legal procedures which are part of institutional unification need not be reduplicated. Most important, however, is the fact that a wider range of theological perspectives is brought to bear on the negotiation process, thus enabling, though not guaranteeing, a more adequate doctrinal basis to be developed.

Unity and Truth. The issues mentioned above were selected because they have provided the most difficulty in union negotiations, not because they are the most important factors in the life of the Church. But, because they loom so large in discussion, the most important aspect of the movement towards church unity is put into shadow. Discussions with Christians from different churches have had the effect of deepening and broadening many people's Christian faith. Negotiations force one to delve deeper into one's own tradition, and dialogue with others often opens one's eyes to facets of Christian truth of which one was heretofore unaware. For the most part union schemes, and records of negotiations, evince commitment to discover a fuller version of Christian faith rather than to compromise on a "lowest common denominator".

However, the "historic distinctives" of the various denominations cannot always be woven into a beautiful fabric! Also involved in dialogue and debate is *Krisis*, judgment. For almost everyone involved this means a decision that some aspects of their traditional denominational life have, for the very sake of truth, to be judged wrong or inadequate—and this is not humanly easy. In short, separation from error and evil is involved in seeking unity: but all seeking unity have humbly to acknowledge that error and evil may possibly be uncovered in their own position—not merely in that of others.

Conclusion. This essay can but point to the bare statistics and a few of the many issues involved in that movement among the churches to seek the unity of the Church "in each place" in such a way that they are "at the same time united with the whole Christian fellowship in all places and all ages" and that "ministry and members are accepted by all, and that all can act and speak together as occasion requires for the tasks to which God calls His people". (*New Delhi Statement on Unity*)

For those who wish more detailed knowledge, especially of particular unions or negotiations, a list of church union surveys is given at the end of this essay. Lists of unions and negotiations may be obtained from the Secretariat of the Commission on Faith and Order, the World Council of Churches, Geneva, Switzerland.

List of Surveys

A Decade of Objective Progress in Church Unity: 1927–1936, by H. Paul Douglass (New York: Harper and Brothers, 1937).

Towards Church Union: 1937–1952, by Stephen Neill (London: S.C.M. Press, 1952).

The Ecumenical Review, April 1954
The Ecumenical Review, October 1955
The Ecumenical Review, April 1957
The Ecumenical Review, January 1960
The Ecumenical Review, April 1962
The Ecumenical Review, July 1964
The Ecumenical Review, July 1966

Note: These surveys in *The Ecumenical Review* are compiled and published by the Faith and Order Secretariat biennially.

ANALYSIS OF CHURCH UNIONS BY AREAS

Area	Countries	Unions	Churches	Trans-confessional	Confessional
Africa	4	8	31	2	6
Asia	6	8	34	6	2
Australasia	1	1	2	–	1
Europe	4	7	17	1	6
Near East	1	1	2	1	–
Latin America	2	2	9	1	1
North America	3	17	42	3	14
	21	44	137	14	30

ANALYSIS OF CHURCH UNIONS BY CHURCHES INVOLVED

Confession	Total number	Transconfessional
Anglican	1	1
Reformed	43	17
Methodist	17	7
Lutheran	42	1
United	5	5
Congregational	12	9
Disciples	3	2
Baptists	5	3
Friends	2	–
Brethren	2	5
	137	50

CHURCH UNIONS CONSUMMATED SINCE 1925

Date

United Church of Canada   1925
  The Congregational Churches
  The Methodist Church
  The Presbyterian Church

Church of Christ in China   1927
  Presbyterian Churches
  Congregational Churches
  Baptist Churches
  The Methodist Church
  Reformed Churches
  United Brethren Church
  United Church of Canada

United Evangelical Church of the Philippines   1929
  United missions of Presbyterian Church, U.S.A.
        Congregational Churches
        United Brethren

Church of Scotland   1929
  Church of Scotland
  United Free Church of Scotland

Korean Methodist Church   1930
  United missions of Methodist Episcopal Church, U.S.A.
        Methodist Episcopal Church, South, U.S.A.

American Lutheran Church (U.S.A.)   1930
  Lutheran Synod of Buffalo
  Evangelical Lutheran Synod of Iowa and Other States
  Evangelical Lutheran Synod of Ohio and Other States

The Methodist Church of Mexico   1930
    United missions of Methodist Episcopal Church, U.S.A.
              Methodist Episcopal Church, South, U.S.A.

Congregational Christian Churches (U.S.A.)   1931
    Congregational Churches
    Christian Churches

Iglesia Evangélica de Puerto Rico   1931
    Congregational Churches
    Christian Churches
    United Brethren

The Methodist Church (England)   1932
    The Wesleyan Methodist Church
    The Primitive Methodist Church
    The United Methodist Church

The Church of Christ in Siam (Thailand)   1934
    Siamese Presbyterian Church
    Chinese Presbyterian Church
    Chinese Baptist

The Evangelical Reformed Church   1934
    Evangelical Synod of North America
    Reformed Church in the United States

The Reformed Church of France   1938
    The Reformed Church of France
    Reformed Evangelical Church of France
    Evangelical Methodist Church of France
    Union of Evangelical Free Churches

The Methodist Church (U.S.A.)   1939
    The Methodist Episcopal Church
    Methodist Episcopal Church, South
    Methodist Protestant Church

The Church of Christ in Japan (*Kyodan*)   1941
    Methodist Churches
    Presbyterian Churches
    Congregational Churches
    Disciples of Christ
    Baptists (some)
    Other churches forced into union during the war have subsequently left the *Kyodan*

The Reformed Evangelical Church of Neuchâtel (Switzerland)   1943
    National Church of Neuchâtel
    Evangelical Church of Neuchâtel, Independent of the State

The Church of Central Africa in Rhodesia   1945
   Congregational Churches (London Miss. Soc.)
   Presbytery of Livingstonia
   Union Church of Copperbelt

The Dutch Reformed Church   1946
   The Dutch Reformed Church
   The Reformed Churches in the Netherlands (in Restored
    Connection)

The Evangelical United Brethren Church   1946
   The Evangelical Church
   The Church of the United Brethren in Christ

The Church of South India   1947
   Dioceses of the Church in India, Pakistan, Burma, and Ceylon
   South India United Church (Congregational, Presbyterian,
    Reformed)
   The Methodist Church of South India

The Evangelical Lutheran Church (Netherlands)   1947
   The Evangelical Lutheran Church
   The Restored Evangelical Lutheran Church

The United Church of Christ   1948
   The United Evangelical Church of the Philippines
   The Philippine Methodist Church
   The Evangelical Church (United Brethren, Disciples of
    Christ, Independent Methodist Episcopal Church)

The Synodal Federation of Lutheran Churches in Brazil   1950
   Evangelical Church of the Rio Grande do Sul
   Lutheran Church in Brazil
   Evangelical Synod of Santa Catarina and Paranà
   The Synod of Central Brazil

The Malagasy Lutheran Church   1950
   Norwegian Mission
   Mission of Evangelical Lutheran Church in America
   Mission of the Lutheran Free Church in America

Philadelphia Yearly Meeting of the Religious Society of Friends   1955
   Philadelphia Yearly Meeting of Friends (Race Street)
   Yearly Meeting of the Religious Society of Friends of Phila-
    delphia and Vicinity (Arch Street)

	Date
United Church of Christ	1957
Congregational-Christian Churches	
Evangelical and Reformed Church	

United Church of Christ   1957
  Congregational-Christian Churches
  Evangelical and Reformed Church

United Presbyterian Church in the U.S.A.   1958
  Presbyterian Church in the U.S.A.
  United Presbyterian Church

American Baptist Convention   1958
  American Baptist Convention
  Danish Baptist General Conference

Evangelical Lutheran Church of the Zulu-Xhose and Swazi
  District (South Africa)   1960
  Evangelical Lutheran Zulu Church (Sweden)
  Zuly-Xhose-Swazi Synod (Berlin Mission)
  Mankankana Synod (American Mission)
  Norwegian Lutheran Zulu Synod

Unitarian-Universalist Association (U.S.A.)   1961
  Unitarian Church
  Universalist Churches

American Lutheran Church   1961
  American Lutheran Church
  Evangelical Lutheran Church
  United Evangelical Lutheran Church
  (Lutheran Free Church included in 1963)

Church of South Arabia (Aden)   1961
  Church of Scotland Mission
  Church of Denmark Mission

Lutheran Church in America   1962
  American Evangelical Lutheran Church
  Augustana Evangelical Lutheran Church
  Finnish Evangelical Lutheran Church
  United Lutheran Church in America

United Dutch Reformed Church (South Africa)   1962
  Union of the five provincial churches in South Africa: Cape
    Province, Orange Free State, Natal, Transvaal, South West
    Africa

United Bantu Reformed Church of South Africa   1963
  Union of Bantu Churches in Natal, Orange Free State, Cape
    Province, and Transvaal

Evangelical Lutheran Church in Tanganyika   1963
    Lutheran Churches of Northern, Central and Southern Tanganyika
    Tanganyika
    Usambara-Digo Lutheran Church
    Lutheran Church of Uzaramo-Uluguru
    Evangelical Lutheran Church of North Western Tanganyika
    Iraqw Lutheran Church

Japan Evangelical Lutheran Church   1963
    Japan Evangelical Lutheran Church
    Tokai Lutheran Church
    Missions of American Lutheran Church, Lutheran Church in America, Lutheran Evangelical Association of Finland, Danish Missionary Society, Christian Mission to the Buddhists, Mission of North Germany

Lutheran Church—Missouri Synod (U.S.A.)   1964
    Lutheran Church—Missouri Synod
    National Evangelical Lutheran Church (Finnish)

United Bantu Church joined by Dutch Reformed Mission
    (South Africa)   1965
    Church of the Transvaal

United Church of Zambia   1965
    Church of Central Africa in Rhodesia
    Church of Barotseland
    Free Churches in the Copperbelt
    Methodist Church

Eglise évangélique réformée du Canton de Vaud   1965
    Eglise nationale évangélique réformée (Switzerland)
    Eglise évangélique libre

United Evangelical Church of Ecuador   1965
    Missions of United Presbyterian Church, U.S.A.
        Presbyterian Church, U.S.
        Evangelical United Brethren Church
        United Church of Christ
        Church of the Brethren

Reformed Presbyterian Church-Evangelical Synod   1965
    Reformed Presbyterian Church in North America (U.S.A.)
    Evangelical Presbyterian Church

Lutheran Church of Australia
Evangelical Lutheran Church
United Evangelical Lutheran Church

ANALYSIS OF CHURCH UNION NEGOTIATIONS BY AREAS

Area	Countries	Negotiations	Churches	Trans-confessional	Confessional
Africa	10	13	36	9	4
Asia	5	6	21	5	1
Australasia	2	2	8	2	–
Europe	3	11	20	9	2
Near East	3	1	4	1	–
Latin America	4	3	8	3	–
North America	2	10	24	2	8
Totals	29	46	121	31	15

ANALYSIS OF CHURCH UNION NEGOTIATIONS BY CHURCHES INVOLVED

Confession	Total number	Transconfessional
Anglican	16	16
Reformed	30	18
Methodist	28	19
Lutheran	13	4
United	9	9
Congregational	11	10
Disciples	5	5
Baptists	4	4
Moravian	3	1
Friends	1	1
Waldensians	1	1

NEGOTIATIONS FOR ORGANIC UNION NOW UNDER WAY

AFRICA

Cameroon
    Presbyterian Church in West Cameroon
    Eglise évangélique du Cameroun
    Eglise Presbytérienne Camerounaise

Ghana*
    Diocese of Accra (Church of the Province of West Africa, Anglican)
    Methodist Church
    Evangelical Presbyterian Church
    Presbyterian Church of Ghana

Kenya-Tanzania*
  Methodist Church in Kenya
  Presbyterian Church in East Africa
  Anglican Church of the Province of East Africa
  Moravian Provinces in Tanzania
  Evangelical Lutheran Church of Tanzania

Madagascar
  Church of Christ
  Evangelical Church
  Malagasy Friends Church

Malawi
  Church of Central Africa, Presbyterian
  Churches of Christ
  Anglican Church

Nigeria*
  Anglican Dioceses of the Province of West Africa
  Methodist Church
  Presbyterian Church in Nigeria

Rhodesia
  Anglican Dioceses of Mashonaland and Matabeleland
  Methodist Church
  Presbyterian Church

South Africa
  Church of the Province of South Africa (Anglican)
  Methodist Church

  Church of the Province of South Africa (Anglican)
  Presbyterian Churches

  United Congregational Church of South Africa*
    Congregational Union of South Africa
    Congregational Church in Africa
    London Missionary Society Churches in South Africa, Bechuana-
      land and Rhodesia

  United Presbyterian Church of Southern Africa*
    Presbyterian Church of South Africa
    Bantu Presbyterian Church
    Tsonga Presbyterian Church

  United Lutheran Church in Southern Africa
    German Churches of South West Africa, Cape and Transvaal
    Other Lutheran Churches both white and non-white

43

Zambia
United Church of Zambia
Anglican Church of Zambia

ASIA

Burma
Methodists in Upper Burma
Methodists in Lower Burma

Ceylon*
Church of India, Pakistan, Burma and Ceylon (Anglican)
Methodist Church
Baptist Church
Presbyterian Church
Jaffna Diocese of the Church of South India

North East India*
Baptist Churches
Presbyterian Church
United Church of North India
Lutheran Churches
Church of India, Pakistan, Burma and Ceylon (Anglican)

North India and Pakistan*
Church of India, Pakistan, Burma and Ceylon (Anglican)
Baptist Churches
Disciples of Christ
Methodist Church-British and Australasian Conference
Methodist Church in Southern Asia (Episcopal)
United Church of North India

Papua
The United Church of Melanesia
The Papua Ekalesia
The United Church in North Australia and the Territories
The United Methodist Synod in Melanesia

South India*
Church of South India
Federation of Evangelical Lutheran Churches

AUSTRALASIA

Australia*
  The United Church of Australia
    Congregational Union of Australia
    Methodist Church of Australasia
    Presbyterian Church of Australia

New Zealand*
  United Church of New Zealand
    Presbyterian Church of New Zealand
    Methodist Church of New Zealand
    Congregational Union of New Zealand
    Associated Churches of Christ in New Zealand
    Church of the Province of New Zealand (Anglican)

EUROPE

Germany
  Die Methodistische Evangelische Freikirche
    Methodist Church
    Evangelical Community

  Evangelisch-Lutherische (Altlutherische) Kirche
  Selbständige Evangelisch-Lutherische Kirche
  Evangelisch-Lutherische Freikirche
  Evangelisch-Lutherische Bekenntniskirche in Deutschland

United Kingdom and Ireland
  Church of England*
  Methodist Church

  Church of England*
  Presbyterian Church of England
  Church of Scotland
  Episcopal Church in Scotland

  Church of Scotland
  Congregational Union of Scotland

  Presbyterian Church of England
  Congregational Church of England and Wales

  Church of Wales
  Methodist Church

  Presbyterian Church of Ireland
  Methodist Church in Ireland

United Kingdom and Ireland—*continued*
  Church of Ireland (Anglican)
  Methodist Church in Ireland
  Presbyterian Church of Ireland

  Baptist Union of Wales*
  Congregational Church of England and Wales
  Presbyterian Church of Wales
  Methodist Church
  Union of Welsh Independents

NEAR EAST

  Evangelical Episcopal Church (Diocese of Jordan, Lebanon, and
    Syria)
  Evangelical Synod of Syria and Lebanon (Presbyterian)
  National Evangelical Church of Beirut (Congregational)
  Lutheran Evangelical Church in Jordan

LATIN AMERICA

Argentina-Uruguay
  Methodist Conference of Argentina
  Methodist Conference of Uruguay
  Waldensian Church (of Argentina and Uruguay)
  Disciples of Christ (Argentina)

Jamaica
  The Church in Jamaica in the Province of the West Indies (Anglican)
  The Methodist Church

Netherlands Antilles
  Verenidge Protestantse Gemeente van Curaçao
  The Methodist Church

NORTH AMERICA

Canada
  Lutheran Church in America (Canada Section)
  American Lutheran Church (Canada Section)
  Lutheran Church-Canada (Missouri Synod affiliate)

  United Church of Canada*
  Anglican Church of Canada

United States of America
 African Methodist Episcopal Church
 African Methodist Episcopal Church Zion
 Christian Methodist Episcopal Church

 Cumberland Presbyterian Church
 Second Cumberland Presbyterian Church

 Moravian Provinces (North and South)

 Pilgrim Holiness Church
 Wesleyan Methodist Church

 Presbyterian Church in the United States
 Reformed Church in America
 Reformed Presbyterian Church, Evangelical Synod
 Orthodox Presbyterian Church

 United Methodist Church*
 The Methodist Church
 Evangelical United Brethren Church

 Consultation on Church Union*
 Protestant Episcopal Church in the U.S.A.
 United Presbyterian Church, U.S.A.
 Evangelical United Brethren Church
 The Methodist Church
 United Church of Christ
 International Convention of Christian Churches (Disciples)
 Presbyterian Church in the United States
 African Methodist Episcopal Church

(* Basis of Union, Constitution or other documentation is available)

World Council of Churches
Division of Studies
COMMISSION ON FAITH AND ORDER
May 1966

WORLD CHRISTIAN STATISTICS

—SOME WARNINGS, AND DISCUSSION ON THEIR FUTURE COLLECTION

by

FRANK WILSON PRICE

STATISTICS are an important feature of our modern world, and most Christians would not deny a place for statistical studies in the records of the Church's life and development. "The science of organizing facts, as in tables or graphs, to reveal or elucidate their significance" is necessary in all fields of human endeavour, including religion. Both the values and the limitations of factual surveys need to be recognized. The assembling of significant numerical data should be followed by careful analysis and interpretation. Effective interpretation depends upon the accuracy and credibility of the data collected and the skilfulness and wisdom of the methods employed. One must always ask, "*Whose* facts are being evaluated?" Otherwise the familar taunt will be invited, "Figures never lie but figurers do."

Opinions differ in religious circles as to the time, effort and money that should be spent on statistical research. We sometimes hear King David's ill-advised census of his valiant men of war used as a warning. David's sin and punishment (according to the story in II Samuel ch. 24 and I Chronicles ch. 21) took place because he was moved by a desire for military and national glory. Other countings, somewhat exaggerated, of the Hebrew tribes were permitted, (for example, Exodus ch. 20, Numbers chs. 1 and 2, Nehemiah ch. 6).

In the New Testament and Early Church period not much emphasis is placed on numbers. Jesus met the needs of individuals and had compassion on the crowds without a shepherd. He miraculously fed the 4,000 and the 5,000. There were 12 apostles, and 120 disciples, men and women, in the Jerusalem company after Jesus' ascension. On the day of Pentecost 3,000 persons were converted and baptized. But in the tremendous geographical expansion of Christianity, that began with Paul's missionary journeys, almost no numerical facts are given. Some statistically-minded historians have estimated a Christian population of around one million at the end of the first century. Dr. K. S. Latourette cautiously refers to various conjectures, based on fragmentary evidence, ranging from one-twentieth to one-eighth of the total population at the time of Constantine's accession, and the opinion of the German scholar Schultz that there were then ten million Christians among the one hundred million of the Roman Empire. (*A History of the Expansion of Christianity*, Vol. 1, pp. 108–9).

By the end of the fifth century the Mediterranean world and adjoining lands were nominally Christian. Attempts to determine the numerical strength of Christianity at various periods in history are generally unsatisfactory. The Church has treasured the promise of our Lord that the Gospel seed would bear fruit thirty, sixty and a hundredfold, and John's vision of the assembly of the redeemed: "a great multitude which no man could number, from every nation, from all tribes and peoples and tongues" (Revelation 7:9).

Several factors have stimulated new interest this century in world Christian statistics: the modern missionary movement, the spread of Christian faith to all parts of the earth, advances in inter-church cooperation and international Christian conferences, the growing attention of governments to censuses which include religious information, and the challenge to Christianity of renascent ethnic religions and rapid population growth.

The *Interpretative Statistical Survey of the World Mission of the Christian Church* (International Missionary Council, 1938), published just before the I.M.C. Conference in India, was a high-water mark in statistical research. It reflected, as the 1925 Survey did not, the significant shifting of gravity from the western missionary societies established by them, and revealed many interesting contrasts and trends. This comprehensive and detailed study* has been succeeded by the smaller but valuable Handbooks published by the World Dominion Press, in 1949, 1952, 1957, 1962, and now in 1967. These have depended on questionnaires, correspondence and the study of official reports of missionary societies, national churches and interchurch agencies and research organizations for their material. They are helpful not only for the facts assembled but also for their interpretative articles on changing situations and new development. The editors have not hesitated to correct errors and mistakes in facts or judgments when these are called to their attention.

Government census figures are helpful, especially as in India, where they give percentages of believers in different religions, based upon government surveys and estimates. The year books of the United Nations and other organizations furnish useful information which, of course, must be used with discrimination. It is relatively easy to collect data on institutions—number of Christian schools, hospitals, theological seminaries, social service centres, teachers, students, physicians, nurses, social workers, etc. The number of missionaries engaged in overseas service may be obtained from the missionary societies. It is far more difficult to secure complete and accurate data on the life and work of the national churches, the number of congregations, leaders, officers, members and statistics on finances and the inclusive Christian community. The co-operation of denominational secretaries, national

* (This study was also materially assisted by The World Dominion Press—Ed.)

Christian councils, and special Christian research centres is indispensable. Unless reports are received from 90 per cent or more of the Christian constituency (Protestant, Anglican, Roman Catholic and Orthodox) it is almost impossible to present a rounded picture and to make valid comparisons from one survey to another.

Some of the reasons for our difficulty in collecting world-wide church statistics are quite apparent. (1) The "younger churches" to which responsibilities for leadership and administration are being entrusted do not as yet have all the facilities, personnel, time and experience required for statistical research that the foreign missionary agencies formerly possessed. However, the situation is steadily improving. (2) Not all churches or church associations keep adequate records of their work. It is easier to gather statistical data from highly centralized denominations than it is from loose fellowships of semi-independent congregations. In a number of cases church records and membership lists have been lost or they are not kept up to date. Information on absent members is lacking. On the other hand, some of the new evangelistic sects are tempted to exaggerate their number of converts. If the sources of information are not thoroughly reliable the whole survey suffers; guess-work cannot take the place of facts. (3) There is no uniform terminology. "Organized congregation" is clear; what is the difference between unorganized congregation, branch church or chapel, worship centre, place having regular service, etc.? Various terms are used for Christian disciples—communicants, baptized non-communicants, total baptized (including infants), catechumens (or other name) who are undergoing instruction and preparing for baptism, friends of the Church. *The Christian Handbook of India* lists under each denomination the number of full members (communicants) and the estimated Christian community. The Church of South India in its reports distinguishes communicants, baptized Christians not yet admitted to Holy Communion, and baptized children, each group accounting for about one-third of the total membership of about 1,100,000. The Christian Year Books of Japan, the Philippines, Korea and other countries, give figures for church membership only; this presumably includes baptized and communicant members and in some denominations also baptized infants (similar to Roman Catholic and Orthodox practice). "Members" is not an exact designation in either Occidental or Oriental communions. "Christian community" is another useful but rather hazy term which seeks to take in the concentric circles of Christian discipleship or preference. It may, in many denominations, include occasional attendants at services and even "hidden Christians". (4) Churches are in various stages of growth and development, or sometimes decline, which the statistical data do not show. How many enrolled members are really active and earnest in the work of the Church? How many churches have full-time ordained ministers, or part-time pastoral supervision with help from lay workers, paid or unpaid? Are they strong, self-reliant congregations or are they dependent upon outside grants and subsidies? (5) Wide discrepancies

50

between the data supplied by the national church and the foreign missionary society may lead to misunderstanding. The English *Prayer Calendar of Christian Missions in Korea and General Directory* (1964) gives the "constituency" of the Presbyterian Church in Korea as 348,904, while the baptized membership in the 23 presbyteries is reported by the General Assembly as 89,812 or one-fourth of the constituency. Usually the "community" is not more than twice the baptized membership. (6) For statistics of the Roman Catholic and Orthodox churches and their various orders, rites, or branches, we are dependent upon officials of these communions and their own published reports. The gap at times between their figures and estimates by outside, objective observers makes the work of the statistician trying. The same is true of the estimated number of believers in non-Christian faiths; one must try to judge between various estimates based on uncertain sources. (7) The result of our Christian research is often not seen in relation to the better knowledge of nations and societies given to us by secular agencies population, analyses, changes in rural-urban ratio, new developments in education, community improvement, etc.

A few suggestions might be given for the consideration of those engaged in or interested in Church statistics. (1) Accurate primary data lead to more dependable surveys. Frequent errors or omissions are compounded in the sum totals of various columns and reduce the usefulness of the research effort. (2) It is better not to depend too heavily on written questionnaires. Obtain as much information as possible from annual church reports and other publications, natural channels through which to reach reporters in the field. (3) Give a clear definition of all terms and categories employed in the survey. Some standardization of nomenclature is greatly needed. The word "Christian", I think, should be applied to all followers of Christ, whether Protestant, Anglican, Roman Catholic or Orthodox. From this standpoint the Philippines are a dominantly Christian (Roman Catholic) country in which Protestants and other non-Roman bodies have a minority membership of two to three million persons. (4) Although the reliability may be open to question, statistical information from churches under totalitarian regimes should still be sought. (5) Facts about national churches and foreign missionary societies should be kept in separate tables; institutions and personnel may be included in one or the other category. Believers should not be listed as "belonging" to missionary organizations from abroad.

A vital question today is the proportion of Christians in the rapidly expanding world population and changes taking place in this ratio. For several decades the Christian population of the earth has been about 30 per cent of the world's population. With the present population explosion this proportion has begun to shrink, and if trends today continue, the year A.D. 2000 will see only 20 per cent of the world Christian, divided as follows: Roman Catholic 12 per cent, Protestants and Anglicans 5 per cent, Orthodox and Old Catholics 3 per cent. Assuming that the Christian world population maintains its present

51

spiritual growth rate in the next thirty-five years it will be expanding only one third as rapidly as the whole world's population. The evangelistic and missionary task has only just begun.

This may be an opportune time to establish a world-wide co-operative agency for gathering and making generally available essential information in furtherance of the most vital objects of the world mission. In this enterprise we should seek the help of both the World Council of Churches and the World Evangelical Fellowship, Roman Catholic and Orthodox bureaux of information, World Dominion Press, the Missionary Research Library, and other research agencies. There is need for careful, co-ordinated study, thinking and planning. And, above all, for renewed emphasis on the intangible, immeasurable but ever powerful spiritual forces which must inspire the task of world evangelism and the building of the Christian Church on earth. Our goal is not primarily statistical gains; we offer our deepest thanksgiving when we find that "faith is growing abundantly and the love of everyone for one another is increasing." (II Thessalonians 1:3.)

BIBLE SOCIETIES AND THEIR AREAS OF WORK

I. Members of the United Bible Societies

American Bible Society
Argentine Bible Society
Austrian Bible Committee
Belgian Bible Society
Bible Society of Brazil
Bible Society of India
Bible Society of Mexico
Bible Society of South Africa
British and Foreign Bible Society
British and Foreign Bible Society in Australia
British and Foreign Bible Society: New Zealand
Canadian Bible Society
Danish Bible Society
Finnish Bible Society
French Bible Society
Hibernian Bible Society
Icelandic Bible Society
Indonesian Bible Society
Japan Bible Society
Korean Bible Society
National Bible Society of Scotland
Netherlands Bible Society
Norwegian Bible Society
Philippine Bible Society
Swedish Bible Society
Swiss Bible Society
German Bible Societies

II. Associate Members of the United Bible Societies

Bible Societies in Malaysia, Singapore and Brunei
Bible Society Cameroun-Gabon
Bible Society of Burma
Bible Society of Ghana
Bible Society of Nigeria
Bible Society of West Pakistan
Ceylon Bible Society
Malagasy Bible Society

53

III. Other National Bible Societies

China Bible Society
Hungarian Bible Council
(These two Societies are at their own request temporarily disassociated from membership in the United Bible Societies.)

IV. Bible Society Agencies

Bible Society work in the following countries is the responsibility of two or more national Bible Societies working in co-operation, as indicated in brackets (see key). The Society whose name appears first administers the work of the Agency, of which the headquarters is in the country appearing first in the list.

Africa

Algeria, Gibraltar, Libya, Malta, Morocco, Tunisia   (ABS/BFBS)
Angola ..   ..   (BFBS/ABS)
Burundi, Rwanda   ..   ..   (BFBS/ABS)
Central African Republic, Chad, Congo Republic
   (Brazzaville) ..   ..   (ABS/BFBS)
*Congo Democratic Republic (Kinshasa)   ..   ..   (ABS/BFBS)
*Ethiopia, Aden, Somali Republic, Somaliland   ..   (ABS/BFBS)
Ivory Coast, Dahomey, Guinea, Mali, Mauritania,
   Niger, Senegal, Togo, Upper Volta   ..   ..   (ABS/BFBS)
*Kenya, Mauritius and Seychelles, Tanzania, Uganda   (BFBS/ABS)
*Liberia ..   ..   (BFBS/ABS)
*Malawi ..   ..   (NBSS/ABS/BFBS)
Mozambique ..   ..   (SBS/BFBS/NBSS)
Rhodesia   ..   ..   (BFBS/ABS/NBSS)
*Sierra Leone, Gambia ..   ..   (BFBS/ABS)
Sudan ..   ..   (BFBS/ABS)
U.A.R.—Egypt ..   ..   (ABS/BFBS)
*Zambia ..   ..   (ABS/BFBS/NBSS)

Latin America

Bolivia ..   ..   (BFBS/ABS)
Chile ..   ..   (BFBS/ABS)
Colombia   ..   ..   (ABS/BFBS)
*Cuba ..   ..   (CBS/ABS/BFBS)
Ecuador ..   ..   (ABS/BFBS)
Guatemala, Costa Rica, *El Salvador, *Honduras,
   *Nicaragua, *Panama   ..   ..   (ABS/BFBS)
*Haiti, French Antilles ..   ..   (ABS/BFBS)
Jamaica, Bahamas, Barbados, Bermuda, Guyana,
   British Honduras, Trinidad and Tobago, Windwards
   and Leewards   ..   ..   (CBS/ABS/BFBS)
*Peru ..   ..   (ABS/BFBS)

```
*Puerto Rico, Dominican Republic, Virgin Islands  ..   (ABS/BFBS)
*Uruguay, *Paraguay  ..   ..   ..   ..   (ABS/BFBS/NoBS)
*Venezuela  ..   ..   ..   ..   ..   ..   (ABS/BFBS)
```

Asia

```
Cyprus  ..   ..   ..   ..   ..   ..   ..   (BFBS/ABS)
Hong Kong  ..   ..   ..   ..   ..   (BFBS/ABS/NBSS)
Iran  ..   ..   ..   ..   ..   ..   ..   (BFBS/ABS)
*Lebanon, Iraq, Jordan, *Syria  ..   ..   ..   (ABS/BFBS)
*Pakistan (East) ..   ..   ..   ..   ..   ..   (BFBS/ABS)
*Taiwan  ..  ·  ..   ..   ..   ..   ..   (ABS/BFBS/NBSS)
Thailand, Laos ..   ..   ..   ..   ..   ..   (ABS/BFBS)
Vietnam (South), Cambodia  ..   ..   (ABS/BFBS/BFBSA)
```

Europe

```
Greece  ..   ..   ..   ..   ..   ..   ..   (BFBS/ABS)
Italy  ..   ..   ..   ..   ..   ..   ..   (BFBS/ABS)
Poland  ..   ..   ..   ..   ..   ..   ..   (BFBS/ABS)
Portugal ..   ..   ..   ..   ..   ..   ..   (BFBS/ABS)
Turkey  ..   ..   ..   ..   ..   ..   ..   (BFBS/ABS)
Yugoslavia  ..   ..   ..   ..   ..   ..   (BFBS/ABS)
```

In the following countries and areas, Bible Society work is the responsibility of a single national Society.

```
Israel (Agency)  ..   ..   ..   ..   ..   ..   (NoBS)
Spain (Agency)  ..   ..   ..   ..   ..   ..   (BFBS)
Surinam, Bonaire, Curaçao  ..   ..   ..   ..   ..   (NBS)
French Guiana  ..   ..   ..   (in association with FBS) (NBS)
Marshall, Mariana, Caroline and other islands north of the
    Equator ..   ..   ..   ..   ..   ..   ..   ..   (ABS)
Fiji, Gilbert and Ellice Islands, New Caledonia, New Hebrides,
    Samoa, Tahiti, Tonga ..   ..   ..   ..   ..   (BFBSNZ)
Pacific Islands other than the above  ..   ..   ..   (BFBSA)
New Guinea and Papua (Agency)  ..   ..   ..   (BFBSA)
```

```
Key:   ABS  ..  American Bible Society
      BFBS  ..  British and Foreign Bible Society
     BFBSA  ..  British and Foreign Bible Society in Australia
    BFBSNZ  ..  British and Foreign Bible Society in New Zealand
       CBS  ..  Canadian Bible Society
      NBSS  ..  National Bible Society of Scotland
       NBS  ..  Netherlands Bible Society
      NoBS  ..  Norwegian Bible Society
       SBS  ..  Swiss Bible Society
```

* In countries marked thus a local advisory committee has been set up.

STATISTICS

Notes on the use of the Statistical Section
(*See also* Editor's Foreword and article by Frank W. Price, pp. xiii and 48.)

The following guidance was given to those to whom questionnaires were sent:

1. PLACES OF WORSHIP
   "This figure should include all cathedrals, churches, chapels and other buildings which are regular places of public worship."

2. COMMUNICANTS OR FULL MEMBERS
   "This will include the communicants or full members of the various churches. All who take communion or are recognized as being in full membership of the church in question should be included. If you find this classification inadequate please indicate how you define your answers to this question and also to the next."

3. TOTAL CHRISTIAN COMMUNITY
   "This will include all communicants and full members, as above, and in addition all participants in the life of your church, such as regular worshippers, children of Christian parents, catechumens, and members of functional groups, etc., associated with your own church or denomination."

4. STAFF
   (*a*) *National workers*
   "Under this heading it is hoped to give the numbers who are full-time workers in connection with the church in question, showing also whether they are ordained, recognized priests or pastors, or whether they are laymen. Please indicate how many are men and how many are women. Under this heading do not include 'foreign missionaries'."

   (*b*) *Missionaries*
   "Please indicate here the number of missionaries or other full-time workers you have in your country from other countries or churches, irrespective of the work they do, i.e. evangelistic, medical, educational, etc., or how they are supported."

Despite the above guidance, some churches and missions were unable, for various reasons (political, church laws, etc.), to act upon it. Some were only able to give us figures for category "2", others for category "3", and some, none at all.

5. When no figures for the column "Latest available figure" is given, the 1962 figure is used in the total. When this also is missing for "Total Christian Community" the figure for "Full Members" is used, if given, for totalling.

   In the Statistical sheets for Africa the difference between the sum of figures given and the total is indicated by the letter "N", meaning "Not reported".

6. Roman Catholic figures, Orthodox Churches and African Independent Churches, are not included in these Statistical Tables but are given separately on pages 221 to 228.

7. Key to symbols or abbreviations used.

   Sources of Information:

   A. Direct from the Church or Mission named.
   B. From the Headquarters of the Church, Society or Mission.
   C. From the National Christian Council of the Country concerned.
   D. From a Year Book or other source.
   E. From the 1962 edition of the *World Christian Handbook*, no other source being forthcoming.

   a, b, c., etc.: is used in footnotes to indicate Missions or Societies co-operating with Churches named.

   Est. = Estimate.

   U = Unclassified. A figure in brackets followed by "U" in "Ordained" column, signifies unclassified national and foreign ministries: in "Lay" column, it signifies unclassified men and women and foreign workers. Some returns have made correct classification in either column impossible. In the African Statistical Tables: —=not applicable, O=zero. A blank space=no information is available.

8. POPULATION

   We have endeavoured to give the latest available figures either from the United Nations, *The Statesman's Year Book*, or published census figures.

9. WARNING

   Considerable effort has been made to obtain accurate and complete information regarding the Christian Church in each country. The difficulty, or actual impossibility of receiving this, particularly for some countries, must be accepted.

AFRICA

ALGERIA 919,352 sq. mls. Pop.: 11,600,000 (1963)

Church or Mission N.B. See notes on Statistics, page xiii	Places of Regular Worship	Communicants, Full Members (p. 57)		Total Christian Community (p. 57)		National Workers, full-time			Missionaries from other Churches or countries, full-time		Theolog. Colls., Bible Schools	Source of Information
		1962 Handbook	Latest available figure	1962 Handbook	Latest available figure	Ordained	Laymen	Women	Ordained	Lay-workers		
Eglise Méthodiste en Afrique du Nord a	8	400	234	1,000	1,000	0	2	4	14	25	0	A
Eglise Reformée en Algérie b	10	—	800	—	1,000	—	—	—	2	1	—	B
Mission Adventiste du Septième Jour *	3	647	149	647	200	7	(16)U	—	—	—	—	D
North Africa Mission †	3	22	N 24	130	100 N 2	—	—	—	2	8	0	A
	16	1,071	407	1,779	1,302	8	18 (16)U	4	18	34	0	

* Includes Tunisia. † Including former Algiers Mission Band. N Not reported. U Unclassified.

Co-operating: **a** Eglises Protestantes de Suisse Romande, Metodistkirkens Misjonsselskap. **b** Action Chrétienne en Orient.

Also working: Bible Mission of Ghardaia, Communauté Evangélique Indépendante, Emmanuel Mission, Evangelical Mission of Medea, Mennonite Mission, Mission Evangélique de Ghardaia, Mission Baptiste Evangélique (German), Open Brethren, Rolland Mission, Sahara Desert Mission, Salvation Army, Southern Baptist Convention, Vennenes Samfunn Norge.
Note: Danske Israel Mission no longer at work.

ANGOLA 471,351 sq. mls. Pop.: 5,012,000 (1963)

Church or Mission	Places of Regular Worship	Communicants, Full Members (p. 57)		Total Christian Community (p. 57)		National Workers, full-time			Missionaries from other Churches or countries, full-time		Theolog. Colls., Bible Schools	Source of Information
		1962 Handbook	Latest available figure	1962 Handbook	Latest available figure	Ordained	Laymen	Women	Ordained	Lay-workers		
Igreja de Deus a	77	1,500	—	1,500	—	(78)U	(170)U	—	—	—	—	E
Igreja Adventista do Setima Dia	63	13,298	17,071	13,298	20,000	—	—	—	—	—	—	D
Igreja Baptista Portuguesa	1	217	25	600	50	—	—	0	0	0	0	C
Igreja Evangelica de Angola Central b	730	22,000	50,000	70,000	200,000	52	840	60	10	37	—	A
Igreja Evangelica Metodista c	713	20,000	14,250	30,000	57,137	53	57	0	2	0	—	B

AFRICA

Church or Mission N.B. See notes on Statistics, page xiii	Places of Regular Worship	Communicants, Full Members (p.57)		Total Christian Community (p.57)		National Workers, full-time			Missionaries from other Churches or countries, full-time		Theolog. Colls., Bible Schools	Source of Information
		1962 Handbook	Latest available figure	1962 Handbook	Latest available figure	Ordained	Lay-men	Women	Ordained	Lay-workers		
Igreja Evangelica Portuguesa de Luanda	3	—	200	—	700	4	0	0	0	0	0	A
Igreja Lusitana Catolica Apostolica Evangelica	1	—	50	—	100	1	0	0	0	0	0	A
Missão Baptista ... d	112	10,856	—	39,862	—	—	—	—	—	—	—	B
Missão Evangelica Filafricana em Angola	427	2,167	5,850	3,543	11,000	36	355	20	3	18	1	A
Missão Evangelica de Cabinda ... e	141	1,465	1,000	3,878	10,611	—	—	—	3	18	1	C
Missão Geral da Africa Meridional ... f	164	2,500	3,480	8,100	—	—	(434)U	—	—	—	—	A
Missões Cristas em Muitos Paises ...	—	—	—	—	—	—	—	—	—	—	—	E
North Angola Mission	—	N4,000	N50,462	—	—	—	—	—	—	—	—	C
	2,432	74,003	95,926	170,781	350,060	224 (78)U	1,856 (604)U	80	18	73	2	

N Not reported.   U Unclassified.

Co-operating: **a** Church of God (Cleveland). **b** United Church of Canada, United Church Board for World Ministries. **c** Methodist-kirkens Misjonsselskap. **d** Formerly Baptist Missionary Society (now largely dispersed northwards into Congo). **e** Africa Evangelical Fellowship (SAGM). **f** Christian Missions in Many Lands.

BOTSWANA   275,000 sq. mls.   Pop.: 540,401 (1964)

Church or Mission	Places	1962 Handbook	Latest available figure	1962 Handbook	Latest available figure	Ordained	Lay-men	Women	Ordained	Lay-workers	Theo	Source
Church of the Province of Central Africa (Anglican) ... a	13	—	1,400	—	—	1	14	0	1	0	0	A
Dutch Reformed Church (Mother Church)	10	3,860	—	21,600	—	1	6	7	3	20	0	E

BOTSWANA—*continued*

BOTSWANA — co-operating / statistics table

												C
Apostolic Faith Mission No statistics available	—	—	—	—	—	—	—	—	—	—	—	
Assemblies of God	—	—	—	—	—	—	—	—	—	—	—	
Evangelical Lutheran Church, Tswana Region	100	—	30,000	—	50,000	—	—	—	—	—	—	
United Congregational Church of Southern Africa **b**	180	—	7,481	—	12,128	10	29	0	4	3	1*	A
Methodist Church of South Africa	—	—	4,437	—	6,508	—	—	—	—	—	—	D
Seventh-day Adventist Church	21	—	2,311	—	—	—	—	—	—	—	—	D
Society of Friends	—	—	—	—	—	—	—	—	—	—	—	
United Free Church of Scotland	—	—	2,000 / N 3,860	—	5,000 / N 25,311	—	—	—	—	—	—	D
	324	3,860	51,489	21,600	101,316	12	49	7	8	23	1	

* Member of United Theological Seminary.   N Not reported.   **b** London Missionary Society.
Co-operating: **a** United Society for the Propagation of the Gospel.

BURUNDI   10,797 sq. mls.   Pop.: 2,650,000 (1963)

Eglise Adventiste du Septième Jour	43	—	5,769	—	43,223	21	(474)U	—	1	25	1	D
Eglise Anglicane du Burundi **a**	400	—	10,081	—	158,792	57	427	—	18	50	1	A
Eglises de Pentecôte **b**	441	—	39,698	—	5,176	17	27	0	18	11	4	B
Eglise Libre Méthodiste	—	2,300	4,548	18,000	4,000	—	—	—	—	—	—	B
Mission Evangélique des Amis **c**	30	—	2,700	—	1,711	—	—	—	—	—	—	E
Mission Evangélique Mondiale **d**	84	1,057	876	6,042	7,523	3	160	2	5	19	0	A
Union des Eglises Baptistes…	70	2,207	2,444	8,815	N 5,769	6	127	24	3	10	0	B
	1,068	5,564	66,116	32,857	226,194	104	1,215 (474)U	26	45	115	6	

N Not reported.   U Unclassified.

Co-operating: **a** Ruanda General and Medical Mission (CMS).   **b** Svenska Fria Missionen.   **c** World Gospel Mission.   **d** Danske Baptistsamfunds Ydre Mission.

CAMEROON 166,700 sq. mls. Pop.: 5,008,000 (1963)

Note	Church or Mission (N.B. See notes on Statistics, page xiii)	Places of Regular Worship	Communicants, Full Members (p. 57)		Total Christian Community (p. 57)		Staff					Theolog. Colls., Bible Schools	Source of Information
							National Workers, full-time			Missionaries from other Churches or countries, full-time			
			1962 Handbook	Latest available figure	1962 Handbook	Latest available figure	Ordained	Laymen	Women	Ordained	Lay-workers		
a	Cameroon Baptist Convention	422	—	26,775	—	31,057	36 (26U)	185 (299)U	1	5	16	1	B
	Eglise Adventiste du Septième Jour	39	6,646	9,108	15,894	—			—	11	27	1	D
b	Eglise Evangélique du Cameroun	1,035	80,479	86,000	250,000	250,000	108	1,300	—				A & E
c	Eglise Evangélique Luthérienne du Cameroun	207	—	13,287	—	22,135	9	242	46	17	—	1	D
	Eglise Fraternelle Luthérienne du Nord Cameroun	190	2,000	2,819	2,000	4,500	7	159	—	11	25 (10)U	9	B
d	Eglise Presbytérienne Camerounaise	1,650	85,000	87,942	135,728	200,000	105	1,582	—	9	70	1	A
e	Mission Unie du Soudan	185	6,438	14,486	8,691	34,000	23	240	—			3	A
	Norske Mohammedanermisjon		—	—	—	—	—	—	—			—	D
f	Presbyterian Church in West Cameroun	681	32,400	53,198	66,301	118,098	52	381	1	12	51	2	A
*	Société Missionnaire Baptiste Européenne	54	—	200	—	2,000	0	5	0	8	17	0	A
h	Union Baptiste Camerounaise		—	500	—	—	—	—	—			—	C
i	Union des Eglises Baptistes du Cameroun	165	—	16,000	—	24,000 N116,394	41	150	—	4	2	2	A
		4,628	212,963	310,315	478,614	702,184	407 (26U)	4,543 (299)U	48	77	218 (10)U	20	

* Cameroun du Nord field only.   N Not reported.   U Unclassified.

Co-operating: **a** North American Baptist General Convention. **b** Société des Missions Evangéliques de Paris. **c** Mission au Sudan (American Lutheran Church). **d** United Presbyterian Church in the USA. **e** Sudan United Mission (Norwegian and Swiss Branches). **f** Coopération Evangélique Mondiale. **h** Basel Mission. **i** Société Missionnaire Baptiste Européenne.

CENTRAL AFRICAN REPUBLIC — 238,000 sq. mls. — Pop.: 1,300,000 (1963)

Church / Mission		1	2	3	4	5	6	7	8	9	10	11	
Eglise Adventiste du Septième Jour		1	—	76	—	—	—	—	—	2	—	—	D
Eglise Baptistes	a	319	15,548	40,000	20,693	50,000	—	(200)U	—	4	(123)U	5	A
Eglise Evangélique Centrafricaine	b	100	424	800	5,500	5,000	2	30	0	10	9	0	B
Eglise Evangélique des Frères	c	300	3,000	45,000	6,000	65,000	60	160	—	—	31	1	A
Eglise Evangélique Luthérienne	d	15	—	—	—	—	—	—	—	—	—	—	D
Eglise du Nazarene		1	2	—	246	50	0	0	0	0	0	0	E
Eglise Protestante du Bangui		—	—	40	—	—	—	—	—	—	—	—	C
Mission Evangélique Elim	e	—	100	—	—	—	—	—	—	—	—	—	C
Mission Franco-Suisse de Pentecôte	f	—	—	—	—	—	—	—	—	—	—	—	C
Union des Eglises Baptistes...	g	90	12,736	16,000 N 102	12,736	25,000 N 422	21	206	38	19	46	2	B
		826	31,810	102,018	45,175	145,472	83	596 (200)U	38	35	209	8	

N Not reported. U Unclassified.

Co-operating: a Baptist Mid-Missions. b African Inland Mission. c Brethren Church Mission. d American Lutheran Church. e Central Africa Pioneer Mission. f Coopération Evangélique Mondiale. g Örebro Missionsförening.

CHAD — 495,000 sq. mls. — Pop.: 3,307,200 (1966)

Church / Mission		1	2	3	4	5	6	7	8	9	10	11	
Assemblées Chrétiennes	a	250	2,000	5,000	6,000	15,000	—	(147)U	72	10	12	—	A
Eglises Baptistes du Tchad	b	150	2,000	15,000	6,000	20,000	25	57	—	10	20	2	A
Eglise Evangélique des Frères	c	30	—	2,000	—	3,000	47	291	—	10	77	—	D
Eglise Evangélique au Tchad	d	372	4,500	18,871	28,000	50,000	—	—	—	—	—	—	A
Eglise Fraternelle Luthérienne du Tchad	e	230	2,000	3,778	2,000	5,800	8	125	—	3	4	3	B
Mission Evangélique du Geura	f	7	—	100	—	200	—	—	—	—	(20)U	—	C
Mission Evangélique du Plein Evangile	g	—	—	—	—	—	—	—	—	—	—	—	D
		1,039	10,500	44,749	42,000	94,000	80	620 (147)U	72	33	133	5	

U Unclassified.

Co-operating: a Christian Missions in Many Lands. b Baptist Mid-Missions. c Brethren Church Mission. d French Mennonites, Sudan United Mission, Worldwide Evangelization Crusade. e American Lutheran Brethren. f Assemblées de France, Mission Evangélique Belge. g Coopération Evangélique Mondiale.

CONGO (BRAZZAVILLE) — 139,000 sq. mls. — Pop.: 840,000 (1963)

Church or Mission. N.B. See notes on Statistics, page xiii	Places of Regular Worship	Communicants, Full Members (p. 57) 1962 Handbook	Communicants, Full Members (p. 57) Latest available figure	Total Christian Community (p. 57) 1962 Handbook	Total Christian Community (p. 57) Latest available figure	National Workers, full-time — Ordained	National Workers, full-time — Lay-men	National Workers, full-time — Women	Missionaries from other Churches or countries, full-time — Ordained	Missionaries from other Churches or countries, full-time — Lay-workers	Theolog. Colls., Bible Schools	Source of Information
Armée du Salut	236	—	6,585	—	27,422	79	280	280	15	0	1	A
Eglise Baptiste de la Sangha ... a	100	—	6,000	—	10,000	—	—	—	2	4	—	C
Eglise Evangélique du Congo ... b	575	49,743	59,318	66,378	110,000	52	721	30	19	56	1	A
United World Mission	—	—	500	—	1,000	1	0	0	0	4	0	C
	911	49,743	72,403	66,378	148,422	132	1,001	310	36	64	2	

Co-operating: a Örebro Missionsförening. b Norske Misjonsforbund, Svenska Missionsförbundet.

CONGO (KINSHASA) — 895,348 sq. mls. — Pop.: 15,007,000 (1963)

Church or Mission	Places of Regular Worship	Communicants, Full Members (p. 57) 1962 Handbook	Communicants, Full Members (p. 57) Latest available figure	Total Christian Community (p. 57) 1962 Handbook	Total Christian Community (p. 57) Latest available figure	National Workers, full-time — Ordained	National Workers, full-time — Lay-men	National Workers, full-time — Women	Missionaries from other Churches or countries, full-time — Ordained	Missionaries from other Churches or countries, full-time — Lay-workers	Theolog. Colls., Bible Schools	Source of Information
Africa Christian Mission	11	—	—	—	—	—	—	0	0	0	0	D
Africa Evangelistic Band	345	525	—	1,500	33,186	—	16	2	—	16	—	E
Armée du Salut ... a	56	30,386	13,160	49,635	50,000	—	814	64	8	26	—	C
Assemblées de Dieu au Congo (USA) ... b	21	760	4,710	48,196	30,613	16	317	14	—	2	1	C
Assemblées de Dieu au Congo (GB) ... c	289	8,418	13,456	21,535	—	6	319	—	—	—	—	C
Association des Eglises Baptistes au Congo-Ouest	116	61,907	113,116	61,907	300,000	8	856	—	22	71	—	C
Association des Eglises Libres de Norvège ... d	114	—	12,755	—	31,150	9	237	24	5	21	1	C
Baptist Mid-Missions ... e	8	10,592	1,920	11,794	6,251	—	(179)U	—	—	(10)U	—	C
Congo Gospel Mission	—	2,450	—	2,940	—	—	140	—	—	39	1	E
Disciples du Christ au Congo ... f	841	73,773	139,403	100,000	200,000	22	1,266	—	10	43	1	A

CONGO (KINSHASA)—continued

Church	(1)	(2)	(3)	(4)	(5)	(6)	(7)	(8)	(9)	(10)	(11)	Code
Eglise Anglicane au Congo	110	—	2,950	—	23,189	7	449	8	0	0	—	C
Eglise Baptiste du Bas-Fleuve ... g	556	—	16,420	—	60,000	6	1,387	51	4	19	1	C
Eglise Baptiste du Haut-Congo g	548	—	24,077	—	50,000	—	—	—	—	—	1	A
Eglise Baptiste du Moyen-Fleuve g	158	—	10,413	—	11,500	3	256	8	1	7	1	A
Eglise Baptiste du Maindombe h	194	17,251	19,502	26,300	45,000	25	446	—	5	19	—	C
Eglise Chrétienne Missionnaire Alliance ... i	856	30,716	10,658	56,081	24,807	40	433	—	9	34	1	C
Eglise des Frères Mennonites au Congo	44	5,399	8,875	17,447	—	14	388	12	2	5	—	A
Eglise du Christ au Congo (AIM) j k	2,000	26,306	30,306	245,064	300,000	34	3,658	—	42	80	3	C
Eglise du Christ en Ubangui ... l	368	14,275	22,273	26,000	86,250	30	700	9	6	44	2	C
Eglise du Nord-Sankuru	57	1,105	4,063	3,736	5,785	—	64	—	2	4	—	C
Eglise Evangélique Béréenne au Congo	500	2,000	—	3,500	15,000	7	470	150	—	—	—	C
Eglise Evangélique de la Lulonga m	487	26,000	33,451	50,000	61,800	34	1,495	6	0	16	1	C
Eglise Evangélique de Manianga-Matadi n	347	27,954	22,487	44,114	49,922	12	2,011	27	3	28	—	C
Eglise Evangélique du Bas-Uélé o	200	13,413	16,000	13,413	30,000	—	158	—	1	1	—	C
Eglise Evangélique du Haut-Congo p	300	9,295	13,000	11,962	25,000	9	478	—	4	11	—	C
Eglise Evangélique parmi les Bayaka A	32	7,500	2,936	16,800	8,500	8	161	10	5	13	—	C
Eglise Evangélique Westcott	8	7,660	1,187	8,886	2,242	1	12	—	0	0	—	C
Eglise Libre Méthodiste au Congo Est	154	4,800	9,698	25,000	18,679	11	209	—	1	3	—	C
Eglise Mennonite au Congo q	740	22,876	38,200	50,000	52,750	32	200	—	11	38	—	C
Eglise Méthodiste, Diocèse du Congo	1,833	35,000	41,450	100,000	150,000	99	(590)U	—	35	130	4	C
Eglise Pentecôtiste du Congo ... r	1,012	20,715	46,721	46,000	65,000	119	—	—	4	14	2	A
Eglise Presbytérienne au Congo s	1,172	69,504	144,001	133,174	175,871	80	1,488	—	12	7	3	A
Eglise Presbytérienne à Kinshasa t	14	—	5,153	—	5,823	3	28	5	1	1	1	C&B
Eglises de Pentecôte au Congo... u	233	45,000	23,966	135,000	37,960	21	287	—	6	21	—	C
Evangelization Society Africa Mission v	392	—	—	—	17,776	—	—	—	3	7	—	C
Fundamental Worldwide Mission	—	—	7,126	—	—	10	432	—	0	0	0	C
Garanganze Evangelical Mission w	132	13,625	—	34,813	—	46	268	—	9	23	2	C
Heart of Africa Mission x	500	6,000	6,500	50,000	22,000	—	470	—	16	24	1	C
Mission Baptiste de Kivu y	276	19,402	7,678	29,600	11,500	3	110	—	1	—	—	C
Mission des Baptistes Réguliers du Canada	5	550	—	1,000	—	1	34	4	—	2	—	C

65

CONGO (KINSHASA)—*continued*

Church or Mission N.B. See notes on Statistics, page xiii	Places of Regular Worship	Communicants, Full Members (p. 57)		Total Christian Community (p. 57)		Staff					Theolog. Colls., Bible Schools	Source of Information
		1962 Handbook	Latest available figure	1962 Handbook	Latest available figure	National Workers, full-time			Missionaries from other Churches or countries, full-time			
						Ordained	Laymen	Women	Ordained	Lay-workers		
Mission Luanza... w	94	5,085	4,939	7,804	7,746	—	—	—	—	—	—	C
Mission Emmanuel w		—	—	—	—	—	98	—	2	11	—	C
Mission Evangélique des Adventistes du Septième Jour	306	—	14,134	—	24,342	56	(1,861)U	—	8	10	—	B
Mission Evangélique du Maniema z	103	5,626	3,624 N19,150	11,108	8,653 N57,700	17	248	—	5	4	—	C
	15,532	625,868	909,458	1,444,309	2,105,995	789	23,033 (2,630)U	394	245	812	26	

N Not reported.   U Unclassified.

Co-operating: a Assemblies of God, USA. b UPMGBI. c American Baptist Foreign Mission Society. d Mission Libre Norvégienne. e Baptist International Mission. f United Christian Mission. g Baptist Missionary Society. h Svenska Baptist Missionen. i Christian and Missionary Alliance. j American Mennonite Brethren Mission. k Africa Inland Mission. l Evangelical Covenant Church of America, Evangelical Free Church. m Berean African Missionary Society. n Congo Balolo Mission (RBMU). o Svenska Missionsförbundet. p Norske Baptisters Kongomisjon. q Congo Inland Mission. r Methodist Church, USA. s Congo Evangelistic Mission. t American Presbyterian Congo Mission. u Svenska Fria Missionen. v Pittsburgh Bible Institute. w Christian Missions in Many Lands. x Worldwide Evangelization Crusade. y Conservative Baptist Foreign Mission Society. z Worldwide Grace Testimony Mission. A Unevangelized Fields Mission.

DAHOMEY 44,290 sq. mls. Pop.: 2,250,000 (1963)

													Code
Assemblées de Dieu		251	5,685	100	28,313	31,631	13	49	0	8	6	—	D
Eglise Protestante Méthodiste	a	49	—	7,353	—	1,850	0	54	0	9	29	1	B
Evangelical Church of West Africa	b	—	—	1,775	—	N 100	—	—	—	—	—	4	B
		300	5,685	9,228	28,313	33,581	13	103	0	17	35	5	

N Not reported.

Co-operating: a Methodist Missionary Society. b Sudan Interior Mission.

ETHIOPIA 395,000 sq. mls. Pop.: 21,800,000 (1963)

													Code
American Faith Mission		14	—	—	—	1,000	—	—	—	—	—	—	D
Baptist Bible Fellowship		4	—	77	—	320	0	14	0	11	12	0	C
Baptist Evangelical Church		4	26	59	217	760	0	—	0	8	29	0	B
Baptist General Conference Mission		1	—	—	10,000	—	22	4	0	7	24	0	C
Bethel Evangelical Church	a	139	4,127	3,311	10,000	15,170	—	45	—	15	80	1	A
Bible Churchmen's Missionary Society	*	4	0	0	0	0	0	6	3	1	15	0	C
Chrischona Mission	†	2	—	25	—	30	0	4	1	1	8	0	C
Christian Mission Fellowship		1	—	14	—	14	0	4	0	0	4	0	C
Christian Missions in Many Lands		2	—	17	—	130	0	3	0	0	9	0	A
Church's Ministry Among the Jews		2	100	200	—	1,000	15	15	6	1	4	0	C
Church of Christ		1	—	—	—	—	—	—	—	—	—	0	D
Disciples of Christ		—	—	—	—	—	—	—	—	—	—	—	
Episcopal Church, Diocese of the Sudan		2	45	130	115	250	2	0	0	3	18	0	A
Ethiopian Evangelical Church Mekane Jesus	b	300	12,937	13,611	25,192	59,510	36	425	0	34	178	14	A
Evangelical Church of Eritrea	c	20	—	2,383	—	5,144	7	62	12	8	10	—	D
Evangelical Presbyterian Mission	d	4	4	4	40	40	2	0	15	3	10	0	A
Fellowship of Evangelical Believers	e	988	66,500	100,000	125,000	125,000	—	900	—	29	239	15	D
Jerusalem and the East Mission		—	—	—	—	—	—	—	—	—	—	—	

ETHIOPIA—*continued*

Church or Mission N.B. See notes on Statistics, page xiii	Places of Regular Worship	Communicants, Full Members (p. 57)		Total Christian Community (p. 57)		Staff					Theolog. Colls., Bible Schools	Source of Information
						National Workers, full-time			Missionaries from other Churches or countries, full-time			
		1962 Handbook	Latest available figure	1962 Handbook	Latest available figure	Or-dained	Lay-men	Women	Or-dained	Lay-workers		
Lutheran Church in Ethiopia ... f	8	250	187	1,000	510	7	195	12	0	18	0	C
Lutheran Church of Eritrea ... f	6	—	346	—	821	4	42	5	0	2	0	C
Meserete Christos Church ... g	17	10	225	35	1,000	3	22	0	11	35	0	C
Middle East General Mission ... h	4	—	—	—	—	0	20	10	1	22	0	C
Philadelphia Church Mission	18	—	2,000	—	6,000	0	15	0	3	12	0	C
Red Sea Mission Team	1	—	—	—	—	—	—	—	—	21	0	E
Seventh-day Adventist Church	55	3,208	8,277	3,208	10,209 ‡	10	376	—	9	24	0	C
Swiss Evangelical Nile Mission	1	—	N 26	—	N 217	0	0	0	0	3	0	C
	1,599	87,203	130,892	164,767	227,125	108	2,152	64	145	755	30	

N Not reported.   * Works within Ethiopian Orthodox Church.

† Switzerland: originally with Church's Ministry Among the Jews.   ‡ Medical and educational work only.
Co-operating: **a** United Presbyterian Church in the USA. **b** American Lutheran Mission, Danish Ethiopian Mission, Evangeliska Fosterlands Stiftelson, Hermannsburger Evangelisch-Lutherische Mission, Icelandic Mission Society, Norsk Luthersk Misjonsambund. **c** Evangeliska Fosterlands Stiftelson. **d** Orthodox Presbyterian Church (USA). **e** Sudan Interior Mission. **f** Missionsällskapet Bibeltrogna Vänner. **g** Mennonite Mission in Ethiopia. **h** Svenska Fria Missionen.

FRENCH SOMALILAND   8,492 sq. mls.   Pop.: 70,000 (1963)

None	0	0		0							0	

GABON

102,290 sq. mls. Pop.: 456,000 (1963)

											Code	
Eglise Evangélique de Pentecôte ...	2	—	200	—	1,000	—	—	—	—	—	D	0
Eglise Evangélique du Gabon ... a	310	16,067	17,850	60,000	75,000	22	195	0	5	26	A	2
Eglise Evangélique du Sud Gabon... b	113	2,180	4,507	3,409	N 4,507	8	61	0	10	20	D	1
	425	18,247	22,557	63,409	80,507	30	256	0	15	46		3

N Not reported.

Co-operating: a Société des Missions Evangéliques de Paris. b Christian and Missionary Alliance.

GAMBIA

4,005 sq. mls. Pop.: 315,486 (1963)

											Code	
Diocese of Gambia and the Rio Pongas (Anglican)... a	14	600	—	600	1,900	3	—	—	0	0	C	0
Methodist Church ... b	5	1,102	1,244	1,767	1,876	1	—	—	2	1	C&E	0
Seventh-day Adventist Mission ...	15	1,017	N 1,617	2,341	N 2,341	(10)U	(50)U	—	—	—	B	—
	34	2,719	2,861	4,708	6,117	14 (10)U	(50)U	—	2	1	E	0

N Not reported.   U Unclassified.

Co-operating: a United Society for the Propagation of the Gospel. b Methodist Missionary Society.

GHANA   91,843 sq. mls.   Pop.: 7,340,000 (1963)

Church or Mission — N.B. See notes on Statistics, page xiii	Places of Regular Worship	Communicants, Full Members (p. 57)		Total Christian Community (p. 57)		Staff — National Workers, full-time			Staff — Missionaries from other Churches or countries, full-time		Theolog. Colls., Bible Schools	Source of Information
		1962 Handbook	Latest available figure	1962 Handbook	Latest available figure	Ordained	Lay-men	Women	Ordained	Lay-workers		
African Methodist Episcopal Church	11	5,000	3,000	10,000	6,058	8	—	—	0	0	0	E
African Methodist Episcopal Zion Church	87	5,000	6,560	9,346	10,594	47	142	25	0	0	—	
Apostolic Church of Ghana	120	5,000	15,000	5,000	—	—	22	—	—	2	0	C
Assemblies of God	180	5,193	6,069	9,140	14,490	—	—	0	11	16	—	E
Baptist Mid-Missions	15	58	188	129	238	0	1	0	—	—	0	B
Christian Methodist Episcopal Church (1,160 Communicants)											—	B
Diocese of Accra (Anglican) a	200	15,000	32,188	50,000	100,000	55	2	—	9	—	1	
Evangelical Lutheran Church of Ghana b	4	—	104	—	158	2	—	0	3	23	2	C
Evangelical Presbyterian Church c	342	24,262	3,371	75,332	—	36	1,350	150	5	19	2	B
Ghana Baptist Convention d	180	2,300	—	4,000	11,000	5	(7)U	12	12	9	—	E
Mennonite Board	1,481	45	263	115	700	—	267	—	8	8	2	B
Methodist Church, Ghana e	686	58,422	69,260	159,254	187,870	116	(84)U	5	30	—	2	C
Presbyterian Church of Ghana f	95	46,147	52,547	180,527	244,405	36	32	17	15	16	—	A
Salvation Army	56	3,806	8,351	6,946	—	18	(37)U	—	—	—	—	E
Seventh-day Adventist Church		6,850	10,034	22,365	—	—	—	—	—	—	0	C
Society of Friends	2	—	27	—	—	—	—	—	2	4	—	E
Sudan Interior Mission	25	—	—	—	—	—	3	—	—	19	—	C
Worldwide Evangelization Crusade		69	—	407	N111,077	—	—	—	—	—	—	B
	3,484	177,152	N24,331 / 234,446	532,561	686,545	323	1,947 (128)U	209	95	116	11	

N Not reported.   U Unclassified.

Co-operating: a United Society for the Propagation of the Gospel. b Lutheran Church, Wisconsin and Missouri Synods. c Bremen Mission, Church of Scotland, United Church Board for World Ministries. d Southern Baptist Convention. e Methodist Missionary Society. f Church of Scotland, Evangelische Missionsgesellschaft in Basel.

AFRICA

GUINEA

95,935 sq. mls. Pop.: 3,360,000 (1963)

Diocese of Gambia and the Rio Pongas (Anglican) ... **a**	4	—	—	800	—	6	—	—	4	—	—	E
Evangelical Protestant Church of the CMA ... **b**	144	15	1,350	—	—	1	(48)U	0	16	35	2	B
Open Bible Standard Church ...	2	—	—	50	—	—	—	—	3	3	0	E
Société des Missions Evangéliques de Paris ...	1	—	N 15	—	N 2,200	—	—	—	—	—	—	D
	151	15	1,365	850	2,200	7	(48)U	0	23	38	2	

N Not reported. U Unclassified.

Co-operating: **a** United Society for the Propagation of the Gospel. **b** Christian and Missionary Alliance.

IVORY COAST

127,520 sq. mls. Pop.: 3,665,000 (1963)

Assemblées de Dieu ... **a**	43	1,500	—	3,000	—	0	52	0	—	—	0	E
Eglise Pentecôtiste de la Côte d'Ivoire	—	—	—	—	—	—	—	—	—	—	—	
Eglise Protestante Méthodiste en Côte d'Ivoire ... **a**	491	11,646	14,064	56,501	68,776	15	92	1	6	13	—	B
Eglise Protestante Evangélique de la Côte d'Ivoire ... **b**	338	—	6,739	—	12,000	0	(34)U	—	9	12	1	B
Free Will Baptists ...	4	—	75	300	300	0	(2)U	—	7	8	1	B
Mission Adventiste du Septième Jour	4	194	218	194	—	0	(26)U	—	—	—	—	D
Mission Baptiste ... **c**	63	52	813	230	900	—	2	10	23	37	1	B
Union des Eglises Evangéliques du Sud-Ouest de la Côte d'Ivoire ... **d**	157	988	1,534	6,500	9,450	8	34	1	18	35	1	E
Southern Baptist Convention	—	—	—	—	—	—	—	—	1	1	0	B
Mission Evangélique d'Afrique Occidentale ... **e**	25	150	300 N 1,500	1,200	2,500 N 3,194	—	77	—	5	14	1	B
	1,125	14,530	25,243	67,925	97,120	23	319 (62)U	12	69	120	5	

N Not reported. U Unclassified.

Co-operating: **a** Methodist Missionary Society. **b** Christian and Missionary Alliance. **c** Conservative Baptist Foreign Mission Society. **d** Mission Biblique en Côte d'Ivoire, Unevangelized Fields Mission. **e** Worldwide Evangelization Crusade.

71

KENYA 224,960 sq. mls. Pop.: 8,847,000 (1963)

Church or Mission (N.B. See notes on Statistics, page xiii)	Places of Regular Worship	Communicants, Full Members (p. 57) 1962 Handbook	Communicants Latest available figure	Total Christian Community (p. 57) 1962 Handbook	Total Christian Community Latest available figure	National Workers, full-time Ordained	National Laymen	National Women	Missionaries from other Churches or countries, full-time Ordained	Missionaries Lay-workers	Theolog. Colls., Bible Schools	Source of Information
Africa Gospel Church a	190	1,576	2,800	6,051	15,000	10	150	5	7	24	2	A
Africa Inland Church b	1,000	23,043	30,000	96,980	130,000	45	250	20	66	246	7	A
Baptist Churches of Kenya c	70	32	4,109	180	8,000	2	68	2	15	21	1	A
Church of God in East Africa	175	28,000	—	33,000	—	229	920	—	7	25	1	E
Church of the Province of East Africa:	—	27,140	—	200,000	—	—	—	—	—	—	—	—
Diocese of Maseno d	850	—	20,817	—	46,151	52	626	1	9	20	1	A
Diocese of Mombasa d	100	—	7,000	—	15,000	19	160	0	5	10	1	C
Diocese of Mount Kenya d	321	—	16,844	—	47,970	33	20	4	10	15	1	A
Diocese of Nairobi	18	—	5,000	—	20,000	11	20	6	18	30	2	C
Diocese of Nakuru e	62	—	2,800	—	7,173	22	53	—	17	30	1	A
Dutch Reformed Church (South Africa)	3	—	137	—	170	1	18	0	0	0	0	D
East Africa Yearly Meeting of Friends f	575	30,397	31,100	104,000	76,000	7	632	—	3	12	1	D
Eastern Mennonite Board	1	—	—	—	—	—	—	—	—	—	—	D
Full Gospel Churches of Kenya g	168	1,200	6,885	7,000	—	35	106	0	10	15	0	E
Gospel Furthering Fellowship	85	4,000	—	—	—	10	50	0	4	7	0	D
Independent Board for Presbyterian Foreign Missions	1	—	—	—	—	—	—	—	—	—	—	—
International Missions	—	10	0	20	0	—	—	—	2	10	—	A
Lutheran Church in Kenya h	8	534	4,966	1,000	7,234	4	50	0	2	12	1	A
Methodist Church in Kenya i	249	7,042	11,876	10,852	17,554	16	18	2	12	9	2	A
Pentecostal Assemblies of God j	450	60,000	95,000	90,000	100,000	—	—	—	18	42	1	B
Pentecostal Evangelistic Fellowship of Africa	4	300	320	530	700	0	1	0	2	2	0	B
Presbyterian Church of East Africa k	390	24,000	28,062	44,436	56,975	50	31	0	5	17	2	C
Reformed Church of East Africa l	26	1,200	1,200	—	2,500	3	20	0	1	6	0	B
Salvation Army	581	33,362	50,635	86,010	107,418	28	423	423	55	0	0	A

KENYA—continued

Mission											Code
Seventh-day Adventist Church	713	31,461	50,593	68,048	81,264	59	11	12	46	1	C
Swedish Free Missions … m	8	—	692	—	2,076	8	0	1	3	1	B
World Presbyterian Mission	—	—	N59,150	—	N246,883	—	—	2	4	—	D
	6,048	272,097	402,836	748,107	788,070	644	474	283	606	26	

N Not reported.

Co-operating: **a** World Gospel Mission. **b** Africa Inland Mission. **c** Southern Baptist Convention. **d** Church Missionary Society. **e** Bible Churchmen's Missionary Society. **f** Friends United Meeting. **g** Finnish Free Mission, Norske Pinsevenners Ytremisjon. **h** Missionssällskapet Bibeltrogna Vänner. **i** Methodist Missionary Society. **j** Pentecostal Assemblies of Canada. **k** Elim Missionary Assemblies. **l** Church of Scotland Mission. **m** Svenska Fria Missionen.

LESOTHO

11,716 sq. mls. Pop.: 727,000 (1963)

Mission											Code
Assemblies of God …	29	326	450	608	884	8	0	0	2	0	0	A
Bantu Baptist Church … a	26	—	479	—	—	27	—	0	1	1	0	C
Lesotho Evangelical Church … b	444	58,727	56,000	200,000	—	(46)U	(360)U	—	—	4	1	C
Diocese of Lesotho (Anglican) … c	253	—	37,464	—	—	23	266	—	14	—	—	A
Methodist Church of South Africa…	—	—	2,824	—	5,270	6	2	2	—	—	—	C
Seventh-day Adventist Church …	—	—	—	—	N237,943	—	—	—	—	—	—	
	752	59,053	97,217	200,608	244,097	110 (46)U	628 (360)U	2	17	5	1	

N Not reported.   U Unclassified.

Co-operating: **a** South African Baptist Missionary Society (Mahon Mission Branch). **b** Société des Missions Evangéliques de Paris. **c** United Society for the Propagation of the Gospel.

LIBERIA 43,000 sq. mls. Pop.: 1,030,000 (1963)

Church or Mission N.B. See notes on Statistics, page xiii	Co-op	Places of Regular Worship	Communicants, Full Members (p. 57)		Total Christian Community (p. 57)		National Workers, full-time			Missionaries from other Churches or countries, full-time		Theolog. Colls., Bible Schools	Source of Information
			1962 Handbook	Latest available figure	1962 Handbook	Latest available figure	Ordained	Lay-men	Women	Ordained	Lay-workers		
African Methodist Episcopal Church		—	1,500	—	1,500	—	—	—	—	—	—	—	E
African Methodist Episcopal Zion Church	a	186	2,500	—	2,500	—	—	—	—	—	(37)U	—	E
Assemblies of God	a	—	3,190	5,241	6,483	18,746	—	(227)U	—	—	—	3	B
Church of God in Christ	h	—	—	—	—	—	—	—	1	—	—	—	D
Free Pentecostal Church	b	5	750	766	2,250	2,298	9	—	—	7	13	1	B
Liberia Inland Mission		30	200	1,000	1,000	3,000	—	—	—	17	36	—	D
Liberian Baptist Convention	c	60	1,885	15,314	2,000	20,000	—	—	—	6	11	—	D
Lutheran Church in Liberia	d	223	—	8,334	5,464	10,853	8	(192)U	—	20	34	—	A
Methodist Church	e	292	25,000	16,212	60,000	26,782	75	118	—	5	27	4	B
Mid-Liberian Mission	f	85	129	419	605	4,231	—	(23)U	—	—	(41)U	—	B
New Tribes Mission		—	—	—	—	—	6	2	—	2	—	—	E
Open Bible Standard Mission		12	225	5,000	750	15,000	—	—	—	2	5	—	E
Pentecostal Assemblies of Canada		60	800	—	15,000	—	10	56	—	2	5	—	B
Presbyterian Church	g	8	500	—	1,500	—	32	92	1	6	18	1	E
Protestant Episcopal Church		145	5,806	7,414	8,087	11,149	(8)U	(37)U	1	—	—	—	B
Seventh-day Adventist Church	*	12	1,491	2,024	1,413	0	0	0	0	10	59	0	D
Sudan Interior Mission		1	—	0	—	N 7,663	—	—	—	—	—	—	B
United Pentecostal Church		—	—	N4,725	—	—	—	—	—	—	—	—	E
		1,119	43,976	66,449	108,552	119,722	148 (8)U	747 (479)U	3	77	286 (78)U	9	

* Broadcasting Station ELWA only. N Not reported. U Unclassified.

Co-operating: a Assemblies of God USA. b Worldwide Evangelization Crusade. c Southern Baptist Convention. d United Lutheran Mission. e Methodist Church USA. f Baptist Mid-Missions. g Protestant Episcopal Church in the USA. h Svenska Fria Missionen.

LIBYA

679,338 sq. mls. Pop.: 1,504,000 (1963)

Church of Christ :: b	1	—	100	—	200	—	—	—	—	—	E
Diocese of Egypt with Libya and North Africa (Anglican) ... a	3	20	300	40	500	0	0	1	0	0	A
First Baptist Church ... c	1	—	150	13	300	0	0	2	5	0	D
North Africa Mission	1	3	—	—	—	—	—	—	—	—	E
Seventh-day Adventist Mission	1	—	38	—	100	—	—	—	—	—	D
Tripoli Bible Church	1	—	50	—	—	—	—	—	—	—	D
Union Church of Tripoli	1	—	425	—	1,500	—	—	—	—	—	D
Worldwide Evangelization Crusade	—	—	—	—	—	—	—	—	—	—	D
			N 3		N 51						
	9	23	1,066	53	2,651*	0	0	3	5	0	

Co-operating: a Jerusalem and the East Mission. b Churches of Christ USA. c Southern Baptist Convention.
* This total consists entirely of expatriates; there are no national Christians, and the law forbids mission work.
N Not reported.

MALAGASY REPUBLIC

229,233 sq. mls. Pop.: 5,940,000 (1963)

Eglise Adventiste du Septième Jour	82	2,898	3,754	4,876	40,000	(22)U	(138)U	—	—	—	—	D
Eglise des Amis en Madagascar	314	7,928	7,575	64,505	21,000	62	38	0	5	7	10	A
Eglise du Christ à Madagascar ... a	1,654	62,551	66,245	319,845	352,578	605	137	10	4	3	3	A
Eglise Episcopale de Madagascar ... b	386	10,939	13,500	31,006	37,000	60	115	0	18	3	45	A
Eglise Evangélique de Madagascar... c	1,876	46,634	67,920	280,000	410,000	246	275	—	40	88	7	A
Eglise Luthérienne Malgache ... d	2,024	95,594	136,147	227,285	243,453	305	1,484	153	1	1	0	A
Eglise Pentecôtiste	8	—	2,000	—	9,000	—	—	—	—	—	—	D
	6,344	226,544	297,141	927,517	1,113,031	1,300 (22)U	2,187 (138)U	163	68	99	65	

U Unclassified.

Co-operating: a London Missionary Society. b United Society for the Propagation of the Gospel. c Société des Missions Evangéliques de Paris. d American Lutheran Church, Norske Misjonsselskap.

MALAWI   46,066 sq. mls.   Pop.: 3,753,000 (1963)

Church or Mission — N.B. See notes on Statistics, page xiii	Places of Regular Worship	Communicants, Full Members (p. 57)		Total Christian Community (p. 57)		Staff					Theolog. Colls., Bible Schools	Source of Information
						National Workers, full-time			Missionaries from other Churches or countries, full-time			
		1962 Handbook	Latest available figure	1962 Handbook	Latest available figure	Ordained	Laymen	Women	Ordained	Lay-workers		
Africa Evangelical Church ... a	57	703	682	1,507	2,111	—	(116)U	—	3	10	2	B
Assemblies of God ...	69	743	3,500	1,029	4,337	—	(61)U	—	12	—	1	B
Baptist Mission of Central Africa ...		—	4,000	—	—	—	—	—	—	—	—	C
Church of Central Africa Presbyterian:												
Synod of Blantyre ... b	450	42,311	69,243	126,934	240,000	24	72	4	7	9	2	A
Synod of Mkhoma ... c	862	61,100	83,632	139,000	513,840	46	32	88	13	69	2	A
Synod of Livingstonia ... d	476	—	35,000	—	100,000	40	94	61	4	13	1	A
Church of the Nazarene ...	26	—	193	—	1,611	11	—	1	3	3	1	B
Churches of Christ (Disciples) ...	46	—	5,000	—	10,000	—	—	—	—	—	1	C
Diocese of Malawi (Anglican) ... e	188	23,000	19,209	54,000	54,092	22	243	22	30	35	2	A
Nyasa Evangelical Church ... f	109	2,939	4,000	4,387	8,000	—	(169)U	—	3	2	1	C & E
Seventh-day Adventist Church ...	331	16,388	19,829	33,453	—	(89)U	(301)U	—	—	—	2	D
Seventh-day Baptist Mission ...	50	1,259	2,500	2,500	—	—	—	—	1	18	1	C
Southern Baptist Convention ...	22	—	700	—	970	—	1	—	5	5	1	B
Zambesi Evangelical Church ... g	258	16,697	10,000	30,592	20,000 N39,953	—	50	3	—	12	1	C
	2,944	165,140	257,488	393,402	634,914	232 (89)U	1,139 (647)U	179	81	176	18	

N Not reported.   U Unclassified.

Co-operating: a Africa Evangelical Fellowship (SAGM). b Church of Scotland. c Dutch Reformed Church (South Africa). d Free Church of Scotland. e United Society for the Propagation of the Gospel. f Nyasa Mission. g Zambesi Mission.

MALI

464,873 sq. mls. Pop.: 4,394,000 (1963)

Conservative Baptist Foreign Mission	40	84	—	580	—	2	2	—	26	23	0	E
Evangelical Baptist Mission	—	—	—	—	—	—	—	—	—	—	—	E
Evangelical Christian Church of Mali and Upper Volta ... a	150	—	1,700	—	3,000	—	100	0	10	15	0	D
Gospel Missionary Union ...	40	150	—	2,500	—	2	2	0	13	30	0	E
Société des Missions Évangéliques de Paris	2	100	N 350	300	—	—	—	0	2	2	0	E
United World Mission	—	—	N 334	—	N 3,730	—	—	—	—	—	—	E
	232	334	2,384	3,380	6,730	4	104	0	51	70	0	

N Not reported.

Co-operating: a Christian and Missionary Alliance.

MAURITANIA

419,230 sq. mls. Pop.: 780,000 (1963)

None (1966)	—	—	0	0	0	—	—	0	0	0	—	A

MAURITIUS and SEYCHELLES

Mauritius: 726 sq. mls. Pop.: 736,965 est. (1965)
Seychelles: 156 sq. mls. Pop.: 46,472 est. (1964)

Anglican (Diocese of Mauritius) ... a	31	2,550	2,550	8,000	8,000	13	—	7	—	—	E
Seventh-day Adventists	15	1,219	1,264	2,177	3,742	6	22	1	—	—	B
	46	3,769	3,814	10,177	11,742	19	22	8	—	—	

Co-operating: a United Society for the Propagation of the Gospel.
Also working: Church of Scotland.

MOROCCO   171,305 sq. mls.   Pop.: 13,118,000 (1964)

Church or Mission *N.B.* See notes on Statistics, page xiii	Places of Regular Worship	Communicants, Full Members (p. 57)		Total Christian Community (p. 57)		Staff					Theolog. Colls., Bible Schools	Source of Information
						National Workers, full-time			Missionaries from other Churches or countries, full-time			
		1962 Handbook	Latest available figure	1962 Handbook	Latest available figure	Ordained	Laymen	Women	Ordained	Lay-workers		
Bible Churchmen's Missionary Society	4	60	—	100	—	—	1	—	2	—	0	E
Eglise Evangélique an Maroc	4	—	1,000	—	2,500	—	—	—	—	—	—	D
Emmanuel Mission (no statistics available)	—	—	—	—	—	—	—	—	—	—	—	E
Gospel Missionary Union	6	50	—	200	—	0	2	—	—	12	0	D
Mission Adventiste du Septième Jour	5	247	165	393	—	0	(5)U	—	0	(5)U	0	B & E
North Africa Mission a	10	182	170 N 110	650	350 N 706	0	0	0	4	42	0	D
	27	539	5,458	1,343	6,056	0	8 (5)U	1	7	59 (5)U	0	

N Not reported.   U Unclassified.
a Including former Southern Morocco Mission.
Note: Swedish Israel Mission no longer at work.

MOZAMBIQUE   297,731 sq. mls.   Pop.: 6,789,000 (1963)

Church or Mission	Places of Regular Worship	1962 Handbook	Latest available figure	1962 Handbook	Latest available figure	Ordained	Laymen	Women	Ordained	Lay-workers	Theolog. Colls., Bible Schools	Source of Information
African Methodist Episcopal Church	—	—	—	—	—	—	—	—	—	—	—	D
Assembleias de Deus	17	1,586	4,777	1,586	—	—	—	—	—	—	—	D
Igreja Adventista do Setima Dia	—	—	—	—	—	(5)U	(36)U	—	—	—	—	D
Igreja Anglicana, Diocese of Lebombo a	163	13,800	23,347	25,500	—	28	110	1	3	2	0	A
Igreja Baptista	2	48	120	48	200	—	—	—	—	—	—	C
Igreja Congregacional	60	—	2,459	—	8,000	3	7	0	0	0	0	D

MOZAMBIQUE—continued

Igreja de Cristo em Manica e Sofala **b**	21	600	3,000	2,000	6,000	—	—	16	—	—	—	A
Igreja do Nazareno ...	302	—	4,172	—	16,053	20	178	—	9	9	2	B
Igreja Evangelica de Mocambique... **c**	80	5,864	5,000	7,164	7,000	—	(136)U	0	0	0	0	C
Igreja Evangelica Portuguesa ...	1	47	50	120	80	1	0	0	0	0	0	A
Igreja Metodista Episcopal ... **d**	1,127	9,250	6,723	25,000	27,399	45	1,502	150	3	(21)U	—	B
Igreja Metodista Livre ...	806	3,500	5,385	11,200	7,724	9	450	6	2	9	1	A
Igreja Presbiteriana de Mocambique **e**	185	6,653	—	11,545	—	16	10	—	5	40	1	B
International Holiness Mission ...	70	—	—	—	—	—	—	—	—	—	—	D
Missão Baptista Escandinava ... **f**	100	1,600	2,900	4,500	6,000	7	0	0	3	1	0	A
Missão Metodista Wesleyana ... **g**	200	1,479	2,500	7,500	4,000	4	—	—	1	1	—	A
Pentecostal Assemblies of Canada...		4,000	8,000	4,500		—	—	—	1	2	—	B
	3,134	48,427	N6,653 75,086	100,663	N38,631 125,587	138 (5)U	2,449 (172)U	173	27	84	4	

N Not reported.   U Unclassified.

Co-operating: **a** United Society for the Propagation of the Gospel. **b** Christian Council of Mozambique. **c** Formerly Africa Evangelical Fellowship (SAGM) field. **d** Methodist Church (USA). **e** Mission Suisse dans l'Afrique du Sud. **f** Fribaptist-samfundet. **g** Methodist Church of South Africa.

NIGER

489,180 sq. mls.   Pop.: 3,117,000 (1963)

Coopération Evangélique Mondiale	0	—	0	0	0	0	0	0	0	2	0	D
Eglise Méthodiste ...	2	—	—	—	—	0	—	0	—	0	0	D
Evangelical Baptist Church ... **a**	6	—	30	—	100	0	0	0	—	35	0	D
Evangelical Churches of West Africa **b**	12	39	—	422	—	—	—	—	9	51	0	B
	20	39	N 39 69	422	N 422 522	0	0	0	9	88	0	

N Not reported.

Co-operating: **a** Formerly Mission Chrétienne d'Afrique (Christian Missions). **b** Sudan Interior Mission.

NIGERIA 356,669 sq. mls. Pop.: 55,620,000 (1963)

Church or Mission (N.B. See notes on Statistics, page xiii)	Places of Regular Worship	Communicants, Full Members (p. 57) 1962 Handbook	Communicants Latest available figure	Total Christian Community (p. 57) 1962 Handbook	Total Christian Community Latest available figure	Staff — National Workers, full-time: Ordained	National Workers: Laymen	National Workers: Women	Missionaries from other Churches/countries, full-time: Ordained	Missionaries: Lay-workers	Theolog. Colls., Bible Schools	Source of Information
African Methodist Episcopal Church	—	30,000	30,000	30,000	90,000	—	—	—	—	—	—	E
African Methodist Episcopal Zion Church	—	—	—	—	—	—	—	—	—	—	—	E
Apostolic Church	600	2,500	25,000	10,000	50,000	—	—	—	—	—	—	D
Assemblies of God	583	5,194	10,256	23,377	27,117	—	(423)U	—	45	—	—	B
Christian Methodist Episcopal Church (no statistics available)	—	—	—	—	—	—	—	—	—	—	—	
Church of God [a]	62	2,500	—	2,500	—	—	—	—	—	—	—	E
Church of the Province of West Africa: [b]	—	120,458	—	433,000	—	—	—	—	—	—	—	
Diocese of Benin	527	—	17,661	—	86,366	42	258	—	—	—	—	E
Diocese of Ibadan	436	—	16,285	—	182,828	104	167	—	8	—	—	C
Diocese of Lagos	476	—	19,486	—	73,789	88	124	—	4	4	—	C
Diocese on the Niger	375	—	32,271	—	83,503	56	1,564	868	4	47	—	C
Diocese of the Niger Delta	65	—	25,794	—	107,239	40	365	—	—	—	—	C
Diocese of Northern Nigeria	413	—	16,274	—	25,000	40	75	—	2	17	—	C
Diocese of Ondo	321	—	17,864	—	127,526	105	188	—	4	1	—	A
Diocese of Owerri	500	—	28,311	—	81,379	50	306	440	2	9	—	C
Churches of Christ	40	6,000	—	6,000	—	—	40	—	10	—	—	A
Congregational Holiness Church	—	—	—	—	—	—	—	—	—	3	—	E
Evangelical Churches of West Africa [c]	900	18,000	100,000	54,000	300,000	85	—	—	—	—	5	A
Evangelical Lutheran Church of Nigeria	220	12,132	19,000	30,677	37,000	24	300	100	8	22	2	D
International Church of the Four-Square Gospel	5	500	—	500	—	—	—	—	—	—	—	E

NIGERIA—*continued*

	1	2	3	4	5	6	7	8	9	10		
Methodist Church, Nigeria ... **d**	1,540	47,162	54,332	131,212	146,640	91	288	15	20	44	—	A
New Church in West Africa ...	47	2,000	4,000	5,500	6,000	—	—	—	5	—	—	B
Nigerian Baptist Convention ... **e**	1,400	42,961	65,000	78,352	250,000	125	(25)U	—	73	150	—	C
Pentecostal Holiness Church ...	21	—	1,250	—	2,025	—	—	—	3	—	—	B
Pilgrim Baptist Mission ...	—	—	12,000	—	30,000	—	—	—	—	47	—	C
Presbyterian Church of Nigeria **f**	426	14,564	16,623	90,000	101,600	38	1,506	343	15	7	—	C
Qua Iboe Church ...	853	40,000	40,945	90,000	100,000	20	670	—	3	15	—	C
Salvation Army ...	248	19,321	9,347	41,275	30,000	83	101	86	8	12	—	C
Seventh-day Adventist Church ...	166	13,508	18,774	17,113	—	14	29	—	5	—	—	D
Seventh-day Baptist Church (no statistics available) ...	—	—	—	—	—	—	—	—	—	—	—	
TEKAS (Fellowship of Churches of Christ in the Sudan) ... **g**	3,737	39,339	64,237	170,560	492,237	141	2,161	45	45	—	—	C
United Missionary Church of Africa ... **h**	85	615	1,277 N11,500	5,000	7,285 N36,113	14	79	15	15	2	—	C
	14,046	471,754	657,487	1,274,066	2,523,647	1,160	8,669 (448)U	1,852	279	380	7	

N Not reported.   U Unclassified.

Co-operating: **a** Church of God (Cleveland). **b** Church Missionary Society. **c** Sudan Interior Mission. **d** Methodist Missionary Society. **e** Southern Baptist Convention. **f** Church of Scotland, Presbyterian Church of Canada. **g** Christian Reformed Church Mission, Church of the Brethren Mission, Evangelical United Brethren, Sudan United Mission. **h** United Missionary Society.

PORTUGUESE GUINEA   13,948 sq. mls.   Pop.: 524,000 (1963)

	1	2	3	4	5	6	7	8	9	10		
Worldwide Evangelization Crusade	15	185	220	731	1,320	—	(20)U	—	7	14	0	B
	15	185	220	731	1,320	0	(20)U	0	7	14	0	

U Unclassified.

RHODESIA 150,333 sq. mls. Pop.: 4,140,000 (1964)

Church or Mission (N.B. See notes on Statistics, page xiii)	Places of Regular Worship	Communicants, Full Members (p. 57)		Total Christian Community (p. 57)		Staff					Theolog. Colls., Bible Schools	Source of Information
		1962 Hand-book	Latest available figure	1962 Hand-book	Latest available figure	National Workers, full-time			Missionaries from other Churches or countries, full-time			
						Ordained	Lay-men	Women	Ordained	Lay-workers		
Africa Evangelical Church ... a	39	1,540	1,701	1,740	3,776	—	(80)U	—	4	32	1	B
African Methodist Episcopal Church	—	—	6,000	87,188	93,685	—	—	170	21	165	—	D
African Reformed Church ... b	534	29,484	29,428	250	—	11	2,142	0	0	4	1	B
Apostolic Church ...	12	250	—	250	—	0	6	—	8	—	0	E
Baptist Union of Central Africa ...	12	710	—	2,800	—	—	—	—	20	46	—	E
Brethren in Christ Church ...	146	3,725	3,936	7,661	16,112	4	607	—	2	3	1	B
Church of Central Africa Presbyterian	200	8,000	6,000	16,000	15,000	4	—	—	3	11	—	A
Church of Christ ... c	35	3,600	—	3,600	—	0	8	6	1	1	0	E
Church of the Nazarene ...	1	—	43	—	100	1	0	0	—	—	0	B
Church of the Province of Central Africa: d												
Diocese of Mashonaland ...	365	—	16,700	—	89,000	69	400	—	—	7	—	A
Diocese of Matabeleland ...	257	—	7,041	—	20,000	16	150	—	25	—	—	A
Churches of Christ ... e	100	—	1,000	—	3,000	—	—	—	—	—	—	A
Congregational Union of South Africa ...	12	474	529	1,464	909	2	—	0	—	—	—	D
Dutch Reformed Church (Mother Church) ...	15	—	6,681	—	11,615	—	—	—	—	—	—	D
Elim Church ...	19	403	450	2,550	2,800	2	2	2	4	8	—	B
Evangelical Alliance Mission ...	94	210	1,162	250	4,000	15	200	—	20	30	—	A
Evangelical Lutheran Church in Rhodesia ... f	210	9,471	15,319	12,929	20,262	15	851	414	10	50	1	B
Free Methodist Church ...	30	801	1,286	1,277	4,426	5	70	4	18	11	2	B
Free Presbyterian Church of Scotland ...	28	350	—	4,000	—	—	—	—	—	—	—	E
London Missionary Society ...	153	3,027	3,585	5,783	6,564	5	4	5	6	10	1*	A
Methodist Church (UK) ...	788	26,000	28,014	—	112,500	42	117	1	31	22	2	B
Methodist Church (USA) ...	325	24,000	14,920	—	45,000	35	5	—	—	(88)U	—	B

RHODESIA—continued

Mission												Code
Nederduitsch Hervormde Kerk van Afrika	60	—	723	—	1,311	—	—	—	—	—	—	D
Pentecostal Assemblies of Canada	800	—	5,000	1,200	10,000	—	—	—	4	4	1	B
Presbyterian Church of Southern Africa	—	—	7,375	—	—	—	—	—	—	—	—	A
Salvation Army	410	18,981	—	59,082	—	17	738	179	111	—	—	E
Seventh-day Adventist Church	130	21,841	26,336	36,420	36,222	281 (100)U	(365)U	—	22	26	1	A
Southern Baptist Convention	105	2,214	3,228	2,214	13,549	23	6	—	1	1	—	B
Swedish Alliance Mission	3	—	12	—	275	0	2	—	—	—	—	B
United Church of Christ g	—	1,300	1,668	4,300	N87,407	12	—	1	—	—	—	A
	4,083	157,181	212,028 / N23,891	250,708	597,513	659 (100)U	5,753 (445)U	782	311	519	9	

N Not recorded.   U Unclassified.

Co-operating: **a** Africa Evangelical Fellowship (SAGM).   **b** Nederduitse Gereformeerde Kerk (Suid Afrika).   **c** Churches of Christ in New Zealand.   **d** United Society for the Propagation of the Gospel.   **e** Churches of Christ in the USA.   **f** Svenska Kyrkans Missionstrelse.   **g** United Church Board for World Ministries.

RWANDA

10,166 sq. mls.   Pop.: 2,850,000 (1963)

Mission												Code
Eglise Adventiste du Septième Jour	326	—	58,839	—	85,260	29	(785)U	—	1	—	—	D
Eglise Anglicane du Rwanda ... **a**	826	—	18,566	—	N58,839	—	—	—	8	22	1	A
Eglise Libre Méthodiste ...	—	—	1,929	—	4,356	—	—	—	—	5	0	B
Eglise Presbytérienne au Rwanda ... **b**	214	1,721	4,685	3,736	8,756	2	145	0	4	14	1	A
Eglises de Pentecôte ... **c**	50	—	3,067	—	9,201	5	61	0	5	14	1	B
Union des Eglises Baptistes... **d**	51	—	1,994	—	4,233	2	63	13	1	3	1	B
	1,467	1,721	89,080	3,736	170,645 / N58,839	38	1,054 (785)U	13	19	58	4	

N Not reported.   U Unclassified.

Co-operating: **a** Ruanda General and Medical Mission (CMS).   **b** Société Belge des Missions Protestantes.   **c** Svenska Fria Missionen.   **d** Danske Baptistsamfunds Yare Mission.

AFRICA

ST HELENA 47 sq. mls. Pop.: 4,634 (1964)

N.B. See notes on Statistics, page xiii

Church or Mission	Places of Regular Worship	Communicants, Full Members (p. 57) 1962 Handbook	Latest available figure	Total Christian Community (p. 57) 1962 Handbook	Latest available figure	Staff — National Workers, full-time: Ordained	Lay-men	Women	Missionaries from other Churches or countries, full-time: Ordained	Lay-workers	Theolog., Colls., Bible Schools	Source of Information
Baptist Union of South Africa	4	74	74	280	280	1	—	—	1	1	—	
Church of the Province of South Africa (Anglican): Diocese of St Helena*	5	1,400	1,400	4,300	4,300	3	—	—	—	—	—	
	9	1,474	1,474	4,580	4,580	4	—	—	1	1	—	

* Including islands of Ascension and Tristan da Cunha.

SENEGAL 197,161 sq. mls. Pop.: 3,326,000 (1963)

Church or Mission	Places of Regular Worship	Communicants, Full Members (p. 57) 1962 Handbook	Latest available figure	Total Christian Community (p. 57) 1962 Handbook	Latest available figure	Staff — National Workers, full-time: Ordained	Lay-men	Women	Missionaries from other Churches or countries, full-time: Ordained	Lay-workers	Theolog., Colls., Bible Schools	Source of Information
Assemblées de Dieu	25	40	148	40	1,698	—	(6)U	—	—	(11)U	1	B
Conservative Baptist Foreign Mission Society	2	—	4	—	—	0	0	0	5	5	0	B
Eglise Protestante de Dakar a	5	8	24	30	100	—	—	—	—	—	—	D
Mission Evangélique de l'Afrique Occidentale b	1	—	7	—	30	—	—	—	—	—	—	A
New Tribes Mission	—	—	—	—	N 4	0	0	0	0	17	0	A
United World Mission	—	—	—	—	—	—	—	—	—	—	—	D
	33	48	183	70	1,832	0	(6)U	0	5	33 (11)U	1	

N Not reported.   U Unclassified.

Co-operating: **a** Société des Missions Evangéliques de Paris. **b** Worldwide Evangelization Crusade.

84

SIERRA LEONE 27,925 sq. mls. Pop.: 2,190,000 (1963)

Church												Class
African Methodist Episcopal Church	7	200	—	500	—	—	—	—	—	—	—	E
American Wesleyan Methodist Church	41	481	642	2,500	2,691	6	31	0	10	24	2	D
Assemblies of God	36	681	668	863	2,968	1	17	0	2	2	1	B
Church of God of Prophecy	5	805	—	2,400	—	0	2	0	1	1	0	E
Diocese of Sierra Leone (Anglican) a	56	7,414	11,151	15,000	25,000	35	(234)U	—	—	—	—	E
Evangelical United Brethren Church	164	6,689	8,402	8,300	14,182	28	72	0	9	33	1	D
Methodist Church b	399	8,251	240	16,239	17,592	32	53	—	14	11	1	E
Missionary Church Association	29	196	—	300	1,200	—	13	—	6	15	—	B
Nigerian Baptist Convention	—	—	—	—	—	—	—	—	—	—	—	
Seventh-day Adventist Church *	19	1,017	2,325	3,358	—	(10)U	(50)U	0	1	1	0	D
Sierra Leone Baptist Union c	2	205	228	205	—	0	2	—	—	—	—	C
Sierra Leone Mission d	14	1,200	—	2,000	—	—	(12)U	—	—	—	—	E
Société Missionnaire Baptiste Européenne	1	—	1,726	—	—	—	—	—	—	—	—	
United Brethren in Christ	112	1,592	—	6,818	2,355	25	110	42	2	35	1	A
United Pentecostal Church	6	600	—	800	—	—	24	—	—	8	—	A
West African Methodist Church	—	2,000	—	2,000	—	—	—	—	—	—	—	E
	891	31,331	N12,219 / 37,601	61,283	N11,263 / 77,251	137 (10)U	620 (296)U	42	45	130	6	

* Includes Gambia. N Not reported. U Unclassified.

Co-operating: a Church Missionary Society. b Methodist Missionary Society. c Formerly Baptist Commonwealth Society. d Countess of Huntingdon's Connexion.

SOMALIA — 246,135 sq. mls. — Pop.: 2,300,000 (1963)

Church or Mission — N.B. See notes on Statistics, page xiii	Places of Regular Worship	Communicants, Full Members (p. 57)		Total Christian Community (p. 57)		Staff					Theolog. Colls., Bible Schools	Source of Information
						National Workers, full-time			Missionaries from other Churches or countries, full-time			
		1962 Hand-book	Latest available figure	1962 Hand-book	Latest available figure	Or-dained	Lay-men	Women	Or-dained	Lay-workers		
Episcopal Church, Diocese of the Sudan ... a	1	—	15	—	50	0	0	0	0	0	0	A
Somalia Mennonite Mission ...	8	6	—	30	90	0	5	0	6	22	—	E & B
Sudan Interior Mission ...	3	—	N 6	—	—	0	0	0	3	26	—	B
	12	6	21	30	140	0	5	0	9	48	0	

N Not reported.

Co-operating: a Jerusalem and the East Mission.

SOUTH AFRICA — 472,359 sq. mls. — Pop.: 17,474,000 (1964)

Church or Mission	Places of Regular Worship	1962 Hand-book	Latest available figure	1962 Hand-book	Latest available figure	Or-dained	Lay-men	Women	Or-dained	Lay-workers	Theolog. Colls., Bible Schools	Source of Information
African Evangelical Church ... a	122	2,808	2,905	4,287	8,367	—	(194)U	—	16	58	—	A
African Methodist Episcopal Church ...	318	35,000	41,509	75,000	80,000	215	—	—	—	—	—	D
Apostolic Faith Church ...	535	70,000	100,000	100,000	—	—	100	—	—	—	—	E
Assemblies of God ...	225	—	5,791	15,000	21,676	—	(163)U	—	—	(26)U	1	B
Bantu Evangelical Church ... b	189	7,430	9,581	15,000	17,000	105	33	12	28	68	2	A
Bantu Presbyterian Church of South Africa ...	770	39,676	43,413	45,680	47,520	46	36	1	5	9	1	A
Baptist Union of South Africa c	520	37,015	45,015	150,000	135,000	246	67	25	—	—	4	A
Christian Brethren ... d	9	—	—	2,450	—	—	—	—	—	30	—	D
Christian Churches (Disciples of Christ) ...	20	507	1,650	1,100	3,900	9	—	2	1	0	1	A

SOUTH AFRICA—*continued*

											D & E
Church of Christ Mission	39	3,064	—	4,595	4,700	20	—	—	3	—	—	A
Church of England in South Africa	100	32,500	25,000	97,500	—	(27)U	(57)U	44	16	48	1	B
Church of the Nazarene	125	5,537	—	12,098	20,355	58	33	—	—	—	3	A
Church of the Province of South Africa **e**	3,962	202,402	336,740	597,000	1,456,000	524	2,459	222	225	4	—	C & E
Congregational Church in Africa **f**	392	13,641	—	25,367	70,000	—	—	—	8	—	1*	A
Congregational Union of South Africa	786	64,297	68,281	130,275	130,335	96	23	—	4	8	0	B
Elim Church **b**	19	2,987	450	6,314	2,800	2	2	2	—	—	—	D
Evangelical Bible Church												
Evangelical Lutheran Church in Southern Africa: **g**		300,000		500,000							2	
Cape Orange Region	261	—	21,170	—	44,769	32	464	—	8	6	—	D
South-Eastern Region	1,206	—	51,470	—	81,924	123	1,141	—	46	102	—	D
Transvaal Region	592	—	100,072	—	111,531	65	277	3	14	4	—	D
Tswana Region	380	1,000	81,000	6,000	141,000	29	72	11	24	30	—	D
Free Church of Scotland	46	—	3,000	—	10,000	9	160	1	3	4	—	A
Free Evangelical Lutheran Synod in South Africa **†**	9	1,136	4,030	1,710	5,830	7	1	—	12	—	—	D
Free Methodist Church	11	1,200	866	2,826	1,758	6	77	10	9	8	4	B
Full Gospel Church of God	1,200	69,000	79,000	140,000	141,000	310	619	113	37	8	—	A
Gereformeerde Kerk in Suid Afrika	280	59,408	69,764	100,987	118,101	178	—	—	2	—	—	A
Hannoverian Evangelical Lutheran Free Church Mission **h**	114	7,136	11,323	16,530	28,351	22	30	7	—	(11)U	1	D
Indian Christian Church	22	—	777	—	1,590	—	—	—	2	9	2	B
International Church of the Four-Square Gospel	52	3,867	—	5,611	—	113	(56)U	—	4	2	1‡	E
London Missionary Society	177	—	10,158	—	15,795	10	—	—	—	11	2	A
Methodist Church of South Africa	6,743	315,515	338,604	1,250,000	1,250,000	689	342	896	4	—	2	A
Methodist Church S.E. Conference	115	1,000	1,000	2,061	2,360	6	319	—	—	9	—	C
Moravian Church, Eastern Province	104	—	9,007	—	22,302	13	120	5	—	(5)U	2	A

SOUTH AFRICA—*continued*

Church or Mission — N.B. See notes on Statistics, page xiii	Places of Regular Worship	Communicants, Full Members (p. 57) — 1962 Handbook	Communicants — Latest available figure	Total Christian Community (p. 57) — 1962 Handbook	Total Christian Community — Latest available figure	Staff: National Workers, full-time — Ordained	National Workers — Laymen	National Workers — Women	Missionaries from other Churches or countries, full-time — Ordained	Missionaries — Lay-workers	Theolog. Colls. Bible Schools	Source of Information
Moravian Church, Western Province	127	10,032	14,186	27,665	31,965	21	17	1	7	10	2	A
Nederduitsch Hervormde Kerk van Afrika	221	74,645	90,550	133,485	153,454	—	(85)U	—	—	—	—	D
Nederduitse Gereformeerde Kerk: [i]												
Mother Church	877	691,214	713,533	1,145,747	1,168,632	1,100	750	750	0	0	3	D
Coloured Church	183	95,253	111,420	286,947	341,017	44	38	120	116	134	1	D
NGK in Afrika	334	119,296	132,930	363,053	423,584	12	780	960	213	556	4	A
Indian Church	4	—	262	—	570	0	8	7	6	12	0	B
New Church in South Africa	90	4,247	9,994	5,250	18,500	1	—	—	90	—	1	D
Norwegian Free Evangelical Mission	—	—	—	—	2,000	—	—	—	—	—	—	B
Pentecostal Assemblies of Canada	80	2,500	20,000	60,000	60,000	—	—	—	4	7	1	E
Pentecostal Holiness Church	240	10,000	—	20,000	—	—	72	—	—	16	—	D & E
Pilgrim Holiness Church	96	1,393	—	4,000	700	—	—	—	—	—	—	—
Presbyterian Church of Southern Africa	480	—	44,943	—	100,000	141	—	4	—	—	—	D
Religious Society of Friends	11	167	208	215	300	—	—	—	—	—	—	A
Salem Mission	21	—	571	—	2,375	11	14	9	1	2	1	B
Salvation Army	409	12,563	12,563	27,733	29,200	(327)U	(436)U	(259)U	—	(100)U	—	D
Scandinavian Independent Baptist Union	40	2,200	—	4,000	—	22	(196)U	—	17	(298)U	—	E
Seventh-day Adventist Church	250	14,806	19,118	39,454	—	—	—	—	—	—	—	D
Société des Missions Evangéliques de Paris	45	—	2,666	—	—	(3)U	(8)U	—	—	—	—	C

SOUTH AFRICA—*continued*

Society												Code
South African Baptist Missionary Society ... j	20	14,500	16,335	15,460	20,000	19	325	100	6	25	1	B
Swedish Alliance Mission ... §	400	5,385	—	5,385	5,000	86	—	—	12	10	1	B
Swedish Holiness Mission ...	229	6,695	9,787	12,843	21,004	—	33	1	11	—	1	D & E
Tsonga Presbyterian Church ... k	199	—	—	—	—	14	—	—	—	—	—	D
United Evangelical Lutheran Church	—	—	10,000	—	25,000	—	—	25	—	8	—	D
United Free Church of Scotland ... †	16	2,195	—	4,500	—	0	1	—	0	—	0	E
		N117,282	N117,282		N275,792							
	23,905	2,343,217	2,687,924	5,445,499	6,653,147	4,761 (357)U	9,608 (1,195)U	3,590 (259)U	954	1,639 (414)U	45	

* United.   † White congregations only.   ‡ United.   § Figures include Swaziland.

N Not reported.   U Unclassified.

Co-operating: **a** Africa Evangelical Fellowship (SAGM). **b** The Evangelical Alliance Mission. **c** Mahon Mission. **d** South African Evangelization and Missionary Trust. **e** United Society for the Propagation of the Gospel. **f** United Church Board for World Ministries. **g** American Lutheran Mission, Berlin Mission Society, Church of Sweden Mission, Missionsanstalt Hermannsburg, Norwegian Mission Society. **h** Africa Evangelical Fellowship (SAGM). **i** Formerly Bantu Kerk. **j** Mahon Mission Branch. **k** Mission Suisse dans l'Afrique du Sud.

Also working: African Evangelistic Mission, Christian Missions in Many Lands, Christadelphian Church, Church of Jesus Christ of Latter Day Saints, Dorothea Mission, International Holiness Mission, International Mission to Miners, Norwegian Mission Union, Pentecostal Protestant Church, Portuguese Evangelical Church, Reformed Baptist Church, South Africa Compounds and General Mission, Volkskerk van Afrika.

SOUTH WEST AFRICA 318,099 sq. mls. Pop.: 554,000 (1963)

Church or Mission (N.B. See notes on Statistics, page xiii)	Places of Regular Worship	Communicants, Full Members (p. 57) — 1962 Handbook	Communicants, Full Members (p. 57) — Latest available figure	Total Christian Community (p. 57) — 1962 Handbook	Total Christian Community (p. 57) — Latest available figure	National Workers, full-time — Ordained	National Workers, full-time — Lay-men	National Workers, full-time — Women	Missionaries from other Churches or countries, full-time — Ordained	Missionaries from other Churches or countries, full-time — Lay-workers	Theolog. Colls., Bible Schools	Source of Information
African Methodist Episcopal Church	21	—	3,389	—	6,000	—	—	—	—	—	—	D
Congregational Union of South Africa	4	255	567	405	667	—	—	—	—	—	—	D
Diocese of Damaraland (Anglican) ... a	119	600	18,850	4,300	38,000	9	55	6	12	—	—	A
Evangelical Lutheran Church in SWA (Rheinische Missionskirche) ... b	43	51,700	45,308	98,300	102,422	32	71	2	20	14	1	A
Evangelical Lutheran Ovambokavango Church ... c	126	48,137	61,021	113,007	156,204	83	552	444	9	97	1	D
Gereformeerde Kerk	11	—	1,659	—	3,150	—	—	—	—	—	—	C
Methodist Church	—	—	1,589	—	2,015	8	0	1	0	0	0	D
Nederduitsch Hervormde Kerk van Afrika	—	—	840	—	1,578	—	—	—	—	—	—	D
Nederduitse Gereformeerde Kerk in SWA (Mother Church)	38	17,985	18,318	34,476	33,135	33	6	—	0	0	—	D
Nederduitse Gereformeerde Kerk vir SWA (Coloured Church)	6	918	886	3,783	2,310	1	58	16	3	22	—	D
NGK Sending Kerk (Bantu)	—	—	—	—	500	—	—	—	—	—	—	D
Seventh-day Adventist Church	5	4,000	500	10,000	12,000	—	—	—	—	—	—	D
United Evangelical Lutheran Church *	—	—	6,000	—	N10,000	—	—	—	—	—	—	A
	373	123,565	158,927	264,271	367,981	166	742	469	44	133	2	

* White congregations only.   N Not reported.

Co-operating: a Protestant Episcopal Church in the USA, United Society for the Propagation of the Gospel. b Rheinische Missionsgesellschaft. c Suomen Lähetysseura.

AFRICA

SPANISH EQUATORIAL AFRICA   10,830 sq. mls.   Pop.: 258,000 (1963)

Iglesia Evangelica Presbiteriana en la Guinea Ecuatorial ... a	95	—	2,583	—	7,500	5	45	0	4	4	0	B
Iglesia Metodista ... b	5	—	300	—	800	0	0	0	1	1	0	D
Worldwide Evangelization Crusade	23	171	500	504	700	3	—	—	1	3	0	D
	123	171	3,383	504	9,000	8	45	0	6	8	0	

Co-operating: **a** United Presbyterian Church in the USA. **b** Methodist Missionary Society (Fernando Poo only).

SPANISH WEST AFRICA   115,780 sq. mls.   Pop.: 83,000 (1963)

None	0	—	0	—	0	—	—	—	—	—	0	
	0	—	0	—	0	—	—	—	—	—	0	

SUDAN   967,500 sq. mls.   Pop.: 13,733,000 (1966)

Africa Inland Church ... a	8	161	300	1,190	3,000				0	0	0	A & E
Church in the East Central Sudan ... b	20	87	500	900	2,000	2	4	0	2	4	0	A
Church of Christ in the Nuba Mountains ... c	90	87	600	900	3,000	3	10	0	0	0	0	B
Church of Christ in the Upper Nile ... d	24	809	3,238	1,500	7,018	6	20	0	0	0	0	A
Episcopal Church in the Sudan ... e	600	45,185	110,000	82,100	150,000	52	600	30	3	10	1	A
Evangelical Church in the Sudan ... d	9	364	600	600	1,000	9	1	0	3	10	1	A
Swiss Evangelical Nile Mission ... *	—	—	—	—	—	—	—	—	—	—	—	
	751	46,693	115,238†	87,190	166,018†	72	635	30	8	24	2	

* Medical work only.   † Half of this membership is estimated to have been driven into dispersion in neighbouring countries, 1964-5.
Co-operating: **a** Formerly Africa Inland Mission. **b** Sudan Interior Mission. **c** Formerly Sudan United Mission. **d** United Presbyterian Church in the USA. **e** Church Missionary Society.

SWAZILAND   6,704 sq. mls.   Pop.: 278,000 (1963)

Church or Mission — N.B. See notes on Statistics, page xiii	Places of Regular Worship	Communicants, Full Members (p. 57) 1962 Handbook	Latest available figure	Total Christian Community (p. 57) 1962 Handbook	Latest available figure	National Workers, full-time — Ordained	Laymen	Women	Missionaries from other Churches or countries, full-time — Ordained	Lay-workers	Theolog. Colls., Bible Schools	Source of Information
African Evangelical Church ... a	24	612	465	1,239	1,477	—	(90)U	—	2	13	0	B
Bantu Evangelical Church ... b	4	—	—	—	—	5	—	—	—	—	—	C
Church of the Nazarene	210	—	1,524	—	12,821	61	84	193	14	50	1	B
Diocese of Swaziland (Anglican) ... c	70	—	2,365	—	—	8	48	0	8	2	0	A
Evangelical Lutheran Church (South-eastern Region)	—	—	—	—	—	—	—	—	—	—	—	C
Full Gospel Church of God	—	—	—	—	—	15	—	—	—	—	—	D
Methodist Church of South Africa	—	—	2,349	—	4,037	6	5	2	—	0	0	C
Seventh-day Adventist Church	—	—	1,769	—	5,458	—	(20)U	—	—	—	—	A
Swedish Alliance Mission	23	—	—	—	N 2,365	—	—	—	—	—	—	C
	331	612	8,472	1,239	26,158	95	247 (110)U	195	24	65	1	

N Not reported.   U Unclassified.

Co-operating: **a** Africa Evangelical Fellowship (SAGM).   **b** The Evangelical Alliance Mission.   **c** United Society for the Propagation of the Gospel.

TANZANIA   362,440 sq. mls.   Pop.: 10,123,000 (1963)

Church or Mission	Places of Regular Worship	Communicants, Full Members 1962 Handbook	Latest available figure	Total Christian Community 1962 Handbook	Latest available figure	National Workers, full-time — Ordained	Laymen	Women	Missionaries — Ordained	Lay-workers	Theolog. Colls., Bible Schools	Source of Information
Africa Inland Church	400	10,400	22,000	27,000	110,000	25	200	—	26	73	1	B
Assemblies of God	174	836	2,869	1,309	6,070	—	(97)U	—	—	(12)U	1	B
Baptist Churches of Tanzania ... a	163	75	2,850	75	5,000	7	109	3	19	32	1	A
Christian Missions in Many Lands	9	—	100	—	450	—	—	—	—	—	—	C
Church of the Province of East												

TANZANIA—continued

Church	(1)	(2)	(3)	(4)	(5)	(6)	(7)	(8)	(9)	(10)	(11)	
Africa:												
Diocese of Central Tanganyika b	899	54,200	21,233	94,500	74,769	65	—	—	13	100	—	A
Diocese of Dar-es-Salaam c	5	—	1,100	—	5,000	6	—	—	4	—	2	A
Diocese of Masasi c	100	—	20,000	—	50,000	51	—	—	12	—	—	A
Diocese of Morogoro b	171	—	6,186	—	14,591	18	154	34	4	—	1*	A
Diocese of South West Tanzania c	220	—	35,000	—	100,000	35	—	—	6	1	—	A
Diocese of Victoria Nyanza b	131	—	6,196	—	17,591	27	—	—	6	—	1*	A
Diocese of Western Tanganyika b	119	—	5,859	—	16,950	17	—	—	2	—	—	A
Diocese of Zanzibar and Tanga c	105	—	10,922	—	24,121	47	—	—	6	—	1*	A
Churches of Christ ... d	—	—	2,000	—	—	—	—	—	—	—	—	D
Evangelical Lutheran Church in Tanganyika:												
Central Synod ...	180	13,912	13,069	21,400	23,986	20	244	53	9	42	5	A
Mbulu Synod ...	30	—	903	—	3,010	2	36	15	4	(15)U	2	B
Northeast Diocese	110	15,691	20,500	18,572	49,750	26	13	25	8	32	2	B
Northern Diocese	383	82,732	90,356	139,141	181,885	86	594	27	9	36	1	A
Northwest Diocese	252	16,500	35,500	50,594	74,166	42	252	5	6	25	—	B
Southern Synod	41	49,232	63,550	74,060	114,409	52	(1,326)U	11	—	(11)U	—	D
Synod of Uzaramo-Uluguru ...	21	—	4,052	—	15,000	12	113	—	—	—	—	D
Gospel Furthering Fellowship ...	1	—	—	—	—	—	—	—	—	—	—	D
Moravian Church ...	400	28,250	42,710	58,511	72,000	34	1,058	206	10	29	0	B
Pemba Yearly Meeting of Friends	3	73	46	145	59	0	0	0	0	0	1	B
Pentecostal Assemblies of God ... e	30	5,000	5,000	15,000	10,000	11	246	9	2	2	2	B
Pentecostal Churches in Tanzania... f	261	—	8,699	—	24,660	—	—	—	36	85	—	D
Pentecostal Evangelistic Fellowship of Africa ... g	20	166	300	—	1,300	4	—	2	2	—	0	A
Presbyterian Church of East Africa	6	901	901	950	300	1	—	0	1	—	—	D
Salvation Army ...	—	—	—	—	1,504	—	—	—	—	—	—	B
Seventh-day Adventist Church ...	103	13,103	18,049	28,451	26,017	17	8	—	—	13	—	
Tanganyika Mennonite Church ...	158	2,298	5,211	8,000	10,000 N 2,000	—	(130)U	—	5	36	2	
	4,489	292,468	445,161 N54,200	537,708	1,034,588	605	4,580 (1,553)U	390	190	544 (38)U	21	

* United.   N Not reported.   U Unclassified.

Co-operating: a Southern Baptist Convention. b Church Missionary Society of Australia, New Zealand Church Missionary Society, Bethel Missionary Society, Breklum c United Society for the Propagation of the Gospel. d Berlin Missionary Society, Evangelical-Lutheran Mission, Danske Missionsselskab, Evangelish Lutherse Kerk in Nederland, Suomen Lähetysseura, Lutheran Church in America, Norwegian Lutheran Mission, Svenska Kyrkans Missionsstyrelse. e Pentecostal Assemblies of Canada. f Svenska Fria Missionen. g Elim Missionary Assemblies.

TOGO 21,853 sq. mls. Pop.: 1,565,000 (1963)

Church or Mission N.B. See notes on Statistics, page xiii	Places of Regular Worship	Communicants, Full Members (p. 57)		Total Christian Community (p. 57)		Staff					Theolog. Colls., Bible Schools	Source of Information
						National Workers, full-time			Missionaries from other Churches or countries, full-time			
		1962 Handbook	Latest available figure	1962 Handbook	Latest available figure	Ordained	Laymen	Women	Ordained	Lay-workers		
Assemblées de Dieu ...	255	982	2,000	5,121	16,199	4	77	—	22	—	1	B
Eglise Apostolique ...	—	—	5,000	—	—	—	—	—	5	—	—	D
Eglise Evangélique du Togo ... a	252	10,618	—	50,000	45,000	23	194	—	5	16	—	D
Eglise Méthodiste ...	—	10,000	4,000	30,000	—	2	—	—	—	—	—	E
Southern Baptist Convention ...	5	—	65	—	745	0	1	0	1	1	0	B
			N10,618		N35,000							
	512	21,600	21,683	85,121	96,944	29	272	0	28	17	1	

N Not reported.

Co-operating: a Société des Missions Evangéliques de Paris, United Church Board for World Ministries, Northern German Missionary Society (Bremen).

TUNISIA 48,195 sq. mls. Pop.: 4,494,000 (1963)

Church or Mission	Places of Regular Worship	Communicants, Full Members		Total Christian Community		National Workers, full-time			Missionaries		Theolog. Colls., Bible Schools	Source of Information
		1962 Handbook	Latest available figure	1962 Handbook	Latest available figure	Ordained	Laymen	Women	Ordained	Lay-workers		
Christian Missions in Many Lands...	1	20	—	20	—	—	—	—	—	—	—	E
Eglise Pentecôtiste ...	1	35	—	50	—	—	—	—	—	—	—	E
Englise Anglicane* ...	—	—	50	—	150	—	—	—	—	—	—	
Eglise Méthodiste en Afrique du Nord ...	2	50	40	1,000	100	0	0	0	1	4	0	E
Eglise Reformée en Tunisie ...	2	647	200	647	300	(7)U	(16)U	0	—	—	0	D
Mission Adventiste du Septième Jour ...	3	149	5	175	20	0	0	0	—	—	—	E
North Africa Mision ...	3	25			N 1,717							E
	19	777	757	1,892	1,737	(7)U	(16)U	0	1	4	0	
			N752		N 1,717							

N Not reported.

Co-operating: * Church's Ministry to the Jews.

UGANDA

93,981 sq. mls. Pop.: 7,189,600 (1963)

Baptist Churches of Uganda	a	9	—	80	—	200	1	4	0	5	5	0	B
Church of Uganda	b	6,500	180,839	200,000	825,641	1,500,000	369	—	—	52	100	2	A
Conservative Baptist Foreign Mission Society		11	—	25	—	300	0	—	0	5	5	0	A
Pentecostal Assemblies of God	c	100	—	6,000	—	10,000	—	—	—	2	2	0	B
Presbyterian Church of East Africa		2	—	—	—	300	0	—	0	0	0	0	D
Salvation Army		—	—	1,210	—	2,017	—	—	—	—	—	—	A
Seventh-day Adventist Church		51	4,112	6,272	10,080	8,152	—	—	—	—	—	—	A
		6,673	184,951	213,587	835,721	1,520,969	370	4	0	64	112	2	

Co-operating: **a** Southern Baptist Convention. **b** Africa Inland Mission, Bible Churchmen's Missionary Society, Church Missionary Society. **c** Pentecostal Assemblies of Canada.

UNITED ARAB REPUBLIC

386,198 sq. mls. Pop.: 27,963,000 (1963)

Armenian Evangelical Congregational Church		5	30	—	160	—	—	—	—	0	0	0	E
Assemblies of God		138	5,286	9,105	13,026	15,667	—	—	—	6	—	1	B
Baptist Church		6	20	—	180	—	—	—	—	0	0	0	E
Brethren	a	165	6,500	—	9,000	—	—	(75)U	—	—	—	—	E
Church of God		15	500	700	600	800	9	—	—	1	—	0	A
Coptic Evangelical Church*	b	256	24,665	27,344	75,000	100,000	182	6	—	12	27	1	A
Episcopal Church in Egypt*		10	1,296	800	2,868	1,000	5	300	150	2	6	0	B
Egypt General Mission		5	150	—	400	—	—	—	—	—	—	—	E
Free Methodist Church†		92	—	4,250	—	15,250	65	158	1	8	5	1	B

Co-operating: * Church Missionary Society, Jerusalem and the East Mission. † Peniel American Mission and former Church of the Standard (Canadian Holiness Movement).

UNITED ARAB REPUBLIC—continued

Church or Mission (N.B. See notes on Statistics, page xiii)	Places of Regular Worship	Communicants, Full Members (p. 57) 1962 Handbook	Latest available figure	Total Christian Community (p. 57) 1962 Handbook	Latest available figure	National Workers, full-time Ordained	Lay-men	Women	Missionaries from other Churches or countries, full-time Ordained	Lay-workers	Theolog. Colls., Bible Schools	Source of Information
Pentecostal Church of God ... c	30	4,020	3,000	4,020	5,000	12	13	0	0	0	0	A
Seventh-day Adventist Church ...	22	776	947	1,925	2,000	11	18	0	—	—	—	D
Swiss Evangelical Nile Mission ... *	2	—	N6,750	—	N 9,740	0	12	15	1	13	0	B
	743	43,293	52,396	107,179	149,007	282	592 (75)U	174	28	47	3	

* Medical work only.   N Not reported.

Co-operating: a Christian Missions in Many Lands. b United Presbyterian Church in the USA. c Church of God (Cleveland). Also working: Armenian Brotherhood, Baptist Evangelical Church, Church of Christ, Church of Faith, Church of Grace, Day of Pentecost Church, First Baptist Biblical Church, Greek Evangelical Church, Open Brethren, Pentecostal Grace Church.

UPPER VOLTA

105,900 sq. mls.   Pop.: 4,650,000 (1963)

Church or Mission	Places of Regular Worship	Communicants, Full Members (p. 57) 1962 Handbook	Latest available figure	Total Christian Community (p. 57) 1962 Handbook	Latest available figure	National Workers, full-time Ordained	Lay-men	Women	Missionaries from other Churches or countries, full-time Ordained	Lay-workers	Theolog. Colls., Bible Schools	Source of Information
Assemblées de Dieu ... a	199	2,710	16,000	6,333	24,009	—	(188)U	—	—	(35)U	2	B
Eglise Pentecôtiste ... b	—	—	—	—	—	—	—	—	—	—	—	D
Evangelical Christian Church of Mali and Upper Volta ... c	150	—	1,700	147	3,000	—	100	—	10	15	1	B
Evangelical Churches of West Africa d	9	37	175	100	2,500	0	—	0	5	17	1	B
Worldwide Evangelization Crusade	6	11	25	—	150	0	0	0	6	8	0	B
	364	2,758	17,900	6,580	29,659	0	288 (188)U	0	21	75	4	

N Not reported.   U Unclassified.

Co-operating: a Assemblées de Dieu (France), Assemblées of God (USA). b Canadian Pentecostal Mission. c Christian and Missionary Alliance. d Sudan Interior Mission.

ZAMBIA 208,130 sq. mls. Pop.: 3,545,200 (1963)

Church	(1)	(2)	(3)	(4)	(5)	(6)	(7)	(8)	(9)	(10)	(11)	
African Methodist Episcopal Church	500	—	7,500	—	—	25	—	—	—	—	—	D
African Reformed Church a	12	18,101	20,000	60,000	59,000	7	243	73	8	81	1	B
Baptist Mission of Zambia b	41	1,209	3,000	—	—	2	35	0	12	9	0	C
Baptist Union of Central Africa	50	735	1,124	4,800	4,593	—	(116)U	—	4	12	1	E
Brethren in Christ Church	200	1,500	—	1,838	—	—	200	—	7	16	0	A
Christian Missions in Many Lands	27	1,300	—	13,500	—	5	—	—	—	104	1	E
Church of Christ (Disciples)	—	—	—	4,000	—	—	45	12	10	11	2	E
Church of the Nazarene	—	—	—	—	—	—	—	—	—	—	—	C
Diocese of Zambia (Anglican) c	—	—	—	—	—	—	—	—	—	—	—	A
Dutch Reformed Church (Mother Church)	120	20,000	23,000	40,000	45,000	15	247	22	30	55	0	B
Evangelical Church in Zambia d	1	2,926	1,113	7,090	2,417	—	(565)U	—	10	72	1	B
Full Gospel Church	209	—	4,635	—	16,670	—	—	—	—	—	—	C
Lambaland Baptist Church e	2	—	1,200	—	—	—	—	—	—	—	—	D
Lutheran Church	16	—	60	—	60	6	2	6	2	—	—	B
New Apostolic Church	—	—	—	—	—	—	—	—	—	—	—	C
Pentecostal Assemblies of Canada	40	—	800	—	2,500	—	—	—	1	1	1	A
Pilgrim Holiness Church	—	—	—	—	—	—	—	—	—	—	—	C
Presbyterian Church of Southern Africa	—	—	—	—	—	—	—	—	—	—	—	C
Reformed Baptist Mission of Canada	—	—	—	—	—	—	—	—	—	—	—	C
Salvation Army	—	—	—	—	—	—	—	—	—	—	—	C
Scandinavian Independent Baptist Union	15	—	1,000	1,000	2,000	—	—	—	—	—	—	D
Seventh-day Adventist Church	114	550	13,510	29,043	33,729	14 (45)U	(111)U	—	4	3	0	D
United Church of Zambia f	648	8,762	23,702 N4,009	—	N63,043	92	50	34	41	55	1	A
	1,995	55,083	104,653	161,271	229,012	211 (45)U	1,614 (792)U	147	129	419	7	

N Not reported.   U Unclassified.

Co-operating: a Dutch Reformed Church (South Africa). b Southern Baptist Convention. c United Society for the Propagation of the Gospel. d Africa Evangelical Fellowship (SAGM). e South African Baptist Missionary Society. f Church of Scotland Mission, London Missionary Society, Methodist Missionary Society, Société des Missions Evangéliques de Paris, United Church Board for World Ministries, United Church of Canada.

AFRICAN INDEPENDENT CHURCHES

Adherents and Bodies by Nation and Region, 1966

Nation	Year[a]	Distinct[b] Bodies	Average size of body	Adherents[c]
WEST AFRICA	1862	588	1,559	917,100
Dahomey	1899	4	1,100	4,500
Gambia	–	0	–	nil
Ghana	1862	50	4,000	200,000
Guinea	–	0	–	nil
Ivory Coast	1913	20	10,000	200,000
Liberia	1947	10	1,000	10,000
Mali	–	0	–	nil
Niger	–	0	–	nil
Nigeria	1888	500[d]	1,000	500,000[e]
Portuguese Guinea	–	0	–	nil
Senegal	–	0	–	nil
Sierra Leone	1947	2	1,000	2,000
Togo	1930[c]	1	500	500
Upper Volta	1959	1	100	100
CENTRAL AFRICA	1888	563	2,126	1,197,050
Angola	1949	2	5,000	10,000
Cameroun	1888	7	7,000	50,000
Cabinda	1953	1	1,000	1,000
C.A.R.	1956	2	2,500	5,000
Chad	1951	2	1,000	2,000
Congo-Brazzaville	1921	5	4,000	20,000
Congo-Kinshasa	1921	500[f]	2,000	1,000,000
Gabon	1928	3	3,300	10,000
Spanish Equat. Africa	1948	1	50	50
Zambia	1900	40	2,500	100,000
EASTERN AFRICA	1894	291	3,522	1,025,000
Burundi	1959	2	10,000	20,000
Ethiopia	1955	5	10,000	20,000
French Somaliland	–	0	–	nil
Kenya	1914	120[g]	5,000	600,000
Malawi	1900	40	1,250	50,000
Madagascar	1894	20	10,000	200,000
Mozambique	1921	80	600	50,000
Rwanda	–	0	–	nil
Somalia	–	0	–	nil
Sudan	1937	2	–	nil[h]
Tanzania	1925	25	1,000	25,000
Uganda	1914	2	5,000	10,000
SOUTHERN AFRICA	1872	3,152	1,177	3,710,000
Botswana	1904	10	1,000	10,000
Lesotho	1872	10	5,000	50,000
Rhodesia	1910[c]	100	5,000	500,000
South Africa	1882	3,000	1,030	3,100,000[i]
S.W. Africa	1946	2	10,000	20,000
Swaziland	1904	30[j]	1,000	30,000
AFRICA TOTAL		4,594	1,500	6,849,050

Notes: a. Date of first indigenous independent church movement in nation or region.
   b. Total all bodies with a distinct name, including the few bodies now defunct (less than 10 per cent of the total).
   c. These estimates of total community are based on claimed or estimated totals for individual bodies (see pp. 227, 228 for a selection).
   d. In 1964, 78 bodies were registered with the Nigerian Government, but there were scores of unregistered small bodies.
   e. In the year 1921 there were 90,233 adherents in the nation.
   f. In 1966, some 200 bodies had applied for government *personnalité civile*; in only two cases had it been granted, and of these one was proscribed for subversion during the year.
   g. In 1966, 70 bodies were registered with the Kenya Government.
   h. Former adherents had rejoined mission churches by 1966.
   i. Estimate for 1966 based on 1960 Census figure of 2,188,303.
   j. In the 1936 Census, 20 bodies with 20,000 adherents were reported.

BAHAMAS 4,404 sq. mls. Pop.: 131,428 estimate (1963)

Church or Mission — N.B. See notes on Statistics, page xiii	Places of Regular Worship	Communicants, Full Members (p. 57)		Total Christian Community (p. 57)		Staff — National Workers, full-time			Staff — Missionaries from other Churches or countries, full-time		Theolog. Colls., Bible Schools	Source of Information
		1962 Handbook	Latest available figure	1962 Handbook	Latest available figure	Ordained	Laymen	Women	Ordained	Lay-workers		
Assemblies of God	12	362	150	862	1,050	(16)U	—	—	(4)U	—	—	B
Baptist Mid-Missions	2	—	60	—	85	1	—	—	—	—	—	B
Church of England (a)	93	7,459	8,000	13,289	15,000	17	153	8	19	—	—	A
Church of God (Anderson)	—	—	3,983	—	11,949	(96)U	—	—	—	—	—	D
Church of God (Cleveland)	58	1,360	3,130	1,360	18,130	—	80	—	—	—	—	B
Church of God of Prophecy	43	4,060	4,060	9,000	9,000	—	—	—	—	—	—	E
Church of Scotland	—	—	250	—	250	—	—	—	—	—	—	B
Christian Missions in Many Lands	—	—	2,774	—	8,322	5	—	2	12	1	—	D
Methodist Church	39	2,910	3,171	4,661	6,859	(9)U	(17)U	—	—	—	—	B
Seventh-Day Adventists	29	1,103	1,274	1,675	2,364	2	3	—	5	5	1	B
Southern Baptist Convention	17	166	281	178	956	—	—	—	—	2	—	B
United Baptist Mission	70	—	6,000	—	14,000	—	—	—	—	—	—	D
	363	29,982	33,133	71,022	87,965	146 (121)U	253 (17)U	10	40 (4)U	8	1	

Figures supplied by the Bahamas Christian Council (1965). Estimated Total Christian Community:

Anglicans	...	31,481
Baptists	...	38,630
Methodists	...	10,754
Presbyterians	...	600
Roman Catholics	...	26,413
Orthodox Community	...	55
Pentecostal Groups and Seventh-day Adventists	...	15,000 Grand Total 121,933

U Unclassified

Co-operating: a United Society for the Propagation of the Gospel.
Also working: Bahamas United Baptist Mission; Church of Christ Scientist; Salvation Army.

BARBADOS 166 sq. mls. Pop.: 240,468 estimated (1963)

Anglican Church ... a	55	—	23,628	—	150,000	55	63	—	—	2	1	A
Church of God (Cleveland)	47	—	2,533	—	12,533	(78)U	—	1	—	—	—	B
Church of the Nazarene	32	1,180	1,283	—	7,116	15	—	1	8	4	—	B
Methodist Church*	89	—	14,613	2,560	67,850	21	—	—	8	2	—	B
	223	1,180	42,057	2,560	237,499	169 (78)U	63	2	16	8	1	

* Figures include Trinidad.

Co-operating: a Community of the Resurrection; United Society for the Propagation of the Gospel.
Also working: Church of Christ Scientist.

BERMUDA 21 sq. mls. Pop.: 47,230 (1963)

Anglican: Diocese of Bermuda	16	3,500	3,500	19,000	19,000	16	3	—	—	E
Church of God (Cleveland)	4	150	173	150	673	8	—	—	—	B
Church of God of Prophecy	1	17	17	17	17	—	—	—	—	E
Church of Scotland ...	—	—	460	—	460	—	—	—	—	B
Church of the Nazarene	1	—	17	—	124	—	—	1	1	B
Seventh-day Adventists	4	—	920	—	1,666	3	—	6	—	B
	26	3,667	5,087	19,167	21,740	27	3	7	1	

BRITISH HONDURAS   8,866 sq. mls.   Pop.: 90,343 (1960)

Church or Mission N.B. See notes on Statistics, page xiii	Places of Regular Worship	Communicants, Full Members (p. 57) 1962 Hand-book	Latest avail-able figure	Total Christian Community (p. 57) 1962 Hand-book	Latest avail-able figure	National Workers, full-time Or-dained	Lay-men	Women	Missionaries from other Churches or countries, full-time Or-dained	Lay-workers	Theo-log. Colls., Bible Schools	Source of Information
Anglican Church	23	3,000	8,000	10,000	15,000	7	—	2	(2)U	—	—	A
Assemblies of God	11	66	54	191	755	(7)U	—	—	1	8	1	B
Belize Mennonite Mission	3	—	16	357	50	—	(34)U	—	(13)U	—	1	B
Church of the Nazarene	23	450	493	1,396	1,993	3	1	—	(4)U	—	1	D
Methodist Church	17	464	1,801	3,600	14,505	1	2	1	—	—	—	D
Pentecostal Church of God	12	100	800	100	800	—	18	—	1	—	1	B
Seventh-day Adventists	16	954	954	1,566	1,056	—	—	—	—	—	—	D
	105	5,164	12,118	17,524	34,159	18 (7)U	55 (34)U	3	21 (19)U	8	3	

U Unclassified

CANADA   3,560,238 sq. mls.   Pop.: 19,237,000 (1964)

Church or Mission	Places of Regular Worship	Communicants 1962 Hand-book	Latest avail-able figure	Total Christian Community 1962 Hand-book	Latest avail-able figure	Or-dained	Lay-men	Women	Miss. Or-dained	Lay-workers	Theo.	Source
Anglican Church of Canada	3,602	664,729	686,552	1,300,029	1,365,313	n.a.	56	111	—	—	10	A
Apostolic Church of Pentecost of Canada	125	5,000	5,000	5,000	5,000	—	140	30	—	79	—	E
Baptist Federation of Canada	2,000	136,371	138,866	436,371	436,371	842	10	40	35	11	5	A
Brethren in Christ Church	27	—	1,307	—	3,117	30	1	4	6	—	4	B
Canadian Lutheran Council	1,090	—	177,367	—	287,148	743	75	20	—	—	1	A
Christian and Missionary Alliance	156	—	15,855	—	15,855	183	—	—	—	—	1	B
Churches of Christ (Disciples)	81	7,000	8,909	9,000	14,000	69	—	—	—	—	1	A
Church of the Nazarene	148	—	6,954	—	26,937	234	—	—	—	—	1	B

CANADA—continued

Evangelical Lutheran Church	343	—	45,110	—	100,000	215	—	—	—	12	26	3	A
Evangelical United Brethren Church	66	10,095	10,095	29,364	29,364	30	12	—	—	—	—	—	E
Fellowship of Evangelical Baptist Churches	326	23,000	30,000	50,000	100,000	268	58	5	—	—	—	—	A
Free Methodist Church	142	—	4,752	—	12,220	191	—	—	—	—	—	—	A
Mennonite Brethren Church	112	—	15,315	—	65,000	86	24	20	4	—	—	2	B
Moravian Church*	9	1,167	1,167	1,696	1,696	6	—	—	—	—	—	5	E
North American Baptist General Conference	91	—	11,820	—	11,820	84	—	1	1	—	—	1	B
Pentecostal Assemblies of Canada	650	50,000	98,000	100,000	150,000	700	—	—	—	—	—	10	A
Presbyterian Church	1,178	198,000	198,000	781,747	781,747	766	—	—	—	—	—	—	E
Reformed Presbyterian Church	—	—	—	—	—	—	—	—	—	—	—	—	
Evangelical Synod	2	—	120	—	120	3	—	—	—	—	—	—	B
Salvation Army‡	1,304	26,321	26,189	92,158	92,158	1,687†	3,213	1,076	—	—	—	—	E
Seventh-day Adventists	179	14,347	16,189	25,874	33,392	123	478	—	—	—	—	—	E
United Church of Canada	6,011	980,461	980,461	2,989,000	2,989,000	3,294	220	291	—	—	—	—	E
Yearly Meeting of Society of Friends	23	623	779	623	779	—	4	4	—	—	—	—	A
	17,665	2,196,494	2,478,939	6,237,944	6,521,037	9,554	4,966	1,602	58	118	43	

Estimated Total Christian Community from Canadian Council of Churches:

Protestants and Anglicans	...	9,212,000
Roman Catholics	...	8,530,000
Orthodox Community	...	350,000

n.a. Not available.

* Includes Labrador. † Total number of Officers. ‡ Includes Bermuda.

Also working: Church of Christ, Scientist; International Grenfell Association.

CAYMAN ISLANDS — 100 sq. mls. — Pop.: 8,803 (1960)

Church or Mission (N.B. See notes on Statistics, page xiii)	Places of Regular Worship	Communicants, Full Members (p. 57)		Total Christian Community (p. 57)		National Workers, full-time			Missionaries from other Churches or countries, full-time		Theolog. Colls., Bible Schools	Source of Information
		1962 Handbook	Latest available figure	1962 Handbook	Latest available figure	Ordained	Laymen	Women	Ordained	Lay-workers		
World Presbyterian Missions ...	1	—	46	—	175	1	3	—	—	—	—	A
	1	—	46	—	175	1	3	—	—	—	—	—

Also working: Reformed Presbyterian Church Evangelical Synod; United Society for the Propagation of the Gospel (with Anglican Church).

COSTA RICA — 19,653 sq. mls. — Pop.: 1,369,659 (1963)

Church or Mission	Places of Regular Worship	Communicants, Full Members (p. 57)		Total Christian Community (p. 57)		National Workers, full-time			Missionaries from other Churches or countries, full-time		Theolog. Colls., Bible Schools	Source of Information
		1962 Handbook	Latest available figure	1962 Handbook	Latest available figure	Ordained	Laymen	Women	Ordained	Lay-workers		
Asambleas de Dios (Assemblies of God)	35	524	915	970	3,680	10	38	—	7	—	2	A
Asociacion Bautista Centroamericana	7	90	90	300	300	2	3	—	1	1	—	E
Asociacion de Iglesias Biblicas Costarricenses	40	1,022	1,500	2,000	3,000	7	16	—	—	—	—	C
Asociacion de Iglesias Evangelicas Centroamericanas ...	33	529	700	1,000	1,500	9	18	3	—	—	—	C
Central American Mission ...	33	—	1,050	—	3,500	9	9	2	6	19	—	B
Church of God of Prophecy	—	130	130	130	130	—	—	—	—	—	—	E
Church of God (Cleveland) ...	10	—	632	—	1,054	(10)U	—	—	—	—	—	B
Companerismo Bautista Mundial (World Baptist Fellowship) ...	2	new	—	new	—	—	—	—	2	2	—	C
Convencion Bautista del Sur (Southern Baptist Convention) ...	19	540	1,031	540	2,699	19	—	—	6	6	1	A
Iglesia de Dios (Anderson, Ind.) ...	5	10	56	50	300	1	—	—	2	—	—	C

COSTA RICA—*continued*

Iglesia de Dios (Cleveland, Tenn.) ...	14	700	700	700	800	—	7	—	1	2	—	B
Iglesia de Dios (Universal) ...	2	new	36	new	80	—	1	—	—	1	—	C
Iglesia del Nazareno (Church of the Nazarene) ...	5	new	63	new	185	2	—	—	3	2	—	B
Iglesia Episcopal (Episcopal Church) a	15	20	943	50	2,374	1	25*	—	11	1	1	B
Iglesia Evangelica Nacional ...	2	—	20	50	50	—	2	—	—	—	—	E
Iglesia Luterana (Alejan) German Lutheran Church ...	1	20	20	40	40	—	—	—	1	—	—	B
Iglesia Luterana, Sinodo de Misuri (Lutheran Church Missouri Synod)	1	—	—	—	630	—	—	—	—	—	—	B
Iglesia Metodista (Methodist Church) (U.S.A.) ...	36	504	874	762	2,725	7	7	—	(19)U	—	—	B
Iglesia de la Santidad Pentecostal (Pentecostal Holiness Church) ...	8	36	284	175	979	(13)U	1	—	(4)U	64	1	B
Latin America Mission, Inc. ...	42	934	934	3,400	3,400	3	—	4	22	5	—	C&E
Limon Baptist Church ...	15	50	375	200	500	—	—	2	13	5	—	C
Limon Methodist Church ...	6	—	—	—	500	—	—	—	1	—	—	C
Methodist Church (Gt. Britain) ...	15	—	2,399	—	3,701	4	—	—	2	—	—	D
Mision Evangelica Menonita (Mennonite Church) ...	9	new	12	new	100	—	—	—	3	16	—	C
Mision del Evangelio Cuadrado (International Church of the Four-square Gospel) ...	19	100	100	109	109	—	—	—	—	—	—	E
Seventh-day Adventists ...	31	954	2,126	1,566	5,772	6	(23)U	—	(23)U	—	—	B
Union Church ...	1	—	98	—	1,000	—	—	—	1	—	1	C
	406	12,218	15,089	22,902	39,008	103 (23)U	149 (23)U	11	104 (23)U	124	6	

* For all Central America.

Co-operating: a Protestant Episcopal Church in the U.S.A.

Also working: Navigators; Salvation Army; World Baptist Fellowship Mission Agency.

CUBA   44,206 sq. mls.   Pop.: 7,022,300 (1962)

Church or Mission (N.B. See notes on Statistics, page xiii)	Places of Regular Worship	Communicants, Full Members (p. 57)		Total Christian Community (p. 57)		Staff					Theolog. Colls., Bible Schools	Source of Information
		1962 Handbook	Latest available figure	1962 Handbook	Latest available figure	National Workers, full-time			Missionaries from other Churches or countries, full-time			
						Ordained	Laymen	Women	Ordained	Lay-workers		
American Baptist Home Mission Societies	227	6,537	6,537	35,000	35,000	—	—	—	—	—	—	E
American Friends Board of Missions	11	381	381	1,092	1,092	7	—	—	—	—	—	E
Assemblies of God	290	2,441	2,746	3,984	13,408	(121)U	—	—	—	—	—	B
Berean Mission	12	1,000	1,000	5,000	5,000	—	—	—	12 (13)U	—	—	E
Church of God (Anderson)	10	—	200	—	500	3	—	—	—	—	—	D
Church of God (Cleveland)	12	—	411	230	911	23	—	—	—	—	—	B
Church of God of Prophecy	11	230	305	230	915	12	—	—	—	—	—	D
Church of the Nazarene	20	190	190	1,128	1,128	2	7	—	1	—	1	B
Christian Reformed Church	1	—	200	—	600	—	15	—	—	—	—	D
Congregational Holiness Church	34	1,000	1,000	3,000	3,000	—	—	—	—	2	1	E
Conservative Baptists a	210	—	4,200	—	12,000	25	15	4	—	—	4	D
Evangelical Association	91	—	3,000	—	3,000	—	—	—	1	1	—	B
Free Will Baptists	26	2,000	2,000	6,000	6,000	(13)U	—	17	1	1	1	B
Iglesia Episcopal b	55	—	3,712	69,981	74,422	23	62	—	—	—	—	E
Iglesia Presbyteriana	—	—	—	—	—	—	—	—	—	—	—	
International Church of the Foursquare Gospel	30	4,000	4,000	21,000	21,000	—	—	—	—	—	—	E
Lutheran Church of Cuba (Missouri Synod)	6	1,000	1,000	1,000	1,000	—	—	—	—	—	—	B
Methodist Church (U.S.A.)	129	8,000	10,000	35,000	50,000	38	3	—	1 (50)U	3	—	D
Open Bible Standard Missions	10	305	305	2,500	2,500	9	36	—	3	—	—	E
Pentecostal Church of God	7	—	300	—	300	—	28	—	—	—	—	B
Pentecostal Evangelical Church	—	15,000	15,000	15,000	15,000	(32)U	—	—	—	—	—	E
Pentecostal Holiness Church	20	—	397	500	1,996	—	—	—	—	—	—	B
Seventh-day Adventists	82	5,464	6,517	11,401	14,364	16	(69)U	—	5	—	—	B

106

CUBA—continued

Southern Baptist Convention	84	—	8,750	—	26,250	—	—	—	(166)U	—	—	D
United World Mission	16	—	800	—	2,400	—	(18)U	—	(13)U	—	—	D
West Indies Mission	36	2,800	925	9,000	2,775	13	41	—	(19)U	—	1	D
	1,440	85,222	74,063	264,927	295,727	344 (166)U	300 (87)U	21	290 (261)U	7	8	

U Unclassified.

Co-operating: a West Indies Mission.   b Protestant Episcopal Church in the U.S.A.

Also working: Salvation Army.

DOMINICAN REPUBLIC   18,700 sq   Pop.: 3,451,700 (1964)

African Methodist Episcopal Church ...	5	500	500	1,800	1,800	4	4	—	5	—	—	E
Assemblies of God	314	2,211	3,352	5,211	10,436	(81)U	—	—	(6)U	—	—	B
Baptist Mid-Missions	9	38	118	102	360	(6)U	—	—	—	—	—	B
Board for Christian Work in Santo Domingo	38	—	2,825	—	12,155	12	14	—	2	—	—	D
Church of God (Anderson)	18	—	435	—	1,300	—	—	—	(38)U	—	—	D
Church of God (Cleveland)	34	700	1,583	1,300	2,539	(40)U	—	—	(20)U	—	—	D
Church of God of Prophecy	21	837	996	837	2,000	—	—	—	(9)U	—	—	D
Christian Missions in Many Lands...	27	—	550	—	1,100	—	2	—	(18)U	—	—	D
Dominican Evangelical Church ...	66	2,702	2,702	11,905	11,905	11	14	—	1	1	—	E
Evangelical Mennonite Church ...	11	233	236	485	890	3	12	—	6	—	—	D
Free Methodist Church	19	1,450	1,479	5,800	3,452	12	114	3	3	4	—	B
Iglesia Episcopal ... ... a	14	1,318	1,266	2,394	2,871	4	6	155	3	—	1	B
Missionary Church Association ...	15	68	191	100	955	—	11	—	3	3	—	B
Mission Evangelizadora ... b	14	48	150	97	300	—	2	—	3	9	—	B

DOMINICAN REPUBLIC—continued

Church or Mission N.B. See notes on Statistics, page xiii	Places of Regular Worship	Communicants, Full Members (p. 57)		Total Christian Community (p. 57)		Staff						Source of Information
						National Workers, full-time			Missionaries from other Churches or countries, full-time		Theolog. Colls., Bible Schools	
		1962 Handbook	Latest available figure	1962 Handbook	Latest available figure	Ordained	Laymen	Women	Ordained	Lay-workers		
Moravian Church ...	2	120	120	640	640	—	2	—	—	—	—	D
Seventh-day Adventists ...	54	3,381	7,903	6,735	24,185	9	(100)U 7	—	(18)U	—	—	B
West Indies Mission ...	7	—	226	—	545	—	—	—	—	—	—	D
	668	20,172	23,749	43,765	77,433	183 (127)U	242 (100)U	158	138 (109)U	17	1	

U Unclassified.

Co-operating: **a** Protestant Episcopal Church in the U.S.A.   **b** Unevangelized Fields Mission.
Also working: Moravian Church in America; Worldwide Evangelization Crusade; Southern Baptist Convention.

EL SALVADOR   8,236 sq. mls.   Pop.: 2,723,040 estimate (1963)

Church or Mission	Places of Regular Worship	1962 Handbook	Latest available figure	1962 Handbook	Latest available figure	Ordained	Laymen	Women	Ordained	Lay-workers	Theolog. Colls., Bible Schools	Source of Information
American Baptist Home Mission Societies ...	23	1,911	2,036	—	4,040	4	32	—	(7)U	—	—	D
Assemblies of God ...	1,088	6,203	9,052	8,780	41,291	(1,058)U	—	5	(11)U	19	1	B
Central American Mission ...	63	2,300	2,540	5,000	6,500	24	37	—	3	—	1	B
Central American Mission of the Lutheran Church (Missouri Synod) ...	24	65	459	231	985	2	4	—	7	—	—	B
Church of God (Cleveland) ...	72	2,200	3,187	2,200	4,499	(88)U	—	—	—	2	—	B
Church of the Nazarene ...	2	—	—	—	224	—	—	1	2	—	—	B
Evangelical Lutheran Church	—	—	97	—	97	—	—	—	—	—	—	

EL SALVADOR—continued

Iglesia Episcopal ... ... a	1	—	69	—	206	1	—	—	2	—	—	B
Pentecostal Churches ...	—	10,000	10,000	10,000	10,000	—	—	—	—	—	—	E
Seventh-day Adventists ...	26	1,659	3,171	5,680	7,239	4	24	6	32 (18U)	21	2	B
	1,299	29,019	30,611	57,691	75,081	1,181 (1,146U)	97	6				

Co-operating: a Protestant Episcopal Church in the U.S.A.

U Unclassified.

GUATEMALA   42,042 sq. mls.   Pop.: 4,278,341 (1964)

Assemblies of God	576	3,964	6,827	6,582	27,661	(448)U	—	—	(12)U	—	2	B
Central American Mission (Iglesia Evangelica) ...	355	—	6,609	—	22,000	79	27	6	19	50	4	B
Church of God (Cleveland)* ...	216	—	6,923	—	10,979	(252)U	—	—	—	(2)U	—	B
Church of God of Prophecy ...	22	1,030	1,030	1,030	2,060	(33)U	—	—	—	—	—	D
Church of the Nazarene ...	54	1,814	1,859	4,646	8,236	45	3	3	—	8	8	B
Evangelical Presbyterian Church ... b	241	5,700	8,300	15,300	21,500	(67)U	—	—	9	—	3	B
Friends, California Yearly Meeting...	123	1,432	7,000	7,881	12,000	11	(21)U	—	(6)U (15)U	—	—	D
Iglesia Episcopal c	6	—	303	541	541	3	—	—	2	—	—	B
Iglesia Metodista Primitiva ... a	34	691	1,800	2,500	2,100	8	4	1	5	6	1	D
Lutheran Church (Missouri Synod) ...	4	—	813	—	1,660	—	2	3	(7)U	—	—	B
Pentecostal Church of God ...	1	—	85	—	85	—	—	—	—	—	—	D
Seventh-day Adventists ...	31	2,835	5,285	4,865	15,793	7	(21)U	—	3	—	—	B
Southern Baptist Convention ...	53	1,703	2,093	—	6,476	20	14	—	9	9	2	B
	1,716	19,169	48,927	43,345	131,091	973 (800)U	92 (42)U	13	87 (40)U	75 (2)U	15	

* Figures for Central, North and West Guatemala.

Co-operating: a Primitive Methodist Church. b United Presbyterian Church in U.S.A. c Protestant Episcopal Church in U.S.A. U Unclassified.

Also working: Christian Nationals' Evangelism Commission. Independent Board of Presbyterian Foreign Missions. Source of Light Mission. Wycliffe Bible Translators.

HAITI 10,700 sq. mls. Pop.: 4,000,000 estimate (1961)

Church or Mission (N.B. See notes on Statistics, page xiii)	Places of Regular Worship	Communicants, Full Members (p. 57) 1962 Handbook	Communicants Latest available figure	Total Christian Community (p. 57) 1962 Handbook	Total Christian Community Latest available figure	National Workers, full-time Ordained	National Workers Lay-men	National Workers Women	Missionaries from other Churches or countries, full-time Ordained	Missionaries Lay-workers	Theolog. Colls., Bible Schools	Source of Information
American Baptist Home Mission Societies	620	30,459	27,178	79,000	92,200	31	—	—	(4)U	—	—	D
American Wesleyan Mission	57	1,456	2,183	6,000	7,000	6	28	—	8	15	3	B
Assemblies of God	57	399	1,143	1,100	7,050	(41)U	—	—	(4)U	—	—	E
Baptist Mid-Missions	18	269	534	1,447	1,132	—	—	—	—	—	1	B
Church of God (Cleveland)	185	20,205	13,421	20,205	54,121	(108)U	—	—	(230)U	(286)U	—	B
Church of God of Prophecy	249	16,208	16,814	16,208	33,650	—	—	—	—	6	—	D
Church of the Nazarene	220	880	2,631	6,417	20,215	55	15	15	4	—	1	B
Conservative Baptists	50	—	3,559	—	12,325	4	(45)U	—	(10)U	5	1	D
Eglise Episcopale b	164	10,615	13,438	30,650	35,330	28	188	—	4	—	1	B
Eglise Evangélique a	2	—	400	—	1,200	1	3	—	—	—	—	B
Faith Holiness Mission	33	160	—	—	—	6	—	—	—	—	1	B
Free Methodist Church	2	—	—	—	160	—	4	—	2	1	2	B
Inter-American Mission	2	—	125	—	750	2	(8)U	—	1	—	—	D
Methodist Church d	114	2,149	2,728	16,693	22,537	4	4	1	(10)U	4	—	B
Missionary Church Association	14	731	1,309	731	6,545	1	24	—	4	33	—	E
Mission Evangélique Baptiste c	229	—	9,255	—	35,000	20	—	—	2	6	1	E
Oriental Missionary Society	12	240	240	760	760	1	7	—	15	—	—	B
Pentecostal Church of God	116	—	7,500	9,000	9,000	2	—	2	3	—	1	B
Seventh-day Adventists	55	15,008	23,239	29,414	61,947	18	(93)U	—	1	—	—	B
West Indies Mission	200	10,000	35,000	78,000	100,000	50	100	50	15	35	1	A
	2,399	133,171	160,697	332,714	500,922	378 (149)U	519 (146)U	73	301 (254)U	391 (286)U	13	

U Unclassified.

Co-operating: **a** World Gospel Mission. **b** Protestant Episcopal Church in U.S.A. **c** Unevangelized Fields Mission. **d** Methodist Missionary Society.

Also working: East and West Indies Bible Mission (operates 'The Evangelistic Voice of Haiti' 4–VEH). Salvation Army.

GREENLAND

840,000 sq. mls. Pop.: 36,500 estimate (1965)

												A
												B
												B
Evangelical Lutheran Church … … …	120	28,210	35,000	30,500	35,000	24	135	—	—	—	—
Seventh-day Adventists … … …	1	7	9	7	9	1	2	—	—	—	—
Svenska Fria Missionen … … …	3	3	3	100	100	2	3	—	—	—	—
	124	28,220	35,012	30,607	35,109	27	140	—	—	—	—

HONDURAS

43,227 sq. mls. Pop.: 2,007,990 estimate (1963)

Assemblies of God … … …	94	674	1,017	1,243	4,956	(92)U	—	—	(10)U	—	—	B
Baptist Mid-Missions … … …	4	—	17	—	126	2	—	—	—	—	1	B
Central American Mission … … …	76	—	1,417	—	4,868	26	—	—	8	40	—	B
Church of God (Anderson, Ind.) … …	32	—	1,279	—	2,743	—	(42)U	—	(4)U	—	—	D
Church of God (Cleveland) … …	48	1,157	2,050	1,157	6,675	(72)U	2	—	—	7	—	B
Church of the Nazarene … … …	32	—	385	—	2,083	13	7	17	4	10	1	D
Conservative Baptists … … …	10	—	161	—	1,330	—	—	—	(7)U	—	—	A
Evangelical and Reformed Church c	50	746	1,000	—	2,000	9	(6)U	1	3	7	1	B
Evangelical Lutheran Church … …	—	43	43	43	43	—	3	—	—	—	—	
Friends, Board of Missions, California Yearly Meeting … … …	22	215	1,068	1,882	3,000	—	(10)U	—	(2)U	—	—	D
Iglesia de los Hermanos Unidos en Cristo … … a	13	270	287	300	927	6	—	1	1	2	—	B
Iglesia Episcopal … … b	7	300	323	200	619	—	—	—	3	—	—	B
Iglesia Evangelica Menonita … …	23	75	150	200	650	3	—	—	7	22	1	B
International Church of the Four-square Gospel … … …	7	183	310	262	1,000	(12)U	—	—	1	2	—	D
Methodist Church … … …	35	1,917	2,326	14,400	13,959	7	—	—	3	1	—	B
Moravian Church … … …	25	989	1,722	1,828	2,483	2	18	1	3	3	1	B

E

111

HONDURAS—*continued*

Church or Mission (N.B. See notes on Statistics, page xiii)	Places of Regular Worship	Communicants, Full Members (p. 57)		Total Christian Community (p. 57)		National Workers, full-time			Missionaries from other Churches or countries, full-time		Theolog. Colls., Bible Schools	Source of Information
		1962 Handbook	Latest available figure	1962 Handbook	Latest available figure	Ordained	Laymen	Women	Ordained	Lay-workers		
Seventh-day Adventists	24	—	2,471	—	6,381	6	17	—	1	1	1	B
Southern Baptist Convention	32	136	381	136	1,747	3	4	—	5	5	1	B
Wesleyan Methodist Mission	6	100	105	800	300	—	—	7	1	1	1	B
World Gospel Mission	55	267	300	1,825	1,000	21	11	13	9	16	1	B
	595	9,311	16,812	34,488	56,890	274 (176U)	120 (58U)	40	72 (23U)	116	6	

U Unclassified.

Co-operating: **a** Church of the United Brethren in Christ. **b** Protestant Episcopal Church in U.S.A. **c** United Church Board for World Ministries.

Also working: Missionary Aviation Fellowship. Pioneer Bible Mission. Svenska Fria Missionen. United Society for the Propagation of the Gospel. Wycliffe Bible Translators.

JAMAICA   4,411 sq. mls.   Pop.: 1,737,666 estimate (1964)

Church or Mission	Places of Regular Worship	Communicants, Full Members (p. 57)		Total Christian Community (p. 57)		National Workers, full-time			Missionaries from other Churches or countries, full-time		Theolog. Colls., Bible Schools	Source of Information
		1962 Handbook	Latest available figure	1962 Handbook	Latest available figure	Ordained	Laymen	Women	Ordained	Lay-workers		
African Methodist Episcopal Church	4	—	520	2,500	520	2	—	—	(5)U 1	—	—	D
American Friends, Board of Missions	14	725	725	3,000	2,500	(5)U 2	—	—	—	3	—	E
Apostolic Church	3	1,000	1,000	3,000	3,000	—	—	—	—	—	—	E
Assemblies of God	65	2,673	1,728	3,139	8,728	(54)U	—	—	8	—	1	B
Baptist Mid-Missions	18	—	495	—	1,640	(5)U	—	—	(15)U 3	—	—	B
Baptist Union	265	29,083	29,083	140,000	140,000	46	—	—	3	7	—	D
Church of God	83	2,000	3,000	3,075	6,000	—	—	—	5	—	—	D

JAMAICA—*continued*

Church of God (Cleveland)	240	—	17,598	—	67,598	(192)U	—	—	8	—	—	B
Church of God (Anderson, Ind.)*	93	—	2,180	—	3,480	11	—	—	—	—	—	D
Church of God of Prophecy†	176	—	7,875	—	15,780	—	—	—	(198)U	—	—	D
Church of the Province of West Indies (Diocese of Jamaica) b	128	39,000	39,000	312,000	312,000	59	348	4	18	—	—	E
Congregational Union	50	3,350	3,450	12,500	12,800	8	—	—	4	2	1	A & E
Methodist Church c	188	—	20,106	—	47,063	28	—	7	21	3	1	B
Missionary Bands of the World (Wesleyan)	36	1,415	1,244	400	1,600	14	55	—	3	6	1	B
Missionary Church Association	31	—	1,851	5,394	9,255	14	8	—	3	—	—	D
Moravian Missions	38	984	5,006	—	9,830	7	(3)U	—	(13)U	—	1	D
Open Bible Standard Church	10	1,100	437	4,000	1,475	18	(2)U	2	(11)U	—	1	D
Pentecostal Church of God	45	—	1,500	1,000	1,500	2	—	—	(2)U	3	—	B
Pilgrim Holiness Church	14	—	387	—	1,247	4	(8)U	2	10	—	—	D
Presbyterian Church a	—	13,000	11,956	25,000	12,262	21	(285)U	—	11	1	—	A
Seventh-day Adventists	315	30,319	40,833	47,764	83,612	56	(2)U	1	(5)U	—	—	B
Seventh-day Baptists	21	—	751	—	2,300	5	15	—	1	—	—	D
United Brethren in Christ	17	1,041	1,027	3,100	1,550	3	—	—	(8)U	—	1‡	B
United Christian Missionary Society	45	2,776	5,055	8,000	8,000	(18)U	(22)U	—	(8)U	—	1	A
Wesleyan Methodist	23	—	800	—	1,600	12	—	—	(8)U	—	—	D
	1,922	**128,466**	**197,607**	**570,872**	**755,340**	**579 (269)U**	**755 (327)U**	**16**	**361 (265)U**	**25**	**7**	D

The 1962 Edition gave statistics for the Federation of the West Indies. As that Federation no longer exists comparisons with 1962 figures are often now impossible. Some figures recently received from islands in the Caribbean also prevent correct and distinct classification. (See WEST INDIES, General, p. 000.)

* Includes Cayman Islands.   † Includes Turk Islands.   ‡ United.   U Unclassified.

Co-operating: a United Church of Canada. Church of Scotland. b United Society for the Propagation of the Gospel. c Methodist Missionary Society.

Also working: Baptist Missionary Society. Church of Christ Scientist. Source of Light Mission. Southern Baptist Convention. West Indies Mission.

LEEWARD AND WINDWARD ISLANDS

Br. Virgin Islands: 59 sq. mls. Pop.: 7,338 (1960)
St. Lucia: 238 sq. mls. Pop.: 94,718 (1960)
St. Vincent: 150·3 sq. mls. Pop.: 80,042 (1960)

Church or Mission (N.B. See notes on Statistics, page xiii)	Places of Regular Worship	Communicants, Full Members (p. 57) 1962 Handbook	Communicants, Full Members (p. 57) Latest available figure	Total Christian Community (p. 57) 1962 Handbook	Total Christian Community (p. 57) Latest available figure	National Workers, full-time Ordained	National Workers, full-time Lay-men	National Workers, full-time Women	Missionaries from other Churches or countries, full-time Ordained	Missionaries from other Churches or countries, full-time Lay-workers	Theolog. Colls., Bible Schools	Source of Information
Baptist Mid-Missions *	8	—	50	—	540	(14)U	—	—	(19)U	—	1	B
Baptist Mid-Missions †	16	—	141	—	470	(52)U	—	—	⎰	—	—	
Caribbean Evangelical Lutheran Synod (United Lutheran Church) ‡‡	3	1,173	1,173	2,246	2,246	3	—	—	1	—	—	E
Church of the Nazarene ‡‡‡	4	—	13	—	84	1	—	1	6	1	—	B
Church of God (Cleveland)	19	—	822	—	5,145	(44)U	—	—	—	—	—	B
Church of the Province of West Indies: Diocese of Windward Islands b	50	64,000	64,000	150,000	260,000	20	21	1	12	—	—	A
Methodist Church	81	11,760	14,301	40,596	51,647	13	—	3	—	2	—	B
Moravian Church ‡‡	9	1,592	1,592	3,810	3,810	—	12	13	13	1	—	E
Protestant Episcopal Church ‡a	6	2,650	3,391	6,430	8,998	2	5	—	—	—	—	B
Seventh-day Adventists ‡‡	14	671	671	1,500	1,500	16	20	8	15	8	—	E
West Indies Mission ...	43	75	775	200	775	—	—	—	—	—	1	A
	253	81,921	86,929	204,782	335,215	165 (110)U	58	26	66 (19)U	12	2	

* St. Vincent. † St. Lucia. ‡ Virgin Islands. U Unclassified.

Co-operating: a Protestant Episcopal Church in the U.S.A. b United Society for the Propagation of the Gospel.

LESSER ANTILLES (GUADELOUPE)

Church of God	24	1,180	1,180	2,205	2,205	—	—	—	4	3	—	E
Church of the Nazarene	30	1,180	1,180	2,560	2,560	—	15	3	3	3	—	E
Moravian Church	51	6,418	6,418	46,528	46,528	16	41	14	12	32	—	E
Seventh-day Adventists (British)	59	6,392	6,392	15,294	15,294	(13)U	(45)U	—	—	—	—	E
	164	15,170	15,170	66,587	66,587	29 (13)U	101 (45)U	17	19	38	—	

Also working: West Indies Mission (Guadeloupe).

MEXICO

761,530 sq. mls.   Pop.: 38,400,000 estimate (1963)

American Baptist Home Mission Societies	43	8,257	5,899	28,000	12,621	40	(40)U	—	(11)U	—	1	D
Asociacion de Iglesias Cristianas Evangelicas (Disciples) ...	19	1,100	1,114	1,700	2,228	8	17	1	3	10	2	A
Central American Mission ...	7	—	56	250	250	2	4	2	2	20	1	B
Church of God (Cleveland) ...	377	13,268	17,575	13,268	33,480	(403)U	(623)U	—	—	—	—	B
Church of God (Holiness) ...	512	—	16,155	—	33,542	—	119	—	(1)U	—	2	D
Church of God of Prophecy ...	50	2,200	2,200	2,200	2,200	5	4	1	—	—	—	E
Concordia Conference (Missouri Synod) Lutheran ...	6	382	382	865	1,500	78	86	—	1	—	—	B
Convencion Nacional Bautista (Southern Baptist Convention) ...	506	7,640	11,315	—	31,384	16	(13)U	—	30	34	1	B
Free Methodist Church	22	950	615	2,500	2,000	3	2	2	—	—	—	D
German-speaking Evangelical Congregations (Lutheran) ...	22	—	600	—	2,400	4	—	—	—	—	—	B
Iglesia Alianza Cristiana y Misionera	6	—	166	—	166	—	1	—	—	—	—	B
Iglesia Christiana Nacional las Assemblies de Dios	630	9,650	12,727	14,954	39,948	(714)U	(49)U	—	(10)U	—	5	B
Iglesia del Nazarene	283	5,712	7,345	16,318	31,729	158	—	46	—	—	1	B
Iglesia de los Peregrinos (Pilgrim Holiness Church) ...	77	5,755	5,492	10,000	16,476	23	(49)U	—	—	—	1	D

MEXICO—*continued*

Church or Mission N.B. See notes on Statistics, page xiii	Places of Regular Worship	Communicants, Full Members (p. 57)		Total Christian Community (p. 57)		National Workers, full-time			Missionaries from other Churches or countries, full-time		Theolog. Colls., Bible Schools	Source of Information
		1962 Handbook	Latest available figure	1962 Handbook	Latest available figure	Ordained	Laymen	Women	Ordained	Lay-workers		
Iglesia Episcopal b	80	2,741	5,336	5,484	10,337	28	25	1	3	1	1	B
Iglesia Luterana	15	—	1,758	—	1,758	12	2	—	—	—	—	A
Iglesia Metodista	299	20,975	25,807	37,560	42,162	79	69	—	39	—	1	B
Iglesia Nacional Presbyterian	840	50,000	22,999	—	80,460	(296)U	—	—	(14)U	7	2	B
Iglesias Evangelicas Independientes	600	—	100,000	80,000	140,000	500	1,200	—	4	—	—	D
Independent Churches	150	—	4,882	—	11,391	(73)U	—	—	—	—	—	
International Church of the Four-square Gospel a	19	1,018	1,235	1,338	2,187	4	(15)U	—	(1)U	—	—	D
Junta General Congregational	13	478	478	1,516	1,516	8	6	—	—	—	—	E
Mennonite Brethren Church	6	85	137	—	300	4	4	2	6	4	1	A
Mexican Indian Mission	47	6,000	1,252	10,000	3,951	7	(41)U	—	(12)U	5	1	D
Mexican Lutheran N.W. Synod	3	—	45	—	45	1	2	1	—	—	—	A
Pentecostal Church of God	37	750	1,000	750	1,000	2	—	2	—	—	1	B
Pentecostal Holiness Church	58	1,183	1,900	1,703	3,356	(94)U	—	—	4	—	2	B
Scandinavian Congregations (Lutheran)		—	30	—	200	1	—	—	—	—	—	
Seventh-day Adventists	232	22,764	21,370	52,854	41,023	2	(48)U	—	—	—	—	B
Svenska Fria Missionen	300	50,000	50,000	80,000	150,000	200	300	100	7	7	—	D
United Christian Missionary Society	40	1,100	1,114	1,700	1,700	21	—	18	7	5	1	D
World Gospel Mission	9	43	66	190	200	—	6	5	1	—	—	B
	5,310	243,181	321,050	897,227	701,510	2,786 (1,580)U	2,676 (829)U	272	162 (49)U	93	24	

n.a. not available.   U Unclassified.

Co-operating: a United Church Board for World Ministries. b Protestant Episcopal Church in the U.S.A.
Also working: American Friends Board of Missions. Church of Christ Scientist. Inter-American Missionary Society. Latin American Prayer Fellowship. Missionary Aviation Fellowship. World Baptist Fellowship Mission Agency. Wycliffe Bible Translators.

NETHERLANDS ANTILLES (CURACAO) 394 sq. mls. Pop.: 199,607 (1963)

Methodist Missionary Society	3	—	1,338	—	2,000	2	—	—	(1)U	—	—	D
Seventh-day Adventists	8	—	946	—	2,894	3	(17)U	—	2	18	—	B
The Evangelical Alliance Mission	7	—	450	—	1,350	2	2	2	9	—	—	D
	18	—	2,744	—	6,244	7	19 (17)U	2	12 (1)U	18	—	

The total Protestant population of this group of Islands is estimated as: 8,000.

NICARAGUA 57,143 sq. mls. Pop.: 1,593,007 (1964)

American Baptist Home Mission Societies	23	2,821	2,120	11,200	4,573	12	(12)U	—	—	—	1	D
Assemblies of God	79	678	986	1,179	4,939	—	53	—	7	—	1	B
Brethren in Christ	1	—	—	—	—	—	7	3	1	1	—	B
Central American Mission	50	345	600	1,076	3,000	12	(19)U	—	6	14	1	B
Church of God (Cleveland)	25	—	989	—	2,709	—	2	13	(2)U	10	—	B
Church of the Nazarene	53	571	620	2,207	3,679	34	—	2	6	—	1	B
Convencion Nacional Bautista	—	2,000	1,422	2,000	2,310	—	—	—	—	1	—	E
Iglesia Episcopal [a]	14	500	1,012	1,500	3,198	3	—	—	1	—	1	B
International Church of the Four-square Gospel	6	—	208	—	665	2	(4)U	—	(3)U	5	—	D
Moravian Church [b]	97	7,903	8,686	22,033	26,043	14	77	—	10	—	1	B
Seventh-day Adventists	19	980	1,428	1,760	3,026	4	(30)U	—	1	—	—	B
	367	16,407	18,071	43,606	54,142	81	204 (65)U	18	37 (5)U	31	6	

U Unclassified.

Co-operating: a Protestant Episcopal Church in the U.S.A. b Moravian Church in America.

PANAMA AND CANAL ZONE

Panama: 29,201 sq. mls. **Pop.:** 1,075,541 (1960)
Canal Zone: 647 sq. mls. **Pop.:** 48,000 (38,500 U.S. citizens) (1964)

Church or Mission N.B. See notes on Statistics, page xiii	Places of Regular Worship	Communicants, Full Members (p. 57)		Total Christian Community (p. 57)		National Workers, full-time			Missionaries from other Churches or countries, full-time		Theolog. Colls., Bible Schools	Source of Information
		1962 Hand-book	Latest available figure	1962 Hand-book	Latest available figure	Ordained	Lay-men	Women	Ordained	Lay-workers		
Central American Mission	5	53	120	311	860	2	4	1	4	8	—	B
Church of God (Cleveland)	22	1,568	979	1,568	1,814	(40)U	—	—	(17)U	—	—	B
Church of the Nazarene	7	—	60	—	1,442	3	—	3	1	1	—	B
Church of the Nazarene (Canal Zone)	2	—	53	—	177	—	—	—	2	2	—	B
Convencion Bautista de Panama	118	—	5,500	—	15,000	3	1	2	29	21	—	A
Free Will Baptists	3	—	—	—	—	—	—	—	3	3	—	B
International Church of the Foursquare Gospel	172	8,500	8,500	9,000	9,000	181	3	—	—	4	—	E
Methodist Church	11	1,926	491	2,151	1,679	3	3	—	12	3	—	B
New Tribes Mission	—	—	—	—	—	16	48	1	13	19	1	B
Protestant Episcopal Church *a	19	5,076	4,581	17,674	13,007	—	1	1	7	2	—	B
Redeemer Lutheran Church	—	88	234	123	594	—	—	—	1	—	—	B
Seventh-day Adventists	57	—	5,452	—	12,164	9	(52)U	—	7	—	—	B
Union Church of the Canal Zone	5	1,006	1,006	1,650	1,650	4	1	4	—	—	—	E
	423	23,847	26,976	41,778	57,387	261 (40)U	113 (52)U	12	96 (17)U	63	1	

* Including Canal Zone.

Co-operating: a Protestant Episcopal Church in the U.S.A.

Also working: Salvation Army.

PUERTO RICO

3,423 sq. mls.   Pop.: 2,574,300 estimate (1964)

American Baptist Home Mission Societies	48	6,729	6,521	25,000	30,061	26	26	—	—	—	—	D
American Wesleyan Mission	8	240	475	700	800	1	8	—	—	7	—	B
Assemblies of God	207	—	9,895	—	35,000	—	—	—	(3)U	—	—	D
Baptist Mid-Missions	2	—	—	—	20	—	—	—	2	—	—	B
Church of God (Cleveland)	75	3,456	4,665	3,456	17,505	(108)U	—	—	5	—	—	B
Church of God of Prophecy	15	—	339	—	700	—	—	—	(10)U	—	—	D
Church of the Nazarene	18	422	507	2,254	3,453	13	—	1	4	4	1	B
Congregational Churches	53	4,576	4,576	4,576	4,576	—	—	—	—	—	—	E
Iglesia Alianza Cristiana y Misionera	25	794	1,903	1,996	1,996	23	—	—	1	—	—	B
Iglesia Evangélica Unida	55	4,730	4,906	14,000	10,000	34	8	—	(23)U	—	—	A
Mennonite Church	11	411	290	800	800	48	(237)U	—	3	3	—	D
Methodist Church b	120	9,123	10,500	14,500	14,500	28	(25)U	—	(10)U	—	—	B
Presbyterian Church c	80	4,983	4,983	35,000	32,000	26	27	2	12	7	1	D
Protestant Episcopal Church a	34	3,448	3,826	8,407	7,513	22	(93)U	—	13	—	—	B
Seventh-day Adventists	91	—	7,317	—	17,323	42	1	—	—	1	1	B
United Christian Missionary Society	110	6,283	8,656	10,000	12,000	—	—	—	—	—	—	B
United Lutheran Church	21	—	2,265	—	6,012	—	—	—	—	—	—	D
	973	68,121	71,624	174,707	194,259	371 (108)U	417 (355)U	3	76 (46)U	22	4	

U Unclassified.

Co-operating: a Protestant Episcopal Church in the U.S.A. b Methodist Church U.S.A. Department of Home Missions. c Presbyterian Church in the U.S.A.

Also working: Calvary Baptist Mission. Church of Christ Scientist. Evangelical United Brethren Church.

TRINIDAD AND TOBAGO

Trinidad: 1,864 sq. mls.
Tobago: 116 sq. mls.

Pop.: 827,957 (1960)

African Methodist Episcopal Church	5	—	400	—	553	—	—	—	—	—	—	D
Baptist Church	—	12,000	12,000	12,000	18,522	—	—	—	—	2	—	D
Church of God (Anderson, Indiana)	28	550	550	1,150	785	1	—	—	4	1	1	D

TRINIDAD AND TOBAGO—continued

Church or Mission N.B. See notes on Statistics, page xiii	Places of Regular Worship	Communicants, Full Members (p. 57)		Total Christian Community (p. 57)		Staff					Theolog. Colls., Bible Schools	Source of Information
		1962 Hand-book	Latest avail-able figure	1962 Hand-book	Latest avail-able figure	National Workers, full-time			Missionaries from other Churches or countries, full-time			
						Or-dained	Lay-men	Women	Or-dained	Lay-workers		
Church of God (Cleveland) ...	17	—	635	—	2,138	(18)U	—	—	12	—	—	B
Church of Scotland ...	—	—	700	—	700	—	—	—	—	—	—	D
Church of the Nazarene ...	21	372	517	2,074	6,047	18	4	2	9	8	1	B
Church of the Province of the West Indies: Diocese of Trinidad ...b	60	—	35,000	—	175,000	41	—	1	—	—	—	A
Methodist Church ...c*	89	1,336	14,613	6,936	67,850	21	—	—	8	2	—	B
Moravian Church ...	12	—	1,978	—	5,936	3	(3)U	—	—	—	—	D
Open Bible Standard Church ...	8	3,500	522	3,500	1,573	3	(2)U	—	(7)U	—	1	D
Pentecostal Assemblies ...	75	—	3,500	—	4,031	—	—	—	(6)U	—	—	D
Pilgrim Holiness Church ...	14	—	450	—	930	6	(8)U	—	—	—	—	D
Presbyterian Church ...a	203	4,000	4,000	4,000	32,409	265	204	199	47	—	—	E
Salvation Army ...†	61	6,415	6,415	25,397	25,397	19	(201)U	—	(15)U	—	—	D
Seventh-day Adventists ...	2	9,115	6,963	17,728	12,981	—	—	—	2	2	—	B
Southern Baptist Convention ...	—	—	24	—	129	—	—	—	(18)U	—	—	D
United Church of Canada ...	70	—	2,461	—	20,000	—	—	—	—	—	—	D
	665	37,288	90,728	72,785	374,981	395 (18)U	422 (214)U	202	128 (46)U	14	3	

* Figures include Barbados.　† Figures include Bahamas, Guyana, Cuba and Surinam.　U Unclassified.

Co-operating: a United Church of Canada.　b United Society for the Propagation of the Gospel.　c Methodist Missionary Society.

Also working: Baptist Missionary Society. Board of World Missions of the Lutheran Church in America. Church of Christ Scientist. Norske Pinsevenners Ytremisjon. West Indies Mission.

UNITED STATES OF AMERICA   3,548,974 sq. mls.   Pop.: 192,040,000 Estimate (1964) (incl. Alaska and Hawaii)

Church or Mission N.B. See Notes on Statistics, page xiii	Places of Regular Worship	Total Christian Community		Ordained Clergy	Source of Information
		1962 Hand-book	Latest Available Figure		
Adventist Bodies:					
Advent Christian Church	400	30,586	31,454	511	D
Church of God (Abrahamic Faith)	118	5,400	5,800	79	A
Seventh-day Adventists	3,756	311,535	364,666	2,394	D
African Orthodox Church	24	6,000	6,000	50	D
American Rescue Workers	45	2,310	3,575	50	D
Apostolic Faith	43	—	4,678	75	A
Apostolic Overcoming Holy Church of God	300	75,000	75,000	350	D
Armenian Church, Diocese of N. America and Diocese of California	56	125,000	163,960	68	D
Assemblies of God	8,443	505,703	572,123	10,519	D
Baptist Bodies:					
American Baptist Association	3,227	647,800	726,112	3,150	D
American Baptist Convention	6,119	1,555,360	1,495,326	8,103	A
Baptist General Conference	571	68,930	86,719	700	D
Conservative Baptist Association of America	1,500	275,000	325,000	2,500	D
Duck River (and Kindred) Associations of Baptists	27	3,139	3,201	37	D
Evangelical Baptist Church, Inc. General Conference	31	2,200	2,200	37	A
Free Will Baptists	2,028	400,000	173,275	3,166	D
General Association of Regular Baptist Churches	1,100	130,612	154,767	1,100	D
General Baptists	837	55,637	63,150	1,280	D
National Baptist Convention of America	11,398	2,668,799	2,668,799	28,574	D
National Baptist Convention, U.S.A. Inc.	26,000	5,000,000	5,500,000	27,500	D
National Baptist Evangelical Life and Soul Saving Assembly of U.S.A.	264	57,674	57,674	137	D
National Primitive Baptist Convention of the U.S.A.	1,880	80,983	768,800	575	D
North American Baptist Association	1,450	330,265	174,000	1,800	D
North American Baptist General Conference	329	50,455	53,711	426	A
Primitive Baptists	1,000	72,000	72,000	—	D

UNITED STATES OF AMERICA—continued

Church or Mission N.B. See Notes on Statistics, page xiii	Places of Regular Worship	Total Christian Community		Ordained Clergy	Source of Information
		1962 Hand-book	Latest Available Figure		
Baptist bodies (*Cont.*)					
Progressive National Baptist Convention	487	—	516,400	974	D
Separate Baptists in Christ	84	7,209	7,496	106	D
Seventh-day Baptist General Conference	65	5,963	5,773	73	A
Southern Baptist Convention	33,774	9,485,276	10,770,573	35,000	A
United Baptists	586	63,641	63,641	1,100	D
United Free Will Baptist Church	836	100,000	100,000	784	D
Berean Fundamental Church	35	500	1,621	40	D
Bible Protestant Church	37	2,477	2,668	49	D
Bible Way Churches of Our Lord Jesus Christ World Wide Inc.	155	25,000	45,000	165	D
Brethren (German Baptist):					
Brethren Church (Ashland Ohio)	120	19,474	18,013	149	A
Church of the Brethren	1,067	201,219	194,815	2,118	D
National Fellowship of Brethren Churches	201	25,198	28,495	281	D
Old German Baptist Brethren	54	4,002	4,225	130	D
Plymouth Brethren	665	25,000	33,250	—	D
Brethren (River):					
Brethren in Christ	159	6,698	8,251	302	A
Central Alaskan Missions	9	—	350	7	A
Christadelphians	850	15,000	15,800	—	D
Christian and Missionary Alliance	1,057	67,641	64,586	1,078	A
Christian Catholic Church	5	—	1,555	10	A
Christian Churches (Disciples of Christ) International Convention	8,081	2,242,669	1,918,471	7,609	A
Christian Union	130	7,300	5,821	80	A
Church of Christ (Holiness) U.S.A.	159	9,018	9,289	76	D
Churches of God:					
Church of God (Cleveland, Tenn.)	3,575	162,794	205,465	2,401	D

UNITED STATES OF AMERICA—*continued*

Church of God (Anderson, Ind.)	2,287	135,294	143,231	2,705	D
Church of God (Seventh Day)	7	1,500	2,000	9	D
The (Original) Church of God, Inc.	7	7,000	18,000	60	B
The Church of God ...	1,921	77,000	73,868	2,529	D
The Church of God (Seventh Day) Denver, Colo.	56	3,800	5,500	76	D
The Church of God by Faith	105	2,300	3,470	112	D
The Church of God of Prophecy	1,452	35,000	42,516	3,164	D
Church of God and Saints of Christ	217	38,127	38,127	n.a.	D
Church of God in Christ	4,500	382,679	425,500	6,000	D
Church of Illumination	14	5,000	9,000	60	A
Church of our Lord Jesus Christ of the Apostolic Faith Inc.	155	45,000	45,000	165	A
Church of the Nazarene (American Indian)	4,580	696,512	343,380	6,194	A
Church of the Nazarene (Spanish-speaking people in the U.S.A.)	33	2,270	5,541	48	A
Churches of Christ	93	4,848	7,760	102	A
Churches of Christ in Christian Union	18,500	2,007,650	2,350,000	7,000	D
Churches of God, Holiness	228	11,500	7,514	285	D
Churches of God in North American (General Eldership)	32	25,600	25,600	29	D
Churches of the Living God:					
Church of the Living God (Motto: Christian Workers for Fellowship)	374	37,304	36,550	379	D
House of God which is the Church of the Living God, the Pillar and the Ground of Truth, Inc.	276	25,562	45,320	76	D
Churches of the New Jerusalem:	107		2,350	170	
General Convention of the New Jerusalem in the U.S.A.	63	2,350	4,831	63	D
General Church of the New Jerusalem	35	3,941	1,982	43	A
Congregational Christian Churches, National Association of	300	1,830	110,000	300	A
Congregational Holiness Church	141	—	5,212	308	D
Conservative Congregational Christian Conference	68	4,664	12,307	151	D
Evangelical Congregational Church	163	35,000	29,968	151	D
Evangelical Covenant Church of America	533	155,400	65,780	656	A
Evangelical Free Church of America	438	31,192	43,851	680	D
Evangelical United Brethren Church	4,093	761,858	735,723	645	A

UNITED STATES OF AMERICA—*continued*

Church or Mission *N.B.* See Notes on Statistics, page xiii	Places of Regular Worship	Total Christian Community		Ordained Clergy	Source of Information
		1962 Hand-book	Latest Available Figure		
Evangelistic Associations:					
Apostolic Christian Church (Nazarean) ...	51	1,960	2,347	147	D
Apostolic Christian Churches of America	72	8,400	8,700	30	D
The Christian Congregation ...	245	26,240	43,734	254	D
Church of God as organized by Christ ...	14	2,192	2,192	n.a.	D
Missionary Church Association ...	129	7,577	8,867	193	D
Federated Churches	508	88,411	88,411	n.a.	D
Fire-Baptized Holiness Church (Wesleyan) ...	53	1,007	1,007	82	D
Free Christian Zion Church of Christ ...	740	18,989	19,826	632	D
Friends:					
Five Years Meeting of Friends (Friends United Meeting)	487	68,399	70,167	493	D
Ohio Yearly Meeting of Friends Church (Independent) ...	87	6,540	7,059	157	D
Oregon Yearly Meeting of Friends Church ...	63	5,398	5,972	156	A
Pacific Yearly Meeting of Friends	35	1,055	2,073	—	D
Religious Society of Friends (Conservative) ...	21	1,894	1,696	—	D
Religious Society of Friends, General Conference ...	308	32,124	31,795	25	A
Religious Society of Friends (Kansas Yearly Meeting)	89	8,580	8,227	169	D
Independent Churches	384	40,276	40,276	—	A
Independent Fundamental Churches of America ...	852	148,155	106,572	1,070	D
Independent Negro Churches	50	12,337	12,337	—	A
International Church of the Foursquare Gospel ...	741	133,000	89,215	2,690	D
Italian:					
Christian Church of North America	151	20,200	20,000	131	A
Latter-Day Saints:					
Church of Christ	12	3,000	3,000	211	D
Church of Jesus Christ, Bickertonites ...	43	2,500	2,456	209	D
Church of Jesus Christ of Latter-day Saints ...	4,222	1,457,753	1,789,175	4,504	A
Reorganized Church of Jesus Christ of Latter-day Saints	999	155,391	168,355	14,674	A

UNITED STATES OF AMERICA—continued

Lutherans:					
American Lutheran Church	4,900	1,034,377	2,541,546	635	A
Church of the Lutheran Brethren	71	8,000	5,155	67	B
Church of the Lutheran Confession	59	—	8,128	69	B
Evangelical Lutheran Church in America (Eielsen Synod)	44	4,220	4,220	3	E
Evangelical Lutheran Synod (formerly Norwegian Synod of the American Evangelical Lutheran Church)	75	14,302	14,608	52	B
Finnish Apostolic Lutheran Church of America	58	6,567	6,994	28	B
Lutheran Church in America*	5,639	2,304,962	2,692,889	6,395	B
Protestant Conference (Lutheran)	8	3,000	3,000	15	B
Synod of Evangelical Lutheran Churches (Slovak Evangelical Lutheran Church)	65	19,931	21,656	54	B
Wisconsin Evangelical Lutheran Synod	869	348,725	358,466	789	B
Mennonite Bodies:					
Beachy Amish Mennonite Churches	37	2,217	3,117	99	D
Church of God in Christ (Mennonite)	38	4,156	5,000	38	D
Conference of the Evangelical Mennonite Church	21	2,303	2,516	46	D
Evangelical Mennonite Brethren	16	2,536	1,644	33	D
General Conference, Mennonite Church	190	35,531	35,651	437	D
Hutterian Brethren	77	2,005	7,600	90	D
Mennonite Brethren Church of North America	81	11,582	13,171	173	A
Mennonite Church	963	72,138	80,087	1,722	D
Old Order Amish Mennonite Church	285	17,321	20,416	1,074	D
Old Order (Wisler) Mennonite Church	36	4,391	5,193	80	D
Methodist Bodies:					
African Methodist Episcopal Church	5,878	2,000,000	1,166,301	7,089	D
African Methodist Episcopal Zion Church	4,583	1,500,000	1,100,000	2,983	D
African Union First Colored Methodist Protestant Church Inc.	33	7,500	5,000	40	D
Bible Protestant Church	37	2,668	2,500	49	E
Christian Methodist Episcopal Church	2,598	500,000	466,718	2,259	D
Congregational Methodist Church	223	22,000	14,274	308	D
Methodists:					
Congregational Methodist Church of U.S.A.	100	10,000	7,500	120	D
Evangelical Methodist Church	150	7,000	8,728	300	A

* Including Caribbean Area Synod.

UNITED STATES OF AMERICA—*continued*

Church or Mission *N.B.* See Notes on Statistics, page xiii	Places of Regular Worship	Total Christian Community		Ordained Clergy	Source of Information
		1962 Hand-book	Latest Available Figure		
Methodists (*cont.*)					
Free Methodist Church of North America	1,162	60,000	59,415	1,550	A
Holiness Methodist Church	23	1,000	1,000	35	A
The Methodist Church	38,876	10,970,000	10,331,574	28,981	D
Primitive Methodist Church, ...U.S.A.	86	30,000	11,945	60	A
Reformed Methodist Union, Episcopal Church	21	20,000	16,198	31	D
Reformed Zion Union Apostolic Church	50	20,000	16,000	4	D
Southern Methodist Church	52	10,000	4,025	21	D
Union American Methodist Episcopal Church	256	40,000	27,560	276	D
Wesleyan Methodist Church of America	1,085	119,933	48,326	1,600	D
Moravian Bodies:					
Moravian Church in Alaska*	22	1,767	3,783	1	D
Moravian Church in America (Unitas Fratrum)	174	60,875	62,527	163	D
Unity of the Brethren	32	6,103	6,142	13	D
National David Spiritual Temple of Christ Church Union (Inc.) U.S.A.	66	40,715	40,816	275	D
New Apostolic Church of North America Inc.	165	13,595	17,803	196	D
Open Bible Standard Churches Inc.	257	25,000	27,000	761	D
Pentecostal Assemblies:					
Calvary Pentecostal Church, Inc.	22	20,000	8,000	141	D
Emmanuel Holiness Church	56	1,200	1,200	90	D
Elim Church	75	3,500	4,000	120	D
Free Will Baptists of Pentecostal Faith	176	2,000	10,000	210	A
Independent Pentecostal Association	100	5,000	5,000	150	E
International Pentecostal Assemblies	55	7,000	6,000	135	D
Pentecostal Assemblies of the World (Inc.)	550	50,000	45,000	600	D
Pentecostal Church of Christ	41	1,200	1,158	65	D

* Work among Eskimos

126

UNITED STATES OF AMERICA—continued

Pentecostal Church of God in America, Inc. ... Hawaii	958	103,500	105,000	1,282	B
	2	—	75	2	B
Pentecostal Holiness Church Inc. ... in Alaska	1,338	51,688	63,453	1,156	D
	5	105	479	13*	D
United Pentecostal Church Inc.	2,000	160,000	125,000	2,061	D
Pilgrim Holiness Church	1,431	32,558	56,506	1,588	D
Presbyterian Bodies:					
Associate Reformed Presbyterian Church (General Synod)	143	27,561	27,464	120	D
Cumberland Presbyterian Church	967	87,263	78,917	740	A
Orthodox Presbyterian Church	110	10,648	12,867	150	D
Presbyterian Church in the U.S.	4,008	889,196	950,139	4,082	D
Reformed Presbyterian Church Evangelical Synod	109	16,000	10,400	247	A
Second Cumberland Presbyterian Church in U.S.	121	—	30,000	125	D
The United Presbyterian Church in the U.S.A.	9,026	3,145,733	3,304,321	12,743	D
Protestant Episcopal Church	7,202	3,126,662	3,410,657	10,213	A
Reformed Bodies:					
Christian Reformed Church	624	236,145	272,461	817	A
Hungarian Reformed Church in America	40	11,110	11,110	36	D
Netherlands Reformed Congregations	14	2,300	2,500	4	D
Protestant Reformed Churches in America	19	2,754	2,906	16	D
Reformed Church in America	927	219,770	232,414	1,208	D
Reformed Church in the United States	20	—	2,554	18	D
Reformed Episcopal Church	64	8,928	7,007	81	D
Salvation Army	1,219	245,570	287,991	5,133	D
Schwenkfelder Church	5	2,500	2,300	4	D
Social Brethren	30	1,540	1,540	38	D
Triumph the Church and Kingdom of God in Christ	420	71,089	43,500	1,200	D
Unitarian Churches (Universalist Association)	1,044	185,253	166,622	863	A
United Brethren Bodies:					
United Brethren in Christ	310	20,896	22,586	294	D
United Church of Christ	6,960	(1,076,508)† (1,414,595)	2,070,413	8,692	D
United Holy Church of America, Inc.	470	28,300	28,980	400	D
United Missionary Church	215	10,357	11,013	273	D
Volunteers of America	209	28,234	30,230	341	D
	284,817	62,382,099	65,475,714	318,165	

* Ordained and lay   † Union of Evangelical and Reformed Church and Congregational Christian Churches completed in 1961

UNITED STATES OF AMERICA—*continued*

Church or Mission *N.B.* See Notes on Statistics, page xiii	Places of Regular Worship	Total Christian Community		Ordained Clergy	Source of Information
		1962 Hand-book	Latest Available Figure		
Old Catholic Churches:					
American Catholic Church, Archdiocese of New York ...	18	8,435	4,369	18	D
North American Old Roman Catholic Church	50	71,521	62,575	60	D
Reformed Catholic Church (Utrecht Confession) Province of North America.	20	2,217	2,217	21	D
Polish National Catholic Church of America	162	271,316	282,411	144	D
	250	353,489	351,572	243	

WEST INDIES (GENERAL)*

Church or Mission / N.B. See notes on Statistics, page xiii	Places of Regular Worship	Communicants, Full Members (p. 57)		Total Christian Community (p. 57)		Staff					Theolog. Colls., Bible Schools	Source of Information
						National Workers, full-time			Missionaries from other Churches or countries, full-time			
		1962 Handbook	Latest available figure	1962 Handbook	Latest available figure	Ordained	Laymen	Women	Ordained	Lay-workers		
Church of God (Cleveland) ... †	7	—	94	—	504	8	—	—	1	—	—	B
Church of God of Prophecy ...	210	12,485	12,485	12,584	12,584	—	201	—	—	—	—	E
Disciples of Christ ...	36	4,500	4,500	4,500	4,500	—	—	—	—	—	—	E
International Church of the Four-square Gospel ...	100	6,818	6,818	6,924	6,924	130	—	—	1	1	1	E
Methodist Church ...	260	31,046	31,046	124,449	124,449	44	1	9	24	27	—	E
Moravian Church ...	46	5,037	8,532	9,327	22,825	9	1	—	9	1	1	B
Pentecostal Assemblies of Canada ...	70	—	36,000	36,000	36,000	—	—	—	4	7	1	B
United Christian Missionary Society	31	2,776	2,776	8,000	8,000	—	(18)U	—	(8)U	—	—	E
United Church of Canada ...	70	20,000	20,000	50,000	50,000	—	—	—	—	—	1	E
Wesleyan Methodist Church	25	780	780	3,870	3,870	10	25	3	3	3	1	E
	855	83,442	123,031	219,654	269,656	201	246 (18)U	12	50 (8)U	39		

* Statistics of Churches and Missions in the Caribbean working on more than one island or which have not indicated their exact area of operation.
† Figures for Grenada, Nevis, St. Kitts, St. Martins and Turks Island.

Also working: Southern Baptist Convention (French West Indies).

ARGENTINA 1,084,120 sq. mls. Pop.: 22,186,800 estimate (1964)

Church or Mission (N.B. See notes on Statistics, page xiii)	Places of Regular Worship	Communicants, Full Members (p. 57) 1962 Handbook	Communicants Latest available figure	Total Christian Community (p. 57) 1962 Handbook	Total Community Latest available figure	National Workers, full-time — Ordained	Lay-men	Women	Missionaries from other Churches or countries, full-time — Ordained	Lay-workers	Theolog. Colls., Bible Schools	Source of Information
Armenian Church Brethren	3	—	96	—	450	—	—	—	(6)U	—	—	D
Armenian Evangelical Church	1	—	55	—	500	—	—	—	1	—	—	D
Asambleas de Dios ...U.S.A. (c)	250	13,000	17,000	15,000	19,350	25	200	10	13	13	1	B
Assemblies of God U.S.A.	137	1,737	4,000	3,100	8,626	(120)U	—	—	14	5	1	B
Baptist Mission of N.W. Argentina	3	—	65	22	65	1	3	—	5	—	—	D
Brethren Church Missionary Board	6	150	160	400	389	—	—	—	(6)U	—	—	
Christian Churches (Disciples of Christ)	8	497	426	2,000	2,000	5	—	—	5	—	—	D
Christian and Missionary Alliance	39	1,242	1,022	2,286	2,286	48	12	—	4	5	1	B
Christian Missions in Many Lands	52	—	2,655	—	5,145	—	—	—	(10)U	—	—	D
Church of England	31	2,500	2,500	11,000	5,000	3	—	—	(25)U	—	—	D
Church of God (Cleveland)	79	—	9,680	—	19,424	—	73	—	(4)U	—	2	D
Church of God of Prophecy	11	—	196	—	350	—	—	—	(9)U	—	—	D
Church of the Nazarene	45	831	983	2,870	6,062	27	—	7	12	4	3	B
Church of Scotland		—	1,600	—	1,600	—	—	—	—	—	—	B
Congregational Christian Board	82	7,003	7,003	15,000	15,000	9	2	—	(8)U	—	—	D
Conservative Baptist Foreign Mission Society	42	816	1,017	2,400	2,000	1	2	—	17	17	1	A
Convencion Evangelica Bautista	500	12,813	18,000	40,000	80,000	—	—	—	—	—	—	A
Danish Church	4	20,000	20,000	60,000	60,000	—	—	—	(4)U	—	—	D
Dutch Reformed Church	3	—	540	—	1,600	—	—	—	(2)U	—	—	D
Emmanuel Holiness Church		—	68	—	405	—	—	—	(3)U	—	—	D
Evangelical Union of South America	50	—	600	—	8,000	—	8	—	(16)U	—	—	D
German Evangelical Synod (La Plata Synod)	60	11,239	11,239	100,000	100,000	1	—	—	(22)U	—	—	D
Iglesia Evangelica Luterana Unida	25	1,903	2,581	4,078	5,491	24	7	6	4	1	2	A
Iglesia Evangelica Valdense *	64	7,174	6,461	7,174	17,172	17	—	1	—	—	—	A

130

ARGENTINA—*continued*

Iglesia Metodista	a	130	6,822	7,338	23,900	15,424	68	36	—	28	12	—	B
Iglesia Reformada	b	16	—	1,850	—	5,000	9	8	—	(7)U	—	—	D
Irish Baptist Foreign Mission		10	—	306	—	900	4	1	—	(5)U	—	—	D
Lutheran Church (Missouri Synod)		64	9,752	16,797	16,925	27,679	30	8	—	(4)U	—	—	D
Mennonite Board of Missions and Charities		32	673	664	1,350	1,350	3	17	—	(24)U	—	—	D
New Testament Missionary Union		50	2,000	2,000	4,000	4,000	(18)U	—	—	(18)U	—	—	D
Norske Pinsevenners Ytremisjon		10	3,009	3,009	3,009	9,027	—	—	—	(6)U	—	—	D
Norwegian Church		—	—	300	—	825	—	—	—	(2)U	—	—	B
Pentecostal Assemblies of Canada		130	6,000	20,000	25,000	25,000	4	5	—	2	5	1	B
Pentecostal Holiness Church		6	—	125	—	460	100	30	—	(4)U	12	—	D
Salvation Army		66	4,267	4,211	11,655	8,500	16	68	—	(25)U	—	—	D
Seventh-day Adventists		56	11,104	10,465	18,151	19,390	—	—	—	(11)U	—	—	D
Slavic Gospel Association		2	—	250	—	700	—	—	—	(19)U	—	1	D
South American Missionary Society		6	2,500	1,100	9,000	2,600	3	—	—	(9)U	—	—	D
Southern Baptist Convention		317	—	16,112	—	41,077	147	21	—	36	42	—	B
Swedish Church		2	400	400	2,500	2,500	3	—	—	—	—	—	D
United Lutheran Church		20	1,903	3,995	4,078	4,310	12	5	—	(11)U	—	—	D
		2,412	156,625	196,869	414,323	529,657	695 (138)U	506	24	401 (260)U	112	15	

* Includes figures for Uruguay.   U Unclassified.

Co-operating: **a** Methodistenkirche in der Schweiz.   **b** Gereformeerde Kerken in Nederland.   **c** Svenska Fria Missionen.

Also working: Church of Christ Scientist. Dansk Missionsrad. Presbyterian Church of Brazil. South American Missionary Society. United Church Board for World Ministries.

BOLIVIA 424,160 sq. mls. Pop.: 3,519,532 estimate (1964)

Church or Mission (N.B. See notes on Statistics, page xiii)	Places of Regular Worship	Communicants, Full Members (p. 57)		Total Christian Community (p. 57)		National Workers, full-time			Missionaries from other Churches or countries, full-time		Theolog. Colls., Bible Schools	Source of Information
		1962 Handbook	Latest available figure	1962 Handbook	Latest available figure	Ordained	Laymen	Women	Ordained	Lay-workers		
Asambleas de Dios ... ... a	8	250	354	600	1,065	6	1		6	8	1	B
Assemblies of God	48	796	934	2,002	4,615	(45)U			14		3	B
Bethesda Missions	1		20		390	1			12			D
Bolivian Friends Holiness Mission...	5	30	30	605	605		3		4			D
Bolivian Indian Mission ...	38	1,557	1,278	5,549	5,185		62		(40)U		4	B
Bolivian Lutheran Church ...	18		270		554		11	3	22			D
Canadian Baptist	39	1,100	1,133	8,100	3,435	16	74		(37)U		2	D
Central Yearly Meeting of Friends...	18		400		800		8		(17)U			B
Church of the Nazarene	35	856	930	1,876	4,875	22	21		6	6	1	B
Evangelical Union of S. America ...	22		888		1,593		19		(29)U		2	D
Friends (Oregon Yearly Meeting) ...	19	3,000	700	5,000	2,050	30	35	8	(8)U		1	D
German Speaking Evangelical Lutheran Church	4		70		870	1	1					B
International Church of the Foursquare Gospel	5	510	520	660	1,000	3			(4)U		1	D
Methodist Church	35	742	1,386	1,675	9,000	14	147	1	20	45	2	A
New Tribes Mission									34	44	1	B
Seventh-day Adventists	34	8,083	11,603	11,060	20,725	14	206		(39)U			B
South American Indian Mission ...	13	200	200	1,200	1,200	13			(17)U			B
Union Cristiana Evangélica (Andes Evangelical Mission)	50	1,557	1,940	5,549	8,043	52	3	10	40	52	6	B
World Gospel Mission	45	248	85	868	900	2	18		10	10	1	B
World Mission Prayer League ...	7	214	200	750	500		14		(17)U		2	D
	444	18,897	22,941	43,135	67,405	219 (45)U	623	22	376 (208)U	165	27	

Co-operating: **a** Svenska Fria Missionen.
Also working: American Leprosy Mission. Student Christian Movement. Wycliffe Bible Translators. Church of God (Cleveland).

BRAZIL 3,286,000 sq. mls. Pop.: 82,200,000 estimate (1965)

Alianca das Igreja Cristas Evangelicas do Norte do Brazil	a	30	1,100	1,545	2,250	4,612	12	20	10	23	83	2	A
Assembleias de Deus	d	4,250	700,000	1,400,000	1,000,000	1,700,000	5,250	10,000		5	14	5	B
Assemblies of God		5,000	650,000	800,000	960,000	1,300,000	(5,500)U			(15)U		4	B
Baptist Mid-Missions		61	363	1,167	561	2,627	19			(85)U		2	B
Baptist Missionary Society		8	297	297	1,000	891		29		(6)U			D
Brazil Christian Mission		4	260	260	450	720				(9)U			D
Christian Missions in Many Lands		13		417		902		1		(6)U			D
Christian Reformed Church		2		165		495				(2)U	17	2	A
Church of Christ		23		860		2,500		11		15			D
Church of God		23	900	1,076	1,140	2,610		71		(4)U		2	B
Church of God (Cleveland)		37	1,050	1,776	1,050	4,257	(47)U		1		5		B
Church of the Nazarene		22	14	302	72	2,342	10			5			D
Congregazion Cristao do Brasil		2,500		500,000	500,000	700,000							D
Conservative Presbyterian		104	1,278	1,803	2,185	2,185				109	148	10	A
Convencao Baptista		2,200	175,000	245,000	175,000	500,000	1,100	(500)U					
Convencao das Ingrejas Irmaos Menonitas		17	150	256	1,489	2,000	5	5	2	4	10	1	A
Evangelical Baptist Union		6		125		300		3		7	7		B
Evangelical Church of Lutheran Confession	c	261	112,662	265,630	549,957	837,139	215	4	1	4		1	B
Evangelical Lutheran Church		259	62,489	69,853	109,345	186,449	106						B
Evangelical Union of South America		53	350	401	1,400	1,033	24	28	16	(51)U	5	5	D
Free Methodist Church	b	20	115	1,334	250	2,024	9	228		9	12	1	B
Free Will Baptists		5		145		250		1		10			B
Igreja Crista Reformada		7	3,000	3,000	5,000	5,000	3			1			E
Igreja Evangelica de Confissao Lutherana		1,100		315,000		650,000	6	7	7	235	10	2	A
Igreja Evangelica Congregacional		116	9,428	9,428	30,000	30,000				58	74	1	B
Igreja Evangelica Pentecostal (Elim)		10		330		874	3	3	1	1	1	1	B
Igreja Evangelica Reformada		7		595		1,500	4	(33)U		4	7		A
Igreja Presbyteriana Independent		742	26,000	22,300	56,000	45,400	86	3					D

133

BRAZIL—*continued*

Church or Mission N.B. See notes on Statistics, page xiii	Places of Regular Worship	Communicants, Full Members (p. 57)		Total Christian Community (p. 57)		National Workers, full-time			Missionaries from other Churches or countries, full-time		Theolog. Colls., Bible Schools	Source of Information
		1962 Hand-book	Latest available figure	1962 Hand-book	Latest available figure	Or-dained	Lay-men	Women	Or-dained	Lay-workers		
Independent Board of Presbyterian Foreign Missions	19	—	2,165	—	6,495	10	2	—	7	—	—	D
Inter-American Missionary Society	5	—	322	—	751	3	13	—	(13)U	—	1	D
International Church of the Foursquare Gospel	139	14,640	12,902	26,532	32,626	57	57	—	(10)U	—	1	D
Lutheran Church (Missouri Synod)	503	—	167,871	—	503,613	91	16	—	(6)U	—	—	D
Methodist Church	1,146	45,000	57,171	80,000	117,320	197	151	—	(99)U	28	4	B
Missao Batista Conservadora	87	1,135	1,335	2,000	2,500	5	5	5	24	—	1	B
Missionary Church of Brazil	13	—	809	—	—	9	9	—	24	—	1	A
New Testament Church	18	1,000	1,000	2,300	2,300	(12)U	—	—	(10)U	—	—	E
Orebro Missionsforening Church	35	4,457	4,457	4,457	4,457	22	33	1	18	25	—	E
Oriental Missionary Society	37	1,119	1,119	2,600	2,600	19	16	4	8	11	—	E
Pentecostal Assemblies of Canada	30	—	5,000	—	5,000	—	—	—	1	2	1	B
Pentecostal Church of God	26	—	1,100	—	1,100	3	2	2	—	—	1	B
Presbyterian Church	4,633	95,341	100,511	171,053	502,555	(625)U	—	—	(30)U	—	3	B
Protestant Episcopal Church	153	—	8,466	—	41,433	77	35	—	(41)U	—	—	D
Seventh-day Adventists	279	54,322	59,759	100,000	76,603	176	1,009	—	(27)U	—	1	D
South American Indian Mission	22	500	550	1,800	1,800	17	—	—	115	148	7	B
Southern Baptist Convention	5,995	—	220,000	—	635,118	1,020	(259)U	2	—	8	—	B
West Amazon Mission	3	—	31	—	163	6	3	—	—	6	—	A
West Indies Mission	7	—	42	—	258	—	—	—	4	—	—	A
	30,030	2,093,044	4,287,675	4,071,643	7,922,802	14,748 (6,184)U	12,552 (792)U	51	1,105 (414)U	622	64	

U Unclassified.

134

CHILE 286,397 sq. mls. Pop.: 8,515,023 estimate (1964)

Denomination												
Asambleas de Dios	22	1,500	1,500	4,500	4,500	7	13	3	7	7	1	B
Assemblies of God	60	1,036	1,005	3,421	6,064	(62)U	—	—	(16)U	13	1	B
Christian and Missionary Alliance	175	2,405	2,541	8,911	8,911	39	—	—	10	—	1	B
Christian Missions in Many Lands	11	320	210	320	330	4	(60)U	—	(12)U	—	—	D
Church of God	32	—	1,362	—	3,663	—	—	—	2	—	1	D
Church of God (Cleveland)	65	—	6,829	—	41,829	(92)U	—	—	52	1	—	B
Church of the Nazarene	13	—	50	—	1,039	2	—	—	3	—	—	B
Church of Scotland	—	—	103	—	103	—	—	—	—	—	—	B
Evangelical Lutheran Church	57	6,840	8,000	25,000	25,000	10	—	—	(8)U	—	—	B&D
Iglesia Anglicana	65	10,000	10,000	10,000	10,000	—	—	—	—	—	—	E
Iglesia Evangelica Pentecostal	538	—	100,000	300,000	300,000	80	—	—	(14)U	—	—	D
Iglesia Metodista Pentecostal	800	400,000	400,000	400,000	400,000	—	—	—	—	—	—	E
International Church of the Foursquare Gospel	17	553	931	3,012	1,800	27	(22)U	—	(5)U	—	1	D
Methodist Church	96	7,000	4,900	16,000	7,500	7	16	13	9	27	1	A
National Presbyterian Church	19	406	406	1,500	1,500	(14)U	4	—	5	5	1	A
Presbyterian Church	46	2,259	2,010	8,000	8,000	43	—	—	1	—	1	B
Salvation Army	32	1,375	1,828	3,528	5,000	15	13	—	(26)U	—	1	D
Seventh-day Adventists	82	7,324	7,412	14,862	14,862	11	4	—	3	—	—	D
Soldiers and Gospel Mission	19	360	498	1,850	1,105	56	10	—	(14)U	—	1	D
Southern Baptist Convention	348	7,655	7,973	11,723	36,597	10	10	—	22	31	—	B
Union de Centros Biblicos	75	—	970	—	2,700	10	15	3	15	22	1	A
	2,572	679,559	558,528	834,839	880,503	479 (168)U	157 (82)U	19	221 (95)U	106	11	

Co-operating: **a** Philafricain Mission, Unevangelized Fields Mission. **b** United Board for World Ministries. **c** Lutheran Church Mission Society (Germany). **d** Svenska Fria Missionen.

Also working: American Leprosy Mission. Episcopal Church in the U.S.A. Gereformeerde Kerken in Nederland. Good News Trailer Missionary Fellowship. Hebrew Christian Testimony to Israel. Missionary Aviation Fellowship. Navigators. Presbyterian Church in the U.S. United Church of Canada. World Baptist Fellowship Mission Agency. Wycliffe Bible Translators.

Co-operating: **a** Presbyterian Church of Brazil. **b** Svenska Fria Missionen.

Also working: Association of Baptists for World Evangelism. Board of World Missions, Lutheran Church in America. Church of Christ, Scientist. Dansk Missionsrad. Independent Board for Presbyterian Missions. International Miners Mission. South American Missionary Society. World Presbyterian Missions. Worldwide Evangelization Crusade.

COLOMBIA 455,335 sq. mls. Pop.: 15,434,090 estimate (1964)

Church or Mission N.B. See notes on Statistics, page xiii	Places of Regular Worship	Communicants, Full Members (p. 57)		Total Christian Community (p. 57)		Staff					Theolog. Colls., Bible Schools	Source of Information
						National Workers, full-time			Missionaries from other Churches or countries, full-time			
		1962 Hand-book	Latest available figure	1962 Hand-book	Latest available figure	Or-dained	Lay-men	Women	Or-dained	Lay-workers		
Alianza Christiana y Misionere Colombiana	109	1,711	2,274	5,731	5,731	33	—	—	14	18	2	B
Asambleas de Dios	60	175	488	532	3,998	(35)U	—	—	(12)U	—	1	B
Asociación de Iglesias Evangélicas del Caribe	108	914	1,200	4,115	4,115	3	5	—	—	29	—	C
Asociación de Iglesias Evangélicas del Magdalena	44	361	304	1,136	1,000	—	—	3	20	—	—	E & C
Asociación de Iglesias Evangélicas Interamericanas	81	588	1,063	2,300	1,990	7	14	—	(25)U	—	2	B
Congregaciones Independientes	—	—	158	—	250	—	—	—	—	—	1	C
Convención Bautista de Colombia	54	3,422	4,021	7,552	14,946	22	24	—	17	22	—	B
Cruzada Hispanoamericana	15	164	675	548	1,000*	—	4	—	—	—	—	E & C
Embajadores Christianos de Col. (Asambleas de Jesucristo)	22	100	275	500	750*	—	5	—	—	1	—	E & C
Evangelical Union of Sth. America	18	—	227	—	933	(16)U	—	—	(11)U	—	1	B
Federación Luterana Mundial, Com. para America Latina	6	—	936	—	1,464	2	1	1	21	13	—	B
Hermanos Menonitas	11	100	350	200	1,000	3	6	3	(16)U	—	—	B
Iglesia Adventista del Séptimo Dia	72	10,496	19,213	15,978	19,213	23	65	—	13	21	1	D & C
Iglesia Christiana del Norte	17	574	220	—	500*	3	13	—	19	—	1	B & C
Iglesia Cruzada Evangélica	8	219	1,000	1,320	1,430	3	—	—	2	—	—	B
Iglesia de Dios (Cleveland)	1	125	662	—	664	1	1	—	6	—	—	C & B
Iglesia de Dios Pentecostal	56	1,105	282	135	300*	1	—	—	(10)U	—	—	B
Iglesia Episcopal	9	1,492	1,272	110	1,485	13	16	—	8	—	1	C
Iglesia Evangélica Cuadrangular	16	372	3,620	1,500	5,000*	4	21	—	6	—	—	C & D
Iglesia Evangélica Luterana	3	50	890	616	1,095	—	—	—	—	—	2	E & C
Iglesia Hermanos Cristianos	—	—	408	300	500*	—	—	—	—	—	1	E & C

COLOMBIA—*continued*

												Class
Iglesia Pentecostal Unida	43	3,000	15,352	5,000	20,000*	5	—	—	(9)U	—	—	C
Iglesia Presbiteriana Cumberland	25	900	850	3,000	1,500	3	38	—	—	—	—	D
Iglesia Presbiteriana de Colombia	46	1,684	1,882	3,987	6,650	9	11	—	—	1	—	C&D
Misión a las Tribus Nuevas	2	300	2,900	1,500	3,500*	—	—	—	2	10	1	B
Misión Alianza Evangélica	75	692	1,200	2,015	2,760	17	20	6	6	2	—	A
Misión Evangélica de Colombia	6	57	60	241	360	3	5	—	2	—	—	A
Misión Indígena de Sur América	15	150	156	600	700	6	—	7	14	—	—	B
Misión Menonite Colombiana	6	143	217	345	485*	1	4	—	2	9	—	B
Misión Metodista Wesleyana	10	205	387	712	2,250	—	—	—	4	4	—	B
Misión Panamericana	16	105	862	710	1,500*	1	3	—	—	—	—	B&C
Union Church de Bogotá	2	196	225	200	500*	1	—	—	—	—	1	C
Union Misionera Evangélica	33	1,200	1,325	5,000	3,500	9	10	20	11	26	—	A
	989	36,558	64,954	92,728	111,069	224 (51)U	266	40	250 (35)U	156	13	

* Estimate.   U Unclassified.

ECUADOR   104,505 sq. mls. (U.N.)   Pop.: 4,650,000 estimate (1962)

												Class
Assemblies of God	5	—	166	—	556	(4)U	—	—	(4)U	10	1	D
Church of the Brethren	1	62	35	100	350	—	6	—	—	—	—	D
Evangelical Church of the Christian and Missionary Alliance	54	1,378	1,926	4,924	4,924	(22)U	—	—	21	36	1	D
Evangelical Mission Covenant Church	4	99	96	430	230	1	1	—	(22)U	—	—	D
Free Will Baptists	—	—	—	—	—	—	2	—	1	1	—	B
Gospel Missionary Union b	15	765	534	3,000	1,221	6	11	—	(51)U	1	—	D
Iglesia Episcopal	4	—	111	250	331	1	2	—	4	—	—	B
Iglesia Evangelica Luterana	4	12	150	—	500	—	1	1	2	—	—	A
Inter-American Evangelical Church	8	83	301	83	301	2	3	—	12	—	—	D
Missionary Church Association	32	153	210	291	1,050	3	4	—	5	7	—	B

ECUADOR—*continued*

Church or Mission N.B. See notes on Statistics, page xiii	Places of Regular Worship	Communicants, Full Members (p. 57)		Total Christian Community (p. 57)		Staff					Theolog. Colls., Bible Schools	Source of Information
						National Workers, full-time			Missionaries from other Churches or countries, full-time			
		1962 Handbook	Latest available figure	1962 Handbook	Latest available figure	Ordained	Laymen	Women	Ordained	Lay-workers		
Seventh-day Adventists ...	12	1,319	2,098	1,729	4,567	7	(65)U	—	2	—	—	B
Southern Baptist Convention ...	20	107	455	107	3,797	6	11	—	10	9	1	B
United Andean Indian Mission ...	27	23	120	135	415	—	2	—	3	7	—	B
United Evangelical Church ... a	5	23	61	135	150	6	—	—	1	—	—	B
World Radio Missionary Fellowship	3	—	329	—	770	2	(96)U	—	(111)U	—	—	D
	194	4,087	6,592	11,499	19,162	60 (26)U	204 (161)U	1	249 (183)U	71	4	

U Unclassified.

Co-operating: **a** United Church Board for World Ministries. **b** Protestant Episcopal Church in the U.S.A.

Also working: Missionary Aviation Fellowship. Presbyterian Church in the United States. Wycliffe Bible Translators.

FALKLAND ISLANDS   4,700 sq. mls.   Pop.: 2,102 (1964)

	Places	1962 Hb	Latest	1962 Hb	Latest	Ordained	Laymen	Women	Ordained	Lay-workers	Theolog	Source
Anglican Church: Diocese of the Falkland Islands	15	1,500	1,500	2,000	2,000	2	4	—	8	7	—	E
United Free Church ...	1	50	50	50	50	1	—	—	—	—	—	E
	16	1,550	1,550	2,050	2,050	3	4	—	8	7	—	

FRENCH GUIANA   23,000 sq. mls.   Pop.: 33,698 (1961)

Christian Missions in Many Lands ...	2	21	60	75	150	—	—	—	(2)U	—	—	D
Seventh-day Adventists ...	1	141	150	141	370	1	—	—	(1)U	—	—	D
	3	162	210	216	520	1	—	—	(3)U	—	—	

GUYANA   83,000 sq. mls.   Pop.: 621,368 estimate (1963)

African Methodist Episcopal Church	4	1,000	230	2,000	700	(60)U	—	—	5	—	—	D
Assemblies of God ...	49	306	1,450	481	8,365	1	—	—	(6)U	—	1	B
Baptist Mid-Missions	7	—	68	—	618	—	—	—	6	—	1	B
Church in the Diocese of Guyana (Anglican) ...	122	19,634	21,845	85,329	400,000	42	223	—	—	—	—	A
Church of God (Anderson, Ind.) ...	6	—	475	—	1,250	3	3	—	2	—	—	D
Church of God (Cleveland) ...	8	—	153	—	383	8	—	—	2	—	—	B
Church of the Nazarene ...	25	327	638	2,478	4,754	12	—	—	4	4	—	B
Congregational Union ...	39	3,500	3,500	18,000	18,000	4	—	—	5	—	—	E
Elim Church ...	3	81	95	622	622	—	6	—	1	—	—	B
Evangelical Lutheran Church ...	58	2,677	3,025	9,396	11,258	8	—	—	4	1	—	B
Methodist Church ...	53	5,365	5,428	19,658	5,600	4	202	—	7	6	—	B
Moravian Church ...	10	683	787	2,679	1,060	—	2	1	3	1	—	E
Presbyterian Church in Canada	45	785	785	916	916	(204)U	1	—	(15)U	—	—	D
Salvation Army ...	17	—	1,615	—	3,300	22	—	—	4	—	—	D
Seventh-day Adventists ...	42	4,422	4,422	8,704	8,004	9	77	—	6	2	—	E
Southern Baptist Convention ...	6	133	82	200	457	—	—	—	2	2	—	D
Unevangelized Fields Mission ...	7	160	125	300	300	4	—	—	17	—	—	B
United Lutheran Church ...	42	—	2,501	—	9,396	2	30	—	10	—	1	D
	543	47,083	47,224	179,795	474,983	383 (264)U	544	1	99 (21)U	14	3	

U Unclassified.

Also working: Church of Christ, Scientist. Missionary Aviation Fellowship. United Society for the Propagation of the Gospel.

PARAGUAY 406,752 sq. km. Pop.: 1,816,890 (1962)

Church or Mission *N.B. See notes on Statistics, page xiii*	Places of Regular Worship	Communicants, Full Members (p. 57) 1962 Handbook	Communicants Latest available figure	Total Christian Community (p. 57) 1962 Handbook	Total Christian Community Latest available figure	National Workers, full-time Ordained	National Workers, full-time Lay-men	National Workers, full-time Women	Missionaries from other Churches or countries, full-time Ordained	Missionaries from other Churches or countries, full-time Lay-workers	Theolog. Colls., Bible Schools	Source of Information
Asambleas de Dios [a]	8	200	330	800	990	17	19		1	3	1	B
Assemblies of God	21	501	462	841	1,748	22			8		1	B
Christian Churches (Disciples)	14	63	354	147	450	5	26		16	6		A
Christian Missions in Many Lands	9	254	348	950	540	3			(4)U			B
Church of God	9		246		696		26		2			D
Church of God (Cleveland)	20	50	632	200	1,078	(34)U			(18)U	2		B
Free Methodist Church	5	150	124	600	301	3	20		3			B
German Evangelical La Plata Synod	24	175	614	404	614	2						D
Lutheran Church (Missouri Synod)	4	40	200	4,000	582	1		10		6		D
Mennonite Brethren Church	30	1,500	852	3,000	4,250		10		(7)U			E
New Testament Church	3		1,500		3,000	8	8	10	17	24		B
New Tribes Mission	10	513		893	170				(7)U	6		B
Seventh-day Adventists	6		425	800	1,105		10		5	18		A
South American Missionary Society	20		350		1,000	3	6			13		B
Southern Baptist Convention	9	509	934	1,100	2,845	3	8		9		1	B
	192	3,955	7,371	13,735	19,369	101 (34)U	133	20	97 (36)U	78	3	

U Unclassified.

Co-operating: a Svenska Missionen.

Also working: American Leprosy Mission.

PERU 496,093 sq. mls Pop.: 10,364,620 (1961)

Organisation												Code
Anglican Church	2	560	560	560	560	—	—	—	—	—	—	E
Asambleas de Dios	66	14	970	70	1,940	4	6	—	2	2	—	B
Assemblies of God a	322	4,227	8,000	6,947	26,264	(267)U	—	1	16	—	1	B
Association of Baptists for World Evangelism	21	580	580	1,075	1,075	4	3	—	6	7	—	E
Baptist Faith Missions	4	80	80	530	530	6	—	—	1	2	—	E
Baptist Mid-Missions	16	125	95	500	645	(6)U	—	—	(17)U	—	—	B
Christian Missions in Many Lands	23	—	206	—	700	1	—	—	(17)U	15	1	D
Christian and Missionary Alliance	116	870	1,020	4,350	3,049	16	29	—	11	10	1	B
Church of God	24	—	571	—	1,870	—	—	2	2	12	—	B
Church of God (Cleveland)	40	—	1,006	—	1,006	(50)U	6	2	(23)U	2	1	D
Church of God of Prophecy	14	100	280	100	550	—	10	2	(10)U	2	—	B
Church of the Nazarene	142	1,150	1,795	4,730	10,481	34	8	1	8	—	—	B
Evangelical Union of S. America (Misión Evangelica)	302	—	5,240	—	12,705	2	—	2	(19)U	14	—	D
Free Church of Scotland	37	269	269	1,863	1,863	—	1	—	5	1	1	E
German Evangelical Church in Chile	3	280	280	1,200	1,200	2	11	2	1	3	—	D
Iglesia Evangelica Luterana	1	1,270	965	1,655	2,500	—	40	—	(17)U	—	1	A
Iglesia Evangelica Peruana	309	2,800	7,725	8,000	23,175	10	5	2	2	—	1	D
Iglesias Pentecostales Autonomas	75	1,000	1,000	5,000	5,000	—	—	—	—	—	—	E
Irish Baptist Foreign Mission	30	820	375	1,200	1,300	—	7	1	1	—	—	B
Lima Union Church	1	325	325	600	600	—	—	—	6	—	—	E
Menmonite Brethren	3	50	30	250	250	13	—	—	(34)U	—	—	A
Methodist Church	46	1,825	1,439	9,000	5,337	—	9	3	6	20	—	B
Peru Inland Mission	32	330	330	1,050	1,050	8	1	—	—	10	—	E
Pilgrim Holiness Church	23	900	1,108	2,500	1,830	—	7	—	6	—	—	D
Plymouth Brethren	14	450	450	950	950	—	6	—	—	—	—	E
Regions Beyond Missionary Union U.S.A.	21	329	349	425	916	—	7	—	(18)U	—	—	D
Regions Beyond Missionary Union Gt. Britain	24	—	—	—	—	—	—	—	—	—	—	D
Seventh-day Adventists	26	18,172	6,532	33,463	15,746	10	128	—	(25)U	4	—	B
South American Indian Mission	29	200	490	1,700	2,000	28	—	—	(50)U	—	1	B

PERU—*continued*

Church or Mission N.B. See notes on Statistics, page xiii	Places of Regular Worship	Communicants, Full Members (p. 57)		Total Christian Community (p. 57)		Staff					Theolog. Colls., Bible Schools	Source of Information
						National Workers, full-time			Missionaries from other Churches or countries, full-time			
		1962 Handbook	Latest available figure	1962 Handbook	Latest available figure	Ordained	Laymen	Women	Ordained	Layworkers		
Southern Baptist Convention	16	216	384	1,000	1,497	5	2	—	11	11	—	B
Swiss Indian Mission	5	70	—	100	—	5	—	—	9	16	1	B
World Presbyterian Missions ...	14	440	484	1,148	1,313	1	6	—	8	—	1	D
	1,801	38,439	42,938	94,053	127,902	482 (323)U	472	285	336 (230)U	128	10	

U Unclassified.

Co-operating: **a** Svenska Fria Missionen.
Also working: Church Missionary Society of Australia. Church of Christ Scientist. Good News Trailer Missionary Fellowship. Reformed Presbyterian Church. World Baptist Fellowship Agency. Wycliffe Bible Translators.

SURINAM 62,500 sq. mls. Pop.: 330,000 estimate (1962)

Church or Mission	Places of Regular Worship	Communicants, Full Members (p. 57)		Total Christian Community (p. 57)		Staff					Theolog. Colls., Bible Schools	Source of Information
						National Workers, full-time			Missionaries from other Churches or countries, full-time			
		1962 Handbook	Latest available figure	1962 Handbook	Latest available figure	Ordained	Laymen	Women	Ordained	Layworkers		
Assemblies of God ... ... **a**	95	(New Field)				16	41	9	4	30	—	B
Moravian Church		6,418	6,418	46,528	46,528				12		—	E
Nederlandse Hervormde Kerk ...	9	9,900	9,900	16,000	16,000	2	9	—	1	—	—	D
Seventh-day Adventists	12	333	458	653	1,280	—	(1)U	—	(7)U	—	—	B
West Indies Mission	—	—	50	—	200						—	D
	116	16,651	16,826	63,181	64,008	18	51 (1)U	9	24 (7)U	30	—	

U Unclassified.

Co-operating: **a** Zendingsgenootschap der Evangelische Broedergemeente.
Also working: Dansk Missionsrad. International Missions. Missionary Aviation Fellowship. Salvation Army (*see* Trinidad and Tobago). Swiss Aid for Moravian Missions.

URUGUAY 72,172 sq. mls. Pop.: 2,590,158 estimate (1963)

American Lutheran Mission	3	—	87	—	194	—	15	—	—	—	—	B
Asambleas de Dios a	30	600	1,905	1,500	3,810	8	15	—	6	4	1	B
Assemblies of God	44	400	765	1,000	3,307	(35)U	—	—	4	—	1	B
Augustana Lutheran Church	2	—	75	—	165	—	—	—	8	—	—	D
Church of God (Cleveland)	16	—	1,923	—	4,322	43	—	—	(2)U	—	—	B
Ejercito de Salvacion (Salvation Army)	20	1,200	1,200	3,000	3,000	4	—	4	12	2	1	E
Evangelical Mission to Uruguay	17	—	275	—	550	13	—	12	1	3	1	A
Free Will Baptists	11	—	—	—	43	—	—	1	—	—	—	B
German Evangelical, La Plata Synod	11	2,000	1,328	5,000	4,400	1	—	1	(4)U	4	1	D&B
Iglesia del Nazareno	10	100	132	250	850	6	—	1	6	4	—	B
Iglesia Evangelica Menonita	10	850	850	2,000	2,000	—	—	—	4	4	—	E
Iglesias Cristianos Evangelicas Unidas (de los Hermanos)	23	700	700	2,000	2,000	1	—	—	—	—	—	E
Lutheran Church, Missouri Synod	1	—	192	—	348	17	—	—	(19)U	—	—	D&B
Methodist Church	31	2,000	1,768	5,000	3,591	13	8	8	2	2	—	B
New Testament Church	13	200	200	500	500	7	—	—	5	—	—	E
Seventh-day Adventists	16	2,122	2,614	4,098	4,996	16	49	—	11	11	1	B
Southern Baptist Convention	57	1,100	1,313	2,500	5,384	—	(10)U	—	2	3	1	B
Worldwide Evangelization Crusade	12	—	45	—	230	—	—	—	—	—	—	B
	316	11,272	15,372	26,848	39,690	164 (35)U	97 (10)U	27	87 (25)U	33	7	

U Unclassified.

Co-operating: **a** Svenska Fria Missionen.

Also working: Church of Christ, Scientist. Iglesia Evangelica Valdense del Rio de la Plata (*see* Argentina).

F

143

VENEZUELA 352,143 sq. mls. Pop.: 8,572,946 estimate (1964)

Church or Mission — N.B. See notes on Statistics, page xiii	Places of Regular Worship	Communicants, Full Members (p. 57)		Total Christian Community (p. 57)		Staff					Theolog. Colls., Bible Schools	Source of Information
						National Workers, full-time			Missionaries from other Churches or countries, full-time			
		1962 Handbook	Latest available figure	1962 Handbook	Latest available figure	Ordained	Lay-men	Women	Ordained	Lay-workers		
Asociacion de Iglesias Evangelicas... b	74	1,792	2,200	4,000	9,000	3	9	5	19	29	1	A
Assemblies of God	77	2,357	2,661	2,926	10,486	(95)U	—	—	(17)U	—	1	B
Baptist Mid-Missions	28	537	528	780	1,471	(37)U	—	—	(17)U	—	—	B
Christian Missions in Many Lands	6	250	150	600	300	—	—	—	(15)U	—	—	D
Evangelical Free Church	60	620	760	950	900	10	18	—	13	32	1	B
Evangelical Presbyterian Church a	16	589	817	1,300	2,406	6	—	—	5	—	—	B
Lutheran Church-Missouri Synod	8	—	195	—	405	—	2	—	—	—	—	B
Lutheran Council	7	—	2,216	—	3,000	7	4	1	(3)U	—	—	A
New Tribes Mission Inc.	3	—	—	—	—	—	—	3	—	31	—	B
Seventh-day Adventists E. and W.	41	2,905	5,189	3,420	14,602	15	(69)U	—	21	10	—	B
Southern Baptist Convention	33	620	900	—	5,285	11	—	—	6	38	—	B
The Evangelical Alliance Mission	93	1,200	1,950	2,884	3,800	21	35	7	10	—	1	A
United World Mission	8	—	209	—	430	4	(1)U	—	16	—	—	D
Worldwide Evangelization Crusade	6	107	100	265	295	—	—	—	(4)U	3	8	B
	460	10,977	17,875	26,042	52,380	209 (132)U	138 (70)U	16	146 (56)U	143	12	

U Unclassified.

Co-operating: **a** United Presbyterian Church in the U.S.A. **b** Orinoco River Mission.

Also working: Christian Churches (Disciples). Church of Christ, Scientist. Igreja Presbiteriana do Brasil. Missionary Aviation Fellowship. United Society for the Propagation of the Gospel.

144

ASIA

ADEN

75 sq. mls.   Pop.: 225,000 estimate (1964)

N.B. See notes on Statistics, page xiii

Church or Mission	Places of Regular Worship	Communicants, Full Members (p. 57)		Total Christian Community (p. 57)		Staff					Theolog., Colls., Bible Schools	Source of Information
						National Workers, full-time			Missionaries from other Churches or countries, full-time			
		1962 Handbook	Latest available figure	1962 Handbook	Latest available figure	Ordained	Laymen	Women	Ordained	Lay-workers		
Church of South Arabia ... a	2	—	15	—	22	—	—	1	1	13	—	B
Episcopal Church ... *	6	—	500	—	1,000	—	—	—	10 (Chaplains)		—	A
	8	—	515	—	1,022	—	—	1	11	13	—	

Co-operating: a Church of Scotland.   * The majority are members of H.M. Forces.
Also working: Danish Mission to the Orient. Mission to Mediterranean Garrisons. Jerusalem and the East Mission.

BURMA

261,789 sq. mls.   Pop.: 23,735,000 (1963)

Church or Mission	Places of Regular Worship	Communicants, Full Members (p. 57)		Total Christian Community (p. 57)		National Workers, full-time			Missionaries from other Churches or countries, full-time		Theolog., Colls., Bible Schools	Source of Information
		1962 Handbook	Latest available figure	1962 Handbook	Latest available figure	Ordained	Laymen	Women	Ordained	Lay-workers		
Assemblies of God ...	176	8,806	6,726	18,558	12,961	(103)U	—	—	(5)U	—	2	B
Burma Baptist Convention ...	2,789	207,068	222,673	600,000	600,000	627	1,317	302	13	17	17	A
Church of India, Pakistan, Burma and Ceylon (Diocese of Rangoon) ...	127	18,000	18,000	130,000	130,000	48	10	2	—	—	1	E
Lakher Pioneer Mission ...	50	3,991	3,991	7,448	7,448	6	—	—	—	—	—	E

BURMA—*continued*

Church or Mission N.B. See notes on Statistics, page xiii		Places of Regular Worship	Communicants, Full Members (p. 57)		Total Christian Community (p. 57)		Staff					Theolog., Colls., Bible Schools	Source of Information
							National Workers, full-time			Missionaries from other Churches or countries, full-time			
			1962 Hand-book	Latest avail-able figure	1962 Hand-book	Latest avail-able figure	Or-dained	Lay-men	Women	Or-dained	Lay-workers		
Methodists	a	91	4,687	6,429	9,654	13,382	18	6	11	2	1	1	B
Methodists	b	28	2,000	1,075	3,500	2,124	14	2	—	7	—	—	B
Pentecostalists ...		—	10,000	10,000	10,000	10,000	—	—	—	—	—	—	E
Salvation Army ...		14	211	211	924	924	9	22	—	9	12	—	E
Seventh-day Adventists ...		53	2,307	3,453	3,000	7,889	24	(131)U	—	5	—	—	B
		3,328	257,070	272,558	783,084	784,728	849 (103)U	1,488 (131)U	315	41 (5)U	30	21	

Co-operating: **a** Methodist Missionary Society, London. **b** Board of Missions of Methodist Church, New York.
Also working: American Leprosy Missions Inc. Bible Churchmen's Missionary Society. United Society for the Propagation of the Gospel.

CAMBODIA   71,000 sq. mls.   Pop.: 5,748,842 (1962)

Church or Mission	Places of Regular Worship	Communicants 1962 Hand-book	Latest avail-able figure	Total Christian 1962 Hand-book	Latest avail-able figure	Or-dained	Lay-men	Women	Or-dained	Lay-workers	Theolog.	Source
Christian Alliance of Cambodia ...	29	—	734	—	734	(18)U	—	—	7	8	1	D
Seventh-day Adventists ...	11	810	810	1,238	1,238	(15)U	(51)U	—	—	—	—	E
	40	810	1,544	1,238	1,972	(33)U	(51)U	—	7	8	1	

U Unclassified

CEYLON

25,332 sq. mls. Pop.: 10,624,507 (1963)

Assemblies of God	30	366	366	609	609	37	6	—	2	—	—	E
Church of India, Pakistan, Burma and Ceylon (Dioceses of Colombo and Karunagala)	125	19,000	19,000	42,000	42,000	87	18	2	6	4	—	E
Church of South India:												
Jaffna Diocese **a**	28	3,142	3,142	4,737	4,737	17	5	—	7	—	—	E
Dutch Reformed Church	9	2,500	2,500	4,500	4,500	17	5	—	2	—	—	E
Methodist	146	11,881	13,278	23,876	24,653	48	53	3	9	7	1	B
Presbyterian Church	—	1,000	1,000	1,000	1,000	—	—	(85)U	—	—	—	E
Salvation Army	181	1,792	1,792	5,256	5,256	118	176 (48)U	—	12	—	—	E
Seventh-day Adventists	12	595	775	1,162	2,035	12	—	—	6	—	—	B
Sri Lanka Baptist Sanga Maya **b**	29	1,796	1,796	3,069	3,069	—	—	1	3	7	—	B & E
Svenska Fria Missionen	8	115	210	1,005	756	11	—	—	2	6	—	B
	568	42,187	43,859	87,214	88,635	347	293 (48)U	91 (85)U	49	24	1	

U Unclassified

Co-operating: **a** United Church Board for World Ministries. **b** Baptist Missionary Society. Church of Scotland.

Also working: Church of Scotland Colonial Congregation. Pentecostals.

CHINA 3,768,100 sq. mls. Pop.: 669,000,000 (1958)

Church or Mission N.B. See notes on Statistics, page xiii	Places of Regular Worship	Communicants, Full Members (p. 57)		Total Christian Community (p. 57)		Staff					Theolog. Colls., Bible Schools	Source of Information
						National Workers, full-time			Missionaries from other Churches or countries, full-time			
		1962 Hand-book	Latest avail-able figure	1962 Hand-book	Latest avail-able figure	Or-dained	Lay-men	Women	Or-dained	Lay-workers		
	19,337				*Baptized Member-ship* 1,013,176	2,506	11,485					

No new and reliable figures of the state of the Christian Church in China are available. Most of the statistics given in the 1962 World Christian Handbook were from a Survey by the National Christian Council of China in 1950. We repeat below the totals then given. However, it is estimated that the total Christian Community in China is now below 700,000.

CYPRUS 3,572 sq. mls. Pop.: 590,000 (1963)

Church or Mission	Places of Regular Worship	Communicants 1962 Hand-book	Communicants Latest figure	Total 1962 Hand-book	Total Latest figure	Ordained	Lay-men	Women	Ord. Miss.	Lay-workers	Theolog.	Source
Anglican Church—Jerusalem Bishopric	5	—	160	—	750	—	—	—	2	2	—	A
Church of God of Prophecy	3	104	104	104	104	—	2	—	—	—	—	E

CYPRUS—*continued*

	1	2	3	4	5	6	7	8	9	10	11	
Reformed Presbyterian (Greek Evangelical) Church	3	—	25	—	25	1	2	—	—	2	10	B
Seventh-day Adventists ...	1	23	15	23	37	1	2	—	—	2	—	B
Church of Cyprus (Eastern Orthodox)	650	410,000	304	127	916	1,200	2	—	—	6	12	E

Also working: Brethren. Church of God Pentecostal. Community Church. Jerusalem and the East Mission. Mission to Mediterranean Garrisons, Inc.

ASIA

HONG KONG

398,25 sq. mls.   Pop.: 3,642,500 (1963)

	1	2	3	4	5	6	7	8	9	10	11	
Alliance Church Union ...	25	1,179	2,653	—	2,653	32	—	—	9	11	1	B
American Baptist Foreign Mission ...	5	2,222	2,222	2,222	2,222	2	4	9	2	4	—	E
Assemblies of God ...	15	1,457	1,150	1,806	3,257	(23)U	—	—	11	—	1	B
Baptist Mid-Missions ...	2	—	20	—	20	(3)U	2	—	3	5	1	B
Conservative Baptists ... f	6	—	50	—	400	—	—	4	2	2	—	B
Chinese Methodist ...	7	2,997	4,298	3,064	6,659	8	—	7	5	3	—	A
Chinese Rhenish Church: Hong Kong Synod (Lutheran) ...	9	1,179	2,750	—	4,000	5	10	6	1	4	—	E
Christian and Missionary Alliance ...	13	—	1,179	3,750	3,750	5	(62)U	—	7	10	—	A
Church of Christ in China Hong Kong Council ... a	28	13,984	19,515	13,984	40,000	25	13	11	13	29	1	A
Chung Hwa Sheng Kung Hui (Anglican, Diocese of Hong Kong and Macao) ...	18	7,133	7,133	18,291	18,291	33	—	1	18	1	—	E
Elim Church ...	3	140	120	410	400	—	1	—	1	2	—	B
Evangelical Free Church ...	14	—	1,300	—	1,800	5	5	6	4	16	1	B
Evangelical Lutheran Church ...	30	5,159	5,839	9,387	12,044	18	40	30	15	32	2	A
Free Methodist Church ...	7	—	1,190	—	1,190	2	44	5	4	2	—	B
Heap Gay Mission ... c	6	—	696	696	696	4	5	3	1	1	—	B
Lutheran Missouri Synod ...	24	1,896	3,245	5,966	8,866	12	—	—	9	5	1	A

HONG KONG—*continued*

N.B. See notes on Statistics, page xiii

Church or Mission	Places of Regular Worship	Communicants, Full Members (p. 57)		Total Christian Community (p. 57)		Staff					Theolog. Colls., Bible Schools	Source of Information
						National Workers, full-time			Missionaries from other Churches or countries, full-time			
		1962 Handbook	Latest available figure	1962 Handbook	Latest available figure	Ordained	Lay-men	Women	Ordained	Lay-workers		
Methodist Church ... **e**	7	1,000	1,315	2,000	2,722	8	6	—	17(U.S.A.)	—	—	B
Methodist Church (Gt. Britain)	1	—	150	—	198	2	—	—	1	—	—	B
Norwegian Lutheran Mission	8	575	666	1,066	1,254	(174)U	6	—	—	8	1	B
Nordiske Kristne Buddistmisjon	4	105	105	261	397	2	6	3	1	1	—	B
Oriental Missionary Society	4	628	628	1,425	1,425	1	21	13	3	3	—	E
Overseas Missionary Fellowship	15	—	—	—	—	—	—	—	—	15	1	B
Pentecostal Assemblies of Canada	10	4,000	5,000	4,000	5,000	—	—	—	3	5	—	B
Pentecostal Holiness Church	10	1,626	2,429	3,859	5,484	(18)U	—	(18)U	(7)U	—	1	E
Salvation Army ...	19	1,889	3,163	1,889	3,859	20	95	—	9	—	—	B
Seventh-day Adventists ...	19	438	160	714	7,541	21	—	2	25	2	1	B
Sion Church Mission ... **d**	55	—	—	549	549	1	(214)U	—	—	—	—	E
Southern Baptist Convention ...	55	12,527	15,811	12,527	25,943	29	4	—	23	30	1	B
Tsung Tsin Mission (Hakka Churches) ... **b**	14	2,822	4,650	4,984	6,738	8	(62)U	3	5	4	1	A
United Brethren in Christ ...	6	370	370	1,000	1,000	2	5	6	—	—	1	E
Yan Poon (Grace Rock) ...	3	—	856	—	2,653	4	3	3	25	—	1	B
	370	63,326	90,289	92,705	171,011	467 (218)U	602 (358)U	130 (18)U	224 (7)U	195	14	

U Unclassified.

Co-operating: **a** United Presbyterian Church in the U.S.A. United Church of Canada. Reformed Church in America. United Church Board for World Ministries. Evangelical United Brethren Church. **b** Basel Mission. **c** United Brethren in Christ. **d** Svenska Fria Missionen. **e** Board of Missions of Methodist Church. **f** Conservative Baptist Foreign Mission Society.

Also working: Baptist Missionary Society. Christian Nationals Evangelism Commission. Church Missionary Society of Australia. Church of Christ Scientist. Eastern Mennonite Board of Missions. Hildesheimer Blinden-Mission. Laerinnenes Misjonsforbund. Lee Memorial Mission. Metodistkerkens Misjonsselskap. Oriental Boat Mission. Presbyterian Church of New Zealand. The Navigators.

INDIA   1,262,275 sq. mls.   Pop.: 477 million (estimate mid 1965)

Denomination												
Advent Christian Denomination	25	1,190	1,190	3,013	3,013	5	10	13	(8)U	—	—	E
American Marathi Mission	173	6,925	6,925	14,667	14,667	25	183	144	4	8	—	E
Andhra Evangelical Lutheran Church	2,133	123,591	123,591	257,030	284,998	167	378	264	18	35		B & A
Apostolic Church (United Kingdom)	2	500	500	1,500	1,500	—	1	—	—	4	—	E
Apostolic Church of Pentecost	45	2,500	2,500	2,500	2,500	—	45	—	—	6	—	E
Arcot Lutheran Church k	104	6,413	8,152	11,999	15,182	19	(516)U	—	(33)U	8	2	B
Assemblies of God North India	58	900	1,815	2,000	6,571	(83)U	—	—	(18)U	—	4	B
Assemblies of God South India	146	5,133	4,298	11,527	19,859	(157)U	65	50	3	7	—	B
Australian Churches of Christ	13	1,000	1,000	4,000	4,000	10	—	—	—		—	E
Baptist Church of Mizo District c	204	18,198	24,299	44,303	47,753	16	48	21	—	2	1	A
Baptist General Conference North Bank Mission	205	7,500	8,000	—	8,000	—	—	—	7	22	1	B
Baptist Mid-Missions	12	102	162	246	313	(5)U	—	—	34	—	1	B
Baptist Union of North India i	30	—	—	9,000	9,000	20	—	—	7	—	—	E
Bengal Baptist Union i	93	2,370	2,370	15,000	15,000	12	270	125	6	8	—	E
Bengal-Orissa Baptist Yearly Meeting	60	4,242	4,242	12,000	12,000	10	14	16	4	12	—	E
Bible Crusade Missionary Society	8	322	322	556	556	6	6	2	1	1	—	E
Bible Pattern Church	5	200	200	1,000	1,000	—	2	1	—	2	—	E
Brethren in Christ Mission Church	27	550	700	800	1,000	5	17	11	4	11	1	A
Cambridge Mission to Delhi	43	—	—	18,685	18,685	13	11	14	5	14	—	E
Ceylon and India General Mission	51	2,814	2,909	6,222	6,633	5	30	23	7	50		A
Christian and Missionary Alliance (Maharashtra Field)	65	3,294	3,564	7,252	6,150	10	63	25	15	24	2	A
(Gujarat Field)	21	4,415	1,686	7,607	5,430	5	34	4	19	5	1	A
Christian Churches (Disciples) †	51	11,125	12,385	14,625	15,000	147	(424)U	—	3	5	4	A
Church of God	229		10,000	—	15,000	135	6	12	(54)U	—	3	A
Church of God (Cleveland)	196		10,432		35,932	(236)U	—	—			—	B

INDIA—*continued*

Church or Mission — N.B. See notes on Statistics, page xiii	Places of Regular Worship	Communicants, Full Members (p. 57) 1962 Handbook	Communicants, Full Members (p. 57) Latest available figure	Total Christian Community (p. 57) 1962 Handbook	Total Christian Community (p. 57) Latest available figure	Staff — National Workers, full-time Ordained	National Workers Laymen	National Workers Women	Missionaries from other Churches or countries, full-time Ordained	Missionaries Lay-workers	Theolog. Colls., Bible Schools	Source of Information
Church of India, Pakistan, Burma and Ceylon (Anglican) Diocese of Bombay	65	5,086	9,413	10,326	16,628	46	(305)U	—	30	24	1	A
Church of South India …	8,523	336,405	413,299	1,141,144	1,170,752	1,004	788	541	89	172	3	D&E
Church of the Nazarene …	31	968	1,025	3,258	3,736	34	12	24	6	16	1	B
Churches of Christ in West India	16	956	956	2,870	2,870	9	57	48	4	12	—	E
Convention of Baptist Churches of the N. Circars) (Canadian Baptist Mission)	175	47,217	47,217	110,000	110,000	172	760	131	15	37	—	E
Council of Baptist Churches in North East India …	2,128	158,216	173,640	680,000	680,000	61	715	—	5	18	—	B&E
Dohnavar Fellowship …	3	353	353	889	889	—	—	—	—	—	—	E
Dr Graham's Homes Kalimpong	1	120	120	950	950	—	15	34	2	32	—	E
Elim Church …	5	190	232	625	692	4	9	10	3	7	—	B
Evangelical and Reformed Church …	80	5,545	5,545	10,584	10,584	—	—	—	3	17	—	E
i Evangelical Baptist Fellowship	132	420	1,140	1,250	1,250	—	20	—	8	23	2	B
Evangelical Christian Church of India …	30	—	1,619	—	1,619	19	17	—	(19)U	—	3	B
j Evangelical Lutheran Church in Madhya Pradesh …	22	2,608	3,129	5,108	5,738	17	(243)U	—	2	17	1	B
Fellowship of Free Baptist Churches in North India …	20	638	672	638	1,700	7	9	13	3	14	—	B
Free Church of Scotland …	2	24	40	49	65	1	4	3	1	6	—	A
Free Methodist Church …	13	534	569	1,920	1,236	13	18	5	10	5	1	B
Free Will Baptists …	7	312	290	800	800	(22)U	—	—	2	3	1	B
Friends Service Council	8	266	266	1,170	1,170	—	—	—	—	—	—	E

INDIA—*continued*

Name	Code											
Full Gospel Fellowship (Pentecostal)	A	12	—	500	—	2,000	15	30	5	—	—	—
Garo Baptist Union	E	—	7,092	7,092	12,165	12,165	4	—	—	3	4	—
General Conference Mennonite Church	B	28	1,707	2,739	2,311	5,545	14	19	—	10	29	1
Goalpara Boro Baptist Church **m**	E	21	1,895	3,500	4,954	4,954	—	4	3	1	4	—
Gossner Evangelical Lutheran Church	D	978	111,947	111,947	215,805	212,395	121	1,043	261	2	8	—
Hindustani Covenant Church **h**	B	9	270	330	970	970	3	15	8	4	8	—
India Bible Mission Church	E	120	2,200	2,200	3,200	3,200	11	42	24	—	—	—
Indian Christian Assemblies	A	18	5,000	2,500	6,000	5,000	8	10	—	2	1	—
India Evangelical Lutheran Church	B	289	12,382	13,755	31,856	35,079	114	81	306	(27)U	—	—
India Mission	E	400	14,000	14,000	20,000	20,000	—	150	20	30	42	—
India Mission Society of Tirunelveli	E	244	16,025	16,025	16,025	16,025	—	—	—	—	—	—
India Pentecostal Church of God	E	300	9,000	9,000	30,000	30,000	—	300	75	—	—	—
India United Evangelical Mission	E	4	443	443	1,345	1,345	1	14	5	—	1	1
Jeypore Evangelical Lutheran Church **k**	B	412	14,026	19,616	37,415	43,658	34	104	10	3	6	—
Jungle Tribes Mission (Presbyterian)	E	6	910	910	3,161	3,161	6	20	25	2	4	—
Lakher Independent Evangelical Church	A	94	4,454	11,115	9,344	19,991	13	295	—	1	2	—
Malabar Independent Syrian Church	E	8	1,550	1,550	2,410	2,410	8	—	—	—	—	—
Mar Thoma Syrian Church of Malabar	A	468	184,000	100,000	290,000	300,000	225	—	—	—	—	3
Mennonite Brethren	B	90	23,000	24,554	70,000	100,000	9	25	25	28	23	—
Methodist, Bengal	B	84	—	2,020	—	4,466	12	1	1	10	8	—
Methodist Church in Southern Asia **d**	A	300	137,261	155,819	557,010	591,686	843	1,232	1,298	95	47	3
Methodist, Lucknow and Benares	B	30	—	1,552	—	3,227	11	8	4	8	5	—
Mid-India Yearly Meeting (Friends)	E	7	222	222	1,187	1,187	—	—	—	—	—	—
Mission to Aristocracy of India	A	6	—	100	—	—	—	10	5	—	—	—

153

INDIA—continued

Church or Mission N.B. See notes on Statistics, page xiii	Places of Regular Worship	Communicants, Full Members (p. 57)		Total Christian Community (p. 57)		Staff					Theolog. Colls., Bible Schools	Source of Information
						National Workers, full-time			Missionaries from other Churches or countries, full-time			
		1962 Handbook	Latest available figure	1962 Handbook	Latest available figure	Ordained	Laymen	Women	Ordained	Lay-workers		
Missionary Bands in India	7	500	500	1,100	1,100	8	9	17	1	5	—	E
Native Church (Protestant)	70	—	5,000	—	5,000	12	10	20	5	7	1	A
Nepal Evangelistic Band	1	37	6	46	11	1	—	—	—	—	—	B
North Goalpara Garo Baptist Union	27	420	459	1,000	1,129	—	5	—	1	3	—	A
Northern Evangelical Lutheran Church	284	14,236	17,285	35,049	43,018	60	156	133	16	49	4	A
Norwegian Free Evangelical Mission	31	520	520	1,165	1,165	7	30	8	6	24	—	E
Norwegian Pentecostal	80	1,000	1,000	2,500	2,500	—	80	29	—	33	—	E
Old Church Hebrew Mission	1	50	150	300	300	1	—	—	—	—	—	A
Pentecostal Church of God of Andhra Pradesh	700	20,000	20,000	20,000	20,000	—	725	—	—	—	—	E
Pentecostal Holiness Church	15	500	243	1,250	1,278	21	—	—	10	—	2	B
Poona and Indian Village Mission	8	247	247	607	607	—	5	15	1	35	—	E
Presbyterian Church (in Ireland)	27	4,397	4,397	10,792	10,792	18	116	278	7	34	—	E
Ramabai Mukti Mission	2	360	360	800	800	1	—	31	1	14	—	E
Reformed Episcopal Church	1	80	250	172	250	1	8	12	1	3	—	A
Reformed Presbyterian Church (Evangelical Synod)	5	157	250	340	340	5	—	—	4	1	—	B
Regions Beyond Missionary Union	6	200	160	500	369	—	8	—	2	32	—	A
Sajinipara and Calcutta Lutheran Church a	2	—	79	—	144	2	2	2	1	2	—	A
Salvation Army	4,607	120,288	120,288	227,353	227,353	2,403	104	2 (116U)	1,084	—	—	E
Samaresham of Telugu Baptist Churches e	1,880	—	175,884	—	175,884	107	268	78	6	22	1	A

154

INDIA—continued

Seventh-day Adventists	312	18,454	25,111	30,135	57,022	142	(986)U	—	46	—	—	B
South Andhra Lutheran Church	252	—	6,545	—	14,235	23	35	11	(7)U	15	2	B
Strict Baptist Churches	91	2,250	2,250	10,000	10,000	15	12	—	6	16	2	E
Svenska Fria Missionen	25	—	4,768	—	6,000	88	149	42	8	7	—	B
Swedish Alliance Mission	11	737	764	1,589	1,608	6	39	31	2	7	—	B
Swedish Hindustani Mission	4	272	272	933	933	4	7	5	5	7	—	E
Swedish Pentecostal	155	26,275	26,275	26,275	26,275	155	152	69	10	21	2	E
Tamil Evangelical Lutheran Church	1,172	26,476	30,958	56,202	62,540	72	94	40	6	16	—	A
Telegu Mennonite Brethren Convention	750	23,000	23,000	120,000	120,000	10	200	100	27	—	2	E
The Evangelical Alliance Mission	28	970	970	3,000	3,000	9	70	35	16	42	—	E
Tripura Baptist Christian Union b	185	3,909	4,381	7,747	8,507	17	131	15	5	7	1	A
United Church of North India...*g	424	208,770	208,770	485,976	485,976	455	360	128	161	95	—	E
United Missionary Society	18	635	635	1,021	1,021	3	12	6	5	8	—	E
Uktal Christian Church Central Council	255	13,452	13,452	29,617	29,617	229	200	6	29	17	—	E
Wesleyan Methodist	9	1,075	278	1,700	350	3	7	—	1	1	1	A
World Gospel Mission	4	25	20	635	50	1	10	6	6	11	1	B
	30,639	1,799,820	2,087,927	4,810,075	5,303,206	7,833 (503)U	12,489 (2,474)U	4,857 (116)U	2,166 (166)U	1,348	57	

* Represents 28 Church Councils.   † Figures include Orissa.   U Unclassified.

Co-operating: a Norwegian Mission. b New Zealand Baptist Missionary Society. c Baptist Missionary Society. d Board of Mission of Methodist Church U.S.A. e American Baptist Foreign Missionary Society. g United Presbyterian Church in the U.S.A. Presbyterian Church of Wales. h Svenska Missionsforbundet. i Baptist Missionary Society. j Orebro Missionsforening. k Danske Missionsselskab. l Conservative Baptist Foreign Mission Society. m Australian Baptist Foreign Mission Society.

Also working: Banda Misjonen. Bible Churchmen's Missionary Society. C.M.S. of Australia. Church of Scotland. Dublin University Mission to Chota Nagpur. Laerinnenes Misjonsforbund. Lee Memorial Mission. New Tribes Mission. United Society for the Propagation of the Gospel. Worldwide Evangelization Crusade.

INDONESIA 575,450 sq. mls. Pop.: 97,085,348 (1961)

Church or Mission / N.B. See notes on Statistics, page xiii	Places of Regular Worship	Communicants, Full Members (p. 57) 1962 Handbook	Communicants, Full Members (p. 57) Latest available figure	Total Christian Community (p. 57) 1962 Handbook	Total Christian Community (p. 57) Latest available figure	National Workers, full-time — Ordained	National Workers, full-time — Laymen	National Workers, full-time — Women	Missionaries from other Churches or countries, full-time — Ordained	Missionaries from other Churches or countries, full-time — Lay-workers	Theolog., Colls., Bible Schools	Source of Information
Assemblies of God	86	2,987	2,646	4,245	10,141	(99)U	—	—	(22)U	—	4	B
Banua Niha Keriso Protestan (Sumatra)	312	4,375	4,375	190,000	190,000	45	2	—	4	10	—	E
Baptist Mid-Missions	5	71	186	116	611	(15)U	—	—	1	—	—	B
Bethel Full Gospel Church	200	15,000	15,000	50,000	50,000	—	220	2	—	—	1	B
Calvary Mission [a]	263	—	10,000*	—	10,000	2	—	—	—	—	—	B
Geredja Kalimantan Evangelis	750	—	10,000*	30,442	30,442	85	108	6	18	—	6	E
Geredja-Geredja Kristen Djawa	—	—	20,250	—	46,740	846	17	2	5	7	2	A
Geredja Kristen Indjili di Irian Barat	900	—	160,000	200,000	250,000	—	—	—	4	1	1	A
Geredja Kristen Indonesia Djawa Barat	31	7,994	10,053	14,058	16,733	37	355	2	—	2	—	A
Geredja Kristen Pasundan	32	6,332	6,332	9,500	9,500	27	56	34	—	—	—	E
Geredja Kristen Protestan di Bali	31	—	5,500	2,700	6,000	26	5	—	—	—	—	A
Geredja Kristen Protestan Indonesia	—	—	21,000*	—	64,550	—	—	—	—	—	—	B
Geredja Kristen Protestan Simalungun	—	—	—	—	70,800	—	—	—	—	—	—	B
Geredja Kristen Salawesi Tengah	—	—	28,000*	85,000	85,000	—	—	—	—	—	—	E
Geredja Kristen Toradja Kantepao	332	56,711	56,711	117,367	117,367	(1,829)U	24	51	—	2	—	E
Geredja Masehi Indjili Minahasa	—	—	110,000*	350,000	350,000	—	—	—	—	—	—	E
Geredja Masehi Indjili Sangshe dan Taland	246	132,830	132,830	132,830	132,830	116	177	179	—	—	—	E
Geredja Masehi Indjili du Timor	—	—	650,000	295,000	650,000	—	—	—	—	—	—	D

156

INDONESIA—*continued*

													B
Gospel Tabernacle Christian Church (East and West Kalimantan, East Indonesia and Java)	c	262	23,433	27,308	—	27,308	208	—	—	25	33	3	B
Gospel Tabernacle Christian Church (West Irian)		268	2,313	14,001	—	14,001	295	—	—	21	36	3	B
Huria Kristen Batak Protestan		—	46,059	46,059	691,463	1,000,000	—	—	—	—	—	—	B
Huria Kristen Indonesia		—	—	50,000*	—	150,000	—	—	—	—	—	—	B
Methodist Church (Sumatra)	c	142	4,000	11,031	8,000	28,799	24	57	—	10(U.S.A.)	1	—	B
New Tribes Mission		1	—	—	—	—	—	—	1	1	38	1	B
Overseas Missionary Fellowship		—	—	—	—	—	—	—	—	2	1	—	E
Pentecostal Church of God		60	10,000	10,000	10,000	10,000	—	65	—	5	9	—	B
Perhimpunan Indjil Baptist	d	4	—	500	—	500	—	—	1	—	—	—	B
Regions Beyond Missionary Union, Irian Barat		60	—	14,000	—	14,000	—	—	—	3	25	1	A
Rheinische Missionsgesellschaft		1,872	—	4,697	896,908	896,908	259	9,521	72	8	7	—	E
Salvation Army		169	5,140	300,000*	22,146	22,146	159	683	130	33	—	—	E
Seventh-day Adventists		320	17,978	5,140	30,970	30,970	85	437	—	—	49	—	E
Southern Baptist Convention		51	967	17,978	—	9,888	11	(30)U	—	36	27	1	B
The Evangelical Alliance Mission		42	—	3,104	—	11,400	—	15	1	12	16	1	A
Unevangelized Fields Mission		29	2,000	1,610	7,000	11,400	15	—	—	10	28	6	B
Worldwide Evangelization Crusade		9	168	2,562	450	450	—	—	—	21	—	—	B

Estimate of membership within Dewan Geredja di Indonesia (National Council of Churches) Churches: 3,500,000

Estimate of membership of other Protestant Churches: 1,500,000

5,000,000

(see over)

INDONESIA—*continued*

Church or Mission	Places of Regular Worship	Communicants, Full Members (p. 57)		Total Christian Community (p. 57)		Staff					Theolog., Colls., Bible Schools	Source of Information
N.B. See notes on Statistics, page xiii		1962 Handbook	Latest available figure	1962 Handbook	Latest available figure	National Workers, full-time			Missionaries from other Churches or countries, full-time			
						Ordained	Laymen	Women	Ordained	Lay-workers		
Zending der Gereformeerde Kerken in Nederland												
Central Java	250	18,000	18,000	40,000	40,000	60	150	14	4	28	—	E
Sumba	298	11,430	11,430	17,153	17,153	30	60	82	3	3	—	E
	7,025	367,788	1,766,471	2,910,348	4,371,237	4,273 (1,943)U	11,982 (30)U	576	250 (22)U	323	25	

Co-operating: **a** Basel Mission. **c** Christian and Missionary Alliance; Board of Missions of Methodist Church U.S.A. **d** Conservative Baptist Foreign Mission Society.

Also working: Australian Presbyterian Board of Missions. Church of Christ Scientist. Evangelical United Brethren Church. Eglises Protestantes de Suisse Romande. Presbyterian Church of New Zealand. United Presbyterian Church in the U.S.A. United Church Board for World Ministries.

* Estimate.   U Unclassified.

IRAN

627,000 sq. mls.   Pop.: 22,523,039 (1964)

Church or Mission	Places of Regular Worship	1962 Handbook	Latest available figure	1962 Handbook	Latest available figure	Ordained	Laymen	Women	Ordained	Lay-workers	Theolog., Colls., Bible Schools	Source of Information
Assemblies of God	14	351	704	1,201	1,868	(13)U	1	—	—	—	—	E
Episcopal Church of Iran ... **a**	11	400	400	600	600	5	11	—	4	6	—	A
Evangelical Presbyterian Church	41	2,700	3,000	5,000	5,350	8	10	—	8	1	1	A
Filadelphia Assembly	3	—	100	—	100	2	—	—	1	—	—	A
International Missions	2	50	15	80	40	—	—	—	8	9	—	A
Seventh-day Adventists	7	240	268	452	523	7	(17)U	—	6	—	1	B
	78	3,741	4,487	7,333	8,481	35 (13)U	39 (17)U	—	27	16	1	

U Unclassified.

Co-operating: **a** Church's Ministry among the Jews.

Also working: Church Missionary Society of Australia. Jerusalem and the East Mission. Worldwide Evangelization Crusade.

IRAQ

169,240 sq. mls.   Pop.: 7,150,000 (1963)

Anglican Church—Jerusalem Bishopric	4	—	115	—	320	1	—	—	1	1	A
Assemblies of God	—	4	4	34	34	—	—	—	—	—	E
Lutheran Orient Mission	1	—	—	—	30	2	—	1	—	—	B
National Evangelical Churches	6	—	700	—	2,000	4	—	3	—	—	B
Seventh-day Adventists	4	200	169	630	764	7	—	(14)U	7	—	B
United Missions in Iraq a	11	500	840	1,000	1,500	—	—	(38)U	6	28	D
	26	704	1,828	1,664	4,648	14	—	56 (52)U	14	29	—

Co-operating: a United Presbyterian Church in the U.S.A. Reformed Church in America.
Also working: Evangelical Alliance Mission. Jerusalem and the East Mission. Near East and Arabian Mission. United Church Board for World Ministries.

ISRAEL

7,993 sq. mls.   Pop.: 2,430,100 (1964)

Anglican Church—Jerusalem Bishopric	10	—	500	—	1,200	—	—	—	8	50	A
Assemblies of God	1	7	7	17	40	1	—	—	—	—	B
Bible Evangelistic Mission (Pentecostal)	1	130	130	175	175	—	—	—	—	2	E
British Society for the Propagation of the Gospel among the Jews	1	20	20	50	50	1	—	1	—	—	B
Christian and Missionary Alliance	2	—	17	—	17	4	—	1	2	2	B
Church's Ministry among the Jews	3	200	176	300	320	—	—	—	3	13	A
Church of the Nazarene	3	4	2	34	36	1	—	1	1	1	B
Lutheran Congregations	—	94	94	94	94	1	—	1	—	—	E
Mission of the Finnish Missionary Society	—	—	—	—	18	—	—	—	—	—	B

ISRAEL—*continued*

Church or Mission N.B. See notes on Statistics, page xiii	Places of Regular Worship	Communicants, Full Members (p. 57)		Total Christian Community (p. 57)		Staff					Theolog., Colls., Bible Schools	Source of Information
						National Workers, full-time			Missionaries from other Churches or countries, full-time			
		1962 Handbook	Latest available figure	1962 Handbook	Latest available figure	Ordained	Laymen	Women	Ordained	Lay-workers		
Seventh-day Adventists (including Jordan)	4	183	183	721	721	(7)U	(13)U	—	—	—	—	E
Southern Baptist Convention (Figures include Gaza) ...	9	110	208	228	1,069	—	—	—	14	16	1	B
	34	748	1,337	1,619	3,740	15 (7)U	15 (13)U	—	28	84	1	

Total Estimate from United Christian Council

Greek Orthodox	...	19,000
Roman Catholic: Greek Catholic ...	...	20,000
Maronites	...	2,500
Latins	...	6,500
Protestants (and Anglican)	...	2,400
Armenians	...	10,000
Copts, Abyssinians and other Eastern Rites	...	600
		52,000

Also working: American-European Fellowship. Australian Board of Missions, Church of England. American Association for Jewish Evangelism. Bible Lands Mission. British and Foreign Bible Society. British Jews Society. Christian Missions in Many Lands. Edinburgh Medical Missionary Society. Hebrew Christian Testimony to Israel. Hervormde Raad voor de Verhouding van Kerk en Israel. International Hebrew Christian Alliance. Jerusalem and the East Mission. Geref. Kerken in Nederland. Messianic Assembly in Israel. Laerinnenes Misjonsforbund. Svenska Jerusalemföreningen. Svenska Fria Missionen. Svenska Israelmissionen. Church of Scotland. Lutheran Mission to Israel. Mennonite Board of Missions and Charities. Norske Pinsevenners Ytremisjon. Norwegian Lutheran Mission. American Board of Missions to the Jews.

JAPAN 142,726 sq. mls. Pop.: 98,281,955 estimate (1965)

Organization												
American Baptist Association	4	—	90	—	290	1	2	2	4	7	1	B
Anglican Episcopal Church (Nihon Seiko Kai)	336	40,184	46,566	40,184	59,162	307	18	30	26	22	3	A
Apostolic Christian Church (Nihon Shito Kirisuto Kyokai)	4	—	104	—	329	5	—	—	7	—	—	D
Assemblies of God Church (Nihon Assemblies of God Kyodan)	129	2,124	6,500	5,045	11,875	(145)U	—	—	(28)U	—	1	B
Baptist Bible Fellowship (Nihon Seisho Baputesuto Renmei)	24	835	500	835	500	(26)U	—	—	(21)U	2	—	D
Baptist General Conference (Nippon Kirisuto Baputesuto Rengo Senkyodan)	27	—	240	—	600	10	—	1	10	11	1	B
Baptist Mid-Missions (Zen Nippon Baputesuto Mido Mission Senkyodan)	10	—	63	—	261	1	—	—	12	—	—	B
Bible Institute Mission (Shorisha Iesu Kyodan)	5	—	208	—	208	(6)U	—	—	(4)U	—	—	D
Brethren in Christ (Kirisutokyo Kyodai-Dan)	6	37	83	40	200	—	7	2	3	5	1	B&A
Christian Brotherhood Church (Kirisuto Kyodai-Dan)	162	1,748	566	1,748	862	(118)U	—	—	—	—	—	D
Christian Canaan Church (Kirisutokyo Kana Kyokai)	12	2,884	3,163	2,884	3,163	8	—	—	—	—	—	D
Christian Churches (Kirisuto no Kyokai)	50	2,711	1,000	2,711	2,000	(25)U	—	—	(40)U	—	—	D
Christian Holy Convention (Kirisuto Sei Kyodan)	39	—	1,388	—	2,061	(49)U	—	—	—	—	—	D
Christian Reformed Japan Mission (Kirisuto Kaikakuha Nihon Dendokai)	13	—	425	—	1,205	(8)U	—	—	—	—	—	D
Christian Spiritual Church (Kirisuto Shinshu Kyodan)	25	1,500	1,571	1,500	1,571	(21)U	—	—	(8)U	—	—	
Church of Christ in Japan...[d]	106	—	11,636	—	11,636	112	—	—	—	—	—	B
Church of God (Cleveland)	3	—	106	—	362	5	—	—	4	—	—	B

JAPAN—continued

Church or Mission. N.B. See notes on Statistics, page xiii	Places of Regular Worship	Communicants, Full Members (p. 57)		Total Christian Community (p. 57)		Staff					Theolog. Colls., Bible Schools	Source of Information
						National Workers, full-time			Missionaries from other Churches or countries, full-time			
		1962 Handbook	Latest available figure	1962 Handbook	Latest available figure	Ordained	Laymen	Women	Ordained	Lay-workers		
Church of Jesus Christ of Latter Day Saints (Matsujitsu Seito Iesu Kirisuto Kyokai)	29	2,415	7,435	2,415	7,543	—	—	—	(160)U	—	—	D
Church of the Nazarene (Nihon Nazaren Kyodan)	128	2,880	3,650	6,851	8,773	60	9	66	10	11	2	D
Church of the Resurrected Christ (Fukkatsu no Kirisuto Kyodan)	11	—	566	—	862	(9)U	—	—	—	—	—	B
Conservative Association of Churches	36	586	599	586	1,127	4	9	—	18	28	1	D
Cumberland Presbyterian Church (Kambarando Choro Kyokai)	5	209	269	500	969	3	—	—	4	—	—	B
Evangelical Free Church of Japan (Fukuin Jiyu Kyokai)	14	—	130	—	800	5	4	—	6	7	—	D
Evangelical Missionary Church (Fukuin Dendo Kyodan)	26	565	1,644	1,398	2,773	(29)U	—	—	1	—	—	A
Far East Apostolic Mission (Nippon Pentekosute Kyodan)	8	200	120	500	300	7	3	—	1	—	1	D
Far Eastern Gospel Crusade (Kyokuto Fukuin Juji Gun)	10	148	165	448	516	(4)U	—	—	(57)U	—	—	D
Finnish Free Foreign Mission (Nippon Kirisuto Fukuin Kyokai Rengo)	9	—	350	—	350	(4)U	—	—	(23)U	—	—	D
Free Methodist Church (Nippon Jiyu Mesojisuto Kyodan)	31	3,899	4,246	7,900	5,771	37	267	3	10	5	1	B

JAPAN—continued

Church												Code
General Conference Mennonite Church (Kyushu Menonaito Kirisuto Kyokai)	10	—	316	—	600	1	5	—	9	19	—	B
Gospel of Jesus Church (Iesu Fukuin Kyodan)	14	570	720	570	720	(9)U	—	—	—	—	—	D
Holy Jesus Society (Sei Iesu Kai)	75	1,950	3,732	1,950	5,839	(67)U	—	—	—	—	—	D
Holy Spirit Association for Unification of World Christianity (Sekai Kirisuto Toitsu Shinrei Kyokai)	34	—	10,000	—	10,000	—	—	—	—	—	—	D
Immanuel General Mission (Immanuel Sogo Dendo Dan)	93	4,650	6,682	7,980	7,500	52	2	75	3	3	1	A
Japan Advent Christian Church (Nippon Advent Kirisuto Kyokai)	11	—	200	—	450	(6)U	—	—	(12)U	—	—	O
Japan Alliance Church (Nihon Araiansu Kyodan)	40	1,592	2,481	1,592	2,481	(47)U	—	—	5	7	1	B
Japan Baptist Convention (Nihon Baputesuto Renmei)	216	13,035	18,277	13,035	35,860	98	65	—	45	77	2	A
Japan Baptist Union (Nippon Baputesuto Domei)	57	3,694	4,266	3,694	7,706	(75)U	—	—	(38)U	—	—	D
Japan Christ Society (Nihon Kiri Suto Kai)	8	130	124	130	124	(12)U	—	—	—	—	—	D
Japan Christian Presbyterian Church (Nihon Kirisuto Kai)	9	200	200	200	500	(8)U	—	—	(4)U	—	—	D
Japan Church of God (Nippon Church of God Kyokai)	6	—	82	—	312	(4)U	—	—	(4)U	—	—	D
Japan Church of God Federation (Nippon Kami no Kyokai Renmei)	10	350	500	350	500	(9)U	—	—	(9)U	—	—	D
Japan Covenant Church (Nihon Seikei Kirisuto Kyodan)	18	317	481	—	509	4	4	5	9	15	—	B
Japan Evangelical Lutheran Church (Nippon Fukuin Ruteru Kyokai) [a]	138	10,413	6,210	10,413	14,309	119	10	—	33	17	1	B
Japan Evangelical Mission	13	153	100	645	500	3	1	3	9	26	1	A
Japan Evangelistic Band (Nippon Dendo Tai)	13	153	241	—	241	(17)U	—	—	(24)U	—	—	D
Japan Evangelistic Gospel Church (Nihon Dendo Fukuin Kyodan)	24	153	200	645	520	(8)U	—	—	(41)U	—	—	D

163

JAPAN—*continued*

Church or Mission N.B. See notes on Statistics, page xiii	Places of Regular Worship	Communicants, Full Members (p. 57)		Total Christian Community (p. 57)		Staff					Theolog. Colls., Bible Schools	Source of Information
						National Workers, full-time			Missionaries from other Churches or countries, full-time			
		1962 Handbook	Latest available figure	1962 Handbook	Latest available figure	Ordained	Lay-men	Women	Ordained	Lay-workers		
Japan Fellowship Deaconry Mission	2	—	54	—	78	1	2	—	—	7	—	B
Japan Fellowship Deaconry Mission (Marburger)	26	—	60	29	147	2	16	2	8	—	—	A
Japan Free Will Baptist Mission	9	—	100	—	154	2	5	—	3	3	1	B
Japan Gospel Church (Nippon Fukuin Kyodan)	58	1,201	1,038	1,444	1,038	(102U)	—	—	—	—	—	D
Japan Gospel League Church of Christ (Japan Gosuperu Rigu Kirisuto Kyokai)	12	—	331	—	581	(5)U	—	—	2	—	—	D
Japan Gospel of Christ Church (Nippon Fukuin Kirisuto Kyodan)	2	—	240	—	360	(5)U	—	—	—	—	—	D
Japan Holiness Church (Arahara-ha) (Nippon Holinesu Kyokai)	12	374	423	374	944	(12)U	—	—	—	—	—	D
Japan Holiness Church (Kurumada-ha) (Nihon Horinesu Kyodan)	106	3,052	4,877	3,052	4,877	42	140	—	(14)U	—	1	B
Japan Inland Mission (Nippon Kaitaku Dendo Kyokai)	4	45	120	350	270	1	—	—	3	—	—	D
Japan Jesus Christ Church (Nihon Iesu Kirisuto Kyodan)	62	4,000	6,943	4,000	10,285	59	—	74	—	—	1	A
Japan Mennonite Brethren Conference (Nihon Meninaito Burezaren Kyodan)	12	—	390	—	790	(7)U	—	—	(19)U	—	—	D
Japan Mennonite Church (Nippon Menonaito Kyokai)	18	—	246	—	246	(5)U	—	—	(27)U	—	1	D
Japan New Testament Church (Nihon Shinyaku Kyodan)	7	—	170	—	410	(5)U	—	—	—	—	—	D

JAPAN—*continued*

Japan Rural Mission Emmanuel Christ Church (Nippon Chiho Dendodan Immanueru Kyokai)	15	—	863	—	863	(7)U	—	—	(21)U	—	—	D
Kinki Evangelical Lutheran Church (Free Church Mission) ...	6	—	172	—	441	(5)U	—	—	(6)U	16	—	B
Kinki Evangelical Lutheran Church (Norwegian Missionary Society)	23	410	468	436	909	2	21	5	11	72	2	B
Kokusai Fukuin Senkyoo Dan (O.M.F.) ...	16	—	225	—	275	3	1	3	2	—	1	A
Korean Christian Church (Zainichi Daikan Kirisuto Kyokai) ...	54	—	1,474	—	2,718	(28)U	—	—	(7)U	—	—	D
Liebenzeller Mission (Riibenzera Nippon Dendo Kai) ...	21	—	500	—	500	(15)U	—	—	(27)U	—	—	D
Living Water Christian Church (Kassui Kirisuto Kyodan) ...	14	2,440	2,363	2,440	2,363	(25)U	5	5	—	6	1	B
Lutheran Brethren Church (Ruteru Doho Kyokai) ...	19	175	550	406	657	5	—	—	5	—	—	D
Lutheran Church—Missouri Synod (Nihon Ruteru Kyodan) ...	58	1,404	4,876	1,594	7,437	(15)U	3	—	(39)U	—	—	B
Lutheran Mission of Japan (Wisconsin Synod) ...	11	—	50	—	50	3	—	—	—	—	—	B
Marburg Mission (Lutheran) ...	2	—	44	29	45	—	—	1	—	—	—	B
Mino Mission ...	4	1,765	1,765	1,765	1,765	(3)U	—	—	(3)U	—	—	D
Mission Covenant Church of Sweden (Nippon Seiyaki Kirisuto Kyodan)	14	215	480	1,500	902	(5)U	—	—	(22)U	—	—	D
Nippon Domei Kirisuto Kyodan§	151	2,676	3,240	2,676	6,871	(72)U	—	—	(128)U	—	—	D
Norwegian Evangelical Orient Mission (Noruwei Toyo Fukuin Senkyokai)	7	—	120	—	420	(9)U	—	—	(11)U	—	—	D
Open Bible Church (Nihon Open Bible Kyodan)	28	325	500	650	1,000	(7)U	—	—	(6)U	—	—	D
Orebro Missionary Society of Sweden (Sweden Orebro Senyokai) ...	12	279	313	279	1,200	4	9	4	6	13	2	B
Original Gospel Tabernacle (Kirisuto no Makuya) ...	265	—	14,000	—	14,000	(230)U	—	—	—	—	—	D

165

JAPAN—*continued*

Church or Mission N.B. See notes on Statistics, page xiii	Places of Regular Worship	Communicants, Full Members (p. 57)		Total Christian Community (p. 57)		Staff					Theolog. Colls., Bible Schools	Source of Information
						National Workers, full-time			Missionaries from other Churches or countries, full-time			
		1962 Hand-book	Latest avail-able figure	1962 Hand-book	Latest avail-able figure	Or-dained	Lay-men	Women	Or-dained	Lay-workers		
Pentecostal Church of God (Nihon Pentekosute Kamino Kyokai)	11	200	114	200	114	(6)U	—	—	4	—	—	B
Philadelphia Church Mission (Fuiraderufia Kyokai)	13	—	115	—	535	(4)U	—	—	(8)U	—	—	D
Presbyterian and Reformed Church (Nihon Kirisuto Kyokai)	108	9,714	11,982	9,714	16,293	(121)U	—	—	—	—	—	D
Reformed Church (Nihon Kirisuto Kaikakuha Kyokai)	62	2,904	4,022	3,519	6,285	(72)U	—	—	—	—	—	D
Religious Society of Friends (Kirisuto Yukai Nippon Nenkai)	9	123	275	123	375	—	—	—	—	—	—	D
Salvation Army (Kyusei Gun)	116	6,238	10,100	15,036	13,030	(251)U	—	—	(11)U	—	—	D
Sambi Church (Sambi Kyodan)	6	—	145	—	145	(3)U	6	—	2	7	—	D
Scandinavian Christian Doyukai	2	—	—	—	61	1	—	1	—	—	—	B
Seventh-day Adventists (Nihon Rengo Dendo Bukai)	83	—	5,860	—	15,935	54	316	35	11	29	1	A
Spirit of Jesus Church (Iesu no Mitama Kyokai Kyodan) (Okinawa omitted)	269	37,024	280,074	37,024	280,074	(84)U	—	—	—	—	—	D
Svenska Fria Missionen	14	215	215	1,500	1,632	2	9	—	8	16	—	B
Swedish Alliance Mission Church (Nippon Domei Kurisuto Kyodan)	28	387	227	387	660	3	4	3	8	14	—	B
Swedish Evangelical Mission (Sweden Fukuin Dendo Dan)	6	—	150	—	650	3	6	16	3	6	—	A
Swedish Evangelical Orient Mission (Sweden Toyo Fukuin Dendo Dan)	4	35	61	35	273	2	1	1	2	5	—	A

JAPAN—continued

												Class
Swiss Alliance Japan Mission (Sado Dendo Dan)	3	—	35	—	200	—	2	2	2 (40)U	3	—	A
Tokai Evangelical Lutheran Church	29	—	653	—	991	9 (7)U	2	8	—	—	—	B
Toyo Senkyokai Kiyome Kyokai	24	400	500	400	500	—	—	—	—	—	—	D
True Church of Jesus (Shin Iesu Kyokai Nippon Kyodan)	10	—	205	—	205	(7)U	—	—	—	—	—	A
United Church of Christ (Nihon Kirisuto Kyodan) c	1,608	175,506	186,527	175,506	193,455‡	1,853	—	—	84	242	7	
Universal Evangelical Church (Bankoku Fukuin Kyodan)	31	1,254	1,000	1,254	1,000	(20)U	—	—	—	—	—	D
West Japan Evangelical Lutheran Church	56	—	399	—	711	3	13	19	(10)U	—	—	B
World Wide Evangelization Crusade (Sekai Fukuin Dendo Dan)	11	100	100	115	120	—	—	—	—	—	—	B
Independent Groups	53	—	811	—	1,871	9 (18)U	—	—	5 (26)U	10	—	D
	5,808	355,427	702,093	385,262	818,476	5,129 (1,860)U	972	366	1,148 (728)U	716	36	

* With but few exceptions Churches with a membership of less than 100 are not included.
† Includes Sunday School pupils when number is known.
‡ Does not include children dedicated but not baptized.
§ Includes those of independent churches affiliated with TEAM.
U Unclassified.

Co-operating: a Danske Missionsselskab; Lutheran Evangelical Association of Finland. b Presbyterian Church in the U.S. c Christian Church (Disciples); Methodist Church Board of Missions; Reformed Church in America; United Church of Canada; United Presbyterian Church in the U.S.A. d United Presbyterian Church in the U.S.A. (This Church has 66 missionaries in Japan).

Also working: American Leprosy Mission. Church Missionary Society of Australia. Church of Christ Scientist. International Miners' Mission. Laerinnenes Misjonsforbund. New Tribes Mission. Oriental Boat Mission. Overseas Missionary Fellowship. Reformed Pentecostal Church. Swiss East Asia Mission. United Church Board for World Ministries. United Presbyterian Church. United Society for the Propagation of the Gospel. World Gospel Mission. World Mission to Children. Worldwide Evangelization Crusade.

Where we have not received figures directly from a church or mission, we have used, with kind permission, those given in the *Japan Christian Year Book* (1965).

JORDAN 36,715 sq. mls. Pop.: 1,860,443 (1963)

Church or Mission — N.B. See notes on Statistics, page xiii	Places of Regular Worship	Communicants, Full Members (p. 57) 1962 Handbook	Communicants, Full Members (p. 57) Latest available figure	Total Christian Community (p. 57) 1962 Handbook	Total Christian Community (p. 57) Latest available figure	Staff — National Workers, full-time Ordained	National Workers, full-time Lay-men	National Workers, full-time Women	Missionaries from other Churches or countries, full-time Ordained	Missionaries, full-time Lay-workers	Theolog. Colls., Bible Schools	Source of Information
American Friends Board of Missions	3	80	80	100	100	—	1	3	2	—	—	E
Anglican Church—Jerusalem Bishopric	2	—	50	—	120	—	—	—	5	9	—	A
Assemblies of God	6	—	157	—	663	2	—	—	—	—	—	B
Church of God (Cleveland)	4	30	26	30	721	3	—	—	1	—	—	B
Church of the Nazarene	9	115	68	455	950	13	—	22	2	2	—	B
Conservative Baptists	10	—	100	—	500	12	20	62	2	2	—	B
Evangelical Episcopal Community ...a*	15	—	3,000	—	5,323	12	—	—	—	14	—	A
Evangelical Church of the Christian Alliance ...b	5	—	—	—	121	7	3	3	2	2	—	B
Evangelical Lutheran Church	5	883	936	883	1,476	5	4	—	1	—	—	B
Southern Baptist Convention	10	117	149	117	729	3	7	—	5	10	—	B
Seventh-day Adventists	3	—	151	—	608	4	—	—	2	16	—	B
	74	1,225	4,838	1,585	11,311	49	35	90	22	55	—	

* Diocese of Jordan, Lebanon and Syria.

Co-operating: **a** Church Missionary Society. **b** Jerusalemverein zu Berlin.

Also working: Bible Lands Society; Evangelischer Verein für das Syrische Waisenhaus in Jerusalem (Theodor-Schneller School); Independent Board for Presbyterian Foreign Missions; Jerusalem and the East Mission; Near East Council of Churches, Refugee Committee; Østerlandsmissionen; Protestant Episcopal Church in the U.S.A. Reformed Presbyterian Church, Evangelical Synod; Schweizerische Missionshilfe für die Brüdergemeine.

KOREA

38,452 sq. mls. Pop.: 27,132,176 (1963)

Assemblies of God	47	3,550	2,443	11,392	14,790	(44)U	(168)U	—	(17)U	—	1	B
Baptist Church	192	—	2,500*	8,365	8,365	—	(20)U	—	—	—	—	E
Church of Christ	18	—	700*	2,000	2,000	—	—	—	—	—	—	E
Church of God	8	375	375	1,240	1,240	4	—	—	—	—	—	E
Church of the Nazarene	47	1,850	1,784	3,497	15,042	41	5	4	4	4	1	B
Korea Christian Mission	75	2,000	2,000	3,500	3,500	20	35	18	1	—	1	E
Korea Holiness Church	392	—	45,000	118,029	118,029	249	171	81	15	—	1	E&B
Korea Lutheran Church c	4	—	120	50	425	2	—	—	4	2	1	A
Koryu Presbyterian Church	590	—	30,000*	66,524	66,524	—	(363)U	—	(78)U	—	—	E
Methodist Church	92	60,000	60,021	236,853	221,156	501	814	—	30	44	8	B
Presbyterian Church of Korea... a	2,017	110,788	108,565	535,000	530,707	(1,988)U	—	—	—	—	—	B
Presbyterian Church ROK d	725	—	50,000*	191,238	191,238	—	(853)U	—	—	—	1	E
Presbyterian Church N.A.E.	—	—	125,000*	—	508,722	—	—	97	5	—	—	D
Salvation Army	112	10,145	10,145	29,685	29,685	174	80	—	5	321	1	E
Seventh-day Adventists	229	11,375	28,435	21,877	122,453	120	(402)U	—	39	27	—	B
Southern Baptist Convention	210	3,981	6,600	35,000	31,396	58	139	—	20	—	1	B
Taehan Song-gong-hoe (Anglican) b	60	3,000	4,500	4,630	7,000	22	9	6	4	3	2	A
The Evangelical Alliance Mission (TEAM)	12	—	150	—	500	—	25	—	14	23	2	A
Worldwide Evangelization Crusade	9	—	350	—	350	—	—	—	2	2	—	B
	4,839	207,064	448,688	1,268,880	1,873,122	3,223 (2,032)U	3,084 (1,806)U	206	234 (95)U	424	18	

* Estimate. U Unclassified.

Co-operating: **a** Australian Presbyterian Board; Presbyterian Church in the U.S.A. United Presbyterian Church U.S.A. **b** Australian Board of Missions; United Society for the Propagation of the Gospel. **c** Oriental Missionary Society. **d** United Church of Canada.

Also working: American Leprosy Mission. Bible Lands Society. Navigators. Protestant Church in the U.S.A. Reformed Presbyterian Church, Evangelical Synod. World Presbyterian Missions, Reformed P.C.

KUWAIT 9,375 sq. mls. Pop.: 468,389 (1965)

Church or Mission *N.B.* See notes on Statistics, page xiii	Places of Regular Worship	Communicants, Full Members (p. 57)		Total Christian Community (p. 57)		Staff					Theolog., Colls., Bible Schools	Source of Information
						National Workers, full-time			Missionaries from other Churches or countries, full-time			
		1962 Handbook	Latest available figure	1962 Handbook	Latest available figure	Ordained	Lay-men	Women	Ordained	Lay-workers		
Anglican Church: Bishopric ... Kuwait ...	2 2	— —	770 470	— —	2,000 1,500	— 2	— —	— —	4 2	— —	— —	A A
Church of Christ in Kuwait	4	—	1,240	—	3,500	2	—	—	6	—	—	

Estimated total (including Roman Catholics) ... 6–7,000.

LAOS 88,780 sq. mls. Pop.: 2,200,000 estimate (1962)

Church or Mission	Places of Regular Worship	1962 Handbook	Latest available figure	1962 Handbook	Latest available figure	Ordained	Lay-men	Women	Ordained	Lay-workers	Theolog. Colls.	Source of Information
Christian Missions in Many Lands... a	—	—	1,000	1,000	1,000	15	—	—	12	16	1	E
Gospel Church ... a	82	—	3,086	—	3,086	—	—	—	2	1	1	B
Overseas Missionary Fellowship ...	2	—	24	—	47	—	—	—	—	—	—	A & B
	84	—	4,110	1,000	4,133	15	—	—	14	17	1	

Co-operating: a Christian and Missionary Alliance.
Also working: Missionary Aviation Fellowship.

170

LEBANON

3,400 sq. mls.   Pop.: 1,750,000 estimate (1963)

Denomination													
Assemblies of God	*	3	30	30	90	90	3	1	—	—	—	—	E
Church of God	*	5	100	100	400	400	3	—	—	—	—	—	E
Church of the Nazarene	*	8	—	94	—	669	7	3	12	2	2	1	B
Evangelical Church of the Christian Alliance	c	13	104	527	314	527	12	—	—	1	1	1	B
Friends Service Council	*	1	68	68	100	100	—	—	—	—	—	—	E
Lebanon Evangelical Mission	a	2	—	n.a.	—	n.a.	—	19	40	—	30	1	B
Lebanese Baptist Convention		20	380	450	1,000	1,500	8	8	10	8	12	1	A
Lutheran Church		1	—	106	—	291	2	27	8	1	18	—	A
National Evangelical Synod of Lebanon and Syria	b	35	2,176	1,774	—	9,000	10	8	1	12	25	2	B
Pentecostal Church of God of America		4	210	150	210	210	—	—	—	3	1	1	B
Seventh-day Adventists		6	604	528	1,588	1,890	5	(26)U	—	9	20	—	B
Southern Baptist Convention		22	215	425	583	1,307	1	—	—	9	13	1	B
Syrian Orphanage (Lebanon Branch)	*	1	175	175	175	175	2	15	4	6	7	—	E
United Evangelical Church	*	4	120	120	181	181	—	1	26	2	9	—	E
		125	4,782	4,547	4,641	16,340	43	108 (26)U	101	53	138	8	

* Figures include Syria.   U Unclassified.

Co-operating: a Østerlandsmissionionen.   b United Presbyterian Church in the U.S.A.   c Christian and Missionary Alliance.

Also working: Action Chrétienne en Orient. Anglican Church. Bible Lands Society. Edinburgh Medical Missionary Society. Eglise protestantes de Suisse romande. Kvindelige Missions Arbejdere. Mission to the Druzes. Oeuvres protestantes Françaises de Syria et de Liban. The Navigators. Union of the Armenian Evangelical Churches in the Near East. United Church Board for World Ministries. World Gospel Mission.

MACAO — 6 sq. mls. — Pop.: 169,299 (1960)

Church or Mission	Places of Regular Worship	Communicants, Full Members (p. 57) 1962 Handbook	Latest available figure	Total Christian Community (p. 57) 1962 Handbook	Latest available figure	National Workers, full-time Ordained	Lay-men	Women	Missionaries from other Churches or countries, full-time Ordained	Lay-workers	Theolog. Colls., Bible Schools	Source of Information
Sion Church ... a	2	—	79	—	100	1	1	1	1	3	—	B
Southern Baptist Convention ...	3	—	753	—	1,375	1	4	—	1	—	—	B
	5	—	832	—	1,475	2	5	1	1	3	—	

N.B. See notes on Statistics, page xiii

Co-operating: a Svenska Alliansmissionen.

Also working: Christian Nationals Evangelism Commission.

MALAYSIA, FEDERATION OF (Malaya, N. Borneo (Sabah) and Sarawak) and SINGAPORE

Malaya: 50,700 sq. mls.   Pop.: 7,810,205
Sabah: 29,388 sq. mls.   Pop.: 506,628
Sarawak: 48,250 sq. mls.   Pop.: 819,808
Singapore: 224 sq. mls.   Pop.: 1,844,200

Church or Mission	Places of Regular Worship	Communicants 1962 Handbook	Latest available figure	Total Christian Community 1962 Handbook	Latest available figure	National Workers Ordained	Lay-men	Women	Missionaries Ordained	Lay-workers	Theolog. Colls., Bible Schools	Source of Information
Anglican Church, Diocese of Kuching, Borneo ... b	90	7,000	21,000	18,000	21,000	33	7	7	15	13	—	A
Anglican Church, Diocese of Singapore and Malaya ... b	48	6,107	8,000	15,000	17,000	43	1	7	6	8	—	C
American Lutheran Mission ...	29	—	303	—	752	3	18	5	(21)U	—	—	B
Assemblies of God ... *	18	420	1,077	805	3,900	(22)U	—	—	(16)U	—	1	B
Baptist Churches of Malaysia ...	47	1,501	2,643	2,501	5,000	7	28	17	20	58	1	C
Basel Mission (work among Rungus-Dusun, Sabah) ...	32	607	812	1,195	1,858	—	5	—	6	8	1	B
Borneo-Basel Self-established Church	22	2,633	3,157	5,918	9,680	8	8	—	—	2	—	B

MALAYSIA (Federation of)—continued and SINGAPORE

Church		1	2	3	4	5	6	7	8	9	10	11	Code
Chinese Christian Church, Malaysia Synod	d	48	3,752	5,030	6,676	8,224	17	21	6	9	4	1	A
Christian Assembly	*	2	150	200	350	350	500						C
Christian Brethren		20	1,903	1,903	2,903	2,903							E
Church of Christ		6	374	374	574	574		4		4	4		E
Evangelical Free Church		10	95	80	195	350	5	2	1	6	7	1	B
Evangelical Lutheran Church	a	8	587	671	1,202	1,375							A
Finnish Free Foreign Mission		5	180	180	380	380	4	23	1	12	7	1	E
Lutheran Church in Malaysia		35	228	558	420	907				5	1		A
Mar Thoma Syrian Church	*	27	1,522	1,600	2,522	2,700	101	57		70	30	2	B&C
Methodist Church		191	35,000	26,000	75,000	70,000	3	1		5		1	A
Presbyterian Church		4	990	1,000	1,990	1,000							A
Revival Centre		3	577	577	877	877	40			31	9		E
Salvation Army	*	9	313	532	1,088	1,532	41		1	10			C
Seventh-day Adventists	*	57	1,668	6,917	2,868	6,917		337					C
Sidang Injil Borneo (Evangelical Church)	c	200	2,200	3,000	7,300	32,000	120	700	10	1	52	4	A
Southern Baptist Convention		37	1,626	2,450	2,363	6,422	8	19		16	24	1	B
Syrian Orthodox Church		22	594	594	1,594	1,594	2						E
		970	70,027	88,658	151,521	197,295	957 (22)U	1,231	55	248 (37)U	227	13	

* Figures for Singapore and Malaya only.   **U** Unclassified.

Co-operating: **a** Church of Sweden Mission. **b** United Society for the Propagation of the Gospel. **c** Borneo Evangelical Mission. **d** Presbyterian Church of England; London Missionary Society.

Also working: Bethesda Church (Katong). Bible Presbyterian Church. Christian Nationals Evangelism Commission. Church Missionary Society of Australia. Church of Christ Scientist. Dublin University Far Eastern Mission. International Miners' Mission. Methodist Missionary Society. New Tribes Mission. New Zealand Church Missionary Society. Overseas Missionary Fellowship. Protestant Episcopal Church.

NEPAL

54,600 sq. mls. Pop.: 9,500,000 estimate (1964)

Church or Mission N.B. See notes on Statistics, page xiii	Places of Regular Worship	Communicants, Full Members (p. 57)		Total Christian Community (p. 57)		Staff					Theolog. Colls., Bible Schools	Source of Information
						National Workers, full-time			Missionaries from other Churches or countries, full-time			
		1962 Handbook	Latest available figure	1962 Handbook	Latest available figure	Ordained	Laymen	Women	Ordained	Lay-workers		
Assemblies of God ... ...b	2	30	30	30	30	7	5	—	—	—	—	E
Church of Nepal	19	70	460	100	460	—	2	—	(112)U	29	—	B & A
United Mission to Nepal ...*a	—	—	—	—	—	—	—	—	—	—	—	B
	21	100	490	130	490	7	7	—	(112)U	29	—	

* The U.M.N. is made up of 23 member boards and societies. The U.M.N. has, of itself, no place of worship.   U Unclassified.

Co-operating: a Baptist Missionary Society. Bible and Medical Missionary Fellowship. Central Asian Mission. C.M.S. of Australia. East Himalayan Church Board. Friends Foreign Missionary Society. Japan Overseas Christian Medical Co-operative Service. Mar Thoma Church. Malwa Church Council. Mennonite Board. Methodist Church in W.D.C.S. Mission to Lepers. Norwegian Free Evangelical Mission. Protestant Episcopal Church in the U.S.A. Regions Beyond Missionary Union. Swedish Baptist Church. United Church of Canada. United Presbyterian. United Presbyterian Commission. Wesleyan Methodist Missionary Society. World Mission Prayer League. b Nepal Evangelistic Band.

Also working: Church Missionary Society of Australia. Bibelschule Wiedenen. Good Shepherd Agricultural Mission.

OKINAWA

454 sq. mls. Pop.: 759,000 (1960)

Church or Mission	Places of Regular Worship	Communicants, Full Members (p. 57)		Total Christian Community (p. 57)		National Workers, full-time			Missionaries from other Churches or countries, full-time		Theolog. Colls., Bible Schools	Source of Information
		1962 Handbook	Latest available figure	1962 Handbook	Latest available figure	Ordained	Laymen	Women	Ordained	Lay-workers		
Baptist Convention	7	596	1,129	596	3,054	—	—	—	2	2	—	B
Church of the Nazarene	15	27	156	114	1,161	4	—	7	4	—	—	B
Okinawa Holiness Church	1	40	40	40	40	—	—	—	2	—	—	E
Okinawa Seikokai (Holy Catholic Church) ... ...b	10	1,333	1,174	1,333	1,611	10	—	—	4	4	—	B

OKINAWA—continued

Society												
Seventh-day Adventists ... ... a	10	371	837	1,000	2,541	5	(77)U	—	4	18	—	B
United Church of Christ ...	43	—	1,292	1,429	3,213	18	(34)U	7	10	7	—	B
	86	2,367	4,628	4,512	11,620	37	(111)U	7	26	31	—	

Co-operating: a United Christian Missionary Society (Disciples); United Church Board for World Ministries; Board of Missions of the Methodist Church. b Protestant Episcopal Church in the U.S.A.

Also working: Church of Christ Scientist. The Navigators.

PAKISTAN

365,929 sq. mls. Pop.: 93,720,613 estimate (1961)

Society												
Anglican: Diocese of Karachi (West) b	n.a.	—	—	—	n.a.	(14)U	—	—	—	(14)U	1	B
Assemblies of God ...	19	89	89	988	988	12	75	38	3	10	—	E
Associate Reformed Presbyterian Church ... e	—	—	—	—	—	—	—	—	—	—	—	E & B
Baptist Union ...	29	4,232	4,232	12,670	12,670	23	75	38	3	10	—	E
Bengal Evangelical Mission ...	127	4,952	4,952	312	312	—	15	10	—	32	—	E
Ceylon and India General Mission ...	2	95	95	2,040	2,040	—	4	1	3	14	—	E
Church of God ...	—	162	162	570	570	—	—	—	2	2	—	E
Church of India, Pakistan, Burma and Ceylon (Anglican) Dioceses of Dacca and Lahore f, a	19	170	170	—	—	—	—	—	—	—	—	
Churches of God ... f	72	14,919	14,919	102,000	102,000	11	129	58	3	40	—	E
Dansk Pathanmission ... a	14	399	399	818	818	3	1	—	—	5	—	E
East Pakistan and Garo Baptist Unions ... l	5	515	140	1,263	1,263	2	1	—	2	2	—	B
Evangelical Lutheran Church (East)	108	6,817	6,817	12,594	12,594	5	202	19	5	3	—	B
Full Gospel Assemblies ... g	30	336	336	2,000	1,034	2	27	3	2	1	—	B
Indus Christian Fellowship (West) ... k	25	—	—	6,642	—	25	25	—	25	9	—	B
Lutheran Church ... c	8	35	21	100	250	3	2	—	3	20	—	B
Methodist Church (West) ... h	12	500	500	1,700	1,263	45	105	—	(56)U	20	3	B
New Zealand Baptist Missionary Society (East) ...	—	14,643	17,942	15,245	43,243	1	5	17	3	5	—	B
	6	86	96	220	206	1	5	17	3	5	—	B

Church or Mission N.B. See notes on Statistics, page xiii	Places of Regular Worship	Communicants, Full Members (p. 57)		Total Christian Community (p. 57)		Staff					Theolog. Colls., Bible Schools	Source of Information
						National Workers, full-time			Missionaries from other Churches or countries, full-time			
		1962 Handbook	Latest available figure	1962 Handbook	Latest available figure	Ordained	Laymen	Women	Ordained	Lay-workers		
N.E. India General Mission ... d	30	2,208	2,208	4,796	4,796	—	20	—		1	—	E
Pakistan Christian Fellowship ...	7	—	220	—	2,000	2	3	—	2	19	—	B
Philadelphia Pentecostal Church (West) ... j	4	—	77	—	250	—	2	—	2	2	—	B
Presbyterian Church of Wales ...	38	788	788	1,971	1,971	5	34	—	1	3	—	E
Salvation Army ...	609	23,778	23,778	37,699	37,699	216	50	1,031	10	—	—	E
Seventh-day Adventists ...	45	1,006	3,176	6,646	12,249	21	284	8	55	—	—	B
The Evangelical Alliance Mission (West) ...	7	12	160	—	460	1	8	12	11	26	—	A
United Church of North India: Lahore Church Council ... a	40	1,080	9,633	—	41,347	(38)U	—	—	1	—	—	B
Presbyterian ...	49	1,080	1,080	2,764	2,764	—	24	—	1	9	—	E
Sialkot Church Council (West) ...	26	4,200	26,700	4,200	27,000	32	—	7	5	8	1	A
United Presbyterian ... a	157	69,131	55,835	183,518	137,771	(164)U	—	—	(19)U	—	1	B
World Mission Prayer League (Lutheran) (West) ...	2	—	25	—	25	—	1	1	1	10	1	A
	1,490	150,064	176,754	409,392	472,997	625 (216)U	1,015	1,204	222 (89)U	226	4	A

U Unclassified.

Co-operating: a American Churches of God Mission; Church of Scotland; Gereformeerde Kerken Nederland; United Presbyterian Church in the U.S.A. b New Zealand Anglican Board of Missions; New Zealand Church Missionary Society. c Norske Muhammedanermisjon; Selskabet til støtte for Pakistans Luthererske Kirke. d Ceylon and India General Mission. e Baptist Missionary Society. f United Society for the Propagation of the Gospel. g Svenska Fria Missionen. h Board of Missions of Methodist Church. i Santal Mission of Northern Churches. j Orebromissionen. k Conservative Baptist Foreign Missionary Society. l Australia Baptist Mission.

Also working: American Leprosy Mission. Association of Baptists for World Evangelism. Central Asian Mission. Church Missionary Society of Australia. Indian Church Aid Association. International Missions. Missionshaus Bibelschule Wiedenest. Oxford Mission to Calcutta. Pakistan Bible Society. Suomen Lähetysseura. Worldwide Evangelization Crusade.

PHILIPPINES 115,600 approx. sq. mls. Pop.: 32,000,000 (1966)

Denomination											Code
Advent Christian Denomination	5	99	99	600	600	—	1	2	6	—	—	E
American Baptist Foreign Mission	267	19,018	19,018	75,000	75,000	57	73	67	9	27	—	E
Assemblies of God	936	12,022	9,382	16,162	49,464	(607)U	—	—	(29)U	—	4	D
Baptist General Conference of America	13	300	500	300	500	—	—	—	13	13	1	D
Berean Mission Inc.	4	—	—	2,000	2,000	6	—	—	—	—	—	E
Bumila Fellowship of Baptist Churches c	26	450	375	675	800	4	26	1	4	8	1	A
Christian and Missionary Alliance Churches	593	15,638	17,145	48,398	48,398	292	—	—	18	28	2	D
Church of God (Cleveland)	97	—	3,488	—	6,281	(140)U	—	—	(38)U	—	—	B
Church of the Nazarene	56	195	278	1,645	6,165	34	3	14	10	8	2	D
Conservative Baptist Association	24	117	627	250	950	5	14	—	10	16	—	B
Convention of Philippine Baptist Churches	270	24,000	24,000	85,000	85,000	184	25	14	33	28	—	E
Evangelical Free Church	8	34	70	50	275	1	5	—	5	11	1	D
Free Methodist Church	21	60	425	570	2,131	5	2	5	3	5	1	D
Iglesia Evangelica Metodista	67	25,000	30,000	70,000	70,000	97	199	45	—	—	—	A
Iglesia Filipina Independente	3,010	1,600,000	1,600,000	2,050,000	2,050,000	580	5,000*	2,000*	—	—	—	E
Iglesia ni Kristo	—	100,000	100,000	100,000	100,000	—	—	—	—	—	3	E
Lutheran Church	75	941	1,450	3,281	4,067	6	8	7	(27)U	—	(1)U	B
Methodist Church	643	130,000	73,159	175,000	197,065	314	720	—	19	19	1	D
New Tribes Mission	2	—	—	—	1,000	—	—	—	—	—	2	D
Pentecostal Church of God	62	550	1,000	550	57,021	3	2	—	19	18	1	D
Protestant Episcopal Church b	239	21,399	15,316	46,065	3,888	71	39	9	24	—	—	E
Salvation Army	54	1,051	1,051	3,888	3,888	28	9	201	8	—	—	B
Seventh-day Adventists	1,082	67,423	96,128	110,337	234,300	141	903	—	125	315	2	D
Southern Baptist Convention	217	3,639	8,390	3,639	12,321	29	157	—	35	44	—	B
United Church of Christ in the Philippines a	—	—	—	—	—	—	—	—	—	—	—	D
	1,351	119,347	142,405	298,367	356,012	377	546	377	35	45	4	

177

PHILIPPINES—*continued*

Church or Mission N.B. See notes on Statistics, page xiii	Places of Regular Worship	Communicants, Full Members (p. 57)		Total Christian Community (p. 57)		Staff					Theolog. Colls., Bible Schools	Source of Information
						National Workers, full-time			Missionaries from other Churches or countries, full-time			
		1962 Hand-book	Latest available figure	1962 Hand-Book	Latest available figure	Or-dained	Lay-men	Women	Or-dained	Lay-workers		
Unida Iglesia Evangelica Unida de Christo	—	—	5,000	—	15,000	—	—	—	—	—	—	D
	9,122	2,141,283	2,149,306	3,091,777	3,378,238	2,981 (747)U	7,732	2,742	451 (94)U	585	26	
Total figures supplied by the National Council of Churches in the Philippines for Non-Roman Catholics	10,204	2,192,896	2,306,609	3,228,150	4,195,024	3,451	6,856	2,165	345	489	78	C

* Estimate.   U Unclassified.

Co-operating: a Evangelical United Brethren Church; Reformed Church in America; United Christian Missionary Society (Disciples); United Church Board for World Ministries; United Presbyterian Church in the U.S.A. b Protestant Episcopal Church in the U.S.A.; United Church of Canada. International Missions Inc.

Also working: American Leprosy Mission. Association of Baptists for World Evangelism. Christian Nationals' Evangelism Commission. Church of Christ Scientist. International Missions Inc. Missionary Aviation Fellowship. Overseas Missionary Fellowship. Wycliffe Bible Translators.

SOUTH ARABIA, FEDERATION OF, and PERSIAN GULF STATES (*also see* ADEN)

Federation of S. Arabia: 61,890 sq. mls. Pop.: 771,000 estimate (1965)
Bahrain: 231 sq. mls. Pop.: 182,203 (1965)
Trucial States: 32,300 sq. mls. Pop.: 110,000 estimate (1965)

Anglican Church—Jerusalem									
Bishopric: Abu Dhabi	2	200	—	—	—	1	—	—	A
Bahrain	1	160	—	—	—	1	—	—	A
Danish Missionary Society (Lutheran)	—	17	2	—	8	—	—	—	B
Red Sea Mission Team †	—	—	—	—	—	—	19	—	A
The Evangelical Alliance Mission *	1	18	—	—	—	2	6	—	A
	4	395	2	—	8	4	25	—	

Estimated totals: **Bahrain** 2,000
Abu Dhabi 4,000

* In the Trucial States. † Work mainly among British Armed Forces.

Also working: American Leprosy Missions Inc. Church of Scotland. Danske Missionsselskab. Independent Board for Presbyterian Foreign Missions. Jerusalem and the East Mission. Reformed Church in America. Reformed Presbyterian Church Evangelical Synod. World Presbyterian Missions Inc.

SYRIA   71,210 sq. mls.   Pop.: 5,500,000 estimate (1962)

Anglican Church, Diocese of Jordan, Lebanon and Syria	69	3,000	3,000	6,000	6,000	9	14	64	2	11	E
Assemblies of God **	3	30	30	90	90	3	1	—	—	—	E
Church of God	5	100	100	400	400	4	—	—	2	—	B
Church of God (Cleveland)	—	—	—	160	160	—	—	—	—	—	B
Church of the Nazarene *	15	224	224	816	816	2	22	23	3	3	E
Evangelical Church of the Christian Alliance	(For statistics *see* Lebanon)										

SYRIA—*continued*

Church or Mission N.B. See notes on Statistics, page xiii	Places of Regular Worship	Communicants, Full Members (p. 57)		Total Christian Community (p. 57)		Staff					Theolog. Colls., Bible Schools	Source of Information
						National Workers, full-time			Missionaries from other Churches or countries, full-time			
		1962 Handbook	Latest available figure	1962 Handbook	Latest available figure	Ordained	Laymen	Women	Ordained	Lay-workers		
National Evangelical Synod of Syria and Lebanon ... a	26	—	2,070	—	9,000	8	8	—	—	7	—	A
Seventh-day Adventists ...	4	—	179	—	395	2	3	—	1	—	—	B
United Presbyterian Church ... b	(For statistics *see* Lebanon)											
	69	3,354	5,603	7,306	16,861	31	48	87	8	21	—	

* Includes Lebanon.

Co-operating: **a** United Church Board for World Ministries. **b** United Presbyterian Church of N. America and Presbyterian Church in the U.S.A.

Also working: Action Chrétienne en Orient. Christian and Missionary Alliance. Jerusalem and the East Mission. The Bible Lands Society.

TAIWAN (FORMOSA)   13,890 sq. mls.   Pop.: 12,257,000 (1964)

Church or Mission	Places of Regular Worship	1962 Handbook	Latest available figure	1962 Handbook	Latest available figure	Ordained	Laymen	Women	Ordained	Lay-workers	Theol.	Source
Assemblies of God ...	12	438	464	610	1,492	(18)U	—	—	(17)U	—	1	B
Baptist Bible Fellowship ...	28	—	—	324	700	2	8	—	3	4	1	D
China Evangelical Lutheran Church ...	26	790	805	2,202	1,460	12	1	—	6	—	1	B
China Peniel Church ...	8	90	—	90	206	2	2	2	1	1	—	D
Christian Mission in Many Lands ...	13	—	—	1,200	1,200	3	12	2	—	—	—	D

TAIWAN (FORMOSA)—*continued*

Christian and Missionary Alliance ...	2	150	264	390	390	4	2	—	4	6	—	B
Christian Reformed Church	3	100	75	100	130	—	—	3	2	2	—	D
Chu Hui So. The Little Flock	44	—	8,000	—	8,000	—	69	—	—	—	—	D
Church of the Nazarene ...	17	124	190	812	2,155	14	1	6	5	4	1	B
Conservative Baptist Foreign Missions	9	287	381	—	1,020	1	6	—	11	22	1	B
Covenant Mission Society ...	12	674	540	674	540	—	15	3	4	5	—	D
Elim Church ...	8	508	620	908	800	4	20	—	1	7	—	B
Finnish Free Foreign Missions	24	799	1,359	799	1,359	1	20	—	3	7	1	B
Free Methodist Church ...	37	—	1,448	—	2,580	13	154	7	11	—	—	B
General Conference Mennonite Church	7	—	205	135	630	—	7	3	3	17	—	A
Glad Tidings Temple Missionary Society	9	—	400	350	400	7	1	2	4	6	—	D
Independent Board for Presbyterian Foreign Missions ...	7	—	200	—	300	—	5	—	1	2	—	D
Independent Churches all over Taiwan	51	1,739	1,739	4,085	2,346	2	42	4	4	—	1	D
Lutheran Brethren Mission ...	20	1,400	1,872	4,500	4,500	9	10	1	29	5	—	B
Methodist Church ...	15	1,346	2,985	1,346	4,553	3	5	2	3	4	—	B
Norwegian Lutheran Mission ...	10	480	674	684	1,190	6	7	—	4	—	—	D
Oriental Missionary Society ...	54	2,040	1,072	—	2,021	11	—	5	1	12	(1)U	B
Pentecostal Assemblies of Canada ...	20	—	3,000	3,000	3,000	—	—	—	—	1	1	B
Presbyterian Church of Formosa (a) Taiwanese Churches (Presbyterian) c	447	54,435	38,006	158,848	175,690	159	246	—	31	16	5	B
(b) Mountain Churches (Presbyterian)	392	—	27,576	2,000	—	52	228	100	—	—	—	B
Protestant Episcopal Church ...	16	—	849	10,000	1,992	10	9	—	2	1	1	B
Southern Baptist Convention ...	86	8,013	9,700	—	21,783	26	94	—	21	37	—	B
Svenska Fria Missionen ...	—	—	40	—	120	—	—	—	—	1	—	B
Tai-oan Ki-tok Tiun-lo Kau-hoc (Presbyterian) a	856	54,435	64,564	158,848	179,916	191	487	—	31	72	4	A
Taiwan Fellowship Deaconry Mission	10	—	70	—	600	4	10	4	12	49	—	A
Taiwan Friends Fellowship ...	24	—	676	360	676	—	16	6	4	9	—	D
Taiwan Gospel League ...	7	948	1,090	—	1,090	2	6	2	—	1	—	B
Taiwan Holiness Church ...	53	739	4,858	—	4,858	15	33	—	—	—	—	B
Taiwan Lutheran Church ... b	52	3,525	2,565	8,570	6,130	12	187	—	3	1	1	B

TAIWAN (FORMOSA)—*continued*

Church or Mission N.B. See notes on Statistics, page xiii	Places of Regular Worship	Communicants, Full Members (p. 57)		Total Christian Community (p. 57)		Staff					Theolog. Colls., Bible Schools	Source of Information
						National Workers, full-time			Missionaries from other Churches or countries, full-time			
		1962 Handbook	Latest available figure	1962 Handbook	Latest available figure	Ordained	Laymen	Women	Ordained	Lay-workers		
The Evangelical Alliance Mission ...	28	734	2,000	2,200	2,200	—	22	—	12	45	1	A
True Jesus Church	126	18,799	18,799	18,799	23,183	8	86	23	1	—	—	D
Wesleyan Methodist Church ...	1	25	25	133	133	—	—	—	—	—	—	E
	2,534	152,618	197,111	383,654	459,343	591 (18)U	1,810	177	234 (17)U	338	20	

U Unclassified.

Co-operating: **a** Overseas Missionary Fellowship; Reformed Church in America. **b** Finnish Missionary Society; Danske Missionsselskab. **c** Presbyterian Church in Canada; Presbyterian Church of England; Lutheran Church in America; American Lutheran Church; Presbyterian Church U.S. and the United Presbyterian Church U.S.A.

Also working: American Leprosy Mission. Board of World Missions. Christian Nationals Evangelism Commission. Friends Foreign Missionary Society. Independent Board—U.S.A. Presbyterian. Laerinnenes Misjonsforbund. Liebenzeller Mission. Marburger Mission. Reformed Presbyterian Church. United Board for World Ministries. World Gospel Mission. Worldwide Evangelization Crusade.

Where figures have not been received directly from the Churches or Missions those from the *Taiwan Christian Handbook 1964* have, with kind permission, been used.

THAILAND   198,250 sq. mls.   Pop.: 30,000,000 estimate (1964)

Church of Christ in Thailand	b	213	17,634	18,275	23,635	24,512	(89)U	—	—	(33)U	—	2	D
Marburger Mission		(16)		(1,170)		(2,300)	1	9	4	8	7	2	D
Gospel Church	a	128		1,488		—	125	10	3	25	37	2	D
Overseas Missionary Fellowship		7		200		500	—	—	—	2	4	—	A
Pentecostal Assemblies of Canada		6		2,000		2,000	—	—	—	2	4	—	D
Southern Baptist Convention		32		767		2,210	24	32	—	5	25	1	D
Svenska Fria Missionen		7		137		844	1	4	—	3	5	—	D
United Christian Missionary Society (Disciples)		6		440		600	—	—	—	—	—	—	D
Worldwide Evangelization Crusade		4		60		150	—	—	—	(45)U	—	—	D
		403	17,634	23,367	23,635	30,816	240 (89)U	55	7	121 (78)U	115	7	

Co-operating: **a** Christian and Missionary Alliance. **b** American Baptist Foreign Mission Society; Church of South India; Marburger Mission; Presbyterian Church of Korea; United Christian Missionary Society; United Church of Christ in the Philippines; United Presbyterian Church U.S.A.

Also working: American Mission to Lepers. Christian Nationals' Evangelism Commission. Danske Missionsforbund. New Tribes Mission; United Society for the Propagation of the Gospel.

TURKEY

301,302 sq. mls.

Pop.: **In Europe:** 2,284,625 (1960)
In Asia: 25,470,195
1965 Census (provisional): Total: 31,391,207

Church or Mission N.B. See notes on Statistics, page xiii	Places of Regular Worship	Communicants, Full Members (p. 57)		Total Christian Community (p. 57)		Staff					Theolog. Colls., Bible Schools	Source of Information B
						National Workers, full-time			Missionaries from other Churches or countries, full-time			
		1962 Handbook	Latest available figure	1962 Handbook	Latest available figure	Ordained	Lay-men	Women	Ordained	Lay-workers		
Seventh-day Adventists ...	1	63	60	157	141	1	2	—	—	2	—	B
	1	63	60	157	141	1	2	—	—	2	—	

Also working: Bible Lands Society. Congregationalists. United Church Board for World Ministries. United Society for the Propagation of the Gospel. Worldwide Evangelization Crusade.

Note.—The Missionary Research Library gives the number of Protestants as about 10,000.

VIETNAM

South: 66,263 sq. mls. Pop.: 14,200,000 estimate (1962)
North: 63,344 sq. mls. Pop.: 15,916,955 (1960)

Church or Mission	Places of Regular Worship	Communicants, Full Members		Total Christian Community		National Workers, Ordained	National Workers, Lay-men	National Workers, Women	Missionaries Ordained	Missionaries Lay-workers	Theolog. Colls., Bible Schools	Source of Information
		1962 Handbook	Latest	1962 Handbook	Latest							
Evangelical Church ...	a 339	15,000	40,214	40,000	50,000*	277	—	—	48	70	3	B
Mennonite Mission ...	2	—	27	—	50	1	2	—	5	4	—	B
Overseas Missionary Fellowship ...	—	—	—	—	—	—	—	—	2	2	—	B
Seventh-day Adventists ...	13	400	1,358	400	3,272	5	98	—	1	3	—	B

184

VIETNAM—*continued*

Southern Baptist Convention ...	10	—	130	—	355	5	25	—	10	10	1	B
Worldwide Evangelization Crusade	25	800	1,500	1,200	2,000	(47)U	—	—	(17)U	—	—	B
	389	16,200	43,229	41,600	55,677	340 (47)U	125	—	83 (17)U	90	4	

* Estimate.   U Unclassified.

Co-operating: a Christian and Missionary Alliance.

Also working: American Leprosy Missions. The Navigators. Wycliffe Bible Translators.

YEMEN   75,000 sq. mls.   Pop.: 4,500,000 estimate (1953)

Southern Baptist Convention ...	1	—	—	—	15	—	—	1	1	—	B
	1	—	—	—	15	—	—	1	1	—	

185

EUROPE

AUSTRIA 32,366 sq. mls. Pop.: 7,073,807 (1961)

Church or Mission N.B. See notes on Statistics, page xiii	Places of Regular Worship	Communicants, Full Members (p. 57)		Total Christian Community (p. 57)		Staff — National Workers, full-time			Source of Information
		1962 Handbook	Latest available figure	1962 Handbook	Latest available figure	Ordained	Laymen	Women	
Assemblies of God	19	800	840	1,000	1,210	(21)U	—	—	B
Baptists	4	800	800	1,000	1,000	1	3	3	E
Evangelische Kirche A.u.H.B.	632	200,559	421,976	414,812	421,976	310	—	11	A
Mennonite Brethren	3	—	82	—	200	5	2	2	B
Methodist Church	12	2,091	771	—	1,349	12	—	—	B
North American Baptist General Missionary Society Inc.	25	750	750	1,900	1,900	10	3	2	E
Old Catholic Church	51	37,579	40,000	—	40,000	17	50	1	A
Reformed Helvetic Church of Austria	8	13,628	13,628	25,000	25,000	14	1	—	E
Seventh-day Adventists	42	2,701	2,615	6,000	5,641	22	55	—	B
	796	258,908	481,462	449,712	498,276	412 (21)U	114	19	

From Oekumenischer Rat der Kirchen in Oesterreich:

Estimated totals: Protestant Community ... 438,663
Roman Catholics ... 6,295,046
Other Christian Groups ... 340,069
7,073,778

U Unclassified

Also working: Church of Christ, Scientist. Greater Europe Mission. International Miners' Mission. United Society for the Propagation of the Gospel.

BELGIUM 11,778 sq. mls. Pop.: 9,428,100 estimate (1964)

Assemblies of God	104	847	2,120	1,268	4,210	(46)U	—	—	B
Eglise Baptiste	9	272	272	360	360	6	5	—	E
Eglise Chrétienne Missionnaire Belge	50	3,800	3,800	10,000	10,000	30	14	1	E
Eglise Evangélique Protestante de Belgique	51	—	—	10,738	10,738	48	—	—	E
Eglise Mennonite	6	29	29	29	29	3	—	—	B
Eglise Methodiste	25	1,500	1,336	2,400	3,075	17	2	10	A
Mission Evangélique Belge	62	1,567	1,567	3,611	3,611	6	46	—	B
Pentecostal (European Evangelistic Society)	5	—	—	—	—	3	—	—	
Seventh-day Adventists	17	979	1,093	979	2,222	9	9	—	B
Societé Biblique Belge	—	—	—	—	—	2	11	—	A
Svenska Fria Missionen	4	284	75	475	150	3	4	4	B
	333	9,278	10,292	29,860	34,395	173 (46)U	91	15	
Total figures from the Federation des Eglises Protestantes de Belgique	363	—	29,900	—	52,800	280*	149	28	

* Includes 2 ordained women.   U Unclassified

Also working: Church of Christ, Scientist. Eglise Evangélique de Langue Allemande en Belgique. Eglises Lutheriennes Libres de France et de Belgique (figures included under France). Eglise Reformée Libre. Global Gospel Broadcasts. International Miners' Mission. United Society for the Propagation of the Gospel.

BULGARIA 42,823 sq. mls. Pop.: 8,226,564 (1965)

Assemblies of God	n.a.	5,000	5,000	5,000	5,000	—	—	—	B
Baptists	16	9,000	9,000	9,000	9,000	13	42	—	E
Bulgarian Congregational Church	44	4,300	4,300	4,300	4,300	—	—	—	E
Methodist Church	—	—	632	5,000	5,000	—	—	—	B
Reformed Church	—	4,800	4,800	4,800	4,800	—	—	—	E
Seventh-day Adventists	70	3,197	2,803	5,869	5,743	9	10	—	B
	130	26,297	26,535	33,969	33,843	22	52	—	

Also working: European Evangelistic Society.

CZECHOSLOVAKIA 49,362 sq. mls. Pop.: 14,106,886 (1964)

Church or Mission N.B. See notes on Statistics, page xiii	Places of Regular Worship	Communicants, Full Members (p. 57)		Total Christian Community (p. 57)		Staff National Workers, full-time			Source of Information
		1962 Handbook	Latest available figure	1962 Handbook	Latest available figure	Ordained	Laymen	Women	
Bratrská jednota baptistů	146	4,108	4,086	7,500	7,500	20	110	—	A
Keskobratrská Církev Evangelická	521	100,626	100,300	309,459	290,000	278	8	413	A
Czechoslovak Church	—	950,000	950,000	950,000	950,000	—	—	—	E
Evangelická církev metodistická	35	4,000	3,000	4,000	8,000	15	13	1	A
Jednota Keskobratrská (Unity of Czech Brethren)	29	6,500	6,500	10,000	10,000	30	—	—	E
Moravian Church (Unitas Fratrum)	18	10,000	10,000	10,000	10,000	20	18	1	E
Reformed Christian Church	304	130,000	130,000	150,000	150,000	165	—	—	E
Silesian Evangelical Lutheran of the Augsburg Confession	41	—	21,597	53,000	53,000	25	3	1	A
Slovak Evangelical Church (of the Augsburg Confession)	384	—	300,000	400,000	450,000	350	1,017	150	B
Seventh-day Adventists	50	7,505	8,733	12,524	18,733	33	16	—	B
	1,528	262,739	1,533,916	1,906,483	1,947,233	936	1,185	566	

The Ecumenical Council of Churches in Czechoslovakia estimates the total number of Christian Communicants at 2,100,000.

DENMARK 16,576 sq. mls. Pop.: 4,755,698 (1965)

Church or Mission	Places of Regular Worship	Communicants, Full Members (p. 57)		Total Christian Community (p. 57)		Staff National Workers, full-time			Source of Information
		1962 Handbook	Latest available figure	1962 Handbook	Latest available figure	Ordained	Laymen	Women	
Apostolic Church Assembly	60	—	1,598	6,000	6,000	28	3	9	C
Church of the Nazarene	2	—	31	51	51	1	1	—	B
Danske Baptistsamfund (Baptist Union)	84	7,240	7,264	20,000	20,000	38	8	13	C
Danske Missionsförbund (Mission Covenant Church)	39	1,759	1,954	4,000	4,000	18	8	—	C
Denmark Yearly Meeting Friends (Vennernes Samfund, Quakers)	2	60	53	60	80	—	—	—	A
Den Tysk-reformerte Kirke	1	—	350	—	580	1	6	—	C

DENMARK—continued

Evangelisk Luthereske Kirke (Ch. of Denmark) *	2,313	2,000,000	4,517,000	4,156,500	4,517,000	1,965	—	—	C
German Reformed Church	1	70	70	600	600	1	—	—	E
Hebrew Christian Alliance a	—	—	—	—	30	1	—	—	A
Methodist Church	116	3,500	3,536	—	7,838	19	2	—	B
Moravian Church	1	299	296	380	382	2	2	—	C
Salvation Army	66	—	2,809	—	5,836	151	1	1	C
Seventh-day Adventists	66	3,959	4,030	7,772	7,877	22	48	—	B
	2,751	2,016,887	4,538,991	4,189,312	4,570,274	2,247	79	23	

* Includes Greenland (35,000 members) and Faroe Islands (30,000 members).
Co-operating: a Danske Israels Mission.
Also working: Church of Christ, Scientist. Navigators.

FINLAND   305,396 sq. mls.   Pop.: 4,597,793 estimate (1965)

Finlands Svenske Baptistmission	38	2,089	1,989	4,190	4,190	28	18	4	A
Fria Missionsforbundet (Finnish Free Mission)	30	1,071	1,071	2,000	2,000	19	4	3	E
Methodist Church	27	3,000	1,230	4,000	2,148	17	3	—	B
Pentecostal Assemblies	—	40,000	40,000	40,000	40,000	—	—	—	E
Saalem Seurakunta	200	20,000	20,000	30,000	30,000	300	124	100	E
Seventh-day Adventists	49	5,214	5,275	10,188	10,471	34	—	—	B
Suomen-Adventtikirkko (Adventist Church)	2	1,200	1,200	3,659	3,659	—	—	—	
Suomen Baptistiyhdyskunta	6	650	650	1,883	1,883	—	—	—	E
Suomen Evankelis-Luterilainen-Kirkko	1,280	1,500,000	4,217,088	4,309,095	4,217,088	169	4,044U	56	E
Suomen Kirkon Sisälähetysseura	2	—	14,640	—	14,640	7	(621)U	—	A
Suomen Ortodoksinen Kirkka	25	25,000	25,000	75,539	75,539	—	—	—	A
Suomen Vapaa Evankelis-Luterilainen Kirkka	9	130	130	360	360	—	—	—	E
Suomen Vapaa Evankelis-Luterilainen (Suerakuntaitto)	5	200	200	555	555	—	—	—	E
Suomen Vapaa Vapaakirkko (Free Church of Finland)	82	5,227	5,791	8,798	9,161	77	25	52	A
	1,755	1,603,781	4,334,264	4,490,267	4,411,694	651	4,839 (621)U	215	

U Unclassified

Also working: Church of Christ, Scientist. Salvation Army.
Suomen Luterilainen Evankeliumiyhdistys (Membership figures included with Suomen Evankelis-Luterilainen.

FRANCE 212,919 sq. mls. Pop.: 46,520,271 (1962)

Church or Mission (N.B. See notes on Statistics, page xiii)	Places of Regular Worship	Communicants, Full Members (p. 57)		Total Christian Community (p. 57)		Staff — National Workers, full-time			Source of Information
		1962 Handbook	Latest available figure	1962 Handbook	Latest available figure	Ordained	Laymen	Women	
Action Chretienne en Orient†	24	850	850	2,500	2,500	11	5	2	E
Apostolic Church	8	300	300	300	300	—	—	—	E
Assemblies of God	650	—	29,000	—	29,000	—	(186)U	—	B
Baptist Mid-Missions	7	16	60	45	90	7	(19)U	—	B
Church of God (Cleveland)	2	—	61	—	261	8	—	—	B
Conservative Baptist F.M.S.	—	—	—	—	—	—	8	—	B
Eglise de la Confession d'Augsbourg d'Alsace et de Lorraine	365	80,000	147,800	241,000	235,700	205	86	11	A
Eglise Reformée d'Alsace et de Lorraine	90	22,073	39,000	50,000	49,600	61	10	12	A
Eglises Evangéliques Mennonites	28	2,719	2,719	2,719	2,719	—	—	—	E
Eglises Luthériennes Libres de France	14	570	570	990	990	10	—	—	E
Eglises Methodistes de France ...c	9	1,200	1,200	2,000	2,000	8	—	—	E
Europe Mennonite Mission	1	2	2	—	25	1	2	1	B
Evangelical Lutheran Church of France	70	—	15,000	47,650	42,000	51	4	4	B
Fédération des Communautés de Diaconesses de France	7	355	339	355	339	345*	—	—	A
Fédération des Eglises Evangéliques Baptistes de France	50	1,928	1,928	4,838	4,838	24	5	1	E
Mission Evangélique des Alpes ...b	2	—	—	—	—	19	—	—	B
Mission Populaire Evangélique de France ...a	15	—	600	—	3,000	10	3	4	A
Reformed Church of France	1,315	195,000	195,000	363,000	339,282	514	16	27	A
Seventh-day Adventists	76	3,538	4,730	6,500	9,443	38	76	—	B
Society of Friends	—	80	80	134	134	—	—	—	E
Southern Baptist Convention	7	—	772	—	2,199	2	2	—	B

FRANCE—continued

Svenska Fria Missionen	4	50	50	275	275	2	—	—	B
Union Nationale des Eglises Réformées	90	—	n.a.	—	n.a.	15	20	1	B
	2,835	308,681	440,061	722,306	724,695	1,331	442 (205)U	63	

* Ordained Sisters. † Among Armenians. U Unclassified

Co-operating: **a** United Church Board for World Ministries. **b** Unevangelized Fields Mission. **c** Methodist Missionary Society. Also working: Church of Christ, Scientist. Danish Mission to the Jews. Greater Europe Mission. Hebrew Christian Testimony to Israel. International Miners' Missions. North Africa Mission. Société évangelique-Lutherienne.

GERMANY

Federal Republic: 95,958 sq. mls.   Pop.: 58,587,500 (1964)
Democratic Republic: 41,802 sq. mls.   Pop.: 17,011,931 (1964)

Altreformierte Kirchen in Deutschland ...	14	3,104	3,104	5,225	5,225	—	—	E
Assemblies of God	260	7,145	6,450	9,600	6,450	(155)U	—	B
Baptists Mid-Missions	5	—	30	—	60	—	—	B
Bund Evangelisch-Freikirchlicher Gemeinden in Deutschland (Baptisten)	1,509	96,686	94,813	400,000	400,000	605	15	B
Bund Freier Evangelischer Gemeinden in Deutschland ...	669	21,478	21,478	45,023	45,023	148	11	E
Church of God (Cleveland) ...	44	900	1,049	900	3,049	(41)U	—	B
Church of the Nazarene	8	—	221	—	675	3	—	B
Evangelical Free Church	1	—	16	—	60	—	—	B
Evangelische Brüder-Unitat (Moravians)	19	8,110	8,110	9,961	9,961	5	12	E
Evangelische Gemeinschaft in Deutschland (Evangelical Community in Germany) ...	630	30,101	30,101	160,505	160,505	220	—	E

GERMANY—*continued*

Church or Mission N.B. See notes on Statistics, page xiii	Places of Regular Worship	Communicants, Full Members (p. 57)		Total Christian Community (p. 57)		Staff			Source of Information
		1962 Handbook	Latest available figure	1962 Handbook	Latest available figure	National Workers, full-time			
						Ordained	Laymen	Women	
Evangelische Kirche in Deutschland:									
Member Churches of Evangelische									
Kirche Der Union:									
Berlin—Brandenburg ...*a	1,733	773,994	778,994	4,789,000	4,789,000	1,164	180	32	A
Pommern ... *	327	98,027	98,027	680,000	700,000	175	36	7	A
Schlesien ... *	74	69,914	69,914	230,000	230,000	77	5	2	A
Kirchenprovinz Sachsen *	2,369	553,549	553,549	3,460,000	3,460,000	1,075	173	50	A
Westfalen ...	573	765,987	962,706	3,130,000	3,504,000	1,400	78	22	A
Rheinland ...	823	606,284	845,645	3,250,000	3,900,200	1,406	30	17	A
Other United Landeskirchen:									
Hessen und Nassau ...	1,104	618,763	688,358	2,040,000	2,289,600	1,118	90	18	A
Kurhessen-Waldeck †	970	434,431	407,375	1,085,000	1,102,300	549	25	9	A
Baden ...	539	431,278	481,666	1,140,000	1,375,600	693	44	18	A
Pfalz ...	449	200,716	223,316	680,000	746,300	400	—	9	A
Anhalt ... *	221	54,231	54,231	420,000	420,000	116	7	—	A
Bremen ...	58	41,827	56,412	430,000	516,200	118	1	1	A
Member Churches of United									
Evangelical Lutheran Church of									
Germany:									
Sachsen ... *	1,226	1,096,182	1,096,182	4,430,000	3,800,000	1,152	18	18	A
Hannover ... †	1,652	966,635	1,006,762	3,777,000	3,873,200	1,444	125	32	A
Bayern ...	1,270	1,210,022	1,215,393	2,550,470	2,536,800	1,570	40	23	A
Schleswig-Holstein	473	256,684	286,087	2,477,819	2,344,500	756	14	8	A
Thüringen ... **	1,406	312,832	340,000	1,800,000	1,800,000	656	95	8	A
Mecklenburg ... *	501	157,801	157,801	1,230,000	1,444,651	331	35	8	A
Hamburg ...	75	83,355	115,520	790,000	707,000	234	—	8	A
Braunschweig †	424	123,320	140,533	700,000	653,900	283	12	1	A

GERMANY—*continued*

Lübeck	29	21,851	26,011	205,000	208,200	76	—	5	A
Schaumburg-Lippe ...	21	26,506	25,031	75,240	71,200	23	1	—	A
Other Lutheran Landeskirchen:									
Württemberg	1,261	769,941	801,623	2,500,000	2,521,800	1,618	80	36	A
Oldenburg	107	82,944	92,863	543,000	532,300	179	10	4	A
Eutin	17	11,874	10,124	91,000	86,400	24	1	—	A
Reformed Landeskirchen:									
Lippe	67	37,077	56,364	264,049	243,200	98	4	2	A
Nordwestdeutschland ...	129	27,824	29,041	219,000	214,400	103	11	—	A
Evangelisch-Lutherische Frei-Kirche	159	5,000	3,000	15,000	15,000	48	1	—	B
Evangelisch-Lutherische (altlutherische) Kirche ...	—	12,000	12,000	37,000	37,000	—	—	—	B
Gnadauer Verband ...	4,767	—	50,800	—	146,348	610	5,339	924	A
Independent Evangelical Lutheran Church	120	—	18,900	—	21,000	42	—	—	B
Katholisches Bistum der Alt-Katholiken in Deutschland	207	12,000	30,000	—	30,000	59	—	—	A
Mennonite Brethren ...	2	—	120	—	300	10	3	5	A
Mennoniten Gemeinden ...	40	4,000	7,500	12,078	9,000	13	3	—	A
Methodists	1,555	65,000	63,644	105,000	105,000	331	12	—	B
Religiöse Gesellschaft der Freunde (Quaker) ...	28	475	533	—	800	—	25	—	A
Selbständige Evangelisch-Lutherische Kirche ...	91	21,160	21,160	21,160	21,160	44	—	—	E
Seventh-day Adventists ...	820	42,032	39,788	90,338	83,725	472	—	—	B
Southern Baptist Convention	21	—	1,951	—	5,556	—	—	—	A
	28,867	10,168,020	11,034,296	43,898,368	45,176,668	19,644 (196)U	6,493	1,305	

* No figures available later than 31st December, 1960.   † Figures do not include areas with the D.D.R.

Co-operating: **a** United Church Board for World Ministries.   **U** Unclassified

Also working: Church of Christ, Scientist. Europe Mennonite Mission. Friends of Israel Missionary Society. Greater European Mission. Hebrew Christian Testimony to Israel. International Miners' Mission. Salvation Army.

GREAT BRITAIN 89,038 sq. mls. Pop.: 51,435,567 (1961)

Church or Mission N.B. See notes on Statistics, page xiii	Places of Regular Worship	Communicants, Full Members (p. 57)		Total Christian Community (p. 57)		Staff — National Workers, full-time			Source of Information
		1962 Handbook	Latest available figure	1962 Handbook	Latest available figure	Ordained	Laymen	Women	
Apostolic Church	225	5,000	4,500	7,500	7,000	85	—	—	A
Assemblies of God	534	20,000	28,000	60,000	65,972	540	13	8	A
Baptist Union of Gt. Britain and Ireland	2,218	244,510	226,523	544,510	565,000	2,000	2,400	80	A
Baptist Union of Scotland	159	19,501	18,456	39,847	38,000¶	162	80	—	A
Baptist Union of Wales	733	70,282	70,282	111,722	111,722	285	1	4	E
Brethren	1,795	146,300	100,000	246,000	240,000¶	(181)U	—	—	D
Church in Wales, Representative Body of the	1,780	200,000	165,300	400,000	400,000	1,011	—	2	A
Church of England	20,084	9,750,000	9,887,000*	27,000,000	27,435,000‡	17,814†	6,981	3,193	A
Church of Jesus Christ of Latter Day Saints	93	9,460	9,460	11,460	11,400¶	—	—	—	
Church of God (Cleveland)	60	400	2,593	400	5,491	(107)U	—	—	E
Church of Scotland	3,000	1,306,661	1,259,162	1,364,655	1,364,655	2,750	20	—	E
Church of the Nazarene	99	3,401	3,565	7,926	9,541	121	61	17	A
Churches of Christ in Gt. Britain and Ireland (Disciples)	150	9,500	9,500	12,000	12,000¶	35	3	3	A
Congregational Church in England and Wales	2,799	206,833	198,488	376,527	348,811	1,700	—	—	A
Congregational Union of Scotland	136	34,057	30,133	44,000	44,000¶	157	2	—	A
Countess of Huntingdon's Connexion	37	1,218	1,000	3,500	3,500	20	—	—	A
Elim Church	308	20,000	20,000	25,000	44,800	271	186	10	D
Elim Pentecostal Churches	22	1,000	1,000	2,000	2,000	14	6	1	A
Episcopal Church in Scotland	329	56,725	54,584	97,038	97,175	281	—	4	A
Evangelical Lutheran Church of England	11	—	621	869	1,343	13	1	1	A
Fellowship of Independent Evangelical Churches	291	—	1,500	—	2,500¶	(400)U	(80)U	—	A
Free Church of England	37	—	1,500	8,300	6,514	42	29	—	D
Free Church of Scotland	160	—	4,155	25,000	25,000	111	—	—	D
Free Presbyterian Church of Scotland	64	600	600	4,000	4,000	28	30	2	E

194

GREAT BRITAIN—*continued*

Denomination									
General Church of the New Jerusalem	2	—	179	—	250¶	3	(15)U	—	A
Independent Methodist Connexion	149	7,517	7,926	19,226	16,647	—	2	—	A
International Mission to Miners	5	200	200	400	400	—	7	5	E
Lutheran Council of Great Britain	165	11,030	12,500	30,000	32,000	46	3	4	A
Menmonite Board of Missions	3	10	10	80	80	4	—	—	E
Methodist Church	11,539	733,638	701,306	2,250,000	2,100,000	4,371	150	350	A
Moravian Church	40	2,504	2,793	4,914	5,249	34	15	2	D
New Church, General Conference of the	65	4,081	3,685	7,500	7,500	36	50	—	A
Pentecostal Holiness Church	20	1,000	1,000	1,500	1,500	—	18	—	E
Presbyterian Church of England	333	71,329	67,618	112,436	110,000	291	5	14	A
Presbyterian Church of Wales	1,601	140,489	140,489	187,651	187,651	689	(7,366)§	—	E
Reformed Presbyterian Church of Scotland	5	605	605	1,000	1,000	4	—	—	E
Religious Society of Friends	439	21,222	21,062	30,000	30,198	—	43	47	A
Salvation Army	1,218	8,921	—	—	—	2,458	314	—	E
Seventh-day Adventists	116	—	10,234	12,921	20,106	128	236	—	B
Strict and Particular Baptists	700	—	5,000*	—	10,000†	74†	—	—	D
Union of Welsh Independents	810	—	102,437	—	120,000¶	—	—	—	A
Unitarian and Free Christian Churches	313	28,000	24,000	35,000	30,000¶	247	(93)U	—	A
United Free Church of Scotland	107	23,482	21,779	27,844	26,238	91	11	2	A
Wesleyan Reform Union	155	6,123	5,576	19,000	12,654	20	297	—	A
	52,909	13,165,599	13,224,821	33,131,726	33,556,825	36,624 (688)U	11,152 (188)U	3,749	
Figures supplied by the Free Church Federal Council representing twelve Denominations	13,850	1,521,209	—	4,000,000	—	9,239	248	(656)U	

* Confirmed members, estimated 1964.   † Includes Worker-Priests and Semi-Retired.
‡ Baptized Members of all ages. Figure for regular worshippers not available.
§ 104 unordained preachers, 7,262 elders. || Figures for Home Counties only.   ¶ Estimate.   U Unclassified.
Also working: Church Army. Community of the Resurrection. Hebrew Christian Testimony to Israel. Slavic and Baltic Missionary Society. Society of the Sacred Mission (Church of England). World Protestant Union. Church of Christ, Scientist.

Church Attendance Figures: It is estimated that in the British Isles today regular church attendance figures are:

Roman Catholics	...	5,000,000
Anglicans	...	2,800,000
Non-Conformists	...	4,000,000

GREECE 50,534 sq. mls. Pop.: 8,480,000 estimate (1963)

Church or Mission *N.B.* See notes on Statistics, page xiii	Places of Regular Worship	Communicants, Full Members (p. 57)		Total Christian Community (p. 57)		Staff — National Workers, full-time			Source of Information
		1962 Handbook	Latest available figure	1962 Handbook	Latest available figure	Ordained	Laymen	Women	
Anatolic Apostolic Church ...	6	—	133	—	133	6	2	—	B
Assemblies of God ...	15	567	673	1,247	1,943	(43)U	—	—	A
Church of God (Cleveland)	1	—	79	—	329	3	—	—	B
Church of God of Prophecy	3	360	360	360	360	—	3	—	E
Ekklesia tes Ellados (The Church of Greece)	n.a.	2,500,000	2,500,000	7,500,000¶	7,500,000¶	8,000	2,600	1,300	E
Greater Europe Mission	—	—	—	—	—	12	14	—	A
Greek Evangelical Church ...	19	2,000	2,000	15,000	15,000	11	—	—	E
International Church of the Foursquare Gospel ...	1	105	105	181	181	1	—	1	E
Oriental Missionary Society ...	5	1,000	1,000	1,000	1,000	4	3	1	E
Seventh-day Adventists	9	202	224	443	501	9	6	—	B
	58	2,504,234	2,504,574	7,518,231	7,518,547	8,089 (43)U	2,628	1,302	

Also working: Bible Lands Society. Church of Christ, Scientist. European Evangelistic Society. Svenska Fria Missionen. United Church Board for World Ministries.

HUNGARY

35,912 sq. mls. Pop.: 9,977,870 (1960)

Assemblies of God ...	45	3,000	3,000	5,000	3,000	—	—	B
Church of God (Cleveland) ...	19	—	700	—	3,700	10	—	B
Magyar Baptista Egyház ...	100	20,000	20,000	35,000	35,000	100	—	E
Magyar Methodista Egyház ...	—	1,500	703	2,500	2,000	—	—	B
Magyarországi Evangélikas Egyház (Lutheran) ...	514	144,320	144,320	432,961	432,961	490	—	E & D
Magyarirszági Református Egyház...	2,243	973,393	973,393	1,954,000	1,954,000	1,512	(1,130)U	A
Seventh-day Adventists ...	163	6,225	5,800	14,000	11,968	32	18	B
	3,074	1,148,438	1,147,916	2,443,461	2,442,629	2,144	1,148 (1,130)U	—

Totals given by the *Ecumenical Council of Churches:*

Protestants	...	2,450,000
Roman Catholics	...	5,500,000
Orthodox	...	5,000

Also working: Church's Ministry among the Jews. European Evangelistic Society.

ICELAND

39,758 sq. mls. Pop.: 190,230 (1964)

Free Church ...	—	3,500	3,500	10,000	10,000	—	—	E
National Church (Evangelical Lutheran) ...	295	55,000	114,000	166,000	166,000	106	10	B
Pentecostal Assemblies ...	10	500	510	1,000	1,000	20	16	B	1
Seventh-day Adventists ...	8	403	454	800	972	2	—	B
Southern Baptist Convention ...	2	—	41	—	196	—	—	B
Svenska Fria Missionen ...	10	500	500	1,000	1,000	23	10	E	6
	325	59,903	119,005	178,800	179,168	151	36	7

Also working: Icelandic Bible Society. Salvation Army.

IRELAND—IRISH REPUBLIC AND NORTHERN IRELAND

Irish Republic: 26,600 sq. mls. Pop.: 2,818,341 (1961)
Northern Ireland: 5,462 sq. mls. Pop.: 1,458,000 (1964)

Church or Mission N.B. See notes on Statistics, page xiii	Places of Regular Worship	Communicants, Full Members (p. 57)		Total Christian Community (p. 57)		Staff — National Workers, full-time			Source of Information
		1962 Handbook	Latest available figure	1962 Handbook	Latest available figure	Ordained	Laymen	Women	
Baptist Union of Ireland	77	5,554	6,364	16,191	15,049	54	12	3	A
Church of Ireland	1,374	284,000	284,000	475,000	448,600	800	24	12	A
Congregational Union of Ireland	22	1,931	1,533	8,134	7,500	17	8	—	D
Lutheran Congregations in Dublin, Cork, Belfast and Killarney	6		275	—	300	1	—	—	B
Methodist Church	357	32,904	32,904	75,000	75,000	177	41	1	E
Moravian Church	6	338	338	623	623	5	—	—	E
Presbyterian Church in Ireland	638	137,701	142,182	386,112	397,410	563	60	20	A
Reformed Presbyterian Church	47	3,237	3,207	6,500	6,600	31	2	—	A
Seventh-day Adventists	4	223	269	455	486	4	11	—	B
Society of Friends	—	1,960	1,960	2,500	2,500	—	—	—	E
	2,531	467,848	473,032	970,515	954,068	1,652	158	36	

Also working: Apostolic Church of Pentecost of Canada. Assemblies of God. Barbican Mission to the Jews. Church's Ministry among the Jews. Church of Christ, Scientist. Church of God. Elim Church. Good News Trailer Missionary Fellowship.

ITALY

116,280 sq. mls. Pop.: 50,463,762 (1961)

Church or Mission	Places of Regular Worship	Communicants, Full Members		Total Christian Community		Staff			Source of Information
		1962 Handbook	Latest available figure	1962 Handbook	Latest available figure	Ordained	Laymen	Women	
Assembles di Dio	650	45,000	80,000	55,000	120,000	(280)U	—	—	B
Associazione Miss. Evang.	13	440	500	1,400	1,500	8	4	—	B
Baptist Mid-Missions	3	20	20	29	35	4	—	—	B
Chiesa Apostolica	50	—	1,000	—	1,500	6	25	—	C

ITALY—continued

Chiese Cristiana Avventiste ...	58	2,677	3,050	4,645	3,750	62	248	—	C
Chiese dei Fratelli ...	40	—	7,000	—	10,000	40	100	—	C
Chiesa Evangelica Luterana	21	—	4,500	—	6,000	12	60	—	B
Chiesa Metodista ...	64	4,089	3,669	6,842	6,357	32	—	—	B
Chiesa Valdese ...	150	20,378	21,632	27,595	29,199	85	25	—	A
Church of the Nazarene ...	19	303	266	678	654	7	1	—	B
Conservative Baptist Mission ...	9	—	37	—	50*	11	11	3	B
Church of God (Cleveland)	24	—	1,449	—	4,449	16	—	—	B
	1,101	72,907	123,123	96,189	183,494	563 (280)U	474	3	

* Estimate   U Unclassified

Also working: Bible Lands Society. Church of Christ, Scientist. European Evangelistic Society. Greater Europe Mission. Mennonite Board. United Church Board for World Ministries.

LUXEMBOURG   999 sq. mls.   Pop.: 330,000 (1964)

Eglise Protestante du Grand-Duché (Lutheran)	8	—	850	5,400	5,400	3	—	B
Europe Mennonite Mission ...	3	14	15	25	30	3	3	B
Southern Baptist Convention ...	1	—	17	—	97	1	1	B
	19	14	950	5,425	5,527	7	4	

199

NETHERLANDS 12,908 sq. mls. Pop.: 12,212,269 (1964)

Church or Mission (N.B. See notes on Statistics, page xiii)	Places of Regular Worship	Communicants, Full Members (p. 57)		Total Christian Community (p. 57)		Staff — National Workers, full-time			Source of Information
		1962 Handbook	Latest available figure	1962 Handbook	Latest available figure	Ordained	Laymen	Women	
Algemene Doopsgezinde Societist (Mennonites)	—	39,000	39,000	65,000	62,928	—	—	—	B
Apostolisch Genootschap	—	—	10,000†	—	32,657	—	—	—	C
Assemblies of God	61	—	2,230	—	5,585	—	45	—	B
Baptist Mid-Missions	7	—	55	—	85	—	—	—	B
Bond van Vrije Evangelische Gemeenten *	36	6,326	6,326	18,866	20,155	—	—	—	C&E
Christelijk Gereformeerde Kerk	—	30,000	30,000	69,144	73,751	86	—	—	C&E
Evangelische Broedergemeente (Moravian Church)	5	450	726	700	1,084	3	5	1	A
Evangelisch Luthers.	85	30,421	29,918	58,077	67,112	52	—	—	B
Gereformeerde Gemeenten	—	—	30,000†	—	93,481	—	—	—	C
Gereformeerde Kerken (Reformed Church)	1,200	404,688	430,000	762,982	808,000	1,100	—	—	A
Gereformeerde Kerken (Vrijgemaakt)	—	—	32,000†	—	96,241	—	—	—	C
Horst. Apost. Gem. in de Eenh. de Apost	—	—	3,000†	—	9,841	—	—	—	C
Herst. Apost. Zendingskerk	—	—	1,000†	—	2,726	—	—	—	C
Leger des Heils (Salvation Army)	146	—	6,000†	—	18,497	518	(186)U	—	C&E
Nederlandse Protestantenbond	—	—	9,000†	—	26,210	—	—	—	C
Nederlands Hervormde Kerk	3,937	899,363	899,363	3,233,073	3,233,073	1,550	21	6	E
Oud-Katholieke Kerk van Nederland	29	7,400	7,400	12,600	12,600	30	1	—	E
Oud-gereformeerde	—	—	6,500†	—	19,849	—	—	—	C
Remonstrantse Broederschap Algemene Dienst	52	21,170	21,170	40,059	39,609	45	30	32	C&E
Seventh-day Adventists	45	2,663	3,151	4,241	5,783	46	89	—	B

200

NETHERLANDS—continued

Svenska Fria Missionen	3	900	50	1,300	100	—	—	B
Unie van Baptisten Gemeenten	98	8,247	9,205	22,000	20,000	65	40	A
Waale-hervormd	—	—	1,000†	—	3,058	—	417 (186U)	38 (A)
	5,704	1,450,628	1,577,094	4,288,042	4,652,425	3,495		

* Federation of Free Congregations. † Estimate U Unclassified

Also working: Christengemeenschap. Church of Christ, Scientist. Navigators. Pinkstergemeente. Vrij Katholick.

NORWAY

125,249 sq. mls.   Pop.: 3,707,967 (1965)

Evangelical Lutheran Free Church...	150	6,929	6,806	17,509	18,850	43	15	12	B
Methodist Church	142	9,000	8,251	18,000	17,684	82	4	—	B
Norske Baptistsamfunn	110	7,050	6,650	21,150	21,150	75	27	2	A
Norske Kirke (Church of Norway, Lutheran)	1,234	572,000	572,000	3,155,323	3,500,000	1,050	—	—	B
Norske Misjonsforbund	120	10,500	10,500	20,000	20,500	135	—	—	E
Pentecostal	300	40,000	40,000	70,000	70,000	—	300	—	E
Seventh-day Adventists	70	4,922	5,253	8,778	9,835	20	75	—	B
Vennenes Samfunn i Norge (Friends)	3	—	90	—	100	—	—	—	A
	2,129	650,401	649,550	3,310,760	3,658,119	1,405	421	14	

Also working: Church of Christ, Scientist. Navigators. Salvation Army.

POLAND　　120,359 sq. mls.　　Pop.: 31,340,000 estimate (1965)

Church or Mission _N.B. See notes on Statistics, page xiii_	Places of Regular Worship	Communicants, Full Members (p. 57)		Total Christian Community (p. 57)		Staff — National Workers, full-time			Source of Information
		1962 Handbook	Latest available figure	1962 Handbook	Latest available figure	Ordained	Laymen	Women	
Assemblies of God	45	2,218	2,218	2,973	3,859	(45)U	—	—	B
Kosciol Ewangelicko-Augsburski ...	396	88,687	79,759	115,000	109,259	115	(335)U	—	A
Methodist Church	n.a.	12,000	18,734	25,000	27,000*	79	35	—	B & E
Polski Kosciol Chrzescjan Baptystow	64	2,500	2,500	5,000	5,000	15	5	—	E
Polski Narodowy Kosciol Katolicki	62	100,000	100,000	300,000	300,000	10	5	5	E
Reformed Church	12	2,500	2,500	5,000	5,000	7	—	—	E
Seventh-day Adventists	68	3,387	3,810	6,625	9,010	24	43	—	B
United Evangelical Church	—	—	—	5,000	5,000	—	—	—	E
	647	211,292	211,021	464,598	464,128	295 (45)U	418 (335)U	5	

Also working: European Evangelistic Society.

* Estimate　　U Unclassified

PORTUGAL　　34,831 sq. mls.　　Pop.: 8,889,392 (1960)

Church or Mission	Places of Regular Worship	Communicants, Full Members		Total Christian Community		Staff — National Workers			Source of Information
		1962 Handbook	Latest available figure	1962 Handbook	Latest available figure	Ordained	Laymen	Women	
Assembleias de Deus (Svenska Fria Missionen) ...	110	3,300	4,405	9,900	11,000	—	—	—	B
Alliance Mission (Independent Groups)	16	500	500	500	700†	—	—	—	E
Brethren	117	3,000	3,000	3,000	3,000	—	—	—	E
Congregação Cristã	13	500	500	500	700†	—	—	—	E

PORTUGAL—continued

Covenção Batista, Missao Batista ...	42	2,000	1,200	2,000	1,500	20	2	A
Evangelical Presbyterian Church ...	31	1,488	1,488	2,196	1,800	13	6	A
Igreja Evangélica Metodista Portuguesa ...	14	600	650	2,000	2,000	5	27	A
Igreja Lusitana Catolica-Apostolica Evangélica ... a	17	963	1,200	1,700	4,200	11	9	A
Independent Fellowship ...	31	1,500	1,500	1,500	1,500	—	34	E
Pentecostal Church ...	1	—	75	—	150†	1	—	B
Seventh-day Adventists ... *	35	2,607	3,005	3,129	6,272	15	44	B
	427	16,458	17,528	26,425	32,822	65	111	8

* Figures include the Azores, Cape Verde and Madeira Islands.   † Estimate.

Co-operating: a Spanish and Portuguese Church Aid Society.

Also working: American Leprosy Mission.   Bible Action.   Conservative Baptists.   International Miners' Mission.

RUMANIA   113,918 sq. mls.   Pop.: 18,927,081 (1956)

Baptists ...	420	65,880	65,880	90,000	90,000	370	—	E
Biserica Reformata Din Romania ...	719	380,000	380,000	780,000	780,000	686	—	E
Evangelical Synodal Presbyteral Church of the Augsburg Confession	—	—	10,000	35,000	35,000	—	—	B
Evangelische Kirche Augsburgischen Bekenntnisses ...	283	—	55,689	180,000	183,823	203	138	A
Pentecostals ...	—	5,000	5,000	50,000	50,000	—	—	E
Seventh-day Adventists ...	511	33,989	34,069	66,045	69,841	108	127	B
	1,933	484,869	550,638	1,201,045	1,208,664	1,367	265	57

SPAIN 503,545 sq. mls. Pop.: 30,430,698 (1960)

Church or Mission N.B. See notes on Statistics, page xiii	Places of Regular Worship	Communicants, Full Members (p. 57)		Total Christian Community (p. 57)		Staff — National Workers, full-time			Source of Information
		1962 Handbook	Latest available figure	1962 Handbook	Latest available figure	Ordained	Laymen	Women	
Assemblies of God	9	100	152	281	766	(5)U	—	—	B
Brethren	60	5,849	5,489	8,000	8,000	—	30	—	E
Church of God (Cleveland) ...	3	—	54	—	304	5	—	—	B
Federacion de Iglesias Evangelicas Independientes	54	1,163	1,917	3,008	3,300	29	—	—	A
Iglesia Evangelica Española	50	3,032	3,150	10,000	10,000	30	21	—	A
Mission Cristiana Española	—	693	693	1,200	1,200	—	—	—	E
Seventh-day Adventists ...	21	1,411	2,063	3,000	4,622	14	55	—	B
Spanish Reformed Episcopal Church a	12	697	1,100	1,674	3,000	9	4	—	A
Unione Evangelica Bautista... ... b	88	3,172	4,600	6,000	11,485	38	10	1	B
	297	16,117	19,218	33,163	42,678	130 (5)U	120	1	

Co-operating: **a** Spanish and Portuguese Church Aid Society. **b** Southern Baptist Convention. **U** Unclassified

Also working: Greater European Mission. International Miners' Mission. World Baptist Fellowship Mission Agency. World-wide Evangelization Crusade (Canary Islands).

SWEDEN 173,620 sq. mls. Pop.: 7,695,200 estimate (1964)

Estonian Evangelical Lutheran Church	—	22,000	22,000	66,000	66,000	—	—	—	E
Methodist Church	248	12,000	10,905	15,000	20,826	122	12	—	B
Pentecostal Assemblies	2,000	93,000	91,000	115,000	131,000	2,200	—	—	B
Seventh-day Adventists	68	3,815	3,724	6,323	7,198	32	283	5	A
Svenska Alliansmissionen	338	—	14,042	—	32,505	104	50	—	E
Svenska Baptistsamfundet	525	32,540	32,540	150,000	150,000	336	342	—	
Svenska Kyrkan (Lutheran) (Church of Sweden)	3,085	2,500,000	5,300,000	6,580,000	7,000,000	3,070	1,207	—	A
Svenska Missionsforbundet	2,237	99,844	99,626	245,877	225,100	657	—	11	A
Vännernas Samfund	6	—	125	—	500	—	—	—	A
	8,507	2,763,199	5,566,962	7,178,200	7,633,129	6,521	1,894	16	

Also working: Church of Christ, Scientist. Church of the Nazarene. Greater European Mission. Navigators. Religious Society of Friends. Salvation Army. Svenska Israelsmissionen.

Estimated figures supplied by the Swedish Ecumenical Council:

Population	7,630,000
Places of worship ...	9,800
Protestant Community ...	7,455,000
Roman Catholic Community ...	31,000
Orthodox Community ...	11,000
Latter Day Saints ...	3,000
Total ...	7,500,000

For the Protestant Community, the following estimate is given of full members:

Free Churches	350,000
Church of Sweden	5,525,000
Total ...	5,875,000

SWITZERLAND 15,941 sq. mls. Pop.: 5,429,061 (1960)

Church or Mission N.B. See notes on Statistics, page xiii	Places of Regular Worship	Communicants, Full Members (p. 57)		Total Christian Community (p. 57)		Staff — National Workers, full-time			Source of Information
		1962 Handbook	Latest available figure	1962 Handbook	Latest available figure	Ordained	Laymen	Women	
Apostolic Church	70	1,500	1,500	1,500	1,500	—	—	—	A
Assemblies of God	4	—	100	—	150	—	—	—	B
Brüdergemeine Eglise Morave	4	400	600	600	750	5	—	1	A
Bund Freier Evangelischer Gemein-den in der Schweiz *	28	2,750	2,750	3,500	3,500	—	—	—	E
Bund Schweizerischer Baptist-engemeinden	20	1,483	1,498	2,539	2,600†	15	30	—	A
Cantonal Reformed Churches	1,150	1,250,000	1,250,000	2,555,047	2,555,047	1,396	—	—	E
Christkatholische Kirche der Schweiz (Old Catholic)	44	800	800	2,500	2,500	42	—	—	E
Evangelical Lutheran Congregations in Bern, Geneva and Zürich	14	2,500	2,800	2,500	5,900	6	—	—	B
Mennonites	—	1,900	1,900	1,900	1,900	—	—	1	E
Methodist Church	281	15,000	11,147	20,000	24,494	84	1	—	B
Seventh-day Adventists	60	3,454	3,732	6,513	7,130	34	60	—	B
	1,675	1,279,787	1,277,827	2,596,599	2,605,471	1,582	91	2	

* Union of Swiss Free Churches.   † Estimate.

Also working: American-European Fellowship. Church of Christ, Scientist. Church of the Nazarene. Religious Society of Friends. Salvation Army.

UNION OF SOVIET SOCIALIST REPUBLICS

8,650,000 sq. mls.   Pop.: 232,000,000 estimate (1966) (Europe and Asia)

The question of statistics for Religious Groups in the U.S.S.R. is one of the most perplexing of problems. The figures we quote must be considered as estimates only.

Byzantine Rite Catholic ...	—	—	700,000	—	2,000,000	—	—	—	D
Estonian Evangelical Lutheran Church ...	170	350,000	79,768	350,000	350,000	116	24	3	B
Estonian Methodist ...	12	—	750	—	2,000	107	—	—	D
Latvian Lutheran Church ...	257	—	100,000	600,000	600,000	—	—	3	B
Lithuanian Catholic ...	490	—	500,000	—	1,500,000	—	—	—	D
Lithuanian Lutheran Church ...	—	30,000	10,000	30,000	30,000	—	—	—	B
Mennonites ...	—	—	15,000	40,000	45,000	—	—	—	D
Russian Baptists ...	5,000	1,500,000	1,500,000	3,000,000	2,000,000	—	—	—	D
Russian Orthodox Church ...	10,000	30,000,000	30,000,000	50,000,000	50,000,000	—	—	—	D
Churches in Exile:									
1. Estonian Evangelical Lutheran Church ...	132	—	9,040	—	65,000	50	3	5	B
2. Latvian Evangelical Lutheran Church ...	245	—	48,000	—	120,000	128	—	—	B
3. Lithuanian Evangelical Lutheran Church ...	62	—	7,000	—	12,000	5	1	—	B
	16,368	31,880,000	32,969,558	54,020,000	56,724,000	406	28	11	

Also working: Assemblies of God. Armenian Orthodox. Church of God. Dukohbors, etc. European Evangelistic Society. Georgian Orthodox. Molokans. Pentecostals. Seventh-day Adventists.

The Church of God, Headquarters: Queens Village, N.Y., U.S.A., claims some millions of followers in both the U.S.S.R. and also Red China.

YUGOSLAVIA　　98,725 sq. mls.　　Pop.: 19,279,000 estimate (1964)

Church or Mission N.B. See notes on Statistics, page xiii	Places of Regular Worship	Communicants, Full Members (p. 57)		Total Christian Community (p. 57)		Staff — National Workers, full-time			Source of Information
		1962 Hand-book	Latest available figure	1962 Hand-book	Latest available figure	Or-dained	Laymen	Women	
Assemblies of God	54	1,200	1,200	1,500	1,800	—	40	—	B
Baptists	50	3,176	3,176	4,000	4,000	23	—	—	E
Evangelical Christian Church of the Augsburg Confession in the People's Republic of Slovenia-Yugoslavia	26	10,000	13,500	23,500	23,650	10	10	3	B
Evangelical Church in the People's Republic of Croatia, Bosnia, Herzegovina and the Autonomous Province of Vojvodina	38	—	3,902	—	6,500	6	6	3	B
Evangelical Church in the People's Republic of Serbia	14	4,250	4,800	8,540	7,000	2	5	1	B
Kristora Pentekostna	60	1,600	1,600	3,500	3,500	—	52	—	E
Methodists	—	2,000	2,000	2,800	2,800	—	—	—	E
Református Keresztyén Egyház (Reformed Christian Church) ...	69	25,000	25,000	35,787	30,244	31	—	—	A & E
Seventh-day Adventists	240	8,590	9,562	17,056	19,562	53	36	—	B
Slovak Evangelical Christian Church of the Augsburg Confession in Yugoslavia	65	—	5,321	57,339	57,339	18	22	8	B
	616	55,816	70,061	154,022	156,395	143	171	15	

Also working: Old Catholic Church of Yugoslavia.

OCEANIA

AUSTRALIA (and TASMANIA) 2,967,909 sq. mls. Pop.: 11,359,510 estimate (1965)

Church or Mission (N.B. See notes on Statistics, page xiii)	Places of Regular Worship	Communicants, Full Members (p. 57) 1962 Handbook	Communicants, Full Members (p. 57) Latest available figure	Total Christian Community (p. 57) 1962 Handbook	Total Christian Community (p. 57) Latest available figure	Staff — National Workers, full-time Ordained	Staff — National Workers, full-time Laymen	Staff — National Workers, full-time Women	Source of Information
Antioch Orthodox Church	2	—	2,000	—	3,500	2	—	—	C
Armenian Apostolic Church	2	—	6,000	—	6,000	2	4	2	C
Assemblies of God	140	2,400	4,000	3,100	7,000	130	45	10	C
Aborigines Inland Mission (People's Church of the A.I.M.)	60	—	—	—	—	—	—	—	B
Australia Aborigines Mission	38	—	2,200	—	2,200	2	54	66	A
Baptist Union of Australia	604	37,283	44,251	130,000	149,819	12	20	25	A
Baptist Union of Queensland	(158)	—	(6,844)	—	(15,000)*	646	—	—	A
Baptist Union of Western Australia	(53)	—	(2,682)	—	(9,500)	—	—	—	C
Brethren	—	7,000	—	16,384	15,523	—	—	—	A
Church of the Nazarene	19	—	600	—	3,002	—	—	—	B & C
Churches of Christ	380	26,000	43,149	79,264	95,641	17	20	7	C
Congregational Union	380	16,000	15,195	70,000	73,526	316	3	84	C
Church of England (Australia and Tasmania)	2,500	1,200,000	1,200,000	3,408,850	3,668,931	192	—	9	C
C.M.S. Diocese of Carpentaria	38	—	11,575	—	11,575	39	119	—	B
Evangelical Lutheran Church	446	28,180	32,507	45,166	50,922	151	30	40	B
Greek Orthodox Church	50	—	200,000	—	200,000	50	—	—	C
Liberal Catholic Church	14	—	1,400	—	1,600	36	—	—	C
Methodist Church	3,700	—	172,601	977,933	1,000,000	1,170	119	60	A
Methodist Aborigine Work in M.A.	5	106	106	1,630	1,630	6	59	—	E
Presbyterian Church	685	—	137,549	869,242	976,518	765	—	36	A
Presbyterian Church Aborigines	8	501	653	1,550	1,600	6	27	—	A
Presbyterian Church Chinese	1	—	180	—	180	1	—	—	A
Religious Society of Friends	11	653	901	824	1,101	—	—	—	A
Reformed Churches of Australia	46	—	3,320	—	7,650	35	4	2	C
Russian Orthodox Church	24	—	—	—	60,000	34	20	6	C

209

AUSTRALIA—*continued*

Church or Mission *N.B. See notes on Statistics, page xiii*	Places of Regular Worship	Communicants, Full Members (p. 57)		Total Christian Community (p. 57)		Staff — National Workers, full-time			Source of Information
		1962 Handbook	Latest available figure	1962 Handbook	Latest available figure	Ordained	Laymen	Women	
Salvation Army	897	24,602	24,732	73,371	82,722	2,077	2,242	2,126	C
Serbian Orthodox Church	17	—	1,800	—	13,500*	10	15	5	C
Seventh-day Adventists	845†	23,429	54,098†	53,265	92,639†	707	1,126†	926†	C
Ukrainian Autocephalous Orthodox Church	15	—	11,000	—	25,000	22	34	—	C
United Church in N.A. and the Territories	9	—	760	—	9,000	11	1	10	C
United Evangelical Lutheran Church	496	32,379	37,128	54,515	63,887	162	1	4	A
Finke River Mission	24	480	647	1,200	1,397	—	—	—	B
Hope Vale Mission	2	109	137	380	456	—	—	—	B
Koombha Mission	—	—	342	—	579	—	—	—	B
Yalata Mission	—	—	76	—	229	—	—	—	B
Wesleyan Methodist Church	11	60	250	900	1,000*	12	3	—	B
Protestant (Undefined)	—	45,000	45,000	95,408	98,551	—	—	—	C
	11,469	1,444,182	2,073,732	5,882,982	6,738,453	6,613	2,946	3,418	

(‡ +++++++++ among Aborigines — Finke River, Hope Vale, Koombha, Yalata Missions)

* Estimate. † Figures include Australia, New Guinea, New Hebrides. ‡ Among Aborigines.

Figures in brackets are not included in totals.

Also working: Wycliffe Bible Translators. Church of Christ, Scientist. New Tribes Mission. Christian Radio Missionary Fellowship. Evangelization Society of S. Australia.

COOK ISLANDS 93 sq. mls. Pop.: 20,519 (1964)

Anglican Church in Polynesia	—	80	80	80	80	—	—	—	E
Cook Islands Christian Church :: a	24	2,000	2,000	13,067	13,067	23	—	—	E
Seventh-day Adventists	12	398	399	1,173	1,321	3	26	—	B
	36	2,478	2,479	14,310	14,468	26	26	—	

Co-operating: a London Missionary Society.

FIJI ISLANDS 7,036 sq. mls. Pop.: 456,390 estimate (1964)

Assemblies of God	109	367	925	682	8,562	—	116	—	B
Church of the Province of New Zealand, Diocese of Polynesia :: a	12	4,000	3,500	6,000	6,000*	137	10	734	A
Methodist Church of Australia	739	31,914	31,914	138,784	135,000	12	—	—	A & E
Seventh-day Adventists	39	1,669	3,292	3,463	6,979	—	(83)U	—	B
	899	37,950	39,631	148,929	156,541	149	209 (83)U	734	

* Estimate.   U Unclassified.

Co-operating: a U.S.P.G.

FRENCH POLYNESIA 4,000 sq. mls. Pop.: 84,550 (1962)

Church or Mission N.B. See notes on Statistics, page xiii	Places of Regular Worship	Communicants, Full Members (p. 57)		Total Christian Community (p. 57)		Staff — National Workers, full-time			Source of Information
		1962 Handbook	Latest available figure	1962 Handbook	Latest available figure	Ordained	Laymen	Women	
Seventh-day Adventists	8	453	671	453	1,757	6a	3a	—	B
Société des Missions Evangéliques de Paris	68	4,000	4,000	40,000	40,000	50	3	—	E
	76	4,453	4,671	40,453	41,757	56	6	—	

a National and foreign.

Also working: Church of the Province of New Zealand, Diocese of Polynesia.

GILBERT and ELLICE ISLANDS

Gilbert Islands: 100 sq. mls. Pop.: 38,147 (1963)
Ellice Islands: 9½ sq. mls. Pop.: 6,763 (1964)

Church or Mission	Places of Regular Worship	Communicants, Full Members (p. 57)		Total Christian Community (p. 57)		Staff — National Workers, full-time			Source of Information
		1962 Handbook	Latest available figure	1962 Handbook	Latest available figure	Ordained	Laymen	Women	
Church of God (Cleveland)	3	46	49	179	150	3	—	—	B
Ellice Islands Church	8	2,100	3,822	4,900	5,371	9	6	—	A
Gilbertese Protestant Church	a 124	6,275	6,275	23,848	20,500	101	2	23	A & B
Seventh-day Adventists	2	119	225	400	1,111	2	(28)U	—	B
	137	8,540	10,368	29,327	27,132	115	36 (28)U	23	

U Unclassified.

Co-operating: a London Missionary Society.
Also working: Church of the Province of New Zealand, Diocese of Polynesia (U.S.P.G. co-operating).

GUAM 209 sq. mls. Pop.: 46,993 estimate (1965)

Assemblies of God ...	1	30	25	70	140	—	—	A
Protestant Episcopal Church	1	—	147	—	252	—	—	B
Seventh-day Adventists ...	5	403	403	403	403	6	19	E
Southern Baptist Convention	2	—	225	—	742	—	—	B
	9	433	800	473	1,537	6	19	19

Also working: Church of Christ, Scientist.

MARSHALL ISLANDS 150 sq. mls. Pop.: 18,062 (1965)

Assemblies of God ...	7	—	35	—	272	(5)U	—	B
	7	—	35	—	272	(5)U	—	

U Unclassified.

213

NAURU 5,263 acres. Pop.: 4,914 (1964)

Church or Mission *N.B.* See notes on Statistics, page xiii	Places of Regular Worship	Communicants, Full Members (p. 57)		Total Christian Community (p. 57)		Staff — National Workers, full-time			Source of Information
		1962 Handbook	Latest available figure	1962 Handbook	Latest available figure	Ordained	Laymen	Women	
Anglican Church in Polynesia ... :	—	48	48	148	148	—	—	—	E
Nauruan Protestant Church ... a	8	700	700	2,400	2,400	1	2	—	E
	8	748	748	2,548	2,548	1	2	—	

Co-operating: a London Missionary Society.

NEW CALEDONIA 7,374 sq. mls. Pop.: 86,500 (1963)

	Places of Regular Worship	1962 Handbook	Latest available figure	1962 Handbook	Latest available figure	Ordained	Laymen	Women	Source
Seventh-day Adventists ... :	3	40	112	51	316	1	2	—	B
Société des Missions Evangéliques de Paris ... :	119	3,516	3,516	16,000	16,000	90	3	7	E
	122	3,556	3,628	16,051	16,316	91	5	7	

214

NEW GUINEA 92,160 sq. mls. Pop.: 1,539,076 estimate (1964)

Anglican Church in Australia and Tasmania, Diocese of New Guinea	—	20,000	20,000	20,000	20,000	—	—	—	E
Australian Lutheran Mission	98	3,052	3,590	4,649	6,515	7	3	4	B
Church of the Nazarene	12	200	188	600	3,000	1	11	3	B
Evangelical Lutheran Church ... a	1,871	113,796	164,949	208,222	302,096	36	22	15	A
Methodist Mission ... *	161	—	3,927	—	16,440	4	161	—	B
New Tribes Mission	2	—	—	—	—	—	—	—	B
South Sea Mission	39	65	1,500	1,487	4,500	—	70	3	A
Wabag Lutheran Church	390	—	9,362	—	15,776	—	531	—	B
Wesleyan Mission	21	—	51	—	800	—	(26)U	—	B
	2,594	137,113	203,567	234,958	369,127	48	824 (26)U	25	

* Figures include Papua. U Unclassified

Co-operating: a United Evangelical Lutheran Church in Australia.
Also working: Wycliffe Bible Translators. Liebenzeller Mission. Missionary Aviation Fellowship. Christian Radio Missionary Fellowship. Seventh-day Adventists (see Australia).

NEW HEBRIDES 5,700 sq. mls. Pop.: 65.800 estimate (1964)

Apostolic Church Missionary Movement	2	250	250	500	500	—	—	—	E
Australian Churches of Christ	56	2,000	2,000	3,800	3,800	—	50	20	E
John G. Paton Mission Fund	—	800	800	6,000	6,000	5	—	—	E
Presbyterian Church (Australia) ... a	205	3,750	8,464	11,000	25,000	38	356	1	A
Presbyterian Church (New Zealand)	200	7,662	7,662	24,290	24,290	30	300	5	E
Seventh-day Adventists	14	1,447	2,473	3,000	5,495	10	(77)U	—	B
	477	15,909	21,649	48,590	65,085	83	783 77(U)	26	

U Unclassified.

Co-operating: a Australian Presbyterian Board of Missions.
Also working: Anglican Church of Melanesia. (For figures see Solomon Islands.)

NEW ZEALAND   103,736 sq. mls.   Pop.: 2,640,117 estimate (1965)

Church or Mission N.B. See notes on Statistics, page xiii	Places of Regular Worship	Communicants, Full Members (p. 57)		Total Christian Community (p. 57)		Staff — National Workers, full-time			Source of Information
		1962 Handbook	Latest available figure	1962 Handbook	Latest available figure	Ordained	Laymen	Women	
Apostolic Church	34	—	500†	—	1,399	—	15	—	C
Associated Churches of Christ	51	4,351	4,351	11,937	10,485	39	—	—	C
Baptist Union	162	14,789	14,789	31,518	40,886	—	—	—	C
Brethren	76	8,500	8,500	21,398	25,764	—	—	—	C
Christadelphian	—	—	500†	—	1,498	—	—	—	C
Church of the Nazarene	8	—	127	—	791	7	—	—	D
Church of the Province of N.Z. (Anglican)	877*	75,486	75,486	751,994	835,434	—	—	—	C
Commonwealth Covenant Church	—	—	200†	—	875	—	—	—	C
Congregational Union	26	2,508	3,529	5,039	5,864	24	—	—	C
Eastern Orthodox	—	—	2,100†	—	3,328	12	—	—	A
Evangelical Lutheran Church	48	800	1,400	4,000	4,817	12	—	—	B & C
Latter-Day Saints (Mormons)	—	3,500	3,500	10,008	17,978	—	—	—	A
Methodist Church	658	38,000	32,749	160,000	173,838	297	38	41	A
Presbyterian Church	1,320	85,080	90,542	505,503	566,174	475	56	40	A
Religious Society of Friends (Quakers)	14	418	649	1,200	943	—	—	—	A
Salvation Army	178	6,490	6,490	16,999	15,454	167	225U	352	C
Seventh-day Adventists	60	5,612	6,643	12,600	13,754	44	(113)U	—	B
	3,518	245,534	252,473	1,532,196	1,720,072	1,055	447 (113)U	433	

U Unclassified.

OCEANIA

NEW ZEALAND—continued

Population 167,086. Maoris (1961 Census)

Apostolic	269
Brethren	1,569
Church of England	51,148
Church of Christ	178
Commonwealth Covenant Church	360
Congregational	336
Latter-Day Saints (Mormons)	12,179
Methodist	12,611
Presbyterian	3,947
Ratana	21,954
Roman Catholic	28,656
Salvation Army	153
Seventh-day Adventists	622
	133,982

* Churches—Regular services are also held in 893 other places, i.e. schools, halls, etc.   † Estimate.

Also working: Auckland Missionary Society. Christian Literature Crusade. Church of Christ, Scientist. Church of God of Prophecy. New Tribes Mission. The Navigators.

NIUE

100 sq. mls.   Pop.: 5,145 (1965)

Niuean Church (L.M.S.)	13	500	500	4,188	4,188	12	—	—	E
	13	500	500	4,188	4,188	12	—	—

217

OCEANIA

PAPUA
86,100 sq. mls. Pop.: 561,740 estimate (1964)

Church or Mission (N.B. See notes on Statistics, page xiii)	Places of Regular Worship	Communicants, Full Members (p. 57) 1962 Handbook	Communicants Latest available figure	Total Christian Community (p. 57) 1962 Handbook	Total Latest available figure	Staff Ordained	Laymen	Women	Source of Information
Barnu River Mission	3	30	100	500	600	5	3	4	A
Methodist Mission *	161	—	3,927	—	16,440	4	161	—	A
Methodist Overseas Missions (Australia)	1,108	18,086	18,086	94,380	90,000	11	474	—	E & A
Papua Ekalesia (L.M.S.)	528	15,070	23,182	30,000	62,368	218	279	22	A
Seventh-day Adventists	54	—	7,255	—	23,229	22	175	—	B
Unevangelized Fields Mission	96	—	1,360	—	6,000	—	96	—	A
	1,950	33,186	53,910	124,880	198,637	260	1,187 (96)	26	

* Figures include New Guinea.

Also working: Missionary Aviation Fellowship. Presbyterian Church.

SAMOA
American Samoa: 76 sq. mls. Pop.: 20,051 (1960)
Western Samoa: 1,097 sq. mls. Pop.: 130,000 estimate (1964)

Church or Mission	Places of Regular Worship	Communicants, Full Members 1962 Handbook	Communicants Latest available figure	Total Christian Community 1962 Handbook	Total Latest available figure	Ordained	Laymen	Women	Source of Information
Assemblies of God	11	268	604	526	1,519	15	—	—	B
Church of the Nazarene	1	—	24	—	127	—	—	—	B
Church of the Province of New Zealand (Diocese of Polynesia) ...a	—	—	1,191	—	1,191	—	—	—	E
Congregational Christian Church ...b	244	18,691	18,691	67,735	67,735	300	23	17	B & E
Methodist Overseas Church (Australian)	71	6,140	6,140	17,549	16,000	3	(38)U	—	B
Seventh-day Adventists	10	637	1,207	1,711	2,704	7	—	—	B
	337	25,736	27,857	87,521	89,276	325	61 (38)U	17	

U Unclassified.

Co-operating: a U.S.P.G. b London Missionary Society.

SOLOMON ISLANDS (BRITISH)   Land Area: 11,500 sq. mls.   Pop.: 136,750 estimate (1965)

Anglican Church of the Province of N.Z. Diocese of Melanesia *	650	20,000	20,000	35,000	35,000	118	800	—	A
Methodist Church	252	7,970	7,790	21,339	22,600	25	251	17	B
Seventh-day Adventists	150	8,048	11,059	10,176	31,602	43	(545)U	—	A
South Sea Evangelical Church	285	5,000	7,500	24,853	45,000	—	560	—	A
	1,337	41,018	46,349	91,368	134,202	186	2,155 (544)U	17	

* Figures include New Hebrides.   U Unclassified.

TOKELAU ISLAND   4 sq. mls.   Pop.: 1,835 (1964)

Church in Tokelau	2	256	256	874	874	2	—	—	E
	2	256	256	874	874	2	—	—	

U Unclassified.

TONGA   270 sq. mls.   Pop.: 71,412 estimate (1964)

Church of the Province of N. Zealand (Diocese of Polynesia) a	3	500	500	3,500	3,500	1	2	—	E
Church of Tonga	—	1,719	1,719	6,000	6,000	128	105	—	E
Free Church of Tonga	—	3,200	3,200	10,000	10,000	—	—	—	E
Methodist Overseas Mission (Australian)	147	7,587	7,587	29,403	32,000	57	196	—	B
Seventh-day Adventists	118	514	1,004	1,100	2,331	5	(37)U	—	B
	161	13,520	14,010	50,003	53,831	191	340 (37)U		

Co-operating: a U.S.P.G.

TOTALS BY CONTINENTS

PROTESTANT AND ANGLICAN COMMUNIONS

Continent	Population		Places of Regular Worship	Communicants Full Members (p. 57)	Total Christian Community (p. 57)
	1962 Handbook	1967 Estimate†			
Africa ...	231,000,000	306,173,000	114,790	8,109,106	21,608,509
America, North*	256,000,000	290,730,000	323,047	69,757,555	76,756,443
America, South	134,000,000	167,300,000	40,085	5,286,925	10,311,500
Asia ...	1,591,000,000	1,827,861,000	87,993	8,583,828	18,545,389
Europe	420,000,000	440,303,000	} 137,315	82,902,695	179,415,167
U.S.S.R. in Europe and Asia	208,827,000	231,000,000			
Oceania	15,800,000	18,711,000	23,207	2,761,906	9,649,073
Estimated Totals ...	—	3,280,522,000	726,437	177,402,015	316,286,081
As estimated in the 1962 Handbook ...	2,856,627,000	—	721,717	133,928,540	263,741,783

* The figures given for the U.S.A. are for "Inclusive Church Membership". We have therefore included them in the tables above, both in the "Communicants" and "Community" columns.

† Population figures from, *World Population Prospects*, United Nations (1965).

ESTIMATED WORLD FIGURES FOR SOME OF THE LARGER PROTESTANT COMMUNIONS*

Lutherans ...	Baptized Members 77,948,394	
Baptists ...	55/65,000,000	(Baptized membership 27,183,622)
Presbyterian and Reformed ...	50/55,000,000†	(Adult membership 19,100,000)
Methodists ...	41,500,000	
Anglicans ...	40,000,000	
Congregationalists ...	6,000,000	(Adult membership 3,250,000)
Seventh-day Adventists ...	3,830,000	(Adult membership 1,578,500)

* As more and more Churches throughout the world enter into unions, these classifications become less clearly defined.

† This figure includes both the membership of Churches in the World Alliance of Reformed Churches (WARC) as well as those of the Reformed and Presbyterian Churches outside its membership; these latter would number between 2–4 million members.

ROMAN CATHOLICS

AFRICA	Catholics	Source
Algeria	535,000	H.C.
Angola	1,915,000	A.P.
Basutoland (Lesotho)	322,000	A.P.
Bechuanaland (Botswana)	8,000	A.P.
Burundi	1,570,000	A.P.
Cameroon	950,000	H.C.
Cape Verde Is	212,000	A.P.
Central African Republic	180,000	H.C.
Chad	89,000	H.C.
Comoro Islands	1,000	B.M.
Congo (Brazzaville)	320,000	H.C.
Congo (Leopoldville (Kinshasa)	5,650,000	H.C.
Dahomey	300,000	H.C.
Ethiopia	125,000	H.C.
French Somaliland	5,000	A.P.
Gabon	234,000	A.P.
Gambia	6,000	A.P.
Ghana	740,000	H.C.
Guinea	28,000	H.C.
Ivory Coast	280,000	H.C.
Kenya	1,050,000	H.C.
Liberia	14,000	H.C.
Libya	40,000	H.C.
Madagascar	910,000	H.C.
Malawi (Nyasaland)	580,000	H.C.
Mali	31,000	H.C.
Mauritania: *See* Senegal	*	
Mauritius	236,000	A.P.
Morocco	400,000	H.C.
Mozambique	895,000	H.C.
Niger	32,000	H.C.
Nigeria	2,250,000	H.C.
Portuguese Guinea	27,000	H.C.
Reunion	366,000	A.P.
Rhodesia (Southern Rhodesia)	335,000	H.C.
Rwanda	800,000	A.P.
Saint Helena and Ascension Island ...	‡	C.D.E.W
Sao Tome and Principe	50,000	A.P.
Senegal	147,000	H.C.
Seychelles	43,000	A.P.
Sierra Leone	32,000	H.C.
Somalia	8,000	H.C.
South Africa	1,187,000	C.D.S.A.
South-West Africa	76,000	N.C.
Spanish Equatorial Region	*	
Spanish North Africa	*	
Spanish Sahara and Ifni	*	
Sudan	415,000	H.C.
Swaziland	28,000	A.P.
Tanzania	2,400,000	H.C.
Togo	265,000	H.C.
Tunisia	40,000	H.C.
Uganda	2,250,000	H.C.
United Arab Republic	162,000	H.C.
Upper Volta	180,000	H.C.
Zambia (Northern Rhodesia)	550,000	H.C.
ROUNDED TOTAL	29,100,000	ISS/FERES

221

ASIA (excluding Oceania)	*Catholics*	*Source*
Aden: *See* South Arabia	*	
Afghanistan	‡	B.M.
Bahrain: *See* South Arabia	*	
Bhoutan	‡	B.M.
Brunei	2,000	ISS/FERES
Burma	222,000	H.C.
Cambodia	55,000	H.C.
Ceylon	720,000	H.C.
China: People's Republic	2,200,000	H.C.
China: Taiwan (Formosa)	266,000	H.C.
Cyprus	5,000	C.D.E.W.
Hawaii *See* U.S.A.	†	
Hong Kong	215,000	H.C.
India, Nepal, Sikkim	6,625,000	H.C.
Indonesia (excluding West Irian) ...	1,485,000	H.C. & A.P.
Iran	21,000	H.C.
Iraq	125,000	H.C.
Israel	76,000	H.C.
Japan	315,000	H.C.
Jordan	16,000	H.C.
Korea (North)	*	
Korea (Republic)	650,000	H.C.
Kuwait	5,000	A.P.
Laos	27,000	H.C.
Lebanon	650,000	H.C. & C.D.E.W.
Macao (Port)	36,000	A.P.
Malaysia and Singapore	265,000	H.C.
Maldives	‡	B.M.
Mongolia	*	
Muscat and Oman: *See* South Arabia ...	*	
Nepal: *See* India	*	
Pakistan	341,000	H.C.
Philippines	23,000,000	H.C.
Qatar: *See* South Arabia	*	
Ryu-Kyu Islands (U.S.A.): *See* Japan ...	*	
Saudi Arabia	‡	B.M.
South Arabia Fed.	10,000	H.C.
Sikkim: *See* India	*	
Syria	251,000	H.C.
Thailand	116,000	H.C.
Timor (Port)	122,000	A.P.
Trucial Oman: *See* South Arabia ...	*	
Turkey	20,000	H.C.
Vietnam (North)	680,000	H.C.
Vietnam (Republic)	1,595,000	H.C.
West Irian	90,000	A.P.
Yemen	‡	B.M.
ROUNDED TOTAL	53,200,000	ISS/FERES

ROMAN CATHOLICS—*continued*

EUROPE					*Catholics*	*Source*
Albania	...	...	...	...	75,000	H.C.
Austria	...	...	...	...	6,410,000	H.C.
Belgium	...	...	...	...	8,700,000	H.C.
Bulgaria	...	...	...	...	32,000	H.C.
Canary Is. ...	...	...	...	...	474,000	A.P.
Czechoslovakia	...	...	...	...	6,900,000	H.C.
Denmark	...	...	...	...	27,000	H.C.
Finland	...	...	...	...	2,000	H.C.
France	...	...	...	...	39,500,000	H.C.
Germany: Total	...	...	...	...	27,500,000	H.C.
West	...	...	...	...	*	
East	...	...	...	...	*	
Gibraltar	...	...	...	...	21,000	C.D.E.W.
Great Britain:						
England and Wales		...	...	...	4,000,000	C.D.E.W.
Scotland ...	...	...	...	...	810,000	C.D.E.W.
Greece	...	...	...	...	46,000	H.C.
Hungary	...	...	...	...	6,000,000	H.C.
Iceland	...	...	...	...	1,000	H.C.
Ireland:						
Northern ...	...	...	...	...	498,000	C.D.E.W.
Eire	...	...	...	...	2,673,000	C.D.E.W.
Italy	...	...	...	...	46,300,000	H.C.
Luxembourg	...	...	...	...	309,000	H.C.
Malta	...	...	...	...	319,000	H.C.
Monaco	...	...	...	...	23,000	H.C.
Netherlands	...	...	...	...	4,810,000	H.C.
Norway	...	...	...	...	8,000	H.C.
Poland	...	...	...	...	28,000,000	H.C.
Portugal	...	...	...	...	8,600,000	H.C.
Rumania	...	...	...	...	2,700,000	H.C.
Spain	...	...	...	...	31,200,000	H.C.
Sweden	...	...	...	...	34,000	H.C.
Switzerland ...	...	...	...	...	2,500,000	H.C.
U.S.S.R.	...	...	...	...	3,000,000	H.C.
Yugoslavia ...	...	...	...	...	6,125,000	H.C.
ROUNDED TOTAL					237,500,000	ISS/FERES

NORTH AMERICA					*Catholics*	*Source*
Bermuda	...	...	...	...	4,000	A.P.
Canada	...	...	...	...	7,900,000	H.C.
Greenland ...	...	...	...	...	‡	ISS/FERES
St. Pierre and Miquelon ...		...	...	...	5,000	A.P.
United States of America ...		...	...	...	44,000,000	H.C.
ROUNDED TOTAL					52,000,000	ISS/FERES

ROMAN CATHOLICS—*continued*

CENTRAL AMERICA					*Catholics*	*Source*
Bahamas ...	...	...	...	...	27,000	A.P.
British Honduras ...	...	...	...	64,000	A.P.
British West Indies	...	...	...	320,000	A.P.
Canal Zone: *See* Panama ...	...	...		*	
Costa Rica ...	...	...	...	...	970,000	H.C.
Cuba ...	...	...	...	...	6,000,000	H.C.
Dominican Republic	...	...	...	3,350,000	H.C.
El Salvador ...	...	...	...	...	2,100,000	H.C.
Guadeloupe	...	...	...	...	307,000	A.P.
Guatemala ...	...	...	...	...	4,230,000	H.C.
Haiti ...	...	...	...	...	2,900,000	H.C.
Honduras ...	...	...	...	...	1,500,000	H.C.
Jamaica ...	...	...	...	...	130,000	H.C.
Martinique ...	...	...	...	...	285,000	A.P.
Mexico ...	...	...	...	35,000,000	H.C.
Netherlands Antilles	...	...	...	145,000	A.P.
Nicaragua ...	...	...	...	...	1,350,000	H.C.
Panama ...	...	...	...	...	1,130,000	H.C.
Puerto Rico ...	...	...	...	2,300,000	H.C.
Trinidad and Tobago	...	...	...	340,000	A.P.
Virgin Islands (U.S.)	...	...	...	14,000	A.P.
ROUNDED TOTAL					62,500,000	ISS/FERES

SOUTH AMERICA					*Catholics*	*Source*
Argentina ...	...	...	...	...	20,400,000	H.C.
Bolivia ...	...	...	...	...	3,600,000	H.C.
Brazil ...	...	...	...	...	70,200,000	H.C.
British Guiana (Guyana) ...	...	...	96,000	H.C.
Chile ...	...	...	...	...	6,700,000	H.C.
Colombia ...	...	...	...	...	15,000,000	H.C.
Ecuador ...	...	...	...	...	4,380,000	H.C.
Falkland Islands ...	...	...	...	*	
French Guiana ...	...	...	...	32,000	A.P.
Paraguay ...	...	...	...	...	1,850,000	H.C.
Peru ...	...	...	...	...	10,500,000	H.C.
Surinam (Dutch Guiana) ...	...	...	66,000	A.P.
Uruguay ...	...	...	...	...	2,220,000	H.C.
Venezuela ...	...	...	...	...	7,750,000	H.C.
ROUNDED TOTAL					143,000,000	ISS/FERES

OCEANIA	*Catholics*	*Source*
American Samoa: *See* W. Samoa ...	*	
Australia	2,590,000	H.C.
British Solomon Islands	28,000	A.P.
Cook Islands (N.Z.)	2,000	A.P.
Fiji Islands (Br.)	35,000	A.P.
French Polynesia	27,000	A.P.
Gilbert and Ellice Is.	23,000	A.P.
Guam	55,000	A.P.
Nauru (Austr. Trust): *See* Gilbert and Ellice Is.	*	
New Caledonia	61,000	A.P.
New Guinea (Austr. Trust)	386,000	A.P.
New Hebrides (Fr. and Br.)	11,000	A.P.
New Zealand	365,000	H.C.
Niue (N.Z.): *See* Tonga	*	
Pacific Islands (U.S.A. Trust)	31,000	A.P.
Papua	53,000	A.P.
Tokelau Islands (N.Z.): *See* W. Samoa ...	*	
Tonga (and Niue)	12,000	A.P.
Wallis and Futuna: *See* New Caledonia...	*	
Western Samoa (N.Z. Trust)	33,000	A.P.
ROUNDED TOTAL	3,700,000	ISS/FERES
WORLD TOTAL	581,000,000	

NOTES: These figures are derived from several different sources. Their reliability is very uneven: in many cases there are alternative sources giving higher or lower figures. Most of the figures relate to the middle of 1964.

All figures are rounded.

H.C. *Herder Correspondence*, July 1966 (based mainly on the figures published in the 1965 edition of the *Anuario Pontificio*.)

A.P. *Anuario Pontificio*, 1965 or 1966 edition.

B.M. *Bilan du Monde*, Vol. II, 1964.

C.D.E.W. *Catholic Directory* (England and Wales), 1966.

C.D.S.A. *Catholic Directory of Southern Africa*, 1966.

ISS/FERES. Estimates made by HQ Staff of ISS/FERES Project, London

* Not available.

† Not applicable.

‡ Nil or less than 500.

COMPARATIVE CHRISTIAN STATISTICS

Continent*	Protestant and Anglican Latest available Estimate†	Orthodox and Eastern Latest available Estimate‡		Roman Catholic Latest available Estimate
Africa	21,608,509	17,500,000		29,100,000
America, North	76,756,443	⎫	North	52,000,000
America, South	10,311,500	3,250,000 ⎬	Central	62,500,000
		⎭	South	143,000,000
Asia	18,545,389	1,450,000		53,200.000
Europe (Includes U.S.S.R. in Europe and Asia)	179,415,167	99,000,000§		237,500,000
Oceania	9,649,073	90,770		3,700,000
Totals	316,286,081	122,100,770		581,000,000
Totals as Estimated in 1962 Handbook	263,741,783	96,707,653		493,582,509

* For Population see previous table.
† Total Christian Community.
‡ For further classification see page 11.
§ Includes small groups in various countries.

AFRICAN INDEPENDENT CHURCHES

Membership Statistics for a Selection of Bodies

Notes: 1. The official English, French or Portuguese names are given here, though vernacular versions are often preferred.
2. Statistics either are supplied by the churches themselves, checked as reasonable by observers, or are estimated from government and mission records.
3. The figures are of adherents (i.e. total community), except those followed by **m**, which are full adult members.
4. Most churches have grown rapidly over the years, although a few had lost most of their membership by 1966.
5. Initials are given when frequently used to refer to a body.

Nation	Church	Year Begun	Adherents	Date of Estimate
Angola	Igreja do Nosso Senhor Jesus Cristo	1949	10,000	1963
Burundi	Eglise de Dieu au Burundi	1963	20,000	1964
Cameroun	Eglise Baptiste Camerounaise (EBC)	1888	30,000	1965
	Eglise Protestante Africaine (EPA)	1934	10,000	1965
Central African Republic	Comité Baptiste	1956	5,000 m	1966
Congo-Kinshasa	Eglise de Jésus-Christ sur la terre par le Prophète Simon Kimbangu (EJCSK)	1921	200,000 m	1966
	Eglise des Noirs	1939	15,000	1966
	Mission des Fidèles Protestants	1957	7,535	1966
	Eglise Protestante Baptiste du Kivu (EPROBA)	1960	9,000 m	1960
Dahomey	Mission d'Union Africaine	1899	1,400	1965
Ethiopia	Kambatta Evangelical Church	1955	10,000 m	1966
Ghana	Army of the Cross of Christ Church	1923	19,800	1959
	The Saviour Church	c 1925	7,000 m	1962
	Apostolic Revelation Society	1939	60,000 m	1960
Ivory Coast	Eglise Harriste	1913	68,776	1965
	Eglise Déimatiste	1923	90,000	1958
	Eglise Adaïste	1932	5,000	1948
Kenya	African Orthodox Church (AOC)	1935	23,000 m	1965
	African Israel Church (AIC)	1942	60,000	1965
	African Brotherhood Church (ABC)	1945	30,000 m	1966
	African Christian Church and Schools (ACC & S)	1949	14,000	1962
	Church of Christ in Africa (CCA)	1957	75,000	1965
	Legion of Mary Church	1963	90,000	1964

227

Membership Statistics for a Selection of Bodies—continued

Nation	Church	Year Begun	Adherents	Date of Estimate
Madagascar	Eglise Protestante Malgache Tranozozoro Antranobiriky (FMTA)	1894	4,000	1966
	Eglise Baptiste Biblique à Madagascar (FBMB)	1930	5,000 m	1966
	Eglise du Réveil (Disciples du Seigneur)	1955	50,000 m	1966
	Eglise Réformée Indépendante de Madagascar (MET)	1955	20,000	1966
	Eglise du Réveil Spirituel Malgache (FPPM)	1958	5,000 m	1966
Malawi	Providence Industrial Mission	1900	25,258 m	1962
	Faithful Church of Christ	1950	1,000 m	1960
Nigeria	United Native African Church (UNAC)	1891	28,130 m	1964
	African Church Inc.	1901	48,168	1964
	Cherubim and Seraphim	1925	50,000 m	1965
	Church of the Lord Aladura	1930	5,000	1966
	Christ Apostolic Church (CAC)	1931	94,000 m	1965
Rhodesia	Apostolic Church of Johane Marangi	1933	50,000 m	1965
	City of Jehovah (Guta ra Jehova)	1952	50,000	1952
	Christian Marching Church of Central Africa	1954	1,200 m	1966
Sierra Leone	God is Our Light Church	1952	1,000	1965
South Africa	Zulu Congregational Church	1896	8,000	1961
	African Presbyterian Church	1898	20,000	1903
	Ethiopian Catholic Church in Zion	1904	18,819	1957
	Church of Christ	1910	120,000 m	1963
	Nazirite Baptist Church	1911	50,000	1961
	Zion Christian Church	1914	200,000	1966
	African Congregational Church	1917	45,000 m	1944
South West Africa	Herero Church	1955	10,000	1966
Tanzania	Church of the Holy Spirit	1954	4,000 m	1960
	Tanganyika African Church (TAC)	1956	3,000 m	1960
Uganda	Society of the One Almighty God (KOAB)	1914	56,952	1960
	African Greek Orthodox Church (AGOC)	1929	10,291	1946
Zambia	Lumpa Church	1954	100,000	1961

WORLD JEWISH POPULATION
Taken from the *American Jewish Year Book*, 1966

AFRICA

Country	Estimated Jewish Population	
	1961 Year Book	1966 Year Book
Algeria	130,000	3,000
Congo	1,000	500
Egypt (U.A.R.)	13,500	2,500
Ethiopia	12,000	12,000
Kenya	1,000	800
Libya	3,750	6,000
Morocco	200,000	70,000
Rhodesia	5,000	5,500
South Africa	110,000	6,000
Tunisia	65,000	3,000
Zambia	1,500	800
TOTAL ...	542,750	240,100

NORTH AND SOUTH AMERICA

Country	Estimated Jewish Population	
	1961 Year Book	1966 Year Book
Barbados	100	100
Canada	250,000	275,000
Costa Rica	1,500	1,500
Cuba	8,000	2,400
Curaçao	1,000	700
Dominican Republic	600	400
El Salvador	300	300
Guatemala	900	1,200
Haiti	200	150
Honduras	150	150
Jamaica	1,400	1,500
Mexico	26,000	30,000
Nicaragua	200	200
Panama	2,000	2,000
Trinidad	400	400
U.S.A.	5,531,500	5,720,000
Total North America and West Indies	5,824,250	6,036,000
Argentina	400,000	450,000
Bolivia	4,000	4,000
Brazil	125,000	130,000
Chile	30,000	30,000
Colombia	10,000	10,000
Ecuador	2,000	2,000
Paraguay	1,200	1,200
Peru	3,500	4,000
Surinam	1,000	500
Uruguay	45,000	50,000
Venezuela	8,500	8,500
Total South America	630,200	690,200
Total ...	6,454,450	6,726,200

ASIA

Country	Estimated Jewish Population	
	1961 Year Book	1966 Year Book
Aden	800	400
Afghanistan	4,000	800
Burma	500	200
China...	250	200
Cyprus	150	100
Hong Kong	200	200
India	25,400	16,000
Indonesia	200	100
Iran	80,000	80,000
Iraq	6,000	6,000
Israel	1,880,000	2,299,000
Japan	1,000	1,000
Lebanon	7,000	6,000
Pakistan	400	300
Philippines	500	500
Singapore	750	750
Syria	5,000	4,000
Yemen	3,500	2,000
Total ...	2,015,650	2,417,550

EUROPE

Country	Estimated Jewish Population	
	1961 Year Book	1966 Year Book
Albania	300	300
Austria	10,200	12,000
Belgium	35,150	40,500
Bulgaria	7,000	7,000
Czechoslovakia	18,000	18,000
Denmark	6,000	6,000
Finland	1,500	1,500
France...	350,000	520,000
Germany (incl. E. Germany) ...	30,000	31,000
Gibraltar	650	650
Great Britain	450,000	450,000
Greece...	6,500	6,500
Hungary	100,000	80,000
Ireland	5,400	5,400
Italy	35,000	35,000
Luxembourg	1,000	1,000
Malta	50	50
Netherlands	27,000	23,000
Norway	900	800
Poland	40,000	25,000
Portugal	750	750
Rumania	225,000	120,000
Spain	3,000	5,000
Sweden	14,000	13,000
Switzerland	19,050	19,950
Turkey	50,000	40,000
U.S.S.R.	2,268,000	2,486,000
Yugoslavia	7,000	7,000
TOTAL ...	3,711,450	3,955,400

WORLD JEWISH POPULATION—*continued*
AUSTRALIA AND NEW ZEALAND

Country	Estimated Jewish Population	
	1961 Year Book	1966 Year Book
Australia	64,000	67,000
New Zealand	4,500	5,000
TOTAL ...	68,500	72,000

ESTIMATES OF SOME NON-CHRISTIAN RELIGIONS, BY COUNTRIES

Country	Muslims	Buddhists	Hindus	Confucians	Others
AFRICA					
Algeria	9,000,000	—	—	—	—
Cameroon	605,000	—	—	—	—
Central African Republic	50,000	—	—	—	—
Dahomey	270,000	—	—	—	—
Ethiopia	5,000,000	—	—	—	—
Somaliland	70,000	—	—	—	—
Gabon	2,000	—	—	—	—
Gambia	220,000	—	—	—	—
Ghana	400,000	—	—	—	—
Guinea	1,500,000	—	—	—	—
Ivory Coast	680,000	—	—	—	Sikhs 11,000 / Jains 6,500 / Parsees 350
Kenya	70,000	—	46,000	—	—
Liberia	12,000	—	—	—	—
Libya	1,080,000	—	—	—	—
Madagascar	20,000	—	—	—	—
Mali	250,000	—	—	—	—
Malawi	500,000	—	—	—	—
Mauritania	700,000	—	—	—	—
Morocco	9,500,000	—	—	—	—
Mozambique	650,000	—	4,000	—	—
Niger	2,122,000	—	—	—	—
Nigeria	14,000,000	—	—	—	—
Senegal	2,000,000	—	—	—	—
Sierra Leone	740,000	—	—	—	—
Somalia	74,000	—	—	—	—
Sudan	9,000,000	—	—	—	—
Tanzania	40,000	—	21,500	(Tanzania)	Sikhs 3,000 / Jains 700 / Parsees 125
Tunisia	3,750,000	—	—	—	—
Uganda	14,000	—	20,500	—	Sikhs 1,600

NON-CHRISTIAN RELIGIONS BY COUNTRIES—continued

Country	Muslims	Buddhists	Hindus	Confucians	Others
AFRICA (contd.)					
Union of South Africa ...	150,000	2,000	220,000	500	—
United Arab Republic ...	18,000,000	—	—	—	—
Zambia	5,500	—	—	—	—
Zanzibar	200,000	—	—	—	—
AMERICA NORTH a					
Canada	15,000	8,500	—	5,500	—
U.S.A. (Includes Hawaii) ...	—	110,000	—	—	—
Trinidad and Tobago ...	50,000	—	190,500	—	—
AMERICA SOUTH					
Argentina	25,000	—	—	—	Parsis 600
Brazil	3,500	155,000	—	—	—
Chile	1,000	290	—	—	—
Guyana	30,000	—	116,000	—	—
Surinam	74,270	—	77,620	2,500	—
ASIA					
Aden	127,000	—	5,000	—	—
Afghanistan	13,500,000	—	—	—	—
Bahrein	135,000	—	1,000	—	—
Brunei	58,000	—	—	—	—
Cambodia	—	4,750,000	—	—	—
Ceylon	650,000	6,250,000	1,940,000	—	—
China	25,000,000	150,000,000	—	300,000,000	Taoists 30,000,000
Cyprus	105,000	—	—	—	—
India	48,000,000	3,500,000	370,000,000	(India)	Sikhs 8,000,000 / Jains 2,250,000 / Zoroastrians 125,000
Indonesia	84,000,000	1,000,000	—	—	—
Iran	20,000,000	—	—	(Iran)	Sunni Sect 850,000 / Parsis (Ghabrs) 10,000 / Armenians 50,000 / Nestorians 20,000

Country	Muslims	Buddhists	Hindus	Confucians	Others	
ASIA (*contd.*)						
Iraq ...	6,057,000	—	—		Yazidis	56,000
Israel ...	160,000	—	—	(Israel)	Druzes	22,500
Japan **b**	—	55,000,000	—	—	Shintoists	78,000,000
Jordan ...	1,700,000 (Sunnites)		—	—		
Lebanon ...	510,000	—	—	—	Druzes	82,000
Malaysia ...	2,000,000	90,000	800,000	—	—	
Pakistan ...	85,000,000	40,000	575,000	—	—	
Philippines ...	1,300,000	—	—	—	Druzes	117,800
Syria ...	3,300,000	—	—	—	Alawites	410,000
Thailand ...	1,030,000	24,750,000	3,500	465,000	—	
Turkey ...	28,000,000	—	—	—	—	
EUROPE						
Albania ...	1,200,000	—	—	—	—	
Bulgaria ...	750,000	—	—	—	Bulgaro-Muslims (Pomaks)	200,000
Greece ...	110,000	—	—	—	—	
U.S.S.R. ...	20/30,000,000	200,000	—	—	Yesidis	14,500
Yugoslavia ...	2,085,000	—	—	—	—	
OCEANIA						
Fiji ...	30,000	—	138,000	450	Sikhs	2,000

a. Includes Central American and the Caribbean.   **b.** These figures obviously overlap.

In formulating these tables for Non-Christian Religions we are indebted chiefly to *The Statesman's Year Book, 1966/7*; the *Britannica Book of the Year, 1966*; and the *Bilan du Monde, 1964.* Ed.

NON-CHRISTIAN RELIGIONS

Estimated World Membership of the Principal Non-Christian Religions, by Continents.

Religion	Africa	America North*	America South	Asia	Europe	Oceania	World Totals
Muslims ...	97,934,000	40,000	393,000	353,420,000	13,335,000	115,000	465,237,000
Shintoists	—	30,000	109,000	67,621,000	2,000	—	67,762,000
Taoists ...	—	15,000	18,000	52,286,000	12,000	—	52,331,000
Confucians	8,000	93,000	104,000	357,540,000	54,000	56,000	357,855,000
Buddhists	2,000	177,000	148,000	164,769,000	—	—	167,094,000
Hindus ...	312,000	54,000	589,000	406,284,000	157,000	209,000	408,991,000
Zoroastrians	—	—	—	150,000	—	—	150,000
Others, including Primitive and none ...	157,031,000	77,010,000	12,555,000	409,959,000	92,243	4,003,000	758,801,000

These estimates are mainly from the *Britannica Book of the Year, 1966*. It is pointed out that estimates vary considerably. The estimates for Muslims in China, for instance, even before the Communists took over, varied from 12 to 50 millions.

* Includes Central America and the West Indies.

DIRECTORY

Notes on the Directory Section

1. The Directory consists of two sections: (i) a brief list of ecumenical and international organizations; (ii) churches, missions and other organizations grouped alphabetically according to continents and countries. Addresses are given, also telephone numbers and postal code numbers, where these are known.

2. It is realized that some organizations, particularly missionary societies, have work in a large number of countries, but only in exceptional cases have addresses other than those of the headquarters been given.

3. So frequent is the change in the names of officials of many organizations that the use of them would quickly make the Directory Section out-of-date. It is safer for correspondence to be addressed to "The Secretary" or "The Chairman" than to a named person who may no longer hold that office. Therefore, names of persons, except for the officers of Christian Councils or similar organizations, are not given.

4. It may be necessary to refer to the Index to find where a particular organization has been placed.

5. Where the name of an organization usually employs the definite article this has been omitted to help alphabetical classification.

6. Where the year of foundation of an organization is known it appears in brackets after the name.

ECUMENICAL AND INTERNATIONAL CHRISTIAN ORGANIZATIONS

ALLIANCE OF THE REFORMED CHURCHES THROUGHOUT THE
WORLD HOLDING THE PRESBYTERIAN ORDER (World Alliance of
Reformed Churches or World Presbyterian Alliance)
150 route de Ferney, 1211 Geneva 20, Switzerland. Tel.: (022) 33 34 00
Gen. Sec.: Dr. Marcel Pradervand

BAPTIST WORLD ALLIANCE
Hdq.: 1628 16th Street, N.W., Washington, D.C.20009, U.S.A. Tel.: 265–5027
Gen. Sec.: Dr. Josef Nordenhaug
Assoc. Sec. in Europe: Dr. C. R. Goulding, 4 Southampton Row, London, W.C.1,
England. Tel.: 405/3939

EASTERN ORTHODOX EPISCOPATE
Ecumenical Patriarch: His All-Holiness Athenagoras, Archbishop of Constantinople and Ecumenical Patriarch, Phanar, Istanbul, Turkey

FRIENDS WORLD COMMITTEE FOR CONSULTATION
Hdq.: Woodbrooke, Selly Oak, Birmingham 29, England. Tel.: Selly Oak 1769
Gen. Sec.: Mrs. Blanche W. Shaffer
American Section and Fellowship Council: 152A North 15th Street, Philadelphia
2, Pa, U.S.A. (Sec.: Herbert M. Hadley)

INTERNATIONAL CONGREGATIONAL COUNCIL
110 Memorial Hall, Farringdon Street, London, E.C.4. England. Tel.: Central
2191
Sec.: Rev. Ralph F. G. Calder

INTERNATIONAL COUNCIL OF CHRISTIAN CHURCHES
Hdq.: Singel 386, Amsterdam C, The Netherlands. Tel.: (020) 248271
American office: 15 Park Row, New York 38, N.Y., U.S.A.

INTERNATIONAL FELLOWSHIP OF EVANGELICAL STUDENTS
Central Office: Chemin de Chandolin 8, Lausanne, Switzerland.
Tel.: Lausanne (021) 23 32 50
North America: 435 Rowell Building, Fresno, California 93721, U.S.A.
Tel.: 226–5446
Gen. Sec.: C. Stacey Woods (Lausanne)

LAMBETH CONFERENCE
Lambeth Palace, London, S.E.1, England
Exec. Officer of the Consultative Body: Rt. Rev. R. S. Dean, D.D.
Office: 21 Chester Street, London, S.W.1. Tel.: Belgravia 7461

LUTHERAN WORLD FEDERATION
150 route de Ferney, 1211 Geneva 20, Switzerland. Tel.: 33 34 00
Gen. Sec.: Dr. Kurt Schmidt-Clausen (Geneva)

MENNONITE WORLD CONFERENCE
3003 Benham Avenue, Elkhart, Indiana, U.S.A. Tel.: JAckson 3–1385
Exec. Sec.: Cornelius J. Dyck.

PENTECOSTAL WORLD CONFERENCE
1445 Boonsville Avenue, Springfield, Mo., U.S.A.
Chairman: Rev. F. Zimmerman

UNITED BIBLE SOCIETIES
101 Queen Victoria Street, London, E.C.4, England. Tel.: Central 1606
Gen. Sec.: Dr. Olivier Béguin

WORLD ALLIANCE OF YOUNG MEN'S CHRISTIAN ASSOCIATIONS
37 Quai Wilson, Geneva, Switzerland. Tel.: (022) 32 31 00
Gen. Sec.: Fredrik Franklin

WORLD COUNCIL OF CHRISTIAN EDUCATION AND SUNDAY SCHOOL
ASSOCIATION
World Office: 150 route de Ferney, 1211 Geneva 20, Switzerland. Tel. 33 34 00
Gen. Sec.: Rev. Ralph N. Mould
New York Office: Room 732, 475 Riverside Drive, New York 10027, N.Y.,
U.S.A. Tel.: RI 9 4200
Sec.: Loren Walters
London Office: Hillside, Merry Hill Road, Bushey, Herts. Tel.: Bushey Heath 4488

I   239

WORLD COUNCIL OF CHURCHES

Hdq.: 150 route de Ferney, 1211 Geneva 20, Switzerland. Tel.: 33 34 00
New York office: 475 Riverside Drive, New York, N.Y. 10027, U.S.A.
Gen. Sec.: Dr. Eugene Carson Blake (Geneva)
Assoc. Gen. Secs.: (A.G.S.): *see below*
New York office Exec. Sec.: Dr. Eugene L. Smith
Liaison Sec. in London: Miss Sigrid Morden, 10 Eaton Gate, London, S.W.1.
Tel.: SLO 9611

DIVISION OF ECUMENICAL ACTION
Dir.: Fr. Paul Verghese (A.G.S., Geneva)

DIVISION OF INTER-CHURCH AID, REFUGEE AND WORLD SERVICE
Dep. Dir.: Dr. Charles Arbuthnott

DIVISION OF STUDIES
Act. Dir.: Rev. Victor Hayward

COMMISSION AND DIVISION OF WORLD MISSION AND EVANGELISM
Dir.: Rev. Philip Potter (A.G.S., Geneva)

COMMISSION OF THE CHURCHES ON INTERNATIONAL AFFAIRS
Dir.: Dr. O. F. Nolde (A.G.S., New York)

COMMISSION AND DEPARTMENT ON FAITH AND ORDER
Dir.: Dr. Lucas Vischer

DEPARTMENT OF FINANCE AND ADMINISTRATION
Dir.: Frank Northam

DEPARTMENT OF INFORMATION
Dir.:

ECUMENICAL INSTITUTE
Dir.: Prof. Nikos A. Nissiotis

WORLD CONVENTION OF CHURCHES OF CHRIST (DISCIPLES)

Room 448, 475 Riverside Drive, New York 10027, N.Y., U.S.A. Tel.: 870–2751
Gen. Sec.: Dr. Laurence V. Kirkpatrick

WORLD EVANGELICAL FELLOWSHIP

International office: 36 Crossburn Drive, Don Mills, Ontario, Canada.
Tel.: (416) 444–8578
Editorial office: 30 Bedford Place, London, W.C.1, England. Tel.: 01 580 9361
International Sec.: Rev. Dennis Clark

WORLD METHODIST COUNCIL

Box 387, Lake Junaluska, North Carolina, U.S.A. Tel.: 456–9432
Sec.: Dr. Lee F. Tuttle
New York office: 777 U.N. Plaza, New York, U.S.A. Tel.: Oxford 7–8575
London office: 50 Domonic Drive, London, S.E.9. Tel.: Kipling 5177
Sec.: Rev. Max W. Woodward

WORLD'S CHRISTIAN ENDEAVOUR UNION

Hdq.: 1221 East Broad Street, Columbus, Ohio 43216, U.S.A. Tel.: 253–8541
British office: "Sunnydene", Leamington Road, Ryton-on-Dunsmore, Warwicks.,
England
Gen. Secs.: H. E. Westerhoff and W. J. Sharpe

WORLD STUDENT CHRISTIAN FEDERATION

P.B. 206, 1211 Geneva 3 Rive, Switzerland. Tel.: 24 73 54
Gen. Sec.: The Rev. Valdo Galland

WORLD YOUNG WOMEN'S CHRISTIAN ASSOCIATION

Hdq.: 37 Quai Wilson, Geneva, Switzerland. Tel.: 32 31 00
Gen. Sec.: Miss Elizabeth Palmer

AFRICA

ALGERIA

COMMISSION D'ENSEIGNMENT RELIGIEUX D'AFRIQUE DU NORD
(North Africa Council of Religious Education)
La Palmeraie, El-Biar, Algiers

CONSEIL DES MISSIONS EVANGELIQUES EN ALGERIE (Evangelical
Missionary Council of Algeria)
2 rue Palma, Algiers

METHODIST CHURCH IN NORTH AFRICA
78 Chemin Beaurepaire, El-Biar, Algiers. Tel.: 78 32 91

MISSION ROLLAND A TIZI-OUZOU
1 rue Emile Rolland à Tizi-Ouzou, Grande-Kabylie. Tel.: 07 à Tizi-Ouzou

SOCIETE BIBLIQUE "LA BIBLE"
43 rue Benmehidi Larbi, Algiers

ANGOLA

ALIANCA EVANGELICA DE ANGOLA (Angola Evangelical Alliance) (1922)
C.P. 1223—C, Luanda
Sec.: Rev. W. Lawrence Henderson

BURUNDI

ALLIANCE PROTESTANTE DU BURUNDI
B.P. 17, Usumbura. Rev. Hans P. Emming

EGLISE ANGLICANE AU BURUNDI
Ibuye, Ngozi

CAMEROON

ALLIANCE DES UNIONS CHRETIENNES DE JEUNES GENS DU
CAMEROUN
Foyer de Jeunesse, B.P. 89, Douala. Tel.: 48–86

CAMEROON BAPTIST CONVENTION
P.O. Box 1, Bamenda, West Cameroon. Tel.: Bamenda 63

EGLISE EVANGELIQUE DU CAMEROUN
B.P. 89, Douala

EGLISE EVANGELIQUE LUTHERIENNE DU CAMEROUN ET DE LA
REPUBLIQUE CENTRAFRICAINE
B.P. 9, Tibati

FEDERATION EVANGELIQUE DU CAMEROUN ET DE L'AFRIQUE
EQUATORIALE
B.P. 491, Yaoundé. Rev. E. Mallo

LUTHERAN BRETHREN MISSION
B.P. 6, Kaélé

PRESBYTERIAN CHURCH IN WEST CAMEROON
P.O. Box 19, Buea, West Cameroon

SOCIETE BIBLIQUE: CAMEROUN GABON
B.P. 1133, Yaoundé

UNION OF BAPTIST CHURCHES OF CAMEROON
P.O.B. 7, New-Bell, Douala. Tel.: Douala 49–64

CONGO (KINSHASA)

ARMÉE DU SALUT
B.P. 8636, Kinshasa. Tel.: 1 2326

ASSOCIATION OF EVANGELICAL CHURCHES OF THE LULONGA
Baringa, B.P. 30, Basankusu

AFRICA

COMITE CENTRAL DES MENNONITES
B.P. 3101, Kinshasa

CONSEIL PROTESTANT DU CONGO
B.P. 3094, Kinshasa-Kalina Tel.: 29–49
Gen. Sec.: Dr. Pierre Shaumba

EGLISE BAPTISTE DU HAUT CONGO
EGLISE BAPTISTE DU MOYEN FLEUVE
EGLISE BAPTISTE DU BAS FLEUVE
B.P. 205, Kinshasa. Tel.: 2466

EGLISE METHODISTE (Congo)
B.P. 560, Luluabourg. Tel.: 2679

EGLISE ORTHODOXE GRECQUE
B.P. 5007, Kinshasa

FEDERATION NATIONALE DE LA JEUNESSE PROTESTANTE
B.P. 3094, Kinshasa-Kalina

LIBRAIRIE EVANGELIQUE AU CONGO
B.P. 123, Kinshasa

LIGUE POUR LA LECTURE DE LA BIBLE
B.P. 4242, Kinshasa

SOCIETES BIBLIQUES AU CONGO
B.P. 8911, Kinshasa

UNION DES ETUDIANTS CHRETIENS AU CONGO
B.P. 3094, Kinshasa-Kalina

UNION MISSIONNAIRE HOSPITALIERE
B.P. 658, Kinshasa

UNIVERSITE LIBRE DU CONGO
B.P. 4710, Kinshasa

DAHOMEY

ALLIANCE DES UNIONS CHRETIENNES DES JEUNES GENS DU
DAHOMEY (1937)
Foyer Culturel Protestant, B.P. 296, Cotonou

ETHIOPIA (with ERITREA)

BAPTIST EVANGELICAL CHURCH
P.O. Box 2323, Addis Ababa

BETHEL EVANGELICAL CHURCH
P.O. Box 1111, Addis Ababa

BIBLE SOCIETY
41 Haile Selassie Avenue (P.O. Box 130), Addis Ababa

ETHIOPIAN CHURCH
Addis Ababa

ETHIOPIAN EVANGELICAL CHURCH MEKANE YESUS
P.O. Box 2087, Addis Ababa

ETHIOPIAN UNION MISSION OF SEVENTH DAY ADVENTISTS
P.O. Box 145, Addis Ababa

EVANGELICAL CHURCH OF ERITREA
P.O. Box 905, Asmara, Eritrea

INTER-MISSION COUNCIL, ETHIOPIA
P.O. Box 2642, Addis Ababa. Tel.: 12323 Rev. Paul Gingrich

LUTHERAN CHURCH
P.O. Box 56, Harrar

LUTHERAN CHURCH OF ERITREA
P.O. Box 99, Asmara, Eritrea

AFRICA

MESERETE HIWOT CHURCH
P.O. Box 127, Addis Ababa

MESERET CHRISTES CHURCH
P.O. Box 1165, Addis Ababa

YOUNG MEN'S CHRISTIAN ASSOCIATION
P.O. Box 335, Addis Ababa. Tel.: 13455

GABON

ALBERT SCHWEITZER HOSPITAL
Lambarene via Libreville

GHANA

ANGLICAN CHURCH (Church of the Province of West Africa) (1909)
Bishop's House, P.O. Box 8, Accra

BIBLE SOCIETIES IN WEST AFRICA
High Street, Jameston, (P.O. Box 761), Accra

CHRISTIAN SCIENCE COMMITTEE ON PUBLICATION
P.O. Box 3, Accra

EVANGELICAL LUTHERAN CHURCH
P.O. Box 197, Kaneshie

EVANGELICAL PRESBYTERIAN CHURCH (1847)
P.O. Box 18, Ho

GHANA BAPTIST CONFERENCE (1925)
P.O. Box 1933, Kumasi

METHODIST CHURCH, GHANA (1835)
Liberia Road, P.O. Box 403, Accra. Tel.: 62420, 64843

NATIONAL CHRISTIAN COUNCIL OF GHANA (1929)
P.O. Box 919, Accra. Tel.: 76778. Gen. Sec.: Rev. W. G. M. Brandful

PRESBYTERIAN CHURCH OF GHANA (1828)
P.O. Box 1800, Accra

SALVATION ARMY (Ghana: 1922)
Boundary Road (P.O. Box 320), Accra. Tel.: 63005

STUDENT CHRISTIAN MOVEMENT
University College, Legon, Accra

YOUNG MEN'S CHRISTIAN ASSOCIATION
P.O. Box 738, Accra

YOUNG WOMEN'S CHRISTIAN ASSOCIATION
P.O. Box 1504, Accra

IVORY COAST

BIBLE SOCIETY
Rue Lepic, Ancien Cocody (B.P. 1529), Abidjan

KENYA

AFRICA GOSPEL CHURCH
Central Church Council, Box 123, Kericho. Tel.: 123

AFRICA INLAND CHURCH
P.O. Box 13024, Nairobi

BAPTIST CHURCH OF THE EAST AFRICAN BAPTIST MISSION
East African Baptist Assembly of the Baptist Mission of E. Africa, P.O. Box 32, Limuru. Tel.: Tigoni 256

BIBLE SOCIETY IN EAST AFRICA
Bible House, Jeevanjee Street, P.O. Box 12983, Nairobi. Tel.: Nairobi 25587

AFRICA

CHRISTIAN CHURCHES' EDUCATIONAL ASSOCIATION (1958)
P.O. Box 5009, Nairobi. Tel.: Nairobi 22263

CHRISTIAN COUNCIL OF KENYA (1943)
P.O. Box 5009, Nairobi. Rev. John Kamau

CHRISTIAN SCIENCE COMMITTEE ON PUBLICATION
P.O. Box 3476, Nairobi

CHURCH OF GOD IN EAST AFRICA
P.O. Box 410, Kisumu

CHURCH OF THE PROVINCE OF EAST AFRICA
Bishopsbourne, 26 Anderson Road (P.O. Box 502), Nairobi

DUTCH REFORMED CHURCH OF SOUTH AFRICA (in Kenya)
P.O. Box 119, Eldoret. Tel.: 291 (Eldoret)

EAST AFRICAN RELIGIOUS FILMS LIBRARY
P.O. Box 14352, Westlands, Nairobi

EAST AFRICA YEARLY MEETING OF THE RELIGIOUS SOCIETY OF FRIENDS
Dept. of Church Work, P.O. Tiriki, Kisumu

ELIM MISSIONARY ASSEMBLIES
P.O. Box 2627, Mombasa

FRIENDS SERVICE COUNCIL
P.O. Box 6613, Nairobi

FULL GOSPEL CHURCHES
P.O. Box 285, Kericho

GOSPEL FURTHERING FELLOWSHIP
P.O. Box 1141, Nairobi

KENYA STUDENTS CHRISTIAN FELLOWSHIP (1958)
P.O. Box 1718, Nairobi. Tel.: 25539

LUTHERAN CHURCH
P.O. Box 5, Sondu

METHODIST CHURCH
P.O. Box 8268, Nairobi. Tel.: 25095 Nairobi

MISSIONARY AVIATION FELLOWSHIP
Corner Gordon and Hurlingham, Nairobi

NAVIGATORS
P.O. Box 7300, Nairobi

PENTECOSTAL ASSEMBLIES
P.O. Box 25050, Nairobi

PRESBYTERIAN CHURCH OF EAST AFRICA (1898)
P.O. Box 8268, Nairobi. Tel.: 25095

PROTESTANT CHURCHES MEDICAL ASSOCIATION
P.O. Box 360, Nairobi

REFORMED CHURCH OF EAST AFRICA (1963)
P.O. 99, Eldoret

SALVATION ARMY (1921)
Government Road (P.O. Box 575), Nairobi. Tel.: 20320

SCRIPTURE UNION
P.O. Box 717, Nairobi. Tel.: 25539

SEVENTH-DAY ADVENTIST CHURCH, EAST AFRICAN UNION
Box 2276, Nairobi. Tel.: 66025

THIKA BIBLE FELLOWSHIP
P.O. Box 5, Thika

AFRICA

YOUNG MEN'S CHRISTIAN ASSOCIATION
P.O. Box 30330, Nairobi. Tel.: 22217

YOUNG WOMEN'S CHRISTIAN ASSOCIATION
P.O. Box 710, Nairobi. Tel.: Nairobi 20707

LIBERIA

BIBLE SOCIETY
Clay Street (P.O. Box 39), Monrovia

E.L.W.A. RADIO VILLAGE (SUDAN INTERIOR MISSION)
P.O. Box 192, Monrovia

FIRST PRESBYTERIAN CHURCH
Monrovia

LIBERIAN BAPTIST MISSIONARY AND EDUCATIONAL CONVENTION
Monrovia

LIBERIAN INLAND MISSION
Ganta Postal Agency, Ganta

LUTHERAN CHURCH
Monrovia

NATIONAL STUDENT CHRISTIAN COUNCIL (1957)
Y.M.C.A. Building, Box 147, Monrovia

YOUNG MEN'S CHRISTIAN ASSOCIATION
12 Broad Street, Monrovia. Tel.: 21520

YOUNG WOMEN'S CHRISTIAN ASSOCIATION
P.O. Box 118, Monrovia

MALAGASY REPUBLIC

COMITE INTERMISSIONNAIRE
6 rue Georges V, B.P. 538, Tananarive

EKLESIA EPISKOPALY MALAGASY
Misiona Anglikana, Anjohy, Antananarivo. Tel.: Antananarivo 209 13

FIANGONANA LOTERANA MALAGASY
Boîte Postale 61, Fianarantsoa

FIANGONAN' I KRISTY ETO MADAGASIKARA
6 Rue George V, Tananarive. Tel.: 213–68

FIKAMBANANA MAMPIELY BAIBOLY (Society for Distribution of Scriptures)
Mahamasina, Tananarive

FIOMBONAN' NY FIANGONANA PROTESTANTO ETO MADAGASKARA
(Malagasy Christian Council), Ambavahadimitafo, Tananarive. Pastor Daniel
Ratefy

FRIENDS SERVICE COUNCIL
Mission FFMA, Faravohitra, Tananarive

GENERAL SYNOD OF THE CHURCHES ASSOCIATED WITH THE
LONDON MISSIONARY SOCIETY
Lot 11. V. 122, Ampandrana, Tananarive

ISAN-KERIN-TAONA (Malagasy Friends Church)
52 rue George V, Faravohitra, Tananarive

KOMITIN'NY ISAN-ENIM-BOLANA (SYNODE INTERFEDERAL DE
TROIS MISSIONS PROTESTANTES)
Ambavahadimitafo, Tananarive

MALAGASY BIBLE SOCIETY
54 rue George V, Faravohitra (B.P. 922), Tananarive

MALAGASY EVANGELICAL CHURCH
18 ave. Labourdourdonnais, Ambohijatovo, Tananarive

AFRICA

NY ISAN-ENIM-BOLANA (Native Missionary Society)
Tranon'd Rasalama, Andravoahangy, Tananarive
YOUNG MEN'S CHRISTIAN ASSOCIATION
Foyer des Jeunes, B.P. 771, Tananarive
YOUNG WOMEN'S CHRISTIAN ASSOCIATION
F.K.V.Z.M., 81 avenue Maréchal Foch, Tananarive

MALAWI

BIBLE SOCIETIES IN CENTRAL AFRICA
Bible House, Osman Court Building, Sclater Road (P.O. Box 740), Blantyre
CHURCH OF CENTRAL AFRICA, PRESBYTERIAN
Synod of Blantyre (1876): P.O. Box 413, Blantyre
Synod of Livingstonia: P.O. Livingstonia
Synod of Nkhoma (1889): Nkhoma Synod Offices, P.O. Nkhoma. Tel.: Nkhoma 7
CHURCH OF THE PROVINCE OF CENTRAL AFRICA: DIOCESE OF MALAWI
Malosa P.O. Kasupe
CONSULTATIVE BOARD OF FEDERATED MISSIONS IN MALAWI
Mlanje
MALAWI CHRISTIAN COUNCIL (1939)
Churches of Christ Mission, Gowa P.O. Mlangeni
Rev. A. V. Smith
PROVIDENCE INDUSTRIAL MISSION (Baptist)
Chiradzulu

MALI

FEDERATION DES MISSIONS PROTESTANTES EN AFRIQUE OCCI-
DENTALE FRANCAISE
P.O. Box 150, Dakar
YOUNG WOMEN'S CHRISTIAN ASSOCIATION
CIMADE, Centre de Boppe, B.P. 5070, Dakar

MAURITIUS

BIBLE SOCIETY
42 bis, Vandermeersch Street, Rose Hill
YOUNG MEN'S CHRISTIAN ASSOCIATION
Y.M.C.A. House, Beau Bassin

MOROCCO

CHRISTIAN SCIENCE COMMITTEE ON PUBLICATION
Ohana Villa, 58 Boulevard d'Anfa, Casablanca
RAYMOND LULL HOME (1902)
Tangier
SWEDISH ISRAEL MISSION
Foyer du Marin Scandinave, 4 Avenue du Phare, Casablanca
YOUNG MEN'S CHRISTIAN ASSOCIATION "CAZZEFOUR" (1964)
33 rue d'Azilal, Casablanca. Tel.: 2 19 22

MOZAMBIQUE

BIBLE HOUSE (CASA DA BIBLIA)
Avenida Pinheiro Chagas 2678, Lourenço Marques
CHRISTIAN COUNCIL OF MOZAMBIQUE
Rev. Francisco da Cruz, C.P.21, Lourenço Marques

AFRICA

FREE METHODIST CHURCH
c/o Nyamchafu Mission, Inharrime
IGREJA DE CRISTO EM MANICA E SOFALA
C.P. 396, Beira
METHODIST EPISCOPAL CHURCH
C.P. 45, Inhambane
PORTUGUESE EVANGELICAL CHURCH (Presbyterian)
C.P. 21 Lourenço Marques
RONGA-TSONGA PRESBYTERIAN CHURCH
C.P. 21 Lourenço Marques

NIGERIA

AIYANGBA FELLOWSHIP
Via P.O. Idah, N.R.
BASEL MISSION GAVVA
P.A. Gwoza, Sardauna Prov., N. Nigeria
BIBLE SOCIETY
P.O. Box 68, Apapa
CHRIST APOSTOLIC
P.O. Box 11, Akure
CHRISTIAN COUNCIL OF NIGERIA
1 Oil Mill Street, Box 2838, Lagos. Tel.: 21682
Gen. Secretary: Rev. T. A. Adejunmobi
CHRISTIAN SCIENCE COMMITTEE ON PUBLICATION
7 Abeokuta Street, P.O. Box 219, Ebute-Metta, Lagos
CHURCH OF THE PROVINCE OF WEST AFRICA
Ibadan Diocese: Bishopscourt, Oke Are, Box 1075, Ibadan
Lagos Diocese: Bishopscourt, P.O. Box 13, Lagos
Diocese on the Niger: Bishopscourt, Box 42, Onitsha
Niger Delta Diocese: Bishop's House, Box 212, Aba
Northern Provinces: Bishopscourt, Box 72, Kaduna. Tel.: 3220
Ondo-Benin Diocese: Bishop's Lodge, Box 25, Ondo
Owerri Diocese: P.O. Box 31, Owerri. Tel.: 20
EVANGELICAL CHURCHES OF WEST AFRICA AND SUDAN INTERIOR
MISSION
Jos, Northern Nigeria
EVANGELICAL LUTHERAN CHURCH
Obot Idim, Uyo P.O., Uyo Province
KERK VAN CHRISTUS ONDER DIE TIV IN DIE SOEDAN
Mkar, P.M. Bag, Makurdi, Northern Nigeria
LUTHERAN CHURCH OF CHRIST IN THE SUDAN
Box 21, Numan via Jos
METHODIST CHURCH
21/22 Marina, P.O. Box 2011, Lagos. Tel.: Lagos 20916
NIGERIAN BAPTIST CONVENTION
Private Mail Bag, 5113, Ibadan
PRESBYTERIAN CHURCH OF EASTERN NIGERIA (1846)
P.O. Box 14, Afikpo
SALVATION ARMY
West Africa Territory: Box 125, Lagos
STUDENT CHRISTIAN MOVEMENT
P.O. Box 263, Ibadan
SUDAN INTERIOR MISSION
Sudan Interior Mission, Jos. Tel.: 2481

247

AFRICA

WEST AFRICAN GOSPEL PUBLISHING SOCIETY (1945)
P.O. Box 188 (No. 7 Gashash Road), Kaduna. Tel.: 3292 (Kaduna)

YOUNG MEN'S CHRISTIAN ASSOCIATION (1925)
P.O. Box 2106, Lagos. Tel.: 21092

YOUNG WOMEN'S CHRISTIAN ASSOCIATION
8 Moloney Street, Lagos

RHODESIA

BIBLE SOCIETIES IN CENTRAL AFRICA
Bible House, 99 Victoria Street (P.O. Box 1081), Salisbury

CHRISTIAN COUNCIL OF RHODESIA
P.O.B. 904, Salisbury. Rev. H. P. Chikomo

CHRISTIAN SCIENCE COMMITTEE ON PUBLICATION
P.O. Box 540, Salisbury

CHURCH OF THE PROVINCE OF CENTRAL AFRICA
Diocese of Mashonaland: Bishop's Mount, P.O. Box 7, Salisbury. Tel.: 20203
Diocese of Matebeleland: Bishop's House, 46 Park Road, P.O. Box 2422, Bulawayo

CO-OPERATIVE COMMITTEE FOR MISSION WORK IN PORTUGUESE EAST AFRICA
Rusito Mission, Melsetter

DUTCH REFORMED CHURCH MISSION (1891)
P.O. Morgenster, Fort Victoria. Tel.: Fort Victoria 346–18

EVANGELICAL LUTHERAN CHURCH
Mnene Mission, P.O. Mnene, Belingwe. Tel.: 0202 Belingwe

LONDON MISSIONARY SOCIETY IN SOUTHERN AFRICA
Hope Fountain, P.O. Waterford, Bulawayo

SALVATION ARMY
P.O. Box 14, Salisbury

YOUNG MEN'S CHRISTIAN ASSOCIATION, Rhodesia (1959)
P.O. Box 3865, Salisbury. Tel.: 85218

RWANDA

CONSEIL PROTESTANT DU RWANDA
B.P. 79, Kigali. Rev. Ezéchias Gatwaza

EGLISE ANGLICANE AU RWANDA
Gahini, Kigali

SIERRA LEONE

AFRICAN METHODIST EPISCOPAL CHURCH
Freetown

AMERICAN WESLEYAN CHURCH
P.O. Box 33, Makene

ASSEMBLIES OF GOD
P.O. Box 522, Freetown

CHURCH OF THE PROVINCE OF WEST AFRICA (Diocese of Sierra Leone)
Bishopscourt, P.O. Box 128, Freetown

EVANGELICAL UNITED BRETHREN CHURCH
5 Goderich Street, Freetown

METHODIST CHURCH
P.O. Box 64, Freetown

MISSIONARY CHURCH ASSOCIATION
P.O. Box 32, Magburaka

AFRICA

SIERRA LEONE BAPTIST UNION
Fourah Bay College, Freetown

SIERRA LEONE UNITED CHRISTIAN COUNCIL (1924)
P.O. Box 404, Freetown
Rev. S. E. Warratie

STUDENT CHRISTIAN MOVEMENT
39 Westmoreland Street, Freetown

UNITED BRETHREN IN CHRIST CHURCH
P.O. Box 19, Mattru Jong

WEST AFRICAN METHODIST CHURCH
39 Waterloo Street, Freetown

YOUNG MEN'S CHRISTIAN ASSOCIATION
P.O. Box 243, Freetown

YOUNG WOMEN'S CHRISTIAN ASSOCIATION
Brookfields, P.O. Box 511, Freetown

SOUTH AFRICA

AFRIKA EVANGELIESE BOND
"Glenbervie", Epsom Road, Kenilworth, Cape Town

AFRICAN UNITED NATIONAL BAPTIST CHURCH
Swagershoek, P.O. Wolhuterskop, Transvaal

APOSTOLIC FAITH MISSION OF SOUTH AFRICA
Box 1636, Johannesburg

ASSEMBLIES OF GOD IN SOUTHERN AND CENTRAL AFRICA
82 Ford Street, Johannesburg. Tel.: 25.8069; 25.4317

BANTU PRESBYTERIAN CHURCH OF SOUTH AFRICA (1923)
48 Eagle Street, Umtata. Tel.: 454

BAPTIST UNION OF SOUTH AFRICA (1887)
210 Transafrica House, 21 Wolmarans Street, Johannesburg. Tel.: 23–1271

BIBLE SOCIETY OF SOUTH AFRICA
38 Shortmarket Street (P.O. Box 215), Cape Town

CAPE TOWN DIOCESAN MISSION TO MOSLEMS (1849)
Rectory, Pinelands, Cape Province

CHRISTEN-STUDENTEVERENIGING VAN SUID-AFRIKA (1896)
P.O. Box 25, Stellenbosch

CHRISTIAN APOSTOLIC CHURCH IN ZION OF SOUTH AFRICA
P.O. Senekal, Orange Free State

CHRISTIAN CHURCHES (DISCIPLES OF CHRIST)
52–5th Avenue, Linden, Johannesburg, Transvaal. Tel.: 46–9580

CHRISTIAN COUNCIL OF SOUTH AFRICA (1936)
706/707 N.B.S. Building, 11 Greenmarket Square, P.O. Box 2846, Cape Town.
Tel.: 3.5555. Gen. Sec.: Rev. Basil H. M. Brown

CHRISTIAN SCIENCE COMMITTEE ON PUBLICATION FOR CAPE PROVINCE
139a Longmarket Street, Cape Town

CHURCH OF ENGLAND IN SOUTH AFRICA (1806)
Balfour House, St. Georges Street, Cape Town

CHURCH OF THE PROVINCE OF SOUTH AFRICA
Church House, Queen Victoria Street, Cape Town. Tel.: 2–0558

COMMUNITY OF THE RESURRECTION OF OUR LORD (1884)
St. Peter's Home, Box 72, Grahamstown. Tel.: Grahamstown 190

CONGREGATIONAL UNION OF SOUTH AFRICA (1859)
P.O. Box 165, Rondebosch, Cape Town. Tel.: 6–6251

AFRICA

ETHIOPIAN CATHOLIC CHURCH IN ZION
P.O. Box 773, Pretoria

EVANGELICAL LUTHERAN CHURCH IN SOUTH AFRICA (Transvaal Region)
P.O. Box 196, Lynn East, Pretoria

EVANGELICAL LUTHERAN CHURCH IN SOUTH AFRICA (S.E. Region)
ELC BAG, Mapamulo, Natal

EVANGELIES-LUTHERSE KERK, Kaap/Oranje Streek
12 Haberfeld Street, Kimberley, Cape Province

EVANGELIES-LUTHERSE KERK IN SUIDER AFRIKA (Kaapse Kerk)
Hofmeyr Street 26, Stellenbosch, Cape Province

EVANGELIES-LUTHERSE KERK IN SUIDELIKE AFRIKA (Transvaalse Kerk)
100 Barry Hertzog Avenue, Greenside Ext., Johannesburg, Transvaal

EVANGELIES LUTHERSE KERK IN SUIDELIKE AFRIKA (Hermannsburg)
P.O. Pietermaritzburg, Natal

FREE CHURCH OF SCOTLAND (South African Mission) (1843)
14 Frere Street, King William's Town. Tel.: King William's Town 3129

FREE EVANGELICAL LUTHERAN SYNOD IN SOUTH AFRICA
"Kirchendorf", P.O., Wartburg, Natal

FULL GOSPEL CHURCH OF GOD IN SOUTHERN AFRICA
P.O. Box 40, Irene, Transvaal. Tel.: Pretoria 65350

GEREFORMEERDE KERK IN SUID-AFRIKA (1859)
P.O. Box 20004, North Bridge, Potchefstroom. Tel.: 5269

INDIAN REFORMED CHURCH (Dutch Reformed Church—Indian)
101 St. Patrick Road, Pietermaritzburg. Tel.: 2–5122

KEREKE YA LUTHERE YA EFANGELE—AFRICA KWA BORWA (Botswana)
P.O. Box 536, Rustenburg, Transvaal

MAHON MISSION BRANCH OF THE SOUTH AFRICAN BAPTIST MISSIONARY SOCIETY
Etembeni, Kransfontein, Orange Free State. Tel.: Kransfontein 512

METHODIST CHURCH OF SOUTH AFRICA (1806)
Methodist Connexional Office, P.O. Box 2256, Durban. Tel.: Durban 20561

MISSION OF THE EVANGELICAL LUTHERAN FREE CHURCHES
Enhlanhleni, P.O. Pomeroy via Dundee, Natal

MORAVIAN CHURCH (E. PROVINCE)
Moravian Mission, Mvenyane, P.O. Cedarville, East Griqualand

MORAVIAN CHURCH (WESTERN CAPE PROVINCE)
84 Lympleigh Road, Plumstead, Cape Province. Tel.: Capetown 775459

NEDERDUITSE GEREFORMEERDE KERK: General Synod
P.O. Box 1021, Johannesburg. Tel.: 724–6281

NEDERDUITSE GEREFORMEERDE KERK (1652)
Mission Committee of General Synod, P.O. Box 433, Pretoria. Tel.: 3–5691

NEDERDUITSE GEREFORMEERDE KERK IN AFRIKA
Kingfisher Walk 4, Pinelands, Cape. Tel.: 53–6070

NEDERDUITSE GEREFORMEERDE KERK IN DIE ORANJE-VRYSTAAT
Viljoenskroom, Oranje-Vrystaat

NEDERDUITSE GEREFORMEERDE KERK IN SUID-AFRIKA (KAAP)
Alexandalaan 5, Oranjezicht, Cape Town

NEDERDUITSE GEREFORMEERDE KERK VAN NATAL
P.O. Box 649, Pietermaritzburg, Natal. Tel.: 42861/2 Pietermaritzburg

NEDERDUITSE GEREFORMEERDE SENDINGKERK IN SUID-AFRIKA
P.O. Box 169, Worcester. Tel.: 5468

AFRICA

NEDERDUITSE HERVORMDE OF GEREFORMEERDE KERK VAN SUID-AFRIKA (Transvaal)
21 Rhodes Ave., Parktown, Johannesburg

NEDERDUITS-HERVORMDE KERK VAN AFRIKA
Posbus 111, Heidelberg, Transvaal

NEDERDUITS-HERVORMDE SENDINGKERK VAN AFRIKA
Kotzestraat 15, Sunnyside, Pretoria, Transvaal

NEDERDUITSCH HERVORMDE OF GEREFORMEERDE KERK VAN ZUD-AFRIKA IN TRANSVAAL
4 Elm Street, Houghton, Johannesburg

PRESBYTERIAN CHURCH OF SOUTHERN AFRICA
8th Floor, Saambou Building, 112 Commissioner Street, Johannesburg. Tel.: 838.6534

SALVATION ARMY
131 Commissioner Street, Johannesburg. Tel.: 22.4914–15

SOCIETY OF FRIENDS (QUAKERS) IN SOUTHERN AFRICA
c/o 81 Uplands Road, Pietermaritzburg, Natal. Tel.: 21642 Pietermaritzburg

SOUTH AFRICAN BAPTIST MISSIONARY SOCIETY
501 Trans-Africa Building, Wolmarans Street, Johannesburg

SOUTH AFRICAN INSTITUTE OF RACE RELATIONS (INC)
Box 97, Johannesburg

SOUTH AFRICAN NATIONAL SUNDAY SCHOOL ASSOCIATION
P.O. Box 17, Port Elizabeth, Cape Province

SUDAN INTERIOR MISSION
P.O. Box 3017, Cape Town

THE EVANGELICAL ALLIANCE MISSION (TEAM)
57 Commission Street, Vryheid, Natal (Box 121). Tel.: 804

UNITED CHURCH (1956)
54 Langerman Drive, Kensington, Johannesburg

VOLKSKERK VAN AFRIKA (Congregational)
Rosina, Rouwkoop Avenue, Rondebosch, Cape Province

YOUNG MEN'S CHRISTIAN ASSOCIATION
104 Rissik Street, P.O. Box 23221, Joubert Park, Johannesburg. Tel.: 724–4541/2/3

YOUNG WOMEN'S CHRISTIAN ASSOCIATION
Castle Hill, Port Elizabeth

SOUTH-WEST AFRICA

DEUTSCHE EVANGELISCH-LUTHERISCHE SYNODE SUDWEST-AFRIKAS (1926)
P.O. Box 233, Windhoek

EVANGELICAL LUTHERAN CHURCH IN SOUTH-WEST AFRICA (RHENISH MISSION CHURCH)
P.O. Box 21, Windhoek

SUDAN

BIBLE SOCIETY
Bible House, Sharia Khalifa No. 15, Khartoum

EPISCOPAL CHURCH: DIOCESE OF THE SUDAN
All Saints' Cathedral, P.O. Box 135, Khartoum. Tel.: 72121

EVANGELICAL CHURCH IN THE SUDAN
Box 57, Khartoum. Tel.: 70637

SUDAN COUNCIL OF CHURCHES
P.O. Box 317, Khartoum. Rev. Wesley Stasy

CHRISTIAN COUNCIL
P.O. Box 2537, Dar-es-Salaam
Rev. Mahlon Hess

CHURCH OF THE PROVINCE OF EAST AFRICA
Diocese of Central Tanganyika: P.O. Box 15, Dodoma
Diocese of Dar-es-Salaam: P.O. Box 2887, Dar-es-Salaam
Diocese of Masasi: Private Bag, Masasi, Mtwara Region
Diocese of S.W. Tanganyika: P.O. Box 32, Njombe

KANISA LA KIINJILI LA KILUTHERI TANGANYIKA
(Evangelical Lutheran Church in Tanganyika)
P.O. Box 195, Moshi. Tel.: Moshi 2476

PEMBA YEARLY MEETING (RELIGIOUS SOCIETY OF FRIENDS)
Friends Mission, P.O. Box 100, Chake Chake, Pemba

YOUNG MEN'S CHRISTIAN ASSOCIATION
P.O. Box 85, Moshi. Tel.: 2342

TOGO

KRISTOTƆ SUKUVIWO HABƆBƆ (Student Christian Movement)
25 rue Alsace-Lorraine, B.P. 378, Lomé

YOUNG MEN'S CHRISTIAN ASSOCIATION
Secrétariat Synodal, B.P. 2, Lomé

YOUNG WOMEN'S CHRISTIAN ASSOCIATION
B.P. 378, Lomé

UGANDA

BIBLE SOCIETY IN EAST AFRICA—UGANDA
P.O. Box 3621, Kampala

CHURCH OF UGANDA, RWANDA AND BURUNDI
Diocese of Ankole—Kigezi: P.O. Box 14, Mbarara, Ankole
Diocese of Mbale: P.O. Box 473, Mbale
Diocese of Namirembe: P.O. Box 14123, Kampala
Diocese of N. Uganda: P.O. Box 232, Gulu
Diocese of Ruwenzori: P.O. Box 37, Fort Portal

JOINT CHRISTIAN COUNCIL
P.O. Box 2886. Kampala
Rev. Fr. J. Miller

YOUNG MEN'S CHRISTIAN ASSOCIATION
P.O. Box 1702, Kampala. Tel.: 3961

YOUNG WOMEN'S CHRISTIAN ASSOCIATION
3 George Street, Kampala

UNITED ARAB REPUBLIC (EGYPT)

AMERICAN MISSION IN EGYPT
P.O. Box 1422, Cairo

ANGLICAN CHURCH: DIOCESE OF EGYPT AND LIBYA
All Saints' Cathedral, Cairo

ARMENIAN EVANGELICAL CHURCH
14 Bustan al-Kafuri, Faggala, Cairo

ARMENIAN ST. GREGORY CHURCH
179 Avenue El Malika, Cairo

BIBLE SOCIETY IN EGYPT
33 Orabi Street (P.O. Box 724), Cairo

CHALDEAN CATHOLIC CHURCH (in Egypt)
Our Lady of Fatima, 93 rue Nouzah, Eliopolys, Cairo. Tel.: 866274

AFRICA

CHURCH OF GOD (Anderson)
15 Emad el Din 45, Cairo

COPTIC EVANGELICAL CHURCH
P.O. 1422, Cairo. Tel.: 906612

COPTIC ORTHODOX CHURCH
Sharia al-Darb al Wâsa, Clot, Bey, Cairo

EGYPT AND SUDAN SUNDAY SCHOOL UNION
P.O. Box 1422, Cairo

GREEK ORTHODOX PATRIARCHATE OF ALEXANDRIA
Alexandria

MAADI COMMUNITY CHURCH
4 Rd. 11, Maadi

PENTECOSTAL CHURCH OF GOD
8 Ahmed Pacha Kamal, Gayerit Badran, Shoubra, Cairo

ST. ANDREWS UNITED CHURCH (PRESBYTERIAN)
Box 1422, Cairo. Tel.: Cairo 50451

YOUNG MEN'S CHRISTIAN ASSOCIATION
72 Sharia el Gomhouria, Cairo. Tel.: 917360

YOUNG WOMEN'S CHRISTIAN ASSOCIATION
11 Emad el Din Street, Cairo. Tel.: 913466-916932

ZAMBIA

BANTOE GEREFORMEERDE KERK IN NOORD-RHODESIE (1899)
P.O. Box 111, Fort Jameson

CHRISTIAN COUNCIL OF ZAMBIA
Box 8018, "Woodlands", Lusaka
Rev. E. G. Nightingale

CHURCH OF CHRIST MISSIONS (1923)
Namwianga Mission, P.O. Box 22, Kalomo

CHURCH OF THE PROVINCE OF CENTRAL AFRICA: DIOCESE OF ZAMBIA
Bishop's Lodge, P.O. Box 183, Lusaka

COPPERBELT CHRISTIAN SERVICE COUNCIL
P.O. Box 274, Kitwe

LUTHERAN CHURCH OF CENTRAL AFRICA
Box 1141, Lusaka

MINDOLO ECUMENICAL FOUNDATION (1958)
P.O. Box 1192, Kitwe. Tel.: 3380 Kitwe

STUDENT CHRISTIAN MOVEMENT
Munali Secondary School, Box 655, Lusaka

UNITED CHURCH OF ZAMBIA (1965)
P.O. Box R.W.122, Lusaka. Tel.: Lusaka 82486

UNITED SOCIETY FOR CHRISTIAN LITERATURE (Zambia)
P.O. Box 274, Kitwe. Tel.: Kitwe 4346

YOUNG MEN'S CHRISTIAN ASSOCIATION
P.O. Box 1229, Kitwe

YOUNG WOMEN'S CHRISTIAN ASSOCIATION
Y.W.C.A. Centre, Waddington Road, P.O. Box R.W. 115, Lusaka

ZAMBIA BIBLE HOUSE
23 Accra Road, Martindale (P.O. Box 1668), Kitwe

AFRICAN INDEPENDENT CHURCHES

(a small selection)

CAMEROON

EGLISE BAPTISTE CAMEROUNAISE
B.P. 437, Douala

EGLISE PROTESTANTE AFRICAINE
B.P. 26, Lolodorf

CONGO (KINSHASA)

COSSEUJCA (Conseil Supérieur des Sacrificateurs pour Les Eglises-Unies de
Jésus-Christ en Afrique)
Représentant légal, B.P. 985, Luluabourg

DIEU DE NOS ANCÊTRES
Représentant légal, B.P. 607, Luluabourg

EGLISE DES NOIRS
Représentant légal, B.P. 8029, Kinshasa

EGLISE EVANGÉLIQUE BRANCHE INDIGÈNE
B.P. 143, Kaminaville

EGLISE PROTESTANTE BAPTISTE DU KIVU
Représentant légal, B.P. 605, Goma, Nord Kivu

EGLISE DE JÉSUS-CHRIST SUR LA TERRE PAR LE PROPHÈTE SIMON
KIMBANGU (EJCSK)
Représentant légal, B.P. 7069, Kinshasa. Tel.: 8944

EGLISE SAINTE SARA
Représentant légal, B.P. 994, Luluabourg

MISSION DES FIDÈLES PROTESTANTS
Bondo, Bas-Uélé

DAHOMEY

MISSION D'UNION AFRICAINE
Evêque, Porto-Novo

ETHIOPIA

KAMBATTA EVANGELICAL CHURCH
Secretary, c/o P.O. Box 1329, Addis Ababa

GHANA

SACRED CHERUBIM AND SERAPHIM CHURCH OF GHANA
General Superintendent, P.O. Box 2840, Accra

THE HOLY CHURCH OF THE LORD
Senior Prophet, P.O. Box 44, Mamprobi

IVORY COAST

EGLISE HARRISTE
Secretariat, Abidjan

KENYA

AFRICAN BROTHERHOOD CHURCH
Presiding Bishop, P.O. Box 32, Machakos

AFRICAN CHRISTIAN CHURCH AND SCHOOLS
President, P.O. Box 41, Thika

AFRICA

AFRICAN CHURCH OF THE HOLY SPIRIT
High Priest, P.O. Box 183, Kakemega

AFRICAN INTERIOR CHURCH
Minister-in-Charge, P.O. Box 106, Maragoli

AFRICAN ORTHODOX CHURCH
Executive Secretary, P.O. Box 15, Maragoli

CHURCH OF CHRIST IN AFRICA
Presiding Bishop, P.O. Box 782, Kisumu

EAST AFRICAN UNITED CHURCHES AND THE ORTHODOX CHURCHES COMMUNION
Secretary, P.O. Box 9217, Nairobi

LEGION OF MARY CHURCH
Bishop P.O. Box 610, Nairobi

MALAGASY REPUBLIC

EGLISE DU RÉVEIL (Disciples du Seigneur)
Président, Soatanana, B.P. 72, Fianarantsoa

EGLISE DU RÉVEIL SPIRITUEL MALGACHE (FPPM)
Président, Miadampahonina, Mandoa, Betafo

EGLISE REFORMÉE INDÉPENDANTE DE MADAGASCAR (Mission Evangélique de Tananarive)
Président, Ambohimanoro, Tananarive

EGLISE PROTESTANTE MALGACHE TRANOZOZORO ANTRANOBIRIKY (FMTA)
Directeur, V.B–48 Lalana Amiral Pierre, Tananarive

MALAWI

PROVIDENCE INDUSTRIAL MISSION
P.O. Chiradzulo

NIGERIA

APOSTOLIC CHURCH OF CHRIST (SPIRITUAL MOVEMENT)
94 Lagos Street, Benin

CHRIST APOSTOLIC CHURCH
Secretary-General, P.O. Box 530, Ibadan

ETERNAL SACRED ORDER OF THE CHERUBIM AND SERAPHIM
94 Railway Line, Odi-Olowo, Mushin, Lagos

THE AFRICAN CHURCH (Inc)
P.O. Box 2846, Lagos

UNITED NATIVE AFRICAN CHURCH
Archbishop, P.O. Box 519, Lagos

RHODESIA

AFRICAN INDEPENDENT CHURCH
P.O. Box 9027, Harari

AFRICAN METHODIST CHURCH
P.O. Box 89, Selukwe

AFRICAN ZION COLLAR CHURCH OF JESUS
P.O. Box 278, Gwelo

APOSTOLIC CHURCH OF JOHANE MARANGI
Marangi Reserve, P.O. Umtali

APOSTOLIC FAITH AND ACTS CHURCH
B 89–90 Hyde Park Township, Bulawayo

AFRICA

CHRISTIAN MARCHING CHURCH OF CENTRAL AFRICA
P.O. Box 10016, Mabvuku Township, Salisbury

GUTA RA JEHOVA (City of God)
Zimunya Reserve, P.O. Umtali

NEW CHURCH OF AFRICA
P.O. Box 138, Gwelo

SMYRNA AND CROWN OF LIFE MISSION
Room 1145, Mabvuku Township, Salisbury

SOLDIERS OF GOD CHURCH
Commander-in-Chief, Room 3636 S/D, Harari, Salisbury

ZIONIST CHRISTIAN CHURCH
Gumunyu Primary School, N.C. Office, Bikita

SOUTH AFRICA

AFRICAN CONGREGATIONAL CHURCH
President, Pietermaritzburg

AFRICAN INDEPENDENT CHURCHES' ASSOCIATION (AICA)
President, 408 Dunwell, 35 Jorissen Street, Braamfontein, Johannesburg

ASSEMBLY OF ZIONIST AND APOSTOLIC CHURCHES
Secretary, P.O. Box 97, Johannesburg

BANTU AFRICAN HOLY BAPTIST CHURCH IN ZION
Bishop Henry Mthi, c/o ABC Branch, Standard Bank, Adderley Street, Cape Town

ETHIOPIAN CATHOLIC CHURCH IN ZION
34, 10 Avenue, Alexandra Township, Johannesburg

METHODIST CHURCH BANTU PEOPLE
1395 Ngcukana Street, Duncanville, East London

PRESBYTERIAN CHURCH OF AFRICA
P.O. Box 17, Tsomo, C.P.

ZULU CONGREGATIONAL CHURCH
Denver Zoar Mission Station, P.O. Umzumbi, Natal

TANZANIA

CHURCH OF THE HOLY SPIRIT
Secretary, P.O. Bukoba

LEGION OF MARY CHURCH
Bishop, P.O. Tarime

UGANDA

AFRICAN GREEK ORTHODOX CHURCH
Archimandrite, P.O. Box 1487, Kampala

ZAMBIA

AFRICAN INDEPENDENT HOLINESS CHURCH
P.O. Box 493, Lusaka

APOSTOLIC FAITH HOLY GOSPEL CHURCH
P.O. Box 1339, Ndola

WORLDWIDE MISSIONARY CHRISTIAN FELLOWSHIP
P.O. Box 23, Choma

NORTH AMERICA

BAHAMAS

BAHAMAS CHRISTIAN COUNCIL
c/o The Rt. Rev. The Lord Bishop of Nassau and The Bahamas, P.O. Box 107, Nassau

CHRISTIAN SCIENCE COMMITTEE ON PUBLICATION
P.O. Box 810, Nassau

CHURCH OF ENGLAND IN THE BAHAMAS
Diocesan Office, P.O. Box 107, Nassau, N.P. Tel.: 23019

YOUNG MEN'S CHRISTIAN ASSOCIATION
East Street, Nassau, N.P.

YOUNG WOMEN'S CHRISTIAN ASSOCIATION
P.O. Box 1269, Nassau

BARBADOS

CHRISTIAN SCIENCE COMMITTEE ON PUBLICATION
Heatherly, Pine Road, Belleville

CHURCH IN THE PROVINCE OF THE WEST INDIES:
DIOCESE OF BARBADOS
Bishop's Court, Barbados

WEST INDIA CHURCH ASSOCIATION
Diocesan Church House, Bridgetown

YOUNG MEN'S CHRISTIAN ASSOCIATION
Pinfold Street, Bridgetown 3. Tel.: 3910

YOUNG WOMEN'S CHRISTIAN ASSOCIATION
"Weymouth", Roebuck Street, St. Michael

BRITISH HONDURAS

CHURCH IN THE PROVINCE OF THE WEST INDIES : DIOCESE OF BRITISH HONDURAS
Bishopthorpe, Belize City. Tel.: 3029

YOUNG WOMEN'S CHRISTIAN ASSOCIATION
P.O. Box 158, Belize

CANADA

ALL-CANADA COMMITTEE OF THE CHURCHES OF CHRIST (DISCIPLES)
630B St. Clair Avenue W., Toronto 10, Ontario

AMERICAN LUTHERAN CHURCH, Canada Conference
Luther College, Regina, Saskatchewan

ANGLICAN CHURCH OF CANADA
Church House, 600 Jarvis Street, Toronto 5, Ontario. Tel.: 924 9192

AUGUSTANA SYNOD, Canada Conference
222 9th Street, Saskatoon, Saskatchewan

BAPTIST CONVENTION OF ONTARIO AND QUEBEC
190 St. George Street, Toronto 5, Ontario. Tel.: 922–5163

BAPTIST FEDERATION OF CANADA
91 Queen Street, Box 901, Brantford, Ontario. Tel.: 752–7281

BAPTIST UNION OF WESTERN CANADA (1907)
9918 105th Street, Edmonton, Alberta

CANADIAN BAPTIST TESTIMONY TO THE JEWS
635 Markham Street, Toronto 4, Ontario

NORTH AMERICA

CANADIAN BIBLE SOCIETY (1904)
Suite 200, 1835 Yonge Street, Toronto 7, Ontario. Tel.: 485–4446

CANADIAN COUNCIL OF CHURCHES
40 St. Clair Avenue East, Toronto 7, Ontario
Dr. Wilfred Butcher

CANADIAN LUTHERAN COUNCIL
500–365 Hargrave St., Winnipeg 2, Manitoba. Tel.: WH2–0096

CANADIAN YEARLY MEETING OF THE RELIGIOUS SOCIETY OF FRIENDS
60 Lowther Avenue, Toronto 5, Ontario. Tel.: 922–2632

CHRISTIAN SCIENCE COMMITTEE ON PUBLICATION FOR ONTARIO
57 Bloor Street West, Toronto 5

CHURCHES OF CHRIST (DISCIPLES)
695A, St. Clair Ave. W., Toronto 10, Ontario. Tel.: 416–532–3957

COLOMBIA EVANGELISTIC MISSION
16 St. Vincent St., Kitchener, Ontario (P.O. Box 371)

CONVENTION OF REGULAR BAPTISTS OF BRITISH COLUMBIA
834 East 53 Street, Vancouver, British Columbia

EVANGELICAL LUTHERAN CHURCH (Norwegian)
Luther Seminary, Saskatoon, Saskatchewan

EVANGELICAL UNITED BRETHREN CHURCH, Canada Conference
Sebringville, Ontario

FELLOWSHIP OF EVANGELICAL BAPTIST CHURCHES IN CANADA (1953)
15 Spadina Road, Toronto 4, Ontario. Tel.: 925–3273

FELLOWSHIP OF FAITH FOR THE MUSLIMS and ARABIC LITERATURE MISSION (1952)
47 Sussex Avenue, Toronto 4, Ontario. Tel.: 921–0369

INTERNATIONAL GRENFELL ASSOCIATION (1914)
St. Anthony, Newfoundland. Tel.: St. Anthony 2512

LUTHERAN CHURCH, MISSOURI SYNOD (1880)
149 Queen Street, S., Kitchener, Ontario

LUTHERAN FREE CHURCH, Canada District
Standard, Alberta

MISSION TO ORPHANS, INC. (1944)
Three Hills, Alberta

PENTECOSTAL ASSEMBLIES OF CANADA (1917)
10 Overlea Boulevard, Toronto 17. Tel.: 425–1010

PRESBYTERIAN CHURCH IN CANADA (1875)
63 St. George Street, Toronto 5, Ontario
Presbyterian Women's Missionary Society (Western Division) (1914):
100 Adelaide Street W., Room 800, Toronto 1, Ontario

REFORMED EPISCOPAL CHURCH
4034 Gordon Head Road, Victoria, B.C.

SALVATION ARMY
20 Albert Street, Toronto. Tel.: Empire 2–1071

SCRIPTURE GIFT MISSION (CANADA) INC. (1951)
21 Spadina Road, Toronto 4, Ontario

SPANISH CHRISTIAN MISSION
21 Avenue Road, Suite 22, Toronto 5, Ontario

STANDARD CHURCH OF AMERICA (1918)
243 Perth Street, Brockville, Ontario

STUDENT CHRISTIAN MOVEMENT OF CANADA (1920)
1139 Bay Street, Toronto 5, Ontario. Tel.: 925–4291

NORTH AMERICA

SUDAN INTERIOR MISSION
405 Huron Street, Toronto 5, Ontario. Tel.: 925–5955

UNITED BAPTIST CONVENTION OF THE ATLANTIC PROVINCES
112 Princess Street, St. John, New Brunswick

UNITED CHURCH OF CANADA (Union 1925)
The United Church House, 85 St. Clair Avenue E., Toronto 7, Ontario. Tel.: 925–5931

UNITED EVANGELICAL LUTHERAN CHURCH, Canada District
Donalda, Alberta

UNITED LUTHERAN CHURCH IN AMERICA, Canada Synod
237 King Street W., Kitchener, Ontario

WOMEN'S MISSIONARY SOCIETY OF REGULAR BAPTISTS OF CANADA
75 Lowther Avenue, Toronto 5, Ontario

YOUNG MEN'S CHRISTIAN ASSOCIATION
2160 Yonge Street, Toronto 7, Ontario. Tel.: 485–9447

YOUNG WOMEN'S CHRISTIAN ASSOCIATION
571 Jarvis Street, Toronto 5, Ontario

CANAL ZONE

ARMED SERVICES COMMISSION OF THE LUTHERAN CHURCH—MISSOURI SYNOD
830 Balboa Road, Balboa

CHRISTIAN SCIENCE COMMITTEE ON PUBLICATION
Box 221, Balboa Heights

ISTHMIAN RELIGIOUS WORKERS' FEDERATION (PANAMA)
Box J, Christobal

PANAMA BAPTIST CONVENTION
Box 3647, Balboa. Tel.: 2–2865 Canal Zone

UNION CHURCH OF THE CANAL ZONE
Box 261, Curundu

COSTA RICA

ALIANZA EVANGELICA COSTARRICENSE
Apdo. 5134, San José
Sec.: Sra. D. P. de Cabezas

ASAMBLEAS DE DIOS
Apdo. 3608, San José 1

ASOCIACIÓN DE IGLESIAS BIBLICAS COSTARRICENSES
Apdo. 2070, San José 1

ASOCIACIÓN DE IGLESIAS EVANGÉLICAS CENTROAMERICANAS
Apdo. 289, San José1

COMPAÑERISMO BAUTISTA MUNDIAL
Apdo. 3512, San José 1

CONVENCIÓN BAUTISTA DEL SUR
Apdo. 1883, San José 1. Tel.: 6062

IGLESIAS BAUTISTAS (PUERTO LIMÓN)
Apdo 204, Limon

IGLESIA BAUTISTA NACIONAL
Apdo. 4063, San José 1

IGLESIA DE DIOS (Cleveland, Tenn.)
Apdo. 2875, San José 1

IGLESIA DE DIOS (UNIVERSAL)
400 v. Sur Instituto Carit, 100 v. Oeste, Paso Ancho, San José

NORTH AMERICA

IGLESIA DE SANTIDAD PENTECOSTAL
Apdo. 3094, San José 1

IGLESIA EPISCOPAL DE COSTA RICA
Apdo. 288, San José 1

IGLESIA EVANGELICA CRUCEA MORAVIA
Guadalupe

IGLESIA LUTERANA
Apdo. 2159, San José 1

IGLESIA LUTERANA (MISSOURI SYNOD)
Apdo. 2836, San José 1

IGLESIA METODISTA
Apdo. 78, Alajuela

IGLESIA METODISTA (PUERTO LIMÓN)
Apdo. 269, Limon

INTERNATIONAL CHURCH OF THE FOUR-SQUARE GOSPEL
Apdo. 4492, San José 1

MENNONITE CHURCH
Heredia

UNION CHURCH
Apdo. 4456, San José 1

CUBA

BAPTIST CONVENTION OF WESTERN CUBA
Independenzia y Zaragoza, Apdo. 296, Matanzas

CONCILIO CUBANO DE IGLESIAS EVANGELICAS (1941)
Neptuno 629, Havana 2
Prof. Adolfo Ham

CONVENCION BAUTISTA DE CUBA ORIENTAL (Baptist Convention of
Eastern Cuba)
P.O. Box 41, Bayamo, Ote

CUBA YEARLY MEETING, RELIGIOUS SOCIETY OF FRIENDS
Puerto Padre, Ote

IGLESIA LUTERANO DE CUBA—SINODO DE MISURI
Box 1442, Nueva Gerona, Isle of Pines

MOVIMIENTO ESTUDIANTIL CRISTIANO (1960)
Calle K, 502, Vedado, Habana. Tel.: 32-0770

PRESBYTERY OF CUBA
Salud 218, Havana

SOCIEDAD BIBLICA EN CUBA
Neptuno 629, Havana 2

EL SALVADOR

BAPTIST CONVENTION OF THE REPUBLIC OF EL SALVADOR
Templo Bautista, San Salvador

LUTHERAN CHURCH, MISSOURI SYNOD
Apdo. 985, San Salvador

GUATEMALA

ALIANZA EVANGELICA DE GUATEMALA (1953)
Apdo. 4, Guatemala City

ASOCIACION CRISTIANA DE UNIVERSITARIOS
Apdo. 4, Guatemala City

BIBLE SOCIETY IN CENTRAL AMERICA
17 Calle 5-63, Zone 1, (Apdo. 1369), Guatemala City

NORTH AMERICA

IGLESIA EVANGELICA EN GUATEMALA
Apdo. 154, Guatemala City

LUTHERAN CHURCH—MISSOURI SYNOD
Apdo. 1111, Guatemala City

YOUNG MEN'S CHRISTIAN ASSOCIATION
Avenida de la Reform 2–18, Zone 9 (Apdo. 631), Guatemala City. Tel.: 60604

HAITI

BAPTIST UNION OF HAITI
Gonaives

HAITI BIBLE HOUSE
140 rue du Centre, (B.P. 253), Port-au-Prince

HAITI INLAND MISSION (1949)
P.O. Box 994, Port-au-Prince

WEST INDIES MISSION
Box 71, Aux Coyes

HONDURAS

ALIANZA DE LAS MISIONES EVANGELICAS DE HONDURAS (1945)
a/o Alas de Socorro, Suguatepeque, Com

LUTHERAN CHURCH—MISSOURI SYNOD
Apdo. 817, Tegucigalpa

UNITED CHURCH OF CHRIST
Apdo. 17, San Pedro Sula

JAMAICA

BIBLE SOCIETY
40 Duke Street, Kingston

CHRISTIAN SCIENCE COMMITTEE ON PUBLICATION
91 Old Hope Road, Kingston

CHURCH IN THE PROVINCE OF THE WEST INDIES: Diocese of Jamaica
Bishop's Lodge, Oxford Road, Kingston 5

CONGREGATIONAL UNION OF JAMAICA
6 Hope Road, Kingston 10. Tel.: 65636

JAMAICA BAPTIST UNION
6 Hope Road, Half-Way Tree, Kingston 10

JAMAICA COUNCIL OF CHURCHES
6 Hope Road, Kingston 10. Tel.: 65636. Rev. S. A. Webley

JAMAICA YEARLY MEETING, RELIGIOUS SOCIETY OF FRIENDS
Christiana P.O.

PRESBYTERIAN CHURCH OF JAMAICA (1848)
5 Lockett Avenue, Kingston 4. Tel.: 24250

SALVATION ARMY
Corner King Street and N. Parade, Kingston

STUDENT CHRISTIAN MOVEMENT OF JAMAICA
3 Lockett Avenue, Kingston

YOUNG MEN'S CHRISTIAN ASSOCIATION (1920)
21 Hope Road, Kingston 10. Tel.: 67575

YOUNG WOMEN'S CHRISTIAN ASSOCIATION
8 Central Avenue, Kingston Gardens, Kingston 4

MEXICO

ASOCIACION CRISTIANA DE ESTUDIANTES
Apdo. 25327, Gudad Universitaria, D.F.

NORTH AMERICA

ASOCIACION DE IGLESIAS CRISTIANAS EVANGELICAS (DISCIPULOS)
EN MEXICO
Apdo. 351, Aguascalientes, Ags. Tel.: 22–52

BIBLE SOCIETIES IN MEXICO
Liverpool No. 65, Mexico 6, D.F.

CHRISTIAN SCIENCE COMMITTEE ON PUBLICATION
Jamaica 125, Lomas Hipodromo, Mexico 10, D.F.

CONCILIO EVANGELICO DE MEXICO (1928)
Apdo. 1830, Mexico 1, D.F.
Professor Juan Díaz

CONFERENCIA CONCORDIA DE MEXICO
Apdo. 180, H. Matamoros, Tamps

CONVENCION NACIONAL BAUTISTA DE MEXICO
Ave. 16 de Septembre 6, Despacho No. 703, Mexico, D.F.

EVANGELISCHE GEMEINDEN DEUTSCHER SPRACHE IN MEXICO
Guty Gardens, 131, Mexico 20, D.F.

IGLESIA DE LOS PEREGRINOS (Pilgrim Holiness Church) (1920)
Apdo. 17, C. Valles, S.L.P.

IGLESIA DEL NAZARENO (Church of the Nazarene)
5 de Febrero 231, Mexico, D.F.

IGLESIA EPISCOPAL MEXICANA
Mier y Pesado, 212 Colonia del Calle, D.F.

IGLESIA EVANGELICA DE "LOS AMIGOS" DE MEXICO (Evangelical
Church of "The Friends" of Mexico)
Apdo. 446, Monterrey, N.L.

IGLESIA LUTERANA MEXICANA
Zacahuizco num 9, Mexico 13, D.F.

IGLESIA METODISTA DE MEXICO
Balderas 47, Mexico, D.F.

IGLESIA NACIONAL PRESBITERIANA DE MEXICO
616 S.E. Jefferson Street, Brownsville, Texas, U.S.A.

JUNTA GENERAL DE LAS IGLESIAS CONGREGACIONALES DEI
MEXICO
Apdo. 127, Guadalajata, Jalisco

MEXICAN BAPTIST CONVENTION
Jaurez 18, Iguala, Guerrero

MEXICAN INDIAN MISSION INC. (1931)
Tamazunchale, S.L.P.

MEXICAN MISSION OF THE CHURCHES OF CHRIST
Apdo. 817, Rayón 625 Nte., Monterrey, N.L.

MEXICAN CHRISTIAN MISSION (1895)
Apdo. 147, Aguascalientes, Ags

UNION NACIONAL DE SOCIEDADES FEMENILES CHRISTIANAS
Pino Suarez 25, Toluca

YOUNG MEN'S CHRISTIAN ASSOCIATION
Ejercito 253, Mexico 5, D.F. Tel.: 45 72 25

YOUNG WOMEN'S CHRISTIAN ASSOCIATION
Calle Articulo 123, No. 110, Mexico D.F.

NETHERLANDS ANTILLES

EVANGELICAL CHURCH
Box 320, Curaçao. Tel.: 4417

FRENTE EVANGELICO DE UNIVERSITARIOS NICARAGUENSES
Apdo. 9 Léon

PUERTO RICO

BIBLE SOCIETIES IN PUERTO RICO
Calle Robles 54 (P.O. Box 2672), Rio Piedras

CALVARY BAPTIST MISSION OF PUERTO RICO and MISSIONARY
RADIO STATION WIVV
6.8 Curpey Alto Road, Rio Piedras (Box 1904, Hato Rey). Tel.: 767–4232

CHRISTIAN SCIENCE COMMITTEE ON PUBLICATION
1803 Herrera Street, Santurce

CONCILIO EVANGELICO DE PUERTO RICO (1905)
P.O. Box 1788, Hato Rey.
Rev. A. R. Rodriguez

PRESBYTERY OF PUERTO RICO
P.O. Box 354, Mayaguez

PUERTO RICO BAPTIST CONVENTION
Mayaguez St., No. 21, Hato Rey

STUDENT CHRISTIAN FEDERATION
Inter-American University, San German

UNITED EVANGELICAL CHURCH OF PUERTO RICO (1931)
Robles St. 54, Rio Piedras, Puerto Rico 00925. Tel.: 765–3290

YOUNG MEN'S CHRISTIAN ASSOCIATION
Apdo. 2577, San Juan 5

YOUNG WOMEN'S CHRISTIAN ASSOCIATION
P.O. Box 10111, Santurce

TRINIDAD and TOBAGO

BAPTIST UNION OF TRINIDAD AND TOBAGO (1843)
39 Richmond Street, Port of Spain, Trinidad

CHRISTIAN SCIENCE COMMITTEE ON PUBLICATION
"Harroden", Pettit Valley, Four Roads, Trinidad

CHURCH IN THE PROVINCE OF THE WEST INDIES: DIOCESE OF
TRINIDAD
Hayes Court, Port of Spain

FEDERAL COUNCIL OF EVANGELICAL CHURCHES OF TRINIDAD
AND TOBAGO
P.O. Box 248, Port of Spain
Rev. G. O. Maynard

YOUNG MEN'S CHRISTIAN ASSOCIATION OF PORT-OF-SPAIN (1964)
No. 16/17 Victoria Square North, Port of Spain. Tel.: 32055

YOUNG WOMEN'S CHRISTIAN ASSOCIATION
25 Alexandra Street, Port of Spain

UNITED STATES

ADVENT CHRISTIAN CHURCH (1860)
917 Hardin Street, Aurora, Ill.

AFRICA INLAND MISSION (1895)
253 Henry Street, Brooklyn 1, N.Y.

AFRICAN METHODIST EPISCOPAL CHURCH (1787)
1724 Villa Street, Nashville, Tenn.

AFRICAN METHODIST EPISCOPAL ZION CHURCH (1796)
1326 "U" Street, N.W., Washington 9, D.C.

NORTH AMERICA

AFRICAN ORTHODOX CHURCH (1921)
122 W. 129th Street, New York, N.Y. 10026

AFRICAN UNION FIRST COLORED METHODIST PROTESTANT CHURCH, INC. (1805)
602 Spruce Street, Wilmington, Del.

ALBANIAN ORTHODOX ARCHDIOCESE IN AMERICA
529 East Broadway, Boston 27, Mass.

ALBERT SCHWEITZER FELLOWSHIP
297 Park Avenue, South, New York 10, N.Y.

AMERICAN ADVENT MISSION SOCIETY
1339 St. Julian Street, Charlotte, N.C. 28205. Tel.: (704) 376 7152

AMERICAN BAPTIST ASSOCIATION (1905)
214 East Broad Street, Texarkana, Ark.—Tex.

AMERICAN BAPTIST CONVENTION
Valley Forge, Pa.

AMERICAN BIBLE SOCIETY (1816)
Bible House, 450 Park Avenue, New York, N.Y. 10022

AMERICAN CARPATHO-RUSSIAN ORTHODOX GREEK CATHOLIC CHURCH
249 Butler Avenue, Johnstown, Pa.

AMERICAN COUNCIL OF CHRISTIAN CHURCHES
15 Park Row, New York 38, N.Y. 10038. Tel.: DI-9-0935

AMERICAN-EUROPEAN FELLOWSHIP FOR CHRISTIAN ONENESS AND EVANGELIZATION INC. (1926)
15 Philipse Place, Yonkers, New York 10703. Tel.: YOnkers 9-5170

AMERICAN FRIENDS BOARD OF MISSIONS, INC. (1894)
101 Quaker Hill Drive, Richmond, Ind.

AMERICAN FRIENDS SERVICE COMMITTEE
160 North 15th Street, Philadelphia, Pa. 2

AMERICAN LEPROSY MISSIONS, INC. (1906)
297 Park Avenue, South, New York, N.Y. 10010. Tel.: GR 5-5854

AMERICAN LUTHERAN CHURCH (1960)
422 S. 5th Street, Minneapolis, Minn. 55413. Tel.: 338-3821

AMERICAN McALL ASSOCIATION
110 East 23rd Street, New York 10, N.Y.

AMERICAN MISSION TO GREEKS, INC. (1942)
801 Broad Avenue, Ridgefield, N.J. 07657. Tel.: 201-943-4733

AMERICAN RESCUE WORKERS (1896)
2827 Frankford Avenue, Philadelphia 34, Pa.

AMERICAN SUNDAY-SCHOOL UNION
1816 Chestnut Street, Philadelphia 3, Pa.

AMERICAN TRACT SOCIETY, INC. (1825)
Oradell, N.J.

ANTIOCHIAN ORTHODOX ARCHDIOCESE OF TOLEDO AND DE-PENDENCIES IN NORTH AMERICA (1936)
532 Bush Street, Toledo, Ohio

APOSTOLIC CHRISTIAN CHURCH (NAZAREAN)
P.O. Box 5233, Akron 13, Ohio

APOSTOLIC CHRISTIAN CHURCHES OF AMERICA (1847)
410 E. Jefferson Street, Morton, Ill.

APOSTOLIC FAITH
N.W. Sixth and Burnside, Portland, Oregon. Tel.: 222 9761

APOSTOLIC LUTHERAN CHURCH OF AMERICA (1872)
86 Third Street, Laurium, Mich.

NORTH AMERICA

APOSTOLIC OVERCOMING HOLY CHURCH OF GOD (1919)
950 St. Madar Street, Mobile, Ala.

ARMENIAN CHURCH (U.S.A.: 1889)
630 Second Avenue, New York 16, N.Y.

ASSEMBLIES OF GOD, GENERAL COUNCIL (1914)
1445 Booville Avenue, Springfield, Missouri, 65802. Tel.: UN-2-2781

ASSOCIATE REFORMED PRESBYTERIAN CHURCH (GENERAL SYNOD)
508 Boulevard, Anderson, S.C.

ASSOCIATED CHURCH PRESS
875 N. Dearborn Street, Chicago 10, Ill.

ASSOCIATION OF BAPTISTS FOR WORLD EVANGELISM, INC. (1927)
1505 Race Street, Philadelphia, Pa. 19102. Tel.: LOcust 7-0274

BACK TO THE BIBLE BROADCAST (1939) (The Good News Broadcasting Association)
12th and "M" Streets, Lincoln, Nebraska 68501. Tel.: 435-2171

BAPTIST GENERAL CONFERENCE OF AMERICA (1879)
5750 North Ashland Avenue, Chicago, Ill. 60626. Tel.: 312-275-3590

BAPTIST MID-MISSIONS (1920)
4205 Chester Avenue, Cleveland, Ohio 44103. Tel.: 431-5222

BETHEL BAPTIST ASSEMBLY, INC.
701-705 Main, Evansville, Ind.

BETHEL MISSION OF CHINA
249 S. Sierra Bonita Avenue, Pasadena, Calif. 91106. Tel.: (213) SY 6-1300

BIBLE MEDITATION LEAGUE (1923)
957 E. Broad Street, (P.O. Box 477), Columbus, Ohio 43216. Tel.: 252-4700

BIBLE PRESBYTERIAN CHURCH
World Presbyterian Missions Inc.: 1617 W. 14th Street, Wilmington 6, Del.

BIBLE PROTESTANT MISSIONS, INC. (Methodist) (1944)
340 Doughty Boulevard, Inwood 96, N.Y.

BIBLE WAY CHURCH OF OUR LORD JESUS CHRIST WORLD WIDE, INC. (1957)
1132 New Jersey Avenue, N.W., Washington, D.C. 20001. Tel.: Republic 7-2179

BRETHREN CHURCH (ASHLAND, OHIO) (1881)
524 College Avenue, Ashland, Ohio 44895. Tel.: Ashland 2-1766

BRETHREN CHURCH (PROGRESSIVE) (1882)
Box 245, Winona Lake, Ind.

BRETHREN IN CHRIST (RIVER BRETHREN) (1778)
2001 Paxton Street, Harrisburg Pa. Tel.: 717-232-7836

BRETHREN IN CHRIST WORLD MISSIONS (1895)
Box 171, Elizabethtown, Pa. 17022. Tel.: 717 367 7045

BULGARIAN EASTERN ORTHODOX CHURCH
312 W. 101st Street, New York 25, N.Y.

CALVARY PENTECOSTAL CHURCH, INC. (1931)
416 S. 12th Avenue, Seattle, Wash.

CENTRAL ALASKAN MISSIONS INC.
P.O. Box 5, Glennallen, Alaska. Tel.: Talbot 2-3231

CENTRAL AMERICAN MISSION (1890)
3611 Congress Avenue, P.O. Box 6945, Dallas, Tex. 75219. Tel.: Riverside 2-4819

CEYLON AND INDIA GENERAL MISSION (1893)
107 North Hale Street, Wheaton, Ill. Tel.: MOntrose 8-8569

CHILD EVANGELISM FELLOWSHIP INTERNATIONAL (1935)
44 Ionia Street, S.W., Grand Rapids, Mich. 49502. Tel.: 459-4291

CHRISTADELPHIANS (1844)
507 Mitchell Avenue, Waterloo, Iowa

NORTH AMERICA

CHRISTIAN AND MISSIONARY ALLIANCE (1887)
260 West 44th Street, New York, N.Y. 10036. Tel.: LAckawanna 4–9282

CHRISTIAN CATHOLIC CHURCH (1896)
Administration Building, Zion, Ill.

CHRISTIAN CHILDREN'S FUND, INC. (1938)
108 South 3rd Street, Richmond, Va.

CHRISTIAN CHURCH OF NORTH AMERICA (ITALIAN) (1927)
241 Shady Avenue, Pittsburgh, Pa. 15206. Tel.: 242–7996

CHRISTIAN CHURCHES (DISCIPLES OF CHRIST) INTERNATIONAL
CONVENTION
221 Ohmer Avenue, P.O. Box 19136, Indianapolis 19, Ind.

CHRISTIAN CONGREGATION, THE (1887)
143 S. Gregg Street, Charlotte 8, N.C.

CHRISTIAN LITERATURE CRUSADE (1941)
701 Pennsylvania Avenue, Fort Washington, Pa. Tel.: Mitchell 6–2366

CHRISTIAN MEDICAL SOCIETY (1946)
1122 Westgate, Oak Park, Ill. Tel.: (312) 898 9510

CHRISTIAN METHODIST EPISCOPAL CHURCH (1870)
6432 S. Green Street, Apt. 1, Chicago 21, Ill.

CHRISTIAN MISSIONS IN MANY LANDS, INC. (Plymouth Brethren) (1921)
16 Hudson Street, New York 13, N.Y. Tel.: Cortlandt 7– 0306

CHRISTIAN NATIONALS' EVANGELISM COMMISSION, INC.
321 Bradley Avenue, San Jose, California. Tel.: 298–0965

CHRISTIAN REFORMED CHURCH (1857)
2850 Kalamazoo Avenue, Grand Rapids 8, Mich. Tel.: Cherry 5–0988

CHRISTIAN RURAL FELLOWSHIP (1935)
475 Riverside Drive, New York 27, N.Y.

CHRISTIAN UNION (1864)
Grover Hill, R.R.1, Ohio

CHURCHES OF CHRIST IN CHRISTIAN UNION (1909)
459 E. Ohio Street, Circleville, Ohio

CHURCHES OF GOD, HOLINESS (1914)
170 Ashby Street, N.W., Atlanta, Ga.

CHURCHES OF GOD IN NORTH AMERICA (GENERAL ELDERSHIP)
(1825)
13th and Walnut Streets, Harrisburg, Pa.

CHURCH OF CHRIST (HOLINESS) U.S.A.
329 E. Monument Street, Jackson, Miss.

CHURCH OF CHRIST, SCIENTIST (1879)
107 Falmouth Street, Boston, Mass. 02115. Tel.: (617)262–2300

CHURCH OF CHRIST, TEMPLE LOT (Latter Day Saints)
1011 South Cottage, Independence, Mo.

CHURCH OF GOD (1903)
9305, 244th Street, Queens Village, N.Y. 11428. Tel.: 212 HO–5 0756

CHURCH OF GOD (ABRAHAMIC FAITH) (1921)
Box 231, Oregon, Ill. 61031. Tel.: (815) 732–2761

CHURCH OF GOD (ANDERSON, IND.)
Box 2420, Anderson, Ind.

CHURCH OF GOD AND SAINTS OF CHRIST (1986)
Belleville, Portsmouth, Va.

CHURCH OF GOD BY FAITH (1919)
3220 Haines Street, Jacksonville, Fla.

CHURCH OF GOD (CLEVELAND, TENN.)
922–1080 Montgomery Avenue, Cleveland, Tenn. 37312. Tel.: (615)476–4512

NORTH AMERICA

CHURCH OF GOD IN CHRIST (1895)
958 Mason Street, Memphis, Tenn.
Board of Home and Foreign Missions: 1222 E. 35th Street, Los Angeles, Calif.

CHURCH OF GOD IN CHRIST (MENNONITE) (1859)
Lahoma, Okla.

CHURCH OF GOD OF PROPHECY (1903)
Bible Place, Cleveland, Tenn.

CHURCH OF GOD (SEVENTH DAY) (1933)
Box 328, Salem, W. Va.

CHURCH OF GOD (SEVENTH DAY), DENVER, COLORADO
1510 Cook Street, P.O. Box 2370, Denver, Colo.

CHURCH OF ILLUMINATION (1908)
"Beverley Hall", Clymer Road, Quakertown, Pa.

CHURCH OF JESUS CHRIST (BICKERTONITES) (1862)
6th and Lincoln Streets, Monongahela, Pa.

CHURCH OF JESUS CHRIST OF LATTER-DAY SAINTS
47 E. South Temple Street, Salt Lake City, Utah 84111. Tel.: 364–2511

CHURCH OF OUR LORD JESUS CHRIST OF THE APOSTOLIC FAITH, INC.
112–118 East 125th Street, New York 35, N.Y.

CHURCH OF REVELATION, THE (1930)
216 E. 11th Street, Hanford, Calif.

CHURCH OF THE BRETHREN (1708)
General Offices, Elgin, Ill.

CHURCH OF THE EAST AND OF THE ASSYRIANS
750 Gonzalez Drive, San Francisco, Calif.

CHURCH OF THE LIVING GOD (Christian Workers for Fellowship) (1889)
2440 Roman Street, Beaumont, Tex.

CHURCH OF THE LUTHERAN BRETHREN (1900)
Fergus Falls, Minn. Tel.: (218) 736–5758

CHURCH OF THE NAZARENE (1908)
6401 The Paseo, Kansas City, Mo. 64131. Tel.: DElmar 3–7000

CHURCH OF THE UNITED BRETHREN IN CHRIST
Department of Missions: 407 U.B. Building, Huntington, Ind. Tel.: (219) 356–6620

COMMITTEE ON CHRISTIAN LITERATURE FOR WOMEN AND CHILDREN IN MISSION FIELDS, INC. (1912)
475 Riverside Drive, New York, N.Y. 10027. Tel.: 212–870–2376

CONGO INLAND MISSION (Mennonite) (1911)
251 West Hively Avenue, Elkhart, Ind. 46517. Tel.: 523–4511

CONGO PROTESTANT RELIEF AGENCY (1960)
475 Riverside Drive, New York, N.Y. 10027 (Room 627). Tel.: (212) 860–2826

CONGREGATIONAL CHRISTIAN CHURCHES, NATIONAL ASSOCIATION OF,
176 W. Winconsin Avenue, Milwaukee, Wisc.

CONGREGATIONAL HOLINESS CHURCH (1921)
Lincolnton, Ga.

CONGREGATIONAL METHODIST CHURCH (1852)
5237 Terry Avenue, Dallas 10, Tex.

CONGREGATIONAL METHODIST CHURCH OF U.S.A. (1852)
Decatur, Miss.

CONSERVATIVE BAPTIST ASSOCIATION OF AMERICA
Home Mission Society: P.O. Box 328, Wheaton, Ill. 60188. Tel.: (312)665–1828
Foreign Mission Society: P.O. Box 5, Wheaton, Ill. 60188. Tel.: MOntrose 5–1200

NORTH AMERICA

CONSERVATIVE CONGREGATIONAL CHRISTIAN CONFERENCE (1948)
New Salem, Mass.

COUNCIL OF COMMUNITY CHURCHES
3598 Riverside Drive, Columbus 21, Ohio

CUMBERLAND PRESBYTERIAN CHURCH
1978 Union Avenue, Memphis, Tennessee. Tel.: 276–9032
Board of Foreign Missions (1880): Box 4746, Crosstown Station, Memphis 4, Tenn.

DUCK RIVER (AND KINDRED) ASSOCIATIONS OF BAPTISTS
R.F.D.2, Christiana, Tenn.

EASTERN EUROPEAN MISSION
35 North Raymond Avenue, Pasadena, Calif. 91101. Tel.: (213) SY 6–5425

EASTERN MENNONITE BOARD OF MISSIONS AND CHARITIES (1914)
Oak Lane and Brandt Boulevard, Salunga, Pennsylvania 17538. Tel.: 717–898–2251

ELIM MISSIONARY ASSEMBLIES (1947)
Lima, N.Y.

EVANGELICAL BAPTIST CHURCH INC., GENERAL CONFERENCE (1935)
1601 East Rose Street, Goldsboro, N.C.

EVANGELICAL BAPTIST MISSIONS (formerly Christian Missions, Inc.) (1949)
146 North 7th Street, Paterson 2, N.J.

EVANGELICAL CONGREGATIONAL CHURCH
1005 Barberry Road, Reading, PA. 19602. Tel.: 215–372–1976

EVANGELICAL COVENANT CHURCH OF AMERICA (1885)
5101 N. Francisco Avenue, Chicago 25, Ill.

EVANGELICAL FOREIGN MISSIONS ASSOCIATION (1945)
1405 G. Street N.W., Washington, D.C. 20005. Tel.: 628–7911

EVANGELICAL FREE CHURCH OF AMERICA (1887)
1515 East 66th Street, Minneapolis, Minnesota 55423. Tel.: 866–3343

EVANGELICAL LITERATURE OVERSEAS
P.O. Box 275, Wheaton, Ill. 60188. Tel.: (312) 668–4747

EVANGELICAL LUTHERAN CHURCH IN AMERICA (EIELSON SYNOD) (1846)
Lodi, Wisc.

EVANGELICAL LUTHERAN SYNOD (formerly Norwegian Synod) (1918)
Waterville, Iowa

EVANGELICAL LUTHERAN SYNODICAL CONFERENCE OF NORTH AMERICA
Missionary Board: 210 No. Broadway, St. Louis 2, Mo.

EVANGELICAL MENNONITE CHURCH
Commission on Missions: 3100 Addison Avenue, Fort Wayne, Ind.

EVANGELICAL METHODIST CHURCH
3036 North Meridian, Wichita, Kansas 67204. Tel.: Temple 8–4237

EVANGELICAL MISSION TO URUGUAY, INC. (1946)
P.O. Box 1353, Ft. Pierce, Fla. Tel.: 461–8199

EVANGELICAL PRESS ASSOCIATION
P.O. Box 41076, Los Angeles 41, Calif.

EVANGELICAL UNION OF SOUTH AMERICA (1911)
78 W. Hudson Avenue, Englewood, N.J.

EVANGELICAL UNITED BRETHREN CHURCH
601 W. Riverside Avenue, Dayton, Ohio 45406. Tel.: 222–2531

EVANGELICAL UNITY OF CZECH MORAVIAN BRETHREN
P.O. Box 5, Fairfield, Texas

EVANGELICAL FAITH MISSIONS
Box 267, Bedford, Ind. 47421. Tel.: (812) BR 5–7531

NORTH AMERICA

FAR EAST BROADCASTING COMPANY, INC. (1945)
Box 1, Whittier, Calif. 90601. Tel.: (213) Ox 8–0438

FAR EASTERN GOSPEL CRUSADE, INC.
14625 Greenfield Road, Detroit, Mich. Tel.: (313) 273–6460

FREE CHRISTIAN ZION CHURCH OF CHRIST (1905)
Nashville, Ark.

FREE METHODIST CHURCH OF NORTH AMERICA (1860)
Winona Lake, Ind. 46590. Tel.: 267–7161 (219)

FREE WILL BAPTIST CHURCH
1134 Murfreesboro Road, Nashville, Tennessee 37217. Tel.: 244–3470

FRIENDS, BOARD OF MISSIONS OF KANSAS YEARLY MEETING
615 E. 6th Avenue, Emporia, Kansas 66801

FRIENDS, BOARD OF MISSIONS OF OREGON YEARLY MEETING (1930)
N.6117 Maple Street, Spokane, Wash. 99208

FRIENDS, BOARD OF MISSIONS OF CALIFORNIA YEARLY MEETING
126 N. Washington Avenue, Whittier, Calif. (P.O. Box 389)

FRIENDS, FOREIGN MISSIONARY SOCIETY OF THE OHIO YEARLY
MEETING (1884)
Memorial Building, Damascus, Ohio 44619. Tel.: (216) 537–2040

FRIENDS GENERAL CONFERENCE OF THE RELIGIOUS SOCIETY OF
FRIENDS (1900)
1520 Race Street, Philadelphia, Pa. 19102. Tel.: LOcust 7–1965 (215)

FRIENDS, KANSAS YEARLY MEETING
1800 University Avenue, Wichita 13, Kansas

FRIENDS UNITED MEETING (FIVE YEARS MEETING OF FRIENDS)
101 Quaker Hill Drive, Richmond, Ind.

FRIENDS OF ISRAEL MISSIONARY AND RELIEF SOCIETY, INC. (1938)
1218 Chestnut Street, Philadelphia, Pa. 19107. Tel.: MA 7–2676

GENERAL ASSOCIATION OF REGULAR BAPTIST CHURCHES (1932)
608 S. Dearborn Street, Suite 1246, Transportation Bldg., Chicago 5, Ill.

GENERAL BAPTISTS
1629 Stinson, Evansville 12, Ind.

GENERAL CHURCH OF THE NEW JERUSALEM (1897)
Bryn Athyn, Pa. 19009. Tel.: Wilson 7–1375

GENERAL CONVENTION OF THE NEW JERUSALEM IN THE U.S.A.
(SWEDENBORGIAN)
5710 South Woodlawn Avenue, Chicago, Illinois, 60637. Tel.: 523–2966

GIDEONS INTERNATIONAL
2900 Lebanon Road, Nashville, Tennessee 37214

GOOD NEWS PUBLISHERS
9825 W. Roosevelt Road, Westchester, Ill. 60155. Tel.: Fillmore 5–6823

GOSPEL FILMS, INC. (1950)
2735 Apple Avenue, (P.O. Box 455) Muskegon, Michigan. Tel.: 773–3361

GOSPEL RECORDINGS INC. (1939)
122 Glendale Boulevard, Los Angeles 26, Calif. Tel.: 684–7461

GREATER EUROPE MISSION (1949)
214 North Hale Street, Wheaton, Illinois. Tel.: 312–665–0404

GREEK ORTHODOX CHURCH (GREEK ARCHDIOCESE OF NORTH
AND SOUTH AMERICA)
10 E. 79th Street, New York 21, N.Y.
Holy Cross Missionary Society: Greek Orthodox Theological School, Brooklyn,
Mass.

HINDUSTANI BIBLE INSTITUTE (1950)
P.O. Box 2815, Los Angeles, Calif. 90054. Tel.: 241–2654

269

NORTH AMERICA

HOLY CROSS LIBERIAN MISSION (1922)
Holy Cross Monastery, West Park, N.Y. 12493. Tel.: (914) 686–5553

HOUSE OF GOD, WHICH IS THE CHURCH OF THE LIVING GOD, THE
PILLAR AND THE GROUND OF TRUTH, INC. (1919)
41 N. 50th Street, Philadelphia, Pa.

HUNGARIAN REFORMED CHURCH IN AMERICA (1904)
180 Home Avenue, Trenton 10, N.J.

HUTTERIAN BRETHREN
Alexandria, S.D.

INDEPENDENT BOARD FOR PRESBYTERIAN FOREIGN MISSIONS
(1933)
286 W. Walnut Lane, Philadelphia, Pa. 19144. Tel.: Germantown 8–0511

INDEPENDENT FUNDAMENTAL CHURCHES OF AMERICA (1930)
542 So. Dearborn Street, Chicago, Ill. 6065. Tel.: (312) 427–7439

INTERDENOMINATIONAL FOREIGN MISSION ASSOCIATION OF
NORTH AMERICA (1917)
54 Bergen Avenue, Ridgefield Park, N.J. 07660. Tel.: (201) 489–8070

INTERNATIONAL CHURCH OF THE FOURSQUARE GOSPEL
1100 Glendale Boulevard, Los Angeles 26, Calif.

INTERNATIONAL CONVENTION OF CHRISTIAN CHURCHES (DIS-
CIPLES OF CHRIST)
221 Ohmer Avenue, (P.O. Box 19136), Indianapolis, Ind. 46219. Tel.: Fleet-
wood 9–9568

INTERNATIONAL FELLOWSHIP OF EVANGELICAL STUDENTS (1947)
1519 N. Astor, Chicago, Ill. 60610. Tel.: (312) WH 4–7840

INTERNATIONAL MISSIONS INC. (1930)
234 Bergen Avenue, Jersey City 5, N.J. Tel.: 433–3166

INTERNATIONAL PENTECOSTAL ASSEMBLIES (1914)
892 Berne Street, S.E., Atlanta 16, Ga

INTERNATIONAL SOCIETY OF CHRISTIAN ENDEAVOR (1881)
1221 E. Broad Street, Columbus, Ohio 43216. Tel.: 253–8541

INTERNATIONAL STUDENT SERVICE
291 Broadway, New York 7, N.Y.

INTER-VARSITY CHRISTIAN FELLOWSHIP OF THE U.S.A. (1940)
1519 N. Astor Street, Chicago, Ill. 60610. Tel.: WHitehall 4–7840

JAPAN INTERNATIONAL CHRISTIAN UNIVERSITY FOUNDATION,
INC. (1949)
475 Riverside Drive, New York, N.Y. 10027. Tel.: Riverside 9–6734

JOHN MILTON SOCIETY (World-wide Ministry to the Blind) (1928)
475 Riverside Drive, New York 27, N.Y.

LATIN AMERICA MISSION INC. (1921)
285 Orchard Terrace, Bogota, N.J. 07603. Tel.: (201) HU 9–6171

LATIN AMERICAN LUTHERAN MISSION (1939)
Winger, Minn.

LIBERAL CATHOLIC CHURCH
P.O. Box 295, Miranda, Calif.

LUTHERAN CHURCH IN AMERICA, BOARD OF WORLD MISSIONS (1919)
231 Madison Avenue, New York, N.Y. 10016. Tel.: (212) LE 2–3410

LUTHERAN CHURCH, MISSOURI SYNOD (1847)
The Lutheran Building, 210 N. Broadway, St. Louis 2, Mo.

MAHON MISSION
1415 27th Street, Zion, Ill. 60099. Tel.: (312) TR 2–2486

MENNONITE BOARD OF MISSIONS AND CHARITIES (1882)
1711 Prairie Street, Elkhart, Ind.

MENNONITE BRETHREN CHURCH OF NORTH AMERICA
315 South Lincoln, Hillsboro, Kansas 67063. Tel.: (316) 947-3151

MENNONITE CHURCH (1683)
Mennonite Building, Scottdale, Pa.

MENNONITE CHURCH, GENERAL CONFERENCE (1860)
722 Main Street, (Box 347), Newton, Kansas. Tel.: (316) ATwater 3-5100

METHODIST CHURCH, THE (1784)
General Conference: 5250 Santa Monica Boulevard, Los Angeles, Calif.
Council of Bishops: 1115 So. Fourth Street, Louisville, Ky.
Board of Missions: 475 Riverside Drive, New York, N.Y. 10027. Tel.: RIVerside 9-0700

METROPOLITAN CHURCH ASSOCIATION, INC. (1899)
Box 156, Dundee, Ill.

MEXICAN LUTHERAN NORTHWEST SYNOD (World Mission Prayer League Inc.)
228 Clifton Avenue, Minneapolis, Minnesota

MEXICAN MILITANT MISSION
P.O. Box 636, Pharr, Tex. 78577. Tel.: (512) ST 7-3543

MISSIONARY AND SOUL WINNING FELLOWSHIP
350 East Market Street, Long Beach, California 90805

MISSIONARY AVIATION FELLOWSHIP (1945)
P.O. Box 32, Fullerton, Calif. Tel.: 714-525-8206

MISSIONARY CHURCH ASSOCIATION (1904)
Board of Foreign Missions (1898): 3901 South Wayne Avenue, Fort Wayne, Ind., 46807. Tel.: 744-9339

MISSIONARY STRATEGY AGENCY (ASIA FOR CHRIST) (1964)
1054 North Saint Andres Place, Los Angeles, California 90038. Tel.: 465-0067

MISSION TO EUROPE'S MILLIONS (1927)
17650 Old Summit Road, Los Gatos, Calif. 95030

MOODY LITERATURE MISSION (MOODY BIBLE INSTITUTE)
820 N. LaSalle Street, Chicago, Ill. 60610. Tel.: MI 2-1570

MORAVIAN CHURCH IN AMERICA (Unitas Fratrum) (1742)
Northern Province: 69 West Church Street, Bethlehem. Pa. Tel.: 215 867-7566
Southern Province: 500 South Church Street, Winston-Salem, 2, N.C.

NATIONAL ASSOCIATION OF EVANGELICALS (1942)
N. Main Street at Gundersen Dr., Wheaton, Ill.

NATIONAL ASSOCIATION OF FREE WILL BAPTISTS
1134 Murfreesboro Road, Nashville, Tennessee 37217. Tel.: 244-3470
Foreign Mission Dept. (1930): P.O. Box 1088, Nashville, Tennessee 37217. Tel.: (615) 244-3470

NATIONAL BAPTIST CONVENTION OF AMERICA (1880)
1215 Church Street, Georgetown, S.C.

NATIONAL BAPTIST CONVENTION, U.S.A., INC.
3101 S. Parkway, Chicago 16, Ill.

NATIONAL BAPTIST EVANGELICAL LIFE AND SOUL SAVING ASSEMBLY OF U.S.A. (1921)
441 Monroe Avenue, Detroit 26, Mich.

NATIONAL COUNCIL OF THE CHURCHES OF CHRIST IN THE UNITED STATES OF AMERICA
475 Riverside Drive, New York, N.Y. 10027. Tel.: 870-2561
Gen. Sec.: R. H. Edwin Espy

 DIVISION OF CHRISTIAN LIFE AND MISSION
 Assoc. Gen. Sec.: Rev. Jon L. Regier

DIVISION OF CHRISTIAN EDUCATION
Assoc. Gen. Sec.: Rev. Gerald E. Knoff
Dept. of Educational Development, Exec. Dir.: Rev. Eli F. Wismer
Dept. of Higher Education, Exec. Dir.: Rev. Hubert C. Noble
Dept. of Education for Mission, Exec. Dir.: Rev. J. Allan Ranck
Dept. of Ministry, Vocation and Pastoral Services, Exec. Dir.: Rev. Ralph E. Peterson

DIVISION OF OVERSEAS MINISTRIES
Assoc. Gen. Sec.: Rev. David M. Stowe
Dept. of Church World Service, Exec. Dir.: James MacCracken
Dept. of Specialized Ministries, Exec. Dir.: Irene A. Jones
Missionary Research Library, Dir.: Rev. Herbert C. Jackson

DIVISION OF CHRISTIAN UNITY
Assoc. Gen. Sec.: Mrs. Theodore O. Wedel

OFFICE OF PLANNING AND PROGRAM
Assoc. Gen. Sec.: Rev. Rufus Cornelsen

OFFICE OF COMMUNICATION
Assoc. Gen. Sec.:

OFFICE OF ADMINISTRATION
Assoc. Gen. Sec.: Rev. H. Leroy Brininger

NATIONAL DAVID SPIRITUAL TEMPLE OF CHRIST CHURCH UNION (INC.) U.S.A. (1921)
2503 E. 20th Street, Kansas City 20, Mo.

NATIONAL HOLINESS ASSOCIATION
Box S-111, Marion, Ind.

NATIONAL LUTHERAN COUNCIL
50 Madison Avenue, New York, N.Y. 10010. Tel.: MUrray Hill 6-8860
Division of American Missions: 327 S. LaSalle Street, Chicago 4, Ill.

NATIONAL PRIMITIVE BAPTIST CONVENTION OF THE U.S.A. (1907)
2116 Clinton Avenue, W., Huntsville, Ala.

NATIONAL STUDENT CHRISTIAN FEDERATION (1959)
475 Riverside Drive, New York, N.Y. 10027. Tel.: (212) 870-2366

NAVIGATORS, THE (1933)
Colorado Springs, Colo. 80901. Tel.: 634-2861

NEAR EAST COLLEGE ASSOCIATION INC. (1927)
548 Fifth Avenue, New York 36, N.Y.

NETHERLANDS REFORMED CONGREGATIONS (1907)
1610 Main Street, Rock Valley, Iowa

NEW APOSTOLIC CHURCH OF NORTH AMERICA, INC. (1863)
3753 N. Troy Street, Chicago 18, Ill.

NEW TRIBES MISSION INC. (1942)
Woodworth, Wisc. 53194. Tel.: (414) 857-2861

NORTH AFRICA MISSION (1948 in U.S.)
241 Fairfield Avenue, Upper Darby, Pa. Tel.: FL2-2003

NORTH AMERICAN BAPTIST ASSOCIATION (1950)
716 Main Street, Little Rock, Ark.

NORTH AMERICAN BAPTIST GENERAL CONFERENCE (1865)
7308 Madison Street, Forest Park, Ill. Tel.: PResident 1-8700 (312)

OBERLIN SHANSI MEMORIAL ASSOCIATION
Wilder Hall, Oberlin, Ohio

OHIO YEARLY MEETING OF FRIENDS CHURCH (INDEPENDENT)
355 W. 7th Street, Salem, Ohio

OLD GERMAN BAPTIST BRETHREN (1881)
R.D. 4, Box 219, Delphi, Ind.

NORTH AMERICA

OLD ORDER AMISH MENNONITE CHURCH
Mennonite Year Book: Scottdale, Pa.

OPEN BIBLE STANDARD CHURCHES INC. (1932)
851 19th Street, Des Moines, Iowa 50314. Tel.: (515) CH 4-2251

OREGON YEARLY MEETING OF FRIENDS CHURCH
600 E. Third Street, Newberg, Oregon. Tel.: (503) 538-4448

ORIENTAL BOAT MISSION (1909)
P.O. Box 428, Chicago 90, Ill. Tel.: Greenleaf 5-3449

ORIENTAL MISSIONARY SOCIETY (1901)
Box 27000A, Indianapolis, Indiana, 46227. Tel.: (317) 881-6751

ORIGINAL CHURCH OF GOD, INC., THE (1886)
2214 E. 17th Street, Chatanooga 4, Tenn.

ORINOCO RIVER MISSION (1920)
30 North Raymond Avenue, Pasadena, Calif. 91101. Tel.: (213) 796-0673

ORTHODOX PRESBYTERIAN CHURCH
7401 Old York Road, Philadelphia 26, Pa.

OVERSEAS CRUSADES, INC. (1950)
265 Lytton Avenue, Palo Alto, California. Tel.: 321-8587

OVERSEAS MISSION SOCIETY INC. and LAYMEN INTERNATIONAL (1953)
Mount Saint Alban, Washington D.C. 20016. Tel.: 363-1683

PENTECOSTAL ASSEMBLIES OF THE WORLD, INC. (1919)
3040 North Illinois Street, Indianapolis, Ind. 46208. Tel.: Wa 3-3371

PENTECOSTAL CHURCH OF GOD OF AMERICA, INC. (1919)
312-316 Joplin Avenue, Joplin, Mo. 64801. Tel.: MAyfair 4-7050

PENTECOSTAL FELLOWSHIP OF NORTH AMERICA
P.O. Box 966, Dunn, N.C.

PENTECOSTAL FREE WILL BAPTIST CHURCH
Box 966, Dunn, N.C. Tel.: 892-5572

PENTECOSTAL HOLINESS CHURCH, INC.
P.O. Box 295, Franklin Springs, Georgia. Tel.: 245-6111

PHILADELPHIA YEARLY MEETING OF RELIGIOUS SOCIETY OF FRIENDS
1515 Cherry Street, Philadelphia 2, Pa.

PILGRIM HOLINESS CHURCH
226-230 East Ohio Street, Indianapolis 4, Ind. Tel.: (317) ME 9-6415

PILLAR OF FIRE (1901)
Zarephath, N.J.

PIONEER MISSION AGENCY, INC. (1921)
Keswick Grove, (Whiting P.O.), N.J. 08759. Tel.: 201-657-7187

PLYMOUTH BRETHREN
Mt. Carmel Road, Parkton, Md.

POCKET TESTAMENT LEAGUE, INC. (1893)
49 Honeck Street, Englewood, N.J. 07631. Tel.: (201) LO 7-2332

POLISH BAPTIST ASSOCIATION OF THE UNITED STATES AND CANADA
2624 North Fairfield Avenue, Chicago 47, Ill. Tel.: SP 2-3161

POLISH NATIONAL CATHOLIC CHURCH OF AMERICA (1897)
529 E. Locust Street, Scranton 5, Pa.

PRESBYTERIAN CHURCH IN THE U.S. (1861)
341 Ponce de Leon Avenue, N.E., Atlanta 8, Ga.
Board of World Missions: 2400 21st Avenue, S., P.O. Box 330, Nashville 1, Tenn.
Tel.: 298-3351

PRIMITIVE BAPTISTS
c/o Mrs. C. H. Cayce, Thornton, Ark.

273

NORTH AMERICA

PRIMITIVE METHODIST CHURCH, U.S.A. (1889)
310 Steele Road, Feasterville, Pennsylvania. Tel.: Elmwood 5–1832 (215)

PROGRESSIVE NATIONAL BAPTIST CONVENTION, INC. (1961)
630 Glenwood Avenue, Cincinnati, Ohio

PROTESTANT EPISCOPAL CHURCH IN THE U.S.A., DOMESTIC AND
FOREIGN MISSIONARY SOCIETY (1835)
Episcopal Church Center, 815 Second Avenue, New York, N.Y. 10017

PROTESTANT REFORMED CHURCHES OF AMERICA
1139 Franklin, S.E., Grand Rapids 7, Mich.

RAMABAI MUKTI MISSION (1929)
American Council of the Ramabai Mukti Mission,
6869 North 19th Street, Philadelphia, Pa. 19126. Tel.: Waverley 4–4339

REFORMED CHURCH IN AMERICA
475 Riverside Drive, New York, N.Y. 10027. Tel.: (212) 870–2452

REFORMED CHURCH IN THE U.S.
Rt. 3, Manitowac, Wisc.

REFORMED EPISCOPAL CHURCH (1873)
232 Wendover Drive, Havertown, Pa.
Board of Foreign Missions: 25 So. 43rd Street, Philadelphia, Pa. 19104. Tel.:
Baring 2–5158 (215)

REFORMED METHODIST UNION EPISCOPAL CHURCH (1885)
Route 1, Box 107, Pinewood, S.C.

REFORMED PRESBYTERIAN CHURCH IN NORTH AMERICA,
EVANGELICAL SYNOD
1818 Missouri Avenue, Las Cruces, New Mexico 88001. Tel.: 505 –524–9277

REFORMED PRESBYTERIAN CHURCH OF NORTH AMERICA (OLD
SCHOOL) (Church of the Covenanters)
2007 Crest Dr., Topeka, Kan.

REFORMED PRESBYTERIAN (GREEK EVANGELICAL) CHURCH OF
CYPRUS
Empire Building, 537 Liberty Street, Pittsburgh, Pa. 15222. Tel.: 281–5658

REFORMED ZION UNION APOSTOLIC CHURCH (1869)
1st Episcopal District, High Street, South Hill, Va.

RELIGION IN AMERICAN LIFE, INC.
184 Fifth Avenue, New York 10, N.Y.

REORGANIZED CHURCH OF JESUS CHRIST OF LATTER SAINTS (1844)
The Auditorium, Independence, Mo. Tel.: 816–831–1000

ROMANIAN ORTHODOX EPISCOPATE OF AMERICA (1929)
2522 Grey Tower Road, R.F.D. 7, Jackson, Mich. 49201. Tel.: Grass Lake 5286

RUSSIAN ORTHODOX CATHOLIC CHURCH IN AMERICA PATRI-
ARCHAL EXARCHATE
15 E. 97th Street, New York 29, N.Y.

RUSSIAN ORTHODOX CHURCH OUTSIDE RUSSIA
75 E. 93rd Street, New York 28, N.Y.

RUSSIAN ORTHODOX GREEK CATHOLIC CHURCH OF AMERICA
59 East 2nd Street, New York 3, N.Y.

SALVATION ARMY (U.S.A.: 1880)
120–130 West 14th Street, New York 11, N.Y. Tel.: Chelsea 3–8700

SANTAL MISSION OF THE NORTHERN CHURCHES, AMERICAN
BRANCH
122 West Franklin Avenue, Minneapolis, Minnesota 55404. Teo.: 322–2571

SCHWENKFELDER CHURCH MISSION BOARD (1895)
Pennsburg, Pa.

SECOND CUMBERLAND PRESBYTERIAN CHURCH IN U.S.
630 E. Matthew Street, Union City, Tenn.

NORTH AMERICA

SEPARATE BAPTISTS IN CHRIST
Fonthill, Ky.

SERBIAN ORTHODOX CHURCH IN THE U.S.A. AND CANADA
8347 W. Summerdale Avenue, Chicago 56, Ill.

SEVENTH-DAY ADVENTISTS, GENERAL CONFERENCE (1863)
6840 Eastern Avenue, N.W. Takoma Park, Washington D.C. 20012. Tel.:
RAndolph 3-0800

SEVENTH-DAY BAPTIST GENERAL CONFERENCE (1671)
510 Watchung Avenue, Plainfield, N.J. 07061. Tel.: 756-1325
Missionary Society: 403 Washington Trust Bldg., Westerly, R.I.

SLAVIC MISSIONARY SERVICE (1933)
P.O. Box 307, South River, N.J.

SLAVIC MISSIONARY SOCIETY, INC. (1907)
11122 S. State Street, Chicago, Ill. 60628. Tel.: 264-2300

SOURCE OF LIGHT MISSION (1952)
P.O. Box 8, Madison, Ga. 30650. Tel.: 786

SOUTH AMERICAN INDIAN MISSION, INC. (1914)
5217 South Military Trail, Lake Worth, Florida. Tel.: (305) 965-1833

SOUTHERN BAPTIST CONVENTION (1845)
460 James Robertson Parkway, Nashville, Tennessee. Tel.: 254-0272
Foreign Mission Board: 3806 Monument Avenue, Richmond, Va. 23230. Tel.:
353-0151

SOUTHERN METHODIST CHURCH (1939)
3913 Cambridge Avenue, Nashville, Tenn.

SPANISH WORLD GOSPEL BROADCASTING INC. (1958)
Box 335, Winona Lake, Ind. 465 90. Tel.: 267-8821

SUMMER INSTITUTE OF LINGUISTICS (1934) (Wycliffe Bible Translators)
P.O. Box 1960, Santa Ana, California 92702. Tel.: 714-547-6526

SYNOD OF EVANGELICAL LUTHERAN CHURCHES (1902)
1 Sutton Place, Cranford, N.J.

SYRIAN ANTIOCHIAN ORTHODOX CHURCH (Archdiocese of New York
and All North America)
239 85th Street, Brooklyn 9, N.Y.

SYRIAN ORTHODOX CHURCH OF ANTIOCH (Archdiocese of the U.S.A. and
Canada)
293 Hamilton Place, Hackensack, N.J.

THE EVANGELICAL ALLIANCE MISSION (TEAM)
2500 North Main Street, P.O. Box 969, Wheaton, Illinois 60187. Tel.: 312/653-
5300

TRANS WORLD RADIO
354 Main Street, Chatham, N.J. 07928. Tel.: (201) ME 5-5775

TRIUMPH THE CHURCH AND KINGDOM OF GOD IN CHRIST (1902)
213 Furrington Avenue, S.E., Atlanta, Ga.

UKRAINIAN ORTHODOX CHURCH OF AMERICA (1928) (Ecumenical
Patriarchate)
1410 Vyse Avenue, New York 59, N.Y.

UKRAINIAN ORTHODOX CHURCH OF U.S.A. (1919)
P.O. Box 595, South Bound Brook, N.J.

UNION AMERICAN METHODIST EPISCOPAL CHURCH (1813)
774 Pine Street, Camden 3, N.J.

UNITARIAN UNIVERSALIST ASSOCIATION OF NORTH AMERICA
25 Beacon Street, Boston 8, Mass. 02108. Tel.: Ri 2-2100

UNITED ANDEAN INDIAN MISSION (1945)
16th Floor, 475 Riverside Drive, New York, N.Y. 10027. Tel.: 212-870-2616

UNITED BAPTISTS (1801)
8640 Brazil Road, Jacksonville, Fla.

UNITED BOARD FOR CHRISTIAN HIGHER EDUCATION IN ASIA (1932)
475 Riverside Drive, New York, N.Y. 10027. Tel.: 212–870–2601

UNITED BRETHREN IN CHRIST
United Brethren Building, Huntingdon, Ind. Tel.: (219)356–7622

UNITED CHRISTIAN MISSIONARY SOCIETY (Disciples of Christ) (1919)
222 South Downey Avenue, Indianapolis, Ind. 46207. Tel.: 353–1491

UNITED CHURCH BOARD FOR WORLD MINISTRIES (1810)
475 Riverside Drive, 16th Floor, New York, N.Y. 10027. Tel.: (212)870–2637

UNITED CHURCH OF CHRIST
297 Park Avenue, S., New York 10, N.Y.

UNITED FREE WILL BAPTIST CHURCH
Kinston College, 1000 University Street, Kinston, N.C.

UNITED HOLY CHURCH OF AMERICA, INC. (1886)
500 Gulley Street, Goldsboro, N.C.

UNITED MISSION IN IRAQ, JOINT COMMITTEE FOR THE
Room 622, 475 Riverside Drive, New York, N.Y. 10027. Tel.: 870–2445

UNITED MISSIONARY CHURCH (1883)
1819 S. Main Street, Elkhart, Ind. Tel.: (219)JA 4–0526

UNITED PENTECOSTAL CHURCH, INC.
3645 S. Grand Boulevard, St. Louis 18, Mo.

UNITED PRESBYTERIAN CHURCH IN THE UNITED STATES OF AMERICA
510 Witherspoon Building, Philadelphia 7, Pa.
Commission on Ecumenical Mission and Relations: 475 Riverside Drive, New York, N.Y. 10027. Tel.: 870–2312

UNITED STATES CONFERENCE FOR THE WORLD COUNCIL OF CHURCHES
475 Riverside Drive, Room 439, New York, N.Y. 10027. Tel.: (212) 870–2533

UNITED WORLD MISSION
P.O. Box 8000, St. Petersburg, Fla. 33738. Tel.: (813)391–2398

UNITY OF THE BRETHREN
5905 Carleen Dr., Austin 3, Tex.

VOICE OF CHINA AND ASIA MISSIONARY SOCIETY (1946)
P.O. Box 15-M, Pasadena, Calif. Tel.: 796–3117

WESLEYAN METHODIST CHURCH OF AMERICA (1843)
P.O. Box 2000, Marion, Ind. Tel.: 674–3301

WEST INDIES MISSION, INC. (1928)
Box 279, Route One, Homer City, Pa. 15748. Tel.: 479–8380

WISCONSIN EVANGELICAL LUTHERAN SYNOD (1850)
3512 West North Avenue, Milwaukee 8, Wisc.
General Board for World Missions: 4960 Academy Street, San Diego, Calif.

WOMEN'S CHRISTIAN TEMPERANCE UNION
1730 Chicago Avenue, Evanston, Ill.

WORLD BAPTIST FELLOWSHIP MISSION AGENCY (1928)
3001 W. Division, Arlington, Texas 76010. Tel.: CR 4–7161

WORLD GOSPEL CRUSADES
P.O. Box 42188, Los Angeles, Calif. 90042. Tel.: (213) CL 7–8285

WORLD GOSPEL MISSION (1910)
123 West Fifth Street, Marion, Ind. 46953. Tel.: North 4–7331

WORLD LITERATURE CRUSADE (1946)
Box 1313, Studio City, Calif. Tel.: 766–3766

WORLD MISSION PRAYER LEAGUE, INC. (LUTHERAN)
228 Clifton Avenue, Minneapolis, Minnesota 55403. Tel.: FE–8–2433

WORLD MISSIONS, INC. (1958)
P.O. Box 2, Philadelphia, Pa.

WORLD MISSIONS TO CHILDREN, INC. (1950)
Box 1048, Grants Pass, Oregon. Tel.: 479–3731

WORLD PRESBYTERIAN MISSIONS, INC.
901 North Broom Street, Wilmington 6, Delaware. Tel.: OL 2–3204

WORLD RADIO MISSIONARY FELLOWSHIP, INC. (1931)
2741 N.W. 75th Street, Miami, Florida. Tel.: 691–3352

WORLD VISION, INC. (1950)
919 W. Huntington Dr., Monravia, Calif.

WORLDWIDE EVANGELIZATION CRUSADE (1914)
P.O. Box A, Fort Washington, Pa. Tel.: Mitchell 6–2323

WORLDWIDE PRAYER AND MISSIONARY UNION, INC. (1931)
4714 North Spaulding Avenue, Chicago, Ill. 60625. Tel.: 463–0264

WYCLIFFE BIBLE TRANSLATORS, INC. (1942)
P.O. Box 1960, 219 West Walnut, Santa Ana, Calif. Tel.: 547–6526

YOUNG MEN'S CHRISTIAN ASSOCIATION, NATIONAL COUNCIL OF
291 Broadway, New York, N.Y. 10097. Tel.: Digby 9–0700

YOUNG WOMEN'S CHRISTIAN ASSOCIATION, U.S.A., NATIONAL
BOARD
600 Lexington Avenue, New York 22, N.Y.

YOUTH FOR CHRIST INTERNATIONAL (1944)
North Main Street, Wheaton, Illinois 60188. Tel.: 668–6600

SOUTH AMERICA

ARGENTINA

ANGLICAN CHURCH
Calle 25 de Mayo 282, Buenos Aires

CHRISTIAN SCIENCE COMMITTEE ON PUBLICATION
San Martin 551, 8° piso, depto. 78, Buenos Aires

CONVENCIÓN EVANGÉLICA BAUTISTA (1908)
Rivadavia 3476, Buenos Aires. Tel.: 88–8938 and 88–8924

FEDERACIÓN DE EGLESIAS EVANGÉLICAS
Tucumán 358–6° 'L', Buenos Aires
Rev. Luis P. Bucafusco

IGLESIA CONGREGACIONALISTA EN LA REPUBLICA ARGENTINA
San Martin 119, Concordia, Entre Rios, F.N.G.U.

IGLESIA EVANGÉLICA DEL RIO DE LA PLATA
Esmeralda 162, Buenos Aires

IGLESIA EVANGÉLICA LUTERANA ARGENTINA
P. de Mendoza 1249, Hurlingham, F.C.S.M.

IGLESIA EVANGÉLICA LUTERANA UNIDA
Cuenca 3285, Buenos Aires, 17. Tel.: 50–6483

IGLESIA METODISTA CONFERENCIA DEL RIO DE LA PLATA
Rivadavia 4044, Buenos Aires

LIGA ARGENTINA DE MUJERES EVANGÉLICAS
Balcarce 260, Piso 2, Dep.E., Buenos Aires

MOVIMENTO ESTUDIANTIL CRISTIANO
Reconquista 439, Piso 5, Buenos Aires

NEW TESTAMENT MISSIONARY UNION (1902)
Estevez Correa 139, Temperley, F.C.N.G.R., Buenos Aires

SALVATION ARMY
Avda Rivadavia 3253, Buenos Aires

SOCIEDAD BAUTISTA CONSERVADORA (1947)
Carlos Gerow, Huacalera, Provincia de Jujuy

SOCIEDADES BIBLICAS EN LA ARGENTINA
"Casa de la Biblia", Tucumán 352–358, Buenos Aires

UNION EVANGÉLICA DE LA ARGENTINA
Calle Mitre 647, Tandil

YOUNG MEN'S CHRISTIAN ASSOCIATION
Reconquista 439, Buenos Aires

YOUNG WOMEN'S CHRISTIAN ASSOCIATION
Calle Tucumán 844, Buenos Aires

BOLIVIA

ANDES EVANGELICAL MISSION (1907)
Cajon 514, Cochabamba. Tel.: 2840

BOLIVIAN BAPTIST UNION
Casilla 86, Cochabamba

BOLIVIAN FRIENDS' HOLINESS MISSION (1924)
Sorata

BOLIVIAN INDIAN MISSION
Cajón 514, Cochabamba

BOLIVIAN LUTHERAN CHURCH
USIS, La Paz

EVANGELISTIC MISSIONARY FELLOWSHIP (1948)
Casilla 1448, La Paz

278

SOUTH AMERICA

IGLESIAS EVANGÉLICAS UNIDAS (1955)
Casilla 1597, La Paz

LIGA DE ORACIÓN EN MISSION MUNDIAL
Casilla 226, La Paz

METHODIST BAPTIST CHURCH
Landaeta 423, Casilla 356, La Paz. Tel.: 2–4113

MOVIMIENTO ESTUDIANTIL CRISTIANO (1965)
Avenida 16 de julio 1796, La Paz. Tel.: 12702

SOCIEDADES BÍBLICAS EN BOLIVIA
Hamiraya 5313, (Casilla 329) Cochabamba

YOUNG MEN'S CHRISTIAN ASSOCIATION
Primo Rios C., ACJ, Aven. 20 de Octubre 1839 (Casilla 963), La Paz

YOUNG WOMEN'S CHRISTIAN ASSOCIATION
Calle Landaeta 289, La Paz

BRAZIL

ALIANCA BIBLICA DO BRASIL
Caixa Postal 2350, Porto Alegre, R.S.

ALIANCA DAS IGREJA CRISTAS EVANGÉLICAS DO NORTE DO
BRASIL
Caixa 72, São Luis, Maranhão

ASSEMBLÉIAS DE DEUS
Caixa Postal 2277, Rio de Janeiro

ASSOCIAÇÃO EVANGÉLICA DE CATEQUESE AOS INDIOS CUYUAS (1929)
Dourãdos, via Campo Grande, Matto Grosso, Noroeste

CHRISTIAN SCIENCE COMMITTEE ON PUBLICATION
Caixa Postal 3845, São Paulo

CHURCH OF CHRIST (Brazil Christian Mission)
Caixa Postal 201, Goiania, Goias

CONFEDERAÇÃO EVANGÉLICA DO BRASIL (1934)
Av. Erasmo Braga 277, (Caixa Postal 260) Rio de Janeiro
Gen. Sec.: Rev. Rodolfo Anders

CONGREGACIONI CHRISTIANI
São Paulo City, São Paulo

CONSELHO EVANGÉLICO DE EDUCAÇÃO RELIGIOSA DO BRASIL
Erasmo Braga 12, Rio de Janeiro

CONVENÇÃO BATISTA BRASILEIRA
Rua Senador Furtado 56, (Caixa Postal, 1770–ZC–00), Guanabara, Rio de
Janeiro. Tel.: 34–3902 Rio de Janeiro

CONVENÇÃO BRASILEIRA DAS IGREJAS IRMAOS MENONITAS
Caixa Postal 1559, Curutiba, Paraná. Tel.: 4–5822

FEDERAÇÃOS DAS ESCOLAS EVANGÉLICAS DO BRASIL (1917)
Colégio Bennett, Marques de Abrantes 55, Rio de Janeiro

GERMAN LUTHERAN CHURCH, CENTRAL BRAZILIAN SYNOD
Rua Carlos Campio 46a, Rio de Janeiro

IGREJA EVANGÉLICA LUTERANA DO BRASIL
Caixa Postal 47, Canoas, Rio Grande do Sul

IGREJA CRISTÃ EVANGÉLICA BRASILEIRA
Rua Parecis 43, São Paulo

IGREJA CRISTÃ EVANGÉLICA DO BRASIL
Catalão, Est. Goias

IGREJA CRISTÃ REFORMADA DO BRASIL
Caixa Postal 2808, São Paulo

SOUTH AMERICA

IGREJA EPISCOPAL BRASILEIRA
Caixa 88, Porto Alegre, Rio Grande do Sul

IGREJA EVANGÉLICA CONGREGACIONAL DO BRASIL
Caixa Postal 334, Ijui, Rio Grande do Sul

IGREJA EVANGÉLICA DE CONFISSÃO LUTHERANA NO BRASIL
São Leopoldo—Rio Grande do Sul. Tel.: 131

IGREJA EVANGÉLICA REFORMADA (1962)
Caixa Postal 7315, São Paulo-Capital

IGREJA HOLINESS DO BRASIL
Caixa 3919, São Paulo

IGREJA LUTERANA (Missouri)
Rua Conçalves Crespo 103, Rio de Janeiro

IGREJA METODISTA DO BRASIL
Rua João Pessoa 106, Apt. 21, Petropolis

IGREJA PRESBITERIANA DO BRASIL (1865)
Rua Alzira Brandão, 135 Tijuca, Rio de Janeiro

IGREJA PRESBITERIANA INDEPENDENTE DO BRASIL (1903)
Rua Tiradentes 310, Muzambinho, C.M., Estado de Minas Gerais

MISSÃO EVANGÉLICA LUTERANA
C.P. 28, Cianorte, via Marianga, Est do Parana

SALVATION ARMY
Rua Tagua 209, São Paulo

SOCIEDADE BIBLICA BRASIL (1948)
Rua Buenos Aires 135, Rio de Janeiro. Tel.: 43–4910

UNIÃO CRISTÃ DE ESTUDANTES DO BRASIL
Caixa Postal 416, São Paulo

UNIÃO DE IGREJAS EVANGÉLICAS CONGREGACIONAIS E CRISTÃS
Rua Camerino 102, Rio de Janeiro

YOUNG MEN'S CHRISTIAN ASSOCIATION
Rua da Lapa 86 (Caixa Postal 254–ZC–00), Rio de Janeiro. Tel.: 22–9860

YOUNG WOMEN'S CHRISTIAN ASSOCIATION
Av. Franklin Roosevelt 84, 10° andar, Rio de Janeiro

CHILE

CHILEAN BAPTIST CONVENTION
Casilla 3388, Santiago

CHRISTIAN SCIENCE COMMITTEE ON PUBLICATION
Elvira Garces 1944, Santiago

COMITÉ CONSULTOR DE COOPERACION EN LA OBRA CRISTIANA EN CHILE
Casilla 2037, Santiago

CONCILIO EVANGÉLICO DE CHILE (1941)
Clasificador 682, Compania 1560, Bombero Salas 1351, Santiago
Rev. Luis Alvarez

EJERCITO DE SALVACIÓN (1910)
Casilla 3225, Santiago

IGLESIA ANGLICANA (1870)
Casilla 675, Santiago

IGLESIA CRISTIANA APOSTOLICA
Hipodromo Chile 1632, Santiago

IGLESIA DE DIOS
Avda, Salvador 1806, Santiago

SOUTH AMERICA

IGLESIA EVANGÉLICA LUTERANA EN CHILE
Casilla 2000, Santiago

IGLESIA EVANGÉLICA PENTECOSTAL DE CHILE (1909)
Casilla 2, Curico

IGLESIA METODISTA (1885)
Casilla 67, Santiago. Tel.: 83956

IGLESIA METODISTA PENTECOSTAL (1909)
Jotaveche 40, Santiago

IGLESIA WESLEYANA NACIONAL
Lota

MISIÓN EVANGÉLICA DE LOS HERMANOS
Calle Libertad 961, Santiago

MISIÓN EVANGÉLICA NACIONAL
Calle Carmen 1858, Santiago

MISIÓN EVANGÉLICA PENTECOSTAL
Casilla 7033, Santiago

MOVIMIENTO ESTUDIANTIL CRISTIANO DE CHILE (1948)
Avenida Bernardo O'Higgins 723, Depto. 79, Santiago. Tel.: 381433

NATIONAL PRESBYTERIAN CHURCH
Casilla 5596, Santiago

SOCIEDADES BIBLICAS EN CHILE
San Francisco 54, Casilla 784, Santiago

SOLDIERS' AND GOSPEL MISSION OF SOUTH AMERICA
Casilla 507, Temuco

UNION DE CENTROS BIBLICOS
Casilla 43 D, Temuco. Tel.: 33612 (Temuco)

YOUNG MEN'S CHRISTIAN ASSOCIATION
Compania 1360, Casilla 1717, Santiago

YOUNG WOMEN'S CHRISTIAN ASSOCIATION
Modena 1640, Santiago. Tel.: 61608

COLOMBIA

ALIANZA CRISTIANA Y MISIONERA COLOMBIANA
Apdo. aéreo. 4583, Cali, Valle

ASAMBLEAS DE DIOS
Apdo. aéreo 7739, Bogotá, D.E.

ASAMBLEAS DE JESUCHRISTO
Apdo. aéreo 315, Cartagena, Bolivar

ASOCIACIÓN BAUTISTAS DE LA SELVA
Leticia, Amazonas

ASOCIACIÓN DE IGLESIAS EVANGÉLICAS DEL ORIENTE COLOMB-
IANO
Ave. 6A, No. 13–48 (Apdo. aéreo 576), Cucuta

COLOMBIAN BAPTIST CONVENTION
Apdo. aéreo 4742, Bogotá, D.E.

COLOMBIAN EVANGELISTIC MISSION
Apdo. aéreo 224, Sincelejo, Bolivar

CONFEDERACIÓN EVANGÉLICA DE COLOMBIA
Apdo. aéreo 3604, Bogotá
Mr. A. W. de Leon

CONFERENCIA DE LOS HERMANOS MENONITAS
Apdo. aéreo 4172, Cali, Valle

SOUTH AMERICA

CONGREGACION SAN MATEO BOGOTA
Apdo. aéreo 21450, Bogota 2

CRUZADA HISPANOAMERICANA
Carrera 38 No. 72–22, Bogotá, D.E.

IGLESIA DE DIOS
Calle 11 No. 11–59, Sogamoso, Boyaca

IGLESIA EVANGÉLICA LUTERANA
Sinodo de Colombia: Apdo. aéreo 20038, Bogotá

IGLESIA EVANGÉLICA PENTECOSTAL
Apdo. aéreo 8307, Bogotá, D.E.

IGLESIA EVANGÉLICA PRESBITERIANA
Apdo. 4, Ibague

IGLESIAS EVANGÉLICAS DEL CARIBE
Apdo. aéreo 297, Cartagena, Bolivar

IGLESIA INTERNACIONAL DEL EVANGELIO QUADRANGULAR
Apdo. 40, Barrancabermeja, Santander

IGLESIA PENTECOSTAL UNIDA
Apdo. aéreo 1006, Barranquilla

IGLESIA PRESBITERIANA CUMBERLAND
Apdo. aéreo 173, Cali, Valle

IGLESIA PRESBITERIANA
Apdo. aéreo 653, Medellin, Antioquia

MENNONITE (GENERAL CONFERENCE)
Colegio Americano, Cachipay, Cand. Tel.: 08

MOVIMIENTO ESTUDIANTIL CRISTIANO
Apdo. aéreo 9691, Bogotá, D.E.

PLYMOUTH BRETHREN
Apdo. aéreo 209, Pasto, Narino

SEVENTH-DAY ADVENTISTS
Apdo. aéreo 609, Medellin, Antioquia

SOCIEDADES BIBLICAS EN COLOMBIA
Avenida Caracas 28–27 (Apdo. aéreo 4931), Bogotá

UNION CHURCH OF BOGOTA
Carrera 4 No. 69–06, Bogotá, D.E. Tel.: 485–115

UNION MISSIONERA EVANGÉLICA
Carrera 21 No. 29–54 Palmira, Valle
(Apdo. aéreo 244, Apdo. Nacional 16). Tel.: 2588 and 5688

ECUADOR

EGLESIA EVANGÉLICA LUTERANA DEL ECUADOR
Casilla 2736, Quito. Tel.: 34391 Quito

INTER-MISSION FELLOWSHIP OF ECUADOR
Casilla 1030, Quito
Sec.: J. Theodore Kelly

JUNTA EVANGÉLICA NACIONAL
Casilla 137, Quito

MISIÓN EVANGÉLICA LUTERANA
Casilla 1334, Cuenca. Tel.: 23–33

SOCIEDADES BIBLICAS EN EL ECUADOR
Casilla 1030, Quito. Tel.: 34–642

SUMMER INSTITUTE OF LINGUISTICS
Casilla 1007, Quito

YOUNG MEN'S CHRISTIAN ASSOCIATION
Casilla 1177, Quito

UNITED FREE CHURCH OF THE FALKLAND ISLANDS
The Tabernacle, Stanley

GUYANA

CHRISTIAN SCIENCE COMMITTEE ON PUBLICATION
16 Eping Avenue, Bel Air Park, East Demerara

CHURCH IN THE PROVINCE OF THE WEST INDIES
Austin House, Georgetown 1. Tel.: GN 4239
Diocese of Guyana: Diocesan Office, Church House, Church and Carmichael
Streets, Georgetown 2. Tel.: GN 4775

CONGREGATIONAL UNION
The Manse, Bagotville, West Bank, Demerara

LUTHERAN CHURCH
Lutheran Courts, New Amsterdam, Berbice

YOUNG MEN'S CHRISTIAN ASSOCIATION
P.O. Box 13 Georgetown

YOUNG WOMEN'S CHRISTIAN ASSOCIATION
106 Brickdam, Georgetown

PARAGUAY

CONVENCIÓN EVANGÉLICA BAUTISTA DEL PARAGUAY
Casilla 1194, Asunción

LUTHERAN CHURCH, MISSOURI SYNOD
Hohenauer 111, via Encarnación

SOUTH AMERICAN MISSIONARY SOCIETY
Casilla 1124, Asunción

YOUNG MEN'S CHRISTIAN ASSOCIATION
Casilla 672, Asunción

PERU

ASAMBLEAS DE DIOS
Apdo. 4550, Lima

ASOCIACIÓN MISIONERA EVANGÉLICA NACIONAL
Apdo. 479, Huancayo

CHRISTIAN SCIENCE COMMITTEE ON PUBLICATION
Apdo. 2151, Lima

CONCILIO NACIONAL EVANGÉLICO DEL PERU (1940)
Apdo. 2566, Lima
Gen. Sec.: Dr. Herbert Money

IGLESIA EVANGÉLICA DE CRISTO
Galvez 866, Chimbote

IGLESIA EVANGÉLICA LUTERANA EN EL PERU (1899)
Las Magnolias 495, (Urb. El Jardin), San Isidro, Lima. Tel.: 24.452

IGLESIA EVANGÉLICA PERUANA
Apdo. 5028, Lima

IGLESIAS PENTECOSTALES AUTONOMAS
Apdo. 18, Callao

INSTITUTO BIBLICO PERUANO
Apdo. 664, Lima

MOVIMIENTO ESTUDIANTIL CRISTIANO
Apdo. 1386, Lima

SOUTH AMERICA

SOCIEDADES BIBLICAS EN EL PERU
Avenida Petit Thouars 133 (Apdo. 448), Lima

YOUNG MEN'S CHRISTIAN ASSOCIATION
Carabayo 664, Apdo. 2411, Lima. Tel.: 7.78.27

SURINAM

MORAVIAN CHURCH
Dominastreet 48, P.O.B. 219, Paramaribo. Tel.: 3073

YOUNG WOMEN'S CHRISTIAN ASSOCIATION
Heerenstraat 24 (P.O. Box 1404), Paramaribo. Tel.: 2089

URUGUAY

CHRISTIAN SCIENCE COMMITTEE ON PUBLICATION
26 de Marzo 1266, Apt. 801, Montevideo

CONVENCIÓN EVANGÉLICA BAUTISTA
Sierra 1741, Montevideo

EJERCITO DE SALVACIÓN (Salvation Army)
Hocquart 1886, Montevideo

FEDERACIÓN DE LA JUVENTUD EVANGÉLICA DEL URUGUAY
Quito 1618, Montevideo

FEDERATION OF EVANGELICAL CHURCHES OF URUGUAY
San José, Montevideo. Tel.: 4 42 36. Dr. A. Fernández Arlt

IGLESIAS CRISTIANAS EVANGÉLICAS
A. Gallinal 1441, Montevideo

IGLESIA EVANGÉLICA ARMENIA
Duvimioso Terra 1690, Montevideo

IGLESIA EVANGÉLICA DEL RIO DE LA PLATA
Colonia Valdense, Dpto. de Colonia. Tel.: 311

IGLESIA METODISTA
Médanos 1310, Montevideo

MISIÓN EVANGÉLICA DEL URUGUAY
Av. Garibaldi 2804, Montevideo

MISIÓN EVANGÉLICA MENONITA
Av. Millan 4392 (or Casilla Correo 1633), Montevideo

MOVIMIENTO ESTUDIANTIL CRISTIANO DEL URUGUAY
Médanos 1310, Montevideo

SOCIEDADES BIBLICAS EN EL URUGUAY
Calle Constituyente 1540, Montevideo

SOUTH AMERICAN CONFEDERATION OF Y.M.C.As. (1914)
Colonia 1864 p. 2, Montevideo. Tel.: 4.71.94

YOUNG WOMEN'S CHRISTIAN ASSOCIATION
Calle Paraguay 1438, Montevideo

VENEZUELA

BAPTIST CONVENTION
Ave. 99, 95-20, Valencia, Carabobo

CHRISTIAN SCIENCE COMMITTEE ON PUBLICATION
Apdo. 4109, Este, Caracas

CIRCULO DE CRISTIANOS UNIVERSITARIOS
Apdo. 5151 Este, Caracas

SOUTH AMERICA

CONSEJO LUTERANO DE VENEZUELA
Apdo. 4559, Chacao, Caracas. Tel.: 337352

IGLESIA EVANGELICA PRESBITERIANA
Apdo. 212, Caracas

SOCIEDADES BIBLICAS EN VENEZUELA
Principal a Conde, Edif. la Previsora (Apdo. 222), Caracas

THE EVANGELICAL ALLIANCE MISSION (TEAM)
Apdo. 402, Maracaibo. Tel.: 2864; 3669

YOUNG MEN'S CHRISTIAN ASSOCIATION
Avenida Guaicaipuro, San Bernardino (Apdo. 2914), Caracas. Tel.: 55 97 88

ASIA

BURMA

BIBLE SOCIETY
262 Sule Pagoda Road, Rangoon

BURMA BAPTIST CONVENTION
143 St. John's Road, Rangoon. Tel.: 12419

BURMA CHRISTIAN COUNCIL (1949)
549 Merchant Street, Rangoon
Hon. Gen. Sec.: Rev. U. John Thetgyi

CHURCH OF INDIA, PAKISTAN, BURMA AND CEYLON: DIOCESE OF RANGOON
Bishopscourt, 140 Halpin Road, Rangoon

EAST ASIA CHRISTIAN CONFERENCE (1959)
140 Pyi-daungsu-yeiktha Road, Rangoon
Assoc. Gen. Sec.: U Kyaw Than

SALVATION ARMY
176/8 Anawrahta Street, East Rangoon

STUDENT CHRISTIAN MOVEMENT
601 Prome Road, Kamayut P.O., Rangoon

YOUNG MEN'S CHRISTIAN ASSOCIATION
326 Maha Bandoola Street, Rangoon. Tel.: Auto 12110

YOUNG WOMEN'S CHRISTIAN ASSOCIATION
119 Bogalay Zay Road, Rangoon

CAMBODIA

BIBLE SOCIETIES IN VIETNAM, CAMBODIA AND LAOS
Box 545, Phnom-Penh

CEYLON

BIBLE SOCIETY (CEYLON AUXILIARY)
The Bible House, 293 Galle Road, Colombo 3. Tel.: Colombo 4483

CEYLON NATIONAL MISSIONARY SOCIETY (1913)
Dandagamuwa, Kurunagala Dist.

CEYLON PENTECOSTAL MISSION
71 Baseline Road, Colombo 8

CHURCH OF INDIA, PAKISTAN, BURMA AND CEYLON (1845)
Diocese of Kurunagala: Bishop's House, Kurunagala
Diocese of Colombo: Bishop's House, Colombo 3

CHURCH OF SOUTH INDIA
Bishop's House, Araly, Vaddukoddai

DUTCH REFORMED CHURCH
Verdley, Inner Flower Road, Colombo

EVANGELICAL FELLOWSHIP OF CEYLON (1952)
P.O. Box 66, Colombo

METHODIST CHURCH
Methodist Headquarters, Colpetty, Colombo 3

NATIONAL CHRISTIAN COUNCIL (1945)
61 Sir James Peiris Mawata, Colombo 2
Rev. C. L. Abeynaike

PRESBYTERIAN CHURCH, PRESBYTERY OF LANKA
The Manse, Tricomalie Street, Kandy

SALVATION ARMY
61 General's Lake Road, Slave Island, Colombo

ASIA

SRI LANKA BAPTIST SANGAMAYA (1932)
46 Kynsey Road, Colombo 8

STUDENT CHRISTIAN MOVEMENT (1920)
c/o Y.M.C.A. Colombo 1. Tel.: 5238

YOUNG MEN'S CHRISTIAN ASSOCIATION
P.O. Box 381, Colombo. Tel.: 5238–9

YOUNG WOMEN'S CHRISTIAN ASSOCIATION
171 General's Lake Road, Colombo 2

CHINA

CHINA BAPTIST COUNCIL
169 Yuen Ming Yuen Road, Shanghai

CHINA BIBLE SOCIETY
Bible House, 58 Hong Kong Road, Shanghai (O)

CHINESE CHRISTIAN THREE-SELF MOVEMENT
128 Museum Road, Shanghai

CHUNG-HUA CHI-TU CHIAO-HUI (Church of Christ in China)
128 Museum Road, Shanghai

CHUNG-HUA SHENG KUNG HUI (Holy Catholic Church in China)
169 Yuen Ming Yuen Road, Shanghai

HUA PEI KUNG LI HUI (North China Congregational Church)
29 Teng Shih Kou, Peking

LUTHERAN CHURCH OF CHINA
176 Sheng Li Kai, Hankow

NATIONAL CHRISTIAN COUNCIL OF CHINA (1922)
169 Yuen Ming Yuen Road, Shanghai

YOUNG MEN'S CHRISTIAN ASSOCIATION
National Committee: Huchiu Lu 131, Shanghai

YOUNG WOMEN'S CHRISTIAN ASSOCIATION
133 Yuen Ming Yuen Road, Shanghai

CYPRUS

ANGLICAN CHURCH
Chaplain's House, 2 Afxentiou Street, Nicosia

BIBLE HOUSE
8a–8c Said Pasha Street (P.O. Box 1066), Nicosia

CHURCH OF CYPRUS
Archbishopric, Nicosia

HONG KONG

ASSEMBLIES OF GOD, SOUTH CHINA DISTRICT
Corner Argyle Street and Kadoorie Avenue, Kowloon

AUDIO VISUAL EVANGELISM COMMITTEE (1954)
Room 401, 191 Prince Edward Road, Kowloon. Tel.: 814759

BIBLE SOCIETIES IN HONG KONG (1950)
22 Hennessy Road, 3rd Floor, Wanchai (P.O. Box 1725), Tel.: 735505

CHINA MISSIONARY AND EVANGELISTIC ASSOCIATION
c/o Ebenezer Home for Blind Girls, 135 Pokfulam Road

CHINA SUNDAY SCHOOL ASSOCIATION
23a Granville Road, Kowloon

CHINESE CHRISTIAN EVANGELISTS ASSOCIATION
5 Irving Street, Causeway Bay

CHINESE CHRISTIAN LITERATURE COUNCIL (1951)
2 Upper Albert Road, Hong Kong. Tel.: 238527

CHINESE METHODIST CHURCH
36 Hennessy Road, Wanchai

CHINESE RHENISH CHURCH, HONG KONG SYNOD (Lutheran)
Tat Chee Avenue, Yau Yat Chuen, Kowloon. Tel.: 811945

CHRISTIAN AND MISSIONARY ALLIANCE
23 Kent Road, Kowloon Tong, Kowloon

CHRISTIAN SCIENCE COMMITTEE ON PUBLICATION
Chi Lok Villa, 19th Milestone, Castle Peak (N.T.)

CHUNG HWA SHENG KUNG (Anglican Church of China)
Diocese of Hong Kong and Macao (1849): Bishop's House, Hong Kong

CHURCH OF CHRIST IN CHINA, HONG KONG COUNCIL (1919)
Morrison Memorial Centre, 191 Prince Edward Road, Kowloon. Tel.: 802371

COUNCIL ON CHRISTIAN LITERATURE FOR OVERSEAS CHINESE
(1951)
1 Upper Albert Road, Hong Kong

EVANGELICAL FREE CHURCH OF CHINA
41–43 Hau Wong Road, 1st Floor, Kowloon City

EVANGELICAL LUTHERAN CHURCH OF HONG KONG
1 Minden Avenue, 1st Floor. Kowloon. Tel.: 669923

HONG KONG CHRISTIAN COUNCIL (1954)
23 Waterloo Road, Kowloon. Tel.: 846016
Sec.: Mr. Calvin Ngai

HONG KONG CHRISTIAN WELFARE AND RELIEF COUNCIL (1955)
c/o Chinese Y.M.C.A. 23 Waterloo Road, Kowloon. Tel.: 846692

HONG KONG DOCTORS' CHRISTIAN ASSOCIATION (1958)
c/o Alice Ho Miu Ling Nethersole Hospital, Hong Kong

LUTHERAN CHURCH—MISSOURI SYNOD
68 Begonia Road, Kowloon. Tel.: 806909

PENTECOSTAL HOLINESS CHURCHES (1909)
6 Dorset Crescent, Kowloon

SALVATION ARMY
547–549 Nathan Road, Kowloon

SEVENTH-DAY ADVENTISTS
17 Ventris Road, Hong Kong

STUDENT CHRISTIAN MOVEMENT
23 Waterloo Road, Kowloon

TSUNG TSIN (HAKKA) CHURCH OF HONG KONG
Kau Yan Church, 97 High Street, Kowloon

TSUNG TSIN MISSION
59 Hong Keung St., 2nd Floor Front Block, San Po Komg, Kowloon. Tel.: 824589

UNITED HONG KONG CHRISTIAN BAPTIST CHURCHES ASSOCIATION
36 Jordan Road, 1st Floor, Kowloon

WEI LI HUI
North Point Methodist Church, Cheung Hong St., North Point

WESTERN CHINA EVANGELISTIC BAND
4a Somerset Road, Kowloon

YOUNG MEN'S CHRISTIAN ASSOCIATION
11 F, On Lok Yuen Bldg., 25 Des Voeux Road, Hong Kong. Tel.: 222322

YOUNG WOMEN'S CHRISTIAN ASSOCIATION (1920)
1 Macdonnell Road, Hong Kong. Tel.: 223101–4

ALL-INDIA FELLOWSHIP TRAINING ASHRAM (1950)
Pirumadara P.O., Nainital Dist., Uttar Pradesh

AMERICAN MARATHI MISSION
364 Dr. Dadabhai Naoroji Road, P.B. 92, Fort, Bombay 1

ANDHRA EVANGELICAL LUTHERAN CHURCH
Post Box 205, Guntur, Andhra Pradesh

APOSTOLIC LEGATION OF THE HOLY SEE OF ANTIOCH IN MALABAR
Omallur, Kaipattur P.O., Kerala

ARCOT LUTHERAN CHURCH (1899)
Carmel, Tiruvannamalai, N., Arcot Dist., Madras

ASSEMBLIES OF GOD, NORTH INDIA
Tiljala Road, Calcutta 17

BANGALORE CHRISTIAN COUNCIL OF ACTION
Binnypet, Bangalore 2, Mysore

BAPTIST CHURCH OF MIZO DISTRICT (1904)
Lungleh, South Mizo Dist., Assam

BAPTIST UNION OF INDIA (BURMA AND CEYLON)
Theological College, Ramapatnam, Nellore Dist., Andhra Pradesh

BAPTIST UNION OF NORTH INDIA
Bankipur, Patna 4, Bihar

BEHAT VILLAGE MISSION (1946)
Mission House, Behat, Saharanpur, Uttar Pradesh

BENGAL BAPTIST UNION (1935)
95 Elliott Road, Calcutta 16

BENGAL-ORISSA BAPTIST YEARLY MEETING
P.O. Bhimpore, Midnapore Dist., W. Bengal

BHARAT EVANGELICAL MISSION
41 Main Road, St. Thomas' Mount, Madras 16

BHARAT KHRIST SANGH (Kristapanthi Ashram)
129 Dashashmedh, Varanasi, Uttar Pradesh

BHAROSA GHAR MISSION
Bhagalpur P.O., Deoria Dt., Uttar Pradesh

BIBLE CRUSADE MISSIONARY SOCIETY
Uizianagaram Cantt, Vizag Dist., Andhra Pradesh

BIBLE PRESBYTERIAN CHURCH OF INDIA (1950)
Post Box 347, Kanpur, Uttar Pradesh

BIBLE SOCIETY OF INDIA (1944)
A/1 Mahatma Gandhi Road, Bangalore 1, Mysore. Tel.: 24657

BOMBAY TRACT AND BOOK SOCIETY
84 Sanki Street, Byculla, Bombay 8

BOYS' CHRISTIAN HOME MISSION
Dhond, Poona Dist., Maharashtra

CEYLON AND INDIA GENERAL MISSION
Mizpah, Pottery Road, Richards Town, Bangalore 5, Mysore

CHALDEAN SYRIAN CHURCH (*See* CHURCH OF THE EAST)

CHILDREN'S SPECIAL SERVICE MISSION
18 Clive Road, Allahabad 1, Uttar Pradesh

CHOWPATTA AGRICULTURAL AND INDUSTRIAL MISSION
Berenag P.O., Via Almora, Kumaon, Uttar Pradesh

CHRISTA PREMA SEVA SANGHA
St. John's House, Colaba, Bombay 5

CHRISTA SEVA SANGHA
Poona, Maharashtra

ASIA

CHRISTA SEVA VIDYALAYA
7/2 College Road, Nangambakkam, Madras

CHRISTA SISHYA ASHRAM
Tadagam P.O., Coimbatore Dist., Madras

CHRISTA YESUDASI SANGHA
36 Pottinger Road, Tandiewadi, Ahmednatar Dist., Maharashtra

CHRISTIAN AND MISSIONARY ALLIANCE OF INDIA
Gujarat: 20 Camp, Ahmedabad 3. Tel.: 6194
Maharashtra: P.O. Box 5, Akola. Tel.: 530

CHRISTIAN EDUCATIONAL COUNCIL OF SOUTH INDIA
Madras Christian College, Tambaram, Madras

CHRISTIAN INSTITUTE FOR THE STUDY OF RELIGION AND SOCIETY (1957)
Devanandan House, P.O. Box 1504, 17 Millers Road, Bangalore 6, Mysore

CHRISTIAN LITERATURE SOCIETY
P.O. Box 501, Park Town, Madras 3

CHRISTIAN MEDICAL ASSOCIATION OF INDIA (1925)
Christian Council Lodge, Nagpur 1, Maharashtra. Tel.: 2864

CHRISTIAN MEDICAL COLLEGE AND HOSPITAL ASSOCIATION
Christian Medical College, Vellore, North Arcot Distr., Madras. Tel.: 22

CHRISTIAN SCIENCE COMMITTEE ON PUBLICATION
85 Tardeo Road, Bombay 34

CHRISTIAN TRACT AND BOOK SOCIETY
Duff Church, 129 Manicktollah Street, Calcutta 6

CHRISTU DAS ASHRAM
Olive Mount P.O., Palghat Dist., Kerala

CHURCH OF GOD
Vakilwadi, Camp Satara North, Maharashtra

CHURCH OF GOD, AUTONOMOUS CHURCHES IN ASSAM, W. BENGAL AND ORISSA
Mountain View, Chapel Road, Shillong, Assam

CHURCH OF GOD IN INDIA
Mount Zion, Mulakuzha, Kerala

CHURCH OF GOD IN SOUTH INDIA
Girideepam, Chengannur, Kerala

CHURCH OF INDIA, PAKISTAN, BURMA AND CEYLON
Bishop's House, 51 Chowringhee Road, Calcutta 16
Diocese of Bombay: 19 Wandby Road, Bombay 1. Tel.: 263904

CHURCH OF SOUTH INDIA
Diocesan Office, Cathedral P.O., Madras 6

CHURCH OF THE EAST (Chaldean Syrian Church)
Trichur, Kerala

CONFERENCE OF CHURCHES OF CHRIST IN WESTERN INDIA
P.O. Box 26, Baramati, Dist. Poona, Maharashtra

CONVENTION OF CHURCHES OF CHRIST
Jabalpur P.O., Madhya Pradesh

CONVENTION OF THE BAPTIST CHURCHES OF THE NORTHERN CIRCARS
Kakinada, E. Godavari Dist., Andhra Pradesh

COUNCIL OF BAPTIST CHURCHES IN ASSAM AND IN MANIPUR
A.B. Mission, Gauhati, Assam

COUNCIL OF BAPTIST CHURCHES IN NORTHERN INDIA
44 Lower Circular Road, P.O. Park Street, Calcutta 16

DIPTI MISSION (Mission of Light) (1920)
Sahibgunj, Bhagalpur Dist., Bihar

ASIA

DR. GRAHAM'S HOMES (1900)
Kalimpong, Darjeeling Dist., W. Bengal. Tel.: Kalimpong 27

DOHNAVUR FELLOWSHIP (1901)
Dohnavur, Tirunelveli Dist., Madras

EVANGELICAL FELLOWSHIP OF INDIA
Jhansi, Uttar Pradesh

EVANGELICAL LITERATURE DEPOT (1936)
11/1 Mission Row, Calcutta 1

EVANGELICAL LITERATURE FELLOWSHIP OF INDIA (1951)
E.F.I. Civil Lines, Jhansi, Uttar Pradesh

EVANGELICAL LITERATURE SERVICE
158 Purasawalkam High Road, Vepery, Madras 7. Tel.: 62722

EVANGELICAL LUTHERAN CHURCH IN MADHYA PRADESH (1923)
Post Box 1, Swedish Mission, Chhindwara, Madhya Pradesh

FEDERATION OF EVANGELICAL LUTHERAN CHURCHES IN INDIA (1926)
Tranquebar House, Tiruchirapalli, Madras

FREE CHURCH OF SCOTLAND (India) 1915)
Lakhnadon, Seoni Dist., Madhya Pradesh

FREE GOSPEL MISSION (1928)
Faizabad, Uttar Pradesh

FRIENDS SERVICE COUNCIL
Friends Centre, 211 Park Street, Calcutta 17

FULL GOSPEL FELLOWSHIP OF INDIA (PENTECOSTAL)
Bharosa Ghar Mission, P.O. Bhagalpur, Deorie Dt., Uttar Pradesh

GARO BAPTIST UNION
Bagpara P.O., Bongaigaon, Goalpara Dist., Assam

GENERAL CONFERENCE MENNONITE CHURCH
Jagdeeshpur P.O., Via Mahasamund, Raipur Dist., Madhya Pradesh

GOALPARA BORO BAPTIST CHURCH UNION
Village Tukrajhar P.O., Via Bongaigaon, Goalpara Dist., Assam

GOOD SHEPHERD AGRICULTURAL MISSION (1948)
Tanakpur (Naini Tel Dist.), Uttar Pradesh

GONDWANA MISSION
Patpara, Mandha, Madhya Pradesh

GORAKPHUR NURSERIES' FELLOWSHIP (1935)
Gorakphur, Uttar Pradesh

GOSSNER EVANGELICAL LUTHERAN CHURCH (1845)
Ranchi, Bihar

HENRY MARTYN INSTITUTE OF ISLAMIC STUDIES (1930)
Jabalpur, Madhya Pradesh

HINDUSTANI COVENANT CHURCH
29 Souter Street, Bombay 8

HOME MISSIONARY SOCIETY OF INDIA (1905)
22 Stephens Road, Frazer Town, Bangalore 5, Mysore

INDIAN BIBLE CHRISTIAN COUNCIL
P.O. Box 347, Juhi, Kanpur, Uttar Pradesh

INDIA BIBLE MISSION (1938)
Sharon House, Rajahmundry, Andhra Pradesh

INDIA CHRISTIAN ASSEMBLIES (Pentecostal)
Chilakalapudi P.O., Krishna Dist., Andhra Pradesh

INDIAN CHRISTIAN MISSION
Champawat P.O., Almora Dist., Uttar Pradesh

291

ASIA

INDIA EVANGELICAL LUTHERAN CHURCH
Immanuel Lutheran Church, Ambur, N. Arcot Dist., Madras

INDIA GOSPEL FELLOWSHIP MISSION
Union Church Manse, Ootacamund, Madras

INDIA INDUSTRIAL MISSION (PRIVATE) LTD. (1925)
Cossipore, Calcutta 12, W. Bengal

INDIA SUNDAY SCHOOL UNION (1876)
Coonoor, Nilgiris Dist., Madras

INDIA UNITED EVANGELISTIC MISSION
5 Clive Road, Cooke Town, Bangalore 5, Mysore

INDIAN FORCES' SCRIPTURE READERS' FELLOWSHIP
46 Maiganandadeva Mudr. Road, Fraser Town P.O., Bangalore 5, Mysore

INDIAN MISSIONARY SOCIETY OF TIRUNELVELI
Palamcottah, Madras

INTERIOR INDIA MISSION, INC. (1930)
Bahraic, Uttar Pradesh

INTER-MISSION BUSINESS OFFICE
Oriental Building, Flora Fountain (P.O. Box 92), Bombay 1. Tel.: 251651

JEYPORE EVANGELICAL LUTHERAN CHURCH
Jeypore, Koraput Dist., Orissa

KOTAGIRI MEDICAL FELLOWSHIP
St. Margaret's, Kotagiri, Nilgiris Dist., Madras

LAKHER INDEPENDENT EVANGELICAL CHURCH
P.O. Serkawr, South Mizo Dis., Assam

LEE MEMORIAL MISSION (1894)
13 Raja Sobodh Mullick Square (P.O. Box 8968), Calcutta 13. Tel.: 24-4755

LITERATURE MISSION
Kalimpong, W. Bengal

MALABAR INDEPENDENT SYRIAN CHURCH
Episcopal Palace, Thozhiyoor, Kottapadi P.O., S. Malabar, Kerala

**MALABAR MAR THOMA SYRIAN CHRISTIAN EVANGELISTIC ASSOCIA-
TION OF THE MAR THOMA CHURCH (1888)**
M.T.E. Association Office, P.O. Tiruvalla, Kerala. Tel.: 13 Tiruvalla

MALANKARA JACOBITE SYRIAN CHURCH
Thrikkunnathu Seminary, Alwaye, Kerala

MANDLIYON KI PRATNIDHI KAUNSIL (Churches of Christ)
Rerhma, Daltoganj, Palamau Dist., Bihar

MAR THOMA SYRIAN CHURCH OF MALABAR (52 A.D.)
Sabha Office, Tiruvalla, Kerala. Tel.: Tiruvalla 13

MARANATHA MISSIONARY FELLOWSHIP (1912)
Bethamangala, Kolar Gold Fields, Mysore

MASIHI MANDLI (Pentecostal)
Dehra Dun, Uttar Pradesh

MENNONITE BRETHREN CHURCH OF INDIA
Mahabubuagar, Andhra, Pradesh

MENNONITE CHURCH IN INDIA
Dhamtari P.O., Raipur Dist., Madhya Pradesh

METHODIST CHURCH OF NORTH INDIA
P.O. Gahr-Raipur, Bankura Dist., W. Bengal

METHODIST CHURCH IN SOUTHERN ASIA
Robinson Memorial, 13 Sankli Street, Byculla, Bombay 8, 'BC'. Tel.: Bombay
74870 (Episcopal Residence)

MID-INDIA YEARLY MEETING OF THE SOCIETY OF FRIENDS
59 Deshbandhupura, Mission Colony, Itarsi, Madhya Pradesh

ASIA

MID MISSIONS
Makunda, Hatikhira P.O., Cachar Dist., Assam

MISSION TO INDIAN VILLAGES
Latur, Osmanabad, Andhra Pradesh

MISSION TO LEPERS
Purulia, S.E. Rly., W. Bengal. Tel.: 210

MISSION TO THE ARISTOCRACY OF INDIA
Gandhinagar (Box 57), Kakinada, Andhra Pradesh

MULAG MISSION
C.S.I., Mulag, Via Kasipet, Warangal Dist., Andhra Pradesh

MYSORE MISSIONARY SOCIETY
Shanti Sadana, Mission Road, Bangalore 2, Mysore

NASRAPUR SPIRITUAL LIFE CENTRE FELLOWSHIP (1928)
Nasrapur, Poona Dist., Maharashtra

NATIONAL CHRISTIAN COUNCIL OF INDIA
Christian Council Lodge, Nagpur 1, Maharashtra. Tel.: 2864
Exec. Sec.: Mr. M. A. Z. Rolston

NATIONAL MISSIONARY SOCIETY OF INDIA (Bharat Christya Sevak Samaj) (1905)
N.M.S. House, 102–3 Peter's Road, Royappettah, Madras 14. Tel.: 83477

NATIVE CHURCH (PROTESTANT)
Sharon House, Rajahmundry-3, Andhra Pradesh. Tel.: 539

NEPAL EVANGELISTIC BAND
Christian Dispensary, Nautanwa, Gorakhpur Dist., Uttar Pradesh

NEW ZEALAND FULL GOSPEL MISSION
Karmala, Sholapur Dist., Maharashtra

NORTH BANK BAPTIST ASSOCIATION
Biswanathghat, Darrang, Assam

NORTH GOALPARA GARO BAPTIST UNION
Boghpara Union Compound, P.O. Khagarpur via, Bongaigaon Dist., Assam

NORTH INDIA CHRISTIAN TRACT AND BOOK SOCIETY (1848)
18 Clive Road, Allahabad 1, U.P. Tel.: 2733

NORTHERN EVANGELICAL LUTHERAN CHURCH (1950)
P.O. Benagaria, Santal Parganas, Bihar

NORWEGIAN TIBETAN MISSION
2 Macintosh Road, Darjeeling, W. Bengal

OLD CHURCH CHINESE MISSION (Ling Liang Chinese Church)
11 Mission Row, Calcutta, W. Bengal

OLD CHURCH HEBREW MISSION
51 R.N. Mukherjee Road, Calcutta 1. Tel.: 22-2429

ONE-BY-ONE BAND
Udipi, S. Kamara, Mysore

OPEN BIBLE CHURCH OF GOD
Site No. 141, Tatabad, Coimbatore Dist., Madras

ORTHODOX SYRIAN CHURCH
Old Seminary, Kottayam, Kerala

OXFORD MISSION TO CALCUTTA
Oxford Mission House, 111 Vivekananda Road, Calcutta 6. Tel.: 34–3005
(Calcutta)

PAKHAL MISSION
Nekonda, Warangal Dist., Andhra Pradesh

PENTECOSTAL HOLINESS CHURCH
Madhupur, Santal Parganas, Bihar

POONA AND INDIAN VILLAGE MISSION (1893
10 Napier Road, Poona 1, Maharashtra

ASIA

RAMABAI MUKTI MISSION (1896)
Kedgaon, Poona Dist., Maharashtra

RURAL GOSPEL AND MEDICAL MISSIONS OF INDIA
Mission House, Khardi, Thana Dist., Maharashtra

ST. THOMAS EVANGELICAL CHURCH
Tiruvalla, Kerala

SAJINIPARA AND CALCUTTA LUTHERAN CHURCH OF NORWEGIAN
MISSION
Sajinipara Mission, P.O. Chhabghati, Dist. Murshidabad, W. Bengal

SALVATION ARMY
37 Dharamtola Street, Calcutta 13, W. Bengal; Morland Road, Byculla, Bombay
8; 1c Ritherdon Road, Madras 7; New Rhotah Road, Karol Bagh, Delhi 8;
Kowdiyar P.O., Trivandrum 3, Kerala

SAMAVESAM OF TELUGU BAPTIST CHURCHES
A.B.M. Secondary and Training School, Bapatla, Gunter Dist., Andhra Pradesh

SCRIPTURE GIFT MINISTRY OF INDIA
13 Cubbon Road, Bangalore, Mysore

SCRIPTURE UNION AND CHILDREN'S SPECIAL SERVICE MISSION
IN INDIA (1901 in India)
"Omacheril", Temple Road, Lakasserry, Chengannur, Kerala State

SEPARATE BAPTISTS IN CHRIST INDIA MISSION
Vambori, Ahmednagar Dist., Maharashtra

SERVANTS OF THE CROSS (Missionary Brotherhood of Orthodox Syrian
Church of Malabar) (1924)
Mulanlthuruthi, Kerala

SOCIETY OF ST. THOMA
Manganam, Kottayam Dist., Kerala

SOUTH ANDHRA LUTHERAN CHURCH
Renigunta, Chittoor Dist., Andhra Pradesh

SOUTH INDIA ASSEMBLIES OF GOD
Bethal Bible School, Punalur P.O., Kerala

SOUTH INDIA MISSION OF THE CHRISTIAN REFORMED CHURCH
Adoni, Kurnool Dist., Andhra Pradesh

STUDENT CHRISTIAN MOVEMENT OF INDIA (1912)
S.C.M. House, 2 Mission Road, Bangalore 2, Mysore. Tel.: 72937

TAMIL EVANGELICAL LUTHERAN CHURCH
Tranquebar House, Tiruchirapalli, Madras. Tel.: 798

TELEGU MENNONITE BRETHREN CONVENTION
Medical Centre, Jadcherla, Andhra Pradesh

THE EVANGELICAL ALLIANCE MISSION (TEAM)
Amalner, Jalgaon Dist., Maharashtra

TRIPURA BAPTIST CHRISTIAN UNION
P.O. Arundhutinagar, Agartala, Tripura. Tel.: Agartala 234

UNION OF EVANGELICAL STUDENTS OF INDIA (1954)
22 Clemen's Road, Madras 7

UNITED BASEL MISSION CHURCH OF SOUTH KANARA AND BOMBAY
Naregal, Dharwar Dist., Mysore

UNITED CHURCH OF NORTHERN INDIA AND PAKISTAN
Church House, Mhow, Madhya Pradesh

UNITED PENECOSTAL CHURCH
Mission Bungalow, Adur P.O., Quilon Dist., Kerala

UTKAL CHRISTIAN CHURCH CENTRAL COUNCIL (1933)
Madhusudan Road, Cuttack, Orissa

WESLEYAN METHODIST CHURCH—INDIA CONFERENCE
Pardi, Bulsar Dist., Gujarat

ASIA

WIDOWS' AND ORPHANS' SPECIAL SERVICE MISSION
Narasapur, West Godavari Dist., Andhra Pradesh

WOMEN'S UNION MISSIONARY SOCIETY
Broadwell Hospital, Fatehpur, Uttar Pradesh

YOUNG MEN'S CHRISTIAN ASSOCIATION, NATIONAL COUNCIL (1891)
Massey Hall, Jai Singh Road (P.O. Box 14), New Delhi 1. Tel.: 45769

YOUNG WOMEN'S CHRISTIAN ASSOCIATION
Parliament Street, New Delhi. Tel.: 45294

YOUTH FOR CHRIST, INDIA
Mherwan Bldg., Sir P.M. Road, Bombay 1

INDONESIA

AGRICULTURAL TRAINING CENTRE
Tumbang Zehang, Djalan Tugu 6, Bandjarmasin, Kalimantan

BADAN PENERBIT KRISTEN (Christian Literature Society)
Kwitang 22, Djakarta, Java

BALA KESLAMATAN (Salvation Army)
Djalan Djawa 16, Bandung, Java

BANUA HINA KERISO PROTESTANT (Protestant Church on Nias) (1936)
Gunungsitoli, Nias, Sumatra

CHRISTIAN SCIENCE COMMITTEE ON PUBLICATION
Djalan Palem 18, Djakarta 11/15

DEWAN GEREDJA-GEREDJA DI INDONESIA (National Council of Churches in Indonesia)
Djalan Salemba Raya 10, Djakarta IV/3, Java
Gen. Sec.: Rev. Simon Marantika

GERAKAN MAHASISWA KRISTEN INDONESIA (Student Christian Movement)
Djalan Salemba 10, Flat 21, Djakarta IV/3, Java

GEREDJA BATAK KARO PROTESTANT (Karo Batak Church)
Kabandjahe, via Medan, Sumatra

GEREDJA-GEREDJA KRISTEN DJAWA (Christian Javanese Churches)
Djl. Dr. Sumardi 5, Salatiga. Tel.; Sa 126

GEREDJA-GEREDJA KRISTEN SUMBA (Christian Churches on Sumba)
Pajeti, Sumba

GEREDJA-GEREDJA KRISTEN TIONGHOA DJAWA TENGAH (Chinese Christian Churches, Central Java)
149 Imam Bondjol, Semarang, Java

GEREDJA GEREFORMEERD DI INDONESIA (Reformed Church in Indonesia)
Kwitang 28, Djakarta, Java

GEREDJA KALIMANTAN EVANGELIS (Evangelical Kalimantan Church)
Djan Tugu 6, Bandjarmasin, Kalimantan

GEREDJA KRISTEN DJAWA SEKITAR MURIA (Mennonite Church in Northern Central Java)
Djalan Kawedanan 56, Kudas, Java

GEREDJA KRISTEN DJAWI WETAN (Christian Church in East Java)
Sukun 18, Malang, Java

GEREDJA KRISTEN DI IRIAN BARAT (G.K.I.) (Evangelical Christian Church in West Irian)
Kantor Pusat G.K.I. Djalan Argapura, West Irian. Tel.: Sukarnapura 190

GEREDJA KRISTEN INDJILI DI NEDERLANDS NIEUW GUINEA (1956)
Kamtoor Berg en Dal, Hollandia

ASIA

GEREDJA KRISTEN INDONESIA DJAWA BARAT (Formerly Chinese
Christian Church in West Java)
Djalan 1c H. Djuanda 102 E, Bandung, Java

GEREDJA KRISTEN INDONESIA DJAWA TIMUR (Indonesian Christian
Church, East Java)
Djalan Olahraga 19, Bondowoso, Java

GEREDJA KRISTEN PASUNDAN (Christian Church in West Java)
93 Pasirkaliki, Bandung, Java

GEREDJA KRISTEN PROTESTANT BALI (Christian Protestant Church on
Bali)
P.O. Box 220, Penjobekan, Denpasar, Bali. Tel.: 2914

GEREDJA KRISTEN PROTESTAN INDONESIA (Indonesian Protestant
Christian Church)
Djalan Abdullah Lubis No. 48, Medan, Sumatra

GEREDJA KRISTEN PROTESTAN SIMALUNGUN (Simalungun Protestant
Christian Church)
Djalan Djendeval Sudiman 24, Pematang Siantar, Sumatra

GEREDJA KRISTEN SULAWESI SELATAN (Christian Church in South
Celebes)
c/o Rumah Sakit Labuang Badji, Makasar

GEREDJA KRISTEN SULAWESI TENGAH (Christian Church in Central
Celebes)
Tentena, Poso, Sulawesi Tengah, Central Celebes

GEREDJA KRISTEN SULAWESI TENGGARA (Christian Church in S.E.
Celebes)
Kendari, Sulawesi Tenggara

GEREDJA KRISTEN TIONGHOA DJAKARTA (Chinese Christian Church in
Djakarta).
Djalan Taman Djatibaru 7, Djakarta, Java

GEREDJA KRISTEN TIONGHOA DJAWA TIMUR (Chinese Christian Church
East Java)
Djalan Klenteng 61, Modjokerto, Java

GEREDJA KRISTEN TORADJA MAMASA (Toradja Church in Mamasa)
Mamasa, via Makasar

GEREDJA MASEHI INDJILI BOLAANG-MONGONDOW (Christian
Evangelical Church in Bolaang-Mongondow, N. Celebes)
Kotamobagu, via Menado

GEREDJA MASEHI INDJILI HALMAHERA (Christian Evangelical Church in
Halmahera)
Tobelo, Halmahera

GEREDJA MASEHI INDJILI MINAHASA (Christian Evangelical Church in
Minahasa)
Tomohon, Minahasa

GEREDJA MASEHI INDJILI SANGIHE DAN TALAUD (Christian
Evangelical Church in Sangihe and Talaud) (1947)
Tahuna-Sangihe, via Menado

GEREDJA MASEHI INDJILI TIMOR (Christian Evangelical Church in Timor)
Kupang, Timor

GEREDJA METHODIST SUMATRA (Methodist Church in Sumatra)
Djalan Sumatra 74, Medan, Sumatra

GEREDJA PROTESTAN DI INDONESIA (Protestant Church in Indonesia)
Medan Merdeka Timur 10, Djakarta, Java

GEREDJA PROTESTAN MALUKU (Protestant Church of the Moluccas)
2 Djalan Geredja Batugantung, Ambon, Maluku

GEREDJA TORADJA (RANTEPAO) (Toradja Church) (1947)
Djalan Tarulangi 11, Rantepao, Sulawesi

ASIA

HURIA KRISTEN BATAK PROTESTAN (Batak Protestant Christian Church)
Kantor Besar Pearadja, Tarutung, Sumatra

KOMISI KESAHATAN DAN SOSIAL (Medical and Social Commission) (1950)
Salemba Raja 10, Djakarta IV/3, Java

KOMISI PEKABARAN INDJIL (National Missionary Commission in Indonesia)
Djalan Teuku Umar 17, Djakarta, Java

KOMISI SEKOLAH MINGGU (Sunday School Commission)
Djalan Mangga Besar VIII/6, Djakarta, Java

LEMBAGA ALKITAB INDONESIA (1954) (Indonesian Bible Society)
P.O. Box 255/DKT, 12 Djalan Raya Salemba, Djakarta

LEMBAGA AUDIO-VISUAL AIDS (Commission on Audio-Visual Aids)
Medan Merdeka Timur 10, Djakarta, Java

MADJELIS PEMUDA KRISTEN OIKUMENIS (National Ecumenical Youth
Council in Indonesia)
Djalan Teuku Umar 17, Djakarta, Java

MADJELIS PUSAT PENDIDIKAN KRISTEN (Central Council of Christian
Education)
Salemba 10, Djakarta, Java

PERSERIKATAN PEMUDA KRISTEN INDONESIA (Union of Indonesian
Christian Youth)
Djalan Kramat Raya 65, Djakarta, Java

PROTESTANTSE KERK IN INDONESIA (Protestant Church in Indonesia)
P.O. Box 57, Djakarta, Java

THE EVANGELICAL ALLIANCE MISSION (TEAM) (in West Irian)
Manokwari, West Irian

YOUNG MEN'S CHRISTIAN ASSOCIATION, NATIONAL BOARD
Djalan Segara 3, Djakarta. Tel.: 41699

IRAN

ARMENIAN ORTHODOX CHURCH
Teheran

BIBLE SOCIETIES
7/3-4 Ghavam-ol-Saltanch Street (P.O. Box 1412), Teheran

CHURCH COUNCIL OF IRAN (1951)
Box 1505, Teheran

EPISCOPAL CHURCH OF IRAN
No. 87 Sevvom-i-Isfand Street, Teheran

EVANGELICAL CHURCH OF IRAN (Presbyterian)
Box 1505, Teheran. Tel.: 69750

FILADELFIA ASSEMBLY (Armenian Pentecostal)
P.O. Box 2314, Teheran

INTERNATIONAL MISSIONS INC.
P.O. Box 5, Kermanshah

JERUSALEM BISHOPRIC (Anglican): Diocese of Iran
Bishop's House, Isfahan

SYNOD OF THE EVANGELICAL CHURCHES OF NORTH IRAN
Assyrian Evangelical Church, Khiaban-i-Shapur, Khiaban-i, Aramenah, Teheran

IRAQ

ANGLICAN CHURCH—JERUSALEM BISHOPRIC (Iraq)
Chaplain's House, St. George's Church, Baghdad West, Baghdad. Tel.: 31481

BIBLE SOCIETY
321/1 Rashid Street, Baghdad

ASIA

NATIONAL PROTESTANT CHURCH
Basrah

SYRIAN ORTHODOX CHURCH
Baghdad

YOUNG MEN'S CHRISTIAN ASSOCIATION
Sa'Doon Street, Baghdad. Tel.: 81362

YOUNG WOMEN'S CHRISTIAN ASSOCIATION
Damascus Road, Harithyia, Baghdad

ISRAEL

AMERICAN ASSOCIATION FOR JEWISH EVANGELISM
P.O. Box 376, Ramat-gan

AMERICAN INSTITUTE OF HOLY LAND STUDIES
52 Street of The Prophets, Jerusalem

BAPTIST CONVENTION
P.O. Box 154, Jerusalem

BIBLE EVANGELISTIC MISSION
P.O. Box 216, Jerusalem

BIBLE SOCIETY
Hechaluz Street 10 (P.O. Box 525), Haifa

BRITISH SOCIETY FOR THE PROPAGATION OF THE GOSPEL AMONG
THE JEWS
P.O. Box 206, Haifa

CHRISTIAN AND MISSIONARY ALLIANCE
P.O. Box 50, Jerusalem

CHURCH OF SCOTLAND
52 Yefet Street, Jaffa

CHURCH OF THE NAZARENE
P.O. Box 1070, Jerusalem

CHURCH'S MINISTRY AMONG THE JEWS
82 Prophets Street, Jerusalem. Tel.: 28133

EDINBURGH MEDICAL MISSIONARY SOCIETY
P.O. Box 11, Nazareth

EVANGELICAL EPISCOPAL COMMUNITY IN ISRAEL
P.O. Box 1796, Haifa

FINNISH MISSIONARY SOCIETY
25 Shivtei Israel Street, Jerusalem

FRIENDS OF ISRAEL
P.O. Box 2773, Tel-Aviv

INTERNATIONAL HEBREW CHRISTIAN ALLIANCE
P.O. Box 191, Jerusalem

JERUSALEM AND EAST MISSION
P.O. Box 191, Jerusalem

MINISTRY FOR RELIGIOUS AFFAIRS
P.O. Box 1167, Jerusalem

NORWEGIAN LUTHERAN MISSION
P.O. Box 525, Haifa

ST. ANDREW'S (SCOTS MEMORIAL) CHURCH
Jerusalem

UNITED CHRISTIAN COUNCIL IN ISRAEL
P.O. Box 116, Jerusalem. Tel.: (02)37638 Rev. Dr. Maas Boertien

YOUNG MEN'S CHRISTIAN ASSOCIATION (1878)
P.O. Box 294, Jerusalem. Tel.: 2-4437

ASIA

YOUNG WOMEN'S CHRISTIAN ASSOCIATION
P.O. Box 27 Nazareth

JAPAN

ANGLICAN EPISCOPAL CHURCH OF JAPAN (Nihon Seikokai)
23 Tokiwamatsu-cho, Shibuyaku, Tokyo. Tel.: 401-2314

APOSTOLIC CHRISTIAN CHURCH OF JAPAN (Nihon Shito Kirisuto Kyokai)
1384 Kaneko-machi, Chofushi, Tokyo. Tel.: 0424-82-4344

APOSTOLIC CHURCH OF PENTECOST OF CANADA, INC. (Nippon
Pentekosute Fukuin Kyodan)
Unuma, Kagamihara-shi, Gifuken. Tel.: Inuyama 1186

APOSTOLIC FAITH (Shinto no Shinko Dendo Dan)
1017, 1-chome Kugahara-cho, Ota-Ku, Tokyo. Tel.: 751-4211

ASSEMBLIES OF GOD CHURCH OF JAPAN (Nihon Assemblies of God
Kyodan)
430, 3-chome, Komagome, Toshima-Ku, Tokyo. Tel.: 982-4925

ASSOCIATION OF BAPTISTS FOR WORLD EVANGELISM (Bankoku
Baputesuto Fukuin Dendo Kyokai)
11 Nakajima, 3-chome, Fukiai-Ku, Kobe-shi. Tel.: 078-22-0537

ASSOCIATION OF CHRISTIAN PUBLICATIONS AND SALES (Nippon
Kirisutokyo Shuppan Hanbai Kyokai)
c/o Shinkyo Shuppan Sha, 1, 3-chome, Shin Ogawa-machi, Shinjuku-ku, Tokyo.
Tel.: 260-6148

AUDIO VISUAL ACTIVITIES COMMISSION OF NATIONAL CHRISTIAN
COUNCIL OF JAPAN (Nihon Kirisutokyo Kyogikai Shichokaku Jigyobu)
22 Midorigaoka, Shibuya-ku, Tokyo. Tel.: 401-4123

BAPTIST BIBLE FELLOWSHIP OF JAPAN (Nihon Seisho Baputesuto Renmei)
11-3, 1-chome, Matsunamicho, Chiba-shi. Tel.: 0472-51-2929

BAPTIST GENERAL CONFERENCE (Nippon Kirisuto Baputesuto Rengo
Senkyodan)
475 Kushimoto-cho, Nishimuro-gun, Wakayama-ken. Tel.: Kushimoto 718

BAPTIST MID-MISSION IN JAPAN (Zen Nippon Baputesuto Mido Mission
Senkyodan)
21 Bancho, Shiroishi-shi, Miyagi-ken.

BIBLE INSTITUTE MISSION (Shorisha Iesu Kyodan)
2163 Karuizawa-machi, Kitasaku-gun, Nagano-Ken. Tel.: 02674-2302

BRETHREN IN CHRIST MISSION (Kirisutokyo Kyodai Dan Kyokai)
11 Tokaichi Suji, Hijihara, Hagi-shi, Yamaguchi-ken. Tel.: Hagi 444

CATHOLIC CHURCH (Nihon Katorikku Kyokai)
Information Center: National Catholic Committee of Japan, 10 Rokubancho,
Chiyoda-ku, Tokyo. Tel.: 262-3691

CENTRAL JAPAN PIONEER MISSION (Cho Nihon Fukuin Senkyodan)
16-16 Nanatsu Ike-machi, Koriyama-shi, Fukushima-ken. Tel.: 02492-2-7992

CHRISTIAN BROTHERHOOD CHURCH (Kirisuto Kyodai Dan)
448 Tabata-cho. Kita-ku, Tokyo. Tel.: 821-0210

CHRISTIAN CANAAN CHURCH (Kirisutokyo Kanan Kyodan)
36, 1-chome, Kushiya-machi, Higashi, Sakai-shi

CHRISTIAN CATHOLIC CHURCH (Kirisuto Kodo Kyokai)
21-2, 2-chome, Tsukigaoka, Chikusa-ku, Nagoya-shi. Tel.: 052-71-9654

CHRISTIAN CHURCHES (Kirisuto no Kyokai)
1-52 Arai-machi, Nakano-ku, Tokyo. Tel.: 386-5171

CHRISTIAN HOLY CONVENTION (Kirisuto Seikyodan)
539 Tsubakimori-cho, Chiba-shi. Tel.: 0472-51-8510

CHRISTIAN LITERATURE SOCIETY OF JAPAN (Kyo Bun Kwan)
Kyobunkwan Building, 2 Ginza, 4-chome, Chuo-ku, Tokyo. Tel.: 561-8446

ASIA

CHRISTIAN ORIENTAL SALVATION CHURCH (Kirisutokyo Toyo Kyurei Dan)
27, 4-chome, Izumi-dori, Nada-ku, Kobe-shi. Tel.: 078–86–2462

CHRISTIAN SCIENCE COMMITTEE ON PUBLICATION
11, 4, 4-chome Jungumae Shibuya-ku, Tokyo

CHRISTIAN SPIRITUAL CHURCH (Kirisuto Shinshu Kyodan)
8602, Shimoyoshida, Fujiyoshida-shi, Yamanashi-ken. Tel. 0555–2–0367

CHURCH EDUCATION DEPT. OF THE NCC (Kyokai Kyoiku Jigyo BU, NCC)
Christian Center Building, 2 Ginza, 4-chome, Chuo-ku, Tokyo. Tel.: 561–6318

CHURCH OF CHRIST (Kirisuto no Kyokai)
Ibaraki Christian College, Omika, Hitachi-shi, Ibaraki-ken (2215)

CHURCH OF JESUS CHRIST OF LATTER DAY SAINTS (Matsujitsu Seito Iesu Kirisuto Kyokai)
14–2, Hiroo-cho, Azabu, Minato-ku, Tokyo. Tel.: 473–1613

CHURCH OF THE NAZARENE IN JAPAN (Nihon Nazaren Kyodan)
235 Oyama-cho, Tamagawa, Setagaya-ku, Tokyo. Tel.: 701–4667

CHURCH OF THE RESURRECTED CHRIST (Fukkatsu no Kirisuto Kyodan)
Fukkatsu no Kirisuto Nagano, Kyokai, 416, Nishi Nagano, Nagano-shi

COUNCIL OF CHRISTIAN EVANGELISM FOR THE BLIND IN JAPAN, NCC (Nippon Mojin Kirisutokyo Dendo Kyogikai)
c/o NCC, 2 Ginza, 4-chome, Chuo-ku, Tokyo. Tel. 561–5003

COUNCIL OF CO-OPERATION (Naigai Kyoryoku Kai)
Kyobunkwan Building, 2 Ginza, 4-chome, Chuo-ku, Tokyo. Tel.: 561–6131/0921

CUMBERLAND PRESBYTERIAN CHURCH (Kanbarando Choro Kyokai)
3366–3 Minami Rinkan, Yamato-shi, Kanagawa-ken. Tel.: 0462–61–4371

EDUCATION ASSOCIATION OF CHRISTIAN SCHOOLS IN JAPAN (Kirisutokyo Gakko Kyoiku Domei)
Kyobunkwan Building, 2 Ginza, 4-chome, Chuo-ku, Tokyo. Tel.: 561–7643

EVANGELICAL BOOKSELLERS ASSOCIATION (Fukuinteki Shoten Kyoryokukai)
c/o Christian Literature Crusade, 1–3, 2-chome, Surugadai, Kanda, Chiyoda-ku, Tokyo. Tel.: 294–0775

EVANGELICAL FREE CHURCH OF JAPAN (Nihon Fukuin Jiyu Kyokai)
Kyoto Christian Center, 33, 2-chome, Higashi, Ono-cho Koyama, Kita-ku, Kyoto-shi. Tel.: 075–45–4961

EVANGELICAL MISSIONARY ASSOCIATION OF JAPAN (Nippon Fukuin Senkyoshi Dan)
104, 1-chome, Akebono-cho, Tachikawa-shi, Tokyo. Tel.: 0452–4224

EVANGELICAL MISSIONARY CHURCH (Fukuin Dendo Kyodan)
124 Seioji-machi, Maebashi-shi. Tel.: 0272–2–7922

EVANGELICAL PUBLISHERS FELLOWSHIP (Fukuin Shuppan Kyoryokukai)
c/o Inochi no Kotoba sha, 6, Shinao-machi, Shinjuku-ku, Tokyo

FAR EAST APOSTOLIC MISSION (Nippon Pentekosute Kyodan)
Tawaraguchi, Ikoma-cho, Ikoma-gun, Nara-ken. Tel.: 0437–3821

FAR EASTERN GOSPEL CRUSADE (Kyokuto Fukuin Juji Gun)
111 Hakuraku, Kanagawa-ku, Yokohama-shi. Tel.: 045–49–9017

FINNISH FREE FOREIGN MISSION (Nippon Kirisuto Fukuin Kyokai Rengo)
91 Higashi, Okazaki Tenno-cho, Sakyo-ku, Kyoto

FREE METHODIST CHURCH OF JAPAN (Nihon Jiyu Mesojisuto Kyodan)
81, 1-chome, Maruyama-dori, Abeno-ku, Osaka-shi. Tel. 06–661–7989

FRIENDS OF JESUS SOCIETY (Iesu no Tomo no Kai)
859, 3-chome, Kami-Kitazawa, Setagaya-ku. Tokyo. Tel.: 321–2855

GENERAL CONFERENCE MENNONITE MISSION (Kyushu Mennonaito Kyokai Kyogikai)
10853 Kamezaki, Hyuga-shi, Miyazaki-ken. Tel.: 3871

ASIA

GIDEONS INTERNATIONAL IN JAPAN (Nihon Kokusai Gideon Kyokai)
Toko Building, 12 Tomeo-cho, Nishikubo, Shiba, Minato-ku, Tokyo. Tel.: 434-1010

GOSPEL OF JESUS CHURCH (Iesu Fukuin Kyodan)
1548 Shimo Hoya, Hoya-shi, Tokyo

HOLY JESUS SOCIETY (Sei Iesu Kai)
880, 3-chome, Totsuka-cho, Shinjuku-ku, Tokyo. Tel.: 368-8278

HOLY SPIRIT ASSOCIATION FOR UNIFICATION OF WORLD CHRIST-
IANITY (Sekai Kirisutokyo Toisu Shinrei Kyokai)
1200, 1-chome, Kitazawa, Setagaya-ku, Tokyo. Tel.: 421-2889

HOREMCO (Hokkaido Radio and Mass Communication Evangelism)
Box 202, Sapporo

IMMANUEL CHURCH (Immanueru Sogo Dendo Dan)
Kotsu Kyokai Bldg., 4, 3-chome, Marunouchi, Chiyoda-ku, Tokyo. Tel.: 271-0418

INTERNATIONAL CHRISTIAN BODY (Kokusai Kirisuto Kyodan)
29, 1-chome, Yoyogi, Shibuya-ku, Tokyo. Tel.: 371-1967

INTERNATIONAL CHRISTIAN LEADERSHIP (Aishin Kai)
c/o Ocean Cable Co. Ltd., 18 Kamiya-cho, Shiba, Minato-ku, Tokyo. Tel.: 431-2240

INTERNATIONAL CHURCH OF THE FOURSQUARE GOSPEL (Kokusai
Fosukuea Kyodan)
806, Higashi Ooizumi-cho, Nerima-ku, Tokyo. Tel.: 997-4520

INTERNATIONAL GOSPEL LEAGUE (Kokusai Fukuin Renmei)
93 Uyama, Sumoto-shi, Awajishima, Hyogo-ken. Tel.: 1028

INTERNATIONAL INSTITUTE FOR THE STUDY OF RELIGIONS (Kokusai
Shukyo Kenkyujo)
National YMCA Building, 2-1 Nishi Kanda, Chiyoda-ku. Tokyo. Tel.: 291-4231

INTER-VARSITY CHRISTIAN FELLOWSHIP (Kirisutosha Gakusei Kai)
1-3, 2-chome, Surugadai, Kanda, Chiyoda-ku, Tokyo. Tel.: 201-9081

JAPAN ADVENT CHRISTIAN CHURCH (Nippon Adobento Kirisuto Kyokai)
2276 Higashi Iwakura-machi, Kurayoshi-shi, Tottori-ken

JAPAN ALLIANCE CHURCH (Nihon Araiansu Kyodan)
255, Itsukaichi-machi, Saekigun, Hiroshima-ken. Tel.: 21-2514

JAPAN BAPTIST CONFERENCE (Nippon Baputesuto Senkyo Dan)
175 Tsujikuru-cho, Ise-shi, Mie-ken. Tel.: 8-4846

JAPAN BAPTIST CONVENTION (Nihon Baputesuto Renmei)
350, 2-chome, Nishi-okubo, Shinjuku-ku. Tokyo. Tel.: 351-2166

JAPAN BAPTIST UNION (Nihon Baputesuto Domei)
2, 1-chome, Misaki-cho, Kanda, Chiyoda-ku, Tokyo. Tel.: 291-9445

JAPAN BIBLE CHRISTIAN COUNCIL (Nippon Seisho Kirisutokyo Kyogikai)
273 Horinouchi, 1-chome, Suginami-ku, Tokyo. Tel.: 311-5510

JAPAN BIBLE SOCIETY (Nippon Seisho Kyokai)
2 Ginza, 4-chome, Chuo-ku, Tokyo. Tel.: 561-1081/5806

JAPAN CHRIST SOCIETY (Nihon Kirisuto Kai)
25-6, 1-chome, Shoto-cho, Shibuya-ku, Tokyo

JAPAN CHRISTIAN ACADEMY (Nihon Christian Academy)
12-9, 2-chome, Sanno, Ota-ku, Tokyo. Tel.: 771-4341

JAPAN CHRISTIAN MEDICAL ASSOCIATION (Nippon Kirisuto-sha Ika
Renmei)
National YMCA Building, 2, 1-chome, Nishi Kanda, Chiyoda-ku, Tokyo.
Tel.: 201-4659/291-5201/4

JAPAN CHURCH OF GOD (Nippon Church of God Kyokai)
3412 Shimokawai-machi, Hodogaya-ku, Yokohama-shi. Tel.: KAWAI 206

JAPAN CHURCH OF GOD FEDERATION (Nihon Kami no Kyokai Renmei)
93, 3-chome, Okusawa-machi, Tamagawa Setagaya-ku, Tokyo. Tel.: 701-4321

ASIA

JAPAN CHURCH WORLD SERVICE, INC. (Nihon Kirisutokyo Hoshi Dan)
Kyobunkwan Building, 2 Ginza, 4-chome, Chuo-ku, Tokyo. Tel.: 561–4774/5257

JAPAN CONSERVATIVE BAPTIST MISSION (Tohoku Seisho Baputesuto
Kyokai)
c/o Sendai Seisho Baputesuto Kypkai, 31 Naka Sugiyamadori, Sendai-shi.
Tel.: 0222–22–4488

JAPAN COUNCIL OF EVANGELICAL MISSIONS (Nippon Fukuin Senkyo-shi
Renmei)
1–832 Yoshihara, Mihama-cho, Hidaka-gun, Wakayama-ken. Tel.: GOBO 2134

JAPAN COVENANT CHURCH (Nippon Seikei Kyodan)
Seikei Shin-Gakko, 990, 3-chome, Nakameguro, Meguro-ku, Tokyo. Tel.: 712–
8746

JAPAN EVANGELICAL FELLOWSHIP (Nippon Fukuin Renmei)
1–13 Kakigara cho, Chuo-ku, Tokyo. Tel.: 671–4906

JAPAN EVANGELICAL LUTHERAN CHURCH (Nihon Fukuin Ruteru
Kyokai)
3–303, Hyakunin-cho, Shinjuku-ku, Tokyo. Tel.: 361–7550

JAPAN EVANGELISTIC BAND (Nippon Dendo Tai)
11 of 6 Sumauradori, 6-chome, Suma-ku, Kobe-shi. Tel.: 078–71–5651

JAPAN EVANGELISTIC GOSPEL CHURCH (Nihon Dendo Fukuin Kyodan)
4–3 Shimo-Nakajima-cho, Nagaoka-shi, Nigata-ken

JAPAN FREE WILL BAPTIST MISSION (Fukuin Baputesuto Kyodan)
c/o Fred Hersey, American Village, 2143 Unoki, Sayama-shi, Saitama-ken

JAPAN GOSPEL CHURCH (Nippon Fukuin Kyodan)
3, 1-chome, Hachichobori, Chuo-ku, Tokyo

JAPAN GOSPEL FEDERATION (Nippon Fukuin Renmei)
c/o Suginami Chubu Church, 76 Higashi-ogi-cho, Suginami-ku, Tokyo. Tel.:381–
5401

JAPAN GOSPEL LEAGUE (Japan Gosuperu Riigu)
56 Itakura-cho, Koyama, Kita-ku, Kyoto-shi

JAPAN GOSPEL OF CHRIST CHURCH (Nippon Fukuin Kirisuto Kyodan)
2500, Shimoishihara, Chofu-shi, Tokyo. Tel.: 0424–82–2457

JAPAN HOLINESS CHURCH (ARAHARA-HA) (Nihon Horinesu Kyokai-
Arahara-ha)
40, 2-chome, Tamagawanaka-machi, Setagaya-ku, Tokyo. Tel.: 701–1880

JAPAN HOLINESS CHURCH (KURUMADA-HA) (Nihon Horinesu Kyodan-
Kurumada-ha)
1–477, Megurita, Higashimurayama-shi, Tokyo. Tel.: 0423–91–3075

JAPAN JESUS CHRIST CHURCH (Nippon Jesu Kirisuto Kyodan)
Mizugaska 959, Nishitarumi cho, Tarumi-ku, Kobe. Tel.: Kobe (078) Tarumi (77)
4169

JAPAN KESWICK CONVENTION (Nippon Keswick Convention)
Room 42, Student Christian Center, 1, 2-chome, Kanda Surugadai, Chiyoda-ku,
Tokyo. Tel.: 291–1910

JAPAN MENNONITE BRETHREN CONFERENCE (Nippon Mennonaito
Burezaren Kyodan)
59 Sompachi-cho, Ikeda-shi, Osaka-fu. Tel.: 0727–6–8969

JAPAN MENNONITE CHURCH (Nippon Mennonaito Kyokai)
Nishi 7-jo, Minami 17-chome, Obihiro-shi, Hokkaido. Tel.: 3282

JAPAN MISSIONARY BAPTIST ASSOCIATION (Nippon Baputesuto Rengo)
1137 Shimo-Nagaya-cho, Minami-ku, Yokohama-shi. Tel.: 045–74–2586

JAPAN NEW TESTAMENT CHURCH (Nihon Shinyaku Kyodan)
854, 3-chome, Kamitakaido, Suginami-ku, Tokyo

JAPANESE ORTHODOX CHURCH (Nihon Hari utosu Sei Kyokai)
1–3, 4-chome, Surugadai, Kanda, Chi oda-ku, Tokyo. Tel.: 291–1885

ASIA

JAPAN OVERSEAS CHRISTIAN MEDICAL CO-OPERATIVE SERVICE
(Nihon Kirisutokyo Kaigai Iryo Kyoryokukai)
c/o National YMCA Building, 1–2 Nishi Kanda, Chiyoda-ku, Tokyo. Tel.:
201–4659/291–5201

JAPAN PROTESTANT CONFERENCE (Nippon Protestant Seisho Shinko
Domei)
1, 2-chome, Kanda Surugadai, Chiyoda-ku, Tokyo. Tel.: 299–4304

JAPAN REGULAR BAPTIST MISSION (Nihon Regyura Baputesuto Mission)
6 Ou-machi, Toyama-shi. Tel.: 0764–3–6829

JAPAN RURAL MISSION (Nippon Chiho Dendo Dan)
2640 Jonan-ku, Saiki-shi, Oita-ken. Tel.: 2238

JAPAN SOCIETY OF CHRISTIAN STUDIES (Nippon Kirisutokyo Gakkai)
c/o The Theology Dept. of Kanto Gakuin, Mutsuura, Kanazawa-ku, Yokohama-
shi. Tel.: 045–70–8281

JAPAN SUNDAY SCHOOL UNION (Nihon Nichiyo Gakko Josei Kyokai)
36 Mita Matsuzaka-cho, Shiba, Minato-ku, Tokyo. Tel.: 477–4871/2

JAPAN UNION OF CHRISTIAN ENDEAVOUR (Nippon Rengo Kirisutokyo
Kyoreikai)
Niishima Kaikan, Teramachidori, Kamikyo-ku, Kyoto-shi. Tel.: 075–23–5403

KINKI EVANGELICAL LUTHERAN CHURCH (Kinki Fukuin Ruteru Kyokai)
c/o Minami Osaka Church, 420 Kamisumiyoshi-cho, Sumiyoshi-ku, Osaki-shi.
Tel.: 06–691–4398

KOREAN CHURCH OF CHRIST IN JAPAN (Zainichi Taikan Kirisuto Kyokai)
24 Wakamiya-cho, Shinjuku-ku, Tokyo. Tel.: 260–8891

LIEBENZELLER MISSION (Riibenzera Nippon Dendo Kai)
1933, Nakanoshima, Kawasaki-shi, Kanagawa-ken. Tel.: 044–91–2334

LIVING WATER CHRISTIAN CHURCH (Kassui Kirisuto Kyodan)
587 Ogikubo, Odawara-shi, Kanagawa ken. Tel.: 0465–22–6891

LUTHERAN BRETHREN MISSION OF JAPAN (Nippon Ruteru Doho Senkyo
Dan)
10 Ishiwaki Tajiri, Honjo-shi, Akita-ken. Tel.: 5749

LUTHERAN CHURCH, MISSOURI SYNOD (Nihon Ruteru Kyodan)
16, 1-chome, Fujimi-cho, Chiyoda-ku, Tokyo. Tel.: 331–5266

MINO MISSION (Mino Misshon)
Tomidahama, Yokkaichi-shi, Mie-ken. Tel.: 6–0096

MISSION COVENANT CHURCH OF SWEDEN (Nippon Seijaku Kirisuto
Kyodan)
360 Aminohama, Okayama-shi. Tel.: 0862–72–1829

NATIONAL CHRISTIAN COUNCIL OF JAPAN (Nihon Kirisuto-kyo Kyogikai)
Kyobunkwan Building, 2 Ginza, 4-chome, Chuo-ku, Tokyo. Tel.: 561–5003/5571
General Sec.: Rev. Chuzo Yamada

NORWEGIAN EVANGELICAL ORIENT MISSION (Noruei Toyo Fukuin
Senkyo Kai)
6 Machigashira, Yotsukura-machi, Ishiki-gun, Fukushima-ken

OMI BROTHERHOOD (Omi Kyodaisha)
Omi Hachiman-shi, Shiga-ken. Tel.: 3131

OPEN BIBLE CHURCH (Nihon Opun Baiburu Kyodan)
76, 5-chome, Koshien-guchi, Nishinomiya-shi. Tel.: 4–3452

OREBRO MISSION SOCIETY OF SWEDEN (Sueden Oreburo Senkyo Kai)
1–254 Hiraoka-cho, Sakai-shi, Osaka-fu. Tel.: 0722–7–0367

ORIGINAL GOSPEL TABERNACLE (Kirisuto no Makuya)
88 Karashima-cho, Kumamoto-shi

PACIFIC BROADCASTING ASSOCIATION (Taiheiyo Hoso Kyokai)
1433, 2-chome, Setagaya, Setagaya-ku, Tokyo. Tel.: 420–3166

ASIA

PENTECOST CHURCH OF GOD IN JAPAN (Nihon Pentekosute Kami no Kyokai Kyodan)
1580 Ajimashinyama, Kusunoki-cho, Kita-ku, Nagoya-shi. Tel.: 052–98–8280

PHILADELPHIA CHURCH MISSION (Firaderufla Kyokai)
205 Ozato-cho, Honmoku, Naka-ku, Yokohama-shi. Tel.: 045–62–0888

PLYMOUTH BRETHREN (Kirisuto Shinto no Shukai)
77, 1-chome, Narimune, Suginami-ku. Tokyo

PRESBYTERIAN AND REFORMED CHURCH IN JAPAN (Nihon Kirisuto Kyokai)
c/o Nihon Kirisuto Kyokai Shin Gakko, 2, 3-chome, Tsurumaki-cho, Setagaya-ku, Tokyo. Tel.: 420–7047

REFORMED CHURCH IN JAPAN (Nihon Kirisuto Kaikakuha Kyokai)
20, 5-chome, Shimo-dori, Shibuya-ku, Tokyo. Tel.: 461–4616

RELIGIOUS SOCIETY OF FRIENDS (Kirisuto Yukai Nippon Nenkai)
12, 1-chome, Mita Dai-machi, Shiba, Minato-ku, Tokyo. Tel.: 451–7002

SALVATION ARMY (Kyusei Gun Nippon Honei)
17, 2-chome, Jinbo-cho, Kanda, Chiyoda-ku, Tokyo. Tel.: 261–7311

SAMBI CHURCH (Sanbi Kyodan)
14–8 Kako-machi, Hiroshima-shi. Tel.: 0822–41–8957

SEVENTH-DAY ADVENTIST (Nippon Rengo Dendo Bukai)
11–5, 1-chome, Jingumae, Shibuya-ku, Tokyo. Tel.: 401–1171

SOCIETY OF HISTORICAL STUDY OF CHRISTIANITY (Kirisutokyo Shigaku Kai)
c/o Kanto Gakuin, 4 Miharudai, Minami-ku, Yokohama-shi. Tel. 045–23–0305

SPIRIT OF JESUS CHRIST CHURCH (Iesu no Mitama Kyokai Kyodan)
152, 3-chome, Ogikubo, Duginami-ku, Tokyo. Tel.: 391–5925

STUDENT CHRISTIAN FELLOWSHIP (Gakusei Kirisutokyo Yuai Kai)
30 Shinanomachi, Shinjuku-ku, Tokyo. Tel.: 351–2432

SWEDISH EVANGELICAL MISSION IN JAPAN (Zainichi Sueden Domei Dendo Dan)
273–33 Aza Raiba, Noboribetsu-cho, Horobetsu-gun, Hokkaido. Tel.: 182

THE EVANGELICAL ALLIANCE MISSION (The Nihon Domei Kirisuto Kyodan)
15–15, 3-chome, Daizawa, Setagaya-ku, Tokyo. Tel.: 421–3442

TOKYO CHRISTIAN MISSION (Cunningham Mission)
77 Kogai-cho, Azabu, Minato-ku, Tokyo. Tel.: 401–3386

TOYO SENKYOKAI KIYOME KYOKAI
971, 4-chome, Kashiwagi, Shinjuku-ku, Tokyo. Tel.: 369–6646

TRUE CHURCH OF JESUS IN JAPAN (Shin Iesu Kyokai Nippon Kyodan)
178 Minami, Kagaya-cho, Sumiyoshi-ku, Osaka-shi

UNITARIAN CHURCH (Nihon Jiyu Shukyo Renmei)
Seisoku Koko, 24, Shibakoen, Minato-ku, Tokyo. Tel.: 431–0912

UNITED CHURCH OF CHRIST IN JAPAN (Nippon Kirisuto Kyodan)
2 Ginza, 4-chome, Chuo-ku, Tokyo. Tel.: 561–6131–5

UNITED PENTECOSTAL CHURCH MISSION (Yunaito Pentekosute Kyodan)
163 Yamate-cho, Ashiya-shi, Hyogo-ken. Tel.: 0797–2–6669

UNIVERSAL EVANGELICAL CHURCH (Bankoku Fukuin Kyodan)
162 Hon-cho, Matsumoto-shi, Nagago-ken. Tel.: 0263–2–2347

UNIVERSALIST CHURCH (Kirisutokyo Dojin Shadan)
50 Takada-Oimatsu-cho, Bunbyo-ku, Tokyo

WEST JAPAN EVANGELICAL LUTHERAN CHURCH (Nishi Nihon Fukuin Ruteru Kyokai)
8, 2-chome, Nakajima-dori, Fukiai-ku, Kobe-shi. Tel.: 078–22–9706

WORLDWIDE EVANGELIZATION CRUSADE (Sekai Fukuin Dendo Dan)
1–57 Maruyama-cho, Kitashirakawa, Sakyo-ku, Kyoto-shi. Tel.: 075–78–6524

ASIA

YOUNG MEN'S CHRISTIAN ASSOCIATION (Nippon Kirisutokyo Seinenkai Domei)
2, 1-chome, Nishi Kanda, Chiyoda-ku, Tokyo. Tel.: 291–5201/4

YOUNG WOMEN'S CHRISTIAN ASSOCIATION (Nippon Kirisutokyo Joshi Seinenkai)
15, 4-chome, Kudan, Chiyoda-ku, Tokyo. Tel.: 331–7176

JORDAN

ANGLICAN CHURCH—Jerusalem Archbishopric
St. George's Close, P.O. Box 18, Jerusalem. Tel.: 2253

BIBLE SOCIETIES
Bible House, azZahrah Street (P.O. Box 627), Jerusalem

EVANGELICAL EPISCOPAL COMMUNITY, Diocese of Jordan, Lebanon and Syria
P.O. Box 122, Jerusalem. Tel.: 96 Jerusalem

EVANGELICAL LUTHERAN CHURCH
P.O. Box 4076, Jerusalem Old City, Via Amman

GREEK ORTHODOX PATRIARCHATE OF JERUSALEM
P.O. Box 4074, Jerusalem, Via Amman

YOUNG MEN'S CHRISTIAN ASSOCIATION
P.O. Box 23, Jerusalem. Tel.: 79

YOUNG WOMEN'S CHRISTIAN ASSOCIATION
Herod's Gate, Jerusalem

KOREA

ANGLICAN CHURCH IN KOREA (Taehan Song-Gong-Hoe) (1889)
3 Chong Dong, Seoul. Tel.: 2–3587

KOREA LUTHERAN MISSION
Jedong Building, 2-Ka Tae-Pyung Ro, Choung Ku, Seoul. Tel.: 22–7993

KOREAN BAPTIST CONVENTION
Central P.O. Box 51, Seoul

KOREAN BIBLE SOCIETY (Daiban Sungsuh Kong Hoi)
92 2-Ka, Chongo (I.P.O. Box 1030), Seoul

KOREAN METHODIST CHURCH
34 Chung Dong, Methodist Mission, Seoul

NATIONAL CHRISTIAN COUNCIL
Room 308, Christian Literature Society Building, 91 Chong-No. 2-Ka, Seoul
Rev. Greenfield C. Kiel

PRESBYTERIAN CHURCH
91, 2 Street, Chongo, Seoul

SALVATION ARMY (Koo Sei Kun)
P.O. Box 1192, 1 Chong Dong, Seoul

THE EVANGELICAL ALLIANCE MISSION (TEAM) (Work in Korea)
P.O. Box 2, Yong Dung Po Gu, Seoul. Tel.: 6–1364

UNITED CHINESE CHRISTIAN CHURCH
11 Little West Gate Street, Seoul

YOUNG MEN'S CHRISTIAN ASSOCIATION
112 Sokong Dong, Choong Ku (P.O. Box 1056), Seoul. Tel.: 3–3441

YOUNG WOMEN'S CHRISTIAN ASSOCIATION
1–3 First Street, Myong Dong, Seoul

ANCIENT ORTHODOX SYRIAN CHURCH
Homs

ARMENIAN ORTHODOX CATHOLICOSSATE OF CIS
Antelias

BIBLE LANDS UNION FOR CHRISTIAN EDUCATION
Box 235, Beirut

BIBLE SOCIETY
Bible House, Place de l'Etoile (P.O. Box 747), Beirut

FRIENDS SERVICE COUNCIL
Jurdack Building, off rue Saadat, Beirut

J. L. SCHNELLER SCHULE
Khirbet Kanafar. Tel.: Khirbet Kanafar-Lebanon No. 3

LEBANESE BAPTIST CONVENTION
Box 2026, Beirut. Tel.: 223089

MIDDLE EAST LUTHERAN MINISTRY
P.O. Box 2496, Beirut

NATIONAL EVANGELICAL SYNOD OF SYRIA AND LEBANON (1920)
P.O. Box 235, Beirut. Tel.: 229 603

NEAR EAST COUNCIL OF CHURCHES
P.O. Box 5376, Beirut. Rev. Albert Isteero. Tel.: 25 75 41

NEAR EAST YEARLY MEETING OF FRIENDS
rue du Liban, Beirut

UNION OF ARMENIAN EVANGELICAL CHURCHES
Box 582, Beirut

UNITED CHRISTIAN COUNCIL OF SOUTH WEST ASIA
Box 235, Beirut
Sec.: Paul S. Seto

UNIVERSITY CHRISTIAN CENTER
P.O. Box 235, Beirut. Tel.: 24 30 35

YOUNG MEN'S CHRISTIAN ASSOCIATION
Jabbour Building, Rue Clémenceau (P.O. Box 5520), Beirut. Tel.: 255099

YOUNG WOMEN'S CHRISTIAN ASSOCIATION
Ain el Mreissen, Beirut

MALAYSIA

ANGLICAN CHURCH: DIOCESE OF KUCHING (1848)
Bishop's House, Kuching, Sarawak. Tel.: 2303 Kuching

BASEL CHRISTIAN CHURCH OF MALAYSIA
P.O. Box 868, Jesselton, Sabah

BORNEO-BASEL SELF-ESTABLISHED CHURCH
P.O. Box No. 462, Sandakan, Sabah

EVANGELICAL LUTHERAN CHURCH IN MALAYA
21 Jalan Abdul Samad, Kuala Lumpur. Tel.: 80939

LUTHERAN CHURCH IN MALAYSIA
P.O. Box 747, Kuala Lumpur. Tel.: 69469

OVERSEAS MISSIONARY FELLOWSHIP
3A Jalan Nipah, Jalan Ampang, Kuala Lumpur. Tel.: 72187

SIDANG INJIL BORNEO (Evangelical Church in Borneo)
Lawas, Sarawak. Tel.: Lawas 16

TAMIL EVANGELICAL LUTHERAN CHURCH
21 Rosaria Street, Kuala Lumpur

ASIA

YOUNG MEN'S CHRISTIAN ASSOCIATION
Anderson Road, Ipoh
Brickfields Road, Kuala Lumpur
211 Macalister Road, Penang

YOUNG WOMEN'S CHRISTIAN ASSOCIATION
Room 701, China Insurance Building, 174 Batu Road, Kuala Lumpur

NEPAL

CHURCH OF NEPAL
Pokhra

UNITED MISSION TO NEPAL (1954)
P. Box 126, 1/29, Thapathali, Kathmandu. Tel.: 11206

OKINAWA

CHRISTIAN SCIENCE COMMITTEE ON PUBLICATION
P.O. Box 26, Koza

OKINAWA CHRISTIAN COUNCIL (1958)
3–194 Maysuo, Naha (Box 276, Naha Central P.O.)
Rev. Seijin Higa

YOUNG MEN'S CHRISTIAN ASSOCIATION
P.O. Box 222, Miebashi

PAKISTAN

AFGHAN BORDER CRUSADE (1944)
145 Nicholson Lines Road, Jungle Khiel, Kowat, W. Pakistan

ALL PAKISTAN CHRISTIAN COUNCIL
P.O. Box 357, Lahore, W. Pakistan
Exec. Sec.: Rev. Inayat Masih

CHURCH OF INDIA, PAKISTAN, BURMA AND CEYLON
St. Thomas' Church, Victoria Park, Dacca 1, E. Pakistan
Bishop's House, Trinity Close, Karachi, W. Pakistan
Bishopsbourne, Cathedral Close, Lahore, W. Pakistan

EAST BENGAL BAPTIST UNION
Mission House, Pabna P.O., E. Pakistan

EAST PAKISTAN EVANGELICAL LUTHERAN CHURCH
Auliapur Mission, P.O. Pulhat, Dist. Dinajpur, E. Pakistan

FRIENDS SERVICE COUNCIL
Friends Centre, 21 Nurfata Lane, Dacca, E. Pakistan

MASIHI ISHA'AT KHANA INC. (Christian Publishing House)
36 Ferozepore Road, Lahore 4, E. Pakistan

METHODIST CHURCH IN PAKISTAN
113 Qasim Road, Multan Cantonment, West Pakistan. Tel.: 3847

MYMENSINGH GARO BAPTIST UNION
Birisiri, P.O. Hatshibgunj, Dist. Mymensingh, E. Pakistan

PAKISTAN BIBLE SOCIETY (EAST)
38 Hatkhola Road, P.O. Wari, Dacca 3, E. Pakistan

PAKISTAN BIBLE SOCIETY (WEST) (1871)
Bible House, Anarkali, Lahore 2, W. Pakistan. Tel.: 3421

PAKISTANI LUTHERAN CHURCH
Bishop Manzal, Mardan, W. Pakistan

SALVATION ARMY
35 Queens Road, Lahore, W. Pakistan

SIALKOT CHURCH COUNCIL, UNITED CHURCH IN PAKISTAN (1857)
St. Columba's Church, Hospital Road, Sialkot 2, West Pakistan. Tel.: 2397

ASIA

SOCIETY OF ST. HILDA, LAHORE (1896)
St. Hilda's Deaconess House, Cathedral Close, Lahore, W. Pakistan

SOUTHERN REGIONAL CONFERENCE
c/o Y.M.C.A., Havelock Road, Karachi 3, W. Pakistan

STUDENT CHRISTIAN MOVEMENT OF PAKISTAN
Ewing Hall, Nila Gumbad, Lahore, W. Pakistan

TECHNICAL SERVICES ASSOCIATION
20 Queens Road, Lahore, W. Pakistan

THE EVANGELICAL ALLIANCE MISSION (TEAM) (West Pakistan)
24 Pine View Road, Abbottabad, Hazara, E. Pakistan. Tel.: Abbottabad 481

UNITED CHURCH IN PAKISTAN (Presbyterian)
3 Empress Road, Lahore 5, W. Pakistan

UNITED PRESBYTERIAN SYNOD
Chak 85/M.L., P.O. Bahl, Tehsil Leiah, Dist. Muzaffargarh, W. Pakistan

YOUNG MEN'S CHRISTIAN ASSOCIATION
P.O. Box 7417, Saddar, Karachi 3, W. Pakistan. Tel.: 47262

YOUNG WOMEN'S CHRISTIAN ASSOCIATION
14 Queen's Road, Lahore, W. Pakistan

PHILIPPINES

BUMILA FELLOWSHIP OF BAPTIST CHURCHES, INC. (Philippine Mission of International Missions Inc.)
Talakag, Bukidnen

CHRISTIAN SCIENCE COMMITTEE ON PUBLICATION
P.O. Box 3209, Manila

CHURCHES OF CHRIST OF THE PHILIPPINES
Box 841, Manila

CONVENTION OF PHILIPPINE BAPTIST CHURCHES (1935)
Box 263, Iliolo City

IGLESIA CATOLICA FILIPINE INDEPENDIENTE (1902)
1320 V. Concepcion, Santa Cruz, Manila

IGLESIA EVANGELICA METODISTA EN LAS ISLAS FILIPINAS
640 Penalosa, Tondo, Manila. Tel.: 2-67-76

IGLESIA EVANGELICA UNIDA DE CRISTO
250 Moriones, Tondo, Manila

LUTHERAN CHURCH
P.O. Box 507, Manila

NATIONAL COUNCIL OF CHURCHES IN THE PHILIPPINES
941 Epifanio de los Santos Avenue, Quezon City (P.O. Box 1767, Manila). Tel.: 7-99-57. Dr. Jose A. Yap

PHILIPPINE BIBLE HOUSE
890 United Nations Avenue (P.O. Box 755), Manila

SALVATION ARMY
1414-1416 Pennsylvania Avenue, Ermita, Manila

STUDENT CHRISTIAN MOVEMENT
1648 Taft Avenue (P.O. Box 4130), Manila. Tel.: 5-47-69

UNITED CHURCH OF CHRIST IN THE PHILIPPINES (1948)
939 Epifanio do los Santos Avenue (P.O. Box 718), Quezon City. Tel.: 7-83-43; 7-88-74; 7-94-90

YOUNG MEN'S CHRISTIAN ASSOCIATION (1911)
350 Arroceros Street, Manila. Tel.: 3-21-67

YOUNG WOMEN'S CHRISTIAN ASSOCIATION
921 Lepanto Street, Manila

ANGLICAN CHURCH
Diocesan Office, South Porch, St. Andrew's Cathedral, Singapore 6. Tel.: 28204

ASSEMBLIES OF GOD
83 J, Chancery Lane, Singapore 11. Tel.: 56022

BAPTIST CHURCHES OF MALAYSIA
510 Shaw House, Singapore 9. Tel.: 29953

BETHESDA CHURCH (Katong)
17 Pennegather Road, Katong, Singapore 15

BIBLE SOCIETIES IN MALAYSIA
7 Armenian Street, Singapore 6

CHRISTIAN ASSEMBLY
17 Wilkie Terrace, Singapore 9. Tel.: 35990

CHRISTIAN SCIENCE COMMITTEE ON PUBLICATION
5C Wilmer Court, Singapore 9

EVANGELICAL FREE CHURCH
8 Yarwood Ave., Singapore 21. Tel.: 60584

MALAYAN CHRISTIAN COUNCIL
St. Andrew's Cathedral, Singapore 6. Tel.: 30134
Sec.: Rev. Chung Chi-An

MALAYSIA SYNOD OF THE CHINESE CHRISTIAN CHURCH (1901)
(Presbyterian)
47 Koon Seng Road, Singapore 15. Tel.: 40514

MAR THOMA SYRIAN CHURCH
20 Jalan Semerbak, Singapore 12. Tel.: 83521

METHODIST CHURCH
23B Coleman Street, Singapore 6. Tel.: 27366

OVERSEAS MISSIONARY FELLOWSHIP
2 Cluny Road, Singapore 10. Tel.: 642292

PRESBYTERIAN CHURCH
The Manse, 95 Cavenagh Road, Singapore 9. Tel.: 34132

SALVATION ARMY
207 Clemenceau Avenue, Singapore 9. Tel.: 30122

SEVENTH-DAY ADVENTISTS
251 Upper Serangoon Road, Singapore. Tel.: 89293

STUDENT CHRISTIAN MOVEMENT OF MALAYA
9 Hill Street, Singapore 6

SYRIAN ORTHODOX CHURCH IN MALAYA
c/o 10 Chempaka Avenue, Singapore 13

YOUNG MEN'S CHRISTIAN ASSOCIATION
c/o The Chinese Y.M.C.A., 16 South Pier, Singapore 2

SYRIA

BIBLE SOCIETY
Rue el-Abed, Salhieh, Damascus

GREEK ORTHODOX PATRIARCHATE OF ANTIOCH (with membership in Lebanon)
Patriarch of Antioch, Damascus

MISSION MEDICALE EVANGELIQUE DU LEVANT (1925)
B.P. 317, Aleppo

NATIONAL EVANGELICAL CHURCH OF DAMASCUS
Damascus

SYRIAN ORTHODOX PATRIARCHATE
Patriarch of Antioch and All the East, Damascus

UNITED EVANGELICAL CHURCH
Nebk

ASIA   TAIWAN

BIBLE SOCIETIES
180–1 Nanking East Road, Section 3 (P.O. Box 3401), Taipei

CHINA EVANGELICAL LUTHERAN CHURCH
62 Shan Tzu Ting, Chia Yi

CHINA SUNDAY SCHOOL ASSOCIATION (1910)
105 Chung Shan Road, No., Sec. 2, Taipei. Tel.: 45518

CHINESE CHRISTIAN LUTHERAN CHURCH
Box 5050, Taipei

COUNCIL OF THE CHURCH OF SOUTH-EAST ASIA (Anglican): DIOCESE OF TAIWAN
12 Lane 161 So. Hangchow Road, Sec. 1, Taipei

FELLOWSHIP DEACONRY MISSION, TAIWAN
84 Chung Hsueh Lu, Hwalien

FORMOSA EVANGELICAL FELLOWSHIP
14 Lane 125, Chiu Cheng Hsi Lu, Yi Lan.
Rev. J. K. McGillivray

OVERSEAS MISSIONARY FELLOWSHIP
26–5 Victory Road, Tainan

PRESBYTERIAN CHURCH OF FORMOSA
94/2 Chung Shan North Road, Section 2, Taipei. Tel.: 46956

TAIWAN BAPTIST CONVENTION
P.O. Box 427, Taipei

TAIWAN LUTHERAN CHURCH
Hsin Sheng South Road, Sec. 3, No. 86–1, Taipei

TAIWAN MISSIONARY FELLOWSHIP
No. 2, Iong Hu Li, Shih-lin, Taipei

THE EVANGELICAL ALLIANCE MISSION (TEAM)
Box 5100, Taipei. Tel.: 22879

YOUNG MEN'S CHRISTIAN ASSOCIATION
19 Hsu Chang Street, Taipei. Tel.: 26686

THAILAND

CHURCH OF CHRIST IN THAILAND
138 Sathorn Road, Bangkok
681 Pahon Yotin Road, Phayao, Chiengrai Prov.

NATIONAL CHRISTIAN COUNCIL (1929)
14 Pramuan Road, Bangkok
Rev. Charoon Wichaidist

OVERSEAS MISSIONARY FELLOWSHIP
South Thailand: 42 Kanjana 1 Road, Yala. Tel.: 2238
Laos: c/o Postmaster, Mukdahan, Thailand

STUDENT CHRISTIAN MOVEMENT
328/1 Phy Thai Road, Bangkok

THAILAND BIBLE HOUSE
150 Sathorn Road, Bangkok

YOUNG MEN'S CHRISTIAN ASSOCIATION
27 Sathorn Road, Bangkok. Tel.: 30709

TURKEY

OECUMENICAL PATRIARCHATE OF CONSTANTINOPLE
Fener, Istanbul

310

ASIA

YOUNG MEN'S CHRISTIAN ASSOCIATION
23 Alemdar Caddesi, Istanbul

YOUNG WOMEN'S CHRISTIAN ASSOCIATION
24 Ozoqul Sokak, Cihangir, Istanbul

VIETNAM

BIBLE SOCIETIES IN VIETNAM, CAMBODIA AND LAOS
418 Hai Ba Trung Street (P.O. Box 716), Saigon

YOUNG MEN'S CHRISTIAN ASSOCIATION
5/13 duong Hoa Hung, Saigon

EUROPE

AUSTRIA

BAPTISTENGEMEINDEN IN OESTERREICH (Baptist Churches in Austria)
Margaretenguertal 24/IV/4, Vienna V

CHRISTIAN SCIENCE COMMITTEE ON PUBLICATION
Quellenplatz 6, Vienna X

ECUMENICAL COUNCIL OF CHURCHES IN AUSTRIA
Schellinggasse 12, Vienna I
Dr. Karl Pickel

EVANGELICAL CHURCH A.B. (LUTHERAN)
Dorotheegasse 18, Vienna I

EVANGELICAL CHURCH H.B. (REFORMED)
Dorotheegasse 16, Vienna I

EVANGELISCHE KIRCHE A.u.H.B. IN OESTERREICH (Evangelical Church
of the Augsburgian and Helvetic Confession)
Schellinggasse 12, Vienna I. Tel.: 52–23–11

EVANGELISCHE STUDENTENGEMEINDE IN OESTERREICH (Evangelical
Students' Congregation in Austria)
Mozartgasse 9, Graz

FRIENDS' SERVICE COUNCIL
Quakerhaus, Jauresgasse 13, Vienna III

MENNONITE BRETHREN
a.l. Zaun 90, Linz/Donau

MENNONITE CENTRAL COMMITTEE
Cottagegasse 16, Vienna XVIII

METHODIST CHURCH
Trautsohngasse 8, Vienna VIII

OLD CATHOLIC CHURCH
Schottenring 17, Vienna 1. Tel.: 34–83–94

OESTERREICHISCHES BIBELKOMITEE (Austrian Bible Committee) (1947)
Breitgasse 8, Vienna VII. Tel.: 93–82–40

YOUNG MEN'S CHRISTIAN ASSOCIATION
Kenyongasse 15, Vienna VII. Tel.: 44–63–04

BELGIUM

ARMEE DU SALUT (Salvation Army)
15 rue Duquesnoy, Brussels 1. Tel.: (02)13.39.04

BELGIAN GOSPEL MISSION INC. (Mission Evangelique Belge) (1918)
7 rue du Moniteur, Brussels 1

BUREAU DES EGLISES ET MISSIONS PROTESTANTES EN AFRIQUE
CENTRALE, CONGO–BURUNDI–RUANDA
5 rue du Champ-de Mars, Bruxelles 5. Tel.: 12.64.07
Rev. D. Ericson

CHRISTIAN SCIENCE COMMITTEE ON PUBLICATION
151 Av. de Tervueren, Brussels 4

EGLISE CHRETIENNE MISSIONNAIRE BELGE (1837)
119 av. Coghen, Uccle, Brussels 18

EGLISE EVANGELIQUE PROTESTANTE LUTHERIENNE
46 rue de la Loi, Brussels

EGLISE METHODISTE
5 rue du Champ de Mars, Brussels

FEDERATION BELGE DES ASSOCIATIONS CHRETIENNES D'ETU-
DIANTS
208 Avenue Armand Huysmans, Brussels 5

EUROPE

FEDERATION DES EGLISES PROTESTANTES DE BELGIQUE (Federation of Belgian Protestant Churches)
5 rue du Champ-de-Mars, Brussels 5. Tel.: 11.44.71 and 74.31.54
Rev. P. Regard

GEREFORMEERDE KERKEN IN NEDERLAND EN BELGIE
Begynhoflaan 23, Gent

GLOBAL GOSPEL BROADCASTS, INC.
69 Ave. Devoer, Vilvorde

LIQUE POUR LA LECTURE DE LA BIBLE
255 Kievitlaan, Vilvorde

MISSION EVANGELIQUE BELGE (Belgian Gospel Mission)
7 rue du Moniteur, Brussels 1. Tel.: (02) 17.23.83

MISSION MENNONITE BELGE
1 Place Communale, Ohain

SOCIETE BIBLIQUE BELGE—BELGISCH BIJBELGENOOTSCHAP (1946)
34 rue d'Arlon, Brussels 4, Tel.: (02) 13.28.61

UNION DES EGLISES EVANGELIQUES BAPTISTES DE BELGIQUE
51 rue de l'Academie, Liege

UNION DES EGLISES EVANGELIQUES PROTESTANTES DE BELGIQUE
80 Bld. Louis Schmidt, Brussels 4

YOUNG MEN'S CHRISTIAN ASSOCIATION
31 rue Duquesnoy, Brussels. Tel.: 11.07.77

YOUNG WOMEN'S CHRISTIAN ASSOCIATION
43 rue St. Bernard, Brussels 6

CZECHOSLOVAKIA

BRATRSKA JEDNOTA BAPTISTU V CESKOSLOVENSKU (Baptist Union in Czechoslovakia) (1919)
Vinohradská 68, Prague 3. Tel.: 251286

CESKOBRATRSKA CIRKEV EVANGELICKA (Evangelical Church of Czech Brethren) (Presbyterian) (1781)
Jungmannova 9, Prague 1. Tel.: 247101, 247102

EKUMENICKA RADA CIRKVI V CESKOSLOVENSKU (Ecumenical Council of Churches in Czechoslovakia)
Jungmannova 9, Prague 2. Tel.: 24.88.66
Sec.: Rev. J. N. Ondra

EVANGELICKA CIRKEV METODISTICKA (Methodist Church)
Jecná ul. 19, Prague 2. Tel.: 230623

JEDNOTA BRATRSKA (Moravian Church in Czechoslovakia)
Hálkova 5, Prague 2

JEDNOTA CESKOBRATRSKA (Unity of Czech Brethren)
Soukenická 15, Prague 1

KRESTANSKA REFORMOVANA CIRKEV NA SLOVENSKU (Reformed Christian Church in Slovakia)
Bishop's Office, Rimarská Sobota

SLEZSKA CIRKEV EVANGELICKA AUGSBURSKEHO VYZNANI (Silesian Evangelical Church of the Augsburg Confession)
Na Nivách 7, Cesky Tesin, Okres Karviná. Tel.: 356 Cesky Tesin

SLOVENSKA EVANJELICKA A.V. CIRKEV V CESKOSLOVENSKEJ SOCIALISTICKEJ REPUBLIKE (Slovak Evangelical Church of the Augsburg Confession in the CSR)
Palisády 52, Bratislava

BRØDREMENIGHEDENS DANSKE MISSIONSFORENING (Danish Union for Moravian Missions) (1843)
Christianfeld

CHRISTIAN SCIENCE COMMITTEE ON PUBLICATION
Mosevangen 45, Birkerød

DANSKE BAPTISTSAMFUND (Danish Baptist Union) (1839)
Vallovej 19, Copenhagen

DANSKE BAPTISTSAMFUNDS YDRE MISSION (1916) (Danish Baptist Foreign Mission)
Marsalavej 14, Copenhagen S. Tel.: 01 55 53 25

DANSKE BIBELSELSKAB (Danish Bible Society) (1814)
Købmagergade 67, Copenhagen K. Tel.: Palae 823

DANSKE ETHIOPERMISSION (Danish Ethiopian Mission) (1948)
Betu, Oddervej, Skanderborg

DANSKE ISRAELSMISSION (Danish Jewish Mission) (1885)
Lipkesgade 5, Copenhagen Ø. Tel.: ØB 6282

DANSKE LAERERES MISSIONSFORENING (Danish Teachers' Mission Association) (1912)
Adiget 12, Vanløse. Tel.: 70 44 48

DANSKE MISSIONSFORBUND (Missionary Covenant)
Vilh. Becksvej 86, Aarhus

DANSKE MISSIONSSELSKAB (Danish Missionary Society) (1821)
Strandagervej 24, Hellerup. Tel.: 911

DANSKE FORENET SUDAN MISSION (1911) (Sudan United Mission, Danish Branch)
11 Frodesgade, Arhus C. Tel.: Arhus 40840 and 40277

DANSKE MISSIONSRAD (1912) (Danish Missionary Council)
Nørregade 11, Copenhagen K. Tel.: 145949
The Rev. Henning Talman

DANSK PATHANMISSION (1903) (Danish Pathan Mission)
Gothersgade 115 A, Copenhagen. Tel.: Palae 6661

DANSK SANTALMISSION (Danish Santal Mission) (1867)
Nørregade 11, Copenhagen K

EVANGELISK LUTHERSKE FOLKEKIRKE I DENMARK (Church of Denmark) (1536)
Nørregade 11, Copenhagen K. Tel.: 145949

FRELSENS HAER (Salvation Army)
Frederiksberg Alle 9, Copenhagen V. Tel.: Central 4192

KHERWARA-MISSIONEN
Ved Bellahøj 28B, Brønshøj

KRISTELIGE STUDENTERBEVAEGELSE (Student Christian Movement)
Ny Østergade 23, Copenhagen K. Tel.: BY 8518

KRISTNE LAEGMANDSBEVAEGELSE (Laymen's Movement) (1912)
Sankt Hans Plads 5, Odense. Tel.: 09 122074

KVINDELIGE MISSIONS ARBEJDERE (Women Missionary Workers) (1900)
Mynstersvej 3, Copenhagen V

LAERERINDERNES MISSIONSFORBUND (Teachers' Missionary Association) (1902)
Rolighedsvej 31, Copenhagen V

LUTHERAN CHURCH OF GREENLAND (1721)
Bispegaden, Nørregade, Copenhagen K
Dean of Greenland, Godlhäb, Greenland

LUTHERSK MISSIONSFORENING (Danish Lutheran Missionary Society) (1861)
Nansengade 94, Copenhagen K

EUROPE

METODISTKIRKENS MISSIONSRAAD (Methodist Missionary Council)
Møntergade 22, Copenhagen

NORDISK MISSIONSRAAD (Scandinavian Missionary Council) (1923)
Strandagervej 24, Hellerup
Sec.: Erik W. Nielsen

NORDISKE KRISTNE BUDDHIST MISSION (Scandinavian Mission to Buddhists)
Svinget 12, Copenhagen S

ØKUMENISKE FAELLESRAD I DANMARK (Ecumenical Council of Denmark)
Vendersgade 28, Copenhagen K

ØKUMENISKE UNGDOMSRAD (Ecumenical Youth Council)
Vendersgade 28, Copenhagen K

ØSTERLANDSMISSIONEN (1898) (Danish Mission to the Orient)
Kerteminde. Tel.: Kerteminde 320

PORTO NOVO MISSIONEN (1909)
Aale

SELSKABET TIL STØTTE FOR PAKISTANS LUTHERSKE KIRKE (Society for support of Lutheran Church in Pakistan)
Wibrandtsvej 41, Copenhagen S

VENNERNES SAMFUND (KUÆKERNE) (1875) (Society of Friends) (Quakers)
Danish Quaker Centre, Vendersgade 29 IV, Copenhagen K. Tel.: PA 8248

YOUNG MEN'S CHRISTIAN ASSOCIATION
Amaliegade 24, Copenhagen K. Tel.: Byen 9363

YOUNG WOMEN'S CHRISTIAN ASSOCIATION
Amaliegade 24, Copenhagen K

FINLAND

BAPTIST CHURCH IN FINLAND
Enåsvägen 5A, Drumsö, Helsingfors

CHRISTIAN SCIENCE COMMITTEE ON PUBLICATION
Gyldenintie 1 B 28, Lauttasaari, Helsinki

FINLANDS SVENSKA BAPTISTMISSION (Swedish Baptist Union of Finland) (1856)
Rådhusgatan 44, Vaasa. Tel.: 11559

FRIA MISSIONSFORBUNDET (Free Missionary Society) (1889)
Högbergsgatan 22, Helsinford

HELLUNTAI-YSTÄVÄT (FINNISH PENTECOSTAL MISSION)
Rehbinderintie 4, Helsinki

HERÄTTÄJÄ-YHDISTYS (Pietists Association)
Lapua

ISRAELS VÄNNER (Friends of Israel)
Apollonkatu 5, Helsinki

PELASTUSASMEIJA (FRALSNINGSARMEN) (Salvation Army)
Pursimiehenkatu 6, Helsinki. Tel.: 14844

SAALEM SEURAKUNTA (Salem Assembly) (1928)
Pengerkatu 9, Helsinki

SUOMEN BAPTISTIYHDYSKUNTA (Baptist Union of Finland)
Pallaksentie 4, Vaasa

SUOMEN EVANKELIS-LUTERILAINEN KIRKO (Evangelical-Lutheran Church of Finland)
Agricolankatu 2, Turku. Tel.: Turku 15300

SUOMEN KIRKON SISALAHETYSSEURA (Inner Mission Society of the Church of Finland)
Töölonkatu 55, Helsinki. Tel.: 90–440561

EUROPE

SUOMEN KRISTILLINEN YLIOPPILASLITTO (FINLANDS KRISTLIGA STUDENTFORBUND) (Student Christian Movement of Finland)
Meritullinkatu 13 C. 80, Helsinki. Tel.: 633 763

SUOMEN LÄHETYSNEUVOSTO (Finnish Missionary Council)
Tähtitorninkatu 18, Helsinki. Tel.: 13305

SUOMEN LÄHETYSSEURA (Finnish Missionary Society) (1859)
Tahtitorninkatu 18, Helsinki. Tel.: 13305

SUOMEN LUTERILAINEN EVANKELIUMIYHDISTYS (Lutheran Evangelical Association of Finland) (1873)
Malminkatu 12, Helsinki 10. Tel.: 639 369

SUOMEN NUORTEN MIESTEN KRISTILLISTEN YHDISTYSTEN LITTA (National Council of the Y.M.C.As. of Finland)
Liisank 9 D.35, Helsinki. Tel.: 19983

SUOMEN NUORTEN NAISTEN KRISTILLISTEN YHDISTYSTEN LITTO (National Council of the Y.W.C.As. of Finland)
P. Rautatienkatu 23 A. Helsinki

SUOMEN ORTODOKSINEN KIRKKO (Orthodox Church of Finland)
Kuopio

SUOMEN PIPLIASEURA (Finnish Bible Society) (1812)
Yliopistonkatu 29, Turku

SUOMEN VAPAAKIRKKO (Free Church of Finland) (1889)
Annankatu 1, Helsinki

SUOMEN YLEISKIRKOLLINEN TOIMIKUNTA (Ecumenical Council of Finland) (1919)
Raakelinkatu 4, Helsinki—Pasila
Gen. Sec.: Dr. Seppo A. Teinonen

FRANCE

ACTION CHRETIENNE EN ORIENT (Christian Work in the Orient)
7 rue du Général Offenstein, Strasbourg-Meinau

ALLIANCE BIBLIQUE FRANCAISE (French Bible Alliance) (1946)
58 rue de Clichy, Paris IXe

ALLIANCE DES EQUIPES UNIONISTES DE FRANCE
47 rue de Clichy, Paris IXe

ALLIANCE EVANGELIQUE FRANCAISE (French Evangelical Alliance) (1954)
47 rue de Clichy, Paris IXe

ARMEE DU SALUT (Salvation Army)
76 rue de Rome, Paris VIIIe. Tel.: Europe 387. 41–19

ASSOCIATION AUXILLIARE DES MISSIONS LUTHERIENNES
47 rue Dulong, Paris XVIIe

CENTRE MISSIONNAIRE D'ORIENTATION
156 rue de Longechamp, Paris XVIe
Sec.: Rev. Olle Berglund

CHRISTIAN SCIENCE COMMITTEE ON PUBLICATION
7 Boulevard Flandrin, Paris XVI

C.I.M.A.D.E. (Ecumenical Agency of the Protestant and Orthodox Churches and Youth Movements in France)
176 rue de Grenelle, Paris VIIe. Tel.: 705–93–99

COMITE PROTESTANT DES AMITIES FRANCAISES A L'ETRANGER (Protestant Committee for Friendship Overseas)
47 rue de Clichy, Paris IXe. Tel.: TRI. 25–72

CONSEIL PROTESTANT DE LA JEUNESSE (C.P.J.)
25 rue Blanche, Paris IXe

EUROPE

EGLISE DE LA CONFESSION D'AUGSBOURG D'ALSACE ET DE LOR-
RAINE (Evangelical Church of the Augsburgian Confession in Alsace and
Lorraine) (1802)
1 Quai St. Thomas, Strasbourg, (Bas-Rhin). Tel.: 32-45-86

EGLISE EVANGELIQUE LUTHERIENNE DE FRANCE (Evangelical Lutheran
Church in France)
16 rue Chauchat, Paris IXe

EGLISE EVANGELIQUE LUTHERIENNE—SYNODE DE FRANCE ET DE
BELGIQUE
6a place d'Austerlitz, Strasbourg (Bas-Rhin)

EGLISES LUTHERIENNES LIBRES DE FRANCE ET DE BELGIQUE
(Lutheran Free Churches of France and Belgium)
6 Place d'Austerlitz, Strasbourg

EGLISE REFORMEE D'ALSACE ET DE LORRAINE (Reformed Church of
Alsace and Lorraine)
Commission Synodale: 2 rue du Bouclier, Strasbourg (Bas-Rhin). Tel.: (88)
32.16.17

EGLISE REFORMEE DE FRANCE (Reformed Church of France)
47 rue de Clichy, Paris IXe. Tel.: 874-90-92

FEDERATION DES COMMUNAUTES DE DIACONESSES DE FRANCE
(1841)
95 rue de Reuilly, Paris XIIe. Tel.: 343-54-33

FEDERATION DES EGLISES EVANGELIQUES BAPTISTES DE FRANCE
(1911)
48 rue de Lille, Paris VIIe

FEDERATION FRANCAISE DES ASSOCIATIONS CHRETIENNES
D'ETUDIANTS
11 rue Jean-de-Beauvais, Paris Ve

FEDERATION PROTESTANTE DE FRANCE (Protestant Federation of France)
47 rue de Clichy, Paris IXe
Pres.: Pasteur Marc Boegner

FRIENDS SERVICE COUNCIL
110 Avenue Mozart, Paris XVIe

MISSION BIBLIQUE EN COTE D'IVOIRE (Ivory Coast Bible Mission) (1927)
613 bis, rue Belliard, Paris XVIIIe. Tel.: Mar. 43-12

MISSION POPULAIRE EVANGELIQUE DE FRANCE (1872)
47 rue de Clichy, Paris IXe. Tel.: 874-98-58

MOUVEMENT EVANGELIQUE RUSSE (Russian Evangelical Movement)
1 rue Jacques-Offenbach, Paris XVIe

OEUVRES PROTESTANTES FRANCAISES DE SYRIE ET DU LIBAN
(French Protestant Work in Syria and Lebanon) (1925)
47 rue de Clichy, Paris IXe

RUSSIAN STUDENT CHRISTIAN MOVEMENT OUTSIDE RUSSIA
91 rue Olivier de Serres, Paris XVe

SOCIETE BIBLIQUE FRANCAISE (French Bible Society)
58 rue de Clichy, Paris IXe

SOCIETE CENTRALE D'EVANGELIZATION (Central Evangelical Society)
47 rue de Clichy, Paris IXe

SOCIETE DES MISSIONS EVANGELIQUES DE PARIS (Paris Evangelical
Missionary Society) (1822)
102 Boulevard Arago, Paris XIVe

SOCIETE EVANGELIQUE LUTHERIENNE DE MISSION INTERIEURE ET
EXTERIEURE D'ALSACE ET DE LORRAINE (1849)
67 Neuwiller-lès-Saverne. Tel.: 91.00.19

UNION DES ELISES EVANGELIQUES LIBRES DE FRANCE (Union of Free
Evangelical Churches of France)
Rouillac (Charente)

EUROPE

UNION NATIONALE DES EGLISES REFORMEES EVANGELIQUES IN-
DEPENDANTES DE FRANCE
11 rue Racine, Nimes (Gard 30). Tel.: 68–89 à Nimes (Gard)

YOUNG MEN'S CHRISTIAN ASSOCIATION
13 Avenue Raymond Poincaré, Paris XVIe. Tel.: Passy 92–96

YOUNG WOMEN'S CHRISTIAN ASSOCIATION
47 rue de Clichy, Paris IXe

GERMANY

ALLIANZ-MISSION-BARMEN eV (1889) (German Alliance Mission)
Falkenhaynstr. 11, (Postfach 149), 5600 Wuppertal-Vohwinkel. Tel.: (012121)
780991

ALTKATHOLISCHE KIRCHE IN DEUTSCHLAND (Old Catholic Church
in Germany) (1870)
Gregor-Mendel-Str. 25, 53 Bonn/RH.

ALTREFORMIERTE KIRCHEN IN DEUTSCHLAND (Old Reformed Churches
in Germany) (1834)
4459 Veldhausen, Kr. Bentheim

ARBEITGEMEINSCHAFT CHRISTLICHER KIRCHEN IN DEUTSCHLAND
(Council of Christian Churches in Germany) (1948)
Bockenheimer Landstrasse 109, 6 Frankfurt/Main. Tel.: 770521
Dr. Hanfried Krüger

ARBEITSGEMEINSCHAFT DER EVANG. JUGEND DEUTSCHLANDS
Gerokstr. 21, 7 Stuttgart O

BASLER MISSION DEUTSCHER e.V. (Basel Mission, German Branch) (1815)
Vogelsangstr. 62, 7 Stuttgart 1

BERLINER MISSIONSGESELLSCHAFT (1824)
Georgenkirchstr. 70, 1017 Berlin. Tel.: 53 02 46 (East Berlin)
Prinzregentenstr. 82, 1 Berlin 31. Tel.: 862944, 861982 (West Berlin)

BERLINER MISSIONSHILFE e.V. (Auxiliary Association for the Berlin Missionary Society)
Katzbachstr. 15, Berlin S.W.61

BETHEL MISSION (1886)
4813 Bethel bei Bielefeld (P.O. Box 41). Tel.: Bielefeld 541.3883

BUND DEUTSCHER EVANGELISCHER MISSIONARE (Federation of German
Evangelical Missionaries) (1921)
4961 Lauenhagen üb. Stadthagen Nr. 90

BUND EVANGELISCH-FREIKIRCHLICHER GEMEINDEN IN DEUTSCH-
LAND
Loisenstr. 121. 638 Bad Homburg v.d.H.

BUND FREIER EVANGELISCHER GEMEINDEN IN DEUTSCHLAND
(Federation of Free Evangelical Churches in Germany) (1874)
Goltenkamp 2, 581 Witten/Ruhr

CHRISTIAN SCIENCE COMMITTEE ON PUBLICATION
58 Leerbachstr., Frankfort/Main

CHRISTOFFEL BLINDENMISSION IM ORIENT e.V. (Christoffel Mission to
the Blind in the Orient) (1908)
Bahnhofsweg 15, 3423 Bad Sachsa/Brd (Postfach 59). Tel.: (05323)536

DEUTSCHE ADVENT-MISSIONSGESELLSCHAFT (German Seventh-day
Adventist Missionary Society) (1928)
Niklsstr. 19, Berlin-Zehlendorf

DEUTSCHE EVANGELISCHE MISSIONS-HILFE (German Evangelical Missions Fund) (1913)
Mittelweg 143, Hamburg 13

EUROPE

DEUTSCHE GESELLSCHAFT FÜR MISSIONSWISSENSCHAFT (German Society for the Study of Missions) (1918)
Mörikestr. 22, 74 Tübingen. Tel.: 2182 Tübingen

DEUTSCHE MISSIONSGEMEINSCHAFT e.V. (1951) (German Missionary Fellowship Inc.)
Ganzenstr. 13, 7000 Stuttgart-Möhringen. Tel.: 71 11 78

DEUTSCHE OSTASIEN-MISSION (German East Asia Mission) (1884)
Madgeburger Str. 19, 64 Fulda. Tel.: Fulda 891

DEUTSCHER EVANGELISCHER MISSIONS-TAG (German Missionary Council)
Mittelweg 143, 2 Hamburg 13. Tel.: 41 70 21 23
Hauptpastor D. Hans Heinrich Harms

DEUTSCHER FRAUEN-MISSIONS-GEBETSBUND (German Women's Missionary Prayer Union) (1899)
Goethestrasse 7, 25 Rostock. Tel.: 22679

DEUTSCHER HILFSBUND FÜR CHRISTLICHES LEIBESWERK IM ORIENT (Frankfurter Missionsgesellschaft) (German Aid Society for Christian Charity in the East—Mission Society of Frankfurt) (1896)
Parkstr. 6, Frankfurt/Main

DEUTSCHER VERBAND FÜR EVANGELISATION UND GEMEIN-SCHAFTSPFLEGE e.V (GNADAUER VERBAND) (German Federation for Promoting Evangelical Fellowship and Evangelisation)
Löfflerstrasse 4, 2 Hamburg-Altona. Tel.: 384159

DEUTSCHES INSTITUT FÜR ARZTLICHE MISSION (German Institute for Medical Missions) (1906)
Paul Lechlerstr. 24, 74 Tübingen, Württ

DEUTSCH-MENNONITISCHES MISSIONSKOMITEE (German Mennonites Missionary Committee)
Ibersheim/Rhein
Mennonite Central Committee (1920): Eysseneckstr. 54, Frankfurt/Main

DIAKONISSENANSTALT KAISERSWERTH (1836)
4 Düsseldorf-Kaiserswerth

"DIENSTE IN UBERSEE", ARBEITSGEMEINSCHAFT EVANGELISCHER KIRCHEN IN DEUTSCHLAND e.V (1960) (Committee of Protestant Churches in Germany for Service Overseas)
Gerokstrasse 17, 7 Stuttgart 0. Teol.: 24 70 81

DR LEPSIUS' DEUTSCHE ORIENT-MISSION (Dr. Lepsius' German Oriental Mission) (1895)
Periusstr. 13, Potsdam

EUROPIASCHE BAPTISTISCHE MISSIONSGESELLSCHAFT (European Baptist Missionary Society) (1954)
Luisenstr. 121, 638 Bad Homburg v.d.H. Tel.: 2.43.54

EVANGELISCHE AKADEMIKERSCHAFT IN DEUTSCHLAND (Federation of Christians in Professional Life)
Paulinestr. 40, Stuttgart-W

EVANGELISCHE ALLIANZ (Evangelical Alliance)
Goetheplatz 8, Berleburg, Krs. Wittgenstein/Westfalen

EVANGELISCHE ARBEITSGEMEINSCHAFT FÜR WELTMISSION (1963)
Mittelweg 143, 2000 Hamburg. Tel.: 45 64 24

EVANGELISCHE GEMEINSCHAFT IN DEUTSCHLAND (Körperschaft öffentlichen Rechts) (Evangelical United Brethren Church) (1850)
Hagstrasse 2, 741 Reutlingen

EVANGELISCHE KARMELMISSION e.V (Evangelical Mt. Carmel Mission) (1904)
Schlichtenerstr. 61, 706 Schorndorf/Württemberg

EVANGELISCHE KIRCHE DER KIRCHENPROVINZ SACHSEN
Am Dom 2, Madgeburg

EUROPE

EVANGELISCHE KIRCHE DER UNION (E.K.U.) (Evangelical Union Church)
(1832)
Jebensstr. 3, 1 Berlin 12

EVANGELISCHE KIRCHE IN DEUTSCHLAND (E.K.i.D.) (Evangelical
Church in Germany) (1945)
Kirchenkanzlei: Herrenhäuser Str. 2A, 3 Hannover—Herrenhausen. Tel.: 0511/
710246
Kirchliches Aussenamt: Bockenheimer Landstr. 109, 6 Frankfurt/Main
(Postfach 4025). Tel.: 0611/770521

EVANGELISCHE KIRCHE IM RHEINLAND
Inselstrasse 10, Düsseldorf

EVANGELISCHE KIRCHE IN BERLIN-BRANDENBURG
Postfach 79, Berlin-Charlottenburg 2

EVANGELISCHE KIRCHE IN HESSEN UND NASSAU
Postfach 669, 61 Darmstadt

EVANGELISCHE KIRCHE VON WESTFALEN
Ahstädter Kirchenplatz 5, Bielefeld

EVANGELISCHE LANDESKIRCHE IN WURTTEMBERG
Postfach 92, 7 Stuttgart 1

EVANGELISCHE MISSION IN OBERAGYPTEN (Evangelical Mission to
Upper Egypt) (1900)
Walkmühlstr. 8, 6200 Wiesbaden. Tel.: 40196

EVANGELISCHE VEREIN FUR DAS SYRISCHE WAISENHAUS IN
JERUSALEM (Evangelical Association for the Syrian Orphanage) (1860)
Mauspfad 131, Köln-Dellbrück. Tel.: Köln 68.21.60

EVANGELISCHES BIBELWERK (WEST) (Evangelical Bible Societies)
Wittensteinstr. 114, 56 Wuppertal-Barmen. Tel.: Wuppertal 55 56 55

EVANGELISCHES BIBELWERK (OST)
Irisgrund 3, DDR, 1513 Potsdam—Wilhemsherst

EVANGELISCHES STUDENTENGEMEINDE IN DEUTSCHLAND (German
Student Christian Movement) (1895)
Mercedesstrasse 5–7, 7 Stuttgart-Bad, Cannstatt. Tel.: 56 23 03 Stuttgart

EVANGELISCHE WEIBLICHE JUGEND DEUTSCHLANDS (1893)
Herzbachweg 2, 646 Gelhausen. Tel.: 2603/4

EVANGELISCH-FREIKIRCHLICHE GEMEINDEN (Evangelical Free Church
Union—German Baptist Union)
Louisenstr. 121, 6380 Bad Homburg v.d.H. Tel.: 2 30 51

EVANGELISCH-LUTHERISCHE FREIKIRCHE (Evangelical Lutheran Free
Church) (1946)
Provinzstr. 108, 1 Berlin 51

EVANGELISCH-LUTHERISCHE KIRCHE IN BAYERN
Meiserstrasse 13, 8 Munich 2

EVANGELISCH-LUTHERISCHE LANDESKIRCHE HANNOVERS
Calenbergerstrasse 34, Hannover

EVANGELISCH-LUTHERISCHE LANDESKIRCHE SACHSENS
Lukasstrasse 6, 8032 Dresden A 27

EVANGELISCH-LUTHERISCHE LANDESKIRCHE SCHLESWIG-HOL-
STEINS
Dänische Strasse 27–35, Kiel; and Plessenstrasse 5b, Schleswig

EVANGELISCH-LUTHERISCHE MISSIONSANSTALT
8806 Neuendettelsau/Mfr

EVANGELISCH-LUTHERISCHE MISSION ZU LEIPZIG (Leipzig Mission)
(1836)
Burgbergstr. 40, 852 Erlangen

EUROPE

EVANGELISCH-LUTHERISCHER ZENTRAL-VEREIN FÜR MISSION UNTER ISRAEL (Evangelical Lutheran Central Union for the Mission to Israel) (1871)
Melcherstr. 23, 44 Münster/Westfalen

FRAUENARBEIT DER EVANG KIRCHE IN DEUTSCHLAND
Westendstrasse 89, 6 Frankfurt/M

FRAUENMISSION MALCHE e.V. (Women's Mission Malche) (1898)
Bad Freienwalde/Oder

GERMAN BAPTIST UNION
Luisenstr. 121, Bad Homburg v.d.H.

GESSELLSCHAFT FÜR INNERE UND AUSSERE MISSION IM SINNE DER LUTHERISCHEN KIRCHE e.V. (1841) (Lutheran Church Mission Society)
Evang.-Luth. Missionsanstalt, 8806 Neuendettelsau, Bavaria. Tel.: 225

GESSELLSCHAFT FÜR BEFORDERUNG DES CHRISTENTUMS UNDER DEN JUDEN (Society for Promoting Christianity Among the Jews) (1822)
Kastanienallee 22, Berlin N.58

GOSSNERS MISSION (1836)
Handjerystr. 19/20, Berlin Friedenau

GUSTAV-ADOLF-WERK DER EVANGELISCHE KIRCHE IN DEUTSCH-LAND
Kirchweg 68/11, 35 Kassel

HEILSARMEE (Salvation Army)
Salierring 23, 5 Köln. Tel.: 23 47 47

HERMANNSBURGER EVANGELISCH-LUTHERISCHE MISSION (Hermann-burg Evangelical Lutheran Mission) (1849)
3102 Hermannsburg, Kreis Celle. Tel.: Hermannsburg 305

HERRNHUTER MISSIONS-DIREKTION (Moravians) (1722)
BRD: 7325 Bad Boll, über Göppingen, Württ. Tel.: (0 71 64)341
DDR: 10a Herrnhut/O.L.

HILDESHEIMER BLINDEN-MISSION (1890)
32) Hildesheim, Neustädter Markt 37. Tel.: Hildesh. 4594

INNERE MISSION UND HILFSWERK DER EVANGELISCHEN KIRCHE IN DEUTSCHLAND—HAUPTGESCHAFTSSTELLE
Alexanderstrasse 23, 7000 Stuttgart 1. Tel.: 24 69 51

JERUSALEMVEREIN (Jerusalem Union) (1852)
Reichensteinerweg 24, 1 Berlin 33

JUGENDKAMMER DER EVANGELISCHEN KIRCHE IN DEUTSCH-LAND (National Christian Youth Council)
Kornbergstr. 28A, Stuttgart-W

LEITERKREIS DER EVANG. AKADEMIEN IN DEUTSCHLAND
Evang. Akademie, 7325 Bad Boll/ü, Göppingen

LIEBENZELLER MISSION (1899)
7267 Bad Liebenzell/Wurttemberg (Postfach 21). Tel.: 387

MANNERARBEIT DER EVANG. KIRCHE IN DEUTSCHLAND
Kantstrasse 9/11, 605 Offenbach/Main

MARBURGER MISSION GmbH (1929)
Stresemannstr. 22, 3550 Marburg/Lahn (Postfach 600). Tel.: 2723

MENNONITEN BRUDERGEMEINDE
Herweghstrasse 20, 6103 Griesheim/Darmstadt

METHODISTENKIRCHE IN DEUTSCHLAND (Methodist Church in Germany)
Grillparzer Strasse 34, 6 Frankfurt/M

MISSION DER FRAUEN-UND-MADCHEN-BIBEL-KREISE e.V. (M.B.K. Mission) (Mission of the Women's and Girls' Bible Union) (1925)
Hermann-Löns-Str. 14, 4902 Bad Salzuflen/Lippe. Tel.: 4545

EUROPE

MISSION EVANGELISCH-LUTHERISCHER FREIKIRCHEN (BLECK-MARER MISSION) (Hanover Evangelical Lutheran Free Church Mission) (1892)
3041 Bleckmar über Soltau (Hanover)

MISSIONSBUND ZUR AUSBREITUNG DES EVANGELIUMS (Mission Fellowship for the Propagation of the Gospel)
Staudstr. 19, Korntal bei Stuttgart

MISSIONSGESELLSCHAFT DER METHODISTENKIRCHE IN DEUTSCH-LAND (Missionary Society for the Methodist Church in Germany) (1930)
Grillparzer Strasse 34, Frankfurt/M

MISSIONHAUS BIBELSCHULE WIEDENEST (Mission House and Bible School of Wiedenest) (1911)
Kölnerstr. 8, 5281 Wiedenest, Bez, Köln. Tel.: 00261/53133

MORGENLANDISCHE FRAUENMISSION (Women's Association for Christian Education of Girls in Eastern Countries) (1842)
Finckensteinallee 27, 1 Berlin, 45 Lichterfelde (West). Tel.: Berlin 73 57 27

NORDDEUTSCHE MISSIONSGESELLSCHAFT (North German Mission Society) (1836)
Vahrer Strasse 243, 28 Bremen

REFORMIERTER BUND (Reformed Alliance) (1884)
Bleichstrasse 40, 6 Frankfurt/M

RELIGIOSE GESELLSCHAFT DER FREUNDE (Society of Friends)
Planckstr. 20, 108 Berlin W. Tel.: 20 15 25

RHEINISCHE MISSIONSGESELLSCHAFT (Rhenish Missionary Society) (1828)
Rudolfstr. 137/139, 56 Wuppertal-Barmen

SCHLESWIG-HOLSTEINISCHE EVANGELISCH-LUTHERISCHE MISSIONS-GESELLSCHAFT ZU BREKLUM (Schleswig-Holstein Evangelical Lutheran Missionary Society at Breklum) (1876)
Kirchenstr. 36, 2257 Breklum über Bredstedt. Tel.: Bredstedt 04671/315

SELBSTANDIGE EVANGELISCH-LUTHERISCHE KIRCHE (Independent Evangelical Lutheran Church) (1947)
3111 Wriedel üb Velzen

STUDENTENBUND FÜR MISSION (Student Volunteer Movement) (1896)
Paulinenstr. 40, Stuttgart-W

VERBAND DER EVANGELISCHEN BIBELGESELLSCHAFTEN IN DEUTSCHLAND (Union of Evangelical Bible Societies in Germany) (1948)
Wittensteinstrasse 114. 56 Wuppertal-Barmen

VERBAND DEUTSCHER EVANGELISCHER MISSIONSKONFERENZEN (Union of Evangelical Mission Conferences) (1906)
Schloss 1, Marburg/Lahn. Tel.: 73 24 80

VEREINIGTE EVANGELISCH-LUTHERISCHE KIRCHE DEUTSCHLANDS (VELKD) United Evangelical Lutheran Church of Germany) (1948)
Lutherisches Kirchenamt: Böttcherstr. 8, Hanover-Herrenhausen. Tel.: 71 02 46

VEREINIGTE MISSIONSFREUNDE e.V. WEIDENAU (1930)
Wiesenstrasse 19, 5902 Weidenau/Sieg

VEREINIGUNG DER DEUTSCHEN MENNONITEN-GEMEINDEN (1886)
Sekretariat, 6719 Weierhof b. Marnheim/Pfalz. Tel.: Kirchheimbolanden 704

WAISEN UND MISSIONSANSTALT e.V. (Neukirchen Mission) (1878)
Gartenstr. 24, 4133 Neukirchen-Vevyn. Tel.: 4374

WELTWEITER EVANGELISATIONS-KREUZZUG e.V. (1913) (Worldwide Evangelization Crusade)
Missionshaus, 6239 Vockenhausen üb Eppstein/Ts. Tel.: Eppstein 331

YOUNG MEN'S CHRISTIAN ASSOCIATION (CHRISTLICHER VEREIN JUNGER MANNER (C.V.J.M.)
Im Druseltal 8, 35 Kassel-Wilhemshöhe. Tel.: 35001

YOUNG WOMEN'S CHRISTIAN ASSOCIATION (RECHSVERBAND WEIBLICHER EVANGELISCHER JUGEND)
Burckhardthaus, Herzbachweg 2, Gelnhausen

ACTORS' CHURCH UNION
4 Foster Lane, London, E.C.2. Tel.: MONarch 2014

ADVISORY COUNCIL ON MISSIONARY STRATEGY AND THE CON-
SULTATIVE BODY OF THE LAMBETH CONFERENCE
21 Chester Street, London, S.W.1. Tel.: BELgravia 7461

AFGHAN BORDER CRUSADE
95 Malmesbury Road, Chippenham, Wilts.

AFRICA EVANGELICAL FELLOWSHIP (S.A.G.M.) (1889)
30 Lingfield Road, Wimbledon, London, S.W.19. Tel.: WIMbledon 1176

AFRICA INLAND MISSION (1895)
3 John Street, Bedford Row, London, W.C.1. Tel.: HOLborn 8117

ALGIERS MISSION BAND (1888)
92 Gordon Road, Ealing, London, W.13

ANTI-SLAVERY AND ABORIGINES PROTECTION SOCIETY
51 Denison House, 296 Vauxhall Bridge Road, London, S.W.1

APOSTOLIC CHURCH
Penyfroes, Llanelly, Carmarthenshire, Wales. Tel.: Crosshands 349
Missionary Movement (1922): Great Horton Road, Bradford, Yorkshire

ARABIC LITERATURE MISSION (NILE MISSION PRESS)
22 Culverden Park Road, Tunbridge Wells, Kent

ASIA CHRISTIAN COLLEGES ASSOCIATION (1952)
Annandale, North End Road, London, N.W.11. Tel.: SPEedwell 0510

ASSEMBLIES OF GOD IN GREAT BRITAIN AND IRELAND
51 Newington Causeway, London, S.E.1. Tel.: HOP 1879

ASSOCIATION FOR THE FREE DISTRIBUTION OF THE SCRIPTURES
10 Grange Road, Bushey, Hertfordshire. Tel.: WATford 28055

AUSTRIAN BIBLE MISSION (1948) (Oesterreichische Bibel Mission)
111 Churchfield, Harlow, Essex. Tel.: Harlow 24821

BAPTIST COMMONWEALTH SOCIETY (1910)
Baptist Church House, 4 Southampton Row, London, W.C.1. Tel.: HOLborn 2045

BAPTIST MISSIONARY SOCIETY (1792)
93–97 Gloucester Place, London, W.1. Tel.: WELbeck 1482

BAPTIST UNION OF GREAT BRITAIN AND IRELAND (1812)
Baptist Church House, 4 Southampton Row, London, W.C.1. Tel.: HOLborn 2045

BAPTIST UNION OF SCOTLAND (1869)
113 West Regent Street, Glasgow, C.2, Scotland. Tel.: City 5438

BAPTIST UNION OF WALES (Undeb Bedyddwyr Cymru) (1866)
Ilston House, 94 Mansel Street, Swansea, Wales

BARBICAN MISSION TO THE JEWS
Seven Trees, Lubbock Road, Chislehurst, Kent. Tel.: IMPerial 3080

BEREAN BAND (1905)
Dawson Lodge, 30 Woodville Gardens, Ealing, London, W.5. Tel.: PERivale 5140

BIBLE AND MEDICAL MISSIONARY FELLOWSHIP
39 Ladbroke Grove, Holland Park, London, W.11. Tel.: PARk 4131

BIBLE CHURCHMEN'S MISSIONARY SOCIETY (1922)
153–187 Waterloo Road, London, S.E.1. Tel.: WATerloo 4668

BIBLE LANDS SOCIETY (1854)
The Old Kiln, Hazelmere, High Wycombe, Bucks. Tel.: Penn 2144

BIBLE-PATTERN CHURCH FELLOWSHIP
114 Arden Road, Acocks Green, Birmingham 27

BIBLE READING FELLOWSHIP
12 Buckingham Palace Gardens, London, S.W.1. Tel.: SLOane 9181

BOLIVIAN INDIAN MISSION (1907)
262 West Green Road, Tottenham, London, N.15

BORNEO EVANGELICAL MISSION
59 Somerset House, Blagrave Street, Reading, Berkshire

BOYS' BRIGADE (1883)
Abbey House, 2 Victoria Street, Westminster, London, S.W.1. Tel.: ABBey 5285

BOY SCOUTS ASSOCIATION
25 Buckingham Palace Road, London, S.W.1. Tel.: VICtoria 6005

BRITISH AND FOREIGN BIBLE SOCIETY (1804)
Bible House, 146 Queen Victoria Street, London, E.C.4. Tel.: CITy 4751–6

BRITISH COUNCIL OF CHURCHES (1942)
10 Eaton Gate, London, S.W.1. Tel.: SLOane 9611
Gen. Sec.: Rt. Rev. Dr. C. Kenneth Sansbury
Assoc. Gen. Sec.: Rev. John Weller
CHRISTIAN AID DEPARTMENT: Dir.: Miss Janet Lacey
EDUCATION DEPARTMENT:
FAITH AND ORDER DEPARTMENT: Sec.: Rev. John Weller
INTERNATIONAL DEPARTMENT: Secs.: Mr. Noël Salter and Rev. Paul
Oestreicher
SOCIAL RESPONSIBILITY DEPARTMENT: Sec.: Rev. J. Kenneth Lawton
YOUTH DEPARTMENT: Sec.: Rev. Thorley Roe

BRITISH PENTECOSTAL FELLOWSHIP (1948)
50 Medway Crescent, Leigh-on-Sea, Essex

BRITISH YOUTH FOR CHRIST (1946)
St. Mark's Church, Kennington Park Road, London, S.E.11. Tel.: RELiance 9301

CALVARY HOLINESS CHURCH
3 Cross Street, Bargoed, Glamorgan, Wales
Missionary Society: 455 Blackburn Road, Accrington, Lancashire

CAMBRIDGE MISSION TO DELHI (1877)
114 Great Peter Street, London, S.W.1. Tel.: ABBey 6681

CENTRAL ASIAN MISSION (1895)
39 Victoria Street, London, S.W.1. Tel.: ABBey 1607

CENTRAL JAPAN PIONEER MISSION
9 Kent Road, St. Andrews, Bristol 7

CEYLON AND INDIA GENERAL MISSION: PAKISTAN CHRISTIAN
FELLOWSHIP (1893)
73 Mildmay Park, London, N.1. Tel.: CANonbury 2325

CHRISTIAN ACTION
2 Amen Court, London, E.C.4. Tel.: CITy 6869

CHRISTIAN AID
See British Council of Churches

CHRISTIAN ALLIANCE OF WOMEN AND GIRLS (1920)
16 Dartmouth Street, London, S.W.1. Tel.: WHItehall 4721

CHRISTIAN CINEMA AND RELIGIOUS FILM SOCIETY
6 Eaton Gate, London, S.W.1

CHRISTIAN COLPORTAGE ASSOCIATION
25 Beulah Hill, London, S.E.19. Tel.: SLOane 2143

CHRISTIAN ENDEAVOUR UNION OF GREAT BRITAIN AND IRELAND
(1896)
31 Lampton Road, Hounslow, Middlesex. Tel.: HOUnslow 9215

CHRISTIAN FRONTIER COUNCIL
34 Brook Street, London, W.1. Tel.: HYDe Park 7176

CHRISTIAN LITERATURE CRUSADE (1941)
201 Church Road, Upper Norwood, London, S.E.19. Tel.: LIVingstone 3132

CHRISTIAN MISSIONS IN MANY LANDS
1 Widcombe Crescent, Bath, Somerset

CHRISTIAN SCIENCE COMMITTEE ON PUBLICATION
30 Norfolk Street, Strand, London, W.C.2. Tel.: TEMple Bar 2808

EUROPE

CHRISTIAN TEAMWORK INSTITUTE OF EDUCATION (1957)
1 Whitehall Place, London, S.W.1. Tel.: WHItehall 6364

CHURCH ARMY (1882)
185 Marylebone Road, London, N.W.1. Tel.: AMBassador 3211

CHURCHES' COUNCIL OF HEALING
16 Lincolns Inn Fields, London, W.C.2. Tel.: HOLborn 0354

CHURCHES OF CHRIST IN GREAT BRITAIN AND IRELAND
26 Shipley Road, Leicester
Missionary Committee: 61 Oxford Road, Moseley, Birmingham 13

CHURCHES' TELEVISION CENTRE (1959)
Hillside, Merry Hill Road, Bushey, Herts. Tel.: BUShey Heath 4426

CHURCH IN WALES, REPRESENTATIVE BODY OF THE
39 Cathedral Road, Cardiff, Glamorganshire, Wales. Tel.: Cardiff 31638

CHURCH MISSIONARY SOCIETY (1799)
153–187 Waterloo Road, London, S.E.1. Tel.: WATerloo 8681

CHURCH OF ENGLAND (c. 597)
Church Assembly, Church House, Dean's Yard, London, S.W.1. Tel.: ABBey 9011

CHURCH OF JESUS CHRIST OF LATTER-DAY SAINTS
50 Princes Gate, London, S.W.7. Tel.: KNIghtsbridge 8867

CHURCH OF SCOTLAND
121 George Street, Edinburgh 2, Scotland. Tel.: Caledonian 5172

CHURCH OF THE NAZARENE
48 Loxley Road, London, S.W.18 Tel.: VANdyke 8284

CHURCH PASTORAL-AID SOCIETY (1836)
Falcon Court, 32 Fleet Street, London, E.C.4. Tel.: FLEet 4341

CHURCH PUBLICITY AND SERVICE CENTRE (1902)
27 Tavistock Square, London, W.C.1. Tel.: EUSton 8413

CHURCH'S MINISTRY AMONG THE JEWS
16 Lincoln's Inn Fields, London, W.C.2. Tel.: CHAncery 2149

COMMONWEALTH AND CONTINENTAL CHURCH SOCIETY (1823)
7 York Buildings, London, W.C.2. Tel.: WHItehall 1563

COMMONWEALTH MISSIONARY SOCIETY (1836)
202 Memorial Hall, Farringdon Street, London, E.C.4. Tel.: CENtral 6368

COMMUNITY OF ST. MARY THE VIRGIN
St. Mary's Convent, Wantage, Berkshire

COMMUNITY OF THE RESURRECTION
House of the Resurrection, Mirfield, Yorkshire. Tel.: Mirfield 3318

CONFERENCE OF MISSIONARY SOCIETIES IN GREAT BRITAIN AND IRELAND (1912)
Edinburgh House, 2 Eaton Gate, London, S.W.1. Tel.: SLOane 9611
Sec.: Rev. R. K. Orchard

CONGO EVANGELISTIC MISSION (1915)
355 Blackpool Road, Preston, Lancashire. Tel.: 77830

CONGREGATIONAL CHURCH IN ENGLAND AND WALES (1831)
Memorial Hall, Farringdon Street, London, E.C.4. Tel.: CITy 8801

CONGREGATIONAL UNION OF SCOTLAND
217 West George Street, Glasgow, C.2, Scotland. Tel.: Central 0169

COUNTESS OF HUNTINGDON'S CONNEXION (SIERRA LEONE MISSION) (1792)
136a Pack Lane, Kempshott, Basingstoke, Hants.

CRUSADERS' UNION
1 Ludgate Hill, London, E.C.4. Tel.: CITy 5983
Girls' Association: 1 Ludgate Hill, London, E.C.4. Tel.: CITy 7049

DIPTI MISSION
c/o 58 Palewell Park, East Sheen, London, S.W.19

EUROPE

DOHNAVUR FELLOWSHIP
33 Church Road, Wimbledon, London, S.W.19. Tel.: WIMbledon 4787

EAST AND WEST FRIENDSHIP COUNCIL (1921)
101 Gower Street, London, W.C.1. Tel.: EUSton 8525

ECHOES OF SERVICE OFFICE
1 Widcombe Crescent, Bath, Somerset

EDINBURGH MEDICAL MISSIONARY SOCIETY (1841)
12 Mayfield Terrace, Edinburgh 9, Scotland. Te.: New. 2518

EGLWYS BRESBYTERAIDD CYMRU (Presbyterian Church of Wales)
Gwynfryn, Y Felinheli, Sir Gaernarfon (Port Dinorwic, Caernarvonshire)

ELIM CHURCH
297–299 High Street, Cheltenham, Glos. Tel.: Cheltenham 53440 (STD OCH2)

ELIM MISSIONARY SOCIETY (1943)
297–299 High Street, Cheltenham, Glos. Tel.: Cheltenham 53440/53449 (STD OCH2)

ELIM PENTECOSTAL CHURCHES
79 Mildmay Road, Chelmsford, Essex

EMMANUEL HOLINESS CHURCH
1 Palm Grove, Birkenhead, Cheshire

EMMAUS BIBLE SCHOOL (1951)
102 Eastham Rake, Eastham, Wirral, Cheshire. Tel.: EAStham 1172

EPISCOPAL CHURCH IN SCOTLAND
13 Drumsheugh Gardens, Edinburgh 3, Scotland. Tel.: Caledonian 6357

EUROPEAN BAPTIST FEDERATION
4 Southampton Row, London, W.C.1. Tel.: HOLborn 3939

EUROPEAN CHRISTIAN MISSION (1904)
Heightside, Newchurch, Rossendale, Lancashire. Tel.: Rossendale 4583

EUROPEAN EVANGELISTIC SOCIETY (1953)
8 Sydney Grove, Slough, Bucks. Tel.: Slough 28986

EUROPEAN MISSIONARY FELLOWSHIP
128 Hempstead Road, Watford, Herts.

EVANGELICAL ALLIANCE
30 Bedford Place, London, W.C. 1. LANgham 9361

EVANGELICAL LIBRARY (1928)
78A Chiltern Street, London, W.1. Tel.: WELbeck 6997

EVANGELICAL LUTHERAN CHURCH OF ENGLAND
117 Golden Lane, London, E.C.1

EVANGELICAL MISSIONARY ALLIANCE
30 Bedford Place, London, W.C.1. Tel.: LANgham 9361

EVANGELICAL TAPE FELLOWSHIP and EVANGELICAL FELLOWSHIP (1961)
"Kedron", 165 Brackley Square, Woodford Green, Essex. Tel.: BUChurst 0083

EVANGELICAL UNION OF SOUTH AMERICA (1911)
6 Novar Road, London, S.E.9. Tel.: ELTham 8615

FACT AND FAITH FILMS (1948)
Falcon Court, 32 Fleet Street, London, E.C.4. Tel.: FLEet Street 6147

FELLOWSHIP OF FAITH FOR THE MUSLIMS (1915)
53 Charles Road, Small Heath, Birmingham 10. Tel.: Vic 0010

FELLOWSHIP OF INDEPENDENT EVANGELICAL CHURCHES
136 Rosendale Road, West Dulwich, London, S.E.1

FELLOWSHIP OF RECONCILIATION
29 Great James Street, London, W.C.1. Tel.: CHAncery 7130

FREE CHURCH FEDERAL COUNCIL (of England and Wales) (1896)
27 Tavistock Square, London, W.C.1. Tel.: EUSton 8413

EUROPE

FREE CHURCH OF ENGLAND
3 Bristol Avenue, Liscard, Wallasey, Cheshire

FREE CHURCH OF SCOTLAND
15 North Bank Street, Edinburgh 1, Scotland. Tel.: Caledonian 4978

FREE PRESBYTERIAN CHURCH OF SCOTLAND (1893)
Free Presbyterian Manse, Wick, Caithness, Scotland
Foreign Missions Committee (1905): Glendale, Isle of Skye, Scotland

FRIENDS OF VELLORE (1940)
Vellore House, Claverley Villas, London, N.3. Tel.: FINchley 2241

FRIENDS, RELIGIOUS SOCIETY OF (QUAKERS)
Friends House, Euston Road, London, N.W.1. Tel.: EUSton 3601
International Centre: 32 Tavistock Square, London, W.C.1

GIRL GUIDES ASSOCIATION
17 Buckingham Palace Road, London, S.W.1. Tel.: VICtoria 6242

GIRLS' LIFE BRIGADE (1902)
8 Upper Belgrave Street, London, S.W.1. Tel.: BELgravia 5303

GOOD NEWS TRAILER MISSIONARY FELLOWSHIP (1959)
Jersey Gardens, Wickford, Essex. Tel.: Wickford 3729

GOSPEL MISSION OF SOUTH AMERICA
The Manse, 15 Ranfurley Road, Sutton, Surrey

GREATER WORLD CHRIST MISSION AND CHRISTIAN SPIRITUALIST LEAGUE
3 Lansdowne Road, Holland Park, London, W.11. Tel.: PARk 7264

GREEK ORTHODOX METROPOLIS OF THYATEIRA AND GREAT BRITAIN
5 Craven Hill, London, W.2. Tel.: PADdington 4787

HEBREW CHRISTIAN TESTIMONY TO ISRAEL (1893)
189 Whitechapel Road, London, E.1. Tel.: BIShopsgate 5270

HEBREW EVANGELIZATION SOCIETY (1929)
92–94 Amhurst Park, London, N.16. Tel.: STAmford Hill 7315

INDEPENDENT METHODIST CONNEXION (1805)
21 Ashley Drive, Swinton, nr. Manchester, Lancs. Tel.: Swinton 2441

INDIAN CHURCH AID ASSOCIATION (1880)
2 Eaton Gate, London, S.W.1. Tel.: SLOane 9611

INDUSTRIAL CHRISTIAN FELLOWSHIP (1919)
St. Katharine Cree, Leadenhall Street, London, E.C.3. Tel.: AVEnue 5733/34

INSTITUTE OF RURAL LIFE AT HOME AND OVERSEAS (1949)
3 Hendon Avenue, London, N.3. Tel.: FINchley 662

INTERNATIONAL BIBLE READING ASSOCIATION (1882)
Robert Denholme House Nutfield, Redhill, Surrey. Tel.: Nutfield Ridge 2411

INTERNATIONAL HEBREW CHRISTIAN ALLIANCE (1925)
Memorial House, 19 Draycott Place, Chelsea, London, S.W.3. Tel.: KENsington 3121

INTERNATIONAL MINERS' MISSION
"May Trees", Davenham Avenue, Northwood, Middlesex. Tel.: Northwood 21737

INTERNATIONAL SOCIETY FOR THE EVANGELIZATION OF THE JEWS (1842)
7 Great James Street, Holborn, London, W.C.1. Tel.: HOLborn 2954

INTER-VARSITY FELLOWSHIP OF EVANGELICAL UNIONS
39 Bedford Square, London, W.C.1. Tel.: MUSeum 5935

JAPAN EVANGELISTIC BAND (1903)
26 Woodside Park Road, London, N.12. Tel.: HILlside 4622

JERUSALEM AND THE EAST MISSION (1887)
12 Warwick Square, London, S.W.1. Tel.: VICtoria 3232

EUROPE

JOHN G. PATON MISSION FUND (1890)
c/o Kidston's & Co., 86 St. Vincent Street, Glasgow, C.2, Scotland

LAST REAPERS UNLIMITED (1964)
29 Palfrey Road, Bournemouth, Hants. Tel.: Northbourne 4412

LEBANON EVANGELICAL MISSION (1860)
16 Swain's Lane, Highgate, London, N.6. Tel.: GULliver 3034

LEPROSY MISSION (1874) (Formerly Mission to Lepers)
7 Bloomsbury Square, London, W.C.1. Tel.: CHAncery 2601

LONDON CITY MISSION (1835)
6 Eccleston Street, London, S.W.1. Tel.: SLOane 0141/2

LONDON MISSIONARY SOCIETY (1795)
Livingstone House, 11 Carteret Street, Westminster, London, S.W.1. Tel.: WHItehall 0061

LORD'S DAY OBSERVANCE SOCIETY (1831)
Lord's Day House, 55 Fleet Street, London, E.C.4. Tel.: FLEet Street 3157/8

LORD WHARTON'S CHARITY (1696)
12 Hasluck Gardens, New Barnet, Herts. Tel.: BARnet 4957

LUDHIANA BRITISH FELLOWSHIP (1951)
32 Fleet Street, London, E.C.4. Tel.: FLEet Street 5516

LUTHERAN COUNCIL OF GREAT BRITAIN LTD. (1948)
8 Collingham Gardens, London, S.W.5. Tel.: FRE 9604

MEDICAL MISSIONARY ASSOCIATION (1878)
6 and 7 Canonbury Place, London, N.1. Tel.: DICkens 1313

MENNONITE BOARD OF MISSIONS AND CHARITIES
London Mennonite Centre: 14 Shepherd's Hill, Highgate, London, M.6. Tel.: MOUntview 8775

METHODIST CHURCH (1738)
Conference Office: 1 Central Buildings, Westminster, London, S.W.1. Tel.: WHItehall 7608
Methodist Missionary Society (1786): 25 Marylebone Road, London, N.W.1. Tel.: WELbeck 2541

MIDDLE EAST GENERAL MISSION (Formerly Egypt General Mission)
137 Upper Grosvenor Road, Tunbridge Wells, Kent

MILDMAY MISSION TO THE JEWS (1876)
214 Mile End Road, London, E.1. Tel.: STEpney 2079

MISSIONARY AVIATION FELLOWSHIP (1945)
37 Eastwood Road, London, E.18. Tel.: WANstead 0838

MISSIONS TO SEAMEN (1856)
Radnor House, Norbury, London, S.W.16

MISSION TO MEDITERRANEAN GARRISONS (INCORPORATED) (1883)
402 Sauchiehall Street, Glasgow, C.2, Scotland. Tel.: Douglas 2438-9

MORAL RE-ARMAMENT
4 Hay's Mews, London, W.1. Tel.: GROsvenor 3443

MORAVIAN CHURCH IN GREAT BRITAIN AND IRELAND (1457)
5-7 Muswell Hill, London, N.10. Tel.: TUDor 3409

MOVEMENT FOR WORLD EVANGELIZATION (1930)
10 Cuthbert Road, West Croydon, Surrey

NATIONAL BIBLE SOCIETY OF SCOTLAND (1861)
5 St. Andrew Square, Edinburgh 2, Scotland. Tel.: WAVerley 5745

NATIONAL FREE CHURCH WOMEN'S COUNCIL (of England and Wales) (1908)
27 Tavistock Square, London, W.C.1. Tel.: EUSton 8413

NEPAL EVANGELISTIC BAND (1940)
5 Langton Avenue, Ewell, Surrey

EUROPE

NEW CHURCH, GENERAL CONFERENCE OF THE (Swedenborgian) (1789)
20 Bloomsbury Way, London, W.C.1. Tel.: CHAncery 8574
Overseas Missions Committee: 4 Brooklyn Avenue, Manchester 16

NEW ENGLAND COMPANY (1649)
6 Woburn Square, London, W.C.1. Tel.: MUSeum 4762

NILE MISSION PRESS (*see* ARABIC LITERATURE MISSION)

NORTH AFRICA MISSION (1881)
Marsh Memorial House, 34 Bisham Gardens, Highgate, London, N.6. Tel.: MOUntview 3823

NORTH KASAI MISSION
Bishopton Mill, Whitton, Stockton-on-Tees. Tel.: Stillington 341

NORTH SANKURU MISSION
10 Elmsleigh Road, Weston-super-Mare, Somerset

NYASA MISSION
2 Lyminge Gardens, London, S.W.18

ORIENTAL MISSIONARY SOCIETY
1 Sandileigh Avenue, Manchester, 20

OVERCOMER LITERATURE TRUST (1909)
3 Munster Road, Parkstone, Poole, Dorset. Tel.: Parkstone 4551

OVERSEAS MISSIONARY FELLOWSHIP (1865) (China Inland Mission)
Newington Green, London, N.16. Tel.: CANonbury 6831

OXFORD MISSION TO CALCUTTA (1880)
35 Great Peter Street, London, S.W.1. Tel.: ABBey 3608

PENTECOSTAL JEWISH MISSION (BIBLE EVANGELISTIC MISSION) (1931)
"The Boundary", Cameron Road, Bromley, Kent

PIONEER MISSION (1920)
13 Vowler Street, London, S.E.17

PLYMOUTH BRETHREN
1 Widcombe Crescent, Bath, Somerset

POONA AND INDIAN VILLAGE MISSION
75 Mildmay Park, London, N.1. Tel.: CANonbury 6509

POST OFFICE CHRISTIAN ASSOCIATION (1887)
Drayton House, Gordon Street, London, W.C.1. Tel.: EUSton 3350

PRESBYTERIAN CHURCH OF ENGLAND
86 Tavistock Place, London, W.C.1. Tel.: TERminus 0862

PRESBYTERIAN CHURCH OF WALES
Foreign Mission (1840), 16 Falkner Street, Liverpool 8

QUEEN VICTORIA SEAMEN'S REST (1843)
121/131 East India Dock Road, Poplar, London, E.14. Tel.: East 2995

RED SEA MISSION TEAM
35 The Grove, Finchley, London, N.3

REFORMED PRESBYTERIAN CHURCH OF SCOTLAND (1743)
Reformed Presbyterian Manse, Polton Road, Loanhead, Midlothian, Scotland

REGIONS BEYOND MISSIONARY UNION (1878)
Harley House, 99 Thurleigh Road, London, S.W.12. Tel.: KELvin 1288

ROYAL NATIONAL MISSION TO DEEP SEA FISHERMEN (1881)
43 Nottingham Place, London, W.1. Tel.: WELbeck 6823–4

ROYAL SAILORS' RESTS (1876)
31 Western Parade, Southsea, Hampshire. Tel.: Portsmouth 23126

RUANDA MISSION (1921)
St. Mark's Church, Kennington Park Road, London, S.E.11. Tel.: RELiance 7091

RUSSIA AND BORDER STATES MISSION
56 King George Street, London, S.E.10

EUROPE

SAHARA DESERT MISSION (1953)
34 The Avenue, Loughton, Essex

SALVATION ARMY (1865)
International Headquarters: Queen Victoria Street, London, E.C.4. Tel.: CENtral 5222

SCRIPTURE GIFT MISSION (1888)
Radstock House, Eccleston Street, London, S.W.1. Tel.: SLOane 2155

SCRIPTURE UNION AND CHILDREN'S SPECIAL SERVICE MISSION (1867)
47 Marylebone Lane, London, W.1. Tel.: HUNter 2561

SENTINELS MISSIONARY UNION
Clive Court, Ashdown Avenue, Saltdean, Sussex

SLAVIC AND BALTIC MISSIONARY SOCIETY (1907)
104 Upper Walthamstow Road, London, E.17. Tel.: COPpermill 7266

SLAVIC AND EUROPEAN EVANGELISTIC SOCIETY (1952)
30 Bloomfield Villas, London, W.2

SLAVIC AND ORIENTAL MISSION (1932)
13 Wollaston Road, Dorchester, Dorset

SOCIETY FOR PROMOTING CHRISTIAN KNOWLEDGE (1698)
Holy Trinity Church, Marylebone Road, London, N.W.1. Tel.: EUSton 5282

SOCIETY OF ST. JOHN THE EVANGELIST (English Congregation) (1866)
The Mission House, Marston Street, Oxford

SOCIETY OF THE SACRED MISSION
Kelham, Newark, Nottinghamshire. Tel.: Newark 4461

SOUTH AFRICAN CHURCH INSTITUTE (1924)
15 Tufton Street, Westminster, London, S.W.1. Tel.: ABBey 1033

SOUTH AMERICAN MISSIONARY SOCIETY (1844)
20 John Street, Theobalds Road, London, W.C.1. Tel.: HOLborn 9368

SPANISH AND PORTUGUESE CHURCH AID SOCIETY (1880)
c/o G. F. Wallace, 4 Stone Buildings, Lincolns Inn, London, W.C.2. Tel.: CHAncery 5716

SPANISH GOSPEL MISSION
56 Dorset Road, Bexhill-on-Sea, Sussex

SPANISH PIONEER MISSION
79 Colebrook Road, Liverpool 17

SPEZIA MISSION FOR ITALY (1866)
31 Earlsthorpe Road, Sydenham, London, S.E.26. Tel.: SYDenham 7979

STRICT AND PARTICULAR BAPTIST TRUST CORPORATION
7 Bedford Road, London, N.15

STRICT BAPTIST MISSION (1861) and LADIES' ZENANA AUXILIARY (1906)
61 Breakspears Road, London, S.E.4. Tel.: TIDeway 1841

STUDENT CHRISTIAN MOVEMENT OF GREAT BRITAIN AND IRELAND
Annandale, North End Road, Golders Green, London, N.W.11. Tel.: SPEedwell 2311

SUDAN INTERIOR MISSION (1893)
84 Beulah Hill, Upper Norwood, London, S.E.19. Tel.: LIVingstone 3953

SUDAN UNITED MISSION (1904)
21 Granville Road, Sidcup, Kent. Tel.: Footscray 1109

THONAN EVANGELISTIC MISSION
21 Oakdene Road, Orpington, Kent

TOC H (1915)
15 Trinity Square, London, E.C.3. Tel.: ROYal 0472
Toc H Women's Association: Crutched Friars House, London, E.C.3. Tel.: ROYal 5586

EUROPE

TRINITARIAN BIBLE SOCIETY (1831)
7 Bury Place, London, W.C.1. Tel.: HOLborn 9460

UNEVANGELIZED FIELDS MISSIONS (1931)
9 Gunnersbury Avenue, Ealing, London, W.5. Tel.: ACOrn 1293

UNION OF WELSH INDEPENDENTS INC. (Undeb yr Annibynwir Cymraeg) (Corforedig)
11 St. Helen's Road, Swansea, Glamorgan, Wales. Tel.: 52542

UNITARIAN AND FREE CHRISTIAN CHURCHES, GENERAL ASSEMBLY
1–6 Essex Street, London, W.C.2. Tel.: COVent Garden 2384

UNITED BIBLE SOCIETIES
101 Queen Victoria Street, London, E.C.4. Tel.: CENtral 1606

UNITED FREE CHURCH OF SCOTLAND, GENERAL ASSEMBLY
11 Newton Place, Glasgow, C.3, Scotland. Tel.: DOU 3425

UNITED SOCIETY FOR CHRISTIAN LITERATURE (1799)
4 Bouverie Street, London, E.C.4. Tel.: FLEet 3853

UNITED SOCIETY FOR THE PROPAGATION OF THE GOSPEL
15 Tufton Street, London, S.W.1. Tel.: SULlivan 1701–8

WALDENSIAN CHURCH MISSIONS, English Committee (1830)
"White Close", Clawton, Holsworthy, Devonshire

WESLEYAN REFORM UNION OF CHURCHES
Wesleyan Reform Church House, 123 Queen Street, Sheffield 1, Yorks. Tel.: Sheffield 21938

WEST AMAZON MISSION (1953)
67 Sandringham Road, Swindon, Wiltshire. Tel.: Swindon 21674

WESTCOTT MISSION
22 Denewell Avenue, Low Fell, Gateshead 9, Durham

WORLD DOMINION PRESS (SURVEY APPLICATION TRUST)
34 Brook Street, London, W.1. Tel.: HYDe Park 7176

WORLD PROTESTANT UNION (1891)
Clive Court, Ashdown Avenue, Saltdean, Brighton, Sussex. Tel.: Rottingdean 4381

WORLD REVIVAL CRUSADE
8–10 Clarence Avenue, Clapham Park, London, S.W.4. Tel.: TULse Hill 3175

WORLDWIDE EVANGELIZATION CRUSADE (1913)
Bulstrode, Gerrards Cross, Bucks. Tel.: Gerrards x 84631

WYCLIFFE BIBLE TRANSLATORS
17 Downs Court Road, Purley, Surrey

YOUNG MEN'S CHRISTIAN ASSOCIATION
112 Great Russell Street, London, W.C.1. Tel.: MUSeum 8954
10 Palmerston Place, Edinburgh 12, Scotland. Tel.: Caledonian 5022
53 Park Place, Cardiff, Wales. Tel.: Cardiff 20761

YOUNG WOMEN'S CHRISTIAN ASSOCIATION
Y.M.C.A. Central Building, Great Russell Street, London, W.C.1. Tel.: LANgham 4827

ZAMBESI MISSION (INC.) (and Zambesi Industrial Mission) (1892)
92 Romford Road, Stratford, London, E.15. Tel.: MAR 4019

GREECE

BIBLE SOCIETY
18 Philhellinon Street, Athens 118

CHRISTIANIKOS OMILOS FITITON (Student Christian Association)
3 Souliou Street, Athens

CHRISTIAN SCIENCE COMMITTEE ON PUBLICATION
10 Saripolou Street (Museum), Athens

EUROPE

EKKLESIA TES ELLADOS (Church of Greece)
His Beatitude the Archbishop of Athens and All Greece, Athens

FRIENDS SERVICE COUNCIL
Quaker School for Rural Girls, P.O. Box 102, Thessaloniki

GREEK EVANGELICAL CHURCH
50 Amalias Avenue, Athens

NEAR EAST MISSION OF THE A.B.C.F.M.
43 Aioleon Street, Ano Petralona, Athens

YOUNG MEN'S CHRISTIAN ASSOCIATION
Academy and Homer Streets 28, Athens. Tel.: 626-970

YOUNG WOMEN'S CHRISTIAN ASSOCIATION
Odos Amerikis 11, Athens

HUNGARY

MAGYAR BAPTISTA EGYHÁZ (Baptist Church of Hungary)
Aradi utca 48, Budapest VI

MAGYAR BIBLIANTANÁCS (Hungarian Bible Council) (1949)
Abonyi-utca 21, Budapest XIV. Tel.: 226-408

MAGYAR EVANGELIUMI KERESZTYEN DIAKSZOVETSEG
Harsfa-utca 59/b, Budapest VII

MAGYAR METHODISTA EGYHÁZ (Methodist Church of Hungary)
Havas u.6, Budapest V

MAGYARORSZÁGI EGYHÁZAK ÖKUMENIKUS TANÁCSA (Ecumenical
Council of Churches) (1944)
Szabadság tér 2, Budapest V. Tel.: 114-862
Bishop Dr. Tibor Bartha

MAGYARORSZÁGI EVANGELIKUS EGYHÁZ (Lutheran Church of Hungary)
Ullöi-tuca 24, Budapest VIII

MAGYARORSZÁGI REFORMATUS EGYHÁZ (Reformed Church of Hungary)
(1531)
Abonyi-utca 21, Budapest XIV. Tel.: 226-408

YOUNG WOMEN'S CHRISTIAN ASSOCIATION
35 Bocskay-ut, Budapest XI

ICELAND

ICELANDIC BIBLE SOCIETY
Biskopsskrifstafan, Arnarhvoli, Reykjavik

ICELANDIC MISSION SOCIETY
Asyallagatan 13, Reykjavik

KRISTILEGT STUDENTAFELAG (Student Christian Association)
P.O. Box 651, Amtmannsstig 2B, Reykjavik

THJÓDKIRKJA ISLANDS (National Church of Iceland, Lutheran)
Reykjavik

YOUNG MEN'S CHRISTIAN ASSOCIATION
P.O. Box 211, Reykjavik

YOUNG WOMEN'S CHRISTIAN ASSOCIATION
K.F.U.K., Amtmannsstig 2, Reykjavik

IRELAND

ACRE GOSPEL MISSION (1937)
13 Willowbank Drive, Belfast, Northern Ireland. Tel.: Belfast 642272

BAPTIST UNION OF IRELAND
3 Fitzwilliam Street, Belfast 9, Northern Ireland. Tel.: 22303

EUROPE

CHRISTIAN SCIENCE COMMITTEE ON PUBLICATION FOR COUNTY DUBLIN
Castlenock Lodge, Castlenock, Irish Republic

CHURCH OF IRELAND
52 St. Stephen's Green East, Dublin 2, Irish Republic. Tel.: 61131
Church of Ireland Jews Society (1810): 28 Molesworth Street, Dublin S.4, Irish Republic

CONGREGATIONAL UNION OF IRELAND
130 Woodvale Road, Belfast 13, Northern Ireland

DUBLIN MISSIONARY COUNCIL
Norville, Galtrim Road, Bray, Co. Wicklow, Irish Republic

DUBLIN UNIVERSITY FAR EASTERN MISSION (1885)
22 Trinity College, Dublin, Irish Republic. Tel.: 72941

DUBLIN UNIVERSITY MISSION TO CHOTA NAGPUR (1891)
Trinity College, Dublin, Irish Republic. Tel.: 341015

HIBERNIAN BIBLE SOCIETY (1806)
Irish Republic: 41 Dawson Street, Dublin 2
Northern Ireland: 27 Howard Street, Belfast

IRISH AND SCOTCH REFORMED PRESBYTERIAN MISSION IN SYRIA
Pine Hill Manse, Knockahollet, Co. Antrim, Northern Ireland

IRISH BAPTIST FOREIGN MISSION (1924)
3 Fitzwilliam Street, Belfast 9, Northern Ireland. Tel.: 22303

LUTHERAN CHURCH
21 Merlyn Park, Dublin, Irish Republic

METHODIST CHURCH IN IRELAND
Grosvenor Hall, Belfast, Northern Ireland

PRESBYTERIAN CHURCH IN IRELAND
Church House, Fisherwick Place, Belfast 1, Northern Ireland. Tel.: 22284

QUA IBOE MISSION (1887)
108 Scottish Provident Buildings, Donegal Square West, Belfast, Northern Ireland

REFORMED PRESBYTERIAN CHURCH OF IRELAND
Cameron House, 98 Lisburn Road, Belfast 9, Northern Ireland. Tel.: Belfast 21872

YOUNG MEN'S CHRISTIAN ASSOCIATION
22 Howard Street, Belfast, Northern Ireland

ITALY

CHIESA EVANGELICA LUTERANA IN ITALIA (Evangelical Lutheran Church in Italy)
Via Toscana 7, Rome

CHIESA EVANGELICA METODISTA D'ITALIA (Evangelical Methodist Church of Italy)
Via Firenze 38, Rome

CHIESA EVANGELICA VALDESE (Waldensian Church)
Via IV Novembre 107, Roma. Tel.: 674.662

CHRISTIAN SCIENCE COMMITTEE ON PUBLICATION
Via G.Fara 39, Milan

CONSIGLIO FEDERALE DELLE CHIESA EVANGELICHE D'ITALIA
(Federal Council of the Evangelical Churches of Italy) (1946)
Via IV Novembre 107, Rome

LIBRERIA SACRE SCRITTURE (Bible Society)
Via Dell'Umittà 33, Rome

MOVIMENTO CHRISTIANO STUDENTI (Student Christian Movement)
Via Pietro Cossa 42, Rome

EUROPE

SALVATION ARMY
Via Ariosto 32, Rome. Tel.: 734.214

UNIONE CRISTIANA EVANGELICA BATTISTA D'ITALIA (Christian Evangelical Baptist Union of Italy) (1871)
Piazza San Lorenzo in Lucina 35, Rome

YOUNG MEN'S CHRISTIAN ASSOCIATION
23 Piazza Indipendenza 1, Rome. Tel.: 471.476

YOUNG WOMEN'S CHRISTIAN ASSOCIATION (1894)
Via C. Balbo 4, Rome. Tel.: 474.525

LUXEMBOURG

EGLISE PROTESTANTE DU GRAND-DUCHE DE LUXEMBOURG
1 rue Jules Wilhelm, Luxembourg

NETHERLANDS

ALGEMENE DOOPSGEZINDE SOCIETEIT (General Mennonite Society)
Doopsgezinde Kerk, Singel 452, Amsterdam C

BOND VAN VRIJE EVANGELISCHE GEMEENTEN IN NEDERLAND
(Union of Free Evangelical Congregations)
Oldeobroek, Prov. Gelderland

CHRISTIAN SCIENCE COMMITTEE ON PUBLICATION
42 Oranje Nassaulaan, Amsterdam Z

COMMISSIE TOT VERTEGENWOORDIGING IN NEDERLAND VAN DE PROTESTANTSE KERK IN INDONESIE (Commission in the Netherlands for the Affairs of the Protestant Church in Indonesia) (1815)
Koninginnegracht 81, The Hague

DOOPSGEZINDE VERENIGING TOT EVANGELIEVERBREIDING (Mennonite Union for the Propagation of the Gospel) (1847)
Noolseweg 14a, Blaricum (N.4)

DOOPSGEZINDE ZENDINGSRAAD
Snekerstraat 30, Bolsward

EVANGELISCHE BRODERGEMEENTEN IN NEDERLAND (Moravian) (1746)
Broederplein 33, Zeist. Tel.: 03404–12213

EVANGELISCH-LUTHERSE KERK IN HET KONINKRIJK NEDER-LANDEN (Evangelical Lutheran Church in the Kingdom of the Netherlands) (1818)
Fuutlaan 4, The Hague
Mission Council (1852): Provincialeweg 32, Zaandam. Tel.: 02980–66735

GEREFORMEERDE KERKEN IN NEDERLAND (Reformed Churches in the Netherlands) (1892)
Algemeen Kerkelijk Bureau, Wilhelminapark 2, Utrecht. Tel.: 030–10441

GEREFORMEERDE ZENDINGSBOND (Reformed Missions League)
Utrechtseweg 117, Zeist

HERVORMDE RAAD VOOR DE VERHOUDING VAN KERKEN ISRAEL
Von Weberstraat 41, Utrecht

LEGER DES HEILS (Salvation Army)
Prins Henrikkade 49–51, Amsterdam C. Tel.: 241703

NEDERLANDSCH BIJBELGENOOTSCHAP (Netherlands Bible Society) (1814)
366 Heerengracht, Amsterdam C. Tel.: 020–24 37 98

NEDERLANDSE HERVORMDE KERK (Reformed Church of the Netherlands) (1571)
Carnegielaan 9, The Hague

EUROPE

NEDERLANDSE CHRISTEN-STUDENTEN VERENIGING (Netherlands Christian Student Union) (1896)
Woudschoten, Zeist. Tel.: 03439-226

NEDERLANDSE ZENDINGSHOGESCHOOL (Netherlands Missionary Training Institute)
Leidsestraatweg 11, Oegstgeest bij Leiden

NEDERLANDSE ZENDINGSRAAD (Netherlands Missionary Council) (1929)
37 Prins Hendriklaan, Amsterdam 7. Tel.: (020) 71 76 54

NEDERLANDS LUTHERS GENOOTSCHAP VOOR INWENDIGE EN UITWENDIGE ZENDING (Netherlands Lutheran Society for Home and Foreign Missions) (1852)
3 Gerard Schaepstraat, Amsterdam W

NETHERLANDS YEARLY MEETING, RELIGIOUS SOCIETY OF FRIENDS
Quaker Centrum, Vossiusstraat 20, Amsterdam Z

OECUMENISCHE RAAD VAN KERKEN IN NEDERLAND (Ecumenical Council of Churches in the Netherlands)
Maliebaan 88, Utrecht. Miss S. M. Holsteijn

OUD-KATHOLIEKE KERK VAN NEDERLAND (Old Catholic Church) (7th Century)
Emmalaan 8, Utrecht

RAAD VOOR DE ZENDING DE NEDERLANDSE HERVORMDE KERK (Board of Foreign Missions of the Dutch Reformed Church) (1951)
Leidsestraatweg 11, Oegstgeest bij Leiden

REMONSTRANTSE BROEDERSCHAP ALGEMENE DIENST (Dutch Remonstrant Brotherhood)
Mathenesserlaan 3, Rotterdam 2

SAMOSIR ZENDING
Van Breestraat 96, Amsterdam

STICHTING MORGENLAND ZENDING (Missions in the Orient)
Buys Ballotstraat 46, Utrecht

UNIE VAN BAPTISTEN GEMEENTEN IN NEDERLAND (Union of Baptist Churches in the Netherlands) (1881)
Dalweg 77, Arnhem. Tel.: 23007
Zendingscommisie: Orionweg 261, Ijmuiden

VERENIGING VOOR GEMEENSCHAPPELIJKE ZENDING VAN DE VRIJE EVANGELISCHE GEMEENTEN IN NEDERLAND: SAMOSIR-ZENDING (Union for the Joint Missionary Work of the Free Evangelical Congregations: Missions in Samosir, Sumatra) (1926)
Andr. Mulder van Breestraat 96, Amsterdam

VERENIGING TOT ONDERSTEUNNING VAN DE ZENDELINGEN DER SALATIGA-ZENDING (Union for the Support of the Missionaries of the Salatiga Mission) (1889)
Admiraal van Gentstraat, Utrecht

VERENIGING TOT UITBREIDING VAN HET EVANGELIE IN EGYPTE (Society for the Propagation of the Gospel in Egypt) (1886)
Harry Koningsbergstraat 77, Amsterdam W.2

YOUNG MEN'S CHRISTIAN ASSOCIATION
Singel 58, Bondsgebouw, Amsterdam C. Tel.: 222.833

YOUNG WOMEN'S CHRISTIAN ASSOCIATION
F.C. Donderstraat 23, Utrecht. Tel.: 030-715525

ZENDING DER CHRISTELIJKE-GEREFORMEERDE KERK (Mission of the Christian Reformed Church) (1920)
Honthorststraat 6, Amsterdam Z

ZENDING DER GEREFORMEERDE KERKEN IN NEDERLAND (Mission of the Reformed Churches in the Netherlands) (1896)
Zendingscentrum, Wilheminalaan 3, Baarn. Tel.: 02954-4051

M   335

EUROPE

ZENDINGSGENOOTSCHAP DER EVANGELISCHE BROEDERGEMEENTE
(Mission Society of the Moravian Church) (1793)
27 Broederplein, Zeist

NORWAY

AKADEMISKE FRIVILLIGES MISJONSFORBUND (Norwegian Student
Volunteer Movement) (1896)
Norges Kristelige Student-og Gymnasiastlag, Holbergs pl.4, Oslo 1. Tel.: 33.15.13

BANDA MISJONEN (Norwegian Evangelical Mission) (1915)
P.O. Box 1707, Vika, Oslo 1. Tel.: 42.70.40

CHRISTIAN SCIENCE COMMITTEE ON PUBLICATION
Sorgenfrigaten 7B, Oslo

EGEDE INSTITUTTET (Egede Institute of Missionary Study and Research)
Theresegt, 51B, Oslo 3. Tel.: 60 68 17

KARMEL INSTITTUT
Storgt. 38, Oslo

KONTAKTKRETSEN (Contact Circle) (1950)
Røahagan 25, Røa, Oslo

KRISTELIG LAEGEFORENING (Christian Medical Association) (1936)
Tellinsgt. 4, Oslo

KVINNELIGE MISJONS ARBEIDERE (Women Missionary Workers) (1902)
Storgaten 38, Oslo

LAERERINNENES MISJONSFORBUND (Women Teachers' Missionary
Association) (1902)
Theresegt. 51B, Oslo. Tel.: 46 41 12

LUTHERSKE AFRIKAMISJON (Lutheran Africa Mission) (1900)
Ebbelsgt. 5, Oslo

METODISTKIRKEN I NORGE (Methodist Church, Norway)
Thv. Meyersgt. 56, Oslo

METODISTKIRKENS MISJONSSELSKAP (Board of World Missions of the
Methodist Church, Norway) (1907)
St. Olavsgt. 28, Oslo 1. Tel.: 200847

NORDISKE KRISTNE BUDDHISTMISJON (Christian Mission to Buddhists)
(1926)
Elisenbergvn. 6, Oslo 2. Tel.: 44 62 75

NORGES KRISTELIGE STUDENTERBEVEGELSE (Norwegian Student
Christian Movement) (1899)
Universitetsgt. 20, Oslo 1. Tel.: 41 11 44

NORGES KRISTELIGE STUDENT OG GYMNASIASTLAG (Norwegian
Christian Student Association)
Holbergspl. 4, Oslo 1. Tel.: 33 15 13

NORSKE BAPTISTSAMFUNN (Baptist Union of Norway) (1860)
Hausmannsgt. 22, Oslo. Tel.: 42 27 10

NORSKE BAPTISTSAMFUNNS KONGOMISJON (1915) (Mission Baptiste
Norvegienne)
Hausmannsgt. 22, Oslo

NORSKE BIBELSELSKAP (Norwegian Bible Society) (1816)
Munchsgt. 2, Oslo 1. Tel.: 20 34 77

NORSKE EVANGELISK-LUTHERSKE FRIKIRKE (Norwegian Evangelical
Lutheran Free Church)
Josefinegatan 5, Oslo 3

NORSKE EVANGELISK-LUTHERSKE FRIKIRKES CHINA-OG JAPAN-
MISJON (Lutheran Free Church of Norway, China and Japan Mission) (1907)
Wergelandsgt. 4, Moss

EUROPE

NORSKE EVANGELISK ORIENTMISJON (Norwegian Orient Mission)
Möllergt. 20, Oslo

NORSKE ISRAELMISJON (Norwegian Mission to Israel) (1844)
Collettsgt. 43, 2. etg., Oslo 4. Tel.: 69 37 43

NORSKE KIRKE (Church of Norway)
St. Halvards pl. 3, Oslo

NORSKE KIRKES MISJON VED SCHREUDER (Church of Norway Mission
by Schreuder) (1873)
Vei 3453, blokk 2, oppg. 14 Furuseth, Grorud

NORSKE MISJONSALLIANSE (Norwegian Missionary Alliance) (1900)
Munchsgt. 9, Oslo

NORSKE MISJONSFORBUND (Evangelical Covenant Church of Norway) (1899)
Möllergt. 26, Oslo

NORSKE MISJONSSELSKAP (Norwegian Missionary Society) (1842)
Asylgt. 10, Stavanger

NORSKE MUHAMMEDANERMISJON (Norwegian Mission to Muslims) (1940)
Storgt. 38, V.305, Oslo 1. Tel.: 41 06 74

NORSKE PINSEVENNERS YTREMISJON (Norwegian Pentecostal Assemblies,
Foreign Missions) (1910)
"Filadelfia", St. Olavsgt. 24, Oslo

NORSKE TIBETMISJON (Norwegian Tibetan Mission) (1937)
Herm. Gransvei 49, Laksevag

NORSK LUTHERSK MISJONSSAMBAND (Norwegian Lutheran Mission)
(1891)
Grensen 19, Oslo 1. Tel.: 41 76 40

NORSK MELLOMKIRKELIG INSTITUTT (Norwegian Institute for Inter
Church Relations) (1952)
Munchsgt. 2, Oslo 1. Tel.: 20 07 80

NORSK MISJONSRAD (Norwegian Missionary Council) (1921)
Grensen 19, Oslo
Chmn.: T. Vaagen

SALVATION ARMY (Norway and Iceland)
Pilestredet 22, Oslo. Tel.: 33 77 33

SANTAL MISSION
Holbergsgaten 23, Oslo

SCHREUDERMISJONEN
Kvernveien 12, Øvre, Ullern, Oslo 3. Tel.: 24 31 70

SYKEPLEIERSKENES MISJONSRING (Nurses' Missionary Association) (1921)
Johs. Bruns gt. 12.C, Oslo 1. Tel.: 46 56 05

TELEGRAFVERKETS MISJONSFORBUND (1934)
General Birchsgt. 22, Oslo

VENNENES SAMFUNN I NORGE (Society of Friends in Norway) (1818)
Lågardsveien 99, Stavanger. Tel.: 22103

YOUNG MEN'S CHRISTIAN ASSOCIATION
Norges K.F.U.M., Holbergspl. 1, Oslo. Tel.: 33 17 77

YOUNG WOMEN'S CHRISTIAN ASSOCIATION
Norges K.F.U.K., Holbergspl. 1, Oslo. Tel.: 33 17 77

POLAND

BIBLE SOCIETY
Nowy Swiat 40, Warsaw

CHRZESCIJANSKA RADA EKUMENICZNA W POLSCE R.E. (Polish
Ecumenical Council) (1955)
ul. Swierczewskiego 76 a., Warsaw. Tel.: 31 23 83
Rev. Zdzislaw Pawlik

EUROPE

CHRZESCIJANSKA AKADEMICA TEOLOGICZNA (Christian Theological Academy) (1954)
p. Skolimów, ul. Dtuga 43, Chylice—ad Warsaw. Tel.: 564–222

KOSCIOL EWANGELICKO-AUGSBURSKI W POLSKIEJ RZECZYPOS-POLITEJ LUDOWEJ (The Evangelical Church of Augsburg Confession in the Polish Democratic Republic) (16th century)
ul. Miodowa 21, Warsaw

MARIAVITES CHURCH
Dobrzynska 27, Plock

METHODIST CHURCH
Mokotowska 12, Warsaw

POLSKI KOSCIOL CHRZESCIJAN BAPTYSTOW (Polish Baptist Church) (1858)
Chlodna 57/17, Warsaw

POLSKI NARODOWAY KOSCIOL KATOLICKI (Polish National Catholic Church) (1922)
Wilcza 31 m. 1, Warsaw

REFORMED CHURCH
Swierczewskiego 76a, Warsaw

UNITED EVANGELICAL CHURCH
Al. Jerozolimskie 99/37, Warsaw

PORTUGAL

ALIANCA EVANGELICA PORTUGUESA (Portuguese Evangelical Alliance) (1935)
Rua do Arco a S. Mamede n.°9, 3° D, Lisbon 2
Pres.: Guido Oliveira

CONVENCÃO BATISTA PORTUGUESA (Baptist Convention of Portugal) (1920)
Rua Filipe Folque 36, 1°, Lisbon. Tel.: 73 53 62

IGREJA EVANGELICA METODISTA PORTUGUESA (Portuguese Evangelical Methodist Church)
Igreja Evangélica do Mirante, Praça do Coronel Pacheco 23, Porto. Tel.: 27410

IGREJA EVANGELICA PRESBITERIANA EM PORTUGAL (Presbyterian Evangelical Church) (1952)
Rua D. Vasco da Cãmara 8, Carcavelos

IGREJA EVANGELICA PRESBITERIANA DE PORTUGAL, SINODO NACIONAL (Presbyterian Evangelical Church of Portugal)
Rua Febo Moniz 17–19, Lisbon

IGREJA LUSITANA CATOLICA-APOSTOLICA-EVANGELICA (Anglican)
Quinta do Balcalhau, Vila Franca de Xira

JUVENTUDE EVANGELICA PORTUGUESA (Portugese Evangelical Youth)
Avenida dos Combatentes 18–3°, Alges

LIGA EVANGELICA DE ACCÃO MISSIONARIA E EDUCATIONAL (Evangelical League for Missionary and Educational Work) (1934)
Avenida Infante Santo, 4, 2° E, Lisbon

MOVIMENTO ACADÉMICO CRISTÃO (Christian Academic Movement)
Avenida Almirante Reis, 244–2 Esq., Lisbon

SOCIEDADE BIBLICA (in Portugal, 1880) (The British and Foreign Bible Society)
Agencia em Portugal (Agency in Portugal), Rua Passos Manuel, 1–B, Lisbon 1. Tel.: 4 55 34

UNIAO BATISTA DE PORTUGAL (Baptist Union of Portugal)
R. do Bonjardim 1124–1, Porto

UNIAO BIBLICA (Scripture Union)
Rua Santana à Lapa 69–1°, Lisbon

EUROPE

YOUNG MEN'S CHRISTIAN ASSOCIATION
Rua de Sao Bento 329, Lisbon 2
YOUNG WOMEN'S CHRISTIAN ASSOCIATION
Calç Cruz da Pedra 16, Lisbon

RUMANIA

BAPTIST UNION OF RUMANIA
Str. Berzei 29, Bukarest
BISERICA LUTERANA UNGARA DIN ROMANIA (Hungarian Lutheran
Church in Rumania)
Str. Kossuth Lajos 1, Kolozsvár, Cluj
BISERICA REFORMATA DIN ROMANIA (Transylvanian Reformed Church)
Strada 23 August 51, Cluj
EVANGELICAL SYNODAL PRESBYTERAL CHURCH OF THE AUGSBURG
CONFESSION
Bulevardul Lenin Nr. 1, Kolozsvár, Cluj
EVANGELISCHE KIRCHE AUGSBURGISCHEN BEKENNTNISSES IN DER
RUMANISCHEN VOLKSREPUBLIK
Sibiu, Strada General Magheru, Nr. 4, Raion Sibiu, Regiunea Brasov. Tel.:
3079, 1780, 3609

SPAIN

ALIANZA EVANGELICA ESPAÑOLA (Spanish Evangelical Alliance)
calle Verdi 189, Barcelona 12. Tel.: 2276987
FEDERACION DE IGLESIAS EVANGELICAS INDEPENDIENTES DE
ESPAÑA
Rev. José M. Martinez, Calle Verdi 189, Barcelona 12. Tel.: 2276987
IGLESIA ESPAÑOLA REFORMADA EPISCOPAL (Spanish Reformed Epis-
copal Church)
calle Beneficencia 18, Madrid 4. Tel.: 2-575635
IGLESIA EVANGELICA ESPAÑOLA (Spanish Evangelical Church, Reformed)
calle Murillo 16, Palma de Mallorca. Tel.: 31810
SOCIEDAD BIBLICA (Bible Society)
Dup. 133, Joaquin Garcia Morato, Madrid 3
SPANISH BAPTIST MISSION
calle del Dr. Turro 1, Esplugas de Llobreghat, Barcelona
SPANISH REFORMED EPISCOPAL CHURCH
Beneficiencia 18, Madrid. Tel.: 2-575635
UNION EVANGELICA BAUTISTA ESPAÑOLA (Spanish Evangelical Baptist
Union)
calle Trafalgar 32, Madrid 10

SWEDEN

CHRISTIAN SCIENCE COMMITTEE ON PUBLICATION
Kopparormsgatan 6, Gothenburg S
EESTI EVANGEELIUMI LUTERI USU KIRKIK (Estonian Evangelical
Lutheran Church)
Bokbindarvägen 51, IV Hägersten
EVANGELISKA BRÖDRAFÖRSAMLINGEN (Moravian)
Hantverkaregatan 18–20, Stockholm K
EVANGELISKA FOSTERLANDS-STIFTELSEN (Evangelical National Mis-
sionary Society Stockholm) (1856)
Tegnérgatan 34, Stockholm Va. Tel.: 08/34 02 90

EUROPE

FORBUNDET KRISTNA SEMINARISTER OCH LARARE (Society of Christian Seminary Pupils and Teachers) (1946)
Ljungskile

FRÄLSNINGSARMEN (Salvation Atmy)
Östermalmsgatan 71, Stockholm 5. Tel.: 63 17 00

FRIBAPTISTSAMFUNDET (Scandinavian Independent Baptist Union) (1872)
Norevägen 9, Lindesberg. Tel.: 0581/13491

KVINNLIGA MISSIONS ARBETARE (Women Missionary Workers) (1894)
Birger Jarlsgaten 67, Stockholm Va

LÄRARINNORNAS MISSIONSFÖRENING (Women Teachers' Missionary Association)
Vasaplatsen 4, Göteborg C. Tel.: 11 22 20

METODISTYRKAN I SVERIGE (Methodist Church in Sweden) (1867)
Sibyllegatan 18, Stockholm

MISSIONSSÄLLSKAPET BIBELTROGNA (Missionary Society of True Friends of the Bible) (1911)
P.O. Box 6103, Stockholm 6

MISSIONSSÄLLSKAPET HELGELSEFORBUNDET (Swedish Holiness Union)
Stationsgatan 18, Box 61, Kumla

ÖREBROMISSIONEN (Oerebro Mission Society) (1892)
Järnvägsgatan 28 A, Box 330 Örebro. Tel.: 019–11 93 60

SALLSKAPET FOR EVANGELII UTBREDANDE BLAND SLAVISKA (SLAVISKA MISSIONEN) (Slavic Mission) (1903)
Upplandsgaten 28, Stockholm 6

SVENSKA ALLIANSMISSIONEN (Swedish Alliance Mission) (1853)
Västra Storhatan 14, Jönköping. Tel.: 036/11 91 30

SVENSKA AVDELNINGEN AV NORDISKA KRISTNA BUDDHIST-MISSIONEN
Fredr. hofsgatan 3A, Stockholm O

SVENSKA BAPTISTSAMFUNDET (Baptist Union of Sweden)
Norrtullsgatan 10, Stockholm Va

SVENSKA BIBELSALLSKAPET (Swedish Bible Society) (1815)
Storgatan 7, Stockholm O. Tel.: 62 56 12

SVENSKA EKUMENISKA NAMNDEN (Swedish Ecumenical Council)
Väderkvarnsgatan 33 B, Uppsala. Tel.: 018/121133 Docent Lars Thunberg

SVENSKA FRIA MISSIONEN (SVENSKA PINGSTRORELSENS YTTRE MISSION) (Swedish Free Mission)
Rörstrandsgat 5–7, Box 21055, Stockholm 21. Tel.: 08/34 98 50

SVENSKA ISRAELSMISSIONEN (Swedish Church Mission to the Jews) (1875)
Idungatan 4, Stockholm Va

SVENSKA JERUSALEMFORENINGEN (Swedish Jerusalem Society) (1900)
Studentvägen 11, Uppsala

SVENSKA KVINNORS MISSIONSFORENING (Missionary Society of Swedish Women)
Kungsgatan 28, Uppsala

SVENSKA KYRKAN (Church of Sweden)
Archbishop of Uppsala. Tel.: 13 03 40

SVENSKA KYRKANS MISSIONSSTYRELSE (Church of Sweden Mission) (1874)
Kungsgatan 28, Uppsala. Tel.: 018/12 02 04

SVENSKA MISSIONEN I KINA OCH JAPAN (Swedish Evangelical Orient Mission) (1887)
Drottninggatan 55, Stockholm C

SVENSKA MISSIONSFORBUNDET (Mission Covenant Church of Sweden) (1878)
Tegnérgatan 8, Stockholm Va. Tel.: 34 96 80

EUROPE

SVENSKA MISSIONSRÅDET (Swedish Missionary Council) (1912)
Tegnérgatan 8, Stockholm Va. Tel.: 34 96 80
Sec.: Rev. Arvid Stenström

SVENSKA MONGOL-OCH JAPAN MISSIONEN (Swedish Evangelical Mission
in Japan) (1897)
Brunnsgatan 4, Stockholm C. Tel.: 08/10 62 05

SVENSKA PINGSTRORELSENS YTTRE MISSION
Rörstransgatan 5–7, Stockholm

SVERIGES EVANGELISKA STUDENT-OCH GYMNASISTRORELSE
(Evangelical Student and High School Movement of Sweden) (1924)
Hälsingborg

SVERIGES FRIA KRISTLIGA STUDENTFORENING (Free Student Christian
Movement)
Tegnérgatan 8, Stockholm

SVERIGES KRISTLIGA STUDENTRORELSE (Student Christian Movement)
Sigtunastiftelsen, Sigtuna

VANNERNAS SAMFUND I SVERIGE (Religious Society of Friends in Sweden)
Kväkargården, Varvsgatan 15, Stockholm SV. Tel.: 68 68 16

YOUNG MEN'S CHRISTIAN ASSOCIATION
Birger Jarlsgatan 33, Stockholm C. Tel.: 08/24 09 50

YOUNG WOMEN'S CHRISTIAN ASSOCIATION (K.F.U.K.) (1885)
S Riksförbund, 27 Birgejarlasgatan, Stockholm C. Tel.: 08/11 20 57

SWITZERLAND

ACTION BIBLIQUE (1905)
Geneva Bible School, Le Roc, Cologny-Genève

ACTION CHRETIENNE EN ORIENT
5 Chemin des Cèdres, 1000 Lausanne 9. Tel.: (025)24 24 38

ASSOCIATION EVANGELIQUE DES EGLISES BAPTISTES DE LANGUE
FRANCAISE DE FRANCE, BELGIQUE ET SUISSE (Evangelical Association
of French-speaking Baptist Churches of France, Belgium and Switzerland)
rue Dufour, 34, Bienne

BRUDERGEMEINE—EGLISE MORAVE (Moravian Church) (1740)
Leimenstrasse 10, CH-4000 Basel. Tel.: (061)23 74 12

BUND SCHWEIZERISCHER ARMENIERFREUNDE
Staufberg (Aargau)

BUND SCHWEIZERISCHER BAPTISTENGEMEINDEN (Swiss Baptist Union)
(1924)
Gartenstrasse 29, Ch 8180, Bülach. Tel.: 051/96 12 51

CHRISCHONA MISSION IN AETHIOPIEN (Chrischona Mission in Ethiopia)
(1853)
St. Chrischona, Bettingen, near Basle. Tel.: Basle (061)513231

CHRISTIAN SCIENCE COMMITTEE ON PUBLICATION
48 Grange-Falquet, Geneva

CHRISTKATHOLISCHE KIRCHE DER SCHWEIZ (Old Catholic Church)
Willadingweg 39, Berne

DEPARTEMENT MISSIONNAIRE DES EGLISES PROTESTANTES DE
SUISSE ROMANDE
5 Chemin des Cèdres, 1000 Lausanne 9. Tel.: (025)24 24 38

EVANGELICAL LUTHERAN CONGREGATIONS
20 rue Verdaine, Geneva

EVANGELISCHE MISSIONS-GESELLSCHAFT IN BASEL (BASLER
MISSION) (Evangelical Missionary Society, Basel) (1815)
Missionshaus, Missionsstrasse 21, CH 4000 Basel 3. Tel.: 24 39 66

EUROPE

FRIENDS SERVICE COUNCIL
Centre Quaker International, 12 rue Adrien Lachenal, Geneva

HEILSARMEE (ARMEE DU SALUT) (Salvation Army)
Laupenstrasse 5, Berne. Tel.: 25 05 91

LANDLI-MISSION IN RUANDA
Diakonissen-Mutterhaus, Oberägeri, Zug

MISSION BIBLIQUE EN COTE D'IVOIRE
2 Av. des Pléiades, Vevey

MISSION EVANGELIQUE AU LAOS (1902)
Route du Cyprés 13, Corseauz, Vevey

MISSION EVANGELIQUE EN GUYANE FRANCAISE (1930)
2 Route de Bergère, Vevey

MISSION PHILAFRICAINE EN ANGOLA (1897)
7 av. de Cour, 1000 Lausanne. Tel.: (021)27 85 53

MISSIONSGESELLSCHAFT DER METHODISTEN KIRCHE IN DER
SCHWEIZ (Missionary Society of the Methodist Church in Switzerland) (1929)
Badenerstrasse 69, Zürich. Tel.: 064 43 15 62

MISSION SUISSE DANS L'AFRIQUE DU SUD (Swiss Mission in South
Africa) (1875)
5 Chemin des Cèdres, Lausanne

MISSION UNIE DU SOUDAN
Zürichstrasse 131, Küsnacht, Zürich

SCHWEIZER EVANGELIUMSDIENST IN ISRAEL
Pflanzchulstrasse 17, Zürich 4

SCHWEIZER HILFSKOMITEE FÜR DAS SYRISCHE WAISENHAUS
(Syrian Orphanage)
Freiestrasse 41, Zürich 32

SCHWEIZER HILSVEREIN FÜR DAS ALBERT SCHWEITZER-SPITAL IN
LAMBARENE (1949)
Gotthardstrasse 29, Basel

SCHWEIZER INDIANER MISSION (1956)
Postfach 85, CH-9424 Rheineck. Tel.: (071)44 19 72

SCHWEIZERISCHE BIBELGESELLSCHAFT (Swiss Bible Society) (1955)
8303 Bassersdorf. Tel.: 051/935583

SCHWEIZERISCHE CHRISTLICHE STUDENTEN BEWEGUNG (MOUVE-
MENT CHRETIENNE SUISSE DES ETÜDIANTS) (Student Christian
Movement)
Aigle

SCHWEIZERISCHE EVANGELISCHE JUDENMISSION
2 Mommsenstrasse, Zürich

SCHWEIZERISCHE EVANGELISCHE NILLAND-MISSION (Swiss Evangelical
Nile Mission) (1900)
3506 Grosshöchstetten BE. Tel.: 031/68550

SCHWEIZERISCHE MISSIONSGEMEINSCHAFT (Swiss Missionary Community) (1950)
Zürichstrasse 97, Küsnacht, Zürich

SCHWEIZERISCHE MISSIONSHILFE FÜR DIE BRUDERGEMEINE (Swiss
Aid for Moravian Missions) (1934)
Kirchstrasse 11, 2, CH-4127 Birsfeld. Tel.: (061)41 82 00

SCHWEIZERISCHE OSTASIEN-MISSION (Swiss East Asia Mission) (1884)
Webereistrasse 31, Adliswil-Zürich. Tel.: (051) 917481
Biascastrasse 26, Basel

SCHWEIZERISCHE PFINGSTMISSIONS-GESELLSCHAFT (1921)
Biascastrasse 26, Basel

EUROPE

SCHWEIZERISCHER EVANGELISCHER KIRCHENBUND (Swiss Protestant Church Federation) (1927)
Céligny, Geneva

SCHWEIZERISCHER EVANGELISCHER MISSIONSRAT-KOOPERATION EVANGELISCHER MISSIONEN
Zentralsekratariat, Missionsstrasse 21, 4055 Basel. Tel.: Basel 40–381
Mr. J. M. Stettler

SCHWEIZERISCHER HILFSBUND FÜR CHRISTLICHES LIEBESWERK IM ORIENT (1937)
Bubikon Kt., Zürich

SCHWEIZERISCHER VEREIN FÜR EVANGELISCHE MOHAMMEDANER-MISSION (Swiss Evangelical Mission to Mohammedans)
Haus Buchrain, Grosshöchstetten (Berne)

SCHWEIZERISCHE ZIGEUNER-MISSION (Gipsy Gospel Mission of Switzerland) (1918)
1 Wülflingerstrasse, 8400 Winterthur. Tel.: 052/622 79

SCRIPTURE UNION (1867)
Talackerstrasse 15, Winterthur 8404. Tel.: Winterthur (052) 71521

SOCIETE DES MISSIONS EVANGELIQUES DE PARIS
5 Chemin des Cèdres, Lausanne

SUDAN INTERIOR MISSION
Chemin du Devin 95, 1012 Lausanne

SWITZERLAND YEARLY MEETING, RELIGIOUS SOCIETY OF FRIENDS (1939)
Arcangier 3, La Tou-de-Peilz

YOUNG MEN'S CHRISTIAN ASSOCIATION
Sihlstrasse 33, Zürich 1. Tel.: (051)25 86 73

UNION OF SOVIET SOCIALIST REPUBLICS

EESTI EVANGEELIUMI LUTERIUSU KIRIK (Estonian Evangelical Lutheran Church) Raamatukogustr. 8, Quartier K, Tallinn, Estonia

LATVIAN LUTHERAN CHURCH
Kirowstr. 37, Quartier 5, Riga, Latvia

LITHUANIAN LUTHERAN CHURCH
Lietuviu gatve 10, Kaunas, Lithuania

RUSSIAN ORTHODOX CHURCH
His Beatitude Alexii, Patriarch of Moscow and All Russia, Russian Orthodox Patriarch, Chisty Pereulok 5, Moscow 34

SYNOD OF EVANGELICAL CHRISTIAN BAPTIST CHURCHES
Postamt 9, Yashek 520, Moscow

YUGOSLAVIA

BIBLE SOCIETY
Ulica Aleksandra Glisica 6, Belgrade

EV. CRKVA U. N.R. HRVATSKOJ NR BOSNI I HERCEGOVINI (Evangelical Church in the People's Republics of Croatia, Bosnia and Herzegovina)
Gunduliceva 28, Zagreb

EV. CRKVA U. N.R. SRBIJI (Evangelical Church in the People's Republic of Serbia)
P. Kujundrica 17, Subotica

EV. KR. CERKEV AUG. V.V.L.R. SLOVENIJI-JUGOSLAVIJA (Evangelical Christian Church of the Augsburg Confession in the People's Republic of Slovenia-Yugoslavia)
Murska Sobota

EUROPE

REFORMED CHRISTIAN CHURCH OF YUGOSLAVIA
Reformed Episkop, Feketic Feketic-Backa

SLOVENSKA EV. KR. A.V. CIRKEV V. JUHOSLAVII (Slovak Evangelical Christian Church of the Augsburg Confession in Yugoslavia)
Novi Sad

YUGOSLAV BAPTIST UNION
Laze Nancica 64, Novi Sad

OCEANIA

AUSTRALIA

ABORIGINES' FRIENDS' ASSOCIATION, INC. (1858)
Box 716, G.P.O., Adelaide, South Australia

ABORIGINES' INLAND MISSION OF AUSTRALIA
135 Wentworth Road, Enfield, New South Wales. Tel.: 74–5561

ABORIGINES' UPLIFT SOCIETY
Box 1977 R., G.P.O., Melbourne, C.1., Victoria

ANGLICAN CHURCH OF CARPENTARIA (1900)
Church Office, Thursday Island, Queensland

ASSEMBLIES OF GOD IN AUSTRALIA (1937)
79 Moray Street, New Farm, Brisbane, Queensland

AUSTRALIA ABORIGINES MISSIONS AND TORRES STRAIT ISLAND
MISSION (General Synod of the Church of England in Australia)
Box 79, Post Office, Thursday Island, Queensland. Tel.: Thursday Island 56

AUSTRALIAN BAPTIST MISSION INC. (1912)
486 Albert Street, Melbourne, C.2, Victoria

AUSTRALIAN CHRISTIAN YOUTH COUNCIL (1958)
100 Flinders Street, Melbourne, C.1., Victoria. Tel.: 63 5814

AUSTRALIAN CHURCHES OF CHRIST, FOREIGN MISSION BOARD,
INC. (1890)
341 Magill Road, Trinity Gardens, Adelaide

AUSTRALIAN COUNCIL OF CHRISTIAN EDUCATION (1922)
100 Flinders Street, Melbourne, Victoria. Tel.: 63 5814

AUSTRALIAN COUNCIL OF CHURCHES
Room 2, 3rd Floor, 411 Kent Street, Sydney, N.S.W.
Gen. Sec.: The Rev. Harvey L. Perkins

AUSTRALIAN COUNCIL FOR THE WORLD COUNCIL OF CHURCHES
472 Kent Street, Sydney, New South Wales

AUSTRALIAN PRESBYTERIAN BOARD OF MISSIONS (1901)
Assembly Building, Margaret Street, Box 100, G.P.O., Sydney, New South Wales

AUSTRALIAN STUDENT CHRISTIAN MOVEMENT (1896)
Champion House, 57 Swanston Street, Melbourne, C.I., Victoria. Tel.: 63 3825

BAPTIST UNION OF AUSTRALIA
Baptist Church House, 486 Albert Street, Melbourne, C.2, Victoria. Tel.: 32 1046

BAPTIST UNION OF NEW SOUTH WALES
619 George Street, Sydney New South Wales

BAPTIST UNION OF QUEENSLAND
345 Ann Street, Brisbane, Queensland. Tel.: 2 734 3

BAPTIST UNION OF SOUTH AUSTRALIA
61 Flinders Street, Adelaide, South Australia

BAPTIST UNION OF TASMANIA
45 Brisbane Street, Launceston, Tasmania

BAPTIST UNION OF VICTORIA
486 Albert Street, East Melbourne, C.2, Victoria

BAPTIST UNION OF WESTERN AUSTRALIA, INC.
1320 Hay Street, West Perth, Western Australia. Tel.: 21 6072

BORNEO EVANGELICAL MISSION
Southern Cross Chambers, 317 Collins Street, Melbourne, C.1, Victoria

BRITISH AND FOREIGN BIBLE SOCIETY IN AUSTRALIA (1817)
P.O. Box 507, Canberra City, A.C.T. Tel.: 4 5209

CHRISTIAN RADIO MISSIONARY FELLOWSHIP (1946)
Box 5271, G.P.O., Sydney, New South Wales. Tel.: 417283

OCEANIA

CHRISTIAN SCIENCE COMMITTEE ON PUBLICATION FOR NEW SOUTH WALES
Box 3820, G.P.O., Sydney

CHURCH OF ENGLAND IN AUSTRALIA (1872)
Diocesan Church House, St. Andrew's Cathedral, George Street, Sydney, New South Wales
Australian Board of Missions (1850): 109 Cambridge Street, Stanmore, New South Wales. Tel.: Sydney 560 9422

CHURCH MISSIONARY SOCIETY OF AUSTRALIA (1825)
93 Bathurst Street, Sydney, New South Wales. Tel.: 61 9487

CONGREGATIONAL UNION OF AUSTRALIA
Independent Hall, Collins Street, Melbourne, C.1, Victoria

EVANGELICAL LUTHERAN CHURCH OF AUSTRALIA, INC. (1839)
37 Westall Street, Hyde Park, South Australia

EVANGELICAL MISSIONARY SOCIETY IN MAYURBHANJ
77 Merthyr Road, New Farm, Brisbane, Queensland

EVANGELISATION SOCIETY OF AUSTRALIA (1883)
4 Canning Street, Carlton, N.3, Victoria. Tel.: 34 1275

EVANGELISATION SOCIETY OF SOUTH AUSTRALIA INC.
66 Pirie Street, Adelaide, South Australia. Tel.: 23 5428

FEDERAL CONFERENCE OF CHURCHES OF CHRIST IN AUSTRALIA
College of the Bible, Elm Road, Glen Iris, S.E.6, Melbourne, Victoria

LONDON MISSIONARY SOCIETY
Chalmers House, 41 The Boulevard, Petersham, New South Wales

LUTHERAN MISSIONS, SYDNEY, AUSTRALIA
97 Bayview Avenue, Earlwood, Sydney, New South Wales

METHODIST CHURCH OF AUSTRALASIA
139 Castlereagh Street, Sydney, New South Wales. Tel.: 61 5073, 61 7301

METHODIST OVERSEAS MISSIONS (1855)
139 Castlereagh Street, Sydney, New South Wales. Tel.: 61 5073, 61 7301

MISSIONARY AVIATION FELLOWSHIP (1951)
P.O. Box 52, Box Hill, E.11, Victoria. Tel.: 89 4009

MISSIONARY FELLOWSHIP (N.S.W.)
92 Pitt Street, Sydney, New South Wales

MISSION TO THE BLIND OVERSEAS (1918)
United Insurance Buildings, 52 Queen Street, Melbourne. C.1, Victoria. Tel.: 62 6142

NATIONAL MISSIONARY COUNCIL OF AUSTRALIA (1926)
472 Kent Street, Sydney, New South Wales
Hon. Sec.: Rev. E. V. Newman

NEAR EAST AND ARABIAN MISSION
c/o Box 4024, G.P.O., Sydney, New South Wales

PRESBYTERIAN CHURCH OF AUSTRALIA
156 Collins Street, Melbourne, C.1, Victoria. Tel.: 63 9311

QUEENSLAND EVANGELISATION SOCIETY, INC. (1905)
Room 26, Brisbane Arcade, Brisbane, Queensland

RELIGIOUS SOCIETY OF FRIENDS (Quakers General Meeting for Australia)
Friends Home, 133 Orrong Road, Toorak, S.E.2, Victoria. Tel.: Melbourne 24 3595

SALVATION ARMY
140 Elizabeth Street, Sydney, New South Wales. Tel.: 26170
69 Bourke Street, Melbourne, C.1, Victoria. Tel.: 63 4851

SOUTH SEA EVANGELICAL MISSION LTD. (1904)
Eldon Chambers, 92 Pitt Street, Sydney, New South Wales. Tel.: 252 463

OCEANIA

SUDAN INTERIOR MISSION
59 Prospect Road, Summer Hill, New South Wales

UNITED ABORIGINES MISSION OF AUSTRALIA
262 Flinders Lane, Melbourne, C.1, Victoria. Tel.: 63 2506

UNITED CHURCH OF NORTH AUSTRALIA (1956)
Todd Street, Alice Springs, Western Australia

UNITED EVANGELICAL LUTHERAN CHURCH IN AUSTRALIA
54 O'Connell Street, North Adelaide, South Australia
Hope Vale Mission (1886): 12 Sydney Street, Nambour, Queensland. Tel.: Nambour 240
Finke River Mission (1877): 3 Charles Street, Tanunda, South Australia. Tel.: Tanunda 107
Lutheran Mission, New Guinea (1886): 32 Roderick Street, Ipswich, Queensland

VICTORIA ABORIGINAL GROUP (1930)
13 Gladstone Parade, Elsternwick, Melbourne, S.4, Victoria. Tel.: 53 2960

YOUNG MEN'S CHRISTIAN ASSOCIATION
Corner City Road and Sturt Street, Melbourne, S.C.4, Victoria. Tel.: MB 4151

YOUNG WOMEN'S CHRISTIAN ASSOCIATION
68 Powlett Street, East Melbourne, C.2, Victoria

COOK ISLANDS

COOK ISLANDS CHRISTIAN CHURCH
P.O. Box 93, Avarua, Rorotonga

FIJI ISLANDS

ANGLICAN CHURCH IN POLYNESIA (1908)
Bishop's House, Box 35, Suva. Tel.: 23436

FRENCH POLYNESIA

YOUNG MEN'S CHRISTIAN ASSOCIATION
U.C.J.G., Paofai, Papeete, Tahiti

GILBERT AND ELLICE ISLANDS

ELLICE ISLANDS CHURCH
Funafuti, Ellice Islands

GILBERT ISLAND PROTESTANT CHURCH
Antebuka, Tarawa, Gilbert Island

GUAM

CHRISTIAN SCIENCE COMMITTEE ON PUBLICATION
Station 16, Agana

NEW GUINEA

BAMU RIVER MISSION (1936)
Via P.O., Balimo, Western District, Papua

BIBLE SOCIETY
Bible House, Mary Street, Port Moresby, Papua

EVANGELICAL LUTHERAN CHURCH OF NEW GUINEA
Box 80, Lae Territory

PAPUA EKALESIA (1962)
P.O. Box 83, Port Moresby, Papua

WABAG LUTHERAN CHURCH
Wabag

PRESBYTERIAN CHURCH OF THE NEW HEBRIDES (1948)
Lamenu Island, via Vila

NEW ZEALAND

ASSOCIATED CHURCHES OF CHRIST IN NEW ZEALAND (1844)
P.O. Box 1354, Wellington

AUCKLAND MISSIONARY ASSOCIATION (1924)
Institute Place, 427 Queen Street, Box 1176, Auckland, C.1. Tel.: 44730

BAPTIST UNION OF NEW ZEALAND
P.O. Box 1773, Wellington, C.1

BRAZILIAN PRAYER FELLOWSHIP
P.O. Box 1780, Auckland C.1

BRITISH AND FOREIGN BIBLE SOCIETY, NEW ZEALAND, INC.
181–183 Upper Willis Street, (P.O. Box 930), Wellington. Tel.: Wellington 43 242

CHRISTIAN SCIENCE COMMITTEE ON PUBLICATION
P.O. Box 3553, Wellington

CHURCH OF ENGLAND MISSION TO MAORIS
P.O. Box 300, Hastings

CHURCH OF THE PROVINCE OF NEW ZEALAND (Church of England) (1857)
P.O. Box 800, Christchurch, C.1.

CONGREGATIONAL UNION OF NEW ZEALAND
67A Campbell Road, Onehunga, Auckland, S.E.5. Tel.: 566679

EVANGELICAL LUTHERAN CHURCH OF NEW ZEALAND (1907)
31 Hinemoa Street, Whakatane

GREEK ORTHODOX CHURCH OF NEW ZEALAND
3 Lloyd Street, Wellington

MELANESIAN MISSION (Church of the Province of New Zealand) (1894)
National Mutual Life Building, 41 Shortland Street, Auckland

METHODIST CHURCH OF NEW ZEALAND
Methodist Connexional Office: P.O. Box 931, Christchurch 1. Tel.: 79 178
(Christchurch)

METHODIST MISSIONARY SOCIETY OF NEW ZEALAND (1902)
Queen Street, P.O. Box 5023, Auckland. Tel.: 34 525 (Auckland)

NATIONAL COUNCIL OF CHURCHES IN NEW ZEALAND (1941)
P.O. Box 297, Christchurch, C.1. Tel.: 69 274
Gen. Sec.: Rev. David M. Taylor
Commission on Overseas Missions and Inter-Church Aid (1914): P.O. Box 297,
Christchurch C.1

NEW ZEALAND ANGLICAN BOARD OF MISSIONS INC. (1919)
Room 325, D.I.C. Buildings, Lambton Quay, Wellington. (G.P.O. Box 2050,
Wellington). Tel.: 43 923

NEW ZEALAND BAPTIST MISSIONARY SOCIETY (1885)
P.O. Box 6212, Wellington. Tel.: 50630 and 52018

NEW ZEALAND BAPTIST WOMEN'S MISSIONARY UNION
4 Cambourne Road, Sandringham, Auckland, S.W.1

NEW ZEALAND CHURCH MISSIONARY SOCIETY (1893)
167 Wairakei Road, Christchurch 5. Tel.: 516 415

NEW ZEALAND YEARLY MEETING, RELIGIOUS SOCIETY OF FRIENDS
14 Aranoni Track, Sumner, Christchurch 8. Tel.: SUM 6292

PRESBYTERIAN CHURCH OF NEW ZEALAND (1840)
Presbyterian Church Office, 114 The Terrace, P.O. Box 573, Wellington, C.1.
Tel.: 43 196
Overseas Missions Committee (1869): Presbyterian Missions Office, Box 110,
Auckland, C.1. Tel.: 48610
Maori Synod: Box 72, Whakatane, Auckland

OCEANIA

SALVATION ARMY
204 Cuba Street, Wellington. Tel.: 49 021

STUDENT CHRISTIAN MOVEMENT OF NEW ZEALAND (1896)
6 Hill Street, Box 742, Wellington, N.2. Tel.: 45 914

SUDAN INTERIOR MISSION
Institute Place, 427 Queen Street, Auckland, C.1

YOUNG MEN'S CHRISTIAN ASSOCIATION
276 Willis Street, Wellington, C.2. Tel.: 56 717

YOUNG WOMEN'S CHRISTIAN ASSOCIATION
Colonial Mutual Life Building, 123 Custom House Quay, Wellington, C.1

SAMOA

SAMOAN CHURCH
P.O. Box 468, Apia, Western Samoa

SOLOMON ISLANDS

MELANESIAN MISSION (Anglican Church of Melanesia) (1849)
P.O. Box 113, Honiara, Guadalcanal

TOKELAU ISLANDS

CHURCH IN TOKELAU (1861)
Tokelau

TONGA

CHURCH OF TONGA
P.O. Box 43, Nukualofa

INDEX

CONTENTS OF STATISTICAL AND DIRECTORY SECTIONS

The Statistical Section contains the returns of figures from churches and missions; the Directory Section gives the addresses of headquarters. See also the Index, pages 357–378.

Country	Statistics Page	Directory Page
AFRICA (*cont.*)		
Sudan	91	251
Swaziland	92	
Tanzania	92	252
Togo	94	252
Tunisia	94	
Uganda	95	252
United Arab Republic	95	252
Upper Volta	96	
Zambia	97	253
AMERICA, NORTH		
Bahamas	100	257
Barbados	101	257
Bermuda	101	
Br. Honduras	102	257
Canada	102	257
Cayman Islands	104	
Costa Rica	104	259
Cuba	105	260
Dominican Republic	107	
El Salvador	108	260
Greenland	111	
Guatemala	109	260
Haiti	110	261
Honduras	111	261
Jamaica	112	261
Leeward and Windward Islands	114	
Lesser Antilles (Guadeloupe)	115	
Mexico	115	261
Netherlands Antilles	117	262
Nicaragua	117	
Panama and Canal Zone	118	259
Puerto Rico	119	263
Trinidad and Tobago	119	263
United States of America	121	263
West Indies (Islands not listed above)	129	
AMERICA, SOUTH		
Argentina	130	278
Bolivia	132	278
Brazil	133	279
Chile	135	280
Colombia	136	281
Ecuador	137	282
Falkland Islands	138	283
French Guiana	139	
Guyana	139	283
Paraguay	140	283

Country	Statistics Page	Directory Page
Peru	141	283
Surinam	142	284
Uruguay	143	284
Venezuela	144	284
ASIA		
Aden	145	
Burma	145	286
Cambodia	146	286
Ceylon	147	286
China	148	287
Cyprus	148	287
Hong Kong	149	287
India	151	289
Indonesia	156	298
Iran	158	297
Iraq	159	297
Israel	159	298
Japan	161	299
Jordan	168	305
Korea	169	305
Kuwait	170	
Laos	170	
Lebanon	171	306
Macao	172	
Malaysia	172	306
Nepal	174	307
Okinawa	174	307
Pakistan	175	307
Philippines	177	308
Singapore	172	309
South Arabia and Persian Gulf	179	
Syria	179	309
Taiwan	180	310
Thailand	183	310
Turkey	184	310
Viet-Nam	184	311
Yemen	185	
EUROPE		
Austria	186	312
Belgium	187	312
Bulgaria	187	
Czechosolovakia	188	313
Denmark	188	314
Finland	189	315
France	190	316
Germany	191	318

INDEX

The number or numbers which are printed in heavier type indicate
the Directory Section.

The Preface, Introduction and Articles are not included in this Index.

357

American Marathi Mission, 151, **289**
American McAll Association, **264**
American Mission in Egypt, **252**
American Mission to Greeks, **264**
American Rescue Workers, 121, **264**
American Sunday School Union, **264**
American Tract Society, **264**
Anatolic Apostolic Church, 196
Ancient Orthodox Syrian Church, **306**
Andes Evangelical Mission, 132, **278**
Andhra Evangelical Lutheran Church, 151, **289**
Anglican Church, 60, 61, 65, 69, 70, 71, 72, 73, 75, 76, 78, 80, 82, 83, 84, 85, 87, 90, 92, 93, 97, 100, 101, 102, 103, 104, 113, 114, 120, 130, 135, 138, 139, 141, 148, 149, 159, 168, 169, 170, 171, 172, 175, 179, 195, 211, 212, 214, 215, 216, 219, **241,** **243, 244, 246, 247, 248, 249, 252,** **253, 257, 261, 263, 278, 280, 283,** **287, 297, 305, 306, 309, 310, 345,** **347, 348, 349**
Anglican Episcopal Church, 161, **299**
Anglicans, 220
Angola, 59, 60, 221, 226, **241**
Antioch Orthodox Church, 209, **264**
Anti-Slavery and Aborigines Protection Society, **323**
Apostolic Christian Church (Nazarean), 121, 161, **264, 280, 299**
Apostolic Christian Church of America, 124, **264**
Apostolic Church, 70, 82, 94, 112, 151, 188, 190, 194, 198, 200, 206, 215, 216, 217, **323**
Apostolic Church of Pentecost, 102, 151, 198, **299**
Apostolic Faith Church, 86, 121, **264,** **299**
Apostolic Faith Mission, 61, **249**
Apostolic Legation of the Holy See of Antioch in Malabar, **289**
Apostolic Lutheran Church, **264**
Apostolic Overcoming Holy Church of God, 121, **265**
Arabia, 179, 222
Arabic Literature Mission, **323**
Arbeitsgemeinschaft Christlicher Kirchen in Deutschland, **318**
Arbeitsgemeinschaft der Evang. Jugend, **318**
Arcot Evangelical Lutheran Church, 151, **289**
Argentina, 130, 131, 143, 224, 230, 234, **278**
Armenian (Brethren) Church, 9, 130
Armenian Church, 121, 160, 209, **265**
Armenian Evangelical Church, 130, 171, **252, 284**
Armenian Evangelical Congregational Church, 95
Armenian Gregorian Church, **252**
Armenian Orthodox Catholicossate of Cis, **306**
Armenian Orthodox Church, 207, **297**

Armenians, 234
Asambleas de Jesucristo, 136, **281**
Asia, 145–185, 220, 222, 226, 231, 234, 235, **286–311**
Asia Christian Colleges Association, **323**
Asociación Bautistas de la Selva, **281**
Asociación Bautista Centroamericana, 104
Asociación de Iglesias Biblicas Costar-rincenses, 104
Asociación Misionera Evangélica Nacional, **283**
Assemblées de France, 63
Assemblies of God, 61, 64, 66, 67, 70, 71, 73, 74, 76, 78, 84, 85, 86, 92, 94, 95, 96, 100, 102, 104, 106, 107, 108, 109, 110, 111, 112, 115, 117, 121, 130, 132, 133, 135, 136, 137, 139, 140, 141, 142, 143, 144, 145, 149, 151, 156, 158, 159, 161, 168, 169, 171, 172, 174, 175, 177, 179, 180, 186, 187, 190, 191, 194, 196, 197, 198, 200, 202, 204, 206, 207, 208, 209, 211, 213, 218, 219, **248, 249,** **259, 265, 279, 281, 283, 287, 289,** **294, 299, 309, 323, 345**
Associate Reformed Presbyterian Church, 127, 175, **265**
Associated Churches of Christ in New Zealand, **348**
Associated Church Press, **265**
Association Auxilliare des Missions Lutheriennes, **316**
Association des Eglises Libres de Norvége, 64
Association Evangélique des Eglises Baptistes de Langue Française, **341**
Association for the Free Distribution of the Scriptures, **323**
Association of Baptists for World Evangelism, 135, 141, 176, 178, **265,** **299**
Association of Christian Publications, **299**
Association of Evangelical Churches of the Lulonga, **241**
Auckland Missionary Association, 217, **348**
Audio-Visual Evangelism, **287, 299**
Augustana Lutheran Church, 143, **257**
Australia, 209, 210, 225, 232, **345**
Australia Aborigines Mission, 209, **345**
Australian Baptist Mission, 155, 176, **345**
Australian Board of Missions (Anglican), 160, 169
Australian Christian Youth Council, **345**
Australian Churches of Christ, 151, **345**
Australian Council for the World Council of Churches, **345**
Australian Council of Christian Educa-tion, **345**
Australian Presbyterian Board of Mis-sions, 158, 169, 215, **345**
Austria, 186, 223, 232, **312**
Austrian Bible Mission, **323**
Azores, 203

Christian and Missionary Alliance, 65, 66, 69, 71, 96, 102, 115, 119, 122, 130, 135, 136, 137, 141, 149, 151, 158, 159, 170, 171, 177, 180, 181, 183, 185, **266**, **281**, **288**, **290**, **298**

Christian Apostolic Church in Zion of South Africa, **249**

Christian Assemblies, 63, 153, 173, **309**

Christian Brethren, 86, 136, 173

Christian Brotherhood Church, 161, **299**

Christian Canaan Church, 161, **299**

Christian Catholic Church, 122, **266**, **299**

Christian Children's Fund, **266**

Christian Churches (Disciples) (see Disciples of Christ)

Christian Churches' Educational Association, 244

Christian Churches, Japan, 161, **299**

Christian Church of North America, 124, **266**

Christian Cinema and Religious Film Society, 324

Christian Colportage Association, **324**

Christian Congregation, 124, **266**

Christian Council of: (see also Council of Churches in, National Christian Council of, and United Christian Council of): Bahamas, **257**; Burma, **286**; Hong Kong, **288**; Kenya, **244**; Malagasy Rep., **245**; Malawi, **246**; Malaya, **309**; Mozambique, **246**; Nigeria, **247**; Okinawa, **307**; Pakistan, **307**; Rhodesia, **248**; South Africa, **249**; Tanzania, **252**; Uganda, **252**; Zambia, **253**

Christian Educational Council of South India, **290**

Christian Endeavour Union, 303, **324**

Christian Fellowship, 175, 176

Christian Frontier Council, **324**

Christian Holy Convention, 161, **299**

Christian Institute for the Study of Religion and Society, **290**

Christian Literature Crusade, 217, **266**, **324**

Christian Literature Society (or Council), **288**, **290**, **299**

Christian Medical Association, **290**

Christian Medical College, Vellore, **290**

Christian Medical Society, **266**

Christian Methodist Episcopal Church, 70, 80, 125, **266**

Christian Mission Fellowship, 67

Christian Missionary Alliance, 77

Christian Missions in Many Lands, 60, 63, 66, 67, 89, 92, 94, 96, 97, 100, 107, 130, 133, 135, 139, 140, 141, 144, 160, 170, 180, **266**, **324**

Christian Nationals' Evangelism Commission, 109, 150, 172, 173, 178, 182, 183, **266**

Christian Oriental Salvation Church, **300**

Christian Radio Missionary Fellowship, 210, 215, **345**

Christian Reformed Church, 81, 106, 127, 133, 161, 180, **266**

Christian Rural Fellowship, **266**

Christian Scientists (see Church of Christ, Scientist)

Christian Spiritual Body (or Church), 161, **300**

Christian Teamwork, **325**

Christian Tract and Book Society, **290**

Christian Union, 122, **266**

Christkatholische Kirche der Schweiz, 206, **341**

Christoffel Blinden missionim Orient, **318**

Christu Das Ashram, **290**

Chrzescijanska Akademica Teologiczna, **338**

Chung Hua . . ., **287**, **288**

Church Army, 195, **325**

Church Council of Iran, **297**

Churches' Council of Healing, **325**

Churches of Christ (Disciples) (see Disciples of Christ)

Churches of Christ in Christian Union, 123

Churches of Christ in Gt. Britain and Ireland, **325**

Churches of God in N. America (General Eldership), 123, **266**

Churches' Television Centre, **325**

Church in Tokelau, 218, **349**

Church in Wales, 194, **325**

Church Missionary Society, 73, 81, 85, 91, 95, 155, 168, 209, **325**

Church Missionary Society (Australian), 93, 142, 150, 158, 167, 173, 174, 176, **346**

Church of Central Africa (Presbyterian), 76, 79, 82, **246**

Church of Christ, 65, 67, 75, 80, 82, 91, 93, 96, 123, 124, 133, 149, 152, 161, 169, 170, 173, 177, 178, 183, 209, 215, 216, **266**, **279**, **288**, **300**, **308**, **310**

Church of Christ (Holiness), 122, **266**

Church of Christ Missions, 87, **253**

Church of Christ, Scientist, 100, 101, 103, 113, 116, 119, 120, 131, 135, 139, 142, 143, 144, 150, 158, 167, 173, 175, 186, 187, 189, 191, 193, 195, 196, 198, 199, 201, 205, 206, 210, 213, 217, **243**, **244**, **246**, **247**, **248**, **249**, **257**, **258**, **259**, **261**, **262**, **263**, **266**, **278**, **279**, **280**, **283**, **284**, **288**, **290**, **295**, **300**, **307**, **308**, **309**, **312**, **315**, **316**, **318**, **324**, **331**, **333**, **334**, **336**, **339**, **341**, **346**, **347**, **348**

Church of Christ, Temple Lot, **266**

Church of Cyprus, 149, **287**

Church of England (see also Anglican Church), 87, 100, 194, 209, 217, **249**, **257**, **325**, **346**

Church of England Mission to Maoris, **348**

Church of Faith, 96

Church of God, 72, 74, 95, 112, 115, 122, 123, 133, 135, 140, 141, 151, 163, 169, 171, 175, 176, 179, 198, 207, **244**, **259**, **266**, **280**, **282**, **290**, **301**

361

Church of God (Abrahamic Faith), 121, 266
Church of God (Anderson, Ind.), 100, 104, 106, 107, 111, 113, 119, 123, 139, 253, 266
Church of God and Saints of Christ, 123, 266
Church of God as Organized by Christ, 124
Church of God by Faith, 123, 266
Church of God (Cleveland), 59, 60, 80, 81, 96, 100, 101, 104, 105, 106, 107, 108, 109, 110, 111, 113, 114, 115, 117, 118, 119, 120, 122, 129, 130, 132, 133, 135, 136, 139, 140, 141, 143, 151, 161, 168, 177, 179, 190, 191, 194, 196, 197, 199, 204, 212, 259, 266
Church of God (Holiness), 115, 123, 266
Church of God in Christ, 123, 267
Church of God in Christ (Mennonite), 125, 267
Church of God of Prophecy, 85, 100, 101, 104, 106, 107, 109, 110, 113, 115, 119, 123, 129, 130, 141, 148, 196, 217, 267
Church of God (Seventh Day), 123, 267
Church of Grace, 96
Church of Greece, 332
Church of Illumination, 123, 267
Church of India, Pakistan, Burma and Ceylon, 145, 147, 152, 175, 286, 290, 307
Church of Ireland, 198, 333
Church of Jesus Christ (Bickertonites), 124, 267
Church of Jesus Christ of Latter-Day Saints, 89, 124, 162, 194, 205, 216, 217, 267, 300, 325
Church of Nepal, 174, 307
Church of Our Lord Jesus Christ of the Apostolic Faith, 123, 267
Church of Revelation, 267
Church of Scotland, 70, 73, 76, 81, 97, 100, 101, 113, 120, 130, 135, 145, 147, 155, 160, 176, 179, 194, 201, 298, 325
Church of South Arabia, 145
Church of South India, 147, 152, 183, 286, 290
Church of Sweden, 89, 173, 205
Church of the Brethren, 81, 122, 137, 199, 267
Church of the East and of the Assyrians, 267
Church of the East in India, 290
Church of the Living God, 123
Church of the Lutheran Brethren of America, 125, 267
Church of the Nazarene, 63, 76, 79, 82, 87, 92, 97, 101, 102, 105, 106, 108, 109, 110, 111, 114, 115, 117, 118, 119, 120, 123, 130, 132, 133, 135, 139, 141, 143, 152, 159, 162, 168, 169, 171, 174, 177, 179, 181, 188, 191, 194, 199, 205, 206, 209, 215, 216, 218, 262, 267, 298, 300, 325

Church of the Province of . . . (see Anglican Church)
Church of the Resurrected Christ, 162, 300
Church of the United Brethren in Christ (see United Brethren in Christ)
Church of Tonga, 219, 349
Church of Uganda, 95
Church Pastoral Aid Society, 325
Church Publicity and Service Centre, 325
Church's Ministry Among the Jews, 67, 95, 158, 159, 197, 198, 298, 325
Church World Service, 272, 302
C.I.M.A.D.E., 316
Circulo de Cristianos Universitarios, 284
Colombia, 136, 137, 224, 230, 281
Colombia Evangelistic Mission, 258
Comité Consultor de Cooperación en la Obra Cristiana en Chile, 280
Comité Intermissionnaire de Madagascar, 245
Comité Protestant des Amities Françaises a l'Etranger, 316
Commissie tot Vertegenwoordiging in Nederland van de Protestantse Kerk in Indonesie, 334
Commission d'Enseignement Religieux d'Afrique du Nord, 241
Commission of the Churches on International Affairs, 240
Committee on Christian Literature for Women and Children in Mission Fields, 267
Commonwealth and Continental Church Society, 325
Commonwealth Missionary Society, 325
Commonwealth Covenant Church, 216, 217
Community Church, 149, 253
Community of St. Mary the Virgin, 325
Community of the Resurrection, 101, 195, 249, 325
Comoro Islands, 221
Comparative Christian Statistics, 226
Concilio Evangélico de Chile, 280
Concilio Nacional Evangélico del Peru, 283
Confederación Evangélica de Colombia, 281
Conference of Churches of Christ in Western India, 290
Conference of Missionary Societies in Gt. Britain and Ireland, 325
Conference of the Evangelical Mennonite Church, 125
Conferencia Concordia de Mexico, 262
Confucians, 233, 236
Congo (Brazzaville), 64, 221
Congo (Kinshasa), 64, 65, 66, 221, 227, 229, 241, 254
Congo Evangelistic Mission, 66, 325
Congo Gospel Mission, 64
Congo Inland Mission, 66, 267
Congo Protestant Relief Agency, 267
Congregaçao Crista de Portugal, 202

364

Good News Trailer Missionary Fellowship, 135, 142, 198, **327**
Good Shepherd Agricultural Mission, 174, **291**
Gorakpur Nurseries Fellowship, **291**
Gospel Church, 170, 183
Gospel Films, **269**
Gospel Furthering Fellowship, 72, 93, **244**
Gospel Missionary Union, 77, 78, 137
Gospel Mission of South America, **327**
Gospel of Jesus Church, 163, **300**
Gospel Recordings, **269**
Gospel Tabernacle Christian Church, 157
Gossner-Evangelical-Lutheran Church, 153, **291**
Gossners Mission, **321**
Great Britain, 194, 223, 232, **323**
Greater Europe Mission, 186, 193, 196, 199, 205, **269**
Greater World Christian Spiritualist League, **327**
Greece, 196, 223, 232, 235, **331**
Greek Evangelical Church, 96, 196, **332**
Greek Orthodox Church: Patriarchate of Alexandria, **253**; Antioch, **309**; Jerusalem, **305**; Thyateira and Gt. Britain, **327**
Greenland, 111, 189, 223
Guadeloupe, 115, 224
Guam, 213, **347**
Guatemala, 109, 224, 230, **260, 261**
Guinea, 71, 221, 233
Gustav-Adolf-Werk, **321**
Guyana, 120, 139, 224, 234, **283**

Haiti, 110, 224, 230, **261**
Haiti Inland Mission, **261**
Hanover Evangelical Lutheran Free Church Mission, 87, **322**
Heap Gay Mission, 149
Heart of Africa Mission, 65
Hebrew Christian Alliance, 189
Hebrew Christian Testimony to Israel, 135, 160, 191, 193, 195, **327**
Hebrew Evangelization Society, **327**
Helluntai-Ystävät, **315**
Henry Martyn School of Islamic Studies, **291**
Herättäjä-Yhdistys, **315**
Hermannsburger Evangelisch-Lutherische Mission, 68, 89, **321**
Herrnhuter Missions, **321**
Hervormde Raad Voor Kerk en Israel, 160, **334**
Hildesheimer Blinden-Mission, 150, **321**
Hindus, 233, 236
Hindustan Bible Institute, **269**
Hindustani Covenant Church, 153, **291**
Holiness Church, 181, **280**
Holiness Methodist Church, 126
Holy Catholic Church, 174
Holy Cross Liberian Mission, **270**
Holy Jesus Society, 163, **301**
Holy Spirit Association, 163, **301**

Home Missionary Society of India, **291**
Honduras, 111, 112, 224, 230, **261**
Hong Kong, 149, 222, 231, **287**
Hong Kong Christian Welfare, **288**
Hong Kong Doctors Christian Association, **288**
HOREMCO, **301**
House of God, Which is the Church of the Living God, the Pillar and the Ground of Truth, 123, **270**
Hua Pei Chi Tuh Chiao Kung Li Hui, **287**
Hungarian Bible Council, **332**
Hungarian Reformed Church, 127, **270**
Hungary, 197, 223, 232, **332**
Huria Kristen Batak Protestan, 157, **295**
Huria Kristen Indonesia, 157
Hutterian Brethren, 125, **270**

Iceland, 198, 223, **332**
Icelandic Mission Society, 68, **332**
Iglesia Catolica Filipine Independiente, **308**
Iglesia Cristiana del Norte, 136
Iglesia Cruzada Evangelica, 136
Iglesia de Dios (Universal), 105
Iglesia Evangélica Crucea Moravia, **260**
Iglesia Evangélica Espanola, 204, **339**
Iglesia Evangélica Metodista en las Islas Filipinas, **308**
Iglesia Evangélica Nacional, 105
Iglesia Evangélica Unida de Cristo, **308**
Iglesia Evangélica Valdense, 130, 143
Iglesias Evangelicas Unidas, **279**
Iglesias Pentecostales Autónomas, **283**
Igreja Cristã Evangelica Brasileira, **279**
Igreja Cristã Evangelica do Brasil, **279**
Igreja Cristã Reformada do Brasil, **279**
Igreja de Cristo em Manica e Sofala, **247**
Igreja Lusitana Catolica-Apostolica-Evangélica, 60, 203, **338**
Immanual General Mission (or Church), 163, **301**
Independent Baptists, 97
Independent Board for Presbyterian Foreign Missions, 72, 109, 134, 135, 168, 179, 181, 182, **270**
Independent Church(es), 116, 124, 136, 167, 177, 181
Independent Evangelical Church(es), 59, 116, 153, **292**
Independent Evangelical Lutheran, 193
Independent Fellowship, 203
Independent Fundamental Churches of America, 124, **270**
Independent Methodist Churches, 195, **327**
Independent Negro Churches, 124
Independent Pentecostals, 126
Independent Presbyterian Church, 133, **280**
India, 151, 222, 231, 234, **289**
India Bible Christian Council, **291**
India Bible Mission Church, 153, **291**
India Christian Assemblies, **291**
India Christian Mission, **291**

India Gospel Fellowship Mission, **292**
India Industrial Mission, **292**
India Mission, 153
Indian Christian Church, 87
Indian Church Aid Association, 176, **327**
Indian Forces' Scripture Readers' Fellowship, **292**
Indian Missionary Society of Tirunelvelli, **292**
India United Evangelical Mission, 153, **292**
Indonesia, 156, 222, 231, 234, **295**
Industrial Christian Fellowship, **327**
Innere Mission und Hilfswerk der Evangelischen Kirche in Deutschland, **321**
Institute of Rural Life at Home and Overseas, **327**
Instituto Biblico Peruano, **283**
Inter-American Missionary Society (see also Oriental Missionary Society), 110, 116, 134, 137
Interdenominational Foreign Mission Association of North America, **270**
Interior India Mission, **292**
Inter-Mission Business Office, **292**
Inter-Mission Council, **242**
Inter-Mission Fellowship of Ecuador, **282**
International Bible Reading Association, **327**
International Christian Church, **301**
International Christian Leadership, **301**
International Church of the Four-Square Gospel, 80, 87, 105, 106, 111, 116, 117, 118, 124, 129, 132, 134, 135, 136, 196, **260, 270, 282, 301**
International Congregational Council, **239**
International Convention of Christian Churches (see Disciples)
International Council of Christian Churches, **239**
International Fellowship of Evangelical Students, **239, 270**
International Gospel League, **301**
International Grenfell Association, 103, **258**
International Hebrew Christian Alliance, 160, **298, 327**
International Holiness Mission, 79, 89
International Missions, 72, 142, 158, 176, 178, **270, 297**
International Mission to Miners, 89, 135, 167, 173, 186, 187, 191, 193, 195, 203, 204, **327**
International Pentecostal Assemblies, 126, **270**
International Society of Christian Endeavour, **270**
International Society for Evangelization of Jews, **327**
International Students Service, **270**
Inter-Varsity Christian Fellowship, **270, 300**

Inter-Varsity Fellowship of Evangelical Unions, **327**
Iran, 158, 222, 231, 234, **297**
Iraq, 159, 222, 231, 235, **297**
Ireland, 198, 223, 232, **332**
Irian, 156, 157, 222
Irish and Scotch Reformed Presbyterian Mission, **333**
Irish Baptist Foreign Mission, 131, 141
Israel, 159, 222, 231, 235, **298**
Isthmian Religious Workers' Federation, **259**
Italy, 198, 223, 232, **333**
Ivory Coast, 71, 221, 227, 233, **243, 254**

Jains, 223, 234
Jamaica, 112, 113, 224, 230, **261**
Japan, 161, 222, 231, 235, **299**
Japan Advent Christian Church, 163, **300**
Japan Alliance Church, 163, **300**
Japan Bible Christian Council, **301**
Japan Christian Academy, **301**
Japan Christian Medical Association, **301**
Japan Christian Presbyterian Church, 163
Japan Christian Yearbook, 167
Japan Christ Society, 163, **301**
Japan Evangelical Mission, 163, **302**
Japan Evangelistic Band, 163, **302, 327**
Japan Evangelistic Gospel Church, 163, **302**
Japan Gospel Church, 163, **302**
Japan Gospel Federation, **302**
Japan Gospel League Church of Christ, 164, **302**
Japan Gospel of Christ Church, 164, **302**
Japan Holiness Church, 164, **302**
Japan Inland Mission, 164
Japan International Christian University Foundation, **270**
Japan Jesus Christ Church, 164, **302**
Japan Overseas Christian Medical Service, 174, **303**
Japan Rural Mission Emmanual Christ Church, 165, **303**
Japan Society of Christian Studies, **303**
Jednota Ceskobratrska, 188, **313**
Jerusalem and the East Mission, 67, 145, 149, 158, 159, 160, 168, 179, 180, **298, 327**
Jerusalemverein, 168, **321**
Jewish Population, 229, 232
Jeypore Evangelical Lutheran Church, 153, **292**
J. L. Schneller Schule, **306**
John G. Paton Mission, 215, **328**
John Milton Society, **270**
Jordan, 168, 222, 235, **305**
Jugendkammer der Evangelischen Kirche in Deutschland, **321**
Jungle Tribes Mission, 153
Junta Evangelica Nacional, Ecuador, **282**
Juventude Evangelica Portuguesa, **338**

Karmel Institutett, 336
Kenya, 72, 221, 227, 229, 233, **243, 254**
Kerk van Christus onder die Tiv in die Soedan, **247**
Kherwara-Missionen, **314**
Kokusai Fukuin Senkyoo Dan, 165
Komisi Kesahatan dan Sosial, **297**
Komisi Pekabaran Indjil, **297**
Komisi Sekolah Minggu, **297**
Komitin'ny Isan-enim-Bolana, **245**
Kontaktkretsen, **336**
Korea, 169 222 **305**
Korean Christian Church, 165, 169
Korean Church of Christ in Japan, **303**
Korean Holiness Church, 169
Korean Lutheran Mission, 169, **305**
Koryu Presbiterian, 169
Kosciol Ewangelicko-Augsburski W Polse, 202, **338**
Kotagiri Medical Fellowship, **292**
Krestanska Reformovana Cirkev na Slovensku, **313**
Kristelig Laegeforening, **336**
Kuwait, 170, 222
Kvindelige Missions Arbejdere, **314, 336**
Kvinnliga Missionsarbetare, 171, **340**

Labrador, 103
Laegmandsbevaegelse, **314**
Laerinnenes Misjonsforbund, 150, 155, 160, 167, 182, **314, 336**
Lahore Church Council, 176
Lakher Pioneer Mission, 145
Lambeth Conference, **239, 323**
Ländli-Mission in Ruanda, **342**
Laos, 170, 222
Lärarinnornas Missionsförening, **340**
Last Reapers, **328**
Latin America Mission, 105, **270**
Latin American Lutheran Mission, **270**
Latin American Prayer Fellowship, 116
Latter-day Saints (see Church of Jesus Christ of . . .)
Latvian Lutheran Church, 207, **343**
Lebanon, 171, 179, 222, 231, 235, **306**
Lebanon Evangelical Mission, 171, **328**
Lee Memorial Mission, 150, 155, **292**
Leeward and Windward Islands, 114
Leiterkreis der Evang. Akademien, **321**
Lembaga Al Kitab Indonesia, **297**
Lembaga Audio-Visual Aids, **297**
Leprosy Mission, 174, **293, 328**
Lesotho, 73, 221
Lesser Antilles, 115
Liberal Catholic Church, 209, **270**
Liberia, 74, 221, 233, **244**
Liberian Baptist Missionary and Educational Convention, 74, **245**
Liberian Inland Mission, 74, **245**
Librairie Evangélique au Congo, **242**
Libya, 75, 221, 229, 233
Liebenzeller Mission, 165, 182, 215, **303, 321**
Liga Argentina de Mujeres Evangélicas, **278**

Liga de Oración en Missón Mundial, **279**
Liga Evangélica de Acção Missionaria e Educational, **338**
Ligue pour la Lecture de la Bible, **242, 313**
Literature Mission, 292
Lithuanian Lutheran Church, 343
Little Flock Church, 181
Living Water Christian Church, 165, **303**
London City Mission, **328**
London Missionary Society, 61, 75, 82, 87, 97, 173, 211, 212, 214, 218, **245, 248, 328, 346**
Lord's Day Observance Society, **328**
Lord Wharton's Charity, **328**
Luanza Mission, 66
Ludhiana British Fellowship, **328**
Lutheran Brethren of America, 63
Lutheran Brethren Mission (or Church), 62, 63, 165, 181, **241, 303**
Lutheran Church(es), 68, 72, 74, 75, 97, 116, 118, 120, 125, 132, 135, 144, 154, 155, 171, 173, 175, 177, 181, 182, 193, 198, 207, 215, **242, 244, 245, 253, 260, 262, 270, 278, 283, 285, 287, 294, 303, 306, 307, 308, 310, 314, 321, 332, 333, 343, 347**
Lutheran Church of Christ in the Sudan, **247**
Lutheran Church, Missouri Synod, 70, 105, 106, 108, 109, 115, 131, 134, 140, 143, 144, 149, 165, **258, 259, 260, 261, 270, 280, 283, 288**
Lutheran Congregations, Haifa and Tel Aviv, 159
Lutheran Council of Gt. Britain, 195, **328**
Lutheran Evangelical Association, 167
Lutheran Free Church, **258**
Lutheran Missions, 159, 160, 165, 215, **346**
Lutheran World Federation, 136, **239**
Lutheran(s), 220
Luthersk Missionsforening, **314**
Lutherske Afrikamisjon, **336**
Luxembourg, 199, 223, 232, **334**

Macao, 172, 222
Madeira, 203
Madjelis Pemuda Kristen Oikumenis, **297**
Madjelis Pusat Pendidikan Kristen, **297**
Magyar Evangeliumi Keresztyen Diakszovetseg, **332**
Mahon Mission, 89, **250, 270**
Malabar Independent Syrian Church, 153, **292**
Malagasy Friends Church, **245**
Malagasy Republic, 75, 221, 228, 233, **244, 255**
Malankara Jacobite Syrian Church, **292**
Malawi, 76, 221, 228, **246, 255**
Malaya, 172
Malaya Synod of the Chinese Christian Church, **309**

Malaysia, 172, 173, 222, 235, **306**
Mali, 77, 221, 233, **246**
Malta, 223, 232
Malwa Church Council, 174
Mandliyon Ki Pratinidhi Kamiti, **292**
Mannerarbeit der Evang. Kirche, **321**
Maoris, 217
Mariavites Church, **338**
Mar Thoma Syrian Church, 153, 173, 174, **292, 309**
Maranatha Mission, **292**
Marburger Mission, 165, 182, 183, **321**
Marshall Islands, 213
Martinique, 224
Masihi Isha'at Khana, **307**
Masihi Mandli, **292**
Mauritania, 77, 221, 233
Mauritius, 77, 221, **246**
Medical Missionary Association, **328**
Melanesian Mission, **348, 349**
Mennonite(s), 63, 207, **242, 321**
Mennonite Board of Missions and Charities, 70, 131, 160, 174, 195, 199, **270, 328**
Mennonite Brethren Church, 65, 66, 103, 116, 125, 133, 136, 140, 141, 153, 164, 186, 193, **271, 279, 281, 292, 302, 312**
Mennonite Central Committee, **312**
Mennonite Church, 65, 68, 70, 93, 105, 119, 125, 164, 187, 193, 206, **260, 271, 292, 322, 334**
Mennonite Church, General Conference, 125, 153, 163, 181, **271, 282, 291, 300**
Mennonite Mission(s), 59, 68, 102, 137, 184, 190, 193, 199, **313, 319**
Mennonite World Conference, **239**
Meseret Christes Church, **243**
Messianic Assembly in Israel, 160
Methodist Aborigine Work, 209
Methodist Baptist Church, **279**
Methodist Church, 59, 61, 65, 66, 67, 69, 70, 71, 72, 73, 74, 79, 81, 82, 85, 87, 90, 91, 94, 100, 101, 102, 105, 110, 111, 113, 114, 116, 118, 119, 120, 129, 131, 132, 134, 135, 139, 141, 143, 146, 147, 150, 153, 157, 169, 173, 175, 177, 181, 186, 187, 189, 190, 193, 195, 197, 198, 199, 200, 201, 202, 203, 205, 206, 207, 208, 209, 211, 216, 217, 219, **241, 242, 243, 244, 247, 248, 250, 260, 262, 278, 280, 281, 284, 286, 292, 295, 305, 307, 309, 312, 313, 321, 328, 332, 333, 336, 338, 340, 348**
Methodist Church of Australia, 211, **346**
Methodist Church of South Africa, 79, 87, 92, **250**
Methodist Church in the U.S.A. (also see Methodist Church), 74, 79, 82, 105, 106, 119, 126, 146, 150, 155, 158, 167, 174, 175, 176, 182, **271**
Methodist Episcopal Church, 79, **247**
Methodistkirkens Misjonsselskap, 59, 60, 150, **315, 336**

Methodist Mission, 215, 218
Methodist Missionary Society, 67, 69, 70, 71, 73, 81, 85, 91, 97, 110, 113, 117, 120, 146, 173, 191, **328, 348**
Methodist Overseas Church, 218, 219
Methodist Pentecostal Church, 135, **281**
Methodists, 220
Metropolitan Church Association, **271**
Mexican Indian Mission, 116, **262**
Mexican Militant Mission, **271**
Mexican Mission of the Churches of Christ, **262**
Mexico, 115, 230, **261**
Mexico Christian Mission, **262**
Mid-African Mission (see Baptist Mid-Missions)
Middle East General Mission, 68, **328**
Middle East Lutheran Ministry, **306**
Mid-India Yearly Meeting (see also Friends), **292**
Mildmay Mission to the Jews, **328**
Mindolo Ecumenical Foundation, **253**
Mino Mission, 165, **303**
Misión Evangélica de los Hermanos, **281**
Misión Evangélica Nacional, **281**
Misión Evangélica Pentecostal, **281**
Mision Indigena de Sur America, 137
Misión Panamericana, 137
Missionary and Soul-Winning Fellowship, **271**
Missionary Aviation Fellowship, 112, 135, 138, 139, 142, 144, 170, 178, 215, 218, **244, 271, 328, 346**
Missionary Bands of the World, 113, 154
Missionary Church Association, 85, 107, 110, 113, 116, 124, 137, **248, 271**
Missionary Church of Brazil, 134
Missionary Fellowship, **346**
Missionary Research Library, 184, **272**
Missionary Strategy Agency, **271**
Mission Biblique en Côte d'Ivoire, 71, **317, 342**
Mission Covenant Church of Sweden, 165, **303**
Missión Cristiana Española, 204
Mission der Frauen-und-Mädchen-Bibel-Kreise, **321**
Mission Evangélique au Laos, **342**
Mission Evangélique Belge, 63, 187, **313**
Mission Evangélique des Alpes, 190
Mission Evangélique du Maniema, 66
Mission Evangélique Elim, 63
Mission Evangélique en Guyane Française, **342**
Mission Franco-Suisse de Pentecôte, 63
Mission Medicale Evangélique du Levant, **309**
Mission Philafricaine, 60, 135, **342**
Mission Populaire Evangélique de France, 190, **317**
Mission Suisse dans l'Afrique du Sud, 79, 89, **342**
Mission to Europe's Millions, **271**
Mission to Indian Villages, **293**
Mission to Lepers (see Leprosy Mission)

370

371

373

Reformed Church(es)–*cont.*
202, 203, 209, **244, 274, 295, 304,
332, 338**
Reformed Episcopal Church, 127, 154,
204, **258, 274, 339**
Reformed Helvetic Church of Austria,
186
Reformed Methodist Union Episcopal
Church, 126, **274**
Reformed Pentecostal Church, 167
Reformed Presbyterian Church, 103,
104, 127, 142, 154, 168, 169, 179,
182, 195, 198, **274, 329, 333**
Reformed Zion Union Apostolic Church,
126, **274**
Reformierter Bund, **322**
Regions Beyond Missionary Union, 66,
141, 154, 157, 174, **329**
Regular Baptists, 65, **303**
Religion in American Life, **274**
Religious Society of Friends (see
Friends)
Remonstrantse Broederchap, 200, **335**
Reorganized Church of Jesus Christ of
Latter-day Saints, 124, **274**
Reunion, 221
Revival Centre, 173
Rheinische Missionsgesellschaft, 157,
322
Rhodesia, 82, 83, 221, 228, 229, **248, 255**
Rolland Mission, 59, **241**
Roman Catholics, 100, 103, 160, 186,
195, 197, 205, 217, 221, 226
Romanian Orthodox Episcopate in
America, **274**
Ronga Tsonga Presbyterian Church, 247
Royal National Mission to Deep Sea
Fishermen, **329**
Royal Sailors' Rests, **329**
Ruanda Mission, 61, 83, **329**
Rumania, 203, 223, 232, **339**
Rural Gospel Mission, **294**
Russia (see U.S.S.R.)
Russia and Border States Mission, **329**
Russian Orthodox Catholic Church, **274**
Russian Orthodox Church, 207, 209, **343**
Russian Orthodox Church Outside
Russia, **274**
Russian Orthodox Greek Catholic
Church in North America, **274**
Russian Student Christian Movement
Outside Russia, **317**
Rwanda, 82, 221, **248**

Saalem-Seurakunta, 189, **315**
Sabah, 172
Sahara Desert Mission, 59, **330**
Salem Mission, 88
Sällskapet för Evangelii Utbredande
Bland Slaviska, **340**
Salvation Army, 59, 64, 70, 72, 81, 83,
88, 93, 97, 100, 103, 105, 107, 110,
120, 127, 131, 135, 139, 142, 143,
146, 147, 150, 154, 157, 166, 169,
173, 176, 177, 189, 193, 195, 197,
200, 201, 205, 206, 210, 216, 217,

241, 243, 244, 247, 248, 251, 258,
261, 274, 278, 280, 284, 286, 288,
294, 295, 304, 305, 307, 308, 309,
312, 314, 315, 316, 321, 330, 334,
337, 340, 342, 346, 349
Sambi Church, 166, **304**
Samoa, 218, 225, **349**
Samoan Church, **349**
Samosir Zending, 335
Santal Mission of the Northern
Churches, 174, **274, 337**
Sao Tome, 221
Sarawak, 172
Saudi Arabia, 222
Schleswig-Holsteinische Evangelisch-
Lutherische Missionsgesellschaft
zu Breklum, **322**
Schreudermisjonen, 337
Schweizer Evangeliumdient in Israel, **342**
Schweizer Hilfsverein für das Albert-
Schweitzer-Spital, **342**
Schweizer Indianer Mission, 142, **342**
Schweizerische Evangelische Juden-
mission, **342**
Schweizerische Missionsgemeinschaft,
342
Schweizerische Pfingstmissions-Gesell-
schaft, **342**
Schweizerische Zigeuner-Mission, **343**
Schweizerischen Ostasien-Mission, 167
342
Schweizerischer Evangelischer Kir-
chenbund, **343**
Schweizerischer Evangelischer Missions-
rat, **343**
Schweizerischer Evangelischer Nilland-
Mission, 68, 91, 96, **342**
Schweizerischer Hilfsbund für Christ-
liches Liebeswerk im Orient, **343**
Schweizerischer Verein für Evangelische
Mohammedaner Mission, **343**
Schwenkfelder Church in the U.S.A.,
127, **274**
Scots' Memorial Church, **298**
Scripture Gift Mission, **258, 294, 330**
Scripture Union, **244, 294, 330, 338, 343**
Second Cumberland Presbyterian
Church, 127, **274**
Selbständige Evangelisch-Lutherische
Kirche, 193, **322**
Senegal, 84, 221, 233
Sentinels Missionary Union, **330**
Separate Baptists in Christ, 122, **274, 294**
Serbian Eastern Orthodox Church, 210
Servants of the Cross, **294**
Seventh-day Adventists, 59, 61, 62, 63, 66,
68, 69, 70, 73, 74, 75, 76, 78, 81, 83,
85, 88, 90, 92, 93, 94, 95, 96, 97, 100,
101, 102, 103, 105, 106, 108, 109,
110, 111, 112, 113, 114, 115, 116,
117, 118, 119, 120, 121, 131, 132,
134, 135, 136, 138, 139, 140, 141,
142, 143, 144, 146, 147, 150, 155,
157, 158, 159, 160, 166, 168, 169,
171, 173, 175, 176, 177, 180, 184,
186, 187, 188, 189, 190, 193, 195,

374

Suomen Luterilainen Evankeliumiyh-distys, 189, **316**
Suomen Vapaa Evankelis-Luterilainen, 189
Suomen Vapaa Evankelis-Luterilainen Seurakuntaliitto, 189
Suomen Vapaakirkko, 189, **316**
Surinam, 120, 142, 224, 230, 234, **284**
Svenska Alliansmissionen, 83, 89, 92, 155, 166, 172, 205, **340**
Svenska Avdelningen av Nordiska Kristnä Buddhist-Missionen, **340**
Svenska Baptistsamfundet, 205
Svenska Baptistmissionen, 66, 174
Svenska Fria Missionen, 61, 66, 68, 73, 74, 83, 93, 111, 112, 116, 131, 132, 135, 140, 142, 143, 147, 150, 155, 166, 177, 181, 183, 187, 191, 196, 197, 201, **340**
Svenska Israelsmissionen, 160, 205, **246, 340**
Svenska Jerusalemsföreningen, 160, **340**
Svenska Kvinnors Missionsförening, **340**
Svenska Kyrkan, 205, **340**
Svenska Kyrkans Missionsstyrelse, 83, 93, **340**
Svenska Mission I Kina och Japan, **340**
Svenska Missionsforbundet, 64, 66, 155, 205, **340**
Svenska Missionsradet, **341**
Svenska Mongol Missionen, **341**
Svenska Pingströrelsens Yttre Mission, **341**
Sveriges Evangeliska Student-och Gym-nasiströrelse, **341**
Swaziland, 92, 221
Sweden, 205, 223, 232, **339**
Swedish . . . (see Svenska)
Swedish Church (Argentina), 131
Swedish Evangelical Missionary Society, 166, **304**
Swedish Evangelical Orient Mission, 166
Swedish Hindustani Mission, 155
Swedish Holiness Mission, 89
Swedish Pentecostal, 155
Swiss . . . (see Schweizer . . .)
Swiss Alliance Japan Mission, 167
Switzerland, 206, 223, 232, **341**
Sykepleirekenes Misjonsring, **337**
Synod of the Evangelical Christian Baptist Churches, U.S.S.R., **343**
Synod of the Evangelical Churches of North Iran, **297**
Syria, 171, 180, 222, 231, 235, **309**
Syrian Antiochian Orthodox Church, **275**
Syrian Orphanage, 168, 171, **320, 342**
Syrian Orthodox, 173, **275, 298, 309**

Taiwan, 180, 222, **310**
Taiwan Christian Yearbook, 182
Taiwan Friends Fellowship, 181
Taiwan Gospel League, 181
Taiwan Missionary Fellowship, **310**
Tamil Evangelical Lutheran Church, 155, **294, 306**

Tanzania, 92, 221, 228, 233, **252, 256**
Taoists, 234, 236
Tasmania, 209, 210
T.E.A.M. (The Evangelical Alliance Mission), 82, 89, 92, 117, 137, 144, 155, 157, 159, 169, 176, 179, 182, **251, 275, 285, 294, 297, 304, 305, 308, 310**
Technical Services Association, **308**
TEKAS (Fellowship of Churches of Christ in Sudan), 81
Telegrafverkets Misjonsforbund, **337**
Telugu Mennonite Brethren Convention, 155, **294**
Thailand, 183, 222, 235, **310**
Thonan Evangelistic Mission, **330**
Timor, 222
Toc H, **330**
Togo, 94, 221, **252**
Tokelau, 219, 225, **349**
Tonga, 219, 225, **349**
Toyo Senkyokai Kiyome Kyokai, 167, **304**
Trans World Radio, **275**
Trinidad and Tobago, 119, 142, 224, 230, **263**
Trinitarian Bible Society, **331**
Tripura Baptist Church Union, 155, **294**
Triumph the Church and Kingdom of God in Christ, 127, **275**
Trucial States, 179
True Jesus Church, 167, 182, **304**
Tsung Tsin (Hakka) Mission of Hong Kong, 150, **288**
Tunisia, 59, 94, 221, 229, 233
Turk and Caicos Islands, 113
Turkey, 184, 222, 232, 235, **310**
Tysk-reformerte Kirke, 188

Uganda, 95, 221, 228, 233, **252, 256**
Ukrainian Orthodox Church, 210; of America **275**; of U.S.A. **275**
Uktal Christian Church Council, 155, **294**
Unevangelized Fields Mission, 66, 71, 107, 108, 110, 139, 157, 191, 218, **331**
Uniao das Igrejas Evangelicas Congre-gacionais e Cristas do Brasil, **280**
Union American Methodist Episcopal Church, 126, **275**
Union Church(es), 75, 105, 118, 137, 141, **259, 260, 282**
Union de Centros Biblicos, 135, **281**
Union des Eglises Evangéliques Bap-tistes de Belgique, **313**
Union des Eglises Evangéliques Libres de France, **317**
Union des Eglises Evangéliques Protes-tantes de Belgique, **313**
Unión Evangélica Bautista Espanola, **339**
Unión Evangélica de la Argentina, **278**
Unión Misionera Evangélica, 137
Union Missionnaire Hospitaliere, **242**
Union Nacional de Sociedades Femen-iles Cristianas, **262**